ARCANA CŒLESTIA.

ARCANA CÆLESTIA

THE

HEAVENLY ARCANA

CONTAINED IN

THE HOLY SCRIPTURES OR WORD OF THE LORD

UNFOLDED

BEGINNING WITH THE BOOK OF GENESIS

TOGETHER WITH WONDERFUL THINGS SEEN IN THE WORLD OF
SPIRITS AND IN THE HEAVEN OF ANGELS

TRANSLATED FROM THE LATIN OF

EMANUEL SWEDENBORG

Servant of the Lord Jesus Christ

VOL. IV

NEW YORK

AMERICAN SWEDENBORG PRINTING AND PUBLISHING
SOCIETY

20 COOPER UNION

MDCCCLXXXII

Published by THE AMERICAN SWEDENBORG PRINTING AND PUBLISHING SOCIETY, *organized for the purpose of Stereotyping, Printing, and Publishing Uniform Editions of the Theological Writings of* EMANUEL SWEDENBORG, *and incorporated in the State of New York* A. D. 1850.

GENESIS.

CHAPTER THE TWENTY-SIXTH.

3353. THE greatest part of mankind believe, that when the last judgment comes, all things are to be destroyed which are in the visible world, that the earth will be consumed by fire, the sun and the moon will be dissipated, and the stars will vanish away; and that a new heaven and a new earth will afterwards spring forth. This opinion they have conceived from prophetic Revelations, wherein mention is made of such things coming to pass; but that the real case is otherwise, may appear from what was shown above concerning the last judgment, n. 900, 931. 1850, 2117 to 2133; hence it is evident, that the last judgment is nothing else but the end of the Church with one nation, and its beginning with another; which end and which beginning then have place, when there is no longer any acknowledgment of the Lord, or what is the same thing, when there is no faith; and there is no acknowledgment of the Lord, and no faith, when there is no charity, for faith cannot possibly exist but with those who are in charity. That in such case there is an end of the Church, and a translation thereof to others, appears manifest from all those particulars, which the Lord Himself taught and foretold in the Evangelists, concerning that last day, or concerning the consummation of the age, viz. in Matthew, chap. xxiv.; in Mark, chap. xiii.; and in Luke, chap. xxi.: but inasmuch as these particulars cannot be comprehended by any one without a key, which is their internal sense, it is permitted to unfold them in the order in which they stand, according to that sense: we shall begin with these words in Matthew, "*The disciples came to Jesus, saying, Tell us when these things shall be, and what is the sign of thy coming, and of the consummation of the age: and Jesus answering, said unto them, See that no one seduce you; for many shall come in My name, saying, I am Christ, and shall seduce many: but ye shall hear of wars and rumours of wars; see that ye be not disturbed; for all these things must needs be, but the end is not yet. For nation shall be stirred up against nation, and kingdom against kingdom; and there shall be famines and pestilences, and earthquakes. But all these things are the beginning of sorrows,*" xxiv. 3, 4, 5, 6, 7, 8. They who abide in the sense of the letter, cannot know whether these, and the particulars which follow in this chapter, were spoken concerning the destruction of Jerusalem and the dispersion of the Jewish nation, or concerning the end of days, which is called the last judgment; but they who are in the internal sense see clearly, that the subject here treated of is concerning the end of the Church, which end, in this and other passages, is what is called the coming of the Lord, and the consummation of the age; and inasmuch as this end is here understood, it may be known that all the above particulars signify things appertaining to the Church; but what they signify, may appear from each particular in the internal sense; as for example: when it is said, *many shall come in My name, saying, I am Christ, and shall seduce many,* by name here is not signified name, nor by Christ Christ, but name signifies that by which the Lord is worshipped, see n. 2724, 3006; and Christ signifies essential truth, n. 3009, 3010; thus it is signified, that there would come those who would assert, that this or that is an article of faith, or that this or that is true, when yet it is neither an article of faith, nor true, but false: by *hearing of wars and rumours of wars,* is signified, that there would exist disputes and litigations concerning truths, which are wars in the spiritual sense: by *nation being stirred up against nation, and kingdom against kingdom,* is signified, that evil would combat with evil and what is false with what is false; that nation denotes good, but in an opposite sense evil, may be seen, n. 1259, 1260, 1416, 1849; and that kingdom denotes truth, but in an opposite sense what is false, n. 1672, 2547: and by there being *famines, and pestilences, and earthquakes in divers places,* is signified that there would be no longer any knowledges of good and of truth, and thus that the state of the Church would be changed, which is an earthquake (motion of the earth).

3354. From these particulars it is evident, what is meant by these words of the Lord, viz. that they denote the first state of the Church's perversion, which comes to pass when men begin no longer to know what is good and what is true, but dispute with each other on such subjects, whence come falsities: inasmuch as this is the first state, it is said, that *the end is not yet,* and that *these things are the beginning of sorrows,* and this state is called *earthquakes in divers places,* whereby is signified in the internal sense, a change of the state of the Church in part, or at first. By these things being said to the disciples, is signified, that they are said to all who are of the Church, for the twelve disciples represented all such, see n. 2089, 2129, 2130; wherefore it is said, *see that no one seduce you;* also, *ye shall hear* of wars and rumours of wars, *see that ye be not disturbed.*

3355. That earthquake (motion of the earth), in the internal sense, denotes a change in the state of the Church, appears from the signification of earth, as denoting the Church, see n.

566, 662, 1066, 1067, 1262, 1733, 1850, 2117, 2118, 2928, and from the signification of motion, as denoting change of state, in the present case as to things appertaining to the Church, viz. as to good and truth ; it is also manifest from other passages in the Word, as in Isaiah, "It shall come to pass, he that fleeth from the voice of fear shall fall into the pit, and he that cometh up out of the midst of the pit shall be taken in a snare, because the cataracts from the deep are open, and *the foundations of the earth are shaken*, by breaking *the earth is broken*, by moving *the earth is moved*, by reeling *the earth reeleth* as a drunkard, *it staggereth* as a cottage, and the transgression thereof is heavy upon *it*, and it shall fall, and shall not rise again : and it shall come to pass in that day, Jehovah will visit upon the host of height in height, and upon the kings of the *ground* upon the *ground*," xxiv. 18, 19, 20. In this passage, that earth denotes the Church, is very evident, for the subject treated of is concerning the Church, whose foundations are said to be shaken, and itself to be broken and moved, to reel and stagger, when good and truth are no longer known ; the kings of the ground denote truths, in the present case falses, upon which will be visitation ; that kings denote truths, and in an opposite sense falses, see n. 1672, 2015 ; and that ground like earth denotes the Church, but with a difference, n. 566, 1068. Again, in the same prophet, " I will render a man more rare than pure gold, and a man than the gold of Ophir ; therefore I will shake the heaven, *and the earth shall be shaken* (or moved) *out of its place ;* in the indignation of Jehovah of Sabaoth, and in the day of the heating of his anger," xiii. 12, 13 ; speaking of a day of judgment ; in which passage also earth manifestly denotes the Church, which is said to be shaken (or moved) out of its place, when it is changed as to state : that place denotes state, may be seen, n. 1273, 1274, 1275, 1377, 2625, 2837. Again, in the same prophet, "Is this the man that *shaketh* (or moveth) *the earth*, that shaketh (or moveth) *kingdoms*, that maketh the world a desert, and destroyeth the cities thereof?" xiv. 16, 17 ; speaking of Lucifer ; where earth denotes the Church, which he is then said to shake (or move), when he claims to himself all things thereto appertaining ; that kingdoms denote truths of the Church may be seen, n. 1672, 2547. So in Ezechiel, "It shall come to pass in that day, when Gog cometh upon *the land of Israel*, My heat in Mine anger and in My zeal shall rise up, in the fire of My indignation I will speak, if not in that day there shall be a great *earthquake* (motion of the earth) upon the *ground* of Israel," xxxviii. 18, 19, 20 ; where Gog denotes external worship separate from internal, and thereby rendered idolatrous, see n. 1151 ; earth and the ground of Israel denote the spiritual Church ; earthquake (motion of the earth) denotes a change of its state. So in Joel, "Before Him the *earth was moved*, the heavens trembled, the sun and the moon were darkened, and the stars withdrew their brightness," ii. 10; speaking also of the day of a last judgment, where the earth being moved denotes a changed state of the Church; the sun and moon denote the good of love and the truth thereof, see n. 1529, 1530, 2441, 2495, which are said to be darkened, when goods and truths are no longer acknowledged; stars denote the knowledges of good and of truth, n. 2495, 2849. So in David, " *The earth was shaken and was moved*, and the foundations of the mountains trembled and were shaken, because he was wroth," Psalm xviii. 7; where the earth shaken and moved denotes the state of the Church rendered perverse. So in the Apocalypse, " I saw further, when he opened the sixth seal, and lo, there was made a *great earthquake* (motion of the earth), and the sun became black as sackcloth of hair, and the whole moon became as blood, and the stars of heaven fell upon the earth," vi. 12, 13; where the earthquake, the sun, the moon, and the stars signify the same as above in Joel: and again, " In that hour was *made a great earthquake*, and a tenth part of the city fell, and in *the earthquake*, there fell the names of men seven thousand," Apoc. xi. 13. From all these passages it is evident that an earthquake is nothing else but a change of the state of the Church, and that earth, in the internal sense, is nothing else but the Church; and inasmuch as earth is the Church, it is manifest by the new heaven and new earth, which was to succeed instead of the former, as mentioned in Isaiah lxv. 17; chap. lxvi. 22; Apoc. xxi. 1, nothing else is signified but a New Church internal and external, see n. 1733, 1850, 2117, 2118.

3356. The ground and reason why motion denotes change of state, is because motion is effected in space and in time; and in another life there is no idea of space and of time, but instead thereof there is an idea of state; in another life, indeed all things appear as in space, and succeed each other as in time, but in themselves they are changes of state, inasmuch as space and time are thence derived; this circumstance is perfectly well known to every spirit, even to the wicked, who by changes of state induced in others cause them to appear in another place, when yet they are not there; it may also be known to man from this consideration, that in proportion as he is in a state of affections, and of consequent joy, and in proportion as he is in a state of thoughts and consequent absence from the body, in the same proportion he is not in time, for several hours in such case appear to him scarce as one; and this by reason that the internal man, or the spirit, has states, to which spaces and times in the external man correspond; motion therefore, as being successive progression in space and time, is in the internal sense change of state.

CHAPTER XXVI.

1. AND there was a famine in the land, besides the former famine, which was in the days of Abraham; and Isaac went to Abimelech king of the Philistines, to Gerar.

2. And Jehovah appeared to him, and said, Go not down into Egypt, reside in the land, which I say to thee.

3. Sojourn in this land, and I will be with thee, and I will bless thee, because I will give all these lands to thee and to thy seed, and I will establish the oath which I sware to thy father Abraham.

4. And I will make thy seed to be multiplied, as the stars of the heavens, and I will give to thy seed all these lands, and in thy seed shall all the nations of the earth be blessed.

5. Because that Abraham hearkened to my voice, and observed my ordinances, my precepts, my statutes, and my laws.

6. And Isaac dwelt in Gerar.

7. And the men of the place asked him respecting his woman; and he said, She is my sister, because he feared to say, She is my woman, lest perhaps the men of the place may slay me for the sake of Rebecca, because she is good to look upon.

8. And it came to pass, because the days were there prolonged to him, that Abimelech king of the Philistines looked out through a window, and saw, and behold Isaac was laughing with Rebecca, his woman.

9. And Abimelech called Isaac, and said, But behold she is thy woman, and how saidst thou, She is my sister? and Isaac said unto him, Because I said, Perhaps I may die because of her.

10. And Abimelech said, What is this that thou hast done unto us, that one of the people might lightly have lain with thy woman, and thou wouldst have brought guilt upon us?

11. And Abimelech charged all his people saying, He that toucheth this man and his woman, dying shall die.

12. And Isaac sowed in that land, and found in that year an hundred measures, and Jehovah blessed him.

13. And the man increased, and went going and increasing until he became very great.

14. And he had acquisition of flock, and acquisition of herd, and much service, and the Philistines envied him.

15. And all the wells, which his father's servants digged, in the days of his father Abraham, the Philistines stopped them up, and filled them with dust.

16. And Abimelech said to Isaac, Go from being with us, because thou prevailest exceedingly above us.

17. And Isaac departed thence, and pitched his camp in the valley of Gerar, and dwelt there.

18. And Isaac returned, and digged again the **wells of**

waters, which they digged in the days of Abraham his father, and the Philistines stopped them after the death of Abraham ; and he called their names, according to the names which his father called them.

19. And the servants of Isaac digged in the valley, and they found there a well of living waters.

20. And the shepherds of Gerar disputed with the shepherds of Isaac, saying, We have the waters, and he called the name of the well Esek, because they contended with him.

21. And they digged another well, and disputed also over it, and he called the name thereof Sitnah.

22. And he removed thence, and digged another well, and they did not dispute over it, and he called the name thereof Rehoboth, and he said, Because now JEHOVAH hath made us to be dilated, and we shall be fruitful in the earth.

23. And he went up thence to Beersheba.

24. And JEHOVAH appeared to him in that night, and said, I am the God of thy father Abraham. Fear not, because I am with thee, and I will bless thee, and will make thy seed to be multiplied for the sake of Abraham my servant.

25. And he built there an altar, and called on the name of JEHOVAH, and stretched out his tent there, and the servants of Isaac digged a well there.

26. And Abimelech went to him from Gerar, and Ahusath his companion, and Phicol the chief captain of his army.

27. And Isaac said unto them, Wherefore are ye come to me, and ye have hated me, and have sent me away from you?

28. And they said, Seeing we have seen that JEHOVAH was with thee, and we said, Let there be I pray a sacrament between us, between us and between thee, and let us make a covenant with thee.

29. If thou shalt do evil with us, as we have not touched thee, and as we have done with thee nothing but good, and have sent thee in peace : thou art now the blessed of JEHOVAH.

30. And he made them a feast, and they did eat and drink.

31. And in the morning they arose early, and sware a man to his brother ; and Isaac sent them away, and they went from being with him in peace.

32. And it came to pass in that day, and the servants of Isaac came, and told him concerning the reasons of the well which they digged, and they said unto him, We have found waters.

33. And he called it Shebah ; therefore the name of the city is Beersheba even to this day.

* * * * * *

34. And Esau was a son of forty years, and he took a woman Jehudith, the daughter of Beeri, the Hittite, and Basemath, the daughter of Elon, the Hittite.

35. And they were bitterness of spirit to Isaac and to Rebecca.

CONTENTS.

3357. THE subject treated of in this chapter, in the internal sense, is concerning appearances of truth of a threefold degree, how they were adjoined to Truth Divine, in order that truths and the doctrinals thereof might be received, and a Church might exist.

3358. The subject treated of, verses 1, 2, 3, 4, 5, 6, is con cerning appearances of truth of a superior degree which are in the internal sense of the Word, in which appearances the angels are, and in which are Divine Truth and Good. And that Divine Good and Truth cannot be comprehended, consequently cannot be received, unless they are in appearances, verses 7, 8, 9, 10, 11, 12, 13.

3359. The appearances of truth of an inferior degree are also treated of, which are in the interior sense of the Word, in which appearances men may be, who are of the internal Church verses 14, 15, 16, 17.

3360. Afterwards appearances of truth of a still inferior de gree are treated of, which are those of the literal sense of the Word, in which appearances men may be, who are of the exter- nal Church, verses 18, 19, 20, 21, 22, 23. 24, 25 ; and by these may still be effected conjunction with the Lord, verses 26, 27. 28, 29, 30, 31, 32, 33.

3361. Concerning scientific truths adjoined to good therein. verses 34, 35.

THE INTERNAL SENSE.

3362. THE subject treated of in chapter xxi. was concerning Abimelech, in that he made a covenant with Abraham. and that on this occasion Abraham reproved him concerning a well of waters, which his servants had seized upon.   A circumstance nearly similar to this here again occurs between Abimelech and Isaac, alike too in this particular, that as Abraham had said that his wife was his sister, so also does Isaac ; from which con- siderations it is evident that some divine arcanum is contained in these circumstances, otherwise they would never have hap- pened a second time, and been again related, neither would mention have been made of wells on each occasion, concerning which wells information could be of no importance, unless some- what divine was concealed therein.   The internal sense teaches what this divine somewhat is, showing, that the subject treated of is concerning the Lord's conjunction with those who are in

His kingdom, in the heavens and in the earths, by truths, and indeed by appearances of truth of a superior degree with the angels, and by appearances of truth of an inferior degree with men, consequently by the Word, in the internal and external sense whereof are contained those appearances; for essential Truths Divine are such, that they cannot in any sort be comprehended by any angel, still less by any man, inasmuch as they exceed every faculty of the understanding both of men and angels; in order therefore that they may have conjunction with the Lord, Truths Divine flow in with them in appearances, and when Truths Divine are in such appearances, they can both be received and acknowledged. This is effected in a manner adequate to the comprehension of every one, wherefore appearances of truth, that is, truths angelic and human, are of a threefold degree. These are the Divine arcana which are contained in the internal sense, in what was done and related above concerning Abimelech and Abraham, and in what is here done and related concerning Abimelech and Isaac.

3363. Verse 1. *And there was a famine in the land, besides the former famine which was in the days of Abraham; and Isaac went to Abimelech king of the Philistines, to Gerar.* There was a famine in the land besides the former famine which was in the days of Abraham, signifies a deficiency of the knowledges of faith: and Isaac went to Abimelech king of the Philistines, to Gerar, signifies the doctrinals of faith; Abimelech is the doctrine of faith respecting things rational: king of the Philistines, denotes doctrinals; Gerar is faith.

3364. "There was a famine in the land besides the former famine which was in the days of Abraham"—that hereby is signified a deficiency of the knowledges of faith, appears from the signification of famine, as denoting a deficiency of knowledges, see n. 1460; that the knowledges of faith are meant, appears from what presently follows, viz. from the representation of Abimelech, and from the signification of Gerar, as denoting the things which are of faith. The famine in the days of Abraham, which is mentioned chap. xii. 10, and treated of, n. 1460, was a deficiency of the knowledges appertaining to the natural man, but the famine here spoken of is a deficiency of the knowledges appertaining to the rational man, wherefore it is said, that there was a famine in the land besides the former famine which was in the days of Abraham. The subject here treated of, in the internal sense, is concerning the Lord, showing that from His Divine [principle] are derived all the doctrinals of faith; for there is not given a single doctrinal, nor the smallest part of one, which is not from the Lord, inasmuch as the Lord is essential doctrine itself; hence it is that the Lord is called the Word, because the Word is doctrine; but inasmuch as whatever is from the Lord is Divine, and what is Divine cannot be comprehended by any created [subject or being], there-fore the doctrinals which are from the Lord, so far as they ap-pear before created [subjects or beings], are not Truths purely Divine, but are appearances of truth; nevertheless in such ap-pearances are contained Truths Divine, and this being the case the appearances also have the name of truths; the subject treated of in this chapter is concerning these appearances.

3365. "And Isaac went to Abimelech king of the Philis-tines, to Gerar"—that hereby are signified the doctrinals of faith, appears from the representation of Isaac, as denoting the Lord as to the Divine Rational [principle], see n. 1893, 2066, 2072, 2083, 2630; that Isaac is the Lord's Divine Rational [principle] as to Divine Good, see n. 3012, 3194, 3210, and also as to Divine Truth, which is represented by the marriage of Isaac with Rebecca, see n. 3012, 3013, 3077, thus by Isaac is here represented the Lord as to Divine Truth conjoined to Di-vine Good of the Rational [principle], for Rebecca was with Isaac, and was called sister; and from the representation of Abimelech, as denoting the doctrine of faith which has respect to things rational, see n. 2504, 2509, 2510, 2530; and from the signification of king of the Philistines, as denoting doctrinals; that king in the internal sense is truth appertaining to doctrinals, see n. 1672, 2015, 2069, and that the Philistines denote the science of knowledges, which also appertains to doctrinals, see n. 1197, 1198; and from the signification of Gerar, as denoting faith, see n. 1209, 2504; hence it is evident what is signified by Isaac's going to Abimelech king of the Philistines, to Gerar, viz. the doctrine of faith derived from the Lord, and having respect to things rational, or, what is the same thing, having respect to the doctrinals of faith. All those things are called doctrinals which appertain to doctrine, which so far as they can be re-ceived and acknowledged in heaven by angels, and in earth by men, are said to have respect to things rational, for it is the rational principle which receives and acknowledges them; but the rational principle is such, that it can in no wise comprehend things Divine, inasmuch as it is finite, and what is finite cannot comprehend the things which are infinite, therefore Truths Di-vine from the Lord are presented before the rational principle by appearances; hence it is, that doctrinals are nothing else but appearances of Truth Divine, or nothing else but celestial and spiritual vessels, for the containing of what is Divine; and inasmuch as what is Divine, that is, the Lord, is in them, there-fore they affect, and hence the Lord has conjunction with angels and men.

3366. Verses 2, 3. *And Jehovah appeared to him, and said, Go not down into Egypt, reside in the land which I say to thee. Sojourn in this land, and I will be with thee, and will bless thee, because to thee and thy seed will I give all these lands, and I will establish the oath which I sware to Abraham thy father.* Jehovah appeared to him, and said, signifies thought from the Divine [principle]: go not down into Egypt, reside in the land which I say to thee, signifies that he should not look to scientifics, but to rationals, which being illustrated by the Divine [principle] are appearances of truth: sojourn in this land, signifies instruction: and I will be with thee, signifies the Divine [principle]: and will bless thee, signifies that thus would be increase: because to thee, signifies the principle of good: and to thy seed, signifies the principle of truth: will I give these lands, signifies things spiritual: and I will establish the oath which I sware to Abraham thy father, signifies confirmation thereby.

3367. "Jehovah appeared to him and said"—that hereby is signified throughout from the Divine [principle], appears from the signification of appearing, when it is spoken of the Lord, who is Jehovah, as denoting the Essential Divine [principle] which was in Himself; that Jehovah was in the Lord, and that the Lord Himself is Jehovah, has been shown above in many places, see n. 1343, 1725, 1729, 1733, 1736, 1791, 1815, 1819, 1822, 1902, 1921, 1999, 2004, 2005, 2018, 2025, 2156, 2329, 2447, 2921, 3023, 3035, 3061; and that the Lord, so far as He had united the Human essence to the Divine, so far spake with Jehovah as with Himself, n. 1745, 1999; thus by Jehovah appearing to Him, in the internal sense, is signified that it was from the Divine [principle]; that thought is signified, appears from the signification of saying, as denoting to perceive, and also to think, according to what has been frequently shown above.

3368. "Go not down into Egypt, reside in the land which I say to thee"—that hereby is signified that he should not look to scientifics but to rationals, which being illustrated by the Divine [principle] are appearances of truth, appears from the signification of Egypt, as denoting scientifics, see n. 1164, 1165, 1462; and from the signification of land (earth), as here denoting things rational, which illustrated by the Divine [principle] are appearances of truth, for the land (earth), which is here meant, is Gerar, where Abimelech, king of the Philistines, was; and by Gerar is signified faith, and by Abimelech, the doctrine of faith which has respect to things rational, and by king of the Philistines, doctrinals, see n. 3363, 3365; therefore by the land, viz. Gerar, where Abimelech was, nothing else is signified in the internal sense; for the signification of land (or earth) is various, see n. 620, 636, 1067, and signifies the quality of the nation of which it is predicated, n. 1262; but in a proper sense it signifies the Church, see n. 3355, and as signifying the Church, it signifies also those things which appertain to the Church, that is, those things appertaining to man which constitute the Church, consequently the doctrinals of charity and faith; thus also rationals, which illustrated by the Divine [principle], are appearances of truth, for that these appearances are the truths of the Church, consequently its doctrinals, may be seen above, n. 3364, 3365; whether we speak of rationals illustrated by the Divine [principle], or of appearances of truth, or of truths celestial and spiritual, such as are in the Lord's kingdom in the heavens or in heaven, and such as are in the Lord's kingdom in the earths or in earth, it is the same thing; the same are also called doctrinals, but this from the truths which are in them; the angelic and human rational [principle] is and is called rational by virtue of the appearances of truth illustrated by the Divine [principle], and without these it is not rational; thus things rational are these appearances of truth so illustrated. The reason why it is here said that he should not go down to Egypt, that is, should not look to scientifics, is, because scientifics were before treated of, inasmuch as Abraham's sojourning in Egypt represented the Lord's instruction in scientifics, when He was a child, see n. 1502. With respect to this arcanum, that he should not go down into Egypt, but should sojourn in the land of Gerar, that is, that he should not look to scientifics but to rationals, the case is this; all appearances of truth, in which is the Divine [principle], appertain to the rational principle, insomuch that rational truths and appearances of truth are the same thing; whereas scientifics appertain to the natural principle, insomuch that natural truths and scientific truths are the same thing. Rational truths, or appearances of truth, can never be and exist, except from an influx of the Divine into the rational principle, and through things rational into the scientifics appertaining to the natural principle; the things in this case effected in the rational principle appear in the natural, as an image of many things together in a mirror; and thus they are exhibited before man, and also before an angel; nevertheless before an angel they are not exhibited so evidently in the natural principle, but with such as are in the world of spirits, and are in a spiritual-natural principle, and hence they have representatives of truth. The case is the same with every individual man, for, as was before observed, he who is in good is a little heaven, or, what is the same thing, is an image of the greatest heaven, and whereas Divine Truth cannot flow immediately into scientifics, which appertain to the natural man, but must flow thereinto through things rational, therefore it is here said that he should not go down into Egypt, but should reside in the land of Gerar. Nevertheless no clear idea can be formed on this subject, unless the nature and quality of influx, and also the nature and quality of ideas, be first known, wherefore by the Divine Mercy of the Lord, we shall take occasion to speak

concerning these things at the close of the chapters, where
mention is made of particular experiences.

3369. "Sojourn in this land"—that hereby is signified
instruction, appears from the signification of sojourning, as denoting to instruct, see n. 1463, 2025; and from the signification
of land in the present case, as denoting things rational, which
illustrated by the Divine [principle] are appearances of truth,
see above, n. 3368; thus by sojourning in this land is signified
to be instructed in those things.

3370. "And I will be with thee"—that hereby is signified
the Divine [principle], may appear from this consideration, that
it is Jehovah Who speaks, consequently the Divine [principle]
itself, by Whom when it is said, I will be with thee, it signifies
    the series, that thus the Divine [principle] would be in the
tnings spoken of.

3371. "And will bless thee"—that hereby is signified that
thus there would be increase, appears from the signification of
blessing, as denoting to make fruitful in goods, and to multiply
in truths, see n. 1731, 981, 1420, 1422, 2846, 3140; thus denoting increase.

3372. "Because to thee"—that hereby is signified good,
may appear from this consideration, that thee means Isaac, by
whom the Lord is represented as to the Divine Rational principle, according to what has been often shown above; and the
Lord's Divine Rational principle is nothing but good, even the
truth therein is good, because Divine.

3373. "And to thy seed"—that hereby is signified truth,
appears from the signification of seed, as denoting truth, see
n. 29, 255, 1025, 1447, 1610, 1940, 2848, 3310; thus denoting truth which is from the Lord's Divine [principle], which is
thy seed. They who apprehend the Word only according to the
sense of the letter, cannot know otherwise, than that seed denotes posterity, consequently in the present case the posterity
of Isaac descended from Esau and Jacob, but principally from
Jacob, because in that nation the Word was, in which are extant
so many historical relations concerning those of whom the nation
consisted; but in the internal sense is not meant any posterity
descended from Isaac, but all those who are the sons of the
Lord, thus the sons of His kingdom, or, what is the same
thing, who are principled in good and truth which is from the
Lord; and whereas these are seed, it follows that essential good
and truth from the Lord is seed, for hence are sons, wherefore
also essential truths which are from the Lord are called sons of
the kingdom in Matthew, "He who soweth *good seed* is the
Son of Man; the field is the world, the seed are *the sons of the
kingdom*," xiii. 37, 38; hence also in general by sons are signified truths, see n. 489, 491, 533, 1147, 2623. Every one may

know, who thinks somewhat deeper or more interiorly than
common, that by the seed of Abraham, of Isaac, and of Jacob,
which is so often mentioned in the Divine Word, and of which
it is so frequently said that it should be blessed, and this above
all other nations and people in the globe, cannot be signified
their posterity, for these in respect to other nations were least
of all principled in the good of love to the Lord and of charity
towards their neighbour, yea, neither were they principled in
any truth of faith; for what the Lord was, what His kingdom,
thus what heaven was, and what a life after death, they were
altogether ignorant, as well because they were not willing to
know, as because had they known, they would in their hearts
have totally denied such knowledge, and would thereby have
profaned interior goods and truths, as they profaned exterior
by their so often becoming open idolaters; which is the reason
why interior truths are so rarely extant in the literal sense of
the Word of the Old Testament. It was in consequence of their
being such a people, that the Lord said of them out of Isaiah,
" He hath blinded their eyes, and hardened their heart, lest they
should see with their eyes, and understand with their heart, and
should be converted, and I should heal them," John xii. 40;
and when they said, " We are Abraham's seed; Abraham is our
father, Jesus said unto them, If ye were the sons of Abraham,
ye would do the works of Abraham; ye are of your father the
devil, and the desires of your father ye wish to do," John viii.
33, 39, 44; by Abraham here is also meant the Lord, as in
every other passage in the Word. That the Jews were not His
seed, or sons, but of the devil, is said expressly : hence it is
very evident, that by the seed of Abraham, of Isaac, and of
Jacob, in the historical and prophetical Word, are by no means
meant the Jews, inasmuch as the Word throughout is Divine,
but all those who are the Lord's seed, that is, who are principled
in good and the truth of faith in Him : that from the Lord alone
is heavenly seed, that is, all good and truth, may be seen, n.
1438, 1614, 2016, 2803, 2882, 2883, 2891, 2892, 2904, 3195.

3374. " I will give all these lands "—that hereby are signified things spiritual, appears from the signification of lands, as
here denoting things rational, which illustrated by the Divine
[principle] are appearances of truth, see above, n. 3368; which
appearances, that they are truths, was also shown above, n.
3364, 3365, consequently denoting things spiritual, for these
are nothing else but truths derived from the Divine [principle],
as may appear from what has been frequently said above concerning the signification of things spiritual. By what is spiritual
in a genuine sense, is meant the essential light of truth which
is from the Lord, as by what is celestial is meant all the flame
of good from the Lord. Hence it may appear, that inasmuch
as this light flows in from the Lord, both into man's rational

principle and into his natural, spirituality is predicated of each, and that it is the Divine [principle] as to truth which flows in. From these observations it may be known what is signified by spiritual in a genuine sense, and that there is a spiritual-rational principle and a spiritual-natural.

3375. " And I will establish the oath which I sware to Abraham thy father "—that hereby is signified confirmation, appears from the signification of oath, or of swearing, as denoting confirmation, see n. 2842 ; it is not here said, I will establish the covenant which I made with Abraham, but the oath, by reason that covenant is predicated of what is celestial, or of good, whereas oath is predicated of what is spiritual, or of truth, see n. 3037, which are here treated of ; wherefore also in what follows it is not said of Isaac, that he made a covenant with Abimelech, but that he sware a man to his brother, verse 31 ; whereas it is said of Abraham, that he and Abimelech made a covenant, Gen. xxi. 32.   See Psalm cv. 8, 9, 10.   By confirmation here, which is signified by oath, is meant the Lord's conjunction with those who are in His kingdom, for an oath is the confirmation of a covenant, and by covenant is signified conjunction, see n. 665, 666, 1023, 1038, 1864, 1996, 2003, 2021.

3376. The internal sense of these two verses is, that the Divine Truth, when it flows in by things rational, presents appearances of truth, and thus fructifies and multiplies itself as to good and truth, by which the Lord conjoins Himself with angels and men : that this is the sense of these verses, cannot be seen from the first exposition, where things appear scattered, as for instance, from what was said, n. 3366, *that there was thought from the Divine* [principle], *not to look to scientifics but to things rational, which illustrated by the Divine* [principle] *are appearances of truth, and that hence would be instruction from the Divine* [principle], *and increase thus good and truth, which are things spiritual, whereby the Lord has conjunction with the things which are in His Word.*   These things however, which appear scattered before man, are still in their internal sense conjoined together in the most orderly arrangement, and before the angels, or in heaven, appear and are perceived in a most beautiful series, yea, with angelic representatives in a celestial form, and this with a variety inexpressible.   Such is the Word throughout in its internal sense.

3377. Verses 4, 5.   *And I will make thy seed to be multiplied as the stars of the heavens, and I will give to thy seed all these lands, and in thy seed shall all the nations of the earth be blessed.   Because that Abraham hearkened to my voice, and observed my ordinances, my precepts, my statutes, and my laws.*   I will make thy seed to be multiplied as the stars of the heavens, signifies the truths and knowledges of faith : and I will give to thy seed all these lands, signifies Churches thence derived : and in thy seed shall all the nations of the earth be blessed, signifies all those who are principled in good as well within as without the Church : because that Abraham hearkened to my voice, signifies the union of the Divine Essence of the Lord with the Human essence by temptations : and has observed my ordinances, my precepts, my statutes, and my laws, signifies by continual revelations from Himself.

3378. " I will make thy seed to be multiplied as the stars of the heavens "—that hereby are signified the truths and knowledges of faith, appears from the signification of seed, as denoting truths, see above, n. 3373 ; and from the signification of stars, as denoting the knowledges of faith, see n. 2495, 2845.

3379. " And I will give to thy seed all these lands "—that hereby are signified Churches thence derived, appears from the signification of seed, as denoting truths, consequently those who are principled in truths, and are thence called sons of the kingdom, see above, n. 3373 ; and from the signification of lands, as here denoting things rational, which illustrated by the Divine [principle] are appearances of truth, see also above, n. 3368, consequently denoting those who are principled in things rational illustrated by the Divine [principle], or, what is the same thing, who are in heavenly light ; and inasmuch as they only are in such light, who are in the Lord's kingdom in the heavens, that is, who are in heaven, and who are in the Lord's kingdom in the earths, that is, who are in the Lord's Churches, it is therefore evident that by these lands (or earths) are signified Churches ; for Churches are not Churches in consequence of being so called, and of professing the name of the Lord, but in consequence of being principled in the good and truth of faith ; it is the essential good and truth of faith which constitutes the Church, yea, which is the Church, for in the good and truth of faith is the Lord, and where the Lord is there is the Church.

3380. " And in thy seed shall all the nations of the earth be blessed "—that hereby are signified all who are principled in good as well within as without the Church, appears from the signification of being blessed, as denoting to be made fruitful in good and to be multiplied in truths, see above, n. 1731, 981, 1422, 2486, 3140 ; and from the signification of seed, as denoting goods and truths which are from the Lord, see above, n. 3373 ; and from the signification of the nations of the earth, as denoting all who are principled in good, see n. 1259, 1260, 1416, 1849 ; thus by all the nations of the earth being blessed in thy seed, is signified, that by good and truth which are from the Lord all are saved who live in mutual charity, whether they be within the Church or without it ; that the Gentile (nations), who are without the Church, and who are principled in good, are saved alike with those who are within the Church, may be seen, n. 593, 932, 1032, 1059, 1327, 1328, 2049, 2051, 2284, 2589 to 2604, 2861, 2986, 3263.

3381. " Because that Abraham hearkened to My voice "—that hereby is signified the union of the Divine Essence of the Lord with the human essence by temptations, appears from the representation of Abraham, as denoting the Lord even as to the Divine Human [principle], see n. 2833, 2836, 3251; and from the signification of hearkening to My voice, when it is predicated of the Lord, as denoting to unite the Divine Essence to the human by temptations, for it is in relation to temptations that obedience is predicated of the Lord in the Word; what is here said has respect to what is related concerning Abraham, chap. xxii., viz. that God *tempted him*, and said unto him, that he should take his son, and offer him for a burnt-offering, verses 1, 2; and when he hearkened to this voice, it is said, " Now I know that thou fearest God, and hast not withheld thine only son from Me; in Myself have I sworn, saith Jehovah, because thou hast done this word, and hast not withheld thine only son, that in blessing I will bless thee, and in multiplying I will multiply thy seed as the stars of the heavens," verses 12, 16, 17; that by not withholding thine only son from Me, which was hearkening to the voice, is signified the union of the Human with the Divine [principle] by the last state of temptation, may be seen, n. 2827, 2844. That this is meant by hearkening to the voice of Jehovah or the Father, is evident also from the Lord's words in Gethsemane, " My Father, if it be possible, let this cup pass from Me, *nevertheless not as I will but as thou wilt;*" again a second time, " My Father, if this cup may not pass from Me, except I drink it, *Thy will be done*," Matt. xxvi. 39, 42; Mark xiv. 36; Luke xxii. 42; but whereas Jehovah or the Father was in Him, or He in the Father and the Father in Him, John xiv. 10, 11, by hearkening to the voice of Jehovah is meant, that the Lord united the Divine [principle] to the Human by temptations, through His own proper power, which is also evident from the Lord's own words in John, "As the Father knoweth Me, and I know the Father, *and I lay down My soul for the sheep*, for this My Father loveth Me, because *I lay down My soul*, that I may take it again; *I have power to lay it down, and I have power to take it again;* this commandment have I received of My Father," x. 15, 17, 18. That the Lord, by His own proper power, united His Divine Essence to His Human essence by temptations, may be seen, n. 1663, 1668, 1690, 1691, 1725, 1729, 1733, 1737, 1787, 1789, 1812, 1820, 2776, 3318.

3382. " And hath observed My ordinances, My precepts, My statutes, and My laws"—that hereby is signified by continual revelations from Himself, viz. that by temptations so also by those [revelations] He united the Divine Essence to the Human, may appear from this consideration, that to observe ordinances, precepts, statutes, and laws, involves all things appertaining to the Word, viz. ordinances, all things thereof in general; precepts, the internal things thereof; statutes, the external things; and laws, all things thereof in particular: inasmuch as these things are predicated of the Lord, Who from eternity was the Word, and from Whom all those things are, in the internal sense it cannot be signified that He observed those things, but that He revealed them to Himself, when He was in a state of unition of the Human [principle] with the Divine. These things indeed, at first view, appear rather remote from the sense of the letter, yea, even from the proximate internal sense, but still when the words are read by man, this is the sense thereof in heaven; for, as has been occasionally said above, and may be seen from examples, n. 1873, 1874, the sense of the letter in the ascent towards heaven is put off, and instead thereof another heavenly sense takes place, insomuch that this latter sense cannot be known to be from the former; for they who are in heaven, are in the idea that all things of the Word in the internal sense treat of the Lord, and also that all things of the Word are from the Lord; likewise that when He was in the world, He thought from the Divine [principle] and thus from Himself, and acquired to Himself all intelligence and wisdom by continual revelations from the Divine [principle]; therefore they have no other perception from the above words; for to observe ordinances, precepts, statutes, and laws, is not predicable of the Lord, inasmuch as He Himself was the Word, consequently He Himself was what was to be observed. He Himself was the precept, He Himself was the statute, and He Himself was the law; for all these things have respect to Him, as the First from Whom they are derived, and as the Last to Whom they tend; therefore by the above words, in a supreme sense, nothing else can be signified but the unition of the Lord's Divine [principle] with the Human, by continual revelations from Himself; that the Lord thought from the Divine [principle], thus from Himself, otherwise than other men, may be seen n. 1904, 1914, 1935; and that He acquired to Himself intelligence and wisdom by continual revelations from the Divine [pirnciple], n. 1616, 2500, 2523, 2632. That to observe ordinances denotes all things of the Word in general, and that precepts denote the internal things of the Word, statutes the external things, and that laws denote all things of the Word in particular, in a genuine sense, may appear from many passages viewed in the internal sense, some of which we shall here adduce; thus in David, "Blessed are the upright in the way, walking in the *law of Jehovah:* blessed are they that keep *His testimonies:* O that my ways were directed to keep *Thy statutes:* I will keep *Thy statutes:* in my whole heart have I sought Thee, let me not

err from Thy precepts: in my heart have I hid *Thy Word*, that
I may not sin against Thee: blessed art Thou, Jehovah, teach
me *Thy statutes:* with my lips have I told all the *judgments of
Thy mouth:* in the way of *Thy testimonies* I am glad, I medi-
tate in *Thy commandments*, and have respect unto *Thy ways:*
in *Thy statutes* I delight: I do not forget *Thy Word:* recompense
Thy servant, that I may live, and keep *Thy Word:* open mine
eyes that I may see wonderful things out of *Thy law:* hide not
Thy precepts from me: vivify me according to *Thy Word:* teach
me *Thy statutes:* make me to understand the way of *Thy commandments*," Psalm cxix. 1 to 27. The subject treated of throughout this whole Psalm is concerning the Word, and concerning
the things appertaining to the Word, which, it is evident, are
precepts, statutes, judgments, testimonies, commandments, and
ways; but what is specifically signified by each of these expressions, cannot possibly be seen from the sense of the letter, in
which sense they appear only as repetitions of the same thing;
it may nevertheless be seen from the internal sense, in which
sense things altogether different are signified by precepts, by
statutes, by judgments, testimonies, commandments, and ways.
Again, "*The law of Jehovah* is perfect, bringing back the soul;
the *testimony of Jehovah* is sure, rendering the simple wise; the
commandments of Jehovah are right, gladdening the heart; the
precept of Jehovah is pure, enlightening the eyes; the fear of
Jehovah is clean, standing to eternity; the *judgments of Jehovah* are truth," Psalm xix. 8, 9, 10: and in the book of Kings,
"David said to Solomon, Thou shalt *observe the ordinance* of thy
God, to walk in *His ways*, to keep *His statutes*, and *His precepts*, and *His judgments*, and *His testimonies*, according to
what is written in the *law of Moses*," 1 Kings ii. 3; to observe
the ordinance, denotes all things of the Word in general, for it
is mentioned in the first place, and has respect to what follows,
as to what is less general; for to observe the ordinance is the
same thing as to keep what is to be kept. So in Moses, "Thou
shalt love Jehovah thy God, and shalt *observe His ordinance*,
and *His statutes*, and *judgments*, and *precepts*, all days," Deut.
xi. 1; where to observe what was ordained, or to keep what
was to be kept, denotes in like manner all things of the Word
in general; statutes denote the external things of the Word,
such as rituals, and those things which are representative and
significative of the internal sense; but precepts denote the internal things of the Word, such as are the things appertaining to
life and doctrine, especially those which are of the internal
sense; but concerning the signification of precepts and statutes,
by the Divine Mercy of the Lord we shall speak elsewhere.

3383. Verses 6, 7. *And Isaac dwelt in Gerar, and the men
of the place asked him respecting his woman, and he said, She is
my sister, because he feared to say, She is my woman, lest perhaps*

*the men of the place may slay me for the sake of Rebecca, because
she is good to look upon.* Isaac dwelt in Gerar, signifies the
Lord's state as to the things which are of faith in respect to
things rational which were to be adjoined : and the men [*viri*]
of the place asked him respecting his woman, signifies the disquisitions of men [*homines*] concerning Divine Truth : and he
said, She is my sister, signifies truth rational : because he feared
to say, She is my woman, lest perhaps the men of the place
may slay me for the sake of Rebecca, signifies that he could not
open essential Divine Truths, for thus Divine Good would not
be received : because she is good to look upon, signifies that it
may easily be received from this circumstance, that it is called
Divine.

3384. "Isaac dwelt in Gerar"—that hereby is signified the
Lord's state as to the things of faith in respect to things rational
which were to be adjoined, appears from the signification of
dwelling in Gerar, as denoting to be principled in the things
which are of faith, consequently a state as to those things ; for
to dwell signifies to live, see n. 1293 ; and Gerar denotes the
things which are of faith, see n. 1209, 2504, 3365 ; and from
the representation of Isaac, as denoting the Lord as to the Di
vine Rational principle, see n. 1893, 2066, 2072, 2083, 2630 ;
that it is in respect to things rational which were to be adjoined,
appears from what goes before, and from what follows, for the
subject treated of in this chapter throughout is concerning those
things, viz. things rational, which being illustrated by the Divine [principle] are appearances of truth. That to dwell denotes
to be and to live, consequently that it denotes a state, appears
from many passages in the Word, as in David, " *I will dwell in
the house of Jehovah* for length of days," Psalm xxiii. 6 : again,
" One thing have I sought of Jehovah, this I will require, that
I *may dwell in the house of Jehovah* all the days of my life,"
Psalm xxvii. 4 : again, " He that doeth deceit *shall not dwell in
the midst of My house*," Psalm ci. 7 ; where to dwell in the house
of Jehovah denotes to be and to live in the good of love, for
this is the house of Jehovah. So in Isaiah, " They that *dwell
in the land of the shadow of death*, on them hath light shined,"
ix. 2 ; where by dwelling in the land of the shadow of death is
denoted the state of those who are in ignorance of good and of
truth : again, " Babel shall *not be inhabited for ever*," xiii. 20 ;
denoting the state of the damnation of those who are Babel :
again, " Jehovah the God of Israel *inhabiting the cherubim*,"
xxxvii. 16 : " O Shepherd of Israel *inhabiting the cherubim*,
shine forth," Psalm lxxx. 1 ; inhabiting the cherubim denotes
the Lord as to a state of providence, in preventing any one entering into the holy things of love and faith unless he be prepared of the Lord, see n. 308 : so in David, " I lay me down in
peace and sleep, for thou Jehovah alone causest me *to dwell*

secure," Psalm iv. 8; to cause to dwell secure denotes a state of peace: so in Jeremiah, " *Who dwellest upon many waters,* great in treasures, thy end is come, the measure of thy gain," li. 13; speaking of Babel; where to dwell upon many waters denotes being in knowledges concerning truth: so in Daniel, "God Himself revealeth deep and hidden things, He knoweth what is in the darkness, and *light dwelleth* with Him," ii. 22; where to dwell denotes to be: again, in the same prophet, "Under that tree the beasts of the field had shade, *and the fowls of heaven dwelt in its branches,*" iv. 12; and in Ezechiel, "Under its branches every beast of the field brought forth, and *in its shade dwelt all great nations,*" xxxi. 6; where to dwell denotes to be and to live: so in Hosea, "The floor of the wine-press shall not feed them, and the new wine shall lie to her, *they shall not dwell in the land of Jehovah,* and Ephraim shall return to Egypt," ix. 2, 3; where not to dwell in the land of Jehovah denotes not to be in a state of the good of love, consequently not in the Lord's kingdom.

3385. " And the men of the place asked him respecting his woman"—that hereby are signified the disquisitions of men concerning Divine Truth, appears from the signification of asking, as denoting to enter into disquisition; and from the signification of the men of the place, viz. Gerar, as denoting those who are principled in the doctrinals of faith; that Gerar denotes the things of faith, see n. 1209, 2504; thus the men of the place denote men of such a state; and from the signification of the woman, who is here Rebecca, as denoting the Divine Truth of the Lord's Divine Rational principle, see n. 3012, 3013, 3077. The subject treated of in the preceding verses is concerning the appearances of truth, in that they exist by Divine influx from the Lord into man's rationals; the subject here treated of is concerning the reception of those appearances, and this first by those who are principled in the doctrinals of faith, and who are understood by the men of the place or Gerar, and are of the first class of those who are called spiritual; for these, inasmuch as they have not perception, like the celestial, and are respectively in an obscure principle, see n. 1043, 2088, 2669, 2078, 2715, 2718, 2831, 3235, 3241, 3246, enter into disquisitions whether a thing be true or not, and also whether it be Divine Truth; and inasmuch as they have not perception respecting it, there is given them such as appears like truth, and this according to their rational principle, that is according to their apprehension, for thus it is received; it is permitted every one to believe truths as he apprehends them; unless this was the case, there would be no reception, because there would be no acknowledgment: this is the subject now treated of.

3386. " And he said, She is my sister"—that hereby is signified truth rational, appears from the signification of sister, as denoting truth rational, see n. 1495, 2508, 2524, 2556; by truth rational is meant that which appears as true according to the apprehension, or before the rational principle, as was just now said.   Isaac's saying that Rebecca was his sister, as Abraham had before said that Sarah was his sister, first in Egypt, Gen. xii. 11, 12, 13, 19; and afterwards in Gerar, Gen. xx. 2, 5, 12; involves a like arcanum, as may be seen from the explication of those passages; and inasmuch as the like happened three times, and is also three times recorded in the Word, it is evident that it is an arcanum of the greatest moment, which cannot be known to any one but from the internal sense; but what the arcanum is, appears from what follows.

3387. " Because he feared to say, She is my woman, lest perhaps the men of the place slay me for the sake of Rebecca"— that hereby is signified that he could not open essential Divine Truths, because thus Divine Good would not be received, appears from the signification of fearing to say, as denoting not to be able to open; and from the signification of woman, who is here Rebecca, as denoting the Lord's Divine Rational principle as to Divine Truth, see n. 3012, 3013, 3077; and from the signification of slaying me, as denoting that good is not received, for by Isaac, who here is *me*, is represented the Divine Good of the Lord's Rational principle, see n. 3012, 3194, 3210; for good is then said to be slain or to perish, when it is not received. for in such case it becomes none; and from the signification of the men of the place, as denoting those who are principled in the doctrinals of faith, see n. 3385; hence then it is evident what is the internal sense of these words, viz. that if essential Divine Truths were to be opened, they would not be received by those who are principled in the doctrinals of faith, because they exceed all their belief, and consequently nothing of good from the Lord could flow in, inasmuch as good from the Lord, or Divine Good, cannot flow in except into truths, truths being the vessels of good, as has been abundantly shown above.   Truths or appearances of truth are given man to this intent, that Divine Good may form his intellectual principle, and thereby may form the man himself, for truths are to the end that good may flow in, inasmuch as good, without vessels or recipients, does not find place, because it does not find a state corresponding to itself, wherefore where there are not truths, or where they are not received, there is neither rational nor human good, consequently the man has not any spiritual life; nevertheless, in order that man may have truths, and thence have spiritual life, there are appearances of truth given, and this to every one according to his apprehension, which appearances are acknowledged as truths because they are such that Divine things may be in them.   For the better understanding what appearances are, and that they are such things as serve man instead of Truths Divine, the following case may be adduced in the way of illustration : if it should be said that in heaven there is no idea of place, consequently none of distance, but that instead thereof the angels have ideas of state, this could in no wise be apprehended by man, for he would thus be led to conceive that in heaven there was nothing distinct, but all confused, viz. all in one or together, when nevertheless all things therein are so distinct that nothing can be more so ; that places, distances, and spaces, which exist in nature, are states in heaven, may be seen, n. 3356 : hence it is evident that whatever is said in the Word concerning places and spaces, and from them and by them, is an appearance of truth, and unless it was spoken by such appearance, it would in no wise be received, consequently it would scarce be accounted of any reality, for the idea of space and of time is in almost all and singular the things of man's thought during his abode in the world, that is, so long as he is in space and time ; that in the Word it is spoken according to appearances of space, is manifest from almost all and singular the things contained therein, as in Matthew, " Jesus said, How saith David, The Lord to my Lord, Sit *on my right-hand*, until I make thy foes thy *footstool*," xxii. 43, 44 ; where to sit on the right-hand is spoken from the idea of place, thus according to appearance, when nevertheless it is a state of the Divine Power of the Lord which is thus described : so again, " Jesus said, Hereafter shall ye see the Son of Man *sitting on the right-hand of power*, and coming *on the clouds of heaven*," xxvi. 64 ; where to sit on the right-hand, and also to come upon the clouds, are in like manner expressions grounded in the idea of place with men, but in the idea of the Lord's power with the angels ; so in Mark, "The sons of Zebedee said to Jesus, Grant unto us that we may sit one on *Thy right-hand*, and the other on *Thy left*, in Thy glory ; Jesus answered, To sit on *My right-hand*, and on *My left*, is not Mine to give, but to those for whom it is prepared," x. 37, 40 ; from these words it is manifest what sort of an idea the disciples had concerning the Lord's kingdom, viz. that it was to sit on the right-hand and on the left ; and inasmuch as they had such an idea, the Lord also answered them according to their apprehension, thus according to what appeared to them. So in David, " He is as a bridegroom *coming forth from his closet*, he rejoiceth as an hero to run the way, *from the end of the heavens* is his coming forth, and *his circuit* to the *ends thereof*," xix. 5, 6 ; speaking of the Lord, whose state of Divine Power is described by such things as relate to space. So in Isaiah, " How *hast thou fallen from heaven*, O Lucifer, son of the morning ! thou hast said in thine heart, I will *ascend into the heavens*, I will *exalt my throne* above the stars of heaven, *I will ascend above the heights of the clouds*," xiv. 12, 13, 14 ; where to fall from heaven, to ascend the heavens, to exalt the

throne above the stars of heaven, are all expressions grounded
in the idea of space or place, whereby self-love profaning holy
things is described. Inasmuch as things celestial and spiritual
are presented before man by such things as appear, and accord
ing to such things, therefore heaven is also described as being
on high, when yet it is not on high, but within, or in an internal
principle, see n. 450, 1380, 2148.

3388. " Because she is good to look upon"—that hereby is
signified that it might be easily received, from this circumstance
that it is called Divine, appears from the signification of good
to look upon, as denoting that which pleases by its form, thus
what is easily received; the subject treated of is concerning
those who are principled in the doctrinals of faith, and have no
perception of truth from good, but have only a conscience of
what is true grounded in this, that they have been taught so by
their parents and masters; these are they who are called the
men of the place, or of Gerar, n. 3385, 3387; with such persons,
the first principle of the confirmation of truth is, that it is called
Divine, for in this case they have instantly an idea of what is
holy, which gives an universal confirmation to all and singular
the things which are declared, and this, notwithstanding they
do not comprehend such things; but still the things declared
must be adequate to their apprehension; for it is not sufficient
that a man knows a thing to be so, but he is also desirous to
know what it is, and what is its quality, in order that some confirmation may thence accrue to his intellectual principle, and
may be reflected back from that principle: if this be not the
case, a thing may indeed be introduced to the memory, but it
remains there only as a dead thing, or as a mere sound, and unless some confirming proofs infix it, from whatever source they
are derived, it is dissipated like the remembrance only of some
what that made a tinkling noise.

3389. Verses 8, 9. *And it came to pass, because days were
there prolonged to him, that Abimelech, king of the Philistines,
looked out through a window and saw, and behold Isaac was
laughing with Rebecca his woman. And Abimelech called Isaac,
and said, But behold she is thy woman, and how saidst thou, She
is my sister? and Isaac said unto him, Because I said, Perhaps
I may die because of her.* It came to pass because days were there
prolonged to him, signifies a state of reception: Abimelech,
king of the Philistines, looked out through a window, and saw,
signifies the doctrine of faith having respect to things rational
in knowledges: and behold Isaac was laughing with Rebecca
his woman, signifies that Divine Good was present in Divine
Truth: and Abimelech called Isaac and said, signifies the Lord's
perception from doctrine: but behold she is thy woman, and how
saidst thou, She is my sister? signifies if Divine Truth, it was not
also rational : and Isaac said unto him, Because I said, Perhaps

I may die because of her, signifies that he would not be received.

3390. "It came to pass because days were there prolonged to him"—that hereby is signified a state of reception, appears from the signification of prolonging there to him, viz. to Isaac, as denoting that when the Divine Good, which is represented by Isaac, was there for some time, Divine Truth was received, for the subject treated of, in the internal sense, is concerning the reception of truth by the spiritual; and from the signification of days, as denoting states, see n. 23, 487, 488, 493, 893, 2788.

3391. "And Abimelech, king of the Philistines, looked out through a window, and saw"—that hereby is signified the doctrine of faith having respect to things rational in knowledges, appears from the representation of Abimelech, as denoting the doctrine of faith having respect to things rational, see n. 2504, 2509, 2510, 2533; and from the signification of king of the Philistines, as denoting doctrinals, see n. 3365; and from the signification of window, as denoting the intellectual principle, see n. 655, 658; consequently denoting the internal sight, for this formerly was signified by windows; thus to look out through a window is to perceive those things which appear by the internal sight, which things in general are knowledges, such as appertain to the external man; things rational, or, what is the same, appearances of truth, that is, truths spiritual, are not knowledges, but are in knowledges, for they appertain to the rational principle, thus to the internal man, and it is the internal man which has respect to the things of the external, thus to truths in knowledges; for knowledges, inasmuch as they appertain to the natural man, are vessels recipient of things rational; that Truths Divine flow into the rational principle, and through this into the natural, and in this latter are presented as an image of many things in a mirror, may be seen, n. 3368; that windows are such things as appertain to the internal sight, that is, to the intellect, which in one word are called things intellectual, appears from those passages of the Word which were adduced, n. 655, and still further from the following, "They shall run to and fro in the city, they shall run on the wall, they shall climb up into the houses, *they shall enter in by the windows* as a thief," Joel ii. 9; speaking of the evils and falses of the last days of the Church; to climb up into the houses, denotes the destroying the good things appertaining to the will principle: that house denotes such things, see n. 710, 2233, 2234; and to enter in by the windows, denotes the destroying truths and the knowledges thereof appertaining to the understanding. So in Zephaniah, "Jehovah will stretch out His hand over the north, and will destroy Ashur, troops shall lie down in the midst thereof, every wild beast of its nation, the cormorant and bittern shall pass the night in the chapiters of it, *a voice shall sing in the window*, dryness shall be in the threshold, because He hath made bare the cedar," ii. 13, 14; speaking of the destruction of the truths of faith by ratiocinations, which are Ashur, see n. 119, 1186; by a voice singing in the window, is denoted the desolation of truth, thus the desolation of the intellectual faculty as to truth. So in the book of Judges, "The mother of Sisera *looked out through a window*, and cried through *the lattice*, Why is his chariot so long in coming?" v. 28. This is part of the prophetic declaration of Deborah and Barak, concerning the resuscitation (raising up again) of a spiritual Church; by look ing out through a window, are denoted the reasonings of those who deny truths, and thereby destroy the things which apper- tain to the Church, for such reasonings are things intellectual in an opposite sense. So in Jeremiah, "Wo to him that build- eth his house without justice, and his chambers without judg- ment; who saith, I will build for myself an house of measures and spacious chambers; and *he cutteth out for himself win- dows*, and things ceiled with cedar, and he painteth it with ver- milion," xxii. 13, 14. To build a house without justice, and chambers without judgment, denotes religious principles and worship grounded in what is not good and true; that justice and judgment signify good and truth, may be seen, n. 2235; to cut out for himself windows and things ceiled with cedar, and to paint with vermilion, denotes the falsification of intellectual and spiritual truths. The windows of the temple at Jerusalem represented nothing else but what appertains to things intellec- tual, consequently to things spiritual. The same is signified by the windows of the new temple, as mentioned in Ezechiel, chap. xl. 16, 22, 25, 33, 36; chap xli. 16, 26; for that the new tem- ple, the new Jerusalem, and the new earth, as described in that prophet, are nothing else but the Lord's kingdom, every one may see, consequently the things mentioned in regard thereto must be such things as appertain to His kingdom.

3392. "And behold Isaac was laughing with Rebecca his woman"—that hereby is signified that Divine Good was present in Divine Truth, or that Divine Good was adjoined to Divine Truth, appears from the representation of Isaac, as denoting the Divine Good of the Lord's rational principle, see n. 3012, 3194, 3210; and from the signification of laughing, as denoting love or the affection of truth, see n. 2072, 2216; and from the repre- sentation of Rebecca, as denoting the Divine Truth of the Lord's rational principle, see n. 3012, 3013, 3077; hence it is evident, that by Isaac laughing with Rebecca his woman is signified, that Divine Good was present with Divine Truth: the sense of the above words in the series is, that truth spiritual is received at first for this reason, because it is called Divine, afterwards because the Divine [principle] is in it, which is clearly seen by those who are regenerated, and who become men of the spiritual Church; these are they who are meant by Abimelech, that is, they who are principled in the doctrines of faith, and have respect to truths in knowledges, concerning whom, see above, n. 3391.

3393. "And Abimelech called Isaac and said"—that hereby is signified the Lord's perception from doctrine, appears from the representation of Abimelech, as denoting doctrine that has respect to things rational, see n. 2504, 2509, 2510, 2533, 3391; and from the representation of Isaac, as denoting the Lord's Divine Rational principle, concerning which see above, and from the signification of saying, as denoting to perceive, see n. 1898, 1919, 2080, 2862; and whereas Abimelech signifies that doctrine, in which now the Divine [principle] was perceived, therefore also by Abimelech is represented the Lord as to that doctrine; for all and singular the things contained in the Word, in a supreme sense, have relation to the Lord; and the Lord is essential doctrine, that is, the Word, not only as to the supreme sense therein, but also as to the internal sense, and even as to the literal sense, for this sense is representative and significative of the internal sense, as the internal sense is representative and significative of the supreme sense; and that which in the Word is representative and significative, is in its essence that which is represented and signified, consequently it is the Divine [principle] of the Lord; for a representative is nothing else but an image of what is represented, and in the image is the [being] himself who is presented to view; this may appear from man's speech and also from his gestures, these being only images of the things which exist within in man, in his thought and will, so that speech and gesture are thought and will in a form; for if you take away thought and will thence, the remainder would be a mere inanimate somewhat, in which would be nothing human; hence it may appear how the case is with the Word, even in its letter, viz. that it is Divine.

3394. "But behold she is thy woman, and how saidst thou, She is my sister?"—that hereby is signified if Divine Truth, it was not also rational, appears from the signification of woman, who is here Rebecca, as denoting the Divine Truth of the Lord's Divine Rational principle, see n. 3012, 3013, 3077; and from the signification of sister, as denoting truth rational, see n. 3386; thus by these words, "behold she is thy woman, and how saidst thou, She is my sister?" is signified that truth, as being Divine, cannot be rational. With respect to this arcanum, the case is as follows: the spiritual, inasmuch as they have not perception like the celestial, do not know that Divine Truth becomes rational truth with man when he is regenerated; they say indeed that all good and truth is from the Lord, but still, when good and truth exist in their rational principle, they suppose it to be their own, and thus as it were to be from them-

selves, so they cannot be separated from their proprium [pro-
priety, or own proper life of self], which is willing so to think;
with the celestial, however, the case is this: they perceive Divine Good and Truth in the rational principle, that is, in things
rational, which being illustrated by the Lord's Divine [princi-
ple] are appearances of truth, n. 3368, even in the natural principle, that is, in scientifics and things of sense, and inasmuch as
they are in such a state, they can acknowledge that all good
and truth flows in from the Lord, and also that there is a perceptive [faculty or principle] of good and truth, which is communicated and appropriated to them from the Lord, and causes
their delight, blessedness, and happiness; hence it was that the
most ancient people, who were celestial men, in all and singular the objects which they saw with their eyes, perceived
nothing but things celestial and spiritual, see n. 1409: inasmuch
as the subject here treated of is concerning the spiritual man
regenerated, who by regeneration from the Lord receives Divine
Good in a new will, and Divine Truth in a new understanding, and inasmuch as such persons are in no other perception
than that if truth be rational it cannot be Divine, as was said
above, consequently that if it be Divine it has nothing common
with what is rational, therefore it is here said, if Divine Truth,
it was not also rational; this likewise is the reason why such
persons are desirous that the things of faith should be believed
simply, without being viewed from any rational ground, not
being aware, that no article of faith, not even the most mysterious, is comprehended by any man without some rational idea,
and also a natural one, the nature and quality of which idea he
is nevertheless unacquainted with, see n. 3310; hereby indeed
they may secure themselves against those who reason from a
negative principle concerning all and singular things of faith,
whether they be true or not, see n. 2568, 2588; but to those
who are in an affirmative principle concerning the Word, viz.
that it is to be believed, such a position is hurtful, inasmuch as
the freedom of thinking may thus be taken away, which every
one enjoys, and the conscience may be bound even to the most
heretical tenets, and thus dominion established over man's internal and external principles: these are the things signified
by Abimelech saying to Isaac, "Behold she is thy woman, and
how saidst thou, She is my sister?"

3395. "And Isaac said unto him, Because I said, Perhaps I
may die because of her"—that hereby is signified that he would
not be received, appears from what was said above, n. 3387, at
those words, "because he feared to say, She is my woman, lest
perhaps the men of the place may slay me for the sake of Rebecca." That to say, signifies to perceive and to think, appears
more manifestly in this passage than in any other.

3396. Verses 10, 11. *And Abimelech said, What is this*

that thou hast done to us, that one of the people might lightly
have lain with thy woman, and thou wouldst have brought guilt
upon us? And Abimelech charged all the people, saying, He
that toucheth the man and his woman, dying shall die. Abimelech said, What is this that thou hast done to us, signifies indignation: that one of the people might lightly have lain with thy
woman, and thou wouldst have brought guilt upon us, signifies
that truth might have been adulterated and thereby profaned:
and Abimelech charged all the people, saying, signifies a decree from the Lord in the spiritual Church: He that touches
the man and his woman, dying shall die, signifies that Divine
Truth and Divine Good are not to be opened, and are not to be
acceded to by faith, through danger of eternal damnation if
they should be profaned.

3397. "Abimelech said, What is this that thou hast done to
us"—that hereby is signified indignation, may appear without
explication.

3398. "That one of the people might lightly have lain with
thy woman, and thou wouldst have brought guilt upon us"—
that hereby is signified that truth might have been adulterated
and thereby profaned, appears from the signification of lying
with, as denoting to be perverted or adulterated; and from the
signification of one of the people, as denoting some one of the
Church, viz. the spiritual Church, see n. 2928; and from the
signification of woman, who is here Rebecca, as denoting Divine Truth, concerning which see above; and from the signification of guilt, as denoting the blame of the profanation of
truth; hence it is evident, that by these words, "one of the
people might lightly have lain with thy woman, and thou
wouldst have brought guilt upon us," is denoted, that some
one of the Church might easily have adulterated Divine Truth,
and thereby have brought upon himself the blame of profanation. It was said above, n. 3386, that inasmuch as Abraham
on two occasions called his wife Sarah his sister, first in Egypt,
and afterwards in Gerar with Abimelech, and that Isaac in like
manner called his woman Rebecca his sister, when he also was
with Abimelech, and inasmuch as these three cases are likewise
recorded in the Word, there must be some most mysterious
reason for all this. The real mystery appears evidently from
the internal sense, and is this, that since by sister is signified
rational truth, and by woman Divine Truth, therefore this latter was called rational, that is, sister, lest Divine Truth, which is
woman, and which is here Rebecca, should be adulterated, and
thereby profaned. In regard to the profanation of truth, the
case is this: Divine Truth can in no wise be profaned, except by
those who have first acknowledged it; for such, having first entered into truth by acknowledgment and belief, and having thus
been initiated into it, when they afterwards recede from it, there

continually remain with them some traces or footsteps thereof
inwardly impressed, which are recalled whensoever what is false
and evil is present, and hence the truth, by reason of its adhering thereto, is profaned. Such persons therefore, with whom
this is the case, have continually in themselves what condemns
them, consequently their own hell; for the infernals, when they
approach towards the sphere where good and truth is, instantly
are made sensible of their own hell, inasmuch as they come into,
that which they account hateful, consequently into torment ;
whosoever therefore have profaned truth, dwell continually with
that which torments them, and this according to the degree of
profanation.　It is on this account, that the Lord is most especially provident, to prevent the profanation of Divine Good and
Truth ; and His providence herein operates principally in this
way of prevention, that man, who is of such a nature that he
cannot do otherwise but profane, is withheld as far as possible
from the acknowledgment and belief of what is true and good;
for, as was observed, no one can profane, but he who has before acknowledged and believed: this was the reason why internal truths were not discovered to the posterity of Jacob, the
Israelites and Jews, nor was it even openly declared to them
that there was any internal principle in man, consequently
that there was any internal worship, and scarce any thing was
openly said concerning a life after death, and concerning the
heavenly kingdom of the Lord, or of the Messiah whom they expected.　The reason was, because they were a people of such a
nature, that it was foreseen, in case such things had been discovered to them, they could not have done otherwise than profane them, inasmuch as they had no will or inclination for any
thing but what was terrestrial ; and being such a generation in
old time, and also being such at present, it is likewise still permitted that they should remain altogether in a state of unbelief;
for if they had once acknowledged the truth, and afterwards
receded from it, they must needs have occasioned to themselves
the most grievous of all hells.　This was also the reason why
the Lord did not come into the world, and reveal the internal
things of the Word, until there was not any good remaining
with them, not even natural good, for in this case they could no
longer receive any truth to a degree of internal acknowledgment, inasmuch as it is good which so receives, consequently
they could not profane it; this state was what is meant by the
fulness of time, and by the consummation of the age, and also
by the last day so much spoken of by the prophets.　It is for this
same reason, that the arcana of the internal sense of the Word
are now revealed, inasmuch as at this day there is scarce any
faith, because there is not any charity, consequently because it
is the consummation of the age, and when this takes place, then
the arcana of the internal sense of the Word may be revealed

without danger of profanation, because they are not interiorly acknowledged. It is on account of this arcanum, that it is recorded in the Word concerning Abraham and Isaac, that, when in Gerar with Abimelech, they called their wives sisters. See further what was said and shown above on this subject, viz. that they may profane truth who acknowledge it, but not they who do not acknowledge it, and still less they who do not know it, n. 593, 1008, 1010, 1059. What is the danger arising from a profanation of holy things and of the Word, n. 571, 582. That they who are within the Church may profane holy things, but not they who are without the Church, n. 2051. That it is provided of the Lord that there be no profanation, n. 1001, 2426. That worship becomes external to prevent the profanation of internal, n. 1327, 1328. That men are kept in ignorance to prevent the profanation of the truths of faith, n. 301, 302, 303.

3399. That lying with the woman in the internal sense denotes to pervert and adulterate truth, in the present case Truth Divine, because by the woman or Rebecca is represented Divine Truth, as was shown above, may appear from this consideration, that by lying with, by adultery, and by prostitution, in the Word, nothing else is signified but perversions of good, and falsifications of truth, as was shown, n. 2466, 2729; and this by reason that adulteries are altogether contrary to conjugial love, so as to be destructive thereof, and conjugial love is derived from the marriage of good and truth, see n. 2508, 2618, 2727 to 2759, 3132; therefore those things which are contrary to good and truth, or which destroy them, are in the Word called adulteries. But it is to be observed, that they who are of the spiritual Church cannot adulterate good so as to profane it, by reason that they cannot receive good so as to have a perception of it, like the celestial: they are capable however of profaning truth, because this they can acknowledge: but in the last time of the Church, they cannot acknowledge truth, inasmuch as at that time unbelief prevails with them universally concerning the Lord, concerning a life after death, and concerning the internal man; and unbelief, which prevails universally, has this effect, that the truths of faith do not penetrate interiorly; an universal principle of unbelief, prevailing with any one, limits and prevents the interior admission of such truths, though the man be ignorant of it, and though he even fancies that he believes them. But they who are capable of profaning good, are of the celestial Church, for these can receive good even to a degree of perception; this was the case with the antediluvians, who were therefore separated from all others, and confined in a hell separate from the hells of others, see n. 1265 to 1272, and the prevention of any further profanation of good is signified by what is written, when the man was cast out of Eden, that "Jehovah caused to dwell on the east at the garden of Eden, cherubs, and the flame of a sword turning itself, to keep the way of the tree of lives," Gen. iii. 24; on which subject, see n. 308, 310.

3400. That guilt is the blame or imputation of sin and prevarication against good and truth, may appear from the following passages of the Word where guilt is mentioned, and also described, as in Isaiah, "It pleased Jehovah to bruise him, and he made him weak: *if thou shalt make guilt his soul,* he shall see seed, he shall prolong days, and the will of Jehovah shall prosper by his hand," liii. 10; speaking of the Lord, where to make guilt His soul denotes sin imputed to Him, consequently blame by those who hated Him; not that in Himself He contracted any thing of sin, that He should take it away. So in Ezechiel, "By the blood which thou hast shed, *thou hast had guilt,* and by thine idols which thou hast made, thou hast been polluted," xxii. 4; where to shed blood denotes violence offered to good, see n. 374, 376, 1005, whence comes guilt. So in David, "The haters of what is just *shall have guilt.* Jehovah redeemeth the soul of His servants; all that trust in Him *shall not have guilt,*" Psalm xxxiv. 21, 22; thus guilt denotes all sin, which remains; its separation by good derived from the Lord is redemption, which was also represented by the expiation (or atonement) made by the priest, when they offered the sacrifice of guilt, see Levit. v. 1 to 26; chap. vii. 1 to 10; chap. xix. 20, 21, 22; Numb. v. 1 to 8; where also the kinds of guilt are enumerated, which are these, the hearing the voice of cursing and not declaring it: the touching any thing unclean: the swearing to do evil: the sinning by mistake concerning the holy things of Jehovah: the doing any of those things which are forbidden by the commandments: the refusing to a neighbour what was delivered to be kept: the finding what was lost, and denying it and swearing falsely: the lying with a woman that is a bondmaid betrothed to a man, not redeemed, neither made free: the doing of all sins against man by committing trespass against Jehovah.

3401. "And Abimelech commanded all his people, saying" —that hereby is signified a decree from the Lord in the spiritual Church, appears from the signification of commanding, as denoting to make a decree; and from the representation of Abimelech, as denoting those who are in the doctrine of faith, see n. 3392, and in a supreme sense denoting the Lord, see n. 3393; and from the signification of people as denoting those who are of the spiritual Church, see n. 3398; hence it is evident, that by Abimelech's commanding all the people is signified a decree from the Lord in the spiritual Church; the decree itself is what follows, viz that Divine Truth and Divine Good are not to be opened, and not to be acceded to from a principle of faith, for fear of eternal damnation in case they should be profaned; this is the subject next treated of.

3402. "He that toucheth this man and his woman, dying shall die"—that hereby is signified that Divine Truth and Divine Good are not to be opened, and not to be acceded to from a principle of faith, for fear of eternal damnation in case they should be profaned, appears from the signification of touching this man and this woman, as denoting to accede to Divine Truth and Divine Good, which are represented by Isaac and Rebecca; truth is here mentioned in the first place, and good in the second, because the subject treated of is concerning those who are in the spiritual Church, who are capable of adulterating, yea, of profaning truth, but not good, and it is for this reason also that they are called man (*vir*) and woman, see n. 915, 2517; and from the signification of dying to die, as denoting eternal damnation, which is spiritual death, in the present case arising from profanation, which is the subject here treated of. That it is of the Lord's providence, that no one be admitted into good and truth, that is, into the acknowledgment and affection thereof, any further than he can remain steadfast therein through danger of eternal damnation, may be seen, n. 3398. The case with good and truth, as has been said and shown above, is, that they betake themselves to an inner place in man, in proportion as he is in evil and in what is false, consequently the angels who are attendant upon him from heaven, retire in the same proportion, and diabolical spirits from hell in the same proportion come near. The removal of good and truth, consequently of angels from man, who is principled in what is evil and false, does not appear to him, because in such case he is in a persuasion that evil is good, and that what is false is truth, and this by reason of the affection and consequent delight thereof, and when he is in this state, it is impossible for him to know that good and truth are removed from him. Good and truth, or the angels, are then said to be removed from man, when he is not affected with them, that is, when they no longer delight him, being affected contrariwise with the things appertaining to self-love and the love of the world, that is, being delighted solely with such things. To know what is good and true, or to have them in the memory, and to talk about them, is not to possess them, but to be affected with them from the heart, this is to possess them; neither can he be said to possess good and truth, who is affected with them for the sake of gaining thereby reputation and wealth, for in such case he is not affected with good and truth, but with honour and gain, and he makes the former only means of obtaining the latter; with such in another life there is a removal of the goods and truths which they had known, and which they had even preached, during their life in the body, whereas self-love and the love of the world, which were the ruling principles of their lives, remain. From these considerations, it may appear how the case is in regard to good and truth, viz. that no one is allowed to accede thereto with affection and faith, unless he be such, that he can continue steadfast therein to his life's end; but they who profane, cannot possibly be withheld thence.

3403. Verses 12, 13, 14. *And Isaac sowed in that land, and found in that year an hundred measures, and Jehovah blessed him. And the man increased, and went in going and increasing, insomuch that he became exceeding great. And he had acquisition of flock, and acquisition of herd, and much service; and the Philistines envied him.* Isaac sowed in that land, signifies interior truths, which are from the Lord, appearing to the rational principle: and he found in that year an hundred measures signifies abundance: and Jehovah blessed him, signifies as to the good of love therein: and the man increased, and went in going and increasing, insomuch that he became exceeding great, signifies increases: and he had acquisition of flock and acquisition of herd, signifies as to good interior, and as to good exterior: and much service, signifies truth thence derived: and the Philistines envied him, signifies that they who were principled only in the science of knowledges did not comprehend.

3404. "Isaac sowed in that land"—that hereby are signified interior truths, which are from the Lord, appearing to the rational principle, appears from the signification of sowing, as denoting in a supreme sense Divine Truth which is from the Lord Who is the Sower, see n. 3038, and in an internal sense denoting truth and good with man, thence derived, see n. 3373; and from the signification of land, as denoting things rational, which being illustrated by the Divine [principle] are appearances of truth, see n. 3368, or, what is the same thing, interior truths which are from the Lord appearing to the rational principle; which appearances, or which truths, are of a superior degree, being treated of, in the internal sense, even to verse 14; in these appearances of truth the angels are principled, and they are of such a nature as transcend immensely the understanding of man, during his life in the world. In order for the further explaining what is meant by the appearances of truth, it may be illustrated as follows: it is well known that the Divine [being or principle] is infinite as to esse, and eternal as to existere, and that what is finite is not capable of comprehending what is infinite, no, nor of comprehending what is eternal, for what is eternal is infinite as to existere, and inasmuch as the essential Divine [being or principle] is infinite and eternal, therefore all things thence proceeding are also infinite and eternal, and being infinite, it is altogether impossible they can be comprehended by the angels, because the angels are finite; wherefore those things which are infinite and eternal, are presented before the angels in appearances, which are finite, but still in such appearances as are very far above the sphere of man's comprehension. As for example : it is altogether impossible for man to have any idea of what is eternal except from time, and this being the case, it is impossible for him to comprehend what is from eternity, consequently what the Divine [being or principle] was before time, or before the world was created ; and so long as there is in his thought anything of an idea derived from time, he must needs, in thinking on the subject, fall into inextricable errors ; but to the angels who are not in the idea of time, but in the idea of state, it is given to perceive this well, for eternity with them is not the eternity of time, but the eternity of state, without the idea of time. Hence it is manifest in what appearances the angels are principled in comparison of man, and how much their appearances are above those which appertain to man; for man cannot have a single principle of thought even in the smallest degree, but what derives somewhat from time and space, whereas the angels derive nothing thence, but instead thereof they derive their thoughts from the states of things as to esse and existere. From these few considerations it may appear what is the nature of the appearances of truth here treated of, and which are of a superior degree. In what follows, the appearances of truth of an inferior degree are treated of, such as are also adequate to man's apprehension.

3405. "And he found in that year an hundred measures"—that hereby is signified abundance, appears from the signification of year, as denoting the entire state here treated of, see n. 487, 488, 493, 893; and from the signification of hundred, as denoting much and full, see n. 2636; and from the signification of measure, as denoting the state of a thing as to truth, see n. 3104; these things collected into one signify abundance of truth. The subject treated of in this, as in other parts of the Word, in a supreme sense, is concerning the Lord, viz. that He also was in the appearances of truth, when in the maternal human [principle], but that as He put off this human [principle], He put off those appearances also, and put on the essential Divine [principle] infinite and eternal : but the subject treated of, in the internal or respective sense, is concerning appearances of a superior degree with the angels, the abundance whereof is signified by the finding in that year an hundred measures. With respect to appearances of truth, or to truths which are from the Divine [principle], the case is this, that such as are of a superior degree, immensely exceed those which are of an inferior degree, both in abundance and in perfection, for myriads, yea, myriads of myriads of things, which are distinctly perceived by those who are in a superior degree, appear only as one with those who are in an inferior degree, inasmuch as things inferior are nothing but composites of things superior; as may be concluded from the memories appertaining to man, the interior of which, as being in a superior degree, so immensely excels the exterior which is in an inferior degree, see n. 2473, 2474. Hence it may appear in what wisdom the angels are principled in comparison of man, the angels of the third heaven being even in the fourth degree above man, concerning which wisdom therefore, when described to man, nothing can be predicated but that it is incomprehensible, yea, ineffable.

3406. "And Jehovah blessed him"—that hereby is signified as to the good of love therein, appears from the signification of being blessed, as denoting to be enriched with all celestial and spiritual good, see n. 981, 1731, 2846; thus to be blessed of Jehovah denotes to be enriched with celestial good which is of love, for Jehovah is the very esse of love or of good, see n. 1735; therefore when good is treated of, Jehovah is mentioned, but when truth is treated of, the appellation God is applied, see n. 2586, 2769.

3407. "And the man increased, and went in going and increasing, until he became exceeding great"—that hereby are signified increments [increasings], appears from the signification of increasing, of going, and of becoming exceeding great, as denoting increments of good in their order, viz. from truth to good, and from good to truth.

3408. "And he had acquisition of flock and acquisition of herd"—that hereby is signified as to good interior and as to good exterior, that is, as to good rational and as to good natural, appears from the signification of flock, as denoting interior or rational good, see n. 343, 2566; and from the signification of herd, as denoting exterior or natural good, see n. 2566. Good natural, which is signified by herd, is not that which is connate with man, but that which is procured by knowledges of truth joined to affection of good; for good natural, which is connate, is in itself a mere animal principle, having place also with the animals, whereas good natural, which is procured, or with which man is gifted of the Lord, contains in it a spiritual principle, so that it is spiritual good in natural; this latter good is the essential natural human good, whereas the former, viz. that which is connate, although it appears as good, may still not be good, yea, it may be evil, for it may receive even false principles, and believe that to be good which is evil; such natural good is found to exist amongst nations of the worst principles both as to life and faith.

3409. "And much service"—that hereby is signified truth thence derived, appears from the signification of service, as denoting all that which is beneath, which is subordinate and which obeys, see n. 1713, 2541, 3012, 3020, consequently denoting truth, as being derived from good, and ministering to good; on which subject much has been said above.

3410. " And the Philistines envied him"—that hereby is
signified that they who were principled only in the science of
knowledges, did not comprehend, appears from the signification
of envying, as here denoting not to comprehend, as appears from
what follows ; and from the signification of Philisthæa, as de
noting the science of knowledges, consequently by Philistines
are denoted those who are principled in the science of knowledges, see n. 1197, 1198.

3411. Verses 15, 16, 17. *And all the wells, which his
father's servants digged, in the days of Abraham his father, the
Philistines stopped them up, and filled them with dust. And
Abimelech said unto Isaac, Go from being with us, because thou
prevailest exceedingly above us. And Isaac departed thence, and
pitched his camp in the valley of Gerar, and dwelt there.* All
the wells, which his father's servants digged, in the days of
Abraham his father, the Philistines stopped them up, signifies
that they who were principled in the science of knowledges were
not willing to know interior truths which are from the Divine
[principle], and thus obliterated them : and filled them with
dust, signifies by things terrestrial : and Abimelech said unto
Isaac, signifies the Lord's perception concerning that doctrine :
Go from being with us, because thou prevailest exceedingly
above us, signifies that they could not endure those truths by
reason of the Divine [principle] which was in them : and Isaac
departed thence, signifies that the Lord left interior doctrinals :
and pitched his camp in the valley of Gerar, and dwelt there,
signifies that he betook himself to inferior rational things, or
from interior appearances to exterior.

3412. " All the wells which his father's servants digged in
the days of Abraham his father, the Philistines stopped them
up"—that hereby is signified that they, who were principled in
the science of knowledges, were not willing to know interior
truths, which are from the Divine [principle], and thus obliterated them, appears from the signification of wells, as denoting
truths, see n. 2702, 3096 ; in the present case, interior truths,
which are from the Divine [principle], inasmuch as the wells,
by which truths are signified, are said to be digged by his
father's servants, in the days of Abraham his father, for by
Abraham is represented the Lord's essential Divine [principle],
see n. 2011, 2833, 2836, 3251, 3305 ; and from the signification
of stopping up, as denoting not to be willing to know, and thus
to obliterate ; and from the representation of the Philistines, as
denoting those who are principled solely in the science of knowledges, see n. 1197, 1198. The subject now treated of is concerning appearances of truth of an inferior degree, in which they
may be principled who are in the science of knowledges, and who
are here meant by Philistines. With respect to interior truths
which are from the Divine [principle] and are obliterated by

those who are called Philistines, the case is this: in the ancient Church, and afterwards, they were called Philistines, who applied little to life but much to doctrine, and who in process of time even rejected the things appertaining to life, and acknowledged as essentials of the Church the things appertaining to faith, which they separated from life; consequently who made light of the doctrinals of charity, which in the ancient Church were the all of doctrine, and thus obliterated them, and instead thereof professed and taught the doctrinals of faith, and placed the whole of religion therein; and inasmuch as they receded hereby from the life which is of charity, or from charity which is of life, they were particularly called the uncircumcised; for by the uncircumcised were signified all who were not principled in charity, howsoever they might be principled in doctrinals, see n. 2049: such, who receded from charity, removed themselves also from wisdom and intelligence; for no one can be wise and intelligent so as to understand what truth is, unless he be principled in good, that is, in charity, inasmuch as all truth is from good, and has respect to good; thus they who are without good cannot understand truth, and do not even desire to know it. With such, in another life, when they are far from heaven, there sometimes appears a snowy light, but this light is like the light of winter, which, being void of heat, causes no fructification; wherefore also, when such approach towards heaven, their light is turned into mere darkness, and their minds into like darkness, that is into stupor. From these considerations then it may appear, that they who were principled solely in the science of knowledges, were not willing to know interior truths, which are from the Divine [principle], and thus obliterated them.

3413. "And filled them with dust"—that hereby is signified by things terrestrial, that is, by the love of self and of gain, appears from the signification of dust, as denoting such love, see n. 242; the meaning is, that they who are called Philistines, that is, who are not principled in life, but in doctrine, obliterate interior truths by terrestrial loves, which are the loves of self and of gain; in consequence of these loves they were called the uncircumcised, see n. 2039, 2044, 2056, 2632; for they who are in these loves cannot possibly do otherwise than fill the wells of Abraham with dust, that is, obliterate the interior truths of the Word by things terrestrial; for from those loves they can in no wise see things spiritual, that is, the things which are of the light of truth from the Lord, inasmuch as those loves cause darkness, and darkness extinguishes the light of truth, since as was said above, n. 3412, on the approach of the light of truth from the Lord, they who are principled in doctrine only, and not in life, are altogether darkened and confused, yea, become so affected as to be angry, and to desire to dissipate truths by every method possible: for the love of self and of gain is of

such a nature, that it cannot endure anything of truth from the
Divine [principle] to come near unto it; still, however, persons
under the influence of such love can glory and pride themselves
in this, that they know truths, yea, they can preach them from
a kind of zeal, but then it is the fire of those loves which kindles and excites them herein, and their zeal is merely a warmth
thence derived; as may appear plain from this consideration,
that they can preach against their own essential life with a like
zeal or fervour. These are the terrestrial things, with which
the very Word itself, which is the fountain of all truth, is ob-
structed.

3414. "And Abimelech said unto Isaac"—that hereby is
signified the Lord's perception concerning that doctrine, appears
from the signification of saying, as denoting to perceive, con
cerning which see above in many places; and from the repre
sentation of Abimelech, who is here king of the Philistines, as
denoting that doctrine, see n. 3365, 3391; and from the representation of Isaac, as denoting the Lord as to the Divine Rational principle.

3415. "Go from being with us, because thou prevailest over
us exceedingly"—that hereby is signified that they could not
endure interior truths by reason of the Divine [principle] therein, may appear from the signification of the expression, go from
being with us, as denoting not to endure presence; and from
the signification of prevailing exceedingly, as denoting by reason of opulence, in the present case by reason of the Divine
[principle], which was in interior truths; that they who are
called Philistines cannot endure the presence of good, consequently cannot endure the presence of the Divine [principle],
may be seen above, n. 3413.

3416. "And Isaac departed thence"—that hereby is signified that the Lord left interior truths, appears from the signification of departing thence, as denoting to leave, in the present
case to leave interior truths, because these are here treated of;
and from the representation of Isaac, as denoting the Lord as
to the Divine Rational principle. By the Lord's leaving interior truths is signified that He does not open them to persons of
such a character, for there are in the Word throughout internal
truths, but such persons, who are principled in the science of
knowledges, and not at the same time in life, when they read
the Word, do not even see those truths; as may appear from
this consideration, that they who make the essential of salvation to consist in faith, do not even attend to those things which
the Lord so frequently spake concerning love and charity, see
n. 1017, 2373; and they who do attend, call those things the
fruits of faith, which fruits they thus distinguish, yea, separate
from charity, being ignorant of its true nature and quality;
thus the posterior things of the Word appear to them, but not

the anterior things, that is, the exterior things, but not the interior; and to see things posterior or exterior, without seeing anterior or interior things, is to see nothing of what is Divine; this is what is meant by the Lord's leaving interior truths, which is signified by Isaac's departing thence; not that the Lord leaves any, but that they remove themselves from the Lord, inasmuch as they remove themselves from those things which appertain to life.

3417. " And he pitched (or measured out) his camp in the valley of Gerar, and dwelt there"—that hereby is signified that he betook himself to inferior rational things, or from interior appearances to exterior, appears from the signification of pitching (or measuring out) a camp, as denoting to arrange in order; and from the signification of the valley of Gerar, as denoting inferior rational things, or the exterior appearances of truth, for valley signifies inferior things, or, what is the same, exterior things, see n. 1723, and Gerar denotes things appertaining to faith, consequently the things appertaining to truth, see n. 1209, 2504, 3365, 3384, 3385 ; and from the signification of dwelling (or inhabiting), as denoting to be and to live, see n. 3384; hence it is evident, that by pitching his camp in the valley of Gerar and dwelling there, is signified, that the Lord arranged truth, in such order that they might be adequate also to the compre hension and genius of those who are not principled in life, but in the doctrinals of faith; as may appear from the Word, where also truths are thus adapted.   For example: they who are prin cipled in doctrinals and not so much in life, know no other than that the kingdom of heaven is similar to kingdoms on earth in this respect, that authority over others therein constitutes great ness, the delight arising from such authority being the only delight with which they are acquainted, wherefore the Lord spake also according to this appearance, as in Matthew, " Whosoever doeth and teacheth, *he shall be called great in the kingdom of the heavens*," v. 19; and in David, " I have said, *Ye are gods*, and ye are all the sons of the *Highest*," lxxxii. 6; John x. 34, 35; and inasmuch as the disciples themselves had at first no other sentiments respecting the kingdom of heaven, than such as were grounded in earthly greatness and pre-eminence, as appears from Matt. chap. xviii. 1; Mark ix. 34; Luke ix. 46; and also had an idea of sitting on the right-hand and the left of a king, Matt. xx. 20, 21, 24; Mark x. 37; therefore also the Lord replied according to their apprehension and idea, saying (when they disputed which of them should be greatest), " Ye shall eat and drink on My table in My kingdom, and shall *sit on thrones*, judging the twelve tribes of Israel," Luke xxii. 24, 30; Matt. xix. 28; for at this time they did not know that heavenly delight was not a delight grounded in greatness and pre-eminence, but a delight grounded in humiliation and the affection of serving others, consequently in a desire of being the least and not the greatest, as the Lord teaches in Luke, "Whosoever is least among you all, *he shall be great,*" ix. 48. Thus they who are principled in the science of knowledges, and not in the life of charity, cannot know that there exists any delight but what results from pre-eminence; and inasmuch as this is the only delight of which they have any idea, therefore they are altogether ignorant of heavenly delight resulting from humiliation and an affection of being serviceable to others, that is, the delight of love to the Lord and of charity towards their neighbour, consequently of the blessedness and happiness thence derived; this is the reason why the Lord spake in the way of application to their infirmity, that so they might be excited and introduced to good, both to learn, and to teach, and to practise it; nevertheless He teaches what greatness and pre-eminence in heaven is, Matt. xix. 30; chap. xx. 16, 25, 27, 28; Mark x. 31, 42, 43, 44, 45; Luke ix. 48; chap. xiii. 30; chap. xxii. 25, 26, 27, 28: these and such like are the appearances of truth of an inferior degree; it being true in a respective sense, that in heaven all become great, pre-eminent, powerful, and of authority, for one angel has greater power than myriads of infernal spirits, yet not of himself, but from the Lord: and only so far from the Lord, as he believes that he has no power self-derived, and thus that he is least; and this he may believe, so far as he is in humiliation, and the affection of being serviceable to others, that is, so far as he is principled in the good of love to the Lord, and of charity towards his neighbour.

3418. Verse 18. *And Isaac returned, and digged again the wells of waters, which they digged in the days of Abraham his father, and the Philistines stopped them up after the death of Abraham; and he called their names, according to the names which his father called them.* Isaac returned and digged again the wells of waters, which they digged in the days of Abraham his father, signifies that the Lord opened those truths which were known and received amongst the ancients: and the Philistines stopped them up after the death of Abraham, signifies that they who were principled in the science of knowledges only, denied those truths: and he called their names, signifies their quality: according to the names which his father called them, signifies significatives of truth.

3419. "Isaac returned and digged again the wells of waters which they digged in the days of Abraham his father"—that hereby is signified that the Lord opened those truths which were known and received among the ancients, appears from the representation of Isaac, as denoting the Lord as to the Divine Rational principle, concerning which see above; and from the signification of returning and digging again, as denoting to open again; and from the signification of wells of waters, as de-

noting truths of knowledges ; that wells are truths, see n. 2702,
3096, and that waters are knowledges, see n. 28, 2702, 3058 ;
and from the signification of the days of Abraham his father, as
denoting time and state antecedent as to truths, which truths are
signified by the words, *which they digged* at that time, consequently which were known and received amongst the ancients ;
that days denote time and state, see n. 23, 487, 488, 493, 893 ;
when days denote state, then by Abraham the father is repre
sented the essential Divine [principle] of the Lord, before that
He adjoined to it the human [principle], see n. 2833, 2836, 3251 ;
when they denote time, then by Abraham the father are signified the goods and truths which were derived from the Lord's
Divine [principle] before He adjoined to it the Human [prin-
ciple], thus the goods and truths which were known and received
amongst the ancients. The truths which were known and received amongst the ancients, are at this day obliterated, insomuch that it is scarce known to any one that they ever existed,
and that they could be any other than what are taught at this
day ; nevertheless they were totally different : the ancients had
representatives and *significatives* of things celestial and spiritual
appertaining to the Lord's kingdom, consequently to the Lord
Himself, and they who understood such representatives and significatives, were called wise ; and in reality they were wise, for
hereby they were enabled to discourse with spirits and angels,
inasmuch as angelic discourse, which is incomprehensible to
man, as being spiritual and celestial, when it is conveyed down
to man who is in a natural sphere, falls into representatives and
significatives such as exist in the Word, and hence it is that the
Word is a holy code or volume ; for what is Divine cannot be
presented or exhibited otherwise before the natural man, so as
that a full correspondence may exist. And inasmuch as the ancients were principled in representatives and significatives of the
Lord's kingdom, in which kingdom nothing prevails but celestial and spiritual love, therefore they had also *doctrinals* which
treated solely *concerning love to God and charity towards their
neighbour,* by virtue of which doctrinals they were also called
wise ; from these doctrinals they knew that the Lord would
come into the world, and that Jehovah was in Him, and that He
would make the human [principle] in Himself Divine, and would
thereby save the human race ; from the same doctrinals they
knew also what charity is, viz. that it is an affection of being
serviceable to others without having respect to any recompense ;
and also what is meant by the neighbour towards whom charity
is to be exercised, viz. that it means all in the universe, but still
each with discrimination ; these doctrinals are at this day utterly
lost, and instead thereof the doctrinals of faith are adopted,
which the ancients accounted as nothing respectively ; those
doctrinals, viz. of love to the Lord and of charity towards one's

neighbour, are rejected at this day, partly by those who in the Word are called Babylonians and Chaldeans, and partly by those who are called Philistines and also Egyptians, and they are so destroyed, that there scarce remains any trace or vestige thereof; for who knows at this day what that charity is, which is void of all self-respect, and is averse to every thing that merely regards self? and who knows what is meant by neighbour, viz. that it means every individual person with discrimination according to the quantity and quality of good appertaining to each, thus it means good itself, consequently in a supreme sense the Lord Himself, because He is in all good, and all good is from Him, and the good which is not from Him is not good, howsoever it may appear to be so? and inasmuch as it is not known what charity is, and what neighbour, it is not known also who they are that in the Word are signified by the poor, by the miserable, by the needy, by the sick, by the hungry and thirsty, by the oppressed, by widows, by orphans, by captives, by the naked, by sojourners, by the blind, by the deaf, by the halt, by the lame, and by others; when yet the doctrinals of the ancients taught who are to be understood by persons of this description, and to what class of neighbour, and thus of charity, they belonged; according to those doctrinals the whole Word is written as to the sense of the letter, and therefore whosoever is unacquainted with them, cannot possibly know any interior sense of the Word; as in Isaiah, "Is it not to break bread to the *hungry*, and that thou take into thine house the *afflicted outcasts*, when thou seest the *naked* that thou cover him, and that thou hide not thyself from thine own flesh? then shall thy light break forth as the morning, and thy health shall bud forth speedily, and thy righteousness shall walk before thee, the glory of Jehovah shall gather thee," lviii. 7, 8; he who lays stress on the literal sense of these words, believes that if he only gives bread to a hungry person, takes into his house afflicted outcasts or vagabonds, and covers the naked, he shall on that account be admitted into the glory of Jehovah, or into heaven, when nevertheless such are mere external acts, which even the wicked may perform in order to merit heaven; but by the hungry, the afflicted, the naked, are signified those who are spiritually such, consequently different states of misery incident to man, who is the neighbour towards whom charity is to be exercised. So in David, "Doing judgment to the *oppressed*, giving bread to the *hungry*, Jehovah looseth *the bound*, Jehovah openeth the *blind*, Jehovah raiseth up the *bowed down*, Jehovah loveth the just, Jehovah guardeth the *sojourners*, He supporteth the *fatherless* and *widow*," Psalm cxlvi. 7, 8, 9; where by the oppressed, the hungry, the bound, the blind, the bowed down, the sojourners, the fatherless and the widow, are not meant those who are commonly so called, but who are such as to spiritual things,

or as to their souls; who these were, and in what state and
degree they were neighbours, consequently what charity was to
be exercised towards them, was taught by the doctrinals of the
ancients; not to mention many other passages which occur in
the Old Testament throughout; for the Divine [principle], when
it descends to the natural principle appertaining to man, fixes
its descent in such things as works of charity, with discrimination according to genera and species; in like manner also the
Lord spake, because He spake from the essential Divine [prin-
ciple], as in Matthew, "The king shall say to those on the
right-hand, Come ye blessed of My Father, possess the kingdom
prepared for you; for I was an *hungered* and ye gave Me to eat,
I was *thirsty* and ye gave Me to drink, I was a *stranger* and ye
gathered Me, I was *naked* and ye clothed Me, I was *sick* and
ye visited Me, I was in *prison* and ye came to Me," xxv. 34,
35, 36; by the works here recounted are signified universal
genera (kinds) of charity, and in what degree the several genera
are good, or in what degree they are good who are the neighbours towards whom charity is to be exercised, and that the
Lord in a supreme sense is neighbour, for He says, "So much
as ye have done to one of the least of these My brethren, ye
have done to Me," verse 40, of the same chapter. From these
few considerations it may appear what is meant by the truths
taught and received amongst the ancients; but that these truths
are altogether obliterated by those who are principled in the doctrinals of faith, and not in the life of charity, that is, by those
who in the Word are called Philistines, is signified by the Philistines stopping up the wells after the death of Abraham, which
is the subject next treated of.

3420. "The Philistines stopped them up after the death of
Abraham"—that hereby is signified that they who were principled only in the science of knowledges denied those truths,
appears from the signification of stopping up, as denoting not
to be willing to know, and what is the same thing, to deny,
thus to obliterate, concerning which see above, n. 3412; and
from the representation of the Philistines, as denoting those
who are principled only in the science of knowledges, see n
1197, 1198, 3412, 3413. They are principled in the science of
knowledges, who are principled in the doctrinals of faith, and
are not willing to know the truths of knowledges or of doctrinals. The truths of knowledges or of doctrinals are those
which appertain to life, and respect charity towards our neighbour and love to the Lord; doctrine, to which doctrinals and
knowledges appertain, only teaches those truths; he therefore
who teaches what ought to be done, and does not do it, is not
willing to know truths, for they are contrary to his life, and
what is contrary to his life he also denies It is in consequence of such conduct that the doctrinals of love and charity,

which, in the ancient Church, were the all of doctrine, are obliterated.

3421. " And called their names"—that hereby is signified
their quality, appears from the signification of calling names,
as denoting quality, see n. 144, 145, 1754, 1896, 2009, 2724,
3006, 3237; and inasmuch as to call names, or name, denotes
quality, therefore, *to call*, without the addition of name, in the
internal sense of the Word, signifies *to be of such or such a quality*, as in Isaiah, " Hear this, ye house of Israel, called by the
name of Israel, and they have departed from the waters of Judah, because *from the city of holiness are they called*, and stay
themselves upon the God of Israel," xlviii. 1, 2 ; where to be
called from the city of holiness, denotes to be of such a quality :
so in Luke, " Behold thou shalt conceive in the womb, and
shalt bring forth a son, and shalt call His name Jesus, He
shall be great, and *shall be called the Son of the Highest*," i. 31,
32; where to be called the Son of the Highest denotes to be so.

3422. " According to the names which his father called
them"—that hereby are signified significatives of truth, appears
from this consideration, that the names which in ancient times
were given to persons, places, and things, were all significative,
see n. 340, 1946, 2643, thus the names given to fountains and
wells were significative of those things which were formerly
understood by fountains and wells, which things that they had
relation to truth, was shown, n. 2702, 3096 ; and whereas names
were significative, by name also, and by calling by name in
general, is signified the quality either of a thing or state, as was
just now observed above, n. 3421 ; and this being the case, by
names in the Word, in its internal sense, is not signified any
person, or any nation, or any kingdom, or any city, but a thing
in all instances whatsoever. Every one may conclude, that in
the present case by wells is signified somewhat heavenly, for
unless this had been their signification, to mention so many particulars concerning wells would not have been worthy the Divine
Word, because it would have been of no use to be acquainted
with them : as for instance, that the Philistines stopped up the
wells which the servants of Abraham digged ; that Isaac digged
them again, and that he called their names according to their
former names ; and afterwards that the servants of Isaac digged
a well in the valley, about which the shepherds disputed ; and
that they digged again another well, about which they also disputed ; and afterwards another well, about which they did not
dispute ; and again another ; and lastly, that they told him concerning a new well, verses 15, 18, 19, 20, 21, 22, 25, 32, 33 ;
but the heavenly principle, which is signified by these wells, is
now made manifest from the internal sense.

3423. Verses 19, 20, 21. *And the servants of Isaac digged
in the valley, and they found there a well of living waters.*

And the shepherds of Gerar disputed with the shepherds of Isaac, saying, We have the waters: and he called the name of the well Esek, because they contended with him. And they digged another well, and they disputed also over it, and he called the name thereof Sitnah. The servants of Isaac digged in the valley, and they found there a well of living waters, signifies the Word as to the literal sense, in which is the internal sense: and the shepherds of Gerar disputed with the shepherds of Isaac, signifies that they who taught, did not see any such thing therein, because opposite things appear: saying, We have the waters, signifies they are in the truth: and he called the name of the well Esek, because they contended with him, signifies denial on account of those things, also on account of other things, as being contrary to them, and on account of several things besides: and they digged another well, and they disputed also over it, signifies the internal sense of the Word, whether there be such a sense: and he called the name thereof Sitnah, signifies their quality.

3424. "The servants of Isaac digged in the valley, and they found there a well of living waters"—that hereby is signified the Word as to the literal sense, in which is the internal sense, appears from the signification of digging in a valley, as denoting to inquire lower according to truths where they are; for to dig is to inquire, and a valley is what is below, see n. 1723, 3417; and from the signification of a well of living waters, as denoting the Word in which are Truths Divine, thus denoting the Word as to the literal sense in which is the internal sense. That the Word is called a fountain, and indeed a fountain of living waters, is well known; the ground and reason why the Word is also called a well, is, because the sense of the letter is respectively such, and because the Word in respect to the spiritual is not a fountain but a well, see n. 2702, 3096; inasmuch as a valley denotes what is below, or, what is the same thing, somewhat more external, and the fountain was found in a valley, and the literal sense is the lower or more external sense of the Word, therefore it is the literal sense which is understood; but whereas in the literal sense is contained the internal sense, that is, the heavenly and Divine sense, therefore the waters thereof are said to be living, as is said also of the waters which went forth under the threshold of the new house, in Ezechiel, where it is written, "And it shall come to pass, every soul a wild beast which creepeth, to *whichsoever the river there comes, liveth;* and there shall be exceeding much fish, because those waters come thither and are healed, and *every thing liveth whither the river cometh,*" xlvii. 9; where the river is the Word; the waters which cause every thing to live, are the Divine Truths contained in the Word; fish are scientifics, see n. 40, 991. That the Word of the Lord is such, as to give life to him that thirsteth, that is, to him that desires life, and that it is a fountain whose waters are living, the Lord also teaches in John, in these words, speaking to the woman of Samaria at *Jacob's well*, " If thou knewest the gift of God, and who it is that saith to thee, Give me to drink, thou wouldst ask of him, and he would give thee living water; whoso drinketh of the *water* which I shall give him, shall never thirst, but the water which I shall give him shall become in him *a fountain of water springing up unto eternal life*," iv. 10, 14. The ground and reason why the Word is living or alive, and thus gives life, is, because in a supreme sense the Lord is therein treated of, and in the inmost sense His kingdom, in which the Lord is all; and this being the case, there is in the Word essential life, which flows into the minds of those who read it under a holy influence; hence it is that the Lord declares Himself, as to the Word which is from Himself, to be a fountain of water springing up unto eternal life, see also n. 2702. That the Word of the Lord is also called a well, as it is called a fountain, appears from these words in Moses, " Israel sung a song; Rise up, O well, answer ye to it; the *well*, the princes *digged*, the chiefs of the people *digged out* for a lawgiver with their staves," Numb. xxi. 17, 18; these words were spoken at the place Beer, that is, at the place of the well; that by well in this passage is signified the Word of the ancient Church, spoken of above, n. 2897, appears evident from what is there said; princes are primary truths, see n. 1482, 2089; the chiefs of the people are inferior truths, such as are those contained in the literal sense, see n. 1259, 1260, 2928, 3295; that lawgiver is the Lord, is manifest: staves denote the powers which they possessed.

3425. " The shepherds of Gerar disputed with the shepherds of Isaac"—that hereby is signified that they who taught did not see any such thing therein, because opposite things appear, is manifest from the signification of disputing, when the internal sense of the Word is treated of, as denoting to deny it to be such, by thus saying, that they do not see it; and from the signification of shepherds, as denoting those who teach, see n. 343; and from the signification of Gerar, as denoting faith, see n. 1209, 2504, 3365, 3384. Thus the shepherds of the valley of Gerar are those who acknowledge only the literal sense of the Word: the reason why they see no such thing in the Word, viz. no interior sense, is, because opposite things appear, viz. the things which are in the literal sense; nevertheless they are not opposite, although they appear opposite, inasmuch as they altogether correspond; the reason why they appear opposite, is, because they, who thus see the Word, are in an opposite principle. The case in this respect is like that of a man, who is in an opposite principle in himself, that is, whose external or natural man is altogether at disagreement with his internal or spiritual man. Such a person sees the things which are of the internal or spiritual man as it were opposite to himself, when yet he himself, as to the external or natural man, is in the opposite, and if he was not in the opposite, but his external or natural man yielded obedience to the internal or spiritual man, they would entirely correspond. As for example, he who is in an opposite principle, believes that riches are to be absolutely renounced, and all pleasures of the body and of the world, consequently the delights of life, in order to his receiving eternal life, such delights being supposed opposite to spiritual life; whereas they are not opposite in themselves, but correspond: for they are means conducive to an end, which end is, that the internal or spiritual man may enjoy them for the exercises of charity, and moreover may live content in a healthful body. The ends regarded are what alone cause either contrariety between the internal and external man, or correspondence. Contrariety has place, when the riches, pleasures, and delights here spoken of become ends, for in this case, spiritual and celestial things, which appertain to the internal man, are despised and ridiculed, yea, are rejected; whereas correspondence has place, when those things are not made ends, but become means conducive to superior ends, viz. to such things as regard a life after death, consequently which regard the kingdom of heaven and the Lord Himself. In this case, corporeal and worldly things appear to man as scarce any thing respectively; and when he thinks of such things, he values them only as means conducive to ends. Hence it is manifest, that those things which appear opposite, are not opposite in themselves; and that the reason of their appearing so is, because they who judge of them are in an opposite principle. They who are not in an opposite principle, act, and speak, and acquire riches, and also enjoy pleasures, in like manner as they who are in an opposite principle, insomuch that they can scarce be distinguished by their external appearance; the reason is, because what alone distinguishes them is the end regarded, or, what is the same thing, the ruling love, for the ruling love is the end regarded. But although they appear similar in their external form, or as to the body, yet they are altogether dissimilar in their internal form, or as to the spirit; where there is correspondence, that is, where the external man corresponds to the internal, the spirit of the man is fair and beautiful, such as heavenly love is in its form; but where there is opposition, that is, where the external man is opposite to the internal, howsoever there may be a resemblance of the other as to what is external, yet the spirit in this case is dark and deformed, such as is self-love and the love of the world, that is, such as is contempt and hatred of others in its form. The case is similar in respect to very many passages in the Word, viz. that the things of the literal sense appear opposite to what is contained in the internal sense, when yet they are by no means opposite, but correspond entirely; as for example, it is frequently said in the Word, that Jehovah or the Lord is angry, is wroth, causes vastation, and casts into hell, when yet He is never angry, and still less does He cast any one into hell; the former is according to the sense of the letter, but the latter is according to the internal sense; these appear opposite, but the reason is, because man is in an opposite principle. The case in this respect is like that of the Lord's appearing as a sun to the angels in heaven, and thereby as a kind of vernal warmth, and a light as at day-dawn, whereas to the infernals he appears altogether as somewhat opake, and thereby as winter like cold, and as midnight darkness; consequently to the angels He appears in love and charity, but to the infernals in hatred and enmity; thus to the latter according to the sense of the letter, as being angry, being wroth, being the cause of vastation and casting into hell; but to the former according to the internal sense, as in no wise being angry and wroth, and still less as causing vastation and casting into hell. Since therefore in the Word those things are treated of which are contrary to the Divine [principle], they cannot otherwise be exhibited than according to appearance; it is also the Divine [principle] which the wicked change into what is diabolical, and which thus operates; wherefore also in proportion as they approach to the Divine [principle], in the same proportion they cast themselves into infernal torments. The case is the same with the Lord's words in the prayer, " Lead us not into temptation;" it is according to the sense of the letter that He leads into temptation but the internal sense is, that He leads no one into temptation, as is well known, see n. 1875; the same is true in respect to other things as expressed in the literal sense of the Word.

3426. " Saying, We have waters"—that hereby is signified that they are in the truth, or that they have truths, appears from the signification of waters, as denoting knowledges, and also truths, see n. 28, 680, 739, 2702, 3058.

3427. "And he called the name of the well Esek, because they contended with him"—that hereby is signified denial on account of those things, also on account of other things, as being contrary to them, and on account of several things besides, appears from this consideration, that the names, which were given of old, were significative of the thing or state, see n. 3422; hence they were enabled to recollect several particulars concerning such thing or state, especially respecting the quality thereof; in the present case, a name was given to the well from the circumstance of the shepherds of Gerar disputing with the shepherds of Isaac: that to dispute or contend signifies also to deny, may be seen n. 3425. Hence the name Esek, which in the original tongue signifies contention or dispute, and is de-

rived from an expression nearly related thereto, which signifies
oppression and injury; and whereas by well in this passage is
signified the Word as to the literal sense, in which is the internal sense, therefore by Esek, or contention, is signified a denial
of the internal sense of the Word; the causes of denial are also
contained in the same expression, which causes, it is evident,
are grounded in what was said above, n. 3425, viz. that the literal and spiritual senses of the Word appear opposite to each
other.   With respect to the internal sense of the Word, the case
is this: they who are principled merely in the science of knowledges, and are called Philistines, and they who are principled
merely in the doctrinals of faith, and are called the valley of
Gerar, being not principled in any charity towards their neighbour, cannot possibly do otherwise than deny the internal sense
of the Word, inasmuch as the Word in its internal sense treats
of nothing else but love to the Lord, and love towards our
neighbour; wherefore the Lord says, that on these two commandments hang the law and the prophets, that is, the whole
Word, Matt. xxii. 35, 36, 37, 38, 39, 40: how far such persons
deny the internal sense of the Word, was also given me to see
from the state of such in another life, for when it is only mentioned in their presence, that there is an internal sense of the
Word, which does not appear in the literal sense, and that it
treats of love to the Lord and charity towards our neighbour,
there is instantly perceivable not only a denial on the part of
such spirits, but also an aversion, yea, a loathing thereby excited: this is the primary cause of denial; another cause is,
that they altogether invert the Word, setting that above which
is beneath, or, what is the same thing, setting that before (or in
front) which is behind (or in the rear); for they establish it as
a principle that faith is the essential of the Church, and that
the things appertaining to love to the Lord and charity towards
our neighbour, are the fruits of faith; when yet the real case is
this, if love to the Lord be compared to the tree of life in the
paradise of Eden, charity and its works are the fruits thence
derived, whereas faith and all things appertaining thereto are
merely leaves; since therefore they so invert the Word, as to
deduce the origin of fruits not from the tree but from the leaves,
it is not to be wondered at that they deny the internal sense of
the Word, and acknowledge only its literal sense, for from the
literal sense any doctrinal tenet, even the most heretical, may
be confirmed, as is well known.   Moreover, they who are
merely in doctrinals of faith, but not in the good of life,
must needs be in persuasive faith, that is, in preconceived principles, false as well as true, consequently they must be more
stupid than others, for so far as any one is in persuasive faith,
so far he is stupid; but so far as any one is in the good of life,
that is, in love to the Lord and charity towards his neighbour,

so far he is in intelligence, that is, in faith from the Lord; hence also it is, that the former must needs be in the negative respecting the internal sense of the Word, but the latter must needs be in the affirmative; with those also, who are principled merely in doctrinals, and not in the good of life, the interiors are closed, so that light from the Lord cannot flow in, and give them to perceive that it is so; whereas, with those who are principled in love to the Lord, the interiors are open, so that the light of truth from the Lord can flow in, affect their minds, and give a perception that it is so. A further cause is, that they have no other delight in reading the Word, than what arises from the acquirement of honours, and riches, and reputation thereby, which delight is the delight of self-love and the love of the world, and this to such a degree, that in case such acquisitions were not to be derived from the Word, they would entirely reject it; they who are of such a character, not only deny in their heart the internal sense of the Word, when they hear of it, but also the very literal sense, howsoever they may imagine that they believe it; for whosoever regards as an end the delight of self-love and the love of the world, entirely ejects from his heart every thing appertaining to eternal life, and only with his natural and corporeal man makes a show of such things as he calls truths, not for the sake of the Lord and His kingdom, but for the sake of himself and those with whom he is connected. These and several other things operate as causes, why they, who are called shepherds of the valley of Gerar, and Philistines, deny the internal sense of the Word.

3428. "And they digged another well, and disputed also over it"—that hereby is signified the internal sense of the Word, whether there be such a sense, may appear from the signification of another well, and of disputing, concerning which see above, thus from the series of the things treated of; for they who deny any thing, as they who deny the internal sense of the Word, when they again dispute or contend, must needs dispute or contend about the existence of such a thing. It is well known that several disputes at this day go no further than this; but so long as men remain in debate, whether a thing exist, and whether it be so, it is impossible to make any advance into any thing of wisdom; for in the very thing which is the subject of debate, there are innumerable particulars which cannot be seen so long as the thing itself is not acknowledged, inasmuch as all and singular the things appertaining thereto are in such case unknown; modern erudition scarce advances beyond these limits of debate, viz. whether a thing exist, and whether it be so, and of consequence there is an exclusion from the intelligence of truth; as for example, he who merely contends whether there exists an internal sense of the Word, cannot possibly see the innumerable, yea, indefinite things, which

are contained in the internal sense; as again, he who disputes
whether charity be any thing in the Church, and whether or no
the things of faith be not the all thereof, cannot possibly know
the innumerable, yea, indefinite things, which are contained in
charity, but remains altogether in ignorance of what charity is;
the case is the same in regard to a life after death, the resurrection of the dead, the last judgment, the existence of heaven
and hell; they who only dispute whether such things exist,
stand out of the doors of wisdom so long as they dispute, and
are like persons who only knock at the door, and cannot even
look into wisdom's magnificent palaces; and what is surprising,
people of this description fancy themselves wise in comparison
with others, and so much the wiser in proportion to their greater
skill in debating whether a thing be so, and especially in confirming themselves that it is not so; when yet the simple, who
are principled in good, and whom such disputants despise, can
perceive in a moment, without any dispute, much more without
learned controversy, both the existence of the thing, and also
its nature and quality; these latter have a common or general
sense of the perception of truth, whereas the former have extinguished this sense by such things as incline them first to
determine whether the thing exists; the Lord speaks both of the
former, and of the latter, when He says, "I thank thee, Father,
that thou hast hid these things from the wise and intelligent,
and revealed them unto babes," Matt. xi. 25; Luke x. 21.

3429. "And he called the name thereof Sitnah"—that
hereby is signified their quality, appears from the signification
of calling a name, as denoting quality, see n. 144, 145, 1754,
1896, 2009, 2724, 3006, 3421; and from the signification of
Sitnah, as denoting, in the original tongue, aversion, which is
a further degree of denial.

3430. Verses 22, 23. *And he removed thence and digged
another well, and they did not dispute over it, and he called the
name thereof Rehoboth, and said, Because now Jehovah has made
us to be dilated, and we shall be fruitful in the earth. And
he went up thence to Beersheba.* He removed thence, signifies
to things inferior still: and digged another well, and they did
not dispute over it, signifies the literal sense of the Word: and
he called the name thereof Rehoboth, signifies quality thence
derived, as to truth: and said, Because now Jehovah has made
us to be dilated, signifies increments (increasings) of truth thence:
and we shall be fruitful in the earth, signifies increments of
good thence: and he went up thence to Beersheba, signifies
that hence the doctrine of faith was Divine.

3431. "And he removed thence"—that hereby is signified
to things inferior still, appears from the signification of removing (or transferring), as denoting to other things which follow
in the series, therefore in the present case to inferior or exterior

truths, because the subject hitherto in order treated of has been concerning superior or interior truths; inferior or exterior truths are those which are extant in the literal sense of the Word, adequate to the apprehension of the natural man; and these truths now come to be treated of.

3432. "And digged another well, and they did not dispute over it"—that hereby is signified the literal sense of the Word, appears from the signification of well, as denoting the Word, see n. 3702, 3096, 3424; in the present case the Word as to the literal sense, for it is said, that he removed thence, and digged another well, and that they did not dispute over it, by which is signified that sense of the Word which is exterior, and which they do not deny, and it is this which is called the literal sense. The literal sense of the Word is threefold, viz. historical, prophetical, and doctrinal; each whereof is such that it may be apprehended even by those who are in externals. With respect to the Word, the case is this: in the most ancient time, when the Church was celestial, the written Word was not, for the men of that Church had the Word inscribed on their hearts, inasmuch as the Lord taught them immediately through heaven what was good, and thereby what was true, and gave them to perceive each from a principle of love and charity, and to know from revelation. The very essential Word to them was the Lord. After this Church another succeeded, which was not celestial but spiritual, and this in the beginning had no other Word than what was collected from the most ancient people, which Word was representative of the Lord, and significative of His kingdom; thus the internal sense was to this people the essential Word. That they had also a written Word, as well historical as prophetical, which is no longer extant, and that in this Word there was in like manner an internal sense, which had relation to the Lord, may be seen, n. 2686; hence it was the wisdom of that time both to speak and write by representatives and significatives, within the Church concerning things Divine, and out of the Church concerning other things, as is evident from the writings of those ancient people which are come down to us: but in process of time this wisdom perished, insomuch that at length it was not known that there existed any internal sense even in the books of the Word. The Jewish and Israelitish nation was of this character, so that they accounted the prophetic Word holy merely by reason of its resemblance to the ancient Word in sound, and because they heard the name of Jehovah in the sense of the letter, not believing that any thing Divine lay deeper hid within; nor does the Christian world think more holily concerning the Word. Hence it may appear how in process of time wisdom retired from inmost things to outermost, and man removed himself from heaven, and at length descended even to the dust of the earth, wherein wisdom is now made to consist. Forasmuch as this was the case with the Word, viz. that its internal sense was successively obliterated, and this to such a degree, that at this day it is not known that such a sense exists, when yet this sense is the very essential Word in which the Divine [principle] proximately dwells, therefore the successive states thereof are described in this chapter.

3433. "And he called the name thereof Rehoboth"—that hereby is signified the quality thence derived as to truth, appears from the signification of calling a name, as denoting quality, see n. 144, 145, 1754, 1896, 2009, 2724, 3006, 3421; and from the signification of Rehoboth, as denoting truths, for Rehoboth in the original tongue signifies breadths, and that breadths in the internal sense of the Word denote truths, may be seen, n. 1613.

3434. "And he said, Because now Jehovah hath made us to be dilated"—that hereby is signified increments (increases) of truth thence derived, appears from the signification of breadth, as denoting truth, concerning which see immediately above, n. 3433; hence to be dilated is to receive increments of truth.

3435. "And we shall be fruitful in the earth"—that hereby are signified increments of good thence derived, appears from the signification of being fruitful, as denoting increments of good; that to be fruitful is predicated of good, and to be multiplied is predicated of truth, see n. 43, 55, 913, 983, 2846, 2847; and from the signification of earth, as denoting the Church, and whatever is of the Church, concerning which see n. 662, 1066, 1067, 1262, 1733, 1850, 2928, 3325.

3436. "And he went up thence to Beersheba"—that hereby is signified that thence the doctrine of faith was Divine, appears from the signification of Beersheba, as denoting the doctrine of faith Divine, see n. 2723, 2858, 2859: the doctrine of faith which is here signified by Beersheba, is the very literal sense of the Word, for the Word is essential doctrine; and although the Word as to the literal sense is such, that truths may thence be derived, it is also such, that things not true may thereby be confirmed, as is well known from the case of heresies: but whosoever reads the Word to the end that he may grow wise, that is, may do what is good and understand what is true, he is instructed according to such end and according to the affection thereof, for the Lord flows in whilst he knows not, and illuminates his mind, and wherein he hesitates, gives understanding from other passages; moreover, whosoever is in simple good, and in simplicity believes the Word according to its literal sense, he is gifted with the faculty of perceiving truths, when he is instructed in another life by the angels; and in the mean time, the few truths which appertain to him are vivified by charity and innocence, and when charity and innocence are in

truths, then the false principles, which also infused themselves
in the shade of his ignorance, are not hurtful, not being adjoined
to good, but being withheld therefrom as it were in the circumferences, whereby they can easily be cast out : but the case is
otherwise with those who are not principled in the good of
life, for with such, the false principles which by misinterpreta-
tion they have forged from the Word, possess the middle, or as
it were centre, whilst truths possess the circuits or circumferences, wherefore false principles are what are adjoined to the
evil of their life, and truths are dissipated.

3437. Verses 24, 25. *And Jehovah appeared to him in that
night, and said, I am the God of Abraham thy father, fear not
because I am with thee, and I will bless thee, and will make thy
seed to be multiplied for the sake of Abraham My servant. And
he builded there an altar, and called on the name of Jehovah,
and stretched out his tent there ; and the servants of Isaac digged
a well there.* Jehovah appeared to him in that night, and said,
signifies the Lord's perception concerning that obscure principle
(or state) : I am the God of Abraham thy father, fear not because
I am with thee, signifies that the Divine [principle] was also
there : and I will bless thee, and will make thy seed to be multiplied, signifies that hence would be increase of good and of
truth : for the sake of Abraham My servant, signifies from the
Lord's Divine Human [principle] : and he builded there an altar, signifies a significative and representative of the Lord : and
called on the name of Jehovah, signifies worship thence : and
stretched out his tent there, signifies an holy principle therein :
and the servants of Isaac digged a well there, signifies doctrine
thence derived.

3438. "Jehovah appeared to him in that night, and said"
—that hereby is signified the Lord's perception concerning that
obscure [principle or state], appears from the signification of
Jehovah's appearing and saying, when it is predicated of the
Lord, as denoting to perceive from the Divine [principle] ; that
by Jehovah appearing to him is signified from the Divine [prin-
ciple], may be seen, n. 3367, and that to say is to perceive, see
n. 2862, 3395 ; for Jehovah was in Him, consequently so long
as the human [principle] was not yet glorified, the appearing of
Jehovah was perception Divine, or perception from the Divine
[principle], wherefore by Jehovah appearing to him and saying,
nothing else is signified ; and from the signification of night, as
denoting a state of shade or an obscure [principle or state], concerning which see n. 1712 ; by this obscure [principle or state]
is signified the literal sense of the Word, this sense, in respect
to the internal sense, being like shade in respect to light. In
order to show still more clearly how the case is in regard to the
literal sense of the Word, we shall add a few words more on the
subject ; the internal sense is to the literal sense, as man's inte-

rior or celestial and spiritual principles are to his exterior or natural and corporeal principles; his interior principles are in the
light of heaven, whereas his exterior principles are in the light
of the world; what is the nature of the difference between the
light of heaven and the light of the world, consequently between
those things which appertain to the light of heaven, and those
things which appertain to the light of the world, may be seen,
n. 1521 to 1523, 1619 to 1632, 1783, 1880, 2776, 3138, 3167,
3190, 3195, 3222, 3223, 3225, 3337, 3339, 3341, 3413, viz. that
it is like the difference between the light of day and the shade
of night; and whereas man is in this shade, and is not willing
to know that in truth from the Lord there is light, he cannot
believe otherwise than that his shade is light, yea, also on the
other hand that light is shade; for he is in this respect like a
bird of night, which, whilst it flies in the shade of night, thinks
that it is in the light, but whilst in the light of day, it thinks
itself to be in the shade; for the internal eye, that is, the
understanding, by which man sees interiorly, with such a person is no otherwise formed, for he has formed it no otherwise,
inasmuch as he opens it when he looks downwards, that is, to
worldly and corporeal things, and shuts it when he should look
upwards, that is, to spiritual and celestial things; the case is
the same in respect to the Word with persons of this character,
what appears in its literal sense, this they believe to be light,
but what appears in the internal sense, this they believe to be
shade; for the Word appears to every one according to his
quality; when nevertheless the internal sense of the Word, in
respect to its literal sense, is as the light of heaven in respect
to the light of the world, see n. 3016, 3108, that is, as the
light of day in respect to the light of night. In the internal
sense there are singular things, whereof myriads constitute together one particular which is exhibited in the literal sense; or,
what is the same thing, in the internal sense there are particular
things, whereof myriads constitute together one common or
general thing which is in the literal sense, and it is this common
or general thing which appears to man, but not the particular
things which are in it and which constitute it; still however
the order of the particular things in the common or general
thing appears to man, but according to his quality, and this
order is the holy principle which affects him.

3439. "I am the God of Abraham thy father, fear not, because I am with thee"—that hereby is signified that the Divine
[principle] also was therein, viz. in the literal sense of the Word,
appears from the representation of Abraham, as denoting the
Lord's Divine [principle], see n. 2833, 2836, 3251, 3305; hence
Jehovah God of Abraham signifies the Lord's Divine [principle]
which Abraham represents, and whereas the subject treated of
is concerning the Word, which also is the Lord, because all the

Word is from Him, and the all of the Word relates to Him, therefore by these words, "I am the God of Abraham, fear not, because I am with thee," is signified that the Divine [principle] is therein. With respect to the Divine [principle] in the Word, the case is this: the essential. Divine [principle] is in the supreme sense of the Word, because therein is the Lord; the Divine [principle] is also in the internal sense because therein is the Lord's kingdom in the heavens, hence this sense is called celestial and spiritual; the Divine [principle] is also in the literal sense of the Word, because therein is the Lord's kingdom in the earths, hence this sense is called the external and likewise the natural sense, for in it are crass appearances more remote from the Divine [principle]; nevertheless all and singular things therein are Divine. The case is, with respect to these three senses, as it was with the tabernacle; its inmost, or what was within the vail, where the ark was containing the testimony, was most holy, or the holy of holies; but its internal, or what was immediately without the vail, where was the golden table and candlestick, was holy; the external also where the court was, was also holy, the congregation assembled thereat, and hence it was called the tent of the congregation.

3440. " And I will bless thee, and will make thy seed to be multiplied "—that hereby is signified that thence would be an increase of good and of truth, appears from the signification of blessing thee, as denoting an increase of good, see n. 3406; and from the signification of thy seed being multiplied, as denoting an increase of truth, see n. 43, 55, 913, 983, 2846, 2847; that seed denotes truth, of which multiplication is predicated, see n. 1025, 1447, 1610, 2848, 3038, 3373, 3380. The reason why there is an increase of good and truth with man derived from the literal sense of the Word is, because in that sense likewise all and singular things are Divine, as was just now shown above, n. 3439; and because in the literal sense the internal sense is open in many passages; as where it is said in the Old Testament by the prophets, that the Lord would come to be salvation to the human race; that all the law and the prophets teach only to love God and our neighbour; that to commit murder is to bear hatred, for he who hates another commits murder every instant, inasmuch as murder is in his will-principle and in the delight of his life: these are the truths of the internal sense in the literal sense; not to mention several others of a like nature.

3441. " For the sake of Abraham My servant "—that hereby is signified from the Lord's Divine Human [principle], appears from the representation of Abraham, as denoting the Lord's Divine [principle], and also the Divine Human, see n. 2833, 2836, 3251; and from the signification of My servant, when it is predicated of the Lord, as denoting the Divine Human [principle];

not that the Divine Human [principle] is a servant; because this principle is also Jehovah, see n. 1736, 2156, 2329, 2921, 3023, 3035, but because the Lord by this principle is serviceable to mankind; for by this principle man is saved, inasmuch as unless the Lord had united the human [principle] to the Divine, so that man might be enabled with his mind to look upon and adore the Lord's human [principle], and thus have access to the Divine, he could not possibly have been saved; man's conjunction with the essential Divine [principle], which is called the Father, is by means of the Divine Human [principle] which is called the Son; thus it is by the Lord, by Whom is meant the Human [principle] in the apprehension of the spiritual man, but the essential Divine [principle] in the apprehension of the celestial man; hence it is manifest why the Divine Human [principle] is called a servant, viz. because it serves the Divine, in order that man may have access thereto, and because it is serviceable to mankind for their salvation. This then is what is signified by Abraham My servant; as also in David, "Make mention of the wonderful things which He hath done, His wonders and the judgments of His mouth, ye seed of *Abraham His servant*, ye sons of Jacob His elect: He sent Moses *His servant*, Aaron whom He hath chosen: He remembered the Word of His holiness with *Abraham His servant*," Psalm cv. 5, 6, 26, 42; where by Abraham His servant is meant the Lord as to the Divine Human [principle]: in like manner also the Lord as to the Divine Human [principle] is meant by Israel His servant, by Jacob His servant, and by David His servant; by Israel His servant, in this passage, "*Thou Israel My servant*, Jacob whom I have chosen, the seed of Abraham my friend; whom I have laid hold of from the ends of the earth, and from the wings thereof have I called thee, and have said unto thee, *Thou art My servant*, I have chosen thee," Isaiah xli. 8, 9; where Israel My servant in a supreme sense denotes the Lord in respect to the internals of the spiritual Church, and Jacob denotes Him as to the externals of that Church. Again, " He said to me, *Thou Israel art My servant* in whom I will be rendered glorious : it is a light thing *that thou be a servant to Me* to raise up the tribes of Jacob, and to bring back the preserved of Israel, and I have given thee for a light of the Gentiles, that thou mayest be My salvation to the extremity of the earth," xlix. 3, 6; where Israel, in whom I will be rendered glorious, manifestly denotes the Lord's Divine Human [principle]; that he is called servant from being serviceable, is evident, for it is said, that thou be a servant to Me to raise up the tribes of Jacob, and to bring back the preserved of Israel. That the Lord as to His Divine Human [principle] is meant also by Jacob a servant, appears from Isaiah in this passage, " I will give thee the treasures of darkness, and the hidden riches of secret places, for the sake of *Jacob My servant*, and Israel Mine elect," xlv. 3, 4 ; where by My servant Jacob, and Israel Mine elect, is meant the Lord, My servant Jacob having respect to the externals of the Church, and Israel Mine elect to the internals. The same is also signified by David My servant, as in Ezechiel, " I will gather together the sons of Israel from the places around, *My servant David shall be king over them*, and they shall all have one shepherd ; they shall dwell upon the land which I have given to *My servant Jacob ;* and they shall dwell upon it, they and their sons and their sons' sons, even to eternity ; and *David My servant* shall be a prince to them to eternity," xxxvii. 24, 25 ; where David My servant manifestly denotes the Lord's Divine Human [principle], see n. 1888, and this by virtue of Divine Truth, which is signified by king, who in the present case is David, see n. 1728, 2015, 3009 ; that truth itself also is respectively a servant, may be seen, n. 3409 ; and it is on this account that the Lord Himself calls Himself one that serves or ministers, as in Mark, " Whosoever will be great amongst you shall be your minister ; and whosoever will be chief amongst you shall be the servant of all ; even as *the Son of Man came not to be ministered unto, but to minister*," x. 44, 45 ; Matt. xx. 26, 27, 28. And in Luke, " Who is greater, he that sitteth at meat, or he that ministereth ? Is not he that sitteth at meat ? *But I am in the midst of you as he that ministereth*," xxii. 27.

3442. " And he builded there an altar"—that hereby is signified a significative and a representative of the Lord, appears from the signification of altar, as being a principle representative of the Lord, see n. 921, 2777, 2811.

3443. " And called on the name of Jehovah"—that hereby is signified worship thence derived, appears from the signification of calling on the name of Jehovah, as denoting worship, see n. 440, 2724 ; and that the name of Jehovah is all in one complex whereby the Lord is worshipped, see n. 2628, 2724, 3006.

3444. "And stretched out his tent there"—that hereby is signified an holy principle therein, appears from the signification of tent, as denoting the holy principle of worship, see n. 414, 1102, 2145, 2152, 3312.

3445. " And there the servants of Isaac digged a well "—that hereby is signified doctrine thence derived, appears from the signification of well, as denoting the Word, see n. 2702, 3424 ; and whereas the Word is essential doctrine, and thus all doctrine which appertains to the Church is derived from the Word, hence to dig a well signifies doctrine thence derived. viz. from the literal sense of the Word, because this sense is here treated of : howbeit the essential doctrine derived from the literal sense of the Word is one only, viz. the doctrine of charitv and of love, of charity towards our neighbour, and of love to the Lord, for this doctrine and a life according to it is the whole Word, as the Lord teaches in Matthew, chap. xxii. 35, 36, 37, 38.

3446. *Verses 26, 27. And Abimelech went to him out of Gerar, and Ahusath his companion, and Phicol the chief captain of his army. And Isaac said to them, Wherefore are ye come to me, and ye have hated me, and have sent me away from you?* And Abimelech went to him out of Gerar, signifies the doctrine of faith having respect to things rational: and Ahusath his companion, and Phicol the chief captain of his army, signifies the primary principles of the doctrine of their faith: and Isaac said unto them, Wherefore are ye come to me, and ye have hated me, and have sent me away from you? signifies why should they desire the Divine [principle] when they denied it, and were averse to what is contained in the internal sense of the Word.

3447. " Abimelech went to him out of Gerar"—that hereby is signified the doctrine of faith having respect to things rational, appears from the representation of Abimelech, as denoting the doctrine of faith having respect to things rational, see n. 2504, 2509, 2510, 3391, 3393, 3397; and from the signification of Gerar, as denoting faith, see n. 1209, 2504, 3365, 3384, 3385; what is meant by doctrine having respect to things rational, may be seen n. 3368. The subject treated of here, and even to verse 33, is concerning those who are principled in the literal sense of the Word, and thence in the doctrinals of faith, and concerning the agreement of their doctrinals with the internal sense, so far as they are grounded in the literal sense; Abimelech, and Ahusath his companion, and Phicol the chief captain of his army, represent these doctrinals; they are such as make faith essential, not indeed rejecting charity, but postponing it, and thus giving doctrine the preference to life; our Churches at this day are almost all of this character, except that which is in Christian gentilism, where it is permitted to adore saints and their idols. As in every Church of the Lord there are those who are internal men, and those who are external, and the internal are those who are in the affection of good, and the external those who are in the affection of truth ; so also it is with those who are here represented by Abimelech, his companion, and the chief captain of his army. The internal are those who are treated of above, chap. xxi. verse 22 to 33, where it is said of Abimelech, and Phicol the chief captain of his army, that they came to Abraham and made a covenant w.th him in Beersheba, concerning whom see n. 2719, 2720; but the external are those who are here treated of.

3448. " And Ahusath his companion, and Phicol the chief captain of his army"—that hereby are signified the primary principles of the doctrine of their faith, appears from the representation of Abimelech, as denoting the doctrine of faith having respect to things rational; hence his companion, and the chief captain of his army, denote those primary principles, and indeed the primary principles appertaining to doctrine; for a chief captain, like a prince, signifies primary principles, see n. 1482, 2089, and army signifies doctrinals themselves; the ground and reason why army signifies doctrinals, which appertain to truth, or which are inferior truths, is, because by warfare in the Word, and by war, are signified the things appertaining to spiritual warfare and war, see n. 1664, 1788, 2686, as also by arms, viz. by spears, shields, bows, arrows, swords, and the like, according to what has been abundantly shown above; and whereas truths, or doctrinals, are the instruments whereby spiritual combats are waged, therefore by armies are signified such truths, or doctrinals, and also false or heretical principles in the opposite sense. That both the latter and the former are signified in the Word by armies, may appear from several passages; as in Daniel, " One horn of the he-goat grew exceedingly towards the south, and towards the east, and towards honourableness, and grew *even to the army of the heavens*, and cast down *of the army* and of the stars to the earth; and trampled them under foot: yea, he lifted up himself *even to the prince of the army*. *His army* was delivered up continually to transgression, and *he cast truth* to the earth. I heard one holy one speaking, and he said, How long will be this vision, and continually wasting transgression, to give both the holy one and *the army* to be trodden under foot?" viii. 9, 10, 11, 12, 13; where the horn which grew towards the south, towards the east, and towards honourableness, is the power of what is false grounded in evil, see n. 2832; the armies of the heavens are truths; the prince of the army is the Lord as to Divine Truth; and whereas army in a good sense is truth, it is said that he cast down of the army to the earth, and afterwards that he cast truth to the earth. Again, in the same prophet, " The king of the north shall set forth a greater multitude than the former, and at the end of the times of years, he shall come in coming *with a great army*, and with much wealth: afterwards he shall stir up his strength and his heart against the king of the south, *with a great army;* and the king of the south shall mix himself in war *with an army exceedingly great and strong*, but shall not stand; for they that eat his meat shall break him, and *his army* shall overflow, and many shall fall down slain," xi. 13, 25, 26; the subject treated of in this chapter throughout is concerning war between the king of the north and the king of the south, and by the king of the north are meant false principles, as also by his army, and by the king of the south and his army are meant truths; it is prophetic of the Church's vastation. So in the Apocalypse, " I saw heaven open, when lo! a white horse, and he who sat on him was called *faithful and true*, clothed in a vesture tinged with blood, and *his army in heaven* followed Him on white horses, clad in fine linen, white and clean. I saw the beast and the kings of the earth, and *their armies* gathered together to make war with Him who sat on the horse, and *with His army*," xix. 11, 14, 19; he who sat on the white horse denotes the Word of the Lord, or the Lord as to the Word, see n. 2760, 2761, 2762; His armies, which followed Him in heaven, denote truths thence derived, consequently those in heaven who are principled in truths: the beast denotes the evils of self-love; the kings of the earth and their armies denote falses; the combats of the false principle with truth are what are here described. So in David, "By the Word of Jehovah were the heavens made, and the *armies of them* by the breath of his mouth," Psalm xxxiii. 6; the armies of them, or of the heavens, denote truths, and whereas by armies are signified truths, therefore the sons of the kingdom and angels, by virtue of the truths in which they are principled, are called the armies of the heavens, as in Luke, "Suddenly there was present with the angel *a multitude of the heavenly army*, praising God," ii. 13. So in David, "Bless ye Jehovah, *all His armies*, ye ministers of His, that do His will," Psalm ciii. 21: and again, "Praise Jehovah, all ye His angels, praise Him all ye *His armies*," cxlviii. 2. So in Isaiah, "Lift up your eyes on high, and see ye who hath created these things, *He that bringeth out in number their army*, calleth all by name, of the multitude of the powerful and of the mighty a man shall not fail," xl. 26: and again, "I have made the earth, and have created man upon it; I, Mine hands have stretched out the heavens, and *I have commanded all their army*," xlv. 12; where the army of the heavens denotes truths, consequently denotes the angels, because they are principled in truths, as has been already said. So in the first Book of Kings, "I saw Jehovah sitting on His throne, *and the universal army of the heavens* standing beside Him, on His right hand and on His left," xxii. 19: and in Joel, "Jehovah gave His voice *before His army*, because His camp was exceedingly great, because he is numerous that doeth His Word," ii. 11. And in Zechariah, "*I will pitch a camp for My house of the army*, passing and returning, lest the exactor should pass any more over them. Exult exceedingly, O daughter of Zion; shout, O daughter of Jerusalem: behold thy king cometh to thee," ix. 8, 9, speaking of the Lord's coming; His army denotes Truths Divine, and it is on this account, and also because the Lord alone fights for man against the hells which are continually attempting to assault Him, that the Lord in the Word is so often called Jehovah Sabaoth, God Sabaoth, the Lord Sabaoth, that is, of armies; as in Isaiah, "The voice of a tumult of kingdoms of nations gathered together, *Jehovah Sabaoth leads an army of war*," xiii.

4; where kingdoms of nations denote false principles grounded
in evils; to lead an army of war denotes to fight for man.   Inasmuch as the twelve tribes of Israel represented the Lord's heavenly kingdom, and tribes and likewise twelve signified all the
things of faith in one complex, that is, all truths of the kingdom,
see n. 577, 2089, 2129, 2130, 3272, therefore also they were
called the *armies of Jehovah*, as in Exod. vii. 4; chap. xii. 17,
41, 51; and it was commanded that they should be brought out
of Egypt *according to armies*, Exod. vi. 26; and should mete
out the camp *according to armies*, Numb. i. 22; and should be
distributed *into armies*, Numb. ii. 1, to the end.   That by armies
are signified truths, appears also from Ezechiel, "Persia, and
Lud, and Puth were *in thine army*, the men of thy war, they
hung in thee the shield and the helmet, they set forth the honour of thee; the sons of Arwad, and *thine army* upon thy
walls round about, and the Gamadims were in thy towers,"
xxvii. 10, 11; speaking of Tyre, by which are signified interior
knowledges of good and truth, consequently those who are principled therein, see n. 1201; army denotes the truths themselves:
that Lud and Puth are also those who are principled in knowledges, may be seen n. 1163, 1164, 1166, 1195, 1231; shield and
helmet are such things as appertain to combat or spiritual war.
That army in an opposite sense denotes false principles, is evident from the following passages, "It shall be in that day, Jehovah shall visit upon *the army of height* in height, and upon
the kings of the earth upon the earth," Isaiah xxiv. 21; where
army of height denotes false principles grounded in self-love.
So in Ezechiel, "I will bring thee back, and will put hooks in
thy jaws, and will lead thee forth, and *all thine army*, horses
and horsemen, all of them clothed perfectly, a company great
with shield and buckler, all of them handling swords; thou
shalt come out of thy place, out of the sides of the north, thou
and many people with thee, all riding on horses, a great company, *a great army*," xxxviii. 4, 15; speaking of Gog, by whom
is signified external worship separate from internal, thus rendered idolatrous, see n. 1151; the army therefore denotes false
principles.   So in Jeremiah, "I will send against Babel who
draweth, drawing his bow, and lifting up himself in his armour;
spare not the youths, give to the curse *all his army*," li. 2, 3;
where Babel denotes worship, the externals whereof appear
holy, whilst the interiors are profane, see n. 1182, 1283, 1295,
1304, 1306, 1307, 1308, 1321, 1322, 1326; his army denotes the
false principles of such profane interiors, as is also signified by
the army of Babel in other passages, as Jer. xxxii. 2; xxxiv. 1,
2; chap. xxxix. 1.   So in Ezechiel, "Pharaoh shall see them,
and shall be comforted upon all his multitude, the slain with the
sword, Pharaoh and *all his army*, because I will give the terror
of Me in the land of the living," xxxii. 31, 32; speaking of

Egypt, by which are signified those who pervert truths by reasonings grounded in scientifics, see n. 1164, 1165; his army, or the army of Pharaoh, denotes the false principles thence derived; the same is also signified by the army of Pharaoh in other passages, as Jer. xxxvii. 5, 7, 11; chap. xlvi. 2; Ezech. xvii. 17. So in Luke, "When ye shall see Jerusalem encompassed *with armies,* then know ye that devastation is near at hand," xxi. 20; speaking of the consummation of the age, or of the last time of the Church when there is no longer any faith; that by Jerusalem is signified the Church, see n. 2117, which is encompassed with armies when it is beset by false principles. Hence it is manifest that by the armies of the heavens which the Jews and idolaters adored, in the internal sense were signified false principles, concerning which it is thus written in the second Book of the Kings, "They forsook all the commandments of their God, and made to themselves a molten (image), two calves, and they made a grove, and *bowed themselves down to all the army of the heavens,*" xvii. 16; speaking of the Israelites; and in another place, speaking of Manasseh, it is written, "That he built altars to *all the army of the heavens,*" xxi. 5; and that Josias the king brought forth out of the temple all the vessels made for Baal, and for the grove, and for *all the army of the heavens,* xxiii. 4: and in Jeremiah, "That they should spread the bones of the princes, of the priests, and of the prophets, to the sun, to the moon, and to *all the army of the heavens,* which they had loved, and which they had served, and after which they had gone," viii. 1, 2; and in another place, "The houses of Jerusalem, and the houses of the king of Judah shall be as Tophet, unclean as to all the houses, on the roofs whereof they have burned incense to *all the army of the heavens,* and have offered libations to other gods," xix. 13: and in Zephaniah, "I will stretch out mine hand against those who worship *the army of the heavens* on the house tops," i. 5; for the stars are what are principally called the army of the heavens, but that by stars are signified truths, and in an opposite sense falses, may be seen, n. 1128, 1808.

3449. "And Isaac said unto them, Wherefore are ye come unto me, and ye have hated me, and have sent me away from you?"—that hereby is signified why should they desire the Divine [principle] when they denied it, and were averse to what is contained in the internal sense of the Word, may appear from what was said above, verses 15, 16, 19, 20, 21.

3450. Verses 28, 29. *And they said, Seeing we have seen that Jehovah was with thee, and we said, Let there be I pray a sacrament between us, between us and between thee, and let us make a covenant with thee. If thou doest evil with us, as we have not touched thee, and as we have done with thee nothing but good, and have sent thee in peace; thou art now the blessed of Jehovah.* They said, Seeing we have seen that Jehovah was with thee,

signifies that they knew the Divine [principle] was therein:
and they said, Let there be I pray a sacrament between us,
between us and between thee, and let us make a covenant with
thee, signifies that the doctrinals of their faith considered in
themselves sh)uld not be denied: if thou doest evil with us, as
we have not touched thee, and as we have done with thee
nothing but good, and have sent thee in peace, signifies that
they had not violated the internal sense of the Word, and that
they would not violate it: thou art now the blessed of Jehovah,
signifies that it was from the Divine [principle].

3451. "They said, Seeing we have seen that Jehovah was
with thee"—that hereby is signified that they knew that the
Divine [principle] was therein, appears from the signification
of the expression seeing we have seen, as denoting to perceive
and thus to know for certain ; and from the signification of Jehovah being with thee, as denoting that the Divine [principle]
was therein. The subject here treated of, as was said above, n.
3447, is concerning the agreement of the literal sense of the
Word with the internal sense, consequently concerning the
agreement of the doctrinals of faith, which are signified by Abimelech, Ahusath, and Phicol, so far as they are derived from
the literal sense of the Word, with the same, viz. with the internal sense; thus concerning the conjunction of the Lord's kingdom in the earths with the Lord's kingdom in the heavens, consequently with the Lord, by the Word. For the Word, as to
the supreme sense, is the Lord Himself, and as to the internal
sense, it is the Lord's essential kingdom in the heavens, and as
to the literal sense, it is the Lord's essential kingdom in the
earths, as has been also observed above. But with respect to
the Lord's kingdom in the earths, that is, with respect to His
Church, the case is this, that whereas it derives its doctrinals
from the literal sense of the Word, it must needs be various and
diverse as to those doctrinals, viz. one society will profess one
thing to be a truth of faith, because it is so said in the Word,
another society will profess another thing, for the same reason,
and so forth. Consequently the Church of the Lord, inasmuch
as it derives its doctrinals from the literal sense of the Word,
will differ in every different place, and this not only according
to societies in general, but sometimes according to particular
persons in each society. Nevertheless, a difference in doctrinals
of faith is no reason why the Church should not be one, provided only there be unanimity as to willing what is good, and
doing what is good. As for example: if any one acknowledge
for a doctrinal that charity is grounded in faith, and he lives in
charity towards his neighbour, in this case he is not indeed in
the truth as to doctrine, but still he is in the truth as to life,
consequently there is in him the Lord's Church or kingdom.
So again, if any one asserts that good works ought to be done

with a view to recompense in heaven, according to the literal
sense of the Word in Matthew, chap. x. 41, 42; chap. xxv. 34
to 46, and in other places, and yet in doing good works he never
thinks of merit, he in like manner is in the Lord's kingdom,
because as to life he is in the truth, and because being such as
to life, he suffers himself easily to be instructed that no one
can merit heaven, and that works, wherein merit is placed, are
not good; and so in other cases. For the literal sense of the
Word is such, that in many passages it appears opposite to
itself, but the reason is, because in that sense there are appearances of truth accommodated to those who are in external principles, consequently who are also immersed in worldly and corporeal loves. In the present case therefore by Abimelech they
are treated of, who are principled in the doctrinals of faith, and
that these are such as make faith the essential of salvation, was
observed above. The agreement also of their doctrinals with
the internal sense of the Word is treated of, and that conjunction is effected therewith, is manifest, but only with those who
are principled in good, that is, with those who, notwithstanding
they make faith essential as to doctrine, still make charity
essential as to life; for when with such there is confidence or
trust in the Lord, which they call real faith, then they are in
the affection of love to the Lord, consequently as to life they
are in good; but see what was said and shown above on this
subject, viz. that charity, and not doctrinal tenets, constitutes
the Church, n. 809, 916, 1798, 1799, 1834, 1844. That doctrinals are of no account unless the life be according to them, n.
1515. That the Church is various as to truths, but is made one
by charity, n. 3267. That there is a parallelism between the
Lord and man as to the celestial things appertaining to good,
but not as to the spiritual things appertaining to truth, n. 1831,
1832. That there is but one single doctrine, viz. that of love
to the Lord and of charity towards our neighbour, n. 3445. That
the Church would be one if all had charity, notwithstanding
they differed as to worship and doctrinals, n. 809, 1285, 1316,
1798, 1799, 1834, 1844, 2982. That the Church would be as
the Lord's kingdom in the heavens, if all had charity, n. 2385.
That there are innumerable varieties of good and of truth in
heaven, but that by harmony they still make one, like the organs and members of the body, n. 684, 690, 3241.

3452. "And he said, Let there be I pray a sacrament between us, between us and between thee, and let us make a
covenant with thee"—that hereby is signified that the doctrinals
of their faith considered in themselves should not be denied, viz.
so far as they are grounded in the literal sense of the Word,
appears from the signification of a sacrament between us, as
denoting consent of doctrinals with the literal sense of the
Word; and from the signification of between us and between

thee, as denoting agreement with the internal sense; and from the signification of making a covenant, as denoting that thus there might be conjunction; that covenant is conjunction, may be seen, n. 665, 666, 1023, 1038, 1864, 2003, 2021. The sense hence resulting is, that the case being thus, the doctrinals of their faith considered in themselves should not be denied, for, as was observed, all doctrinals whatever, if so be they are derived from the Word, are accepted of the Lord, provided that the person who is principled therein be in the life of charity, for to the life of charity all things which are of the Word may be conjoined; but the interior things of the Word are conjoined to the life, which is in the interior good of charity. See what was said and adduced above on this subject, n. 3324.

3453. "If thou doest evil with us, as we have not touched thee, and as we have done with thee only good, and have sent thee in peace"—that hereby is signified that they had not violated the internal sense of the Word, and that they would not violate it, may appear from the series of things treated of in the internal sense, and from what was said above at verses 11, 22, 23.

3454. "Thou art now the blessed of Jehovah"—that hereby is signified that it was from the Divine [principle], appears from the signification of the blessed of Jehovah, when it is said of the Lord, or, what is the same thing, when it is said of the internal sense of the Word, for the Lord is the Word, as denoting Divine Truth, concerning which see n. 3140; thus that it was from the Divine [principle]; and thus that they had not violated, nor would violate, the internal sense, because it was from the Divine [principle]; but to violate the internal sense is to deny those things which are the principal constituents of that sense, and which are the very essential holy things of the Word, and these are, the Lord's Divine Human [principle], love to Him, and love towards our neighbour. These three are the principal constituents of the internal sense, and are the holy things of the Word; they are also the internal and holy things of all doctrinals which are derived from the Word, and likewise the internal and holy things of all worship, for in them is the Lord's essential kingdom. A fourth is, that the Word, as to all and singular things therein, yea, as to every smallest point or tittle, is Divine, consequently that the Lord is in the Word. This also is confessed and acknowledged by all who derive doctrinals from the Word; nevertheless they deny it in heart who acknowledge no other holy principle in the Word than what appears in the letter, for such can perceive nothing holy in the historical parts, nor in the prophetical, except only a slight external sanctity, in consequence of its being called holy; when yet there must needs be in it an interior holy principle, if it be divine, as to every point and tittle.

3455. Verses 30, 31. *And he made them a feast, and they did eat and drink. And in the morning they arose early, and sware a man to his brother; and Isaac sent them away, and they went from being with him in peace.* He made them a feast, signifies cohabitation: and they did eat and drink, signifies communication: and in the morning they arose early, signifies a state of illustration: and sware a man to his brother, signifies confirmation with those who are principled in the good of truth: and Isaac sent them away, and they went from being with him in peace, signifies that they were content.

3456. "He made them a feast"—that hereby is signified cohabitation, appears from the signification of a feast, as denoting cohabitation, see n. 2341.

3457. "And they did eat and drink"—that hereby is signified communication, appears from the signification of eating, as denoting to have communication as to what appertains to good, see n. 2187, 2343, 3168; and from the signification of drinking, as denoting to have communication as to what appertains to truth, see n. 3089, 3168.

3458. "And in the morning they arose early"—that hereby is signified a state of illustration, appears from the signification of morning, and of rising early, as denoting a state of illustration; for morning and day-dawn, in a supreme sense, is the Lord, and in the internal sense the celestial principle of His love, hence also it is a state of peace, see n. 2333, 2405, 2540, 2780; and to arise, in an internal sense, signifies elevation, see n. 2401, 2785, 2912, 2927, 3171. Hence it is evident, that by their arising in the morning early, is signified a state of illustration.

3459. "And they sware a man to his brother"—that hereby is signified confirmation with those who are principled in the good of truth, appears from the signification of swearing or of an oath, as denoting confirmation, see n. 2842, 3037, 3375; and from the signification of a man with his brother, as denoting the good of truth, or, what is the same thing, those who are principled in that good. That man (*vir*) denotes truth, see n. 265, 749, 1007, 3134, 3309; and that brother denotes good, see n. 2360. What the good of truth is, may be seen, n. 3295, 3332. They are principled in this good who are here represented by Abimelech, or who are represented by the Philistines, whose king Abimelech was, viz. who make faith essential to the Church, and give it the preference to charity. They who are of this character, are principled in no other good than the good of truth, for they extract and draw forth from the Word nothing but what appertains to faith, thus what appertains to truth, and scarce see the things appertaining to good, thus appertaining to life; therefore they confirm themselves in doctrinals of faith, but not in any doctrinals of charity; and when they do good,

it is under the influence of the doctrinals of faith; which good
is called the good of truth. With such as are principled in this
good, the Lord conjoins Himself, but not so as with those who
are principled in the good of charity, for love and charity is
spiritual conjunction, and not faith, unless by love and charity;
and this being the case, it is not said that they made a covenant with Isaac, but that they sware a man to his brother; for
covenant is predicated of good, which appertains to love and
charity, whereas an oath is predicated of truth, which appertains to faith, see n. 3375. Of those who are principled in the
good of truth, is also predicated cohabitation, which is signified
by a feast, see n. 3456. From spirits of this character, in another life, it was given me to know that they are separate from
those who are principled in the good of charity, for these latter
are more nearly conjoined to the Lord than the former; the
good of the former, if I may so express myself, being hard, not
suffering itself to be easily bended, not communicative, thus
not in heaven, but in the entrance into heaven.

3460. "And Isaac sent them away, and they went from being
with him in peace"—that hereby is signified that they were
content, may appear without explication: hence also it is manifest, that with these there was cohabitation, not conjunction,
according to what was just now observed, n. 3459.

3461. Verses 32, 33. *And it came to pass in that day, and
the servants of Isaac came, and told him concerning the reasons
of the well which they digged; and they said unto him, We
have found waters. And he called it Shebah, therefore the name
of the city is Beershebah even to this day.* It came to pass in
that day, signifies that state: and the servants of Isaac came,
signifies things rational: and told him concerning the reasons of
the well which they digged, and said unto him, We have found
waters, signifies interior truths by those things: and he called
it Shebah, signifies the conjunction of confirmed truth by those
things: therefore the name of the city is Beershebah, signifies
the quality of doctrine thence derived: even to this day, signifies the perpetuity of the state.

3462. "It came to pass in that day"—that hereby is signified that state, appears from the signification of day, as denoting
state, see n. 23, 487, 488, 493, 2788, in the present case the state
of the doctrine which is treated of.

3463. "And the servants of Isaac came"—that hereby are
signified things rational, appears from the signification of servants, as denoting things rational, and also scientifics, see n.
2567; and from the representation of Isaac, as denoting the
Lord in regard to the Divine Rational principle, see n. 1893,
2066, 2072, 2083, 2630, 3012, 3194, 3210. From what goes
before it is manifest what [quality or principle] of the Lord is
here represented by Isaac, viz. the Word as to its internal sense;

for by Abimelech, and Ahusath, and Phicol, are signified the doctrinals of faith, which are derived from the literal sense of the Word, such as are the doctrinals of those who are called Philistines in a good sense, that is, those who are principled solely in the doctrinals of faith, and as to life are in good, but in the good of truth, which doctrinals have some conjunction with the internal sense, and thus with the Lord.   For they who are principled solely in the doctrinals of faith, and in a life according thereto, are in a certain kind of conjunction, but remote, by reason that they do not know what charity towards their neighbour is, and still less what love to the Lord is, from any principle of affection, but only from a certain idea of faith; thus neither are they in any perception of good, but in a species of persuasion that what their doctrinals dictate is true and thereby good, in which doctrinals when they are confirmed, it is possible they may be confirmed in what is false as well as in what is true, for nothing else can confirm man what truth is except good; truth indeed teaches what good is, but without perception, whereas good teaches what truth is from perception.   Every one may know how the case herein is, and also what is the nature and quality of the difference here pointed out, solely from this common precept of charity, "All things whatsoever ye would that men should do unto you, do ye even so to them," Matt. vii. 12. He who acts from this precept, does good indeed to others, but then he does good because it is so commanded, and not so much from affection of heart, and as often as he does it, he begins from himself, and also in doing good he thinks of merit; whereas he who does not act from the precept, but from a principle of charity, that is, from affection, acts from the heart, and thus from a free principle, and as often as he acts, he begins from a real will to what is good, thus from a perception of its being delightful to him; and inasmuch as he has recompense in the delight which he perceives, he does not think of merit.   Hence then it may appear what difference there is between doing good from a principle of faith, and from a principle of charity, and that the former are more remote than the latter from essential good, which is the Lord; neither can the former be easily introduced into the good of charity to a degree of perception, inasmuch as they are little principled in truths, for no one can be introduced into that good, unless principles which are not true be first eradicated, and this cannot be effected, so long as such principles are rooted in the mind to a degree of persuasion that they are true.

3464. "And they told him concerning the reasons of the well which they digged, and they said, We have found waters"— that hereby are signified interior truths by those things, appears from the signification of well, as denoting the Word, see n. 3424; and from the signification of waters, as denoting truths,

see n. 2702, viz. such as are from the Word ; thus to tell him
concerning the reasons of the well which they digged, signifies
concerning the Word whence they derived doctrinals : and they
said, We have found waters, signifies that in them, viz. in doctrinals, were interior truths ; for, as was observed above, there are
interior truths in all doctrinals drawn from the literal sense of
the Word, inasmuch as the literal sense of the Word is like a
well wherein is water, for in all and singular parts of the Word
there is an internal sense, which sense is also in doctrinals that
are derived from the Word. In regard to doctrinals derived
from the literal sense of the Word, the case is this, that when
man is principled in them, and at the same time in a life according to them, he has in himself correspondence ; for the angels, who
are attendant on him, are in interior truths, whilst he is in exterior, and thus he has communication by doctrinals with heaven,
but yet according to the good of his life. As for example, when
in the holy supper he thinks simply of the Lord, in consequence
of the words used on the occasion, "This is My body and this
is My blood," then his attendant angels are in the idea of love
to the Lord and charity towards their neighbour, inasmuch as
love to the Lord corresponds to the Lord's body and to bread,
and neighbourly love corresponds to blood and to wine, see n.
1798, 2165, 2177, 2187.   And whereas there is such correspondence, there flows an affection out of heaven through the
angels into that holy principle by which man is influenced at
the time, which affection he receives according to the good of
his life. For the angels dwell with every one in his life's affection, thus in the affection of the doctrinals according to which
he lives, but in no case if the life disagrees therewith ; for if the
life disagrees, as supposing there prevails an affection of gaining honours and riches by means of doctrinals, in such case the
angels retire, and the infernals dwell in that affection, who either
infuse into the man their confirmations for the sake of self and
the world, thus a persuasive faith, which is of such a nature that
he is regardless whether a thing be true or false, provided he
can gain credit thereby, or take away from him all faith, in
which case the doctrine uttered by his lips is only a sound excited and modified by the fire of the above loves.

3465. "And he called it Shebah"—that hereby is signified
the conjunction of confirmed truth by those things, appears
from the signification of calling, viz. by name, as denoting
quality, see n. 144, 145, 1754, 1896, 2009, 3421 ; that names
thus denote a thing or state, see n. 1946, 2643, 3422 ; in the present case therefore is denoted the conjunction of confirmed truth
by those things, viz. by doctrinals ; for Shebah in the original
tongue is an oath, which signifies confirmation, as may be seen,
n. 2842, 3375. It is called the conjunction of confirmed truth,
when interior truths join themselves to truths exterior, which

are doctrinals derived from the literal sense of the Word. That persons of this character have conjunction with the Lord by the truths of faith, and not so much by the good things of charity, was shown above, n. 3463.

3466. "Therefore the name of the city is Beersheba"—that hereby is signified the quality of doctrine thence derived, appears from the signification of name, as denoting quality, see immediately above, n. 3465; and from the signification of city, as denoting doctrine, see n. 402, 2449, 2712, 2943, 3216; hence comes Beersheba, which in the original tongue signifies the well of an oath, thus the doctrine of confirmed truth; that Beersheba is doctrine, may be seen, n. 2723, 2858, 2859. Above, in chap. xxi. verses 30, 31, it is said, "Because thou shalt receive seven ewe-lambs from mine hand, that it may be to me for a witness that I have digged this well, therefore he called *that place Beersheba,* because there they both *sware;*" in which passage by Beersheba was signified the state and quality of doctrine, that it was from the Divine [principle], and that by it conjunction was effected; and whereas the interior things of the Church at that time are treated of in the above passage, it is said that that place was called Beersheba, whereas in the present passage, inasmuch as the exterior things of that Church are treated of, it is said that the city was so called; for of interior things is predicated state, which is signified by place, see n. 2625, 2837, 3356, 3387; but of exterior things is predicated doctrine, which is signified by city, for all doctrine has its state and its quality from its interior things.

3467. "Even to this day"—that hereby is signified the perpetuity of state, appears from the signification of the expression, to this day, as denoting perpetuity of state, see n. 2838.

3468. Verses 34, 35. *And Esau was a son of forty years, and he took a woman Jehudith, the daughter of Beeri the Hittite, and Basemath the daughter of Elon the Hittite. And they were bitterness of spirit to Isaac and Rebecca.* Esau was a son of forty years, signifies a state of temptation as to natural good of truth: and he took a woman, Jehudith, the daughter of Beeri the Hittite, and Basemath the daughter of Elon the Hittite, signifies adjunction of natural truth from another source than from what was real and genuine: and they were bitterness of spirit to Isaac and to Rebecca, signifies that hence at first came grief.

3469. "Esau was a son of forty years"—that hereby is signified a state of temptation as to natural good of truth, appears from the representation of Esau, as denoting natural good of truth, see n. 3300, 3302, 3322; and from the signification of forty years, as denoting a state of temptation; that forty denotes temptations may be seen, n. 730, 862, 2272, and that years denote states, n. 487, 488, 493, 893. The reason why these circumstances concerning Esau are immediately adjoined to what has been related concerning Abimelech and Isaac, is because the subject treated of is concerning those who are in the good of truth, that is, who are principled in life according to doctrinals derived from the literal sense of the Word, for such are signified by Abimelech, and by Ahusath, and by Phicol, as was shown above. They therefore who are in the good of truth, or in a life according to doctrinals, are regenerated as to interiors, which are their rational principles, but not as yet as to exteriors, which are their natural principles, for man is regenerated as to the rational principle before he is regenerated as to the natural, see n. 3286, 3288; inasmuch as the natural principle is altogether in the world, and in the natural principle as in a plane is founded man's thought and will. This is the reason why man perceives during regeneration a combat between the rational or his internal man, and the natural or external man, and the reason also why his external principle is regenerated much later, and likewise with greater difficulty than his internal; for what is nearer to the world and to the body, cannot so easily be constrained to comply with the internal man; a considerable length of time also will be necessary to effect such compliance, and there must be an introduction into several new states, such as states of self-acknowledgment, and of the acknowledgment of the Lord, viz. of the misery of self, and of the Lord's mercy, thus of humiliation by temptation-combats; this being the case, there is here immediately adjoined this relation concerning Esau and his two wives, whereby such things are signified in the internal sense. Every one knows what natural good is, viz. that it is the good into which man is born; but what the natural good of truth is, very few, if any, are acquainted with; natural good, or what is connate with man, is in its kind fourfold, viz. natural good grounded in the love of good, natural good grounded in the love of truth, also natural good grounded in the love of evil, and natural good grounded in the love of what is false. For the good into which man is born, is derived to him from his parents, either father or mother; for whatsoever principle parents have contracted by frequent use and habit, or have become tinctured with by actual life, so as to render it familiar to them till it has the appearance of being natural, this is derived down to their children, and becomes hereditary. Where parents have lived in the good of the love of good, and in so living have perceived their proper delight and blessedness, supposing them to conceive children in such a state of life, the children thence receive an inclination to similar good. Where parents also have lived in the good of the love of truth, concerning which good see n. 3459, 3463, and in so living have perceived their proper delight, supposing them to conceive children in such a state of life, the children thence receive an inclination to similar good. The case is the same in respect to those parents who are in the good of the love of evil, and in the good of the love of what is false, that they also communicate to their offspring such hereditary goods. These latter are called goods, by reason of their appearing in their external form as goods, to those persons who are principled therein, although they have nothing at all of real good in them, but the very reverse; such is the good possessed by several at this day, who appear to be principled in natural good. They who are in the natural good of the love of evil, are flexile and inclinable to evils of every kind, suffering themselves to be easily seduced, and in consequence of that good being compliant and yielding, especially to filthy pleasures, to adulteries, and even to exercises of cruelty; and they who are in the natural good of what is false, are inclinable to false principles of every kind, and in consequence of that good are easily caught by persuasions, especially when urged by hypocrites and cunning people, who are expert at engaging the mind's attention insinuating themselves into the affections, and feigning innocence; into these goods so called, viz. of what is evil and false, several are born at this day in the Christian world, who are in natural good, by reason that their parents have contracted the delight of evil, and the delight of what is false by actual life, and thus have implanted it in their children, and thereby in their posterity.

3470. "And he took a woman, Jehudith, the daughter of Beeri the Hittite, and Basemath, the daughter of Elon the Hittite"—that hereby is signified the adjunction of natural truth from another source than what was real and genuine, appears from the signification of woman, as denoting truth adjoined to good, concerning which see above, where Sarah and Rebecca are spoken of, n. 1468, 1901, 2063, 2065, 2172, 2173, 2198, 2507, 2904, 3012, 3013, 3077; in the present case natural truth adjoined to natural good, this being the subject here treated of; and from the representation of Jehudith the daughter of Beeri the Hittite, and of Basemath the daughter of Elon the Hittite, as denoting truth from another source than what was real and genuine; for the Hittites were amongst the upright Gentiles which were in the land of Canaan, with whom Abraham dwelt, and from whom he bought the cave of Machpelah for a sepulchre, Gen. xxiii. 3, to the end; and by whom is there represented a spiritual Church amongst the Gentiles, see n. 2913, 2986, and as this Church is not in truth derived from the Word, by the same is signified truth not grounded in what is real and genuine; for the nation which represents a Church, signifies also the quality of the truth and good appertaining to the Church, inasmuch as a Church is a Church by virtue of truth and good; whensoever therefore mention is made of a Church, truth and good is understood, and whensoever mention is made of truth and good, a Church is understood.

The case herein is this : natural good of truth is not spiritual good, that is, the good of faith and the good of charity, until it is reformed.   Natural good is from a man's natural parents, as was said above, n. 3469, but spiritual good is from the Lord ; wherefore man must be regenerated in order to receive spiritual good ; whilst this is effecting, there are adjoined to him at first truths from another source than what is real and genuine, which are of such a nature that they do not adhere, but only serve as means of introducing genuine truths, and when these latter are introduced, then truths not genuine are separated.   The case herein is as with boys, who first learn several things, even vain and trifling, such as various kinds of sports and the like, not to be made wise by such things, but to prepare the way to receive the profitable and important things of wisdom ; and when these latter are received, the former are separated, yea, are rejected ; or it is as with fruits which are first filled with sour juice, before they can receive sweet juice, the sour juice, which is not genuine, being the means of introducing the sweet, and when this latter enters the former is dissipated.   Thus also it is with man's natural principle before it is regenerated ; for natural good is such, that of itself it is not willing to obey and serve rational good, as a servant serves a master, but it is desirous to have command.   In order therefore that it may be reduced to a state of compliance and service, it is vexed by states of vastation and temptation, until its concupiscences grow faint, and then by an influx of the good of faith and of charity through the internal man from the Lord it is tempered, until the good received hereditarily is by degrees extirpated, and a new good is implanted in its place, into which goods the truths of faith are then insinuated, which are like new fibres inserted into the heart of man, through which fibres new juice is introduced, until a new heart by degrees grows up to maturity ; the truths which are first introduced cannot be from a genuine fountain, because evil and false principles are in the former or natural good, but they are such resemblances or such appearances of truth, as have a certain affinity with genuine truths, whereby there is gradually given opportunity and place for real genuine truths to insinuate themselves.   Genuine good is as it were the blood in the vessels, or as the juice in the fibres, leading and applying truths into form ; the good which is thus formed in the natural or external man, is a common or general good woven together as it were, or wrought up of the particulars and singulars of spiritual good through the rational or internal man from the Lord, Who alone forms and creates anew; hence it is that the Lord in the Word is so often called Former and Creator.

3471. "And they were bitterness of spirit to Isaac and Rebecca" — that hereby is signified that hence at first came grief, appears from the signification of bitterness of spirit, as denoting grief; and from the representation of Isaac and Rebecca, as denoting the Lord's Divine Rational principle as to Divine Good and Divine Truth ; for the subject treated of in the supreme sense is concerning the Lord, but in the representative it is concerning those who are likenesses or images of Him, viz. in the supreme sense, how the Lord made His Human [principle] Divine, and in the representative sense, how the Lord regenerates man, that is, makes him celestial and spiritual; that the regeneration of man is an image of the Lord's Glorification, may be seen, n. 3043, 3138, 3212, 3296. The ground and reason why there was grief at first is, because when truths are introduced into natural good, they at first cause pain. for they aggravate the conscience, and induce anxieties, inasmuch as concupiscences are present, against which spiritual truth wages combat ; but this first grief by degrees diminishes, and at length vanishes away. Natural good herein is as a weak and sickly body, which is to be restored to health by a painful regimen ; when it is in this state, then at first it has grief.

A CONTINUATION OF THE SUBJECT CONCERNING CORRESPONDEN-CES AND REPRESENTATIONS, ESPECIALLY CONCERNING THOSE WHICH ARE IN THE WORD.

3472. *THAT all and singular things, which are in the literal sense of the Word, are representative of the spiritual and celestial things of the Lord's kingdom in the heavens, may appear from what has been heretofore shown, and from what still remains, by the Divine Mercy of the Lord, to be shown : but inasmuch as man has removed himself so far from heaven, and has immersed himself in the lowest principles of nature, yea, even in such as are terrestrial, therefore it is altogether repugnant to him when it is said, that the Word contains deeper mysteries than what he apprehends from the letter, and more so when it is said, that it contains things incomprehensible, which are adequate only to the wisdom of angels, and still more so when it is said, that it contains things essentially Divine, which infinitely transcend the understanding of angels. The Christian world indeed acknowledges that the Word is Divine, but the Divinity thereof it still denies in heart, if not in tongue ; nor is this to be wondered at, inasmuch as the terrestrial principle, in which man is immersed at this day, has no apprehension of things of a more sublime nature, nor is willing to apprehend them.*

3473. *That the Word in the letter has in it such deep and*

hidden contents, is often exhibited visibly to spirits or souls who come into another life ; and during such exhibitions it has been sometimes granted me to be present, as may appear from the testimonies of experience adduced in the first part of this work, concerning the sacred Scripture or Word, as containing Things Divine, which are made manifest to good spirits and angels, n. 1767 to 1776, and 1869 to 1879, from which testimonies, for the sake of confirmation, it is permitted further to relate what follows.

3474. A certain spirit came to me not long after his decease, as I could conclude from this circumstance, that as yet he was ignorant of his being in another life, imagining that he was still living in the world. It was perceivable that he was studiously inclined, and accordingly I discoursed with him about his studies ; but at that very instant he was suddenly taken up on high, at which I was surprised, and conjectured that he was one of those spirits who are of high and aspiring tempers, for it is usual with such to be carried up aloft ; or that he fancied heaven to be situated on high, and such also are wont to be taken upwards, in order to convince them that heaven is not in what is high, but in what is internal. I presently perceived, however, that he was carried up to the angelic spirits, who are in front a little to the right in the first entrance into heaven. From thence he afterwards discoursed with me, saying, that he saw things more sublime than human minds can possibly conceive ; after this I read the first chapter of Deuteronomy concerning the Jewish people, in that there were some sent to search the land of Canaan, and see what was therein ; and whilst I was reading he said, that he perceived nothing of the sense of the letter, but only the things contained in the spiritual sense, and that these were too wonderful to be described. This was in the first entrance of the heaven of angelic spirits ; what then must have been the case in that heaven itself ? and what in the heaven of angels ? Certain spirits on this occasion, who were attendant upon me, and who had before had no belief in the Word of the Lord as containing such things, began to repent that they did not believe, and said in that state that they did believe, because they heard him assert that he heard, saw, and perceived it to be so. But other spirits still persisted in their unbelief, and said that it was not so, and was mere phantasy, wherefore these also were suddenly taken up, and discoursing with me from their state of elevation they confessed that it indeed was very far from phantasy, for that they really now perceived it to be so, and this by a perception more exquisite than could possibly be communicated to any sense during the life of the body. Presently also others were taken up into the same heaven, and amongst them one with whom I had been acquainted when he was in the body, who testified the same thing, adding to other observations, that through astonishment he was not able to describe the glory of the Word in its internal sense, at the same time saying, and this from a principle of tender pity and compassion, that it was surprising men had no apprehension of such things. On two occasions after this I saw others taken up into another heaven amongst angelic spirits, who thence discoursed with me; I was reading at that time the third chapter of Deuteronomy from beginning to end, whereupon they said, that they were only in the interior sense of the Word, asserting that there was not a single point or tittle, but what contained in it somewhat spiritual most beautifully cohering with the rest, also that names signified things; they likewise had this confirmation granted them, because they had not before believed that all and singular things in the Word were inspired from the Lord: this they were desirous also to confirm before others by an oath, but it was not permitted.

3475. *That there exist in the heavens continual representatives, such as are in the Word, has been occasionally said and shown above; these representatives are such, that spirits and angels see them in a much clearer light than that of the sun of this world at noon-day, and what things they see in an external form, they perceive the signification of in an internal one, and therein things still interior. For there are three heavens; in the first heaven these representatives appear in an external form, with a perception of what they signify in an internal; in the second heaven they appear such as they are in their internal form, with a perception of what they are in a still interior form; in the third heaven they appear such as they are in that still interior form, which is the inmost. The representatives which appear in the first heaven, are the common representatives of those things which appear in the second, and those which appear in the second, are the common representatives of those which appear in the third; thus in those which appear in the first heaven are inwardly those which appear in the second, and in these are inwardly those which appear in the third; and whereas they are thus exhibited according to degrees, it may appear how perfect, and full of wisdom, and at the same time how happy are those representatives which are in the inmost heaven, and that they are altogether ineffable, inasmuch as myriads of myriads exhibit one particular of a general representative. All and singular these representatives involve in them such things as appertain to the Lord's kingdom, and these such things as appertain to the Lord Himself. They who are in the first heaven, in their representatives see such things as exist in the interior sphere of the Lord's kingdom, and therein such things as exist in the sphere still more interior, and thus see representatives of the Lord but remotely; they who are in the second heaven, in their representatives see such things as exist in the inmost sphere of the king-*

dom, and therein see representatives of the Lord nearer; but they who are in the third heaven, see the Lord Himself.

3476. Hence it may be known how the case is in regard to the Word; for the Word was given of the Lord to man, and also to the angels, in order that by it they may be near and present with Him; for the Word is the medium of the union of earth with heaven, and by heaven with the Lord; its literal sense is what unites man with the first heaven; and whereas in the literal there is an internal sense, which treats of the Lord's kingdom, and in this a supreme sense, which treats of the Lord, and these senses are in order within each other; it is hence manifest what is the nature of the union effected with the Lord by the Word.

3477. It was said that there are continual representatives in the heavens, and such as involve the deepest mysteries of wisdom; those which are manifest to man from the literal sense of the Word, are so few respectively, that they are as the waters of a small pool compared with those of the ocean. The nature of representatives in the heavens may appear from those already mentioned above, as having been seen by me, and likewise from the following: there was represented before certain spirits, as I myself saw, a broad way and a narrow way, whereof mention is made in the Word, a broad way which led to hell, and a narrow way which led to heaven; the broad way was beset with trees and flowers, of such a sort as in their external form appeared beautiful and delightful, but there were hidden therein snakes and serpents of various kinds which the spirits did not see; the narrow way was not so decorated with trees and flowers to the sight, but appeared sorrowful and obscure, nevertheless in it there were angel infants most beautifully adorned in paradises and flower gardens most pleasant, which yet the spirits did not see: the spirits were then asked which way they were willing to go? They said, the broad way; when suddenly their eyes were opened, and in the broad way they saw the serpents, but in the narrow way the angels; and they were then again asked, which way they were willing to go? Hereupon they remained silent: and so far as their sight was opened, they said, that they were willing to go the narrow way, and so far as their sight was closed, that they were willing to go the broad way.

3478. There was also represented before certain spirits, the tabernacle with the ark; for they who have been greatly delighted with the Word, during their abode in the world, have such things presented visibly before their view; thus on this occasion there was presented the tabernacle with all its apparatus, viz. with its courts, its curtains round about, its vails within, the golden altar of incense, the table containing the bread, the candlestick, the propitiatory [mercy-seat] with the cherubim; and at the same time it was given to the well-disposed spirits to perceive what each particular signified; the three heavens were what were represented by the tabernacle, and the Lord Himself by the testimony in the ark on which was the propitiatory: and in proportion as their sight was opened, in the same proportion things more celestial and Divine were opened therein, of which they had no knowledge during their life in the body, and what is surprising, there was not the smallest particular therein but what was representative, even to the hooks and rings; to instance only the bread which was on the table, in this, as in a representative and symbol, they had a perception of that food on which angels live, thus they had a perception of celestial and spiritual love with their joys and happinesses, and in that love and these joys and happinesses they had a perception of the Lord Himself, as being the bread or manna from heaven; besides many other particulars arising from the form, position, and number of the loaves, and from the gold encompassing the table, and from the candlestick whence proceeded an illuminating light exhibiting still further representations of things ineffable; and so in other instances: from which it might appear also, that the rituals or representatives of the Jewish Church contained in them all the arcana of the Christian Church, and likewise that they, to whom the representatives and significatives of the Word of the Old Testament are opened, may know and perceive the arcana of the Lord's Church in the earths, whilst they live in the world, and the arcana of arcana which are in the Lord's kingdom in the heavens, when they come into another life.

3479. The Jews who lived before the Lord's coming, as also they who lived afterwards, entertained no other opinion concerning the rituals of their Church, than that Divine Worship consisted solely in such externals, being utterly regardless of what they represented and signified. For they did not know, neither were they willing to know, that there existed any internal principle of worship and of the Word, thus that there was any life after death, consequently that there was any heaven, for they were altogether sensual and corporeal. And whereas they were principled in things external separate from internal, worship with respect to them was merely idolatrous, and therefore they were most prone to worship any gods whatsoever, provided only they were persuaded that such gods could cause them to prosper. But inasmuch as this nation was of such a character that they were capable of being kept in an holy external principle, and thus of possessing holy rituals, whereby were represented the celestial things of the Lord's kingdom, and of having an holy veneration for Abraham, Isaac, and Jacob, and also for Moses and Aaron, and afterwards for David, by whom the Lord was represented, and especially of having an holy reverence for the Word, in which all and singular things were representative and significative of things Divine, therefore in that nation a representative

Church as instituted. But if that nation had known internal things to a degree of acknowledgment, they would in such case have profaned them, and thus, whilst they had been in an holy external principle, they would have been at the same time in a profane internal principle, so that there could have been no communication of representatives with heaven by that nation. Hence it is, that interior things were not discovered to them, not even that the Lord was within, that he might see their souls. Inasmuch as the tribe of Judah was of this character more than the other tribes, and at this day as formerly account the rituals holy which may be observed out of Jerusalem, and also have an holy veneration for their fathers, and a particular reverence for the Word of the Old Testament, and inasmuch as it was foreseen that Christians would almost totally reject that Word, and would likewise defile its internal things with things profane, therefore that nation has been hitherto preserved, according to the Lord's words in Matthew, chap. xxiv. 34; it would have been otherwise if Christians, as they were acquainted with things internal, had also lived internal men; in this case that nation, like other nations, would have been cut off many ages ago. But with regard to that nation, the case is this, that their external holy principle cannot in the least affect the internals of their minds, these being unclean through the sordid love of self and of the world, and also by reason of the idolatrous principle prevailing in them, in that they worship things external separate from internal; thus they have not any thing of heaven in them, nor can they carry any thing of heaven with them into another life, except a few who live in mutual love, and in consequence thereof do not despise others in comparison with themselves.

3480. It was also shown how the unclean principles of that nation did not prevent the interiors of the Word, that is, its spiritual and celestial things, from being still exhibited present in heaven; for those unclean principles were removed so as not to be perceived, and evils were also changed into good, so that the mere external holy principle served as a plane, and thus the internals of the Word were exhibited present before the angels, without the interposition of any hindrances; hence it was made manifest, how that people, though interiorly idolatrous, could represent things holy, yea, the Lord Himself, and thus how the Lord could dwell in the midst of their uncleannesses, Levit. xvi. 16; consequently how He could have somewhat resembling a Church amongst them, for a Church merely representative is but a resemblance of a Church, and not a real Church. With Christians this cannot be the case, because they are acquainted with the interior things of worship, but do not believe them, thus they cannot be in an holy external principle separate from its internal. Moreover, with those who are in the life of faith, communication with heaven is effected by the goods appertain-

ing to them, all evil and false principles being in the mean time removed ; and in this case, what is surprising, all and singular things of the Word, as it is read by them, are made manifest to the angels, and this also notwithstanding they who read do not attend to the sense thereof, as has been evidenced to me by much experience, for the internal principle appertaining to them, which is not so perceivable, serves as a plane of communication.

3481. I have very frequently discoursed with the Jews who are in another life (they appear in front in the lower earth, beneath the plane of the left foot), and once also concerning the Word, concerning the land of Canaan, and concerning the Lord. Concerning the Word, as containing in it the deepest mysteries, which they allowed ; next, that all the mysteries contained therein relate to the Messiah and His kingdom, which also they were willing to allow ; but when I said, that Messiah in the Hebrew tongue is the same as Christ in the Greek, this they were not willing to hear ; again, when I said that the Messiah is the most Holy One, and that Jehovah is in Him, and that no other is meant by the Holy One of Israel and by the God of Jacob ; and that inasmuch as He is most holy, none can be in His kingdom but those who are holy, not in external form but internal ; consequently those who are not principled in the sordid love of the world, and in the exaltation of themselves against other nations, and in hatreds one towards another, this they could not endure to hear. Afterwards, when I told them that the Messiah's kingdom, according to the prophecies concerning it, must be eternal, and that they who are with Him will also inherit the earth for ever ; and that supposing His kingdom to be of this world, and they were to be introduced into the land of Canaan, it would only be for a few years, according to the duration of man's life ; besides that all those who died after that they were driven out of the land of Canaan, did not enjoy such blessedness ; and that hence they might know, that by the land of Canaan was represented and signified the kingdom of heaven, and especially as they now knew that they were in another life, and were to live for ever, and that hereby it was evident that the Messiah had His kingdom there ; and that in case it was given them to discourse with angels, they might know that the universal angelic heaven is His kingdom ; and moreover, that by the new earth, the New Jerusalem, and the new temple spoken of in Ezechiel, nothing else can be signified but such a kingdom of the Messiah : to these things they could make no reply, only that they who were to be introduced into the land of Canaan by the Messiah, and were to die after so few years, and to leave the blessedness which they were to enjoy therein, would weep bitterly.

3482. The language used in the Word, although to man it appears simple, and in some passages unpolished, is yet real

*angelic language, but in its ultimates, for angelic speech or lan-
guage, which is spiritual, when it is conveyed down into human
expressions, cannot be conveyed into any other speech or language than such as occurs in the Word, every singular thing
therein mentioned being representative, and every singular expression being significative.   The ancients, as having commerce
with spirits and angels, had no other speech or language than
this, which was full of representatives, and in every expression
of which was contained an internal spiritual sense.   The books
of the ancients were also thus written, it being the study of their
wisdom so to speak and so to write.   Hence also it may appear
how far man afterwards removed himself from heaven, inasmuch as at this day he does not even know that there is in the
Word any thing else but what appears in the letter, nor that there
is a spiritual sense within ; whatsoever is said beyond the literal
sense is called mystical, and is rejected solely on that account ;
hence also it is, that communication with heaven is at this day
intercepted, and this to such a degree, that few believe there is
any heaven, and what is surprising, fewer amongst the learned
and erudite, than amongst the simple.*

*3483. Whatsoever any where appears in the universe, is re-
presentative of the Lord's kingdom, insomuch that there is not
any thing contained in the universal atmospheric region of the
stars, or in the earth and its three kingdoms, but what in its
manner and measure is representative ; for all and singular the
things in nature are ultimate images, inasmuch as from the
Divine [principle] proceed the celestial things appertaining to
good, and from these celestial things the spiritual things appertaining to truth, and from both the former and the latter proceed natural things.   Hence it may appear how gross, yea, how
terrestrial, and also inverted, human intelligence is, which as-
cribes all and singular things to nature separate or exempt from
influx prior to itself, or from the efficient cause.   They also who
so think and speak, seem to themselves to be wiser than others,
when yet angelic wisdom consists in ascribing nothing to nature,
but all and singular things to the Lord's Divine [principle],
thus to a principle of life, and not to any thing dead.   The
learned know that subsistence is perpetual existence, but still it
is contrary to the affection of what is false, and thereby contrary
to the reputation of learning, to say, that nature continually subsists, as it originally had existence, from the Lord's Divine
[principle].   Inasmuch now as all and singular things subsist
from the Divine [principle], that is, continually exist, and all
and singular things thence derived must needs be representative
of those things whereby they had existence, it follows, that the
visible universe is nothing else but a theatre representative of the
Lord's kingdom, and that this latter is a theatre representative
of the Lord Himself.*

3484. *From very much experience I am instructed, that there is but one single source of life, which is that of the Lord, and that this life flows in and causes man to live, yea, causes both the good and the wicked to live; to this life correspond forms which are substances, and which by continual Divine Influx are so vivified that they appear to themselves to live by or from themselves　This correspondence is that of the recipient organs with the life received; but such as the recipient organs are, such is the life which they live.　Those men who are principled in love and charity, are in correspondence, for the life itself is received by them adequately; but they who are principled in things contrary to love and charity, are not in correspondence, because the life itself is not received adequately, hence they have a life existing with them according to their quality.　This may be illustrated by the case of natural forms, into which the light of the sun is influent; such as the recipient forms are, such are the modifications of that light; in the spiritual world the modifications are spiritual, therefore in that world such as the recipient forms are, such is the intelligence and such the wisdom of the inhabitants; hence it is, that good spirits and angels appear as the very essential forms of charity, whereas wicked spirits and infernals appear as forms of hatred.*

3485. *The representations which exist in another life, are appearances, but living ones, because they are from the light of life; the light of life is the Divine Wisdom, which is from the Lord alone: hence all things which exist from that light are real, not like those things which exist from the light of this world; wherefore they who are in another life have occasionally said, that the things they see therein are real things, and the things which man sees are respectively not real, because the former things live, and thereby immediately affect the life, whereas the latter things do not live, consequently neither do they affect the life, unless so far, and in such a sort, as the things of this world's light conjoin themselves adequately and correspondently with the things of the light of heaven.　Hence then it may appear what representations are, and what are correspondences.*

GENESIS.

CHAPTER THE TWENTY-SEVENTH.

3486. AT the beginning of the preceding chapter, from n. 3353 to 3356, were explained the things which the Lord spake and foretold concerning the consummation of the age, or the end of the days of the Church, in Matt. xxiv. 3 to 7. At the beginning of this chapter, by the Divine Mercy of the Lord, will be explained the things which follow there in order, namely, the things in the same Evangelist, from 8 to 14, where are these words: "*All these things are the beginning of sorrows. Then shall they deliver you into tribulation, and shall kill you, and ye shall be hated of all nations for My name. And then many shall be offended, and shall deliver up one another, and shall hate one another, and many false prophets shall arise and seduce many. And because of the multiplying of iniquity, the charity of many shall wax cold. But he that shall persevere unto the end, the same shall be saved. And this gospel of the kingdom shall be preached in all the inhabited [world], for a testimony to all nations; and then shall the end be.*"

3487. By those words which precede, and are explained, n. 3353 to 3356, was described the first state of the perversion of the Church, which was this, that they began no longer to know what was good and true, but to dispute among themselves concerning goodness and truth, from which falsities originated: by these words is described another state of the perversion of the Church, which is this, that they despised good and truth, and also turned away from them, and thus that faith in the Lord was about to expire, according to the degree in which charity was about to cease.

3488. That the second state of the perverted Church is described in those words of the Lord in the Evangelist, is clear from the internal sense, which is as follows. *All these things are the beginning of sorrows*, signifies those things which precede, namely, the things which are of the first state of the perverted Church; which is, as has been mentioned, when they began no longer to know what was good and what was true, but to dispute about good and truth among themselves, from which spring falsehoods, and thence heresies. That such things perverted the Church before many ages were past, is clear from this, that the Church was divided in the Christian world, and this according to the opinion about good and truth, thus that the perve sion of the Church commenced a long time ago. *Then shall they deliver you into tribulation and shall kill you*, signifies that good and truth were about to perish, first by tribulation, that is, by perversion; afterwards by killing them, that is, by denial; that to kill, when spoken of good and truth, denotes not to receive, that is, to deny, may be seen, n. 3387, 3395; by ye, or by the apostles, are signified all the things of faith in one complex, thus both its good and its truth; that those things are signified by the twelve apostles, may be seen, n. 577, 2089, 2129, 2130, f. 3272, 3354, and here it is manifestly clear, for the subject treated of is not concerning the preaching of the apostles, but the consummation of the age. *And ye shall be hated of all nations for My name*, signifies contempt and aversion for all things relating to good and truth; to hate is to contemn and be averse to, for these are the properties of hatred: by all nations, denotes by those who are in evil; that nations signify such, may be seen, n. 1259, 1260, 1849, 1868, 2588: for My name, is for the Lord, thus for all things which are from Him; that the name of the Lord denotes all in one complex, by which He is worshipped, thus every thing relating to His Church, may be seen, n. 2724, 3006. *Then shall many be offended, and shall deliver up one another, and shall hate one another*, signifies enmities on account of those things: many shall be offended, is the enmity in themselves; the Lord's essential Human [principle] is what excites enmity; that this would be an offence and scandal, is predicted throughout the Word: they shall deliver up one another, is the enmity between themselves arising from the false principle against the true: and they shall hate one another, is the enmity among themselves arising from evil against good. *And many false prophets shall arise and shall seduce many*, signifies preaching of what is false; that false prophets are such as teach false principles, thus that they denote false doctrine, may be seen, n. 2534: and shall seduce many, denotes that thence should be derivations. *And because of the multiplying of iniquity, the charity of many shall wax cold*, signifies the expiration of charity with faith: because of the multiplying of iniquity, denotes according to the falses of faith: the charity of many waxing cold, denotes the expiration of charity; for each keeps pace with the other; where there is no faith there is no charity, and where there is no charity there is no faith; but it is charity which receives faith, and it is no charity which rejects faith; hence the origin of every false principle and every evil. *He who perseveres unto the end, the same shall be saved*, signifies the salvation of those who are in charity; he who perseveres unto the end, is he who does not suffer himself to be seduced, thus he who does not yield in temptations. *And this gospel of the kingdom shall be preached in all the inhabited [world], for a testimony to all nations*, signifies that this shall

first be made known in the Christian world; to be preached is
to be made known: this gospel of the kingdom is this truth
that thus it is; gospel denotes annunciation; kingdom is truth;
that kingdom denotes truth, may be seen, n. 1672, 2547: in all
the inhabited, namely earth, denotes the Christian world; that
earth is the tract where the Church is, thus the Christian world,
may be seen, n. 662, 1066, 1067, 1262, 1733, 1850, 2117, 2118,
2928, 3355; the Church is here called inhabited from the life
of faith, that is, from the good which is of truth; for to inhabit
in the internal sense is to live, and inhabitants are the goods of
truth, n. 1293, 2268, 2451, 2712, 3384: for a testimony, denotes that they may know, and not make ignorance a pretext:
to all nations, denotes evils, n. 1259, 1260, 1849, 1868, 2588;
for when men are principled in what is false and evil, they
no longer know what is true and what is good; they believe
in this case what is false to be true, and what is evil to be
good, and *vice versâ ;* when the Church is in this state, *then will
the end come.* In what follows, which will be explained, by the
Divine Mercy of the Lord, at the beginning of the next chapter
of Genesis, the subject treated of is concerning that state of the
Church, which is called the abomination of desolation, which is
the third state.

3489. That such is the condition of the Church, does not appear to those who are in the Church, namely, that they contemn
and are averse to all those things which are of good and truth,
and that they wage hostilities against them, and especially
against the Lord Himself; for they frequent public worship,
they hear preaching, they are in some degree of holiness when
there, they go to the sacred supper, and occasionally converse
among themselves in a becoming manner concerning those
things; thus do the bad as well as the good. They also live
among themselves in civil charity, or friendship; hence it is,
that in the sight of men no contempt is visible, much less aversion, and least of all enmity against the goods and truths of
faith, and against the Lord: but these things are only external
forms by which one person seduces another; whereas the internal forms of the men of the Church are altogether unlike, even
altogether contrary to the external forms. The internal forms
are those here described, and which are as above-mentioned;
the real quality of which appears to the life in the heavens, for
the angels do not attend to any thing else than things internal,
that is, to ends, or intentions and volitions, and thoughts thence
derived. How far these differ from what is external, may be
clearly seen by those who come from the Christian world into
another life, concerning whom see n. 2121, 2122, 2123, 2124,
2125, 2126: for in another life internal principles are those
alone, according to which they there think and speak, inasmuch as external principles are left behind with the body; in

another life therefore it is clear, that although they appeared peaceable in the world, yet nevertheless they entertained hatred one against another, and against all those things which are of faith, and especially against the Lord, for when the Lord only is named before them in another life, a sphere not only of contempt, but also of aversion and enmity, is manifestly exhaled and diffused from them against Him, even from those who in appearance spake piously of Him, and likewise had preached concerning Him; so also when charity and faith are named. Such is their quality in the internal form, which is there manifested, insomuch that had external restraints been removed, while they lived in the world, that is, had they not feared the penalties of human laws, and especially had they not feared for reputation, on account of the honours which they affected and aimed at, and on account of the wealth which they desired and greedily sought after, they would have rushed one against another with intestine hatred, according to their will-tendencies and thoughts; and would have seized the goods of others without any conscience, and likewise would have murdered one another without any conscience, more especially the innocent. Such are Christians at this day as to their interiors, except a few who are not known; whence it appears what is the quality of the Church.

CHAPTER XXVII.

1. AND it came to pass that Isaac was old, and his eyes were darkened from seeing, and he called Esau his elder son, and said unto him, My son, and he said unto him, Behold me.

2. And he said, Behold I pray thee I am old, I know not the day of my death.

3. And now take I pray thee thy weapons, thy quiver and thy bow, and go into the field, and hunt for me venison.

4. And make me savoury meat, as I have loved, and bring it to me, and I will eat, to the intent that my soul may bless thee before I die.

5. And Rebecca heard Isaac speaking to Esau his son; and Esau went to the field to hunt for venison, to bring it.

6. And Rebecca said unto Jacob her son, saying, Behold I heard thy father speaking unto Esau thy brother, saying,

7. Bring me venison, and make me savoury meat, and I will eat and will bless thee before JEHOVAH before my death.

8. And now, my son, hearken unto my voice, to that which I command thee.

9. Go I pray to the flock, and take for me thence two good

kids of the goats, and I will make them savoury meat for thy father as he loveth.

10. And bring it to thy father, and let him eat, to the intent that he may bless thee before his death.

11. And Jacob said unto Rebecca his mother, Behold my brother Esau is a hairy man, and I am a smooth man.

12. Peradventure my father will feel me, and I shall be in his eyes as one seducing, and I shall bring upon me a curse and not a blessing.

13. And his mother said unto him, Upon me be thy curse, my son, only hearken to my voice, and go take for me.

14. And he went, and took, and brought to his mother, and his mother made savoury meat as his father loved.

15. And Rebecca took goodly raiment [raiment of desires] of her eldest son Esau, which were with her in the house and put them on Jacob her younger son.

16. And she made him put skins of kids of the goats upon his hands, and upon the smooth of his neck.

17. And she gave the savoury meat, and the bread, which she had made, into the hand of Jacob her son.

18. And he came to his father and said, My father; and he said, Behold me, who art thou, my son?

19. And Jacob said unto his father, I am Esau thy first-born, I have done as thou spakest unto me: arise, I pray, sit, and eat of my venison, that thy soul may bless me.

20. And Isaac said unto his son, What is this thou hast hastened to find, my son? and he said, Because JEHOVAH thy God caused [it] to meet my face.

21. And Isaac said unto Jacob, Come near, I pray, and I will feel thee, my son, whether thou be he my son Esau, or not.

22. And Jacob came near to Isaac his father; and he felt him, and said, The voice is Jacob's voice, and the hands are the hands of Esau.

23. And he did not acknowledge him, because his hands were hairy as his brother Esau's hands, and he blessed him.

24. And he said, Art thou he my son Esau? And he said, I (am).

25. And he said, Bring to me, and I will eat of my son's venison, to the intent that my soul may bless thee; and he brought to him, and he did eat, and he brought him wine, and he drank.

26. And Isaac his father said unto him, Come near, I pray, and kiss me, my son.

27. And he came near, and kissed him, and he smelled the smell of his raiment, and blessed him, and said, See the smell of my son is as the smell of a field which JEHOVAH hath blessed.

28. And GOD shall give thee of the dew of heaven, and

of the fatnesses of the earth, and multitude of corn and new wine.

29. People shall serve thee, and people shall bow down themselves to thee; be thou a master to thy brethren, and thy mother's sons shall bow down themselves to thee; cursed are they who curse thee, and blessed are they who bless thee.

30. And it came to pass as Isaac left off to bless Jacob, and Jacob was scarce yet gone out from the presence of Isaac his father, that Esau his brother came from his hunting.

31. And he also made savoury meat, and brought it to his father, and said unto his father, Let my father arise, and eat of his son's venison, to the intent that thy soul may bless me.

32. And Isaac his father said unto him, Who art thou? And he said, I am thy son, thy first-born Esau.

33. And Isaac shuddered with exceeding great horror, and said, Who then is he who hath hunted venison, and brought it to me, and I have eaten of all before thou camest, and blessed him, also he shall be blessed.

34. And Esau heard the words of his father, and he cried with a great and exceeding bitter cry, and said unto his father, Bless me, even I, my father.

35. And he said, Thy brother came in treachery, and hath taken away thy blessing.

36. And he said, Doth he not call his name Jacob? and he hath supplanted me these two times, he hath taken away my birthright, and behold, now he hath taken away my blessing; and he said, Hast thou not reserved a blessing for me?

37. And Isaac answered and said unto Esau, Behold I have placed him a master to thee, and I have given all his brethren to him for servants, and have supported him with corn and new wine, and what then shall I do for thee, my son?

38. And Esau said unto his father, Hast thou but this one blessing, O my father? bless me, even I, O my father; and Esau lifted up his voice, and wept.

39. And Isaac his father answered, and said unto him, Behold thy habitation shall be of the fatnesses of the earth, and of the dew of heaven from above.

40. And on thy sword shalt thou live, and shalt serve thy brother, and it shall be when thou hast dominion, and thou shalt break his yoke from off thy neck.

41. And Esau hated Jacob on account of the blessing with which his father had blessed him; and Esau said in his heart, The days of mourning of my father will approach, and I will kill Jacob my brother.

42. And Rebecca was told the words of Esau her elder son, and she sent and called Jacob her younger son, and said to him, Behold Esau thy brother comforteth himself for thee to slay thee.

43. And now, my son, hearken unto my voice, and arise flee unto Laban, my brother, to Haran.

44. And tarry with him some days, until thy brother's fury turn away.

45. Until thy brother's anger turn away from thee, and he forget what thou hast done unto him, and I will send and receive thee from thence; wherefore should I be deprived of you both in one day?

46. And Rebecca said unto Isaac, I loath my life, because of the daughters of Heth; if Jacob should take a woman of the daughters of Heth, such as are these of the daughters of the land, wherefore have I lives?

CONTENTS.

3490. ABOVE, in speaking of Isaac and Rebecca, the subject treated of in the internal sense is concerning the rational [principle], how the Lord made it Divine in Himself; the subject here treated of in the internal sense is concerning the natural [principle], how the Lord made it Divine in Himself; Esau is the good thereof, and Jacob is the truth; for the Lord, when He was in the world, made His whole Human [principle] Divine in Himself, as well the interior, which is the rational, as the exterior, which is the natural, and also the very corporeal; and this according to Divine Order; according to which the Lord also makes man new or regenerates him; wherefore in a representative sense, the subject here treated of is also concerning the regeneration of man as to his natural [principle], in which sense Esau is the good of the natural [principle], and Jacob is the truth thereof; each nevertheless Divine, because all good and truth, which is in the regenerate, is from the Lord.

THE INTERNAL SENSE.

3491. *AND it came to pass, that Isaac was old, and his eyes were darkened from seeing, and he called Esau his elder son, and said unto him, My son, and he said, Behold me.* It came to pass that Isaac was old, signifies when the state was at hand: and his eyes were darkened from seeing, signifies when the rational was willing to enlighten the natural [principle] with the Divine: and he called Esau his elder son, signifies the affec-

tion of natural good, or the good of life: and he said unto him,
My son, and he said unto him, Behold me, signifies presence by
virtue of being foreseen and provided for.

3492. " It came to pass that Isaac was old "—that hereby is
signified when the state was at hand, appears from the signification of being old, as denoting the presence of a new state, for
old age in the Word signifies both the putting off a former state
and the putting on a new state; and this by reason that old age
is the ultimate of age, when corporeal things begin to be put
off, and therewith the loves of the preceding years, and thus
when the interiors begin to be enlightened, for as the former are
removed, the latter are enlightened; also, because the angels,
who spiritually perceive the things which are in the Word,
have no longer the idea of any old age, but instead of it an idea
of new life, thus an idea in the present case that the state was
at hand, viz. that the Divine Rational principle, which is represented by Isaac, should desire a natural principle corresponding
to itself, that is, which should also be Divine.

3493. " And his eyes were darkened from seeing "—that
hereby is signified when the rational principle was willing to
enlighten the natural with the Divine, appears from the signification of eyes, as denoting interior or rational sight, concerning
which, see n. 2701; and from the signification of seeing, as
denoting to perceive and understand, see n. 2150, 2325, 2807;
hence when the eyes are said to be darkened, it signifies that
there was no more any perception, in the present case no perception of those things which were in the natural principle; and
this being the signification of these words, it signifies that the
rational principle was willing to enlighten the natural with the
Divine. How this case is, may appear from what was above
said and shown concerning the rational and natural principle in
man when he is regenerated, viz. that the rational is regenerated
before the natural, by reason that the rational is interior and
thus nearer to the Divine; and also because it is purer, and
thus fitter to receive the Divine than the natural is; and further,
because the natural is to be regenerated by the rational, as may
be seen, n. 3286, 3288, 3321; when therefore the rational principle is regenerated, and the natural is not, then the former
appears to itself to be darkened, for there is no correspondence;
for the rational principle receives its sight from the light of
heaven, and the natural its sight from the light of the world;
and unless these correspond, the rational can see nothing in the
natural; all therein appears to it as shade, or even as darkness;
but when they correspond, then the rational principle sees things
which are in the natural in light, because in this case the thing
appertaining to the light of the world, are enlightened by those
which are in the light of heaven, and thereby become as it were
transparent; but these things appear more evident from what

has been observed concerning correspondences, n. 2987, 2989, 2971, 2990, 3002, 3138, 3167, 3222, 3223, 3225, 3337, 3485. Hence then it may in some sort be apprehended, that by these words, "The eyes of Isaac were darkened from seeing," is signified that the rational principle was willing to enlighten the natural with the Divine, that is, to make it also Divine, for in the supreme sense the Lord is treated of; which may thus be illustrated by those things which exist with man when he is regenerated, of which mention has been made; for the regeneration of man is an image of the Glorification of the Lord, n. 3043, 3138, 3212, 3296, 3490.

3494. "And he called his elder son Esau"—that hereby is signified the affection of natural good, or the good of life, is manifest from the representation of Esau, as denoting the Divine Good of the natural principle, concerning which see n. 3300, 3302, 3322; and because the good of the natural principle is that which appears in the affection and life, therefore it is the affection of natural good, or the good of life, which is here represented by Esau. The affection of good in the natural principle, and thence the good of life, is what is called the elder son; but the affection of truth, and thence the doctrine of truth, is what is called the younger son. That the affection of good. and thence the good of life, is the elder son, that is, the first-begotten, is clear from this consideration, that infants are first of all in good, for they are in a state of innocence, and in a state of love towards their parents and nurses, and in a state of mutual charity towards other infants their companions; so that good is with every man the first-begotten; this good, into which man is thus initiated when an infant, remains; for whatever is imbibed from infancy assumes life; and because it remains, it is the good of life; for if man was to be without the good which he derives from infancy, he would not be a man, but a wilder beast than any of the forest. This good does not appear indeed to be present, because all that is imbibed in infancy appears no otherwise than as somewhat natural, as is abundantly manifest from the act of walking, and from the other motions of the body, likewise from the manners and graceful carriage required in civil life; also from the speech, and several other particulars; hence it may appear that good is the elder son, that is, the first-born; and also that truth is the younger son, or begotten afterwards; for truth is not learnt till the infant becomes a boy, a youth, and an adult. Each principle, both good and truth, which is in the natural or external man, is a son, viz. a son of the rational or internal man, for whatever exists in the natural or external man, flows in from the rational or internal man, and from that also exists and is born; what does not thence exist and is born, is not a living human [principle]; it would be what might be called a sort of sensual corporeal [principle] without a soul. Hence it is that both good and truth are called sons, and indeed sons of the rational principle. Nevertheless it is not the rational principle which produces and brings forth the natural, but it is an influx through the rational into the natural, which influx is from the Lord. Hence His sons are all infants who are born; and afterwards when they become wise, so far as they are infants at the same time, that is, in the innocence of infancy, in the love of infancy towards their parent, in this case the Lord, and in the mutual charity of infancy towards other infants their companions, in this case their neighbour, so far they are adopted by the Lord as sons.

3495. "And he said unto him, My son, and he said unto him, Behold me"—that hereby is signified presence by virtue of being foreseen and provided for, appears from the signification of calling him, and saying to him, My son, as denoting by virtue of being foreseen and provided for, because it is predicated of the Lord's Divine [principle]; and from the signification of saying unto him, Behold me, which is the reply, as denoting presence.

3496. Verses 2, 3, 4. *And he said, Behold, I pray, I am old, I know not the day of my death. And now take, I pray thee, thy weapons, thy quiver and thy bow, and go into the field, and hunt me venison, and make me savoury meat as I have loved, and bring it to me, and I will eat, to the intent that my soul may bless thee before I die.* And he said, Behold, I pray, I am old, signifies that the state was at hand: I know not the day of my death, signifies life in the natural principle: and now take I pray thy weapons, thy quiver and thy bow, signifies the doctrinals of good which he had: and go into the field, signifies where the ground is good: and hunt me venison, signifies the truth of good: and make me savoury meat as I have loved, signifies pleasant things thence derived because from good: and bring to me and I will eat, signifies appropriation: to the intent that my soul may bless thee, signifies adjunction to his life: before I die, signifies the first state of resuscitation in the natural principle.

3497. "And he said, Behold, I pray, I am old"—that hereby is signified that a state was at hand, appears from what has been said above concerning the signification of growing old, n. 3492.

3498. "I know not the day of my death"—that hereby is signified life in the natural [principle], appears from the signification of day, as denoting state, see n. 23, 487, 488, 493, 893, 2788; and from the signification of death, as denoting to rise again, or to be resuscitated into life, see n. 3326. Thus by the day of death is signified a state of the resuscitation of life, or what is the same thing, is signified life; that this is in the natural principle is clear, because the subject treated of is concerning life in that principle. How this case is, cannot be explained unless it be known how the case is with respect to the life of the rational principle and the life of the natural, or, what is the same thing, with the life of the internal man and the life of the external man. The life of the rational or internal man is distinct from the life of the natural or external man, and indeed so distinct, that the life of the rational or internal man may exist beside the life of the natural or external man; but the life of the natural or the external man cannot exist without the life of the rational or internal; for the external man lives from the internal, insomuch, that if the life of the internal man should cease, the life of the external would be immediately destroyed; for exterior things depend on interior, as posterior things on prior, or as the effect on the efficient cause, for if the efficient cause should cease, the effect would immediately be void; such is the relation between the life of the external man and the life of the internal. This is evident from the case of man, for while he is in this world, or lives in the body, his rational principle is distinct from the natural, insomuch that man may be drawn from the sensual external principles which are of his body, and also in some degree from the interior sensual principles which are of his natural man, and be in his rational principle, thus in spiritual thought. This may still be more evident from this consideration, that when a man dies, he altogether leaves his sensual external principles which are of the body, and then retains the life of his interior man; yea also that the scientifics, which are of the external or natural memory, he has still with him, but does not enjoy them, see n. 2475, 2476, 2477, 2479, 2480, 2481, 2482, 2483, 2485, 2486; whence it is manifest, that the rational or internal man is distinct from the external. But during man's life in the body, his rational principle does not appear distinct from his natural, by reason that he is in the world, or in nature, and this being the case, the rational life appears in the natural, insomuch that there does not appear to be any life in the rational principle, unless it be in the natural at the same time; that life only appears to be in the rational principle, so far as it corresponds with the natural, may be seen above, n. 3493. Hence it may be manifest, that it is life corresponding in the natural principle, which is signified by these words of Isaac unto Esau, "I know not the day of my death;" for the rational principle is represented by Isaac, and the natural by Esau, each as to good therein.

3499. "And now take, I pray, thy weapons, thy quiver and thy bow"—that thereby are signified the doctrinals of good which he had, appears from the signification of weapons, quiver, and bow, as denoting doctrinals, see n. 2686, 2709, in the present case the doctrinals of good which he had, namely, the good of the natural principle, which is represented by Esau.

3500. "And go into the field"—that hereby is signified where the ground is good, is evident from the signification of field, as denoting the good of the Church, also the good of doctrine, concerning which, see n. 2971, 3196, 3310, 3317, thus good ground.

3501. "And hunt me venison"—that hereby is signified the truth of good, is manifest from the signification of hunting, and of venison, as denoting the truth of the natural [principle], from whence is the good of life, concerning which see n. 3309; hence it means truth which is of good, because it is said to Esau, by whom is represented the good of the natural [principle], as has been observed above.

3502. "And make me savoury meat, as I have loved"— that hereby are signified pleasant things thence arising because from good, is clear from the signification of savoury meat, as denoting pleasant things ; and as these are from Esau, by whom is represented the good of the natural [principle], therefore they are from good. Savoury meats in the orignal language are the delights and pleasantnesses of taste, and signify, in the internal sense, the delights which are of good, and the pleasant-nesses which are of truth, because the taste, as well as the other senses of the body, corresponds to celestial and spiritual things, of which correspondence, by the Divine Mercy of the Lord, we shall treat hereafter. It cannot be known how the case herein is, unless it be known in what manner the natural principle is made new, or receives life from the rational, i. e. from the Lord through the rational. The natural principle is not made new, or receives life corresponding with the rational, that is, is not regenerated, unless by doctrinals, or the know-ledges of good and truth ; the celestial man by the knowledges of good first, but the spiritual man by the knowledges of truth first. Doctrinals, or the knowledges of good and truth, cannot be communicated to the natural man, thus cannot be conjoined and appropriated unless by delights and pleasantnesses accom-modated to him, for they are insinuated by an external or sensual way ; whatsoever does not enter by some delight or pleasantness does not inhere, thus does not continue. These are the things which are signified by the truth of good, and the pleasantnesses thence derived, and these are the things which are treated of in what follows.

3503. "Bring it to me that I may eat"—that hereby is sig-nified appropriation, is clear from the meaning of eating, as de-noting appropriation, concerning which see n. 2187, 2343, 3168.

3504. "To the intent that my soul may bless thee"—that hereby is signified adjunction to his life, consequently life cor-responding to the rational, is clear from the meaning of bless-ing, as denoting to be gifted with celestial and spiritual good, concerning which see n. 981, 1731, 2846, 3017, 3406. For the good of infancy, and thence of life, which is the same as the good of the natural principle, and which is represented by Esau, is not spiritual good, for the good of infancy is without science, and without intelligence, and thus without wisdom; the good of infancy becomes spiritual good by the implantation of truth, thus by regeneration, see n. 1616, 1802, 2280, 2290, 2291, 2299, 2304, 2305, 2307, 3494; hence the correspondence between natural and rational things, consequently the adjunction of the natural man to the life of the rational; this adjunction to its life is what is meant by these words, that my soul may bless thee.

3505. "Before I die"—that hereby is signified the first state of resuscitation in the natural [principle], is clear from the signification of dying, as denoting to rise again, or to be raised up into life, concerning which see n. 3326, 3498. That this is the first state, is clear from this consideration, that the good of infancy, and thence the good of life, is that which is the first of regeneration; which state is heretofore represented by Esau. The following states are what are treated of in a series in this chapter.

3506. Verses 5, 6, 7. *And Rebecca heard as Isaac was speaking to Esau his son, and Esau went into the field to hunt for venison, to bring it. And Rebecca said unto Jacob her son, saying, Behold I heard thy father speaking unto thy brother Esau, saying, Bring me venison, and make me savoury meat; and I will eat and bless thee before Jehovah, before my death.* Rebecca heard as Isaac was speaking to Esau his son, signifies the affection of truth, and life from it: and Esau went into the field to hunt for venison, to bring it, signifies the endeavour of the affection of good to procure truth, which might be adjoined to the Divine Rational principle: and Rebecca said to Jacob her son, saying, signifies the perception of the Lord from Divine Truth concerning natural truth: behold I heard thy father speaking unto thy brother Esau, saying, signifies that the Divine Good of the Divine Rational principle willed the affection of good: bring me venison, signifies the truth of good: and make me savoury meat, signifies desire and delight arising from the pleasantness thence derived: and I will eat, signifies appropriation thus: and I will bless thee before Jehovah, signifies conjunction thereby: before my death, signifies thus life in the natural principle.

3507. "Rebecca heard as Isaac was speaking to Esau his son"—that hereby is signified the affection of truth, and life from it, is clear from the representation of Rebecca, as denoting the Divine Rational of the Lord with respect to Divine Truth conjoined with the Divine Good therein, thus denoting the very affection of truth; and from the signification of hearing Isaac speak, as denoting life from thence; for to hear speak, in the

3505—3508.] GENESIS.

internal sense, is influx, by reason that to hear, in a representative sense, is to obey, see n. 2542 ; and to speak is to will and to flow into, see n. 2626, 2951, 3037 ; thus in the supreme sense, hearing speak is life from thence, namely, the life of the Divine Truth from Divine Good; to her son, in the internal sense, denotes concerning the good of the natural [principle], and thence the truth of the natural principle. That this is the sense of these words, does not so plainly appear, because it is in some measure removed from the sense of the letter, which is historical ; nevertheless so it is ; for angelic ideas are altogether different from those of men ; angelic ideas are spiritual, and when they go more inward, they are celestial ; but human ideas are natural, and when derived from things historical, are sensual. Howbeit, such a correspondence is established by the Lord through the Word, between the spiritual things which are of heaven, and the natural things which are of the world, that natural ideas may be changed into spiritual, and this in a moment; hence there is conjunction of heaven with the world by man, and indeed by the Word, consequently by the Church in which is the Word. That there is a correspondence of natural and spiritual things in all and every thing which can be conceived or perceived, will be made clear by the Divine Mercy of the Lord, from the things related from experience concerning the Grand Man at the end of the chapters following.

3508. " And Esau went into the field to hunt for venison, to bring it "—that hereby is signified the endeavour of the affection of good to procure truth which might be joined to the Divine Rational, is clear from the representation of Esau, as denoting the good of the natural [principle], concerning which see above ; hence it denotes the affection of the good of the rational principle in the natural ; for the good which is in the natural, is not of the natural, but is of the rational in the natural, see n. 3498 ; and from the signification of going into the field to hunt for venison, to bring it, as denoting an endeavour to procure truth to itself, for a field is that where there is good ground, see n. 3500 ; venison is truth which is from good, see n. 3501 ; to bring it, is to procure it, thus to adjoin it to the Divine Rational principle. The subject here treated of, as was above observed, in the supreme sense is concerning the Glorification of the Lord's natural principle ; and in the representative sense concerning the regeneration of the natural [principle] in man, see n. 3490. It is according to order that this should be accomplished by truth, that is, by the knowledges of good and truth, for without them, the natural principle cannot be enlightened from the rational, or by the rational ; thus it cannot be regenerated, knowledges being the recipient vessels of good and truth flowing from the rational ; according to the quality and quantity which the vessels receive, such is the illumination.

The vessels which receive good and truth from the rational
principle, are the very truths of the natural, which are only scientifics, knowledges, and doctrinals. From the order of those
things which flow in, and from the order of those things which
are there among themselves, goods are effected; hence the
good of the natural principle.

3509. " And Rebecca said unto Jacob her son"—that hereby
is signified the perception of the Lord from Divine Truth concerning natural truth, is clear from the representation of Rebecca, which is the Divine Truth of the Divine Rational of the
Lord, concerning which see n. 3012, 3013, 3077; and from the
signification of saying, as denoting to perceive, concerning
which see n. 1791, 1815, 1819, 1822, 1898, 1919, 2080, 2506,
2515, 2552, 2619; and from the representation of Jacob, as denoting the natural [principle] of the Lord in respect of truth,
concerning which see n. 3305. Hence it is clear, that by " Rebecca saying unto Jacob her son" is signified the perception of
the Lord from the Divine Truth concerning natural truth. That
the Lord, from the Divine Good of the Divine Rational, which
is represented by Isaac, was willing to procure truth to Himself
by the good of the natural [principle], which is represented by
Esau, whereby He might glorify or make His natural [princi-
ple] Divine; or that the Lord from the Divine Truth of the
Divine Rational principle, which is represented by Rebecca.
was willing to procure truth unto Himself by the truth of the
natural [principle], which is represented by Jacob, by which
the rational might be glorified, or made Divine, cannot be comprehended, unless it be illustrated by those things which exist
in man whilst he is regenerating or creating anew by the Lord;
nor indeed even by this, unless it be known how the case is
with the rational principle in respect of good and truth therein;
wherefore we shall speak a few words on this subject. The
rational mind is distinguished into two faculties, one of which
is called the will, the other the understanding. That which proceeds from the will, whilst man is regenerating, is called good;
that which proceeds from the understanding is called truth.
Before man is regenerated, the will does not act in unity with
the understanding, but the former wills good, whereas the latter wills truth, insomuch that a tendency of the will is perceived
distinct from the tendency of the understanding. This, however, is only perceived by those who reflect and know what the
will is and the things which belong to it, and what the understanding is and the things which belong to it; but it is not perceived by those who do not know these things, and therefore
who do not reflect; and because the natural mind is regenerated by the rational mind, as may be seen, n. 3493, and this
according to order, in such a sort, that the good of the rational
does not immediately flow into the good of the natural and

regenerate it, but through the truth which is of the understanding, thus according to appearance from the truth of the rational. These are the things which are treated of in this chapter in the internal sense ; for Isaac is the rational mind with respect to good, which is of the will ; Rebecca is the same with respect to truth, which is of the understanding ; Esau is the good of the natural principle existing from the good of the rational ; Jacob is the truth of the natural principle existing from the good of the rational by the truth which is therein. From these particulars it may appear what arcana are contained in the internal sense of the Word ; but still there are very few which can be explained to human apprehension ; whilst those which transcend the human intellect, and cannot be explained, are indefinite ; for in proportion as the Word penetrates deeper, that is, more interiorly into heaven, in the same proportion the arcana become more indefinite, and also inexpressible, not only before man, but also before the angels of an inferior heaven, and when they go to the inmost heaven, the angels there perceive that they are infinite, and altogether incomprehensible by them, because they are Divine. Such is the nature of the Word.

3510. " Behold I heard thy father speak unto Esau thy brother, saying"—that hereby is signified that the Divine Good of the Divine Rational principle willed the affection of good, is clear from the representation of Isaac, who is here the father, as denoting the Divine Good of the Divine Rational principle, concerning which see above ; and from the signification of speaking, as denoting to will, concerning which see n. 2626, 2951, 3037 ; and from the representation of Esau, as denoting the affection of good in the natural [principle], concerning which see above, n. 3508.

3511. " Bring me venison"—that hereby is signified the truth of good, is clear from the signification of venison, as denoting the truth of good, see n. 3501.

3512. " And make me savoury meat"—that hereby is signified desire and delight derived from the pleasantness thence arising, is clear from the signification of savoury meat, as denoting pleasantness, concerning which see above, n. 3502, thus denoting desire and delight derived from the pleasantness thence arising, viz. from truth. For in the above passage it is said, that truths are introduced into the natural [principle] of man by the pleasant things agreeing therewith, and those which are not so introduced, do not adhere, and thus are not conjoined to the rational principle by correspondence. Truths also, like all other scientifics, have their place in the memory which belongs to the natural man, according to the agreeablenesses and delights which introduced them, as is evident from this consideration, that when those pleasantnesses and delights return, the things also return which were introduced by them ; and *vice versâ*, when the things are reca.led, at the same time the delights or pleasantnesses are excited to which they are adjoined.

3513. " And I will eat"—that hereby is signified appropriation thus, is clear from the signification of eating as denoting to appropriate, concerning which see n. 2187, 2343, 3168, 3503. Appropriation is effected, when truths, or the knowledges of good and truth, are insinuated by pleasantnesses and delights into the natural [principle], and when these truths are there adjoined to good, then there is effected a communication between truth and good of the rational principle, thus with the rational principle, and this communication is what is called appropriation, for such truth and good are of the rational principle in the natural; for the things which are in the rational principle with respect to those which are in the natural, are as particulars in respect to generals. It is a known thing that particulars compose generals, and that without particulars no generals could exist; the general of the particulars of the rational principle, is what is exhibited in the natural, and inasmuch as it is a general [or common principle], it appears under another form, and this according to the order of the particulars which compose it, thus according to the form thence derived. If the singulars and consequent particulars of celestial good and spiritual truth are what form the general in the natural principle, in this case there exists a celestial and spiritual form, and in a certain image there is represented something of heaven in the singulars of the general. But if the singulars and particulars are not of good and truth, but of what is evil and false, which form the generals in the natural principle, in this case there is represented in an image something of hell in the singulars of the general. Such things also are signified by eating and drinking in the holy supper, where likewise by eating and drinking is signified appropriation; namely, by eating, the appropriation of good; and by drinking, the appropriation of truth. If good, that is, love to the Lord and charity towards our neighbour, form the internal or rational man, and by this the external or natural man corresponding with it, then man becomes in particular and in general an image of heaven, consequently an image of the Lord. But if on the other hand contempt of the Lord, and of the good and truth of faith, and hatred towards our neighbour form the internal man, in this case man becomes in particular and in general an image of hell; and especially if at the same time he is in external sanctity, for hence comes profanation; thus it is that to those who eat and drink worthily, eternal life is appropriated, but that they who eat and drink unworthily, appropriate death unto themselves.

3514. " And will bless thee before Jehovah"—that hereby is signified conjunction thus, is clear from the signification of blessing thee, as denoting adjunction to his life, of which see above, n. 3504; and whereas it is here said, I will bless thee before Jehovah, it denotes conjunction. Adjunction is predicated of the communication of the truth of the natural principle with the good of the rational; but conjunction is predicated of the communication of the good of the natural principle with the good of the rational; for parallelism between the Lord and man is given as to the celestial things which are of good, not as to the spiritual things which are of truth, see n. 1832.

3515. " Before my death"—that hereby is signified life thus in the natural [principle], is clear from the signification of death, as denoting resuscitation to life, of which see above, n. 3498, 3505.

3516. Verses 8, 9, 10. *And now, my son, hearken unto my voice, to that which I command thee. Go I pray unto the flock, and take for me thence two good kids of the goats, and I will make them savoury meat for thy father, as he loveth: and bring it to thy father, and let him eat, to the intent that he may bless thee before his death.* Now, my son, hearken unto my voice, to that which I command thee, signifies the desire and the delight perceived from the Divine Truth in the Divine Rational principle towards natural truth: go I pray unto the flock, signifies to natural domestic good not conjoined with the Divine Rational principle: and take for me thence two good kids of the goats, signifies the truths of that good: and I will make them savoury meat for thy father as he loveth, signifies that he should thence make delights: and bring it to thy father and let him eat, signifies to the Divine Good of the Divine Rational principle, and appropriation: that he may bless thee, signifies conjunction thereby: before his death, signifies resuscitation in the natural [principle].

3517. " And now, my son, hearken unto my voice, to that which I shall command thee"—that hereby is signified desire and delight perceived from the Divine Truth in the Divine Rational principle towards natural truth, is clear from the representation of Rebecca who speaks these things, as denoting the Divine Truth of the Divine Rational principle, concerning which see above; and from the representation of Jacob, to whom these things are said, as denoting natural truth, of which see also above; that it is desire and delight, is clear without explication.

3518. "Go I pray to the flock"—that hereby is signified natural domestic good not conjoined with the Divine Rational principle, is clear from the signification of flock, as denoting good, n. 343, 415, 1565, in this place natural good, because it is spoken to Jacob, and this domestic, because it was at home [or in the house], whereas the field whence Esau brought his venison, by whom the good of the natural [principle] is signified, n. 3500, 3508, was good not domestic. In other cases flock in the Word is predicated of the good of the rational principle, but in such cases herd is predicated of the good of the natural, n. 2566. Natural domestic good is that good which a man receives from his parents, or that in which he is born, very distinct from the good of the natural principle which flows in from the Lord. The nature and quality of natural good may be seen, n. 3470, 3471; wherefore for distinction's sake the one is called *the good of the natural* [principle], but the other *natural good*. Besides, every man receives domestic good from his father and from his mother, which goods are also distinct in themselves; that which he receives from the father is interior; that from the mother is exterior. In the Lord, these goods were most distinct, for the good which He had from the Father was Divine; but that which He had from the mother was contaminated with hereditary evil. That good in the natural principle, which the Lord had from the Father, was his proprium, because it was His very Life, and is that which is represented by Esau; whereas the natural good which the Lord derived from the mother, because it was contaminated with hereditary evil, was evil in itself, and this is what is understood by domestic good; this good, notwithstanding its being of such a quality, yet was serviceable for the reformation of the natural principle, but when it had answered this end, it was rejected. The case is the same with every man who is regenerated; the good, which he receives from the Lord as from a new father, is interior, but the good which he derives from his parents is exterior. The former good, which he receives from the Lord, is called spiritual, but the latter which he derives from his parents is called natural good. The latter good, namely, that which he derives from his parents, is serviceable first of all for his reformation, for by that, as by something pleasing and agreeable, scientifics are introduced, and afterwards the knowledges of truth; but when it has served as a means for this use, then it is separated, and in this case spiritual good comes into view, and manifests itself. This may appear evident from much experience, as from this single consideration, that when a child is first instructed, he is affected with the desire of knowing, at first not for any end manifest unto himself, but from a certain pleasure and delight connate therewith, and arising from other causes. Afterwards as he grows up, he is affected with the desire of knowing on account of some end, viz. that he may excel others, or his rivals; then for some end [or advantage] in the world; but when he is about to be regenerated, he is affected from the delight and pleasantness of truth, and whilst he is regenerating, which is accomplished in mature age, then from the love of truth, and afterwards from the love of good. The ends in this case, which were formerly purposed, and their delights, are separated by little and little, and are succeeded by interior good from the

Lord, which manifests itself in his affection; hence it is clear, that the former delights, which appeared in an external form as good, served for means. Such successions of means are continual. The case herein is comparatively like that of a tree, which in its first age or the beginning of spring adorns its branches with leaves, afterwards as its age or the spring advances, it decorates them with flowers, and next in the summer puts forth the first germs of fruits, which in process of time become fruit, and lastly it produces seeds therein, which contain in them new trees like the parent stock, and indeed whole orchards as to the power of production, and in reality of produce in case the seeds are sown. Such are the comparatives existing in nature, which also are representative; for universal nature is a theatre representative of the kingdom of the Lord in the heavens, hence of the kingdom of the Lord in the earths, or in the Church, and hence of the kingdom of the Lord in every regenerate man. From these considerations it is evident how natural or domestic good, although it is mere external delight, and indeed of a worldly nature, may serve as a means of producing the good of the natural [principle], which may join itself with the good of the rational, and thus become regenerate or spiritual good, that is, good which is from the Lord. These are the things which are represented and signified by Esau and Jacob in this chapter.

3519. "And bring me thence two good kids of the goats" —that hereby are signified the truths of that good, is clear from the meaning of kids of the goats, as denoting the truths of good, of which we shall speak presently; the reason of their being two is, because as in the rational principle, so also in the natural, there are things appertaining to the will and to the understanding; the things in the natural principle which appertain to the will are delights, and those which appertain to the understanding are scientifics; these two must be conjoined in order that they may be something. That kids of the goats denote the truths of good, may appear from those passages of the Word where kids and goats are mentioned. It is to be noted, that all the tame and useful beasts which are named in the Word, signify, in the genuine sense, the celestial things of good, and the spiritual things of truth, as may be seen, n. 45, 46, 142, 143, 246, 714, 715, 2180, 2781, 3218; and because there are various kinds of celestial things or goods, and consequently various kinds of spiritual things or truths, one kind is signified by one beast, and another kind by another, thus one kind is signified by a lamb, another by a kid, another by a sheep, by a she-goat, by a he-goat, by a ram, by a cow, by an ox; another also by a horse and by a camel; another likewise by birds; and also another by the beasts of the sea, as by whales, and by fishes. There are more kinds of celestial and spiritual things than can

be numbered, consequently of goods and truths, although when
the celestial principle or good is named, as also the spiritual
principle or truth, it appears not manifold, but a simple oneness;
but how manifold they both are, or how innumerable their kinds
are, may be evident from the things which are said concerning
heaven, n. 3241, namely, that it is distinguished into innumerable societies, and this according to the kinds of celestial and
spiritual things, or of the goods of love and thence of the truths
of faith ; and moreover every singular kind of good, and every
singular kind of truth, has innumerable species, into which
the societies of each kind are distinguished, and every species
in like manner.   The most universal kinds of good and truth,
are what were represented by the animals which were offered in
burnt-offerings and sacrifices ; and because the kinds are most
distinct in themselves, it is expressly enjoined that such and no
other should be offered ; in some cases, for instance, male and
female lambs, also male and female kids ; in some cases rams
and sheep, and also goats, but in others calves, heifers, and
oxen ; also pigeons and turtle doves, as may be seen, n. 922,
1823, 2180, 2805, 2807, 2830, 3218. What male and female
kids signified, may appear both from the sacrifices in which they
were offered, and also from other passages in the Word · whence
it is evident, that male and female lambs signified the innocence
of the internal or rational man, and that male and female kids
signified the innocence of the external or natural man, thus the
truth and good thereof.   That the truth and good of the innocence of the external or natural man is signified by male and
female kids, is clear from these passages in the Word. In Isaiah,
" The wolf shall dwell with the *lamb*, and the leopard shall lie
down with the *kid*, the calf also, and the young lion, and the
sheep together, and a little child shall lead them," xi. 6 ; the
subject here treated of is concerning the Lord's kingdom, and
therein concerning a state of no fear from evil, or of no dread
from hell, because appertaining to the Lord ; the lamb and the
kid denote those who are in innocence, and because these are
the safest of all, therefore they are first named. When all the
first-born of Egypt were smitten, it was enjoined that they
should slay cattle perfect and male, of the *lambs* or of the *kids*,
and should put the blood on the posts and upon the threshold
of the houses, and thus they should not be smitten with the
plague, Exod. xii. 5, 7, 13 ; the first-born of Egypt is the good
of love and charity extinct, n. 3325 ; lambs and kids are states
of innocence, in which they who are principled are defended
from evil, for all in heaven by states of innocence are defended
of the Lord, and this defence was represented by the slaying of
a lamb or kid, and the blood upon the door and threshold of
the houses. When Jehovah appeared to any one by an angel,
a kid of the goats was sacrified, lest he should die, as when He

appeared to Gideon, Judges vi. 19; and to Manoah, Judges
xiii. 15, 16, 19; the reason was, because Jehovah, or the Lord,
could not appear to any, not even to an angel, unless he, to
whom He appeared, was in a state of innocence; wherefore as
soon as the Lord is present with the angels, they are let into a
state of innocence, for the Lord enters by innocence, even with
the angels in heaven; it is on this account that no one can come
into heaven unless he has somewhat of innocence, according to
the words of the Lord in Matthew, chap. xviii. 3; Mark x. 15;
Luke xviii. 17. That they believed that they should die when
Jehovah appeared, unless they offered a burnt-offering, may be
seen, Judges xiii. 22, 23. Inasmuch as genuine conjugial love
is innocence, see n. 2736, therefore it was a solemn rite in the
representative Church, to enter in unto a wife by a present of
a kid of the goats, as is written of Samson, Judges xv. 1; likewise of Judah when he went in unto Thamar, Gen. xxxviii. 17,
20, 23. That a kid and a she-goat signified innocence, is also
clear from the sacrifices of guilt, which were offered when any
one had sinned through error, Levit. i. 10; chap. xiv. 28; chap.
v. 6; sin through error is a sin of ignorance, in which is innocence. The same is clear from the Divine command in Moses,
"The first-fruits of the first-fruits of thy land thou shalt bring
to the house of Jehovah thy God; thou shalt not seethe a *kid*
in his mother's milk," Exod. xxiii. 19; chap. xxxiv. 26; where
by the first-fruits of the land, which they should bring to the
house of Jehovah, is signified the state of innocence which is in
infancy; and by not seething a kid in its mother's milk is signified that they should not destroy the innocence of infancy;
because these things are signified, one command follows the
other directly in both the passages quoted, which in the literal
sense appear to be altogether different, but in the internal sense
cohere. Because kids and she-goats signify innocence, as has
been said, it was also commanded, that the curtain over the
habitation of the tabernacle should be made of *the wool of
female kids*, Exod. xxv. 4; chap. xxvi. 7; chap. xxiii. 26; chap.
xxxv. 5, 6; chap. xxxvi. 14; for a sign that all the holy things,
which were therein represented, derived their essence from
innocence; by the wool of goats is signified the ultimate or the
outermost principle of innocence, which is in ignorance, such
as has place among the Gentiles, which in the internal sense
are the curtains of the tabernacle. Hence then it is manifest,
what and of what quality the truths of good are which are signified by the two good kids of the goats, concerning which
Rebecca the mother spoke unto Jacob her son, viz. that they
are grounded in innocence or infancy, or those which Esau was
to bring to his father Isaac, concerning which see above, n.
3501, 3508; which indeed were not Jacob's, but appeared so

in the beginning; and hence it is, that by these Jacob pretended to be Esau.

3520. "And I will make savoury meat for thy father, as he
loveth"—that hereby is signified that thence he should make
delights, is clear from the signification of savoury meats, as
denoting agreeablenesses from good, of which see above, n.
3502; here they are called delights, because they are truths
not from genuine good, but from domestic good, n. 3518.

3521. "And bring to thy father, and let him eat"—that
hereby is signified to the Divine Good of the Divine Rational
principle, and appropriation, is clear from the representation of
Isaac, in the present case the father, as denoting the Divine
Good of the Divine Rational principle, of which see above;
and from the signification of eating, as denoting appropriation,
of which see above, n. 3513; but that truth from domestic good
is not appropriated, will be clear from the things which follow.

3522. "To the intent that he may bless thee"—that hereby
is signified conjunction thus, is clear from the signification of
blessing, as denoting conjunction, see n. 3504, 3514.

3523. "Before his death"—that hereby is signified resuscitation in the natural [principle], is clear from the signification
of death, as denoting resuscitation, of which see above, n. 3498,
3505.   That it is in the natural principle is evident.

3524. Verses 11, 12, 13. *And Jacob said unto Rebecca his
mother, Behold my brother Esau is a hairy man, and I am a
smooth man. Perhaps my father may feel me, and I shall be in
his eyes as one who seduceth, and I shall bring a curse upon me,
and not a blessing. And his mother said unto him, Upon me be
thy curse, my son, only hearken unto my voice, and go, take for
me.* Jacob said unto Rebecca his mother, signifies the Lord's
perception from Divine Truth concerning natural truth: Behold
Esau my brother is a hairy man, signifies the quality of natural
good respectively: and I am a smooth man, signifies the quality
of natural truth respectively: perhaps my father may feel me,
signifies an inmost degree of perception: and I shall be in his
eyes as one who seduceth, signifies rejection, because apparently
contrary to order: and I shall bring upon myself a curse and
not a blessing, signifies disjunction: and his mother said unto
him, signifies perception from the Divine Truth: Upon me be
thy curse, my son, signifies that there would be no disjunction:
only hearken unto my voice, and go, take for me, signifies from
the effect.

3525. "And Jacob said unto Rebecca his mother"—that
hereby is signified the Lord's perception from Divine Truth
concerning natural truth, is clear from the signification of saying in the historical parts of the Word, as denoting to perceive,
see n. 3509; and from the representation of Jacob, as denoting

natural truth, n. 3305; and from the representation of Rebecca, as denoting the Divine Truth of the Divine Rational of the Lord, n. 3012, 3013, 3077. The reason why perception from Divine Truth concerning natural truth is signified, not perception from natural truth concerning Divine Truth, according to appearance from the sense of the letter, is, because all apperception, which is of the natural principle, is from the rational: in the present case therefore, as being predicated of the Lord, it is from the Divine Truth of the Divine Rational principle.

3526. "Behold Esau my brother is a hairy man"—that hereby is signified the quality of natural good respectively, is clear from the representation of Esau, as denoting the good of the natural principle, of which see n. 3494, 3504; and from the signification of a hairy man, as denoting the quality of it, viz. of good: that hairy signifies the natural [principle] especially respecting truth, may be seen n. 3301, and from what now follows.

3527. "And I am a smooth man"—that hereby is signified the quality of natural truth respectively, is clear from the representation of Jacob, who is here the person who speaks, as denoting the natural [principle] as to truth, of which see n. 3305, and from the signification of a smooth man, as denoting its quality, of which we shall speak presently. Before it can be known what these things signify, it must be known what is meant by hairy, and what by smooth. The interiors in man exhibit themselves in a certain image in his exteriors, especially in his face and countenance. His inmost principles do not appear therein at this day, but his interiors do in some measure, unless from infancy he has learned to dissemble, for in this case he assumes to himself as it were another soul, and consequently induces another countenance, inasmuch as it is the soul which appears in the face; hypocrites, more than others, have acquired this habit from actual life, thus from custom, and this so much the more, as they are more deceitful; with those who are not hypocrites, rational good appears in their face from a certain fire of life, and rational truth from the light of this fire; man knows these things from a certain innate science, without study, for it is the life of his spirit as to good and as to truth, which thus manifests itself, and because man is a spirit clothed with a body, he has such knowledge from the perception of his spirit, thus from himself; hence it is, that at times man is affected by the countenance of another, although this is not from the countenance, but from the mind which thus shines forth through it; whereas the natural principle appears in the face in a more obscure fire of life, and a more obscure light of life; but the corporeal principle scarce [appears] unless in the warmth and fairness of the complexion, and in the change of their states according to the affections. Inasmuch as the interiors thus manifest themselves in the face especially, as in an image, therefore the most ancient people, who were celestial men, and altogether ignorant of dissimulation, and much more of hypocrisy and deceit, were able to see the minds of one another conspicuous in the face, as in a form, and therefore by the face were signified the things of the will and understanding, or the interior rational principles with respect to good and truth, see n. 358, 1999, 2434, and indeed those interior things with respect to good by the blood and its redness, and the interior things respecting truths by the form thence resulting, and its fairness; but the interior natural things by the excrescences thence arising, such as are the hairs and the scales of the skin, viz. the things from the natural principle that have reference to good by the hairs, and the things from the natural principle which refer to truth by the scales; of course they who were in natural good, were called hairy men; but they who were in natural truth, smooth men; from these considerations it may appear what is meant in the internal sense by these words, "My brother Esau is a hairy man, and I am a smooth man," viz. the quality of natural good respectively, and the quality of natural truth respectively. Hence also it is evident what Esau represents, namely, the good of the natural [principle], for Esau is so called from being hairy, see Gen. xxv. 25; and Edom from being ruddy, Gen. xxv. 30. Mount Seir, where he dwelt, signifies also the same, namely, what is shaggy; and because it had this signification, there was a mountain by which they went up to Seir, which is called a smooth mountain, see Josh. xi. 17; chap. xii. 7; which was also representative of truth ascending to good. That hairy is predicated of good, and thence of truth, and also in an opposite sense of evil, and thence of what is false, may be seen n. 3301; but that smooth is predicated of truth, and in an opposite sense of what is false, is clear from these passages in the Word, in Isaiah, "Waxing warm with their gods under every green tree, in *the smooth things of the valley* is thy portion," chap. lvii. 5, 6; where to wax warm is predicated of evil, and the smooth things of the valley of what is false. Again in the same prophet, "The smith strengthens the melter, *smoothing the hammer* with the stroke of the anvil, saying to the joining, it is good," chap. xli. 7; where the smith strengthening the melter is predicated of evil, and smoothing the hammer of what is false. So in David, "They make *thy mouth smooth* with butter, when his heart approaches, [his] words are softer than oil," Psalm lv. 22, where a smooth or alluring mouth is predicated of what is false, and the heart, and thence soft things, of what is evil. Again, "Their throat is an open sepulchre, they speak *smooth things* with their tongue," Psalm v. 10; the throat an open sepulchre is predicated of evil, the tongue speaking smooth things of what is false. So in

Luke, " Every valley shall be filled, and every mountain and
hill shall be humbled ; and the crooked shall be made straight,
and the rough places *plain ways,*" iii. 4 ; where valley denotes
what is lowly, see n. 1723, 3417 ; mountain and hill what is
elated, see n. 1691 ; the crooked made straight, denotes the
evil of ignorance turned into good, for length, and the things
relating thereto, are predicated of good, n. 1613 ; the rough
places made into plain ways, denotes the falses of ignorance
turned into truths ; that way is predicated of truth, see n. 627,
2333.

3528. "Perhaps my father may feel me"—that hereby is
signified the inmost degree of perception, is clear from the
signification of feeling, and thus of being made sensible, as
denoting the inmost and the all of perception ; and from the
signification of father, as denoting good, in the present case
Divine Good, because it treats of the Lord. That to feel is the
inmost and the all of perception, is from this ground, because
all sensation has reference to the sense of touch, and the touch
is derived and exists from perception, for sensation is nothing
else than external perception, and perception is nothing else
than internal sensation. The nature of perception may be
seen, n. 104, 371, 495, 503, 521, 536, 1383 to 1398, 1616, 1919,
2145, 2171, 2831. Moreover all sensation and all perception,
although it appears so various, has yet reference to one common and universal sense, namely, the touch ; the varieties, as
the taste, the smell, the hearing, and the sight, which are ex
ternal sensations, are no other than the genera thereof, arising
from the internal sensation, that is, from the perception ; this
might be confirmed by much experience, but of this, by the
Divine Mercy of the Lord, we shall treat in its proper place.
Hence it is clear, that to feel is the inmost and the all of perception. Moreover all perception, that is, internal sensation,
exists from good, but not from truth, unless from good by truth,
for the Divine Life of the Lord flows into good, and through
good into truth, and thus produces perception ; hence it may
appear what is signified by this expression, "If my father shall
feel me," viz. the inmost and the all of perception from good,
thus from the Divine [principle] of the Lord.

3529. "And I shall be in his eyes as one seducing"—that
hereby is signified rejection because apparently contrary to
order, is clear from the signification of being in his eyes, as
denoting apperception of the quality, for by the eye is signified
apperception of the internal sight, see n. 212, 2701, 2789, 2829,
3198, 3202 ; and from the signification of seducing, or seducer,
as being contrary to order, in the present case apparently ; all
seduction is nothing else ; and hence would be rejection. But
what is signified by being apparently contrary to order, will
appear evident from what follows.

VOL. IV.	H

3530. " And I shall bring upon me a curse and not a bless-ing"—that hereby is signified disjunction, is clear from the signification of curse, as denoting disjunction or aversion from good, see n. 245, 379, 1423 ; and from the signification of bless-ing as denoting conjunction with good, see n. 3504, 3514.

3531. "And his mother said unto him"—that hereby is signified perception from Divine Truth, is clear from the signi-fication of saying, as denoting to perceive, of which mention has been often made above; and from the representation of Rebecca, here the mother, as denoting the Divine Truth of the Divine Rational of the Lord, concerning which see n. 3012, 3013.

3532. " Upon me be thy curse, my son"—that hereby is signified that there should be no disjunction, is clear from the signification of curse, as denoting disjunction, see n. 3530; and whereas perception was from the Divine principle, see n. 3531, it signifies that there should be no disjunction.

3533. " Only hearken unto my voice, and go, take for me"—that hereby is signified from the effect, may be clear from the signification of hearkening to a voice, as denoting to obey; and from the signification of going and taking for me, as denoting to do ; and because this is spoken to the natural [principle] as to truth, represented by Jacob, from the rational as to truth, in this place the Divine Rational, represented by Rebecca, wherefore nothing else is signified than from the effect; for the natural [principle] sees from the effect, whereas the rational sees from the cause.

3534. Verses 14, 15, 16, 17. *And he went, and took, and brought to his mother, and his mother made savoury meat as his father loved. And Rebecca took goodly raiment [raiment of desires] of her elder son Esau, which were with her in the house, and put them upon Jacob, her younger son. And she made him put the skins of the kids of the goats upon his hands, and on the smooth of his neck. And she gave the savoury meat, and the bread, which she had made, into the hand of Jacob her son.* And he went, and took, and brought to his mother, sig-nifies a state of obedience of natural truth : and his mother made savoury meat as his father loved, signifies delectable things, but not desirable : and Rebecca took goodly raiment [raiment of desires] of her elder son Esau, signifies genuine truths of good : which were with her in the house, signifies which were from the Divine Good by the Divine Truth of the Divine Rational principle : and she put them on Jacob her younger son, signifies the affection of truth, or the life of good from truth : and she made him put on the skins of the kids of the goats, signifies the external truths of domestic good : upon his hands, signifies according to the faculty of receiving : and upon the smooth of his neck, signifies that disjoining truth should not appear: and she gave him savoury meat, signifies delectable things from thence: and bread, signifies good from thence: which she had made, signifies which were from Divine Truth: into the hand of Jacob her son, signifies that such was the affection of natural truth.

3535. "And he went, and took, and brought to his mother" —that hereby is signified a state of obedience of natural truth, may appear from what was said above, n. 3533, thus without further explication.

3536. "And his mother made savoury meat as his father loved"—that hereby are signified delectable things, but not desirable, appears from the representation of Rebecca. who here is mother, as denoting the Divine Rational [principle] as to truth; and from the signification of savoury meats, as denoting the agreeable things which are of truth, of which see above, n. 3502. The reason why the delectable things here spoken of are not desirable, is, because they are not from the hunting of Esau, that is, from the truth of genuine good, see n. 3501, but from the kids of the goats which are of the flock, that is, from the truth of domestic good, see n. 3518, 3519. How these things are, may be clearly understood from what was said above, n. 3502, 3512, 3518, 3519.

3537. "And Rebecca took goodly raiment [raiment of desires] of her elder son Esau"—that hereby are signified genuine truths of good, is clear from the signification of goodly raiment [raiment of desires], as denoting genuine truths; that raiment denotes inferior truths respectively, may be seen, n. 2576; raiment of desires denotes genuine truths, because of genuine natural good, which is represented by Esau the elder son, see n. 3300, 3302, 3322, 3494, 3504, 3527.

3538. "Which were with her in the house"—that hereby is signified which were from the Divine Good by the Divine Truth of the Divine Rational principle, is clear from the representation of Rebecca, who is here understood by her, as denoting the Divine Truth of the Divine Rational [principle], of which see above; and from the signification of house, as here denoting the Divine Good, because it is predicated of the Lord; that house is good, may be seen, n. 710, 2233, 2234, 2559, 3128. The ground and reason why these things are signified by these words, which were with her in the house, is, because by house is signified the rational principle both as to good and as to truth; or, what is the same, both as to the will [principle], this being of good, and as to the understanding, this being of truth; when the rational acts from the will [principle] or good, by means of the intellectual [principle] or truth, then the rational mind is called one house; thence also heaven itself is called the house of God, because therein is nothing but good and truth; and the good acts by means of truth united and

conjoined to itself. This also is represented in marriages between husband and wife who compose one house, by reason
that conjugial love exists from the Divine marriage of good and
truth, see n. 2728, 2729, 3132, and both the husband and wife
have will from good, but with a difference like that of good in
respect to its truth, wherefore also good is signified by the husband, and truth by the wife, for when the house is one, then
good is all therein, and truth, because it is of good, is also good.
The reason why it is said, "with her in the house," not with him
or with them, is, because the subject treated of is concerning
the state of conjunction of truth and good, or concerning the
state before they were fully united or conjoined; which state is
next spoken of.

3539. "And she put [them] on Jacob her younger son"—
that hereby is signified the affection of truth, or the life of good
from truth, is clear from the representation of Rebecca, as
denoting the Divine Truth of the Divine Rational [principle],
and from the representation of Jacob, as denoting the Divine
Truth of the Divine Natural [principle]; and from the signification of putting on, as here denoting to communicate, and to
imbibe, namely, the truths of good which are signified by the
garments of Esau, see n. 3537, thus the affection of natural
truth, which is here the same with the life of good from truth.
How these things are to be understood, may be known from
what was said above, n. 3518; but because they are such things
as are at this day most unknown, it may be proper to explain
them further to common apprehension. The subject treated of
in this chapter is concerning the Lord, how He made His natural [principle] Divine; and in a representative sense, concerning the regeneration of man as to his natural [principle], see n.
3490. The case herein with man is this: the end of regeneration
is that man may be made new as to his internal man, thus as to
his soul or spirit; but man cannot be made new or regenerated
as to his internal man, unless also as to his external; for although
man after death is a spirit, he nevertheless has with him in
another life the things appertaining to his external man, viz.
natural affections, and also doctrinals, and likewise scientifics,
in a word, all things of the external or natural memory, see n.
2475 to 2483; for these are the planes in which his interiors are
terminated. As these therefore are disposed, so interior things,
when they flow in, are formed, for therein they are modified.
Hence it is evident, that man ought not only to be regenerated
or made new as to his internal or rational man, but also as to
his external or natural man; and unless this was effected, there
could be no correspondence. That there is a correspondence
between the internal man and his spiritual [principle], and the
external man and his natural [principle], may be seen, n. 2971,
2987, 2989, 2990, 3002, 3493. The state of the regeneration

of man is described in a representative sense in this chapter by
Esau and Jacob, and here his quality at first, viz. whilst he is
regenerating, or before he is regenerated; for this state is plainly
the inverse of that in which man is when he is regenerated:
for in the former state, viz. whilst man is regenerating, or before he is regenerated, intellectual things, which are of truth,
apparently act first; but when he is regenerated, then the things
of the will, which are of good, act first. That the intellectual
things, which are of truth, apparently act first in the first state,
is represented by Jacob, in that he claimed the birth-right of
Esau to himself, see n. 3325, 3336; also in that he claimed the
blessing, which is here treated of; and that the state is plainly
inverted, is represented by this circumstance, that Jacob feigned
himself to be Esau, viz. in putting on the garments of Esau,
and the skins of the kids of the goats; for in this state, rational
truth not so fully conjoined to rational good, or, what is the
same, the understanding not so fully conjoined with the will,
thus flows in, and acts upon the natural [principle], and thus
inversely disposes the things which are therein. This may also
be manifest from much experience, especially from this, that a
man may perceive in the understanding, and the natural [prin-
ciple] thence know many things which are good and true, but
yet the will may not as yet act according to them: as for instance, that love and charity is the essential [principle] in man,
this his intellectual faculty may see and confirm, but before he
is regenerated, the will-principle cannot acknowledge it. There
are those who have altogether no love to the Lord, and no charity to their neighbour, who are well able to comprehend this.
In like manner, that love is the very life of man, and that as the
love is, such is the life; and likewise that every thing pleasing
and agreeable is from love, consequently all joy and all felicity;
and of course, such as the love is, such is the joy and such the
felicity. Man may also comprehend in his understanding,
(although his will should dissent or even go contrary thereto,)
that the happiest life is from love to the Lord and charity to our
neighbour, because the essential Divine [principle] flows thereinto; and on the other hand, that the most miserable life is
from self-love and the love of the world, because the essential
infernal [principle] flows into it. Hence also it may be perceivable by the understanding, yet not by the will, that love to
the Lord is the life of heaven, and that mutual love is the soul
from that life; wherefore so far as a man does not think from
the life of his will, nor reflects on his life thence derived, so far
he perceives this in his understanding, but so far as he thinks
from the life of his will, so far he does not perceive, nay denies.
The understanding may also clearly comprehend, that the Divine [principle] can only flow into man when he is humble, for
this reason, because when he is in this state the loves of self and

the world, and consequently infernal things which oppose, are removed; but yet, while the will is not new, and the understanding not united to such new will, man cannot be in humiliation of heart; yea, so far as a man is in the life of evil, that is, so far as his will is in evil, so far he cannot be in humiliation; and further, so far the above truth is obscure to him, and he even denies it. Hence also a man may perceive in his understanding, that his humiliation is not for the sake of the love of glory in the Lord, but for the sake of Divine Love, that the Lord with good and truth may thus flow in, and make man blessed and happy; nevertheless, so far as the will is consulted, so much this is obscured; the same is true in several other cases. This faculty, namely, that man may understand what is good and true, although he does not will it, is given to man in order that he may be reformed and regenerated; on which account both the good and bad have this faculty, yea, in the bad it is in some cases more acute, but with this difference, that in the bad there is no affection of truth on account of life, that is, for the good of life from truth, wherefore they cannot be reformed; but with the good there is an affection of truth for life, that is, for the good of life, and therefore these may be reformed. The first state of the reformation of these is, that the truth of doctrine appears to them to be in the first place, and the good of life in the second, for they do good from truth; but their second state is, that the good of life is in the first place, and the truth of doctrine in the second, for they do good from good, that is, from the will of good; and when this is the case, inasmuch as the will is conjoined to the understanding as in a marriage, man is regenerated. These two states are treated of in what is said of Esau and Jacob in the internal sense.

3540. "And she made him put on the skins of the kids of the goats"—that hereby are signified the external truths of domestic good, is clear from the signification of skins, as denoting external things, of which we shall speak presently; and from the signification of kids of the goats, because from the flock at home, as denoting truths of domestic good, of which see n. 3518, 3519; in which passages it is manifest also what is domestic good, and what the truths thence derived. Every particular good has its truths, and all truths have their good, which must be conjoined to each other in order that they may be something. The ground and reason why skins signify things external, is, because skins are the outermost principles of the animal, in which its interiors are terminated, in like manner as the skin or cuticles in man. This significative is grounded in what is representative in another life. There are in the other life those who refer to the province of the skin, concerning whom we shall treat, by the Divine Mercy of the Lord, when we speak concerning the Grand Man at the end of the follow-

:ng chapters; they are such as are only in external good, and in its truths; and hence the skin, and also the hide of beasts, signify things external, which is also manifest from the Word, as in Jeremiah, "Because of the multitude of thy iniquity, thy skirts are revealed, thy heels are violated; can the Ethiopian change *his skin*, and the leopard his spots? ye also may do good, who are taught to do evil," xiii. 22, 23. In this passage, skirts are external truths; heels, outermost goods. That heel and shoes are the lowest natural principles, may be seen, n. 259, 1748; and because those truths and goods were from evil, as it is said, they are compared to an Ethiopian, or a black, and his skin also to a leopard and its spots. So in Moses. "If in pledging thou shalt have pledged unto thee the raiment of thy companion, thou shalt restore it unto him before the sun goes down, because this is his only covering; this *his raiment is for the skin in which he shall lie down*," Exod. xxii. 25, 26. As all laws, even civil and forensic, which are in the Word, have correspondence with the laws of good and truth which are in heaven, and were thence enacted, so also this law, otherwise it would be impossible to discover why they should restore a pledged raiment before the sun set; and why it is said that his raiment is for the skin in which he shall lie down. The correspondence is manifest from the internal sense, which is this, that companions should not be defrauded of external truths which are the docrinals according to which they live, and rituals; that raiment denotes such truths, see n. 297, 1073, 2576. But the sun is the good of love, or of life which is thence, see n. 1529, 1530, 2441, 2495. That this should not perish, is signified by its being restored before the sun set; and because the above things are the externals of the interiors, or their terminations, therefore it is said, that his raiment is for a skin in which he should lie down. Because skins signified things external, it was commanded that the covering of the tent should be of the *skins* of red *rams*, and over these the *skins of badgers*, Exod. xxvi. 14. For the tent was representative of the three heavens, thus of the celestial and spiritual things of the Lord's kingdom. The curtains, which were round about, represented natural things, which are external, see n. 3478, which are the skins of rams and the skins of badgers; and because external things are what cover internal, or natural things what cover things spiritual and celestial, as the body its soul, therefore was this command given. In like manner that Aaron and his sons, when the camp proceeded, should cover the ark of the covenant with the veil of a covering, and should put upon it a covering, the skin of a badger; and upon the table, and the things which were upon it, should spread a cloth of scarlet double dyed, and should cover it with *badger's skin*, as a covering. Likewise they should cover the candlestick and

all its vessels with a covering of *badger's skin ;* and should put
a cloth of blue over all the vessels of the ministry, and should
cover them with a covering of *badger's skin*, Numb. iv. 5, 6,
8, 10, 11, 12.   Whoever thinks religiously concerning the
Word, may know that divine things are represented by all
these particulars, as by the ark, the table, the candlestick, and
the vessels of the ministry, so also by the coverings of scarlet
double dyed and blue, and also by the coverings of the badgers'
skins, and that by these are represented Divine things which
are in externals.   Inasmuch as the prophets represented teachers, and thence the doctrine of good and truth from the Word,
see n. 2534, and Elias the Word itself, see n. 2762, and in like
manner John, who therefore is called the Elias that was to
come, Matt. xvii. 10, 11, 12, 13 ; therefore that they might represent the Word, as it is in its external form, that is, in the
letter, Elias was girded with a *girdle or skin* round his loins, 2
Kings i. 8 ; and "John had a garment of camel's hair, and *a
girdle of skin* round his loins," Matt. iii. 4.   And whereas skin
signified external things, which are natural things in respect of
spiritual and celestial, and in the ancient Church it was customary to speak and write by representations, therefore also in
Job, which is a book of the ancient Church, skin has the same
signification, as may appear from several passages in that book,
as for instance, " I know my Redeemer, He liveth, and at the
last He shall arise over the dust, and these things shall be encompassed with *my skin*, and *out of my flesh* I shall see God,"
xix. 25, 26 ; where to be encompassed with skin, denotes the
natural [principle], such as man has with him after death, concerning which see n. 3539 : out of the flesh to see God, denotes
from a vivified proprium ; that this is flesh may be seen, n.
148, 149, 780.   That the book of Job is a book of the ancient
Church, is evident, as has been mentioned, from the representative and significative style in which it is written, but it is not
of those books which are called the law and the prophets, because it has not an internal sense which only treats of the Lord,
and of His kingdom.   It is this alone which makes a book of
the genuine Word.

3541. " And upon his hands"—that hereby is signified according to the faculty of receiving, is clear from the signification of hand, as denoting power, concerning which see n. 878,
3091 ; thus faculty of receiving.

3542. " And upon the smooth of his neck"—that hereby is
signified that disjoining truth should not appear, is evident from
the predication of smooth or of smoothness, as having respect
to truth, of which see n. 3527 ; and from the signification of
neck, as denoting what conjoins, of which we shall speak presently ; in the present case therefore, because the appearance
was upon the smooth of his neck, it denotes that disjoining

truth should not appear. How this case is, may appear from
what was said and shown above, n. 3539, viz. that the good,
and the truths, which flow from the understanding, and not
from the will at the same time, is not good, and are not truths,
although they should appear so in the external form, and if the
will is of evil, the good and the truths would disunite and not
conjoin ; but if there is any thing of good in the will, in this
case they do not disunite, but conjoin, although they be disposed in an inverted order, for thereby man is regenerated ; and
because when thus disposed, they serve first for the regeneration
of man, it is said that thus disjoining truth should not appear ;
but more of this in what follows. The ground and reason why
the neck signifies the conjoining [principle], is, because the superior things in man, which appertain to the head, communicate
with the inferior things of his body by the interceding neck ;
hence both influx and communication, consequently conjunction, is signified by that intermediate [principle], as may still
better appear from the correspondences of the GRAND MAN
with the various parts of the human body, which are treated of
at the conclusion of the chapters. The same is thence signified
by the neck in the Word ; as in Isaiah, " His spirit, like an inundating stream, *will divide even to the neck,*" xxx. 28 ; where
inundating stream denotes the false principle thus overflowing ;
to divide even to the neck, denotes to check and to intercept
communication, and thence the conjunction of things superior
with things inferior, which is checked and intercepted when
spiritual good and truth is not received. So in Habakkuk,
" Thou hast wounded the head from the house of the wicked,
by making naked the foundation *even to the neck,*" iii. 13 ; where
to wound the head from the house of the wicked, is to destroy
the principles of what is false ; to make naked the foundation
even unto the neck, denotes to intercept the conjunction thereby.
So in Jeremiah, " Prevarications intertwined have *ascended upon
my neck,* he hath thrust at my strength, God hath delivered me
into hands that I cannot rise up," Lam. i. 14 ; where prevarications intertwined ascending upon the neck, denote that falses
ascended towards things interior or rational. Inasmuch as by
neck was signified communication and conjunction, therefore
by the chains of the neck was signified interception, consequently the desolation of truth, which then exists, when spiritual things, which continually flow from the Lord, are not any
longer admitted into the rational [principle] of man, nor of
course into his natural. This interception or desolation is what
is represented in Jeremiah by the injunction, that he should
make unto himself chains and yokes, and should *put them upon
his neck,* and send them to the people, and say, that they should
serve Nebuchadnezzar king of Babylon, and they who did not
yield their necks under his yoke, should be visited by the sword,

famine, and pestilence; but they who *bowed down their neck*, should be left on the earth, Jer. xxvii. 2, 3, 8, 11; where to put the neck under the yoke of the king of Babylon and to serve him, denotes to be desolated as to truth, and to be vastated as to good; that it is Babel which vastates, may be seen, n. 1327; and that they are vastated, lest holy things should be profaned, see n. 301, 302, 303, 1327, 1328, 2426, 3398, 3399, 3402; and because, when the influx of good and truth is intercepted, what is evil and false is served, therefore also to put the neck under the yoke is to serve. Again, in the same prophet, "Jehovah hath said, Within two years of days I will break the yoke of Nebuchadnezzar king of Babylon *from off the neck* of all nations," xxviii. 11; denoting deliverance from vastation. So in Isaiah, "Shake thee from the dust, arise, sit down, O Jerusalem; *open the bands of thy neck*, O captive daughter of Zion," lii. 2; where to open the bands of the neck, is to admit and receive good and truth. So in Micah, "Behold I purpose evil against this family, *from which ye shall not withdraw your necks*, and ye shall not go erect, because that is a time of evil," ii. 3; where not to withdraw the neck from evil, is not to admit truth; not to go erect, is thus not to look to superior things, or those which are of heaven, see n. 248.

3543. "And she gave the savoury meat"—that hereby are signified the delightful things thence derived, is clear from the signification of savoury meat, as denoting things agreeable, and also delightful, of which see above, n. 3502, 3536.

3544. "And bread"—that hereby is signified good thence derived, is clear from the signification of bread, as denoting good, concerning which see n. 276, 680, 1798, 2165, 2177, 3464, 3478.

3545. "Which she had made"—that hereby are signified the things which were from the Divine [principle], is clear from the representation of Rebecca, as denoting the Divine Truth of the Divine Rational of the Lord; and because it is said of Rebecca, that she made them, it signifies that which was from the Divine [principle].

3546. "Into the hand of Jacob, her son"—that hereby is signified that such was the affection of natural truth, is clear from this consideration, that this is a closing period of what precedes, and at this time such was Jacob, by whom is represented natural truth, n. 3305, 3309, 3525, viz. that he was clothed, as to his hands and neck, with the skins of the kids of the goats, and had in his hands savoury meat, which he was to carry to his father Isaac.

3547. Verses 18, 19, 20. *And he came to his father and said, My father; and he said, Behold me, who art thou, my son? And Jacob said to his father, I am Esau thy first-born, I have done as thou spakest to me; arise, I pray, sit, and eat of my venison*

(hunting), to the end that thy soul may bless me. And Isaac
said to his son, What is this thou hast hastened to find, my son?
and he said, Because Jehovah thy God caused it to meet my face.
He came to his father, and said, My father; and he said, Behold
me, who art thou, my son? signifies a state of perception arising
from the presence of that truth : and Jacob said to his father,
signifies the apperception of natural truth : I am Esau thy first-
born, signifies that he believed that he was real natural good :
I have done as thou spakest to me, signifies obedience : arise, I
pray, sit, and eat of my venison (hunting), signifies the truth
of the affection of such good : to the end that thy soul may
bless me, signifies conjunction : and Isaac said to his son, signifies perception : What is this thou hast hastened to find, my
son? signifies production so hasty : and he said, Because Jehovah thy God caused it to meet my face, signifies providence.

3548. " He came to his father, and said, My father, and he
said, Behold me, who art thou, my son?"—that hereby is signified a state of perception arising from the presence of that truth,
may appear from the representation of Isaac, who is here father,
and from the representation of Jacob, who is here son, of which
frequent mention is made above; also from the signification of
saying, as denoting to perceive, concerning which see likewise
above.   Hence, and from the rest of the expressions, it is evident that it is a state of perception arising from the presence of
that truth, which is represented by Jacob.   But what is the quality of the truth which is now represented by Jacob, is manifest
from the internal sense of what goes before and of what follows,
viz. that in an external form it appears like good and the truth
of good, but that it is not such in its internal form.   The natura
principle as to truth with man, who is in the process of regeneration, that is, before regeneration is accomplished, has such
an appearance, not indeed in the sight of man, for he knows
nothing concerning good and truth in himself during regeneration, but in the sight of the angels, who see such things in the
light of heaven.   Man does not even know what the good and
truth of the natural principle is, and inasmuch as he does not
know this, he cannot perceive it ; and inasmuch as he does not
perceive it in general, neither can he perceive it in particular ;
consequently he cannot perceive the differences, and still less
the changes of their state ; and this being the case, he cannot
without difficulty comprehend from any description how this
good and the truth thereof are mutually circumstanced.   But
whereas the subject treated of in this chapter is concerning such
good and truth, therefore in what follows we shall endeavour to
explain it, so far as it is capable of being apprehended.

3549. "And Jacob said to his father"—that hereby is signified the apperception of natural truth, appears from the signification of saying, as denoting to perceive, concerning which see

above ; in the present case denoting to apperceive, because from the natural principle ; and from the representation of Jacob, as denoting natural truth, concerning which see also above.

3550. " I am Esau thy first-born"—that hereby is signified that he believed he was real natural good, appears from the representation of Esau, and from the signification of first-born, as denoting good, and indeed natural good, which is represented by Esau : for thus it is with the truth appertaining to man, before he is regenerated, that it believes itself to be real good. They who have perception know that it is not good, but that it is truth under the form of good ; but they who have not perception, know no other than that it is good. This however will appear more evident from what follows.

3551. " I have done as thou spakest to me"—that hereby is signified obedience, may appear without explication.

3552. " Rise, I pray; sit, and eat of my venison"—that hereby is signified the truth of the affection of such good, appears from the signification of rising, as implying somewhat of elevation, see n. 2401, 2785, 2912, 2927, 3171 ; and from the signification of sitting, as implying somewhat of tranquillity ; and from the signification of eating, as denoting appropriation, see n. 2187, 3168 ; and from the signification of venison (hunting), as denoting truth which is grounded in good, see n. 3501 : hence in the present case denoting the affection of such good from which truth is derived ; for the things signified by rising, sitting, and eating, in the internal sense, have respect to affection, wherefore the term affection alone is used to denote those things.

3553. " To the end that thy soul may bless me"—that hereby is signified conjunction, appears from the signification of being blessed, as denoting conjunction, see n. 3504, 3514, 3530.

3554. " And Isaac said to his son"—that hereby is signified perception, viz. of the rational [principle] represented by Isaac, concerning the natural [principle] which is represented by Jacob, and that to say is to perceive, has been often shown above.

3555. " What is this thou hast hastened to find, my son?"— that hereby is signified production so hasty, appears without explication.

3556. " And he said, Because Jehovah thy God caused it to meet my face"—that hereby is signified providence, may also appear without explication. The providence here treated of is, that good and truths thence derived are thus arranged in order with man, during regeneration, viz. that they appear outwardly, or are exhibited without in such an appearance, as if they were genuine good and genuine truths thence derived, when nevertheless they are not such, but are domestic good and truths thence derived, as was said above, serving only for the regener ation of man, thus for introducing goods and truths of a grosser nature, because such are expedient.

3557. Verses 21, 22, 23. *And Isaac said to Jacob, Come near, I pray, and I will feel thee, my son, whether thou be my son Esau or not. And Jacob came near to Isaac his father, and he felt him, and said, The voice is the voice of Jacob, and the hands the hands of Esau. And he did not acknowledge him, because his hands were hairy as his brother Esau's hands ; and he blessed him.* Isaac said to Jacob, signifies perception concerning this natural principle : Come near, I pray, and I will feel thee, my son, signifies inmost perception from presence : whether thou be my son Esau or not, signifies that it was not natural good : and Jacob came near to Isaac his father, signifies a state of presence : and he felt him, signifies thence all perception : and said, The voice is the voice of Jacob, and the hands the hands of Esau, signifies that the intellectual principle in this case is of truth which is within, but the will-principle is of good which is without, thus of inverted order : and he did not acknowledge him, because his hands were hairy as his brother Esau's hands, signifies that from the will-principle which was without, he perceived that it was natural good : and he blessed him, signifies conjunction thereby.

3558. " Isaac said to Jacob "—that hereby is signified perception concerning this natural principle, appears from the signification of saying, as denoting to perceive, concerning which see above ; and from the representation of Jacob, as denoting the natural [principle] as to truth, in the present case merely the natural [principle], because he also represented apparently, or in an external form resembled Esau, thus also the natural [principle] as to good, which is Esau, and likewise his venison (hunting), which is the truth that is of that good, see n. 3501. The reason of its being so often repeated, He said, is, because thus a new state commences, or a new perception, see n. 2061, 2238, 2260.

3559. "Come near, I pray, and I will feel thee, my son"—that hereby is signified inmost perception from presence, appears from the signification of coming near, as denoting presence ; and from the signification of feeling, as denoting inmost and all perception, see n. 3528.

3560. " Whether thou be my son Esau or not "—that hereby is signified that it was not natural good, appears from the doubt expressed in these words and in those which presently follow ; and whereas it is the rational [principle] which perceives what and of what quality the natural [principle] is, it is a perception that it was not natural good or Esau.

3561. " And Jacob came near to Isaac his father"—that hereby is signified a state of presence, may appear by what goes before, thus without further explication.

3562. " And he felt him"—that hereby is signified all perception, appears from the signification of feeling, as denoting inmost and all perception, concerning which see above, n. 3528, 3559, in the present case all perception, because the perception of all things is from that which is inmost, that is, they who are in inmost perception are in the perception of all things which are beneath, for the things which are beneath are nothing but derivations and consequent compositions, inasmuch as the inmost [principle] is all in all in whatever is beneath it, for whatever is beneath, unless it exists from things interior, or, what is the same, from things superior, as an effect from its efficient cause, has no existence at all. Hence it is evident, why the end regarded renders man happy or unhappy in another life, for the end regarded is the inmost [principle] of all cause, insomuch that unless the end be in the cause, yea, unless it be the all thereof, the cause does not exist; in like manner the end is the inmost [principle] of all effect, for the effect is produced from such cause; and this being the case, whatsoever appertains to man, derives its esse from the end which influences him, and hence in another life his state is such as the end is by which he is influenced, see n. 1317, 1568, 1571, 1645, 1909, 3425. Hence it may appear, that as by feeling is signified inmost perception, it consequently signifies all perception.

3563. " And he said, The voice is the voice of Jacob, and the hands the hands of Esau"—that hereby is signified that the intellectual [principle] in this case is of truth which is within, but that the will-principle is of good which is without, thus of inverted order, appears from the signification of voice, as being predicated of truth, and from the signification of hand, as being predicated of good; that voice is predicated of truth, appears from what was adduced above, 219, 220, and from this circumstance, that it is said, the voice is the voice of Jacob, by whom is represented natural truth, as was shown above; and the reason why hand is predicated of good is, because by hand is signified power and faculty, see n. 878, 3541, which is derived from no other source than good, all power and faculty being hence derived to truth, although it appears to be from truth; the same is evident also from this circumstance, that it is said, the hands are the hands of Esau, by whom is represented natural good, as was likewise shown above. That these principles are of an inverted order, appears from this consideration, that it is according to order that good which is of the will be within, and that truth which is of the understanding be without. These subjects however are of such a nature, as was said above, that they can be explained to the apprehension of very few for want of knowledges respecting them, inasmuch as where such knowledges are wanting, they cannot be comprehended; nevertheless it may be expedient to make some observations in regard thereto, such being the subject here treated of. The good of the natural [principle] has no other source of existence with man but from interior good, that is, the good of the rational [principle]; but influx causes the good therein to have quality agreeable to the quality of the principle; and whereas the good of the natural [principle] is from this source and from no other, the truth of the natural [principle] is also from the same source, for where good is, there is truth, it being necessary that both should exist in order to the existence of either; but influx also causes the truth herein to have a quality agreeable to the quality of the principle. The influx is in this manner: the good of the rational [principle] flows into the natural by a twofold way, viz. by the shortest way, into the essential good of the natural [principle], thus immediately, and through the good of the natural [principle] into its truth; this good and this truth is what is represented by Esau and his venison (hunting); the good of the rational [principle] also flows into the natural by a way less short, viz. through the truth of the rational [principle], and by this influx forms somewhat resembling good, but it is truth. It is thus according to order that the good of the rational [principle] should flow into the good of the natural, and at the same time into its truth, immediately, and also through the truth of the rational [principle] into the good of the natural, thus mediately, and in like manner into the truth of the natural [principle] both immediately and mediately. When this is the case, then the influx is according to order. Such influx has place with those who are become regenerate; but another influx has place before they are regenerate, as was said above, viz. an influx of the good of the rational [principle] not immediately into the good of the natural, but mediately through the truth of the rational, whereby is presented somewhat resembling good in the natural, but it is not genuine good, and consequently not genuine truth, yet it is of such a nature, that it really has good intimately united with it, by virtue of influx through the truth of the rational [principle], but no further. For this reason good also exists therein under another form, namely, outwardly like the good which is represented by Esau, but inwardly like the truth which is represented by Jacob, and as this is not according to order, it is said to be of inverted order; nevertheless, when considered in regard to its expediency, as needful in the process of man's regeneration, it is according to order. I am well aware that these particulars, although they are expressed with clearness, and consequently may be perceived clearly by those who are principled in the knowledge of such things, will still appear obscure to those who are unacquainted with the nature of influx, and more so to those who do not know that the rational [principle] is distinct from the natural, and still more so to those who have not any distinct idea concerning good and concerning truth. But what the quality of natural good is, and of natural truth, in the state previous to regeneration, can only be manifest from the affections which prevail at that time. When man is affected with truth, not for the sake of ends which regard life, but for the sake of other ends, viz. that he may become learned, and this from a certain affection of emulation, or from a certain affection of infantile envy, and also from a certain affection of glory, in such case the good and truth of the natural [principle] is in such an order as is here represented by Jacob, consequently it is in inverted order respectively, that is, the will-principle which is of good is without, and the intellectual principle which is of truth is within; but in the state after regeneration it is otherwise. In this case man is not only affected with truth for the sake of the ends of life, but he is still more affected with essential good of life, and the former affections, viz. of emulation, of infantile envy, and of glory, separate themselves, and this until it appears as if they were dissipated, for in this case good which is of the will is with-in, and truth which is of the understanding is without, yet still in such a manner, that truth acts in unity with good, as being derived from good. This order is genuine; and the former order is to the intent that this order may be formed, for the will principle, which in such case is without, is admissive of several things which are serviceable to regeneration, and like a sponge which imbibes both clear and muddy waters, it also imbibes such things as would otherwise be rejected, which nevertheless serve as mediums, and also for forming ideas concerning goods and truths, besides other uses.

3564. " And he did not acknowledge him, because his hands were hairy as his brother Esau's hands"—that hereby is signified that from the will-principle which was without, he perceived that it was natural good, appears from this consideration, that he did not acknowledge Jacob to be Jacob, that is, the truth which Jacob represents, but that he perceived Esau, that is, the natural good which was without, and this by reason of the influx spoken of above, n. 3563; for between interior good and exterior good there is given a communication, because there is a parallelism, see n. 1831, 1832, 3514, but not between good and truth, unless the influx of good into truth be such as has been just now described above.

3565. " And he blessed him"—that hereby is signified conjunction thence effected, appears from the signification of being blessed, as denoting conjunction, see n. 3504, 3514, 3530; but in this state the conjunction was no other than what was described, n. 3563; there was intimate conjunction, but not middle conjunction, with the truth represented by Jacob, thus it was by the end, which is inmost good, which end was, that thus and no otherwise it could be effected; when there is an end regarded, then first conjunction has place of things inmost with things outermost ; middle conjunction comes by degrees, and is produced by the end regarded, for in the end regarded lies concealed all the progression thereto, inasmuch as the Lord acts by ends, and by them successively arranges intermediate things in order, and hence comes conjunction, which is signified by Isaac blessing Jacob.

3566. Verses 24, 25. *And he said, Art thou he my son Esau ? and he said, I (am). And he said, Bring to me, and I will eat of my son's venison, to the intent that my soul may bless thee ; and he brought to him, and he did eat, and he brought him wine, and he did drink.* He said, Art thou he my son Esau ? and he said, I (am), signifies a state of the affection of natural truth, in that it believed itself then to be natural good, from the external form : and he said, Bring to me, and I will eat of my son's venison (hunting), signifies a desire of conjoining to him-self natural truth by good : to the intent that my soul may bless thee, signifies conjunction : and he brought to him and he did eat, signifies conjunction of good first : and he brought him wine and he did drink, signifies conjunction of truth afterwards.

3567. " He said, Art thou he my son Esau ? he said, I (am)"— that hereby is signified a state of the affection of natural truth, in that it believed itself at that time to be natural good from the external form, may appear from Isaac's inquiry, " Art thou he my son Esau ?" by which nothing else can be signified, in the internal sense, but the influx of the rational [principle] from good into natural truth represented by Jacob ; and from the reply, " He said, I (am)," that he supposed himself at that time to be good, see what is said above, n. 3550.

3568. " And he said, Bring to me, and I will eat of my son's venison"—that hereby is signified a desire of conjoining to him-self natural truth by good, appears from the signification of eating, as denoting to conjoin and to appropriate, see n. 2187, 2343, 3168, 3513 ; and from the signification of my son's veni-son (hunting), as denoting the truth of good, see n. 3309. 3501, 3508 ; that desire is implied, is manifest.

3569. " To the intent that my soul may bless thee"—that hereby is signified conjunction, appears from the signification of being blessed, as denoting conjunction, see n. 3504, 3514, 3530, 3565.

3570. " And he brought to him, and he did eat"—that hereby is signified conjunction of good first ; and that by bring-ing wine to him and he did drink, is signified conjunction of truth afterwards, appears from the signification of eating, as denoting to be conjoined and to be appropriated as to good, concerning which see just above, n. 3568 ; and from the signi-fication of wine as denoting truth which is grounded in good, see n. 1071, 1798 ; and from the signification of drinking, as

denoting to be conjoined and to be appropriated as to truth, see
n. 3168. In regard to this circumstance, that the good of the
rational [principle], which is represented by Isaac, conjoins to
itself good first, and truth afterwards, and this by the natural
[principle], which is Jacob, the case is this : when the natural
[principle] is in that state, that outwardly it is good, and inwardly truth, concerning which see above, n. 3539, 3548, 3556,
3563, it admits at this time several things which are not good,
but which yet are useful, such as are the mediums leading to
good in their order; but the good of the rational [principle]
does not thence conjoin and appropriate to itself any other
things than such as agree with its own good, for good receives
no other, and whatsoever disagrees, it rejects ; the rest of the
things in the natural [principle] it leaves, that they may serve
as means of admitting and introducing several things suitable
to itself. The rational [principle] is in the internal man, and
what is therein transacted is unknown to the natural [principle],
as being above the sphere of its perception. Hence it is, that
man, who lives a mere natural life, cannot know any thing of
what is transacting with him in his internal man, or in his rational [principle], the Lord disposing and ordering such things,
whilst man is altogether ignorant of it. Hence too it is, that
man knows nothing of the manner how he is regenerated, and
scarcely that he is regenerated. But if he be desirous to know
this, let him attend only to the ends of life, which he proposes
to himself, and which he rarely discovers to any one ; if these
ends are directed to good, viz. that he is more attentive to his
neighbour and the Lord than to himself, he is then in a state of
regeneration ; but if the ends are directed to evil, viz. that he
is more attentive to himself than to his neighbour and the Lord,
let him know that in such case he is in no state of regeneration.
Man by the ends of his life is in another life, by ends of good
in heaven with angels, but by ends of evil in hell with devils ;
ends with man are nothing else but his loves, for what a man
loves, that he has for an end ; and inasmuch as ends are his
loves, they are also his inmost life, see n. 1317, 1568, 1571,
1645, 1909, 3425, 3562, 3565. Ends of good with man are in
his rational [principle], and are what is called the rational [prin-
ciple] as to good, or the good of the rational [principle]. By
ends of good, or by good therein, the Lord disposes all things
which are in the natural [principle], for the end is as the soul,
and the natural [principle] is as the body of that soul ; such as
the soul is, such is the body wherewith it is encompassed, thus
such as the rational [principle] is as to good, such is the natural [principle] wherewith it is invested. It is a known thing,
that the soul of man has its beginning in the ovum of the mother, and is afterwards perfected in her womb, and is there encompassed with a tender body, and this of such a nature, that

by it the soul is enabled to act suitably in the world into which
it is born. The case is similar when man is born again, that is.
is regenerated ; the new soul, which he then receives, is the end
of good, which has its beginning in the rat.onal [principle], at
first as in an ovum therein, and afterwards it is there perfected
as in a womb ; the tender body, with which this soul is encompassed, is the natural [principle] and the good therein, which is
such as to act obediently according to the ends of the soul ;
the truths therein are like fibres in the body, for truths are
formed from good, see n. 3470. Hence it is manifest, that an
image of the re-formation of man is exhibited in his formation
in the womb ; and if you are disposed to believe it, celestial
good and spiritual truth, which is from the Lord, is also what
forms him, and at the same time impresses an ability that he
can receive each [principle] successively, and this according to
the manner and degree in which like a man he has respect to
heavenly ends of life, and not like a brute animal to worldly
ends. That the rational [principle] as to good conjoins to itself
good first, and truth afterwards by the natural [principle],
which is signified by Jacob's bringing savoury meat and bread
to Isaac, and he did eat, and bringing him wine and he did
drink, may also be illustrated by the offices which the body
performs for its soul. It is the soul which gives to the body to
appetite food, and which gives also to relish it ; different kinds
of food are introduced by the delight of appetite and by the delight of taste, thus by external good ; but the different kinds of
food which are introduced, do not all enter the life, some serving
as menstruums for digestion, some for tempering, some for
opening, some for introducing into the vessels ; but the good
foods elected are introduced into the blood, and become blood,
and out of the blood the soul conjoins to itself such things as
are of use. The case is similar in regard to the rational [prin-
ciple] and the natural ; the desire and affection of knowing
truth correspond to appetite and relish, and scientifics and
knowledges correspond to different kinds of food, see n. 1480 ;
and it is by reason of this correspondence that the cases are
similar. The soul which is the good of the rational [principle],
gives the faculty of desiring and of being affected with the
things of science and of doctrine, and thus introduces such
things by the delight which is of desire, and by the good which
is of affection ; but the things which it introduces are not all
such as to become the good of life, some serving as means for
a kind of digesting and tempering, some for opening and introducing, but the good things which are of life it applies to itself,
and thereby conjoins them to itself, and from them forms to
itself truths. Hence it is manifest how the rational [principle]
disposes the natural to serve itself as the soul, or, what is the
same thing, to serve the end regarded by man, which is the

soul, and to perfect itself, that it may be of use in the Lord's kingdom.

3571. Verses 26, 27, 28, 29. *And Isaac his father said unto him, Come near, I pray, and kiss me, my son. And he came near, and kissed him, and he smelled the smell of his raiment, and blessed him, and said, See, the smell of my son is as the smell of a field, which Jehovah has blessed. And God shall give to thee of the dew of heaven, and of the fatnesses of the earth, and multitude of corn and new wine. People shall serve thee, and people shall bow down themselves to thee; be a master unto thy brethren, and thy mother's sons shall bow down themselves to thee; cursed are they that curse thee, and blessed are they that bless thee.* Isaac his father said unto him, Come near, I pray, signifies a degree of perception still more inward : and kiss me, my son, signifies whether or no he can be united : and he came near and kissed him, signifies presence and unition : and he smelled the smell of his raiment, signifies what was grateful arising from the truth of good which he perceived : and blessed him, signifies conjunction thus : and said, See, the smell of my son, signifies what was grateful arising from the truth of good . is as the smell of a field, signifies as from good ground out of which is truth : which Jehovah has blessed, signifies that it is multiplied and made fruitful from the Divine [principle] : and God shall give unto thee of the dew of heaven, signifies from Divine Truth : and of the fatnesses of the earth, signifies from Divine Good : and multitude of corn, signifies natural good thence derived : and of new wine, signifies thence natural truth : people shall serve thee, signifies the truths of the Church, or spiritual Churches : and people shall bow down themselves to thee, signifies the truths of good : be a master to thy brethren, signifies dominion at first appearing to be of the affection of natural truth over the affections of natural good : and thy mother's sons shall bow down themselves to thee, signifies over the rest of the affections of truth : cursed are they that curse thee, signifies that whosoever disjoineth himself shall be disjoined : and blessed are they that bless thee, signifies that whosoever conjoineth himself shall be conjoined.

3572. "Isaac his father said unto him, Come near, I pray"— that hereby is signified a degree of perception still more inward, appears from the signification of saying that he should come near, as denoting a degree of more inward perception arising from presence; to come near, can have no other signification.

3573. "And kiss me, my son"—that hereby is signified whether or no he can be united, appears from the signification of kissing, as denoting unition and conjunction from affection. Kissing, which is a thing external, is nothing else but an affection of conjunction, which is a thing internal; there is also a correspondence between them. The subject here treated of, as is manifest from what has been said above, in a supreme sense, is concerning the Glorification of the natural [principle] in the Lord, that is, how the Lord made the natural [principle] in Himself Divine; but in a representative sense it relates to the regeneration of the natural [principle] with man, thus to the conjunction of the natural [principle] with the rational; for the natural [principle] is not regenerated until it is conjoined to the rational. This conjunction is effected by influx immediate and mediate of the rational [principle] into the good and truth of the natural, viz. from the good of the rational [principle] immediately into the good of the natural, and through this good into the truth of the natural [principle]; and mediately through the truth of the rational [principle] into the truth of the natural, and thence into the good of the natural. These conjunctions are here treated of; which conjunctions can in no wise exist but by means provided from the Divine [principle], and indeed by such as are most unknown to man, and of which he can scarce form any idea by those things which are of the world's light, that is, which are of the luminous [principle] naturally appertaining to him, but by those things which are of the light of heaven, that is, which are of rational light. Nevertheless all these means (or mediums) are discoverable in the internal sense of the Word, and are manifest to those who are principled in that sense, consequently to the angels, who see and perceive innumerable things on this subject, whereof scarce a single one can be unfolded and explained adequately to the apprehension of man. But from effects and the signs thereof it is in some measure evident to man how the case is in respect to this conjunction; for the rational mind, that is, the interior will-principle and intellectual [principle] with man, must needs represent itself in his natural mind, as the natural mind represents itself in his face and countenance, insomuch that, as the face is the countenance of the natural mind, so the natural mind must needs be the countenance of the rational mind. When conjunction is effected, as is the case with those who are regenerated, then whatsoever man interiorly wills and thinks in his rational [principle], presents itself conspicuous in his natural [principle], and this latter presents itself conspicuous in his face. Such a face have the angels, and such a face had the most ancient people, who were celestial men; for they were not at all afraid of others knowing their ends and intentions, inasmuch as they willed nothing but good; for whosoever suffers himself to be led of the Lord, in no wise intends and thinks any thing else. When the state is such, then the rational [principle] as to good conjoins itself immediately with the good of the natural [principle], and by this with its truths, and also mediately by truth conjoined to itself in the rational [principle] with truth of the natural [principle], and by this with good in the same [principle]; hence conjunction becomes indissoluble. But how far man at this day is removed from this state, consequently from a celestial state, may appear from this consideration, that it is believed to be a requisite of civil prudence to speak, to act, and also to express by the countenance what is contrary to the thought and intention; yea, even to dispose the natural mind in such a manner, that together with its face, it may act contrary to the things interiorly thought and willed from an end grounded in evil. This was regarded by the most ancient people as enormous, and such persons were rejected from their society as devils. From these considerations, as from effects and their signs, it is manifest what is meant by the conjunction of the rational or internal man, as to good and truth, with the natural or external man; and thus what is the quality of a man-angel, and what the quality of a man-devil.

3574. "And he came near and kissed him"—that hereby is signified presence and conjunction, appears from the signification of coming near, as denoting presence, and from the signification of kissing, as denoting unition or conjunction from affection, see n. 3573. That this is signified by kissing, appears also from the following passages in the Word, "Serve Jehovah in fear, and *kiss the Son*, lest He be angry, and ye perish in the way, because His wrath will kindle shortly; blessed are all they that trust in Him," Psalm ii. 12; speaking of the Lord, Whose Divine Human [principle] is the Son; to kiss Him is to be conjoined to him by faith grounded in love. Again, "Let mercy and truth meet together; let justice and peace *kiss*," Psalm lxxxv. 10; where justice and peace kissing, denotes their conjunction together. So in Hosea, "Ephraim hath spoken horror, and he became guilty in Baal; and now they add to sin, they make them a graven image of their silver, idols in their intelligence, the whole work of artificers, saying to them, sacrificing a man they *kiss* calves," xiii. 1, 2; where Ephraim denotes intelligence, in the present case man's own proper intelligence, that is, of those who believe, and are desirous to believe, that they are wise of themselves and not from the Lord. The graven image of their silver denotes good falsified; the whole work of the artificers denotes self-intelligence. They who are such are said to kiss calves; that is, to embrace magic and to adjoin themselves thereto. So in the first book of the Kings, "Jehovah said to Elijah, I have caused to remain in Israel seven thousand, all the knees which have not bowed themselves to Baal, and every mouth which hath not *kissed him*," xix. 18; where to kiss denotes to join itself from affection, thus to worship.

3575. "And he smelled the smell of his raiment"—that hereby is signified what was grateful arising from the truth of good which he perceived, appears from the signification of smell (odour), as denoting what is grateful, see n. 925, and of smell-

ing, as denoting to perceive what is grateful, and from the signification of raiment, as denoting truth, see n. 297, 1073, 2576;
and as this was Esau's, who is here understood by *his*, and by
Esau is represented natural good, therefore it is the truth of
good which is here signified. Truth of good is that which is
produced in the natural [principle] by influx immediate and
mediate of the rational, concerning which influx see above, n.
3573. This truth was what was desired; but whereas it could
not be produced by immediate influx from the good of the rational [principle], unless at the same time by a mediate one,
that is, through the truth of the rational [principle], and this
could not be produced except by several means (or mediums),
which are what are here described by Esau and Jacob, in the
internal sense; therefore by smelling the smell of his raiment
is signified the truth of good which was perceived.

3576. "And blessed him"—that hereby is signified conjunction thus, appears from the signification of being blessed, as
denoting conjunction, see n. 3504, 3514, 3530, 3565. From
these particulars, which are related concerning Esau and Jacob
it may appear, that the good of the rational [principle] con
joined itself intimately with the good of the natural, and by
good therein with truth; for Isaac represents the rational
[principle] as to good; Rebecca, the rational [principle] as to
truth; Esau, the good of the natural [principle]; and Jacob, the
truth thereof. That the rational [principle] as to good, which
is Isaac, conjoined itself intimately with the good of the natural
[principle], which is Esau, and not with the truth of the natural
[principle], which is Jacob, except mediately, is evident from
this consideration, that Isaac had Esau in mind when he pronounced the blessing on Jacob; nor did he think of Jacob at
that time, but of Esau. Whosoever pronounces a blessing,
blesses him of whom he thinks, and not him at that time of
whom he does not think. All blessing which is uttered with
the mouth, comes forth from an interior principle, having life
in it from the will and thought of him who blesses, and hence
it is essentially his to whom such will and thought are directed.
He who takes it, and thereby makes it his own, is like one who
steals somewhat which is to be restored to another. That Isaac,
when he pronounced blessing, thought of Esau, and not of Jacob, may appear from all and singular the things which precede, as from verses 18, 19, where Isaac says to Jacob, *Who
art thou, my son? and Jacob said to his father, I am thy first-
born Esau;* and from verses 21, 22, 23, *Isaac said to Jacob,
Come near, I pray, and I will feel thee, my son, whether thou be
my son Esau or not;* and after that he felt him, he said, *The
voice is the voice of Jacob, and the hands the hands of Esau,
and he did not acknowledge him;* also from verse 24, *And he
said, Art thou he my son Esau? and he said I (am);* and at

length when he kissed him, *he smelled the smell of his raiment,* namely, Esau's, and when he then blessed him, he said, *See, the smell of my son.* Hence it is manifest, that by the son whom he blessed, no other is understood than Esau; wherefore also when he heard from Esau that it had been Jacob, *Isaac shud-.dered with exceeding great horror,* verse 33, *and said, Thy brother came in treachery,* verse 35. But the reason why Jacob retained the blessing, according to what is said, verses 33 and 37, is, because the truth represented by Jacob was to have dominion apparently as to time, as has been occasionally shown above; but after the stated time of reformation and regeneration, then essential good, which lay intimately concealed, and thence arranged all and singular the things which appeared to be of truth, or which truth had attributed to itself, comes forth and has open dominion; and this is signified by what Isaac said to Esau, *On thy sword thou shalt live, and shalt serve thy brother, and it shall be when thou hast dominion, and thou shalt break his yoke from off thy neck,* verse 40; the internal sense of which words is, that so long as truth is in the process of conjoining to good, good is in an inferior place as to appearance, but that it will be in a superior place, and then there shall be conjunction of the rational [principle] with the good of the natural, and thereby with the truth, and thus truth shall be of good; consequently in such case Esau will represent the essential good of the natural [principle], and Jacob the essential truth thereof conjoined to the rational [principle]; thus in a supreme sense the Lord's Divine Natural [principle], Esau as to Divine Good, and Jacob as to Divine Truth therein.

3577. "As the smell of a field"—that hereby is signified as from good ground out of which is truth, appears from the signification of the smell of a field, as denoting the perception of truth derived from good, like as of an exhalation from ripe corn in a field; that field denotes good ground, may be seen, n. 3500. The ground and reason why smell denotes perception, is, because the delights of good and the pleasantnesses of truth, which are perceived in another life, manifest themselves there by corresponding smells (or odours), see n. 1514, 1517, 1518, 1519; hence, and from the nature of correspondences, it is evident, that smell is nothing else but a perceptive [principle], yet natural, corresponding to the perceptive spiritual [principle].

3578. "Which Jehovah hath blessed"—that hereby is signified that it is multiplied and made fruitful from the Divine [principle], appears from the signification of Jehovah blessing, as denoting to be multiplied as to truth, and to be made fruitful as to good, see n. 2846, 3406.

3579. "And God shall give thee of the dew of heaven"—that hereby is signified of the Divine Truth, and that of the fatnesses of the earth signifies of the Divine Good, appears from the signification of the dew of heaven, as denoting truth, of which we shall speak presently; and from the signification of fatnesses, as denoting good, see n. 353; each Divine, in the supreme sense, in which they are predicated of the Lord. With respect to the multiplication of truth and the fructification of good, the case is this: when the rational [principle] flows into the natural, it there presents its good in a common or general form; by this good it produces truths therein, almost as the life or living [principle] in man composes fibres, and disposes them into forms according to uses. This good, by these truths disposed into a celestial form, produces further good, and by this good further truths, which are derivations; such a natural idea may be had of the formation of truth from good, and further of good by truth, whereby again truth is formed; but a spiritual idea cannot be had except by those who are in another life, for there the ideas are formed from the light of heaven, in which is intelligence. That dew signifies truth, appears also from other passages of the Word, as in Zechariah, "The seed of peace, the vine shall give its fruit, and the earth shall give its produce, and *the heavens shall give their dew*," viii. 12; speaking of a new Church, where by the vine giving its fruit is denoted that the spiritual [principle] of the Church, or the truth of faith, should give good; and by the earth giving its produce, is denoted that the celestial [principle] of the Church, or the good of charity, should give truth; the dew which the heavens should give, denotes these things. So in Haggai, "Because of my house, which is vastated, *the heavens above you is shut from dew*, and the earth is shut from its produce," i. 9, 10; where the dew of the heavens and the produce of the earth, which were checked, have a like signification. So in David, "From the womb of the morning thou hast *the dew of thy nativity*," Psalm cx. 4; speaking of the Lord, the dew of nativity denoting the celestial [principle] of love. So in Moses, "Blessed of Jehovah is his land respecting the precious things of heaven, *respecting the dew*, respecting the abyss also lying beneath," Deut. xxxiii. 13; speaking of Joseph; the precious things of heaven are things spiritual, see n. 3166, which are dew; the abyss lying beneath are things natural. So again, "Israel dwelt securely, solitary at the fountain of Jacob, in a land of corn and new wine, *the heavens also dropped dew*," Deut. xxxiii. 28; where also the dew which the heavens dropped denotes the spiritual things which are of truth. Dew, in a genuine sense, is the truth of good which is from a state of innocence and peace, for by morning or day-dawn, when the dew descends, are signified those states, see n. 2333, 2405, 2780; hence also the manna, which was from heaven, was with the dew which descended in the morning, as may appear from Moses, "In the *morning was the lying of the dew* round about the camp, and when the *lying of the dew* ceased, behold on the faces of the wilderness a bruised round thing, bruised like the hoar-frost on the earth," Exod. xvi. 13, 14. " When *the dew descended upon the camp* in the night, the manna descended upon it," Numb. xi. 9 ; manna, as being heavenly bread, in a supreme sense signified the Lord as to Divine Good, hence the celestial [principle] of love with men, for this is from the Lord's Divine [principle] ; see n. 276, 680, 1798, 2165, 2177, 3464, 3478 ; the dew, in which and with which the manna descended, denotes Divine Truth in a supreme sense, and spiritual truth appertaining to men in a respective sense ; morning is a state of peace in which these good things are found, see n. 92, 93, 1726, 2780, 3170. Inasmuch as dew signifies truth which is from good, or, what is the same thing, the spiritual [principle] which is from the celestial, therefore also spiritual truth in the Word *is compared* to dew, for the things which signify serve also for comparison, as in Isaiah, " Thus said Jehovah to me, I will rest and will look in my habitation, as serene heat upon light, *as a cloud of dew* when the harvest is warm," xviii. 4. And in Hosea, " What shall I do to thee, Ephraim, what shall I do to thee, Judah, because your holiness is as the morning cloud, and *as the dew falling in the morning?*" vi. 4 ; chap. xiii. 3 Again, in the same prophet, " *I will be as the dew unto Israel,* he shall bud as a lily, and shall fix his roots like Lebanon," xiv. 6. And in Micah, " The remains of Jacob shall be in the midst of many people, *as dew* from Jehovah, as drops upon the herb," v. 7. And in David, " As good oil upon the head, which descended upon the border of Aaron's garments, *as the dew of Hermon* which descended upon the mountain of Zion, because there hath Jehovah ordained the blessing of life even to an age," Psalm cxxxiii. 2, 3. And in Moses, " My doctrine shall flow down like rain, *My Word shall drop as dew*, as drops upon the grass, and as drops upon the herb," Deut. xxxii. 2 ; where dew denotes the muliplication of truth from good, and the fructification of good by truth ; and whereas dew is what every morning renders the field and vineyard fruitful, therefore essential good and truth are signified by corn and new wine, which come next to be considered.

3580. " And multitude of corn"—that hereby is signified natural good thence derived, and that by new wine is signified natural truth thence derived, appears from the signification of corn, as denoting good, and from the signification of new wine, as denoting truth; which, when predicated of the natural [principle], signify natural good and truth, and in such case bread and wine are predicated of the rational [principle]. That bread is celestial good, see n. 276, 680, 1798, 2165, 2177, 3464. 3478; and that wine is spiritual truth, thus truth from good, see n. 1071, 1798. That corn and new wine have such a signitication, may appear from the following passages in the Word, " The heavens are shut up from dew, and the earth is shut up from its produce, and I have called dryness upon the earth, and upon the mountains, and *upon the corn, and upon the new wine,* and upon what the earth brings forth," Haggai i. 10, 11 ; where dryness (or drought) denotes a failure of dew and of rain, thus a failure of truth derived from any good ; dryness upon the corn is a failure of good, and dryness upon the new wine is a failure of truth. So in Moses, " Israel shall dwell securely, solitary at the fountain of Jacob, *in a land of corn and new wine,* and the heavens thereof shall drop dew," Deut. xxxiii. 28 ; solitary denotes those who are not infested by evils and false principles, see n. 139, 471; a land of corn and of new wine denotes the good and truth of the Church. So in Hosea, " I will be as the dew unto Israel, he shall bud forth as a lily, and shall fix his roots like Lebanon ; they shall return that dwell in his shade, *they shall vivify the corn,* and shall flourish as a *vine,* his memory shall be as the *vine* of Lebanon," xiv. 6, 7, 8 ; where corn denotes spiritual good, and wine spiritual truth. So in Isaiah, " The curse shall devour the earth, *the new wine shall mourn,* the *vine* shall languish, all the glad in heart shall groan," xxiv. 6, 7 ; speaking of the vastation of the spiritual Church ; the new wine mourning denotes that truth shall cease. So in Jeremiah, " Jehovah hath redeemed Jacob, they shall come and sing in the height of Zion, and shall flow together to the good of Jehovah, *to the corn, and to the new wine,* and to the oil, and to the sons of the flock and of the herd," xxxi. 11, 12 ; where corn and new wine denote good and the truth thence derived ; oil denotes the good out of which they come, and which is derived from them ; the sons of the flock and of the herd denote the truth which is thus thence derived ; and as these things have such a signification, they are called the good of Jehovah. So in Hosea, " She hath not known that I have given her *corn* and *new wine,* and oil, and I have multiplied the silver and gold which they made for Baal ; therefore will I return, and will take *my corn and new wine* in its stated time, and will seize upon my wool and my flax," ii. 8, 9 ; speaking of the Church perverted, where it is evident that by corn is not signified corn, nor by new wine new wine, neither by oil, silver, gold, wool, and flax, such things as are so expressed, but spiritual things, that is, things appertaining to good and truth. In like manner, speaking of a new Church in the same prophet, " I will betroth thee to Myself in faith, and thou shalt know Jehovah, and it shall be in that day I will hear the heavens, and these shall hear the earth, and the earth shall hear the *corn,* and *the new wine,* and the oil, and these shall hear Jesreel," ii. 20, 21, 22 ; Jesreel denotes a new Church. So in Joel, " Rise up ye drunkards and weep, and howl all ye that

drink wine, because of *the new wine* which is cut out from your
mouth. The field is wasted, the earth mourneth, because *the
corn is wasted, the new wine is dried up,* the oil languisheth,"
i. 5, 10. Again, in the same prophet, "Rejoice ye sons of
Zion, and be glad in Jehovah your God, because he hath given
unto you the morning rain for righteousness, and he will cause
to descend upon you the morning and evening rain in the first,
and the floors shall be filled with *pure corn,* and the wine-
presses shall overflow with *new wine,* and oil," ii. 23, 24. Again,
in the same prophet, "It shall come to pass in that day the
mountains shall drop new wine, and the hills shall flow with
milk, and all the rivers of Judah shall flow with waters, and a
fountain shall go forth from the house of Jehovah," iii. 18;
speaking of the Lord's kingdom, where by new wine, by milk,
and by waters, are signified things spiritual, whose abundance
is thus described. So in Zechariah, "Jehovah their God shall
serve them in that day, as a flock His people, for how great is
His goodness, and how great is His beauty! *Corn* shall cause
the young men to bud forth, and *new wine* the virgins," ix. 16,
17. And in David, "Thou visitest the earth, and delightest in
it, thou greatly enrichest it, the river of God is full of water,
thou preparest their *corn,* the pastures are clothed with flocks,
and the valleys are covered with *corn,* they shout for joy, they
also sing," Psalm lxv. 9, 13. Hence then it is evident, what is
signified by corn and new wine.

3581. "People shall serve thee"—that hereby are signified
the truths of the Church; and that by people bowing down
themselves to thee, are signified the truths of good, appears
from the signification of serving, as being predicated of truths,
see n. 2567, 3409; and from the signification of people, as denoting truths, see n. 1259, 1260, 2928, 3295. By people first
mentioned are signified the truths of the Church, which are
called truths, and by people mentioned a second time are signified truths of good, which are spiritual goods, and respectively
are called truths, the goods of charity being such truths; inasmuch as there is this distinction, therefore the people first mentioned are expressed, in the Hebrew tongue, by an expression
not altogether similar, but yet related to that by which they
are expressed in the second place.

3582. "Be a master to thy brethren"—that hereby is signified dominion, at first appearing to be of the affection of natural
truth over the affections of natural good, appears from the signification of being a master, as denoting dominion; and from
the signification of brethren, as denoting the affections of good,
in the present case natural good, see n. 367, 2360, 3303. Concerning the apparent dominion of truth over good, at first, see
n. 3324, 3325, 3330, 3332, 3336, 3470, 3539, 3548, 3556, 3563,
3570.

3583. " And thy mother's sons shall bow down themselves
to thee"—that hereby is signified over the rest of the affections
of truth, appears from tne signification of sons, as denoting also
truths, see n. 489, 491, 533, 1147, 2623, 3373 ; and from the
signification of mother, as denoting the affection of spiritual
truth, and hence denoting the Church, because the Church is a
mother, and is so called by virtue of truth and the affection
thereof, see n. 289, 2691, 2717.

3584. " Cursed are they that curse thee"—that hereby is
signified, that whosoever disjoins himself shall be disjoined;
and that by blessed are they that bless thee, is signified, that
whosoever conjoins himself shall be conjoined, appears from the
signification of cursing, as denoting to be disjoined, and from
the signification of blessing, as denoting to be conjoined, see n.
3504, 3514, 3530, 3565.   These things are predicated of truth,
and by those that curse are signified false principles, which separate themselves from truths ; and by those that bless are signified truths which adjoin themselves to other truths. For with
respect to truths and goods, the case is, that they form a society
between themselves, and at length constitute as it were one
state.   In such manner also they have consociation together ;
which formation and consociation originates in the form of heaven, in which form the angels are arranged according to the
consanguinities and affinities of good and truth, and thus together constitute one kingdom or one state ; and hence truths
and goods flow in with man, and are arranged with him into a
similar form, and this from the Lord alone.   But how this case
is, will appear more evidently from the correspondence of the
GRAND MAN, or heaven, with all and singular the things appertaining to man, concerning which correspondence, by the
Divine Mercy of the Lord, we shall speak at the close of the
chapters.   From these considerations then it is evident what is
involved in the blessing of Isaac pronounced upon Jacob, but
understood as respecting Esau, namely, the fructification of
good by the multiplication of truth, and the fructification again
of this latter.

3585. Verses 30, 31, 32, 33. *And it came to pass, as Isaac
left off to bless Jacob, and Jacob was scarce yet gone out from
the faces of Isaac his father, that Esau his brother came from
his hunting. And he also made savoury meat, and brought it
to his father, and said to his father, Let my father arise, and
eat of his son's venison (hunting), to the intent that thy soul
may bless me. And Isaac his father said unto him, Who art
thou? And he said, I am thy son, thy first-born Esau. And
Isaac shuddered with exceeding great horror, and said, Who
then is he who hath hunted venison, and hath brought to me,
and I have eaten of all before thou camest, and have blessed him,
also he shall be blessed.* It came to pass, as Isaac left off to

bless Jacob, signifies when the first conjunction was thus effected : and Jacob was scarce yet gone out from the faces of Isaac his father, signifies progression and change of state : that Esau his brother came from his hunting, signifies the truth of good, and its arrival : and he also made savoury meat and brought to his father, signifies things desirable and delectable to the Divine Rational [principle] : and said to his father, Let my father arise, and eat of his son's venison, signifies that he should appropriate to himself the truth of natural good : to the intent that thy soul may bless me, signifies that there might be conjunction : and Isaac his father said unto him, Who art thou ? and he said, I am thy son, thy first-born Esau, signifies a state of perception concerning natural good and truth thence derived : and Isaac shuddered with exceeding great horror, signifies a great alteration about the inversion of state : and he said, Who then is he that hath hunted venison (hunting) and hath brought to me ? signifies inquiry concerning that truth : and I have eaten of all before thou camest, signifies that it was appropriated : and I have blessed him, also he shall be blessed, signifies that it was conjoined.

3586. " And it came to pass, as Isaac left off to bless Jacob"—that hereby is signified when the first conjunction was thus effected, appears from the signification of blessing, as denoting conjunction, concerning which see above, n. 3534, 3514, 3530, 3565, 3584; thus by this expression, " As he left off to bless," is signified when conjunction was effected ; that the first conjunction was with truth, which is represented by Jacob, is evident from what has been said above.

3587. " And Jacob was yet scarce gone out from the faces of Isaac his father"—that hereby is signified progression and change of state, appears from the signification of going out from faces, as denoting when those things ceased which were represented by Jacob, thus when the state was changed, for the subject now treated of is concerning Esau, and in an internal sense, concerning the good of the natural [principle], how this comes forth from the inmost [principle], as was said above, and manifests itself, and when re-formation is accomplished by the ministry of truth, has dominion.

3588. " Esau his brother came from his hunting"—that hereby is signified the truth of good and its arrival, appears from the representation of Esau as denoting the good of the natural [principle], concerning which see above ; and from the signification of coming, as denoting arrival ; and from the signification of venison (hunting), as denoting truth which is from good, see n. 3501.

3589. " And he also made savoury meat and brought to his father"—that hereby are signified things desirable and delectable to the Divine Rational [principle], appears from the signification of savoury meat, as denoting the delights which are of good and the pleasantnesses which are of truth, see n. 3502, 3536 ; the delights which are of good are things desirable, and the pleasantnesses which are of truth are things delectable, for the affection of good is what desires, and in such case the affection of truth is what delights.

3590. " And said to his father, Let my father arise, and eat of his son's venison (hunting)"—that hereby is signified that the Divine Rational [principle] should appropriate to itself the truth of natural good, appears from the representation of Isaac, who here is the father, as denoting the good of the rational [principle], concerning which see frequently above ; and from the signification of eating, as denoting to appropriate, see n. 2187, 2343, 3168, 3513 ; and from the signification of venison (hunting), as denoting the truth of natural good, see just above, n. 3588.

3591. " To the intent that thy soul may bless me"—that hereby is signified that conjunction might be effected, appears from the signification of being blessed, as denoting conjunction, see also above, n. 3504, 3514, 3530, 3565, 3584.

3592. " And Isaac his father said unto him, Who art thou? and he said, I am thy son, thy first-born Esau"—that hereby is signified a state of perception concerning natural good and truth thence derived, appears from what was said above, n. 3548, 3549, 3550, at verses 18 and 19, where similar words occur.

3593. " And Isaac shuddered with exceeding great horror" —that hereby is signified a great alteration about the inversion of state, appears from what has been said above concerning the two states of man who is regenerated, the state before he is regenerated, and the state after he is regenerated, namely, that in the state before he is regenerated, truths apparently have the dominion, whereas in the state after he is regenerated, truths give place and good receives the dominion, on which subject see what has often been shown above, n. 1904, 2063, 2189, 2697, 2979, 3286, 3288, 3310, 3325, 3330, 3332, 3336, 3470, 3509, 3539, 3548, 3556, 3563, 3570, 3576, 3579.

3594. " And he said, Who then is he that hath hunted venison (hunting), and hath brought to me ?"—that hereby is signified inquiry concerning that truth, appears from the representation of Jacob, of whom it is here said, who is he, as denoting the natural [principle] in regard to truth, concerning which see above ; and from the signification of venison (hunting), as denoting truth derived from good, see n. 3501 ; in the present case the inquiry concerning that truth was, whether it was derived from good.

3595. " And I have eaten of all before thou camest"—that hereby is signified that it was appropriated, appears from the

signification of eating, as denoting to be appropriated, see n.
2187, 2343, 3168, 3513.

3596. " And have blessed him, also he shall be blessed"—
that hereby is signified that it was conjoined, appears from the
signification of being blessed, as denoting to be conjoined, see
n. 3504, 3514 3530, 3565, 3584. How the case is with respect
to the appropriation and conjunction of the truth represented
by Jacob, may appear from what has been said above; but as
these subjects are of such a nature as to transcend the apprehension of the natural man, and cannot be seen except in the
light in which the rational or internal man is, in which light
few at this day are principled, because few are regenerated,
therefore it is better to illustrate them no further, inasmuch as
the illustration of things unknown, and such as transcend the
apprehension, tends rather to render them obscure than to throw
light upon them. Besides, such things ought to be established
as a superstructure on the ideas of natural truths, whereby they
are to be apprehended, and these also at this day are wanting
and this is the reason why the passages immediately preceding
have been explained so briefly, and only as to the internal sense
of the expressions. From what has been already said it may
appear, what is implied by Isaac's asking venison of his son,
that he might eat of it, before he blessed him, and that he did
not bless him till after he had eaten, and thus that after eating
followed the blessing of him who made the savoury meat and
brought it, as is also evident from Isaac's words spoken here
concerning Jacob, *he hath brought to me, and I have eaten of
all before thou camest, and have blessed him, and also he shall
be blessed.* The reason evidently appears from the internal
meaning of the rituals of the ancient Church, for eating with
them signified appropriation and conjunction, and conjunction
with him with whom they had eaten, or of whose bread they
had eaten; meat in general signified the things which are of
love and charity, that is, the same as celestial and spiritual
meat; bread the things which are of love to the Lord, and wine
the things which are of charity towards our neighbour; when
these things were appropriated, the persons were joined together; thus they spake to each other from affection, and were
consociated together. Feasts (or convivial entertainments)
amongst the ancients were of this nature, nor was any thing
else represented in the Jewish Church by their eating together
of the holy offerings in their sacrifices, nor any thing else implied in the primitive Christian Church by their dinners and
suppers.

3597. Verses 34, 35, 36, 37, 38, 39, 40. *And Esau heard
the words of his father, and he cried out with a great and exceeding bitter cry ; and said to his father, Bless me, even me, my
father. And he said, Thy brother came in treachery, and hath*

*taken thy blessing. And he said, Doth he not call his name
Jacob? and he hath supplanted me these two times; he hath
taken my birth right, and behold now he hath taken my blessing; and he said, Hast not thou reserved a blessing for me?
And Isaac answered and said unto Esau, Behold I have placed
him a master to thee, and I have given all his brethren to him
for servants, and with corn and with new wine have I supported him, and what then shall I do for thee, my son? And
Esau said to his father, Hast thou but this one blessing, my
father? bless me, even me also, my father; and Esau lifted up
his voice and wept. And Isaac his father answered and said
unto him, Behold of the fatnesses of the earth shall be thy habitation, and of the dew of heaven from above. And upon thy
sword thou shalt live, and shalt serve thy brother, and it shall
be when thou hast the dominion, and thou shalt break his yoke
from off thy neck.* Esau heard the words of his father, signifies the perception of natural good derived from Divine Good
and he cried out with a great and exceeding bitter cry, signifies
its great alteration about the inversion of state: and said to
his father, Bless me, even me, my father, signifies that it desired conjunction, although by it truth was conjoined: and he
said, Thy brother came in treachery, signifies the inverse of
order: and hath taken thy blessing, signifies conjunction thus:
and he said, Doth he not call his name Jacob? signifies his
quality: and he hath supplanted me two times, signifies that
he inverted order: he hath taken my birth-right, signifies priority: and behold now he hath taken my blessing, signifies
conjunction: and he said, Hast thou not reserved a blessing for
me? signifies whether he had any thing as to conjunction in
that former state: and Isaac answered and said unto Esau, signifies instruction: Behold I have placed him a master to thee,
signifies that in that state he should have dominion: and all
his brethren have I given to him for servants, signifies that to
the affections of truth in this case the affections of good were
subordinate as to appearance: and with corn and new wine
have I sustained him, signifies, as above, the good and truth
thereof: and what then shall I do for thee, my son? signifies
that good had nothing else in that state: and Esau said to his
father, signifies the perception of natural good: Hast thou but
this one blessing, my father? signifies whether any thing else
could be adjoined from natural good in such case: bless me
also, even me, my father, signifies that natural good desired
conjunction, although by it truth was conjoined: and Esau
lifted up his voice and wept, signifies a further state of alteration: and Isaac his father answered and said unto him, signifies
perception concerning natural good that it would be made
Divine: Behold of the fatnesses of the earth shall be thy habitation, signifies that life is from the Divine Good: and of the

dew of heaven from above, signifies that it is from the Divine
Truth : and upon thy sword thou shalt live, and shalt serve thy
brother, signifies that so long as truth is conjoining to good,
good would be in an inferior place as to appearance : and it
shall be when thou hast dominion, signifies that it shall be in
the prior place: and thou shalt break his yoke from off thy
neck, signifies that in such case conjunction would be by good,
and that truth would be of good.

3598. Inasmuch as the things contained in verses 34, 35, 36,
37, 38, are such as have been explained above, and what is
involved therein may appear from what has been already said,
therefore it is needless to explain them further as to the internal sense. We shall only illustrate what is contained in
verses 39 and 40, relating to the blessing of Esau by his father
Isaac.

3599. "And Isaac his father answered and said unto him"
—that hereby is signified perception concerning natural good,
that it would be made Divine, appears from the signification of
Isaac, as denoting the Lord's Divine Rational [principle] as to
the good thereof, see n. 3012, 3124, 3210 ; and from the signification of saying, in the historical parts of the Word, as denoting to perceive, concerning which see frequently above ;
and from the representation of Esau, to whom he said, as denoting natural good, of which also much has been said above ;
that it should be made Divine, appears from the blessing which
follows. It was said above that Esau represents the Lord's
Divine Natural [principle] as to Divine Good, and Jacob his
Divine Natural [principle] as to Divine Truth ; but here, that
Esau represents natural good which should be made Divine ;
and in what goes before, that Jacob represented natural truth
which should be made Divine. How this is, may appear from
what was said above, n. 3494 and 3576 ; but to render the subject clearer, it may be expedient to add a few words in relation
to it. The natural good, which Esau first represents, is the
natural good of the Lord's infancy, which was Divine from the
Father, but human from the mother ; and so far as it was from
the mother, it was tainted with hereditary evil, and being such,
it could not be instantly in an order capable of receiving the
Divine [principle] which was inmost in it, but had need of being reduced into such order by the Lord. The case is the same
with the truth which is represented by Jacob ; for where good
is, there is truth, each being necessary for the other's existence.
All the thinking principle, even with infants, is of truth adjoined to the will-principle, which is of good ; wherefore after
that the Lord had reduced to order the natural [principle] as to
good and as to truth in Himself, so that it might receive the
Divine [principle], and thus Himself from his Divine [prin-
ciple] might flow in, and after that He had successively ex-

pelled all the human [principle] which was from His mother, in this case Esau represents the Lord's Divine Natural [principle] as to good, and Jacob, his Divine Natural [principle] as to truth. But Esau and Jacob represent the Divine Good and Divine Truth of the Lord's Divine Natural [principle], as conjoined with each other like brethren, which principles, considered in themselves, are nothing else but one power (or potency) together to form and receive actual good and truth. This good and truth, namely, actual, is the subject afterwards treated of. From these considerations, it is evident how great arcana are contained in the internal sense of the Word, which arcana are such, that their most general or common principles are not apprehensible by man's understanding, as is the case possibly with the things here said. How then should the innumerable particulars relating thereto be apprehended? Nevertheless they are adequate to the understanding and apprehension of the angels, who, concerning these and like arcana, receive celestial ideas from the Lord, illustrated by representatives of ineffable pleasantness and blessedness. Hence some conception may be formed of the nature of angelic wisdom, yet but remotely, inasmuch as such arcana are in the shade of the human understanding.

3600. "Behold of the fatnesses of the earth shall be thy habitation"—that hereby is signified that life is from Divine Good, and that by the dew of heaven from above, is signified that it is from Divine Truth, appears from the signification of fatness, as denoting good, see n. 353, in the present case Divine Good, because it is spoken of the Lord; and from the signification of habitation, as denoting life, see n. 1293, 3384; and that habitation is predicated of good, see n. 2268, 2451, 2712 ; and from the signification of the dew of heaven, as denoting truth derived from the good of a state of peace and innocence, see n. 3579, in the present case Divine Truth, because it is spoken of the Lord. Similar words were spoken to Jacob, namely, *God shall give thee of the dew of heaven and of the fatnesses of the earth,* verse 28; but in that passage mention is made of dew, thus of truth, in the first place, and of the fatnesses of the earth, thus of good, in the second place, and also that God should give of them ; whereas here, speaking to Esau, mention is made in the first place of the fatnesses of the earth, thus of good, and in the second place of the dew of heaven, thus of truth ; and not that God would give, but that his habitation should be of them. Hence also it is evident that Jacob represents truth, and Esau good, also that truth apparently in the former place is first, but that this is the inverse of order, according to what has been frequently shown above.

3601. "And upon thy sword thou shalt live, and shalt serve thy brother"—that hereby is signified that so long as truth is conjoining to good, good would be in an inferior place to appearance, is manifest from the signification of sword, as denoting truth combating, see n. 2799. Hence to live upon the sword denotes whilst truth is conjoining to good, for conjunction is effected by combats, that is by temptations, for without them truth is not conjoined; and from the signification of serving thy brother, as denoting to be in an inferior place. That nevertheless good is not in an inferior place, only apparently, is evident from what has been so often said above, see n. 3582.

3602. "And it shall be when thou hast dominion"—that hereby is signified that he should be in a prior place, appears from the signification of having dominion, as denoting to be in a prior place. On this subject see what now follows.

3603. "And thou shalt break his yoke from off thy neck"—that hereby is signified that in such case conjunction would be by good, and that truth would be of good, appears from the signification of breaking a yoke from off the neck, as denoting liberation (setting at liberty). That by neck is signified influx and communication, and thence conjunction, and that by a yoke upon the neck is signified interclusion and interception, may be seen, n. 3542; thus to break the yoke from off the neck denotes liberation (setting at liberty) from interclusion and interception, consequently it denotes conjunction by good, also that truth is become the truth of good, for when there is no longer any interclusion and interception, good flows in and conjoins itself to truth. How this is, may appear from what has been heretofore said and shown; nevertheless it may be expedient to add a few words in the way of further illustration, inasmuch as few comprehend what is meant by the apparent priority of truth, and in the mean while the inferiority of good, and this principally by reason that few reflect on such things, yea, that they do not even reflect upon good, as being distinct from truth. All those also are ignorant what good is, who live a life of self-love and the love of the world, for they do not believe that there can be any good but from this source; and inasmuch as they are ignorant what good is, they are ignorant also what truth is, for truth is of good. They know indeed from revelation that it is good to love God and their neighbour, and that truth consists of doctrinals derived from the Word, but whereas they do not live according to such good and truth, they have no perception thereof, but only of knowledges separate from them; yea, even those who are regenerating do not know what good is before they are regenerated, for before this they suppose truth to be good, and to do according to truth is good, when yet this is not good which in such case they do, but truth; when man is in this state, he is then in the state which is described by Jacob and 'n the blessing given to him; but when he comes into a state to do good from the affection of good,

that is, when he is regenerated, he then comes into the state
which is described in the blessing given to Esau. This may be
illustrated by those things which appear with man in his first
and second age, and afterwards in the third and fourth. Man,
in his first age, knows only by memory the things contained
n the Word, in like manner the things contained in the doctrinals of faith, and he then believes himself to be good, when
he is acquainted with several particulars relating thereto, and
can apply them, not to his own life, but to the lives of others.
In his second age, when he is more grown up, he is not content to know only by memory the things contained in the
Word, and in the doctrinals, but he begins at this time to
reflect thereupon in his own thought, and so much as he superadds thereto from his own thought, this pleases him, and hence
he is in an affection of truth grounded in some kind of worldly
love, which love is also a means of his learning more things,
which without it would have been left unlearnt. But in his
third age, if he be such as to be capable of being regenerated,
he begins to think about use, and in this case to reflect on what
he reads in the Word and imbibes from doctrinals, for the sake
of use; and when he is in this state, the order is inverted,
namely, that truth is no longer placed in the first place as heretofore. But in his fourth age, when it is the age of his regeneration, because then the state is full, concerning which see n.
2636, he loves the Word, and doctrinals which are derived from
the Word, that is truth, for the sake of the good of life, consequently, from the good of life: thus the good comes to be in a
prior place, which until this time was in a posterior place apparently. The ground and reason why good was apparently in
a posterior place, is, because it lay intimately concealed in all
his affection, nor was it able to manifest itself, inasmuch as
such things had place without it as it could not agree with,
namely, vain and empty things, such as are those of self-glory
and the glory of the world; but after he is regenerated, then
these things recede, and the good which lay intimately concealed, comes forth as it were from its place of confinement,
and flows into those things which are without, and makes truth
its own, or truths of good, and thus manifests itself. Good with
man in the mean time, like that involuntary [principle] which
is in his voluntary (or will) [principle], is in all and singular
the things which he thinks, and thence in all and singular the
things which he acts. Man knows not that he has this involuntary [principle], because he perceives nothing else appertaining
to himself but what is his own, that is, the voluntary [principle]
The involuntary [principle] here spoken of is twofold, one is
his hereditary [principle] derived from his father and mother,
the other enters by influx through heaven from the Lord. As
man grows up, then that [principle] which he has hereditarily

from his parents manifests itself more and more, if he be such as not to suffer himself to be regenerated, for thence he takes to himself evils and makes them his own or proper to him; but the involuntary [principle], which is from the Lord through heaven, manifests itself in adult age with those who are regenerated; and in the mean time it has disposed and governed all and singular things of their thought and also of their will, although it had not appeared.

3604. Verses 41, 42, 43, 44, 45. *And Esau hated Jacob on account of the blessing with which his father blessed him, and Esau said in his heart, The days of mourning of my father will approach, and I will slay my brother Jacob. And it was told Rebecca the words of her elder son Esau, and she sent, and called to Jacob her younger son, and said unto him, Behold Esau thy brother comforteth himself for thee to kill thee. And now, my son, hearken to my voice, and arise, flee thou to Laban my brother, to Haran. And tarry with him some days, until thy brother's fury turn away : until thy brother's anger turn away from thee, and he forget that which thou hast done to him, and I will send and receive thee from thence. Why should I be deprived of you both in one day ?* Esau hated Jacob on account of the blessing with which his father blessed him, signifies that natural good was averse to inverted conjunction of truth : and Esau said in his heart, signifies thought : The days of mourning of my father will approach, and I will kill my brother Jacob, signifies the inversion and privation of the self-derived life of truth : and it was told Rebecca the words of her elder son Esau, signifies the Lord's perception from Divine Truth concerning the mind of natural good at that time : and she sent and called to Jacob her younger son, and said unto him, signifies a state of the perception of the affection of truth by virtue of influx through Truth Divine : Behold Esau thy brother comforteth himself for thee to kill thee, signifies a purpose of inverting the state and of depriving truth of self-derived life : and now, my son, hearken to my voice, and arise, signifies staying as yet : flee thou to Laban my brother, to Haran, signifies to the affection of external or corporeal good : and tarry with him some days, signifies what is successive : until thy brother's wrath turn away, signifies until the state is turned : until thy brother's anger is turned away from thee, signifies succession of state with natural good : and he forget that which thou hast done to him, signifies habit acquired from staying : and I will send and receive thee from thence, signifies an end in such case : why should I be deprived of you both in one day? signifies that otherwise conjunction would not be.

3605. "Esau hated Jacob on account of the blessing with which his father blessed him"—that hereby is signified that natural good was averse to the inverted conjunction of truth, appears from the signification of *hating*, as here denoting in the internal sense to be averse to, of which we shall speak presently; and from the representation of *Esau*, as denoting natural good, and of *Jacob*, as denoting natural truth, concerning which see above; and from the signification of *blessing*, as denoting conjunction, see n. 3504, 3514, 3530, 3565, 3584. That in the present case it is an inverted conjunction of truth, which is represented by Jacob, is manifest from what was said and shown above, n. 3539, 3548, 3556, 3563, 3570, 3576, 3603. The ground and reason why hating in the internal sense denotes to be averse to, is, because it is predicated of good, which is represented by Esau, and good does not even know what hatred is, being the direct opposite thereof, and opposites can in no wise exist in one subject; but good, or they who are principled in good, instead of hatred have a species of aversion. Hence it is, that hatred here denotes in the internal sense to be averse to; for the internal sense is principally for those who are in heaven, wherefore when it descends thence, and is derived into the literal sense, then when the historical things are such, the affection of aversion falls into the expression of hatred, but yet in such a sort, that there is no idea of hatred in those who are in heaven. The case herein is like what was related above, n. 1875, concerning these words in the Lord's prayer, "*Lead us not into temptation, but deliver us from evil*," in that temptation and evil are rejected, until what is purely angelical, namely, good, remains without an idea of temptation and of evil, and this with a species of indignation and aversion adjoined, in regard to evil being thought of when the Lord is thought of. The case is the same with all those passages in the Word, wherein it is said of Jehovah or the Lord, that He hates; as in Zechariah, "Think ye not evil in your heart a man of his companions, neither love ye the oath of a lie, *because all these things I hate*, saith Jehovah," viii. 17; and in Moses, "Thou shalt not set up to thyself a statue, *which Jehovah thy God hateth*," Deut. xvi. 22; and in Jeremiah, "Mine inheritance is become unto me as a lion in the forest, it hath uttered against me its voice, *therefore have I hated it*," xii. 8; and in Hosea, "In Gilgal *have I hated them*, by reason of the wickedness of their works I will drive them out of mine house, I will love them no more," ix. 15; in which passages hatred, which is predicated of Jehovah or the Lord, in the internal sense is not hatred, but is Mercy, inasmuch as the Divine [principle] is Mercy; but when this flows in with man who is in evil, and he incurs (or runs into) the punishment of evil, it then appears as hatred, and it it is by reason of its so appearing that in the sense of the letter it is called hatred. In like manner, and for the same reason, anger, wrath, and fury, are in the Word predicated of Jehovah or the Lord, on which subject see n. 245, 592, 696, 1093, 1683, 1874, 2395, 2447

3235. The Jewish and the Israelitish people above all others were of such a nature and quality, that as soon as they observed any thing unfriendly, even amongst those to whom they were allied, they believed it lawful to treat them cruelly, and not only to kill them, but also to expose them to beasts and birds, and thus, because the inflowing mercy of the Lord was changed with them into such hatred, not only against their enemies, but also against those with whom they were allied, therefore they could not believe otherwise but that Jehovah also entertained hatred, was angry, wrathful, and furious, and this was the reason why in the Word it is so expressed according to appearance; for such as man's quality is, such the Lord appears to him, see n. 1861, 2706. But what the quality of hatred is with those who are principled in love and charity, that is, who are principled in good, appears from the Lord's words in Matthew, "Ye have heard that it was said, Thou shalt love thy neighbour, and *shalt hate thine enemy;* but I say unto you, Love your enemies, bless them that speak evil of you, do good to them that hate you, and pray for them that injure and persecute you, that ye may be the sons of your Father Who is in heaven," v. 43, 44, 45.

3606. "And Esau said in his heart"—that hereby is signified thought, appears from the signification of saying in the heart, as denoting thought.

3607. "The days of mourning of my father will approach, and I will kill my brother Jacob"—that hereby is signified the inversion and privation of the self-derived life of truth, appears from the signification of days of mourning, as denoting inversion of state; and from the signification of killing Jacob the brother, as denoting to deprive truth of self-derived life. The case is similar in regard to what is here said, as to what was just now said concerning the signification of hatred in the internal sense, namely, that it is not hatred; and it may also appear from what is the case continually in another life, where all the good, which flows down from heaven to those who are in evil, is changed into evil, and with the infernals into the opposite, in like manner truth is changed into what is false, see n. 2123; wherefore on the other hand, what is evil and false, as appertaining to such spirits, in heaven is good and truth. To the intent also that it may be good, there are spirits in the way who reject the idea of what is evil and false, that so the idea of what is good and true may be presented, concerning which rejection, see n. 1393, 1875; and moreover, when what is evil and false approaches towards those who are principled in good and truth, it does not appear as evil and false, but under another appearance, according to the peculiar quality and state of goodness appertaining to them. Hence also it may be evident, that to kill Jacob the brother in the internal sense does not denote to kill, but denotes a privation of that life which is not competent to truth ; for truth of itself has not life, but receives it from good, inasmuch as truth is only a vessel recipient of good, see n. 1496, 1832, 1900, 2063, 2261, 2269, 2697, 3049, 3068, 3128, 3146, 3318, 3387 ; and in good there is life, but not in truth, except what it receives from good, see n. 1589, and in several other places.   Wherefore the privation of the life of truth from itself is not the extinction of truth, but is its vivification, for when truth appears to itself to have life from itself, in such case it has not life, except such life as in itself is not life, but when it is deprived of that life, it is then gifted with essential life, namely, by good from the Lord, Who is essential Life. This appears manifest from the case of those who are in another life ; with such as are principled in truth alone, the ideas appear closed, so that those things which are of heaven cannot flow in, except only in a manner so general, that the influx is scarce known to be from heaven ; whereas with such as are at the same time principled in good, the ideas appear open, so that the things which are of heaven flow in, as into an heaven in miniature, or as into an image of themselves, namely, by the good appertaining to them through truths, see n. 1869, 2425.   That truth is deprived of self-derived life, when good begins to be in the prior place, or to have dominion, may appear from what has been above said and shown concerning the apparent priority of truth at first, and concerning the priority of good afterwards ; this privation of the life of truth as self-derived, is what is here signified.   The reason why this is called the mourning of a father, is, because days of mourning signify inversion of state, which inversion of state was signified above by the exceeding great horror with which Isaac shuddered, verse 33, n. 3593 ; and by the great and exceeding bitter exclamation with which Esau exclaimed, verse 34, n. 3597.

3608. "And it was told Rebecca the words of her elder son Esau"—that hereby is signified the Lord's perception from Divine Truth concerning the mind (or intention) of natural good at that time, appears from the signification of its being told, as denoting to think and reflect, see n. 2862, thus to perceive ; and from the representation of Rebecca, as denoting the Divine Truth of the Lord's Divine Rational [principle] ; and from the representation of Esau, as denoting natural good, concerning which representations see above.   Hence it is evident, that its being told Rebecca concerning the words of her elder son Esau, denotes the Lord's perception from Divine Truth concerning the intention of natural good at that time.

3609. "And she called to Jacob her younger son, and said unto him"—that hereby is signified a state of perception of the affection of truth from influx through Divine Truth, appears from the representation of Rebecca who called and said, as denoting the Divine Truth of the Lord's Divine Rational [principle] conjoined to Divine Good; and from the representation of Jacob, as denoting natural truth or the affection of truth therein, concerning which representations see above; and from the signification of calling to him and saying to him, as denoting a state of perception, concerning which see also above; in the present case denoting apperception, because the natural [principle] is the subject here treated of.

3610. " Behold Esau thy brother comforteth himself for thee to kill thee"—that hereby is signified a purpose of inverting the state and of depriving truth of self-derived life, appears from the signification of comforting one's self for any one, as denoting to appease restlessness of mind with hope concerning any one, or concerning any thing; *for thee,* implies the inversion of the state of truth; and from the signification of killing thee or Jacob, as denoting to deprive truth of self-derived life, concerning which see just above, n. 3607, where it was shown, that to deprive truth of life is not to extinguish it, but to vivify it.   For the case with respect to truth is this, when they who are principled in truth, or in the affection of truth, do not live according to the truth which they know, and with which they are affected, in such case there is somewhat of pleasure and delight derived from self-love, or the love of the world, which has adjoined itself to the affection of truth, and which appears as good, when nevertheless it is not good, except respectively in regard to use, in that truths may thus be introduced and learnt, which afterwards may be serviceable to essential good and the life thereof. When truth is in this state, that is, they who are in the affection of truth, then truth is said to have self-derived life, which is not life, as may appear from this consideration, that there is no life in self-love and the love of the world, or in their pleasure and delight, but only in celestial and spiritual love, and in their pleasure and delight; wherefore when truth, that is, they who are in the affection of truth, are deprived of that life, they then first receive life, or then first are vivified.   These things cannot possibly be apprehended by those who are in the affection of selfish and worldly love, for they suppose that no other life can be given, consequently that if they should be deprived of that life, they would altogether cease to live, for they who are in that life can in no wise know what spiritual and celestial life is; when yet the real case is this, that when they are deprived of that life, namely, of the affection of selfish and worldly love, then life flows in from the Lord, such as is the angelic and heavenly life, with ineffable wisdom and happiness, from which life, when the former life is viewed, it appears as if it were no life, or as the sordid life of brute animals, inasmuch as there is nothing of a Divine [principle] therein, except the faculty of thinking and speaking, and thus of appearing in an external form like men.　In respect to this circumstance, that good had the purpose of inverting the state and depriving truth of self-derived life, which is signified by Esau comforting himself for thee to kill thee, the case is this : good with man, during regeneration has continually a purpose of inverting the state, and of reducing it to such an order, that truth may not be in the prior place but in the posterior, as it is agreeable to the state of heaven ; this purpose however lies deeply concealed, nor is it perceived until it is effected.　The case herein is as with conjugial love, which does not appear in infancy and childhood, but still lies treasured up, nor does it come forth until all and singular things are so arranged, that it can manifest itself; in the mean time it produces all means suitable to itself, or they are produced.　The case is similar in the vegetable kingdom, in every tree, and in every plant ; there lies intimately hid therein a tendency (*conatus*) to produce fruit or seeds, but this tendency cannot manifest itself until it has first produced all necessary means, namely, branches, leaves, and flowers, and when these are produced, then the tendency comes forth into act.　So also it is with those who are born anew ; the conjugial [principle], which is that of good and of truth, lies secretly treasured up for a long time, but still it is present as a tendency (*conatus*) in the efficient cause and thence in the effect, yet it does not appear until all things are arranged in order, and when they are so arranged, it then first comes forth and manifests itself; this tendency, or effort, is what is meant by the purpose of inverting the state, and depriving truth of self-derived life.　Hence it is evident, that the internal sense is altogether different from what is expressed in the letter, namely, that it is the reduction of truth into order and its vivification, not its destruction and privation of its life.

3611.　" And now, my son, hearken to my voice, and arise"—that hereby is signified staying (or tarrying) as yet, appears from the signification of hearkening to a voice, as denoting to obey, namely, that he should tarry yet in that inverted state, of which we shall speak presently.

3612.　" Flee thou to Laban my brother, to Haran"—that hereby is signified to the affection of external or corporeal good, appears from the representation of Laban, as denoting the affection of good in the natural man, see n. 3129, 3130, 3160 ; and from the signification of Haran, as denoting what is external, and thence respectively obscure, see n. 1430.　But what is here properly signified by Laban and Haran, may appear from what follows, where mention is made of Laban and Haran, namely, that it is the collateral good of a common stock (or stem), for goods and truths have conjunction with each other like the conjunction of parents, brethren, kinsmen, and relations, which has place in families, see n. 685, 917, 2508, 2524, 2556, 2739.

These things, however, are altogether hidden to man, who is not principled in the life of good; he does not even know what good is, and consequently neither what truth is. If he first knew these, namely, from doctrine conjoined to life, or from life conjoined to doctrine, he would then know and perceive innumerable things concerning good and truth, and this successively more and more distinctly, and afterwards their mutual respective conjunctions with each other, and at length their proximities in their series, and in each proximity again things innumerable, thus lastly heaven in its form, that is, in its beauty and felicity.

3613. "And tarry with him some days"—that hereby is signified what is successive, appears from the signification of tarrying, as denoting nearly the same as to dwell, thus the same as to live, see n. 1293, 2268, 2451, 2712, 3384; but to tarry is predicated of the life of truth with good, and to dwell is predicated of the life of good with truth; and from the signification of days, as denoting times and states, see n. 23, 487, 493, 2788, 3462; thus it is the life of subsequent times and states, consequently what is successive, which is here signified by tarrying with him some days. This successive, or tarrying of Jacob with Laban, is treated of in the chapters which follow.

3614. "Until thy brother's wrath turn away"—that hereby is signified until the state changes; and that "until thy brother's anger turn away from thee," signifies succession of state with natural good, appears from the signification of wrath and anger, as denoting states which are repugnant, of which signification we shall speak presently. When these states become such as to be no longer repugnant, but to begin to conjoin themselves, it is then said that wrath turns away, and that anger turns away. Hence it is, that "until thy brother's wrath turn away," signifies until the state changes; and that "until thy brother's anger turn away," signifies succession of state with natural good. That somewhat distinct is implied in the two expressions, wrath and anger, may appear from this consideration, that they are similar words, and that unless they had had a distinct signification, it would have been an idle repetition to say, "until thy brother's *wrath* turn away, and until thy brother's *anger* turn away." What is implied in each expression, appears from the general explication, and also from the predication of wrath and the predication of anger, for wrath is predicated in respect to truth, in the present case in respect to the truth of good which is represented by Esau, whereas anger is predicated in respect to that essential good. Wrath and anger are frequently mentioned in the Word, but in the internal sense they do not signify wrath and anger, but that which is repugnant, and this by reason that whatever is repugnant to any affection produces wrath or anger, so that in the internal sense they are only repugnances; but that is called wrath which is repugnant to

truth, and that anger which is repugnant to good; and in an
opposite sense, it is wrath which is repugnant to what is false
or the affection thereof, that is, to principles of what is false;
and it is anger which is repugnant to evil or its lust, that is, to
self-love and the love of the world. In the former sense, wrath
is properly wrath, and anger is anger; whereas, when predicated of good and truth, wrath and anger is zeal; which zeal
inasmuch as in its external form it appears like wrath and
anger, therefore in the sense of the letter it is so called. That
wrath and anger in the internal sense are only repugnances,
may appear from the following passages in the Word, "The
fervour of Jehovah is against all nations, and *wrath* against all
their army," Isaiah xxxiv. 2; where the fervour of Jehovah
against all nations, denotes repugnance against evil. That nations denote evils, see n. 1259, 1260, 1849, 1868, 2588. Wrath
against all their army, denotes repugnance against the false
principles thence derived. That stars which are called the
army of the heavens, are knowledges, and thus truths, and in
an opposite sense false principles, may be seen, n. 1128, 1808,
2120, 2495, 2849. Again, in the same prophet, "Who hath
given Jacob for a prey, and Israel to them that spoil? hath not
Jehovah to Whom we have sinned? and *He hath poured out
upon him the wrath of His anger*," xlii. 24, 25; where the
wrath of anger denotes repugnance against the false [principle]
of evil. Jacob denotes those who are in evil, and Israel those
who are in the false [principle]. Again, "I have trodden the
wine-press alone, and of the people no man was with Me, and
I have trodden them in *Mine anger*, and have destroyed them
in *My wrath;* and I have trampled down the people in *Mine
anger*, and have made them drunk in *My wrath*," lxiii. 3, 6;
speaking of the Lord and his temptation-victories, where to
tread and trample down in anger denotes victories over evils,
and to destroy and make drunk in wrath denotes victories over
false principles; to trample upon in the Word is predicated of
evil, and to make drunken of what is false. So in Jeremiah,
"Thus saith the Lord Jehovah, Behold *Mine anger* and *My
wrath* is poured out upon this place, upon man and upon beast,
and upon the tree of the field, and upon the fruit of the ground,
and it shall burn and not be extinguished," vii. 20; where
mention is made both of anger and wrath, because the subject
treated of is both concerning what is evil and what is false. It
is usual with the prophets in speaking of evil, to speak also of
the false [principle]; as in speaking of good, to speak also of
truth, and this by reason of the heavenly marriage, which is
that of good and of truth, in all and singular things of the
Word, see n. 685, 793, 801, 2173, 2516, 2712; hence also mention is made both of anger and wrath, otherwise one expression
would have been sufficient. Again, in the same prophet, "I

will fight with you in a stretched-out hand and a strong arm, and *in anger*, and *in wrath*, and in *great fervour*, and I will smite the inhabitants of this city, both man and beast," xxi. 5, 6; where in like manner anger is predicated of the punishment of evil, and wrath of the punishment of what is false, and fervour of the punishment of both.   Anger and wrath, as being repugnant, is also punishment, for things which are repugnant are in collision, and in such case evil and the false [principle] are punished; for in evil there is repugnance to good, and in what is false there is repugnance to truth, and inasmuch as there is repugnance there is also collision; that hence comes punishment, may be seen, n. 696, 967.   So in Ezechiel, "And *Mine anger* shall be consummated, and I will cause *My wrath* to rest in them, and *I will comfort Myself*, and they shall know that I Jehovah have said, and in *My zeal*, in consummating Myself, *My wrath* in them, in doing judgment in thee, in *anger* and in *wrath*, and in the corrections of *wrath*," v. 13, 15; where also anger denotes the punishment of evil, and wrath the punishment of what is false, arising from repugnance, and thence oppugnance (assault).   So in Moses, "It shall not please Jehovah to pardon him, because then the *anger of Jehovah will smoke*, and *His zeal* upon that man, and Jehovah will separate him unto evil out of all the tribes of Israel: sulphur and salt, and a burning shall the whole land thereof be, it shall not be sown, and shall not bud forth, neither shall any herb rise up in it, according to the overthrow of Sodom and Gomorrah, of Admah and Zeboim, which *Jehovah overthrew in His anger and His wrath;* and all nations shall say, Wherefore hath Jehovah done thus to this land, what is *the heat of His great anger?*" Deut. xxix. 20, 21, 23, 24.   Inasmuch as Sodom is evil, and Gomorrah the false [principle] thence derived, see n. 2220, 2246, 2322, and the nation of which Moses here speaks is compared thereto as to what is evil and false, therefore anger is spoken of in respect to evil, and wrath in respect to what is false, and heat of anger in respect to both.   That such things are attributed to Jehovah or the Lord, is according to appearance, because so it appears to man when he runs into evil, and evil punishes itself, see n. 245, 592, 696, 1093, 1683, 1874, 2395, 2447, 3235, 3605.

3615. "And he forget that which thou hast done unto him" —that hereby is signified habit acquired from staying (or tarrying), appears from the signification of forgetting; in the present case, as denoting the successive abolition of repugnance, and as this is effected by staying (or tarrying), and habit thence acquired, therefore such habit is signified by the words, "And he forget that which thou hast done unto him."

3616. "And I will send and receive thee thence"—that hereby is signified the end in such case, appears from what goes before and from what follows; for the end, which is here signified by sending and receiving thee thence, has place, when truth is in agreement with good, and thus truth serves in subordination to good. This end, after the time of Jacob's tarrying with Laban was accomplished, is represented by Esau's *running to meet Jacob, and embracing him, and falling upon his neck, and kissing him, and their both weeping,* Gen. xxxiii. 4; for when the end is, or conjunction, then the good of the rational [principle] flows immediately into the good of the natural, and through the good into its truth, and also mediately through the truth of the rational [principle] into the truth of the natural, and through this into the good therein, see n. 3573. Hence it is evident why it was said by Rebecca, by whom is represented the truth of the rational [principle], to Jacob, by whom is represented the truth of the natural, " I will send and receive thee thence."

3617. " Why should I be deprived of you both in one day?" —that hereby is signified that otherwise conjunction would not be effected, appears from this consideration, that if those things were not done, which are represented in what follows, in the internal sense, by Jacob sojourning with Laban, truth could not have been conjoined with good, thus good could not have been united to truth in the natural [principle], consequently the rational [principle] would be deprived of both; for without the conjunction of truth with good, and the uniting of good with truth in the natural [principle], there is no regeneration, which is the subject treated of in this chapter, in a respective sense. This also is the closing period (*clausula*) of what goes before.

3618. Verse 46. *And Rebecca said unto Isaac, I loathe my life on account of the daughters of Heth; if Jacob take a woman of the daughters of Heth, as they of the daughters of the land, wherefore have I lives?* Rebecca said unto Isaac, signifies the Lord's perception from Divine Truth: I loathe my life on account of the daughters of Heth, signifies the adjunction of natural truth from another source: if Jacob take a woman of the daughters of Heth, signifies that natural truth should not be associated thereto: as they of the daughters of the land, signifies because not from that ground: wherefore have I lives? signifies that thus there would not be conjunction.

3619. " Rebecca said unto Isaac"—that hereby is signified the Lord's perception from Divine Truth, appears from the signification of saying, as denoting to perceive; and from the representation of Rebecca, as denoting the Divine Truth of the Lord's Divine Rational [principle]; and from the representation of Isaac, as denoting the Divine Good therein, concerning which see above; and whereas Divine Good is the very esse, and Divine Truth is life thence derived, on which account the Lord is

the Lord principally by virtue of Divine Good, therefore it is
called the Lord's perception from Divine Truth. Perception
from Divine Truth of the rational [principle], is from the intellectual [principle], whereas perception from Divine Good is
from the will-principle; but perception from the intellectual
principle is not of the intellectual principle, but is of the inflowing will-principle, for the intellectual principle is nothing
else but the will-principle in form. Such is the intellectual principle when it is conjoined to the will-principle, but before it is
so conjoined, the intellectual principle appears to be by itself,
and the will-principle by itself, although it is nothing else but
a separation of what is external from what is internal; for when
the intellectual principle inwardly wills and thinks any thing,
the end regarded is from the will-principle, which constitutes its
life, and governs the thinking principle therein. The reason why
the intellectual principle has life from the end regarded, is be
cause the end regarded with man is his life, see n. 1909, 3570
Hence it may in some sort appear what is meant in a repre
sentative sense by any one's perception from Truth, and what, in
a supreme sense, by the Lord's perception from Divine Truth.

3620. "I loathe my life on account of the daughters of
Heth"—that hereby is signified the adjunction of natural truth
from another source, appears from the signification of loathing
life, as denoting no adjunction, namely, of natural truth to truth
of the rational [principle], for when there is no such adjunction
then to the rational [principle] its life appears as if it was no
life, as may be manifest from what was said above, n. 3493
and from the signification of the daughters of Heth, as deno
ing affections of truth grounded in what is not genuine, in the
present case the affections of natural truth because spoken of
Jacob, by whom natural truth is represented, as has been shown
above. That daughters are affections, see n. 2362; and that
Heth or Hittite is truth grounded in what is not genuine, may
be seen, n. 3470. Hence it appears, that by these words, "I
loathe my life on account of the daughters of Heth," is signified that there should be no adjunction of the natural [principle]
by truth not grounded in what is genuine, consequently that
there should be adjunction of natural truth from another source.
The adjunction of natural truth is treated of in what follows,
where mention is made of Jacob's stay with Laban, namely,
that truths derived from a common stock were adjoined thereto,
and by the truths which the daughters of Heth represent, as
not being from that stock, adjunction could not be effected, be
cause they were in a state of disparity and discordance; for by
the sons of Heth is represented the spiritual Church amongst
the Gentiles, see n. 2913, 2986; and inasmuch as this Church
is not in possession of the Word, therefore truths in this Church
are not from that origin.

3621. "If Jacob take a woman of the daughters of Heth"—
that hereby is signified that natural truth should not be associated thereto, appears from the signification of taking a woman,
as denoting to be associated; and from the signification of the
daughters of Heth, as denoting the affections of truth grounded
in what is not genuine, see above, n. 3620, or, what is the same
thing, denoting truth, for truth without affection is not conjoined, see n. 3066, 3336. How this case is, appears from what
was said above concerning the daughters of Heth.

3622. "As they of the daughters of the land"—that hereby
is signified because not from that ground, namely, from truths
of the genuine Church, appears from the signification of daughters, as denoting Churches; for daughters signify affections of
good and of truth, see n. 2362; and land (or earth) signifies
the tract where the Church is, thus the Church, see n. 662,
1066, 1067, 1262, 1733, 1859, 2117, 2118, 2928, 3355; thus
daughters of the land are the goods and truths of the Church.

3623. "Wherefore have I lives?"—that hereby is signified
that thus there would not be conjunction, appears from the signification of lives, as denoting conjunction by truths and goods;
for when no truth from a common stock, or genuine fountain,
could be adjoined to natural truth, in such case neither would
there be adjunction of the natural principle to truth of the rational; thus to the rational principle its life would appear as no
life, see n. 3493, 3620. Hence by these words, "Wherefore
have I lives?" is signified that thus there would not be conjunction. The reason why in this and in other passages mention is
made of lives in the plural, is, because there are two faculties of
life in man, one of which is called understanding, and which is of
truth, and the other which is called will, and is of good. These
two lives, or faculties of life, make one, when the understanding
is of the will, or, what is the same thing, when truth is of good.
Hence it is that in the Hebrew tongue so frequent mention is
made of life, and also of lives. That frequent mention is made
of lives, is evident from the following passages, "Jehovah God
formed man, dust out of the ground, and breathed into his nostrils the *breath of lives*, and man was made into a living soul,"
Gen. ii. 7: "Jehovah God caused to bud forth out of the ground
every tree desirable to the sight, and good for food, and the *tree
of lives* in the midst of the garden," Gen. ii. 9: "Behold I bring
a flood of waters upon the earth, to destroy all flesh, in which
is the *breath of lives*," Gen. vi. 17: "There entered in to Noah
into the ark, two and two of all flesh in which was the *breath
of lives*," Gen. vii. 15, n. 780: "Every thing expired which
had breath, the *spirit of lives* in his nostrils," Gen. vii. 22. So
in David, "I believe that I shall see the good of Jehovah in
the *land of lives*," Psalm xxvii. 13. Again, "What man
desiring lives, loving days to see good," xxxiv. 12. Again,

"With thee, Jehovah, is the *fountain of lives;* in thy light we see light," Psalm xxxvi. 9 : and in Malachi, "My covenant was with Levi, *of lives* and of peace," ii. 5 : and in Jeremiah, "Thus saith Jehovah, Behold I give before you the *way of lives,* and the way of death," xxi. 8 : and in Moses, "To love Jehovah thy God, to obey His voice, and to cleave to Him, because He is *thy lives,* and the length of thy days, to dwell upon the earth," xxx. 20. Again, "It is not a vain word from you, because it is *your lives,* and by this Word ye shall prolong your days upon the earth," Deut. xxxii. 47; and in other places. Mention is made of lives in the plural, because they are two, as was said, and yet one ; as also mention is made of heavens in the Hebrew tongue, which are several, and yet one. In like manner of waters, which are superior and inferior, Gen. i. 6, 7, 9, which are things spiritual in the rational and natural principles, and which also should be one by conjunction. In respect to lives, they signify in the plural both what is of the will and what is of the understanding, consequently what is of good and what is of truth ; for the life of man is nothing else but good and truth, wherein is life from the Lord ; inasmuch as man, without good and truth, and the life therein, is not man. For man, without these principles, would not be able to will any thing or to think any thing; all his faculty of willing being derived from what is good or not good ; and all his faculty of thinking being derived from what is true or not true. Hence man has lives, which are one life when his thought is derived from his will-principle, that is, when truth, which is of faith, is derived from good, which is of love.

CONCERNING THE CORRESPONDENCE OF ALL MAN'S ORGANS AND MEMBERS, BOTH INTERIOR AND EXTERIOR, WITH THE GRAND MAN, WHICH IS HEAVEN.

3624. *IT is now allowed to relate and describe things wonderful, which, so far as I know, have never as yet come to the knowledge of any one, nor even entered into his mind to conceive, viz. that the universal heaven is so formed as to correspond to the Lord, His Divine Human [principle] ; and that man is so formed as to correspond to heaven in regard to all and singular things appertaining to him, and by heaven to the Lord. This is a great mystery : which is now to be revealed, and of which we shall treat here and at the close of the subsequent chapters.*

3625. *It is from this ground that it has been occasionally asserted above, in speaking of heaven and angelic societies, that*

*they belonged to some province of the body, as to that of the head,
or of the breast, or of the abdomen, or of some particular member
or organ therein; and this by reason of the correspondence
here spoken of.*

*3626. That such a correspondence exists, is a thing most perfectly known in another life, not only to the angels, but also to
spirits, and even to the wicked. The angels are hence acquainted
with the most secret things which are in man, and with the most
secret things which are in the world, and in its universal nature; this was discoverable to me also from this circumstance,
that when I spoke of any part of the human body, they not only
knew all the structure of that part, its manner of acting and use,
but likewise innumerable things besides, more than man is capable of exploring, yea of understanding; and this in their order
and in their series, from intuition into the heavenly order which
they followed, to which the order of that part corresponded, thus,
in consequence of being in principles (or the first rudiments of
things), they thence know the things derived from them.*

*3627. It is a general rule (or law) that nothing can exist and
subsist from itself, but from another, that is, by another, and
that nothing can be kept in form except from another, that is, by
another, as is manifest from all and singular things in nature.
That the human body from without is kept in form by the atmospheres, is a known thing, and unless it was also kept in form
by some acting or living force, it would instantly fall to pieces.
Every thing unconnected with what is prior to itself, and by
things prior with what is prime (or first), immediately perishes.
That the* GRAND MAN, *or influx thence, is that prior thing by
which man, as to all and singular things appertaining to him,
is connected with the First, that is, with the Lord, will be manifest from what follows.*

*3628. On this subject I have been instructed by much experience, whereby it has been evidenced to me, that not only the
things appertaining to the human mind, viz. to its thought and
affection, correspond to things spiritual and celestial, which are
the things of heaven from the Lord, but also that the whole man
in general, and in particular whatever is in man, has such correspondence, insomuch that there is not the smallest part, nor
even the smallest constituent of a part, which does not correspond; also that man thence exists and continually subsists;
and further, that unless there was such a correspondence of man
with heaven, and by heaven with the Lord, thus with what is
prior to himself, and by what is prior with what is prime (or
first), he would not subsist a single moment, but would fall into
annihilation. There are always two forces, which, as was observed, keep every thing in its connection and in its form, viz.
a force acting from without, and a force acting from within, in
the midst of which forces is that which is kept in connection and*

form; thus also man is kept in his connection and form as to singular his parts, even the most minute. That the atmospheres are what keep the whole body in connection, by their continual pressure or incumbence from without, is a known thing; and also that the aerial atmosphere by its influx keeps the lungs in their connection and form, and likewise its organ, which is the ear, with its forms constructed in it, agreeable to the modification thereof. In like manner it is a known thing, that the ethereal atmosphere keeps the interior parts of the body in their connection, for this atmosphere flows in freely through all the pores, and keeps the interior viscera of the whole body inseparable in their forms, by nearly the same pressure or incumbence, and consequent acting force; it also keeps in connection and form its organ, which is the eye, with the forms contained therein and adapted to its modifications. To these forces unless there were correspondent internal forces, which should react against those external ones, and thus keep the intermediate forms in due connection and equilibrium, they would not subsist a moment Hence it is manifest, that there needs must be two forces, in order that any thing may exist and subsist. The forces which flow in and act from within, are from heaven, and by heaven from the Lord, and in themselves have life. This is very evident from the organ of hearing: unless there were interior modifications, which are of life, and to which there corresponded exterior modifications which are of air, hearing would not exist. The same also is evident from the organ of sight: unless there was interior light which is of life, and to which corresponded exterior light which is that of the sun, it would be impossible for vision to exist. The case is the same with all the other organs and members in the human body; there are forces acting from without, which are natural, and in themselves not alive, and there are forces acting from within, in themselves alive, which keep each in its connection, and cause it to live, and this according to the form, such as is given it for use.

3629. That the case is really thus, few can believe, by reason that few are acquainted with what is spiritual and what is natural, and still fewer know how these principles are distinct from each other, also what correspondence is, and what influx, and that the spiritual principle, when it flows into the organical forms of the body, presents living operations such as appear; and that without such influx and correspondence, not even the most minute particle of the body could have life and be moved. In respect to this circumstance, I have been informed by living experience, not only that heaven in general flows in, but also societies in particular; likewise what the societies are and of what quality; what flows into this and that organ of the body, and into this and that member thereof; and further, that it is not one society only which flows into each organ or member, but several,

*and that in each society also there are several; for the more
there are, so much the better and stronger is the correspondence,
inasmuch as perfection and strength arises from unanimity of
many, who act as one in an heavenly form; hence results a
more perfect and stronger tendency of acting* (conatus) *upon
particulars according to plurality.*

3630. *Hence it may appear, that all and singular the viscera and members of the body, or organs of motion and sensations, correspond to societies in heaven, thus to so many as
it were distinct heavens, and that from those societies, that is,
by them, celestial and spiritual things flow in with man, and
this into adequate and suitable forms, and present thus the
effects which are apparent to man; these effects however appear to man no otherwise than as natural, thus altogether under
another form and under another appearance than what they are
in their origin, insomuch that they cannot be known to be from
heaven.*

3631. *It was also once shown me to the life what societies
they are, and of what quality, and how those flow in and act,
which constitute the province of the face, and flow into the muscles of the forehead, of the cheeks, of the chin, and of the neck,
and how they communicate with each other; in order that this
might be presented to the life, it was allowed them to draw an
effigy of a face in various methods, by influx. In like manner
it was shown me what societies, and of what quality, flow into
the lips, into the tongue, into the eyes, and into the ears; and it
was also given me to discourse with them, and thus to be fully
instructed. Hence also it may appear, that all who come into
heaven, are organs or members of the* GRAND MAN; *and also
that heaven is never shut, but in proportion to the numbers who
enter, the stronger is the tendency to action* (conatus), *the stronger
the force, and the stronger the action; and further that the
heaven of the Lord is immense, so as to exceed all belief; the
inhabitants of this earth are very few respectively, and but as a
pool of water in comparison with the ocean.*

3632. *Divine Order, and the celestial order thence derived,
is not terminated but with man, in his corporeal principles,
namely, in his gestures, actions, looks, speech, external sensations, and in the delights thereof; these are the extremes* (outermost principles) *of order, and the extremes of influx, which are
then bounded. But the interior things which flow in, are not
such as they appear in externals, but have altogether a different
appearance, a different countenance, a different sensation, and
a different pleasure; correspondences teach what are their qualities, and also representations, of which see above. That there
is such difference, may appear from actions which flow from the
will, and from discourse which flows from the thought. The
actions of the body are not such in the will, neither are verbal*

discourses such in the thought. Hence also it is manifest, that natural acts flow from spiritual principles, for the things appertaining to will and thought are spiritual; and that these spiritual things are effigied in natural acts correspondently, but still differently from what they are in themselves.

3633. All spirits and angels appear to themselves as men, both in respect to face and body, organs and members; and this by reason that their inmost principle conspires to such a form. As the primitive principle of man, which is from the soul of the parent, has a forcible tendency to the formation of the whole man, in the ovum and the womb, although this primitive principle is not in the form of the body, but in another most perfect form, known only to the Lord; and inasmuch as the inmost principle with every spirit and angel in like manner conspires and has a powerful tendency to such a form, therefore they all appear in the spiritual world as men. Moreover, the universal heaven is such, that every one is as it were the centre of all, for he is the centre of influxes through the heavenly form from all and hence an image of heaven results to every one, and makes him like unto itself, that is, a man; for such as the general (principle or form) is, such is a part thereof, inasmuch as the parts must needs be like unto their general (principle or form) in order to belong thereto.

3634. Man who is in correspondence, that is, who is principled in love to the Lord, and in charity towards his neighbour, and thence in faith, as to his spirit is in heaven, and as to his body in the world; and inasmuch as he thus acts in unity with the angels, he is also an image of heaven; and whereas there is an influx of all, or a general influx, into particulars or parts, as was observed, therefore he is also a little heaven, under a human form; for it is by virtue of good and truth that man is man, and distinct from brute animals.

3635. There are in the human body two (parts or principles), which are the fountains of all its motion, and also of all external or mere bodily action and sensation, namely, the heart and the lungs. These two (parts or principles) correspond in such a manner to the GRAND MAN or heaven of the Lord, that the celestial angels therein constitute one kingdom, and the spiritual another kingdom, for the Lord's kingdom is celestial and spiritual; the celestial kingdom consists of those who are principled in love to the Lord, the spiritual kingdom of those who are principled in charity towards their neighbour, see n. 2088, 2669, 2715, 2718, 3235, 3246. The heart and its kingdom in man corresponds to the celestial angels, the lungs and their kingdom correspond to the spiritual; the celestial and spiritual angels also flow into the things appertaining to the heart and lungs, insomuch that such things exist and subsist by influx thence. But concerning the correspondence of the heart and lungs with the GRAND MAN, *by the Divine Mercy of the Lord, we shall treat particularly.*

3636. *It is a most universal principle, that the Lord is the sun of heaven, and that thence comes all light in another life; and that to angels and spirits, or those who are in another life, nothing at all of the light of the world appears, and also that the light of the world, which is from the material sun, is no other than darkness to the angels. From the sun of heaven, or from the Lord, there is not only light but also heat; howbeit it is spiritual light and spiritual heat; the light in the eyes of the angels appears like light, but it has in it intelligence and wisdom, as being thence derived; and the heat of their senses is perceived as heat, but there is in it love as being thence derived; wherefore also love is called spiritual heat, and likewise constitutes the heat of man's life, and intelligence is called spiritual light, and likewise constitutes the light of man's life; from this universal correspondence the rest are derived; for all and singular things have relation to good which is of love, and to truth which is of intelligence.*

3637. *The* GRAND MAN, *in respect to man, is the universal heaven of the Lord; but the* GRAND MAN, *in a supreme sense, is the Lord alone, for heaven is from Him, and all things therein correspond to Him. Inasmuch as the human race, by the life of evil and the persuasions of what is false thence derived, became altogether perverse, and inasmuch as in this case the inferior principles with man began to have rule over the superior, or his natural principles over his spiritual, so that Jehovah, or the Lord, could no longer flow in through the* GRAND MAN, *that is, heaven, and reduce them into order, therefore hence came a necessity for the Lord's coming into the world, that hereby He might put on the human [principle] and make it Divine, and by it might restore order, so that the universal heaven might have relation to Him as to the only Man, and might correspond to Him alone, those being rejected who were principled in evil and thence in what is false, beneath the feet, that is, out of the* GRAND MAN. *Hence they who are in the heavens are said to be in the Lord, yea, in His body, for the Lord is the all of heaven, wherein all and every one share by distribution their respective provinces and offices.*

3638. *Hence it is, that in another life all societies, how many soever they be, keep their situation constant in respect to the Lord, who appears as a sun to the universal heaven; and what is wonderful, and can scarce be credited by any one, because not apprehended, is, that the societies therein keep the same situation in respect to each individual, wheresoever he may be, and howsoever he may turn himself and move about; as for instance, the societies which appear on the right, are continually to his right-hand, and those which appear on the left, are con*

*tinually to his left-hand, although he changes his direction as
to face and body. This also it has been given me frequently to
observe by a turn of the body. Hence it is evident, that the
form of heaven is such, as to have a constant reference to the
GRAND MAN in respect to the Lord; and that all the angels are
not only with the Lord, but in the Lord, or, what is the same
thing, that the Lord is with them, and in them; otherwise this
circumstance could not have place.*

*3639. Hence all situations in heaven are determined in re-
spect to the human body, according to points of direction (plagas)
from it, that is, to the right, to the left, forwards, and backwards, in whatever position; and also according to planes, as to
the plane of the head and of its parts, as of the forehead, of
the temples, of the eyes, and of the ears: also to the plane of the
body, as to the plane of the shoulders, of the breast, of the abdomen, of the loins, of the knees, of the feet, and of the soles
of the feet; likewise above the head, and beneath the soles of
the feet, in every inclination; to the back, too, and from the
hinder part of the head downwards. It is known from the
situation what the societies are, and to what provinces of man's
organs and members they belong, and this in all cases infal-
libly; but more so from their genius and particular temper as
to affections.*

*3640. The hells, which are very numerous, have also a con-
stant situation, so that from the situation alone it may be
known which they are, and of what quality. With respect to
their situation the case is similar; all things beneath man are
in planes in every direction under the soles of the feet. Some
appear thence also above the head, and dispersed in other places,
not that they have their situations there, for it is owing to a
persuasive phantasy which illudes, and appears to have a situation which in reality it has not.*

*3641. All appear erect, both they who are in heaven and
they who are in hell, with the head upwards and the feet downwards; nevertheless, in themselves, and according to angelic
vision, they are in another position, namely, they who are in
heaven are with the head towards the Lord, who is the sun there,
and thus the common centre, from whom all position and situation is determined; whereas the infernals, when viewed by the
angels, are with the head downwards and the feet upwards,
thus in a position opposite. and also oblique; for, to the infernals, that is beneath which to the celestials is above; and that
is above which to the celestials is beneath. Hence it is in some
degree manifest, how heaven may, as it were, make one with
hell, or how they may together have one aspect as to situation
and position.*

*3642. One morning I was in concert with angelic spirits,
who acted in unity of thought and speech according to custom;*

this penetrated also towards hell, whereunto it was continued, insomuch that they appeared as it were to act in unity with the infernals; but the reason was, that the good and truth appertaining to the angels was changed, by a wonderful turn, into what was evil and false with the infernals, and this by degrees as it flowed down to where hell acted in unity by persuasions of what is false and by lusts of what is evil. The hells, notwithstanding their being out of the Grand Man, *are nevertheless in such a manner reduced as it were into one, and thereby kept in order, according to which are their consociations. Thus the Lord from His Divine [principle] rules also the hells.*

3643. *It was observed, that they who are in the heavens are in a serene aura of light, like as of morning light, and of midday even verging to evening, in like manner that they are in heat, as of spring, of summer, and of autumn; whereas they who are in hell are in an atmosphere gross, cloudy, and dark, and are also in cold. It was further observed, that between these in general there is an equilibrium; also, that in proportion as the angels are in love, charity and faith thence derived, in the same proportion they are in an aura of light and of vernal heat; and in proportion as the infernals are in hatred, and thence in false principles, in the same proportion they are in darkness and in cold. Light in another life, as was said above, has in it intelligence, heat has in it love, darkness insanity, and cold hatred.*

3644. *All men, in the universal orb of the earths, have their situation either in the* Grand Man, *that is, in heaven, or out of the* Grand Man *in hell, as to their souls, or, what is the same thing, as to the spirit, which is to live after the body's decease. Man does not know this during his life in the world, but still such is his situation, and he is thence ruled. All are in heaven according to the good of love and the truth of faith thence derived, and in hell according to the evil of hatred and the false principle thence derived.*

3645. *The universal kingdom of the Lord is a kingdom of ends and uses. It has been given me manifestly to perceive that Divine Sphere, namely, of ends and uses, and certain things at the same time which are inexpressible. All and singular things flow forth from that sphere, and are ruled by it. So far as the affections, the thoughts, and actions have in them an end of doing good from the heart, so far man, spirit, and angel is in the* Grand Man, *that is in heaven; but so far as man and spirit has an end of doing evil from the heart, so far he is out of the* Grand Man, *that is, he is in hell.*

3646. *With brute animals the case is similar as with men as to influxes and correspondences, namely, that with them there is influx from the spiritual world, and afflux from the natural world, by which they are kept in form and order, and*

*live : but the real operation exhibits itself differently according
to the forms of their souls and the forms of their bodies thence
derived. The case herein is as with the light of the world, which
flows into various objects of the earth in a like degree and manner, and nevertheless acts diversely in different forms, producing beautiful colours in some, and colours not beautiful in
others. Thus when spiritual light flows into the souls of brutes,
it is received altogether differently, and thereby acts differently
upon them, than when it flows into the souls of men ; for the
latter are in a superior degree, and in a more perfect state, and
are such that they can look upwards, thus to heaven and to the
Lord, wherefore the Lord can adjoin them to Himself, and give
them eternal life ; but the souls of brutes are such, that they
cannot do otherwise than look downwards, thus to earthly things
alone, and thereby be adjoined solely to such things, in consequence whereof they also perish with the body. The ends regarded are what show the nature and quality of the life which
man has, and the nature and quality of the life which a beast
has. Man may have spiritual and celestial ends, he may see
them, acknowledge them, believe them, and be affected with them,
whereas beasts can have no other than natural ends ; thus man
may be in the Divine Sphere of ends and uses, which is in
heaven and which constitutes heaven, but beasts can be in no
other sphere than that of earthly ends and uses. Ends are
nothing else but loves, for the things which are loved are regarded as ends. The reason why very many men do not know
how to distinguish between their own life and that of beasts, is,
because they in like manner are in things external, and at heart
are solely concerned about terrestrial, corporeal, and worldly objects, and persons of such a character believe themselves also to
be like the beasts in respect to life, and that after death they
shall be dissipated in like manner ; for having no concern about
things spiritual and celestial, they are likewise without knowledge of such things. Hence comes the insane notion of the men
of modern times, in that they compare themselves to brute beasts,
and do not see the internal distinction. But whosoever believes
in celestial and spiritual things, or suffers spiritual light to flow
in and act, he sees altogether according to a different view, and
likewise discovers his superiority above brute animals. But
concerning the life of brute animals, by the Divine Mercy of the
Lord, we shall speak in a treatise apart.*

*3647. How the above case is, was also shown to me. It was
given to see and perceive certain spirits as they were entering
into another life, who in the life of the body regarded only
things terrestrial, and accounted nothing else as an end to be
pursued, nor were they initiated by any knowledges into good
and truth. Their employment had been that of sailors and
husbandmen. They appeared, as it was also perceived, to have*

so little life, that I thought it impossible for them to share eternal life like other spirits, being like machines scarcely animated; but the angels had tender care for them, and by the faculty, which as men they possessed, insinuated into them the life of good and truth, whereby they were more and more restored, from a life resembling that of animals, to human life.

3648. *There is an influx of the Lord through heaven also into the subjects of the vegetable kingdom, as into trees of every kind, and into their fructifications, and into plants of various kinds, and their multiplications.　Unless a spiritual principle from the Lord within continually acted upon their primitive forms which are in the seeds, it would be altogether impossible for them to vegetate and grow in so wonderful a manner and succession; but the forms therein are such, that they do not receive any thing of life.　It is by virtue of this influx, that they have in them an image of what is eternal and infinite, as is evident from this circumstance, that they are in a continual tendency (conatus) to propagate their genera and species, and thus to live as it were for ever, and also to fill the universe; this tendency is in every seed.　Nevertheless man attributes all these things, which are so wonderful, to mere nature, nor believes in any influx from the spiritual world, because in heart he denies it; although he might know, that nothing can subsist except by what it exists, that is, that subsistence is perpetual existence, or, what is the same thing, production is continual creation.　That hence universal nature is a representative theatre of the Lord's kingdom, may be seen, n. 3483.　But on this subject also, and on the correspondence of the vegetable kingdom with the* GRAND MAN, *by the Divine Mercy of the Lord, we shall speak elsewhere.*

3649. *The subject concerning the* GRAND MAN *and correspondence therewith, is continued at the close of the subsequent chapters.*

GENESIS.

CHAPTER THE TWENTY-EIGHTH.

3650. AT the beginning of the preceding chapter was explained what the Lord taught and foretold concerning the last judgment, or concerning the last days of the Church, in Matthew, chap. xxiv. from verse 8 to 14, n. 3486 to 3489; we shall now proceed to explain, by way of introduction to this chapter

as was proposed, the contents of the subsequent verses, 15, 16,
17, 18: " *When therefore ye shall see the abomination of desolation, spoken of by Daniel the prophet, standing in the holy
place, he who readeth let him carefully observe. Then let those
who are in Judea flee into the mountains. Let him who is on
the house-top not come down to take any thing out of his house.
Neither let him who is in the field turn back to take his
clothes.*"

3651. Every one may see that these words contain arcana,
and that without a discovery of such arcana, it cannot possibly
be known what is meant by them who are in Judea fleeing to
the mountains; and by him who is on the house-top not going
down to take any thing out of the house; and by him who is
in the field not returning back to take his clothes. Unless the
internal sense taught what is signified and implied by these
particulars, they who search into and interpret the Word might
be led away and give in to opinions altogether foreign to the
truth; yea, they who in heart deny the sanctity of the Word
might hence maintain, that the above expressions were only
intended to describe flight and escape on the approach of an
enemy, consequently that there is nothing more of sanctity contained therein; when yet by these words of the Lord is fully
described a state of the Church's vastation as to the good
things of love and the truths of faith, as may appear from the
following explication of each expression.

3652. According to the internal sense the signification of the
above passage is this: *When therefore ye shall see the abomination of desolation,* signifies the vastation of the Church,
which then has place, when the Lord is no longer acknowledged,
consequently when there is no love and no faith in Him; also
when there is no longer any neighbourly love or charity; and
consequently when there is no longer any faith of good and
truth. When this is the case in the Church, or rather in the
tract of country where the Word is possessed and read, that is,
when men are such in the thoughts of the heart, although not
such in doctrine of the lips, then there is desolation, and the
particulars just now mentioned are its abomination; hence,
when ye shall see the abomination of desolation denotes, when
any one observes such things; what is to be done in such case,
is told afterwards, verses 16, 17, 18. *Spoken of by Daniel the
prophet,* signifies, in the internal sense, by the prophets; for
where any prophet is mentioned by his name in the Word, it
does not mean that prophet, but the prophetic Word itself, because names in no case penetrate into heaven, see n. 1876,
1888; nevertheless each prophet has a distinct signification.
What is signified by Moses, Elias, and Elisha, may be seen in
the preface to chap. xviii. and n. 2762; but by Daniel is signified every thing prophetical concerning the Lord's coming, and

concerning the state of the Church, in the present case concerning its last state. Vastation is much treated of in the prophets, and by it in the literal sense is signified the vastation of the Jewish and Israelitish Church, but in the internal sense is signified the vastation of the Church in general, thus also the vastation which is now at hand. *Standing in the holy place*, signifies vastation as to all things which are of good and truth, holy place is a state of love and faith; that place in the internal sense denotes state, see n. 2625, 2837, 3356, 3387; the holy principle of that state is the good which is of love, and thence the truth which is of faith, and nothing else is meant in the Word by what is holy, because those things are from the Lord, Who is essential holiness or the sanctuary. *He who readeth let him carefully observe*, signifies that the above things are well to be noted by those who are in the Church, especially by those who are principled in love and faith, who come now to be treated of. *Then let them who are in Judea flee into the mountains*, signifies that they who are of the Church must not look elsewhere than to the Lord, thus to love towards Him, and to charity towards their neighbour; that by Judea is signified the Church, will be shown below; that by mountain is signified the Lord Himself, but by mountains love to Him, and charity towards our neighbour, may be seen n. 795, 796, 1430, 2722. According to the sense of the letter the meaning would be, that when Jerusalem was besieged, as was the case, by the Romans, then they should not betake themselves thither, but to the mountains, according as it is written in Luke, " When ye shall see Jerusalem encompassed about with armies, then know ye that devastation is near; then let them who are in Judea flee to the mountains, and let them who are in the midst of it depart out, and let not them that are in the countries enter thereinto," xxi. 20, 21. But the case is there the same in respect to Jerusalem, namely, that in the sense of the letter it is Jerusalem which is understood, whereas in the internal sense it is the Church of the Lord, see n. 402, 2117; for all and singular the things, which are recorded in the Word concerning the Jewish and Israelitish people, are representative of the Lord's kingdom in the heavens, and of the Lord's kingdom in the earths, that is, of the Church, as has been often shown above. Hence it is, that by Jerusalem in the internal sense is no where meant Jerusalem, nor by Judea, Judea. All and singular things also were such, as to be capable of representing the celestial and spiritual things of the Lord's kingdom, and they were effected in order that they might represent such things; by this means it became possible so to write the Word, that it might be according to the apprehension of man who reads it, and according to the understanding of the angels attendant on man. This likewise was the reason why the Lord spake in like manner, for had He spoken otherwise, His Word would not have been adequate to the understanding of those who read it, especially at that time, nor to the understanding of the angels, thus it would neither have been received by man, nor understood by the angels. *He who is on the house-top, let him not go down to take any thing out of the house,* signifies that such as are principled in the good of charity should not betake themselves to those things which appertain to doctrinals of faith; in the Word the house-top signifies the superior state of man, thus his state as to good; but those things which are beneath signify the inferior state of man, thus his state as to truth, see n. 710, 1708, 2233, 2234, 3142, 3538. With respect to the state of a man of the Church, the case is this: during the progress of regeneration, he learns truth for the sake of good, for he has the affection of truth to this intent; but after that he is regenerated, he then acts from a principle of truth and good. When he is arrived at this latter state, he ought not to betake himself to his former state, for if he should do this, he would reason (*ratiocinate*) from a principle of truth concerning the good in which he is, and would thereby pervert his state; for all reasoning *(ratiocination)* ceases, and ought to cease, when man is in a state to will what is true and good, for in this case he thinks and acts from the will, consequently from conscience, and not from the understanding, as before, and if he was to think and act again from the understanding, he would fall into temptations and sink therein. This then is what is signified by him who is on the house-top not going down to take any thing out of his house. *And he who is in the field, let him not return to take his clothes,* or coat, signifies that such as are principled in the good of truth should not betake themselves from the good thereof to doctrinals of truth; field in the Word signifies that state of man as to good; what is meant by field, may be seen, n. 368, 2971, 3196, 3310, 3317, 3500, 3508; and garment or coat signifies that which clothes good, that is, doctrinals of truth, for these are as clothing or raiment for good; that raiment has this signification, may be seen, n. 297, 1073, 2576, 3301. Every one may see, that things of a deeper nature lie concealed herein, than what appear in the letter, for the Lord Himself spake them.

3653. From these considerations then it may appear, that a state of the Church's vastation, as to the good things of love and the truths of faith, is fully described in these verses, and at the same time they contain an exhortation and direction to those who are principled in such good things and truths, what they ought to do in such case. There are three kinds of men within the Church, namely, those who are principled in love to the Lord, those who are principled in charity towards their neighbour, and those who are in the affection of truth. They

who are in the first class, namely, they who are principled in
love to the Lord, are specifically signified in these words, "*Let
those who are in Judea flee into the mountains.*" They who are
in the second class, namely, they who are principled in charity
towards their neighbour, are specifically signified in these
words, "*He who is on the house-top, let him not go down to take
any thing out of his house.*" They who are in the third class,
namely, they who are in the affection of truth, are specifically
signified in these words, "*He who is in the field, let him not
return to take his clothes.*" See what was said and explained
above on these words, n. 2454, and what is meant by returning
back, and looking behind him.

3654. That Judea, in the internal sense of the Word, does
not signify Judea, nor in like manner Jerusalem, Jerusalem,
may appear from several passages in the Word. In the Word
it is not so often named Judea, but the land of Judah, and by
the land of Judah, as by the land of Canaan, is signified the
Lord's kingdom, consequently also the Church, for the Church
is the Lord's kingdom in the earths; and this by reason that
the Lord's celestial kingdom was represented by Judah or by
the Jewish nation, and His spiritual kingdom by Israel or the
Israelitish people; and inasmuch as it was so represented, therefore also when mention is made in the Word of that nation and
people, nothing else is signified thereby in the internal sense.
That this is the case, will appear manifest from what will be
said in the following passages, by the Divine Mercy of the Lord,
concerning Judah and the land of Judah, and in the mean time
from these few passages out of the prophets : " My beloved
had a vineyard in the horn of a son of oil, he fenced it about,
and gathered the stones out of it, and planted it with a noble
vine, and built a tower in the midst of it, and also hewed out a
wine-press in it, and he expected it would bring forth grapes, but
it brought forth wild grapes ; and now, *O inhabitant of Jerusalem,* and *man of Judah,* judge ye I pray between me and my
vineyard ; I will make it a *desolation,* because the vineyard of
Jehovah of Hosts is the *house of Israel,* and the *man of Judah*
is the plant of his delights ; and he expected judgment, but
behold, a putrid sore ; justice, but behold, a cry," Isa. v. 1, 2,
3, 6, 7. In this passage, in the sense of the letter, the perverse
state of the Israelites and Jews is treated of, but in the internal
sense the perverse state of the Church is treated of as represented by Israel and Judah. The inhabitant of Jerusalem is
the good of the Church. That inhabitant denotes good, or
what is the same thing, those who are principled in good, may
be seen, n. 2268, 2451, 2712, 3613 ; and that Jerusalem is the
Church, see n. 402, 2117. In like manner the house of Israel
is significative ; that house denotes good, may be seen, n. 710,
1708, 2233, 2234, 3142, 3538 ; and that Israel denotes the

Church, n. 3305; in like manner the man of Judah, for by man is signified truth, see n. 265, 749, 1007, 3134, 3310, 3459, and by Judah good, but with this difference, that the man of Judah denotes truth grounded in the good of love to the Lord, which is called celestial truth, that is, it denotes those who are principled in such truth. Again, in the same prophet, " He shall lift up an ensign for the nations, and shall gather together the *outcasts of Israel,* and shall collect the *dispersed of Judah* from the four wings of the earth : then the envy of Ephraim shall depart, and the *enemies of Judah* shall be cut off; Ephraim shall not envy *Judah,* and *Judah* shall not straiten Ephraim ; Jehovah shall destroy the tongue of the sea of Egypt, and shall shake His hand over the river with the vehemence of His spirit: then shall there be a path for the remains of His people which shall be left of Ashur," xi. 12, 13, 15, 16. The subject here treated of in the sense of the letter is concerning the bringing back the Israelites and Jews out of captivity, but in the internal sense it has relation to the New Church in general, and to every individual in particular who is regenerated or becomes a Church The outcasts of Israel denote their truths ; the dispersed of Judah denote their goods ; Ephraim denotes their intellectual principle, in that it will no longer be repugnant; Egypt denotes scientifics, and Ashur reasoning grounded therein, which they have perverted ; the expelled, the dispersed, the remains, and the left (or residue), denote the truths and goods which survive. That Ephraim is the intellectual principle will be shown elsewhere ; that Egypt is the scientific, may be seen, n. 1164, 1165, 1186, 1462, 2588, 3325 ; that Ashur is reasoning, may be seen, n. 119, 1186 ; and that remains are goods and truths from the Lord stored up in the interior man, see n. 468, 530, 560, 561, 660, 661, 798, 1050, 1738, 1906, 2284. Again, in the same prophet, " Hear ye this, O house of Jacob, called by the name of *Israel,* and *from the waters of Judah have they come forth,* because from the city of holiness they are called, and stay themselves upon the God of Israel," xlviii. 1, 2 ; where the waters of Judah denote truths which are grounded in the good of love to the Lord ; those truths so grounded are the essential goods of charity, which are called spiritual goods, and constitute the spiritual Church, the internal Church, which is Israel, and the external, which is the house of Jacob ; hence it is evident what is signified by the house of Jacob called by the name of Israel, and by their coming forth from the waters of Judah. Again, in the same prophet, " I will bring forth seed out of Jacob, and *out of Judah an heir of My mountains,* and Mine elect shall possess it, and My servants shall dwell there," lxv. 9 ; out of Judah an heir of mountains in a supreme sense denotes the Lord, and in a representative sense those who are principled in love to Him, thus in the good of each love; that mountains are those goods, was shown above, n. 3652. So in Moses, "*Judah is a lion's whelp; from the prey, my son, thou hast gone up;* he stooped down, he couched as a lion, and as an old lion, who shall rouse him up?" Gen. xlix 9; where it is very evident, that in a supreme sense by Judah is meant the Lord, and in a representative sense those who are principled in the good of love to Him. So in David, "When Israel went forth out of Egypt, the house of Jacob from a barbarous people; *Judah was made His sanctuary, Israel His dominion*," Psalm cxiv. 1, 2; in this passage also, Judah denotes celestial good, which is the good of love to the Lord, and Israel denotes celestial truth or spiritual good. So in Jeremiah, "Behold the days coming, saith Jehovah, and I will raise up to *David* a righteous germ, who shall reign, a king, and shall prosper, and shall do judgment and justice in the earth; in His days *Judah shall be saved* and *Israel shall dwell securely;* and this is His name whereby He shall be called, Jehovah our Righteousness," xxiii. 5, 6; chap. xxxiii. 15, 16; speaking of the Lord's coming; Judah denotes those who are principled in the good of love to the Lord, Israel those who are in the truth of that good; that by Judah is not meant Judah, nor by Israel, Israel, may appear from this consideration, that Judah was not saved, neither Israel. In like manner, in the same prophet, " I will bring back *the captivity of Judah,* and *the captivity of Israel,* and will build them as heretofore," xxxiii. 7. Again, in the same prophet, " In those days, and in that time, saith Jehovah, shall the *sons of Israel* come, themselves and the *sons of Judah* together, going and weeping they shall go, and shall seek Jehovah their God, and shall seek Zion in their way with their faces thitherward," l. 4, 5. Again, " In that time they shall call Jerusalem the throne of Jehovah, and all nations shall be gathered unto it, on account of the name of Jehovah, to *Jerusalem;* they shall not go any longer after the stubbornness of their evil heart; in those days *the house of Judah shall go to the house of Israel,* and shall come together out of the land of the north upon the earth," iii. 17, 18. Again, " Behold, the days come, saith Jehovah, in which I will sow the *house of Israel* and *the house of Judah* with the seed of man and with the seed of beast; and I will establish a new covenant with *the house of Israel* and with *the house of Judah;* this is the covenant which I will establish with the house of Israel after those days, I will give My law in the midst of them, and will write it upon their heart," xxxi. 27, 31, 33. That Israel or the house of Israel is not here meant, is very evident, because they were dispersed amongst the Gentiles, and were never brought back out of captivity; consequently, neither was Judah or the house of Judah meant, but thereby were signified, in the internal sense, those who are of the Lord's spiritual and celestial kingdoms;

with these is established a new cove ant, and in their hearts is
the law written; new covenant der otes conjunction with the
Lord by good, see n. 665, 666, 1023, 1038, 1864, 1996, 2003,
2021, 2037; the law written in their hearts denotes the perception of good and truth thence derived, and also conscience. So
in Joel, "It shall come to pass in that day, the mountains shall
drop new wine, and the hills shall flow with milk, and *all the
rivers of Judah shall flow with waters*, and a fountain shall
come forth from the house of Jehovah, and shall water the river
of Shittim: Egypt shall be for wasteness, and Edom shall be
for a wilderness of wasteness, by reason of violence to the *sons
of Judah*, whose innocent blood they have shed in their land:
and *Judah shall sit for ever*, and *Jerusalem* to generation and
generation," iv. 18, 19, 20; from all the particulars in this
passage also it is evident, that by Judah is not meant Judah,
nor by Jerusalem, Jerusalem, but that thereby are understood
all those who are in the holy principle of love and charity, for
these shall sit for ever, and to generation and generation. So
in Malachi, "Behold, I send My angel, who shall prepare the
way before Me, and the Lord Whom ye seek shall suddenly
come to His temple, and the Angel of the covenant Whom
ye desire; *then shall the meat-offering of Judah and of Jerusalem be sweet to Jehovah*, according to the days of eternity,
according to former years," iii. 1, 4; speaking of the Lord's
coming; that at that time the meat-offering of Judah and of
Jerusalem was not sweet to Jehovah, is evident; hence it is
plain, that by Judah and Jerusalem are signified such things as
appertain to the Lord's Chruch. The case is the same in other
parts of the Word where mention is made of Judah, of Israel,
and of Jerusalem. Hence then it may appear what is signified
by Judea in Matthew, namely, the Lord's Church, in the present case vastated.

3655. The subject treated of in the preceding verses in the
evangelist was concerning the first and second state of the
Church's perversion. That the first state consisted in their
beginning no longer to know what is good and what is true,
and in disputing about good and truth, whence come falsities,
may be seen, n. 3354; and that the second state consisted in
their despising good and truth, and also in being averse thereto,
and thus in the expiration of faith in the Lord, according to the
degrees of the cessation of charity, may be seen, n. 3487, 3488.
This then is the third state treated of, which is that of the desolation of the Church as to good and truth.

CHAPTER XXVIII.

1. AND Isaac called to Jacob, and blessed him, and com·manded him, and said unto him, Thou shalt not take a woman from the daughters of Canaan.

2. Arise, go to Padan-Aram, the house of Bethuel the father of thy mother, and take to thyself thence a woman from the daughters of Laban thy mother's brother.

3. And GOD Schaddai will bless thee, and will cause thee to be fruitful and to multiply, and thou shalt be for a company of people.

4. And He will give unto thee the blessing of Abraham, to thee and to thy seed with thee, to inherit the land of thy sojournings, which GOD gave to Abraham.

5. And Isaac sent Jacob, and he went to Padan-Aram, to Laban the son of Bethuel the Aramæan, the brother of Rebecca, the mother of Jacob and Esau.

6. And Esau saw that Isaac blessed Jacob, and sent him to Padan-Aram, to take to himself thence a woman, in blessing him, and commanded him, saying, Thou shalt not take a woman of the daughters of Canaan.

7. And that Jacob hearkened to his father and to his mother, and went to Padan-Aram.

8. And Esau saw that the daughters of Canaan were evil in the eyes of Isaac his father.

9. And Esau went to Ishmael, and took Mahalath the daughter of Ishmael Abraham's son, the sister of Nebaioth, over his females to himself for a woman.

*   *   *   *   *

10. And Jacob went out from Beersheba, and went to Haran.

11. And he lighted upon a place, and passed the night there, because the sun was set, and he took of the stones of the place, and placed them for his pillows (*capitalia*, or things of the head), and lay down in that place.

12. And he dreamed, and behold a ladder set on the earth, and its head reaching to heaven, and behold the angels of GOD ascending and descending on it.

12. And behold JEHOVAH standing above it, and He said, I am JEHOVAH, GOD of thy father Abraham, and GOD of Isaac. The land on which thou liest, to thee will I give it, and to thy seed.

14. And thy seed shall be as the dust of the earth, and thou shalt break forth to the sea, and to the east, and to the north, and to the south ; and all the families of the ground shall be blessed in thee, and in thy seed.

15. And behold I am with thee, and will keep thee in all whither thou goest, and will bring thee back to this ground,

because I will not leave thee, until I shall have done what I have spoken to thee.

16. And Jacob awoke out of his sleep, and said, Surely Jehovah is in this place, and I knew not.

17. And he feared, and said, How terrible is this place; this is none other but the house of God, and this is the gate of heaven.

18. And in the morning Jacob arose early, and took the stone which he had placed for his pillows, and set it for a statue, and poured oil upon the head of it.

19. And he called the name of that place Bethel; but the name of the city was Luz at the first.

20. And Jacob vowed a vow, saying, If God shall be with me, and shall keep me in this way wherein I walk, and shall give me bread to eat, and raiment to put on,

21. And I shall return in peace to the house of my father. and Jehovah shall be to me for a God;

22. And this stone, which I have set for a statue, shall be the house of God; and all that Thou shalt give me, I will in tithing tithe it to thee.

THE CONTENTS.

3656. THE subject here treated of in the supreme sense is concerning the Lord, how He began to make His natural principle Divine, as to truth and as to good; and the means by which he effected this are described in general. But the subject treated of in the representative sense, is, how the Lord regenerates, or makes new, man's natural principle as to truth and as to good; the process in general is in like manner described, verse 1 to 10.

3657. In the internal supreme sense is described how the Lord began to make Divine his natural principle as to truth from the ultimate of order, that thereby He might arrange intermediate principles, and might conjoin all and singular to the first, that is, to His essential Divine [principle]. But in the internal representative sense is described how the Lord regenerates the natural human principle also from the ultimate of order, and thereby arranges intermediate principles, that by means of the rational principle He may conjoin them to Himself, from verse 11 to 22.

THE INTERNAL SENSE.

3658. Verse 1, 2. *AND Isaac called to Jacob, and blessed him, and commanded him, and said unto him, Thou shalt not take a woman of the daughters of Canaan. Arise, go to Padan-Aram, the house of Bethuel the father of thy mother, and take to thyself thence a woman from the daughters of Laban thy mother's brother.* Isaac called to Jacob, signifies the perception of quality as to the good of truth from the Lord: and blessed him, signifies that thus conjunction was effected: and commanded him, and said to him, signifies reflection and thence perception: Thou shalt not take a woman of the daughters of Canaan, signifies if so be he should not be conjoined to the affections of what is false and evil: arise, signifies if so be he would elevate that good thence: go to Padan-Aram, signifies knowledges of such truth: the house of Bethuel the father of thy mother, and take to thyself thence a woman from the daughters of Laban thy mother's brother, signifies collateral external good, and thence truth which was to be conjoined.

3659. "And Isaac called to Jacob"—that hereby is signified the perception of quality as to good of truth from the Lord, appears from the signification of calling to any one, as denoting perception of quality, see n. 3609; and from the representation of Isaac, as denoting the Lord in respect to the Divine Good of the Divine Rational principle, see n. 1893, 2066, 2072, 2083, 2630, 3012, 3194, 3210; and from the representation of Jacob, as denoting the Lord in respect to natural truth, see n. 1893, 3305, 3509, 3525, 3546, 3576, 3599. But here, in what follows in this chapter, Jacob represents the good of that truth; hence it is evident, that by these words, "Isaac called to Jacob," is signified the perception of quality from the Lord as to the good of truth. The ground and reason why Jacob here represents the good of that truth is, because now he had taken the birthright of Esau, and also his blessing, and thus thereby put on the person of Esau, but still no further than as to the good of that truth, namely, the truth which he before represented; for all truth, whatsoever be its nature or quality, has in it good, inasmuch as truth is not truth but by virtue of good, it being thence called truth. By the birthright (primogeniture) which he took, and by the blessing, he obtained this privilege over Esau, that his posterity succeeded to the promise made to Abraham and Isaac concerning the land of Canaan, and thus that by him should be represented the Lord's Divine Natural [principle], as by Isaac was represented the Divine Rational, and by Abraham the essential Divine [principle]. In order, therefore, that the representative might fall upon one person, it was permitted that he should thus take from Esau the birthright, and afterwards the blessing. Hence it is that Jacob now represents the good of the natural principle, but here in the beginning the good of that truth, namely, the truth which he just before represented. Esau is also still further treated of, as in the following verses 6, 7, 8, of this chapter ; to the intent that the good of truth, and the interior truth of good, of the Lord's Natural [principle] might be represented, which could not be represented by Jacob. What is the nature and quality of the good, which Jacob here represents, will appear from what follows.

3660. " And blessed him"—that hereby is signified that thus conjunction was effected, appears from the signification of being blessed, as denoting to be conjoined, see n. 3504, 3514, 3530, 3565, 3584. The ground and reason why Isaac the father now blessed Jacob the son, notwithstanding his having come in treachery, and taken the blessing from Esau, and notwithstanding Isaac's having shuddered at that deed, as is evident from the preceding chapter, verses 33 and 35, is, because he now perceived that it was the posterity of Jacob, not of Esau, which should possess the land of Canaan ; hence the blessing from Isaac was confirmed. But the treachery at which Isaac shuddered, signified and predicted what was treacherous in the posterity of Jacob as to representatives, namely, that they were very far from sincerely or in heart representing the Divine or celestial things of the Lord's kingdom, and were thus altogether unlike the ancient Church, being merely in things external separate from any internal principle, and not even this, inasmuch as they so often fell away into open idolatries. What is meant by being conjoined, or by conjunction, which is signified in the internal sense by being blessed, was shown above, namely, that the natural principle as to good and as to truth should be adjoined to the rational, or what is the same thing, the external man to the internal ; for to the intent that the Lord might make His Natural [principle] Divine, He was to implant therein such good and truth as might correspond with the good and truth of the Divine Rational [principle] ; without corresponding goods and truths, no conjunction can have place. The goods and truths of the natural principle, or such as are proper to the natural man, are innumerable, and so innumerable that they can scarce be known by man as to their most common genera, howsoever natural good and truth, when it is mentioned, may appear to man as one simple principle ; for the whole natural principle, and all that is in it, consists of such innumerable genera of goods and truths. And this being the case, it may appear, that there are goods and truths of the natural principle, in which the goods and truths of the rational principle may abide, and that there are goods and truths of the natural principle, in which the goods and truths of the rational cannot abide ; consequently, that there are goods and truths of the natural principle, which may be adjoined to the goods and truths of the rational by correspondence. The subject treated of in this and the following chapters, is concerning such goods and truths. To know these goods and truths, and to distinguish them from each other, and further to examine their qualities, and thus how they are adapted for conjunction, is not so much within the reach of man's capacity, so long as he thinks not from an interior principle, or under the influence of illumination from the light of heaven, for in this case such things appear both obscure and unpleasant to him. Nevertheless they are adequate to the apprehension and understanding of the angels, and also to the apprehension of spirits; for their thoughts are not interrupted with the concerns of worldly, corporeal, and terrestrial things, as heretofore whilst they lived in the world. These latter, namely, angels and spirits, are in the pleasantness of intelligence, and the blessedness of wisdom, when they have a perception of such things from the internal sense of the Word; for in this case the Divine [principle] is resplendent, because the subject treated of in the internal sense is concerning the Lord, and in the representative sense concerning the Church and regeneration; hence they are in the Divine sphere of the Lord, and of His ends and uses.

3661. "And commanded him, and said unto him"—that hereby is signified reflection and perception thence, appears from the signification of commanding in the historical parts of the Word, as denoting to reflect; and from the signification of saying, as denoting to perceive, see n. 1791, 1815, 1819, 1822, 1898, 1919, 2080, 2619, 2862. Reflection is the examination of a thing, as to the circumstances thereof, and also as to its quality, which gives rise to perception.

3662. "Thou shalt not take a woman of the daughters of Canaan"—that hereby is signified if so be he should not be conjoined to the affection of what is false and evil, appears from the signification of taking a woman, as denoting to be associated to or conjoined with; and from the signification of daughters, as denoting affections, see n. 568, 2362, 3024; and from the signification of Canaan, as denoting what is false and evil, see n. 1093, 1140, 1141, 1167, 1205, 1444, 1573, 1574, 1868.

3663. "Arise"—that hereby is signified if so be he would elevate that good thence, appears from the signification of arising, as implying some degree of elevation, see n. 2401, 2785, 2912, 2927, 3171; in the present case an elevation from such things as are signified by the daughters of Canaan to such things as are signified by the daughters of Laban, who are treated of presently.

3664. "Go to Padan-Aram"—that hereby are signified the knowledges of such truth, appears from the signification of Aram or Syria, as denoting knowledges, see n. 1232, 1234,

3249. The ground and reason why Padan-Aram denotes knowledges of truth is, because it was in Syria of Rivers, where Nahor, Bethuel, and Laban dwelt; and that by Syria are signified the knowledges of truth, may be seen, n. 3051. Padan-Aram is also mentioned above, chap. xxv. 20 ; and below, chap. xxxi. 18 ; in which passages it likewise signifies the knowledges of truth.

3665. "The house of Bethuel the father of thy mother, and take to thyself thence a woman from the daughters of Laban thy mother's brother"—that hereby is signified collateral external good, and thence truth which was to be conjoined, appears from the representation of Bethuel, as denoting the good of the Gentiles of the first class, see n. 2685 ; and from the representation of Laban, as denoting the affection of good in the natural man, or the affection of external good, and properly collateral good of a common stock, see n. 3129, 3130, 3160, 3612 ; and from the signification of taking a woman from his daughters, as denoting to be associated to or be conjoined with the affections of truth thence derived. That to take a woman denotes to be conjoined, is evident, and that daughters are affections, may be seen, n. 568, 2362, 3024. Hence it appears what these words signify, namely, that the good of the natural principle, here represented by Jacob, was to be conjoined to truths derived from collateral external good. The case herein is this: in the course of man's regeneration, he is led of the Lord at first as an infant, afterwards as a child, next as a young man, and lastly as an adult. The truths which he learns as an infant child, are altogether external and corporeal, for as yet he is unable to apprehend interior truths ; those truths are no other than knowledges of such things, as contain in their inmost principle things Divine ; for there are knowledges of things, which do not contain any thing Divine in their inmost principle, and there are knowledges which do contain. The knowledges which do contain what is Divine, are such that they can admit interior truths more and more, successively and in order ; whereas the knowledges which do not contain what is Divine, are such that they do not admit, but reject such interior truths ; for the knowledges of good and truth external and corporeal are like ground, which according to its quality admits seeds of such and such a nature, and no other, bringing to maturity one kind of seeds, and suffocating another. The knowledges, which contain in their inmost principle what is Divine, admit in them truth and good both spiritual and celestial, possessing this capacity by virtue of the Divine principle which is within, and which disposes them thereto ; but the knowledges, which do not contain in them what is Divine, admit only what is false and evil, such being their nature. Those knowledges of external and corporeal truth which are admissive of truth and good

spiritual and celestial, are here signified by the daughters of
Laban of the house of Bethuel; but those which are not thus
admissive, are signified by the daughters of Canaan. The
knowledges, which are learnt from infancy to childhood, are as
it were vessels most common (or general) which are designed
to be filled with goods, and in proportion as they are filled, man
is enlightened. If the vessels be such as to admit into them
genuine goods, in this case man is enlightened from the Divine
[principle] which is therein, and this successively more and
more; but if they be such as not to admit of genuine goods,
in this case man is not enlightened, although it may appear as
if he was, such appearance being only the effect of a delusive
light (*lumen*), which is that of the false and evil principle,
whereby he is more and more obscured as to what is good and
true. Such knowledges are manifold, and so manifold that
they can scarce be enumerated as to their genera, still less be
distinguished as to their species, for they are derived in multi
plicity from the Lord through the rational principle into the
natural. Some flow in immediately through the good of the
rational principle, and thence into the good of the natural, and
also into the truth of this good, and thence further into the
external natural or corporeal principle, where they branch off
into various branches. Some also flow in immediately through
the truth of the rational principle into the truth of the natural,
and also into the good of this truth, and thence further into the
external natural or corporeal principle, see n. 3573, 3616. They
are like nations, families, and houses, and like the consanguinities and affinities therein, in that there are some which descend
in a right line from the first father, and some which descend in
an oblique line, or more and more collateral. In the heavens
these things are in the highest degree of distinctness, for all the
societies therein are distinguished according to the genera and
species of good and truth, and the proximities thence derived,
see n. 685, 2508, 2524, 2556, 2739, 3612; which societies, the
most ancient people, who were celestial men, represented by
the circumstance of dwelling together distinguished into nations, families, and houses, see n. 470, 471, 483, 1159, 1246.
Hence also it was enjoined, that they who were of the representative Church, should contract marriages within the families
of their own nation, for thus they might represent heaven, and
conjunction as to good and truth; as was the case here with
Jacob, in that it was enjoined that he should go to the house
of Bethuel the father of his mother, and should take to himself
thence a woman from the daughters of Laban his mother's brother. As to what concerns the knowledges of external or corporeal truth which are from collateral good, and, as was said,
contain in them what is Divine, and thus are admissive of genuine goods, such as are the knowledges with infant children

who are afterwards regenerated, they are in general such as are
contained in the historical parts of the Word, as in what is said
therein of paradise, of the first man, of the tree of life in the
midst of paradise, and of the tree of science, where the deceiv-
ing serpent was.   These are knowledges which contain in them
what is Divine, and admit into them goods and truths spiritual
and celestial, because they represent and signify those goods and
truths.   Such knowledges are also contained in the other historical parts of the Word, as in what is said of the tabernacle,
and of the temple, and of the construction of each.   In like
manner in what is said of the garments of Aaron and of his
sons; also of the feasts of tabernacles, of the first-fruits of harvest, and of unleavened bread, and of other like things.   When
these knowledges are known and thought of by an infant child,
then the attendant angels think of the Divine things which
they represent and signify; and inasmuch as the angels are
affected therewith, their affection is communicated, and causes
the delight and pleasure which the child experiences therein,
and prepares his mind to receive genuine truths and goods.
Such and very many others are the knowledges of external and
corporeal truth derived from collateral good.

3666. Verses 3, 4, 5. *And God Schaddai will bless thee,
and will cause thee to be fruitful and to multiply, and thou
shalt be for a company of people.   And He will give unto thee
the blessing of Abraham, to thee and to thy seed with thee, to
cause thee to inherit the land of thy sojournings, which God
gave to Abraham.   And Isaac sent Jacob, and he went to
Padan-Aram, to Laban the son of Bethuel the Aramæan, the
brother of Rebecca the mother of Jacob and Esau.*   God Schaddai shall bless thee, signifies the temptations of that truth and
good, whereby conjunction was effected: and will cause thee
to be fruitful and to multiply, signifies goods and truths thence
derived: and thou shalt be for a company of people, signifies
plenteousness: and He will give unto thee the blessing of
Abraham, signifies conjunction of the essential Divine [princi-
ple] with the good and truth of the natural principle: to thee
and to thy seed with thee, signifies with the good and truth
thence derived: to cause thee to inherit the land of thy sojournings, signifies the life of instructions: which God gave to
Abraham, signifies which is from the Divine [principle]: and
Isacc sent Jacob, signifies beginning of existence: and he went
to Padan-Aram, signifies here, as above, the knowledges of
that truth: to Laban the son of Bethuel the Aramæan, signifies collateral good: the brother of Rebecca, the mother of Jacob
and Esau, signifies affinity derived from the mother of the good
of truth which is Jacob, with the truth of good which is Esau.

3667. "God Schaddai shall bless thee"—that hereby are
signified the temptations of that truth and good whereby con

junction was effected, appears from the signification of God
Schaddai, as denoting temptations, of which signification we
shall speak presently; and from the signification of being
blessed, as denoting conjunction, concerning which signification, see n. 3504, 3514, 3530, 3565, 3584; inasmuch as by
Jacob is now represented the good of truth, as was shown
above, n. 3659, therefore that good and truth is here understood by *thee*. The ground and reason why God Schaddai signifies temptations, is, because in ancient times they distinguished
the Supreme God, or the Lord, by various names, and this according to His attributes, and according to the goods which
are from Him, and also according to the truths, which every one
knows are manifold. They who were of the ancient Church,
by all these denominations meant to describe one only God,
namely, the Lord, Whom they called Jehovah; but after that
the Church declined from good and truth, and at the same
time from this wisdom, they began to worship as many gods as
there were denominations of the one God, insomuch that every
nation, and at length every family, acknowledged one of them
for its own particular god; hence came the number of gods, of
which mention is made in the Word throughout. The case
was similar in the family of Therah the father of Abraham, and
also in the house of Abraham itself, for that he worshipped other
gods, may be seen, n. 1356, 2559, and especially the God
Schaddai, n. 1992. That the worship of this God remained in
that house, is evident also from these words in Moses, " *I appeared to Abraham, Isaac, and Jacob, in the God Schaddai,
and by My name Jehovah I was not known to them,*" Exod. vi.
3; hence it is that it was said to Abraham, " *I am the God
Schaddai,* walk thou before Me, and be entire," Gen. xvii. 1;
and that it is here said by Isaac to Jacob, " *The God Schaddai*
shall bless thee." That this is the case is also evident from
what follows in this chapter, that after the Lord had said to
Jacob in a dream, "I am Jehovah, God of thy father Abraham,
and God of Isaac," ver. 13, still Jacob afterwards said, " If God
shall be with me, and shall keep me in this way wherein I
walk, and shall give me bread to eat, and raiment to put on,
and I shall return in peace to the house of my father, and *Jehovah shall be to me for a God,*" verses 20, 21; hence it is evident, that neither did the house of Jacob acknowledge Jehovah,
but yet was willing to acknowledge Him, in case he proved a
benefactor; as is exactly the case at this day in Gentile Christendom. As to what concerns God Schaddai in particular, the
Lord was called by this name in the ancient Church with respect to temptations, and to blessings and benefits after temptations, as was shown above, n. 1992; hence then it is that by
the God Schaddai, in the internal sense, are signified temptations. That by temptations is effected a conjunction of good

and truth, see what was said and shown above concerning
temptations, n. 2819.

3668. " And will cause thee to be fruitful and multiply"
—that hereby are signified goods and truths thence derived,
appears from the signification of being fruitful, as being predicated of good, and of being multiplied, as being predicated of
truth, see n. 43, 55, 913, 983, 2846, 2847.

3669. " And thou shalt be for a company of people"—that
hereby is signified plenteousness, may appear without explication ; company of people is especially predicated of truths, for
by people in the Word are signified those who are in truth, see
n. 1259, 1260, 2928, 3581 ; whereas by nations are signified
those who are in good, see n. 1259, 1260, 1416, 1849. The
reason why it is here called a company of people, is, because
the subject treated of is concerning the good of truth represented by Jacob ; for there is a distinction to be made between
good which is derived from truth, and good from which truth
is derived ; the good which is derived from truth is what is here
represented by Jacob, and the good from which truth is derived
is what is represented by Esau ; the good which is derived
from truth is the inverse of the good from which truth is derived ;
in the good which is derived from truth, the regenerate are
principled previous to their regeneration, whereas in the good
from which truth is derived, they are principled when they
become regenerate. That their state is inverted, may be seen,
n. 3539, 3548, 3556, 3563, 3570, 3576, 3603.

3670. " And will give to thee the blessing of Abraham"—
that hereby is signified conjunction of the essential Divine
[principle] with the good and truth of the natural principle,
appears from the signification of blessing, as denoting conjunction, see above, n. 3660, 3667 ; and from the representation of
Abraham, as denoting the Lord's essential Divine [principle],
which is called the Father, see n. 2011, 3251, 3439 ; and inasmuch as these words are spoken to Jacob, by whom will be
represented the Lord's Divine Natural [principle] as to Divine
good and truth therein, therefore the conjunction of the essential Divine [principle] with the good and truth of the natural,
is what is signified, in the internal sense, by these words, " He
will give thee the blessing of Abraham." In the sense of the
letter, it is the possession of the land of Canaan which is meant
by the blessing of Abraham, and also by the words which follow, " to cause thee to inherit the land of thy sojournings, which
God gave to Abraham ;" these words are also conceived according to this sense by all those who do not believe that the
historical parts of the Word contain things more heavenly and
secret, especially by the Jewish nation, which thence claims to
itself privileges above every other nation and people ; their
fathers understood the above words in the same literal sense,

and particularly Jacob, whose nature and quality may appear from what was said just above, n. 3667, namely, that he did not know Jehovah, nor was willing to acknowledge him, unless he would give him things corporeal and worldly; but that neither Abraham, nor Isaac, nor Jacob were understood, but that by Jacob is represented the Lord as to the natural principle which He would make Divine, is abundantly manifest from the explications above. That it is a thing of indifference what be the quality of the man who represents, whether he be evil or good, and that evil men may alike represent, and did represent the Lord's Divine [principle], may be seen, n. 665, 1097, 1361; the same may appear from the representatives which exist even at this day; for all kings, whosover they are, and of whatsoever quality, by virtue of the principle of royalty appertaining to them, represent the Lord; in like manner all priests, whosoever, or of whatsoever quality they are, by virtue of the priestly principle. The principle of royalty (*regium*) and the priestly principle (*sacerdotale*) is holy, whatsoever be the nature and quality of the person who ministers therein; hence it is, that the Word taught by a wicked person is alike holy as when taught by a good person, and also the Sacrament of Baptism and the Holy Supper, and the like; hence also it may appear, that no king can in any sort claim to himself any thing of the holy principle appertaining to his royalty, nor any priest any thing of the holy principle appertaining to his priesthood; in proportion as either claims any thing thereof to himself, or attributes it to himself, he is so far a spiritual thief, and brands himself with the mark and character of spiritual theft; and also in proportion as he does evil, that is, acts contrary to what is just and equitable, and contrary to what is good and true, in the same proportion a king puts off the representative of holy royalty, and a priest the representative of holy priesthood, and represents the opposite. Hence in the representative Jewish Church so many laws were enjoined concerning the holy principle, by which priests especially should be influenced during their ministration; on which subject, by the Divine Mercy of the Lord, more will be said in what follows.

3671. "To thee and to thy seed with thee"—that hereby is signified with the good and truth thence derived, appears from the representation of Jacob, who is here meant by *thee*, as denoting the good of truth, or good which is derived from truth, concerning which, see above; and from the signification of seed, as denoting the good and truth of faith, see n. 1025, 1447, 1610, 2848, 3373; with thee signifies that it was adjoined to the good of truth, which is Jacob. The case is similar, in respect to good and truth, as in respect to seeds and ground; interior good is as the seed which brings forth, but only in good ground; exterior good and truth is as ground in which the seed brings forth, namely, interior good and truth, which cannot otherwise be rooted. Hence it is that man's rational principle is first of all regenerated, for therein are seeds, and afterwards the natural principle that it may serve as ground, see n. 3286, 3288, 3321, 3368, 3493, 3620, 3623, 3576; and whereas the natural principle is as ground, good and truth is capable of being made fruitful and multiplying in the rational principle, which could not be the case, unless it had ground wherein as seed to fix its root: from this comparison, as in a mirror, it may be seen how the case is with regeneration, and with several arcana relating thereto. To understand what is good and true, and to will them, appertains to the rational principle; the perceptions of good and truth thence derived are as seeds, and to know them, and to bring them into act, appertains to the natural principle; scientifics and works are as ground, and when man is affected with the scientifics which confirm good and truth, and especially when he perceives delight in bringing them into act, in this case seeds are therein and grow as in their proper ground; hence good is made fruitful, and truth is multiplied, and they continually ascend from that ground into the rational principle, and perfect it. The case is otherwise when man understands what is good and true, and also inwardly perceives somewhat of inclination of the will thereto, but yet does not love to know them, and still less to do them; for in this case good cannot be made fruitful, nor truth be multiplied in the rational principle.

3672. "To cause thee to inherit the land of thy sojournings" —that hereby is signified the life of instructions, appears from the signification of inheriting, as denoting to have the life of another, see n. 2658, 2851; in the present case, life from the Divine [principle], which is signified by the words which presently follow; and from the signification of sojourning, as denoting instructions, see n. 1463, 2025; land signifies where life is. The life of instruction here treated of, is the life of good derived from truth, which is here represented by Jacob; for when man lives according to the truths in which he is instructed, he is then in the life of instructions.

3673. "Which God gave to Abraham"—that hereby is signified which is from the Divine [principle], appears from the representation of Abraham, as denoting the Lord in respect to the Divine [principle] which is called the father, see n. 2011, 3251, 3439. That by being given of God, is signified that it was appropriated to him, may appear evident; for that which is given is his to whom it is given. Hence it is manifest, that by these words, "which God gave to Abraham," is signified life which is from the Divine [principle].

3674. "And Isaac sent Jacob"—that hereby is signified beginning of existence, appears from this consideration, that

Jacob now comes to represent the good of truth, thus the beginning of the existence of the Lord's Divine natural [principle], for this is contained in what follows concerning Jacob sojourning with Laban. Hence it is that by Isaac sending Jacob is signified beginning of existence.

3675. "And he went to Padan-Aram"—that hereby are signified the knowledges of that truth, appears from the signification of Padan-Aram, as denoting the knowledges of truth, see n. 3664.

3676. "To Laban the son of Bethuel the Aramæan"—that hereby is signified collateral good, appears from the representation of Laban, as denoting collateral good of a common stock, concerning which see also above, n. 3665; and from the representation of Bethuel, as denoting the good of the Gentiles of the first class, see n. 2865, 3665; from which as from a common stock comes the good which is represented by Laban. The reason why Bethuel is here surnamed Aramæan, is, because by Aram or Syria are signified the knowledges of good and truth, see n. 1232, 1234, 3249, which are here treated of. External truth, from which is derived the good here represented by Jacob, is nothing else but knowledges; for these are the truths, which are first of all imbibed, and also are accounted as truths, by those who are in the beginning of regeneration. Nevertheless knowledges are not in themselves truths, but by virtue of the Divine things contained in them, and when these Divine things shine forth, they then first become truths. In the mean time they are as common vessels, by which and in which truths may be received, like those spoken of above, n. 3665, and like all scientifics when they are first learnt.

3677. "The brother of Rebecca, the mother of Jacob and Esau"—that hereby is signified affinity derived from the mother of the good of truth which is Jacob, with the truth of good which is Esau, appears from the representation of Rebecca, as denoting the Lord's Divine Rational [principle] as to Divine Truth, of which frequent mention has been made above; and from the representation of Jacob, as denoting the good of truth, or the good which is derived from truth in the natural principle; and from the representation of Esau, as denoting the truth of good, or the good from whence truth is derived in the natural principle, see above, n. 3669. And whereas all goods and truths, which are in the natural or external man, are conceived and born of the rational or internal man, namely, of the good of the rational man as a father, and of the truth thereof as a mother, see n. 3314, 3573, 3616; therefore by the above words is signified the affinity derived from the mother of the good of truth which is Jacob, with the truth of good which is Esau. There is also herein a real affinity, but to explain it to the apprehension is very difficult, by reason that the most com-

mon [or general] knowledges of the subject are at this day unknown, as for instance, what spiritual good is, and what the
truth thereof, and that there are innumerable genera of such
good and truth, and still more innumerable species, also that
they are conjoined with each other by degrees as it were of
consanguinity and affinity. These most common [or general]
knowledges being unknown, a description of such degrees and
affinities would be altogether obscure, and the more so on this
account, that the learned at this day are not disposed to know
such things, loving only to wander in the bark [the outward
rind or coverings of knowledge] and to dispute, not concerning
the nature and quality of the things, but whether they exist or
not; and so long as they are in this state, they are unwilling
to know any thing concerning the innumerable genera and
species above mentioned.

3678. Verses 6, 7, 8, 9. *And Esau saw that Isaac blessed
Jacob, and sent him to Padan-Aram, to take to himself thence
a woman, in blessing him, and commanding him, saying, Thou
shalt not take a woman of the daughters of Canaan. And
Jacob hearkened to his father, and to his mother, and went to
Padan-Aram. And Esau saw that the daughters of Canaan
were evil in the eyes of Isaac his father. And Esau went to
Ishmael, and took Mahalath the daughter of Ishmael, Abraham's son, the sister of Nebaioth, over his females to himself
for a woman.* Esau saw that Isaac blessed Jacob, signifies
the thought of natural good concerning conjunction by the good
of truth which is Jacob: and sent him to Padan-Aram, signifies
the beginning of existence by the knowledges of that good: to
take to himself thence a woman, signifies thereby conjunction
by the affection of truth: in blessing him, and commanding
him, saying, signifies that conjunction might be effected, reflection, and thence perception: Thou shalt not take a woman of
the daughters of Canaan, signifies that he should not be conjoined to the affections of what was false and evil: and that
Jacob hearkened to his father and to his mother, signifies obedience and affection: and went to Padan-Aram, signifies here,
as above, to imbibe the knowledges of that good and truth: and
Esau saw that the daughters of Canaan were evil in the eyes
of Isaac his father, signifies the Lord's foresight and providence,
that the affections of that truth in which natural good was
heretofore conjoined, would not conduce to conjunction: and
Esau went to Ishmael, and took Mahalath the daughter of
Ishmael, Abraham's son, signifies the conjunction of that good
with truth from a Divine origin: the sister of Nebaioth, over
his females to himself for a woman, signifies the affection of
celestial truth more inwardly.

3679. " Esau saw that Isaac blessed Jacob "—that hereby
is signified the thought of natural good concerning conjunction

by the good of truth which is Jacob, appears from the signification of seeing, as denoting to think; for to think is nothing
else but to see inwardly, or internal sight; and from the representation of Esau, as denoting the good of the natural principle,
see n. 3300, 3302, 3322, 3494, 3504, 3576, 3599; and from the
signification of being blessed, as denoting conjunction, see n.
3504, 3514, 3530, 3565, 3584; and from the representation of
Isaac, as denoting the Lord's Divine rational principle as to
Divine Good, spoken of above; and from the representation
of Jacob, as denoting the good of truth, see n. 3669, 3677.
Hence it is manifest, that by Esau seeing that Isaac blessed
Jacob, is signified the thought of natural good concerning conjunction by the good of truth. What is meant by the thought
of natural good concerning conjunction by the good of truth,
cannot so well be fully explained to the apprehension, nevertheless it may be expedient to attempt a brief explication. The
thought of natural good is the thought of the rational or internal man in the natural or external man, and indeed from the
good thereof; for it is the rational or internal man which thinks,
and not the natural or external man; the former, or the internal
man, being in the light of heaven, in which light there is intelligence and wisdom from the Lord, see n. 3195, 3339, 3636,
3743. Whereas the external man is in the light of the world,
in which is no intelligence, and not even life; wherefore unless
the internal man thought in the external, it would not be possible to think at all. Still however it appears to man, as if
thought was in his external man, inasmuch as he thinks from
those things which have entered in by the senses, and appertain
to the world. The case herein is like that of ocular vision; the
sensual man supposes that the eye sees of itself, when yet the
eye is merely an organ of the body, by which the internal man
sees those things which are out of the body, or which are in the
world. The case is the same also as that of speech; the sensual
man supposes that the mouth and the tongue speak of themselves, and they who think somewhat more deeply, suppose,
that the larynx and interior organs speak by aspiration from
the lungs, when yet it is the thought which speaks through
those organs, inasmuch as speech is nothing else but thought
speaking; there are many such fallacies of the senses. The
case is similar in regard to all apparent life in the external
man, in that it is the life of the internal man therein, as in its
material and corporeal organ. With respect to thought the
case is this: so long as man is in the body, he thinks from the
rational principle in the natural, but with a difference according as the natural principle corresponds to the rational, or does
not correspond. When the natural principle corresponds, then
the man is rational, and thinks spiritually, but when the natural principle does not correspond, then the man is not rational,

neither can he think spiritually; for where the natural principle corresponds to the rational, there communication is opened, so that the light of heaven from the Lord can flow in through the rational into the natural principle, and enlighten it with intelligence and wisdom, hence the man becomes rational and thinks spiritually; but where the natural principle does not correspond to the rational, there communication is closed, and there only flows in somewhat of light in general round about, and through chinks into the natural principle through the rational, hence the man is not rational, and does not think spiritually; for according as man has influx of the light of heaven, so he thinks. Hence it is evident, that every man thinks according to the state of the correspondence of the natural principle with the rational as to good and truth; but spirits and angels do not think as man does; their thought indeed is terminated also in a natural principle, for they have with them all the natural memory and its affections, but they are not allowed to use that memory, see n. 2475 to 2479; and although they are not allowed to use it, still it serves them as a plane, or as a foundation, so that the ideas of their thought are therein terminated. Hence it is that the ideas of their thought are of an interior nature, and their speech is not from forms of expressions, as with man, but from forms of things. Hence it is evident that their thought also is such as is the correspondence of their natural principle with the rational; and that there are spirits who are rational, and think spiritually, and also who are not rational, and do not think spiritually, and this altogether according to their affections and consequent thoughts of things in the life of the body, that is, according to the state of life which they have acquired to themselves in the world. Hence therefore it in some measure appears what the thought of natural good is, namely, that it is thought in the good of the natural principle; (according to the idea of spirits it is called thought of natural good, but according to the idea of men it is called thought in the good of the natural principle.) In this, namely, in the good of the natural principle, the rational thinks, when it respects good as an end; thus the thought of natural good concerning conjunction by the good of truth, is thought in the natural principle concerning the end, namely, how truth can be conjoined thereto, and this according to Divine order, by a common (or general) way, which is, as has been often said above, from such things as are external, and thus such as are the ultimate or last in order; all regeneration of the natural principle commencing from these: such last or ultimate principles are first knowledges, such as are those of infants and children, concerning which see n. 3665. In the beginning the truth of good, which is Esau, is not conjoined in the external form with the good of truth, which is Jacob, for the good of truth is inverted in respect to the truth of good, see n. 3669; but still they are conjoined in the inmost principles, that is, in regard to ends; for the end of truth which is from good is, that truths may be adjoined to itself according to order, and this also is the end of good which is from truth, and inasmuch as the end conjoins, therefore also they are conjoined, see n. 3562, 3565. The inverse of order at first is only a medium, or means, which has respect to the end.

3680. "And sent him to Padan-Aram"—that hereby is signified the beginning of existence by knowledges of that good, appears from the signification of sending him, as denoting beginning of existence, see n. 3674; and from the signification of Padan-Aram, as denoting knowledges of truth, see n. 3664. They are called knowledges of good, because all truths are knowledges of good; and truths are not truths, which are not grounded in good, or which do not respect good as an end; but so far as they respect doctrine, they are called knowledges of truth.

3681. "To take to himself thence a woman"—that hereby is signified conjunction thus by the affection of truth, appears from the signification of woman, as denoting the affection of truth, see n. 1468, 2517, 3236, which to receive is to be adjoined thereto.

3682. "In blessing him, and commanding him, saying"— that hereby is signified that conjunction might be effected, reflection and thence perception, appears from the signification of being blessed, as denoting conjunction, see n. 3504, 3514, 3530, 3565, 3584; and from the signification of commanding and saying, as denoting reflection and thence perception, see n. 3661.

3683. "Thou shalt not take a woman of the daughters of Canaan"—that hereby is signified that he should not be conjoined to the affections of what is false and evil, appears from the signification of taking a woman, as denoting to be associated and to be conjoined; and from the signification of the daughters of Canaan, as denoting the affections of what is false and evil, see above, n. 3662.

3684. "And that Jacob hearkened to his father and to his mother"—that hereby is signified obedience and affection, appears from the signification of hearkening to any one, as denoting to obey, see n. 2542; by hearkening to father and mother is signified obedience from affection.

3685. "And went to Padan-Aram"—that hereby is signified to imbibe the knowledges of that good and truth, appears from the signification of going or departing, as denoting order and institute of life, see n. 1293, 3335 in the present case therefore denoting to imbibe according to order, namely, the knowledges of that good and truth, which are signified by Padan-Aram, see n. 3664, 3675.

3686. "And Esau saw that the daughters of Canaan were evil in the eyes of Isaac his father"—that hereby is signified the Lord's foresight and providence, that the affections of that truth, with which natural good was heretofore conjoined, would not conduce to conjunction, appears from the signification of seeing in the present case, as denoting foresight and providence, see n. 2837, 2839; and from the representation of Esau, as denoting the Lord in regard to the Divine Good of the natural principle, concerning which see above; and from the signification of the daughters of Canaan, in the present case the daughters of Heth, as denoting the affections of truth from a ground not genuine, see n. 3470, 3620, 3621, 3622; and from the signification of being evil in the eyes of Isaac his father, as denoting the not conducing to conjunction, namely, by the good of the natural principle, which is Esau, with the good of the rational principle, which is Isaac. Hence it is manifest, that by these words is signified the Lord's foresight and providence, that the affections of that truth, as not being from a genuine ground, would not conduce to conjunction. How the case herein is, may appear from the explication at chap. xxvi verses 34, 35, where the daughters of Heth are treated of whom Esau had taken to himself for women; and at chap. xxvii. verse 46, where Jacob is treated of, in that he should not take to himself a woman of the daughters of Heth. The ground and reason why by the daughters of Canaan are here signified affections of truth from a ground not genuine, and above by the daughters of Canaan the affections of what is false and evil, n. 3662, 3683, is, because the Hittites were in the land of Canaan of the Church of the Gentiles, and not so much principled in what is false and evil as the other nations therein, namely, the Canaanites, the Amorites, and Perizites. Hence also by the Hittites was represented the Lord's spiritual Church amongst the Gentiles, see n. 2913, 2986. That the most ancient Church, which was celestial, and before the flood, was in the land of Canaan, may be seen n. 567; and that the ancient Church, which was after the flood, was also in that land, and moreover in several other kingdoms, see n. 1238, 2385; hence it came to pass, that all the nations in that land, and likewise all the regions, and all the rivers thereof, became representative; for the most ancient people, who were celestial men, through all objects which they saw, perceived such things as appertain to the Lord's kingdom, see n. 920, 1409, 2896 2897, 2995, thus also through the regions and rivers of that land. These representatives, after their times, remained in the ancient Church, thus also the representatives of the places in that land. The Word in the ancient Church, concerning which see n. 2897, 2898, 2899, had also thence representative names of places, as had also the Word after their time, which is called

Moses and the prophets; and this being the case, Abraham was therefore commanded to go to that land, and a promise made him that his posterity should possess it, and this not by reason of their being better than any other nations, for they were amongst the worst of all, see n. 1167, 3373, but that by 'hem a representative Church might be instituted, in which no attention should be paid to person or to place, but to the things which were represented, see n. 3670, and that thus also the names of the most ancient and of the ancient Church might be retained.

3687. "And Esau went to Ishmael, and took Mahalath the daughter of Ishmael the son of Abraham"—that hereby is signified the conjunction of that good with truth from a Divine origin, appears from the representation of Esau, as denoting the good of the natural principle, see above; and from the representation of Ishmael the son of Abraham, as denoting truth from a Divine origin. That Ishmael represents the Lord's spiritual Church, consequently truth, may be seen n. 1949, 1950, 1951, 2078, 2691, 2699, 3268; and that Abraham represents the Lord's Divine [principle] which is called father, see n. 2011, 3251, 3439. Hence by Mahalath the daughter of Ishmael the son of Abraham, is signified truth from a Divine origin. That to take is to be associated and conjoined, is manifest; hence it is plain, that by Esau going to Ishmael, and taking Mahalath the daughter of Ishmael, the son of Abraham, is signified the conjunction of that good with truth from a Divine origin.

3688. "The sister of Nebaioth over his females for a woman"—that hereby is signified the affection of celestial truth more interior, appears from the signification of sister, as denoting intellectual or rational truth, see n. 1495, 2508, 2524, 2556, 3386; and from the representation of Nebaioth, as denoting good which is of the spiritual Church, see n. 3268; hence the sister of Nebaioth signifies the affection of celestial truth, or what is the same thing, the affection of spiritual good; and from the signification of females or the daughters of Heth, as denoting affections of truth from a ground not genuine, see n. 3470, 3620, 3621, 3622, 3686; and from the signification of taking a woman, as denoting to be associated and conjoined. Hence it is evident, that by these words, together with those immediately preceding, is signified the conjunction of the good represented by Esau with truth from a Divine origin, thus with the affection of celestial truth more interior. How these things are, has been indeed shown above, nevertheless they are such as can scarcely be conceived of intelligibly, so long as the most common [or general] knowledges on the subject are wanting. And moreover the world at this day is little concerned about such things, earthly things and not heavenly being the objects

of its care, inasmuch as, according to the common observation,
they see and know the former things, whereas the latter they
neither see nor know.   But inasmuch as the internal contents
of the Word are not only to be made manifest, but also to be
explained, it may be expedient to illustrate by an example
how the case is in respect to the truth of good which Esau represents, and the good of truth represented by Jacob, and at
the same time in respect to this circumstance, that the good of
truth is inverted in regard to the truth of good, before man is
regenerated, but that afterwards they are conjoined.   Let the
example be this : a man who is such as to be capable of being
regenerated (for the Lord foresees this, and in consequence of
foreseeing he also provides for it) is first like an infant child,
and does not as yet know what are works of charity towards
his neighbour, because he does not as yet know what charity
is, nor what his neighbour ; wherefore since he has learnt from
the Word that he ought to give to the poor, and that whoever
gives to the poor has a reward in heaven, therefore he does
good to common beggars more especially, because he believes
that they are the poor who are meant in the Word, not con
sidering that such as beg in the streets, for the most part, live
an impious and wicked life, despising whatever appertains to
Divine worship, and being totally given up to sloth and idle-
ness.   Nevertheless, he who is in the first state of regeneration
is liberal in his benefactions to such persons ; good actions of
this sort are the goods of external truth from which regeneratio
commences ; the truth of good, which is interior, flows thus int
these acts, and operates according to the knowledges in which
the child is principled ; but afterwards, when he is more en
lightened, he is desirous to do good to all whom he believes to
be in want and distress, and scarce yet makes a distinction between the pious and the impious who fall under this description,
believing every one to be his neighbour in the same respect
and degree.   But when he is further enlightened herein, he
then makes a distinction, and affords help only to the upright
and good, knowing that to afford help to the wicked is to do
evil to many, inasmuch as the wicked are thereby supplied
with more power and opportunity of injuring others.   At
length, when he is regenerated, he does good only to the good
and pious, because then he is not affected with the person of
him to whom he does good, but with the good that is in him ;
and whereas the Lord is present in every thing good and pious,
he thus, by affection towards what is good, testifies love to the
Lord.   When he is principled in this charity from the heart,
he is then regenerated.   Hence it is evident, that his former
state was inverted in respect to this latter state, inasmuch as he
believed that to be good which was not good ; but still he was
bound to do that good in the beginning of regeneration, since

the knowledge of the thing was n)t further opened to him, and
since the interior good of charity cannot flow in any other
truth than what was of the knowledge thereof; and further
since interior good was always at hand, and in operation, and
was not able to manifest itself, until by knowledges the man
was successively enlightened concerning the qualities of goods
and truths. Hence it may in some measure appear what the
good of truth is which Jacob here represents, and what the '
truth of good which Esau represents, and that these at first are
inverted, but afterwards are conjoined.

*　　*　　*　　*　　*

3689. Verses 10, 11. *And Jacob went out from Beersheba,
and went to Haran. And he lighted upon a place, and passed
the night there, because the sun was set, and he took of the stones
of the place, and placed them for his pillows* (capitalia, *or
things of the head*), *and lay down in that place.* Jacob went
from Beersheba, signifies life more remote from Divine Doc
trinals: and went to Haran, signifies good and truth of that
degree: and he lighted upon a place, signifies a state: and
passed the night there, because the sun was set, signifies life ir
an obscure principle: and he took of the stones of the place.
signifies the truths of that state: and placed them for his pillows, signifies communication of a most common or general
nature with the Divine [principle]: and he lay down in that
place, signifies tranquillity of state.

3690. "Jacob went out from Beersheba"—that hereby is
signified life more remote from Divine Doctrinals, appears from
the signification of going, as denoting to live, see n. 3335
3685; thus to go out signifies to live more remotely; and from
the signification of Beersheba, as denoting Divine Doctrine.
see n. 2723, 2858, 2859, 3466; hence it is evident, that by
Jacob going out from Beersheba is signified life more remote
from Divine Doctrinals. Life is said to be more remote, when
it is in external truths, and directed according thereto, as is the
life of infancy and childhood of those who are regenerated,
concerning whom, see above, n. 3688. In order to show further
what that life is, and what is its quality, it may be expedient to
add a few words on the subject. All the historicals of the
Word are truths more remote from essential Divine Doctrinals,
but still they are serviceable to infants and children, in order to
introduce them into the interior doctrinals of truth and good,
by degrees, and at length into the essential Divine Doctrinals;
for within them, in their inmost ground, there is contained a
Divine principle. Whilst infants are reading them, and are
affected by them from innocence, in such case the attendant
angels are in a delighted state, being affected from the Lord
with the internal sense, consequently with those things which
the historicals represent and signify; it is the celestial delight

of the angels which flows in and causes delight with the infants. In order that this first state may be, or the state of infancy and childhood of those who are about to be regenerated, the historicals of the Word were given, and so written, that all and singular the things therein contain in them things Divine. How far these historicals are remote from Divine Doctrinals, may appear from the following example in regard thereto : he who at first knows only that God descended on Mount Sinai, and gave tables to Moses, on which were written the Ten Commandments, and that Moses brake those tables, and that God wrote like Commandments on other tables, whilst he is delighted solely with this historical relation, is in the life of external truth remote from Divine Doctrinals ; but afterwards, when he begins to be delighted and affected with the commandments themselves, or the precepts contained therein, and to live according thereto, he is then in the life of truth, yet still remote from essential Divine Doctrinals ; for a life according to the Ten Commandments is only a moral life, the precepts whereof are known to all who live in human society, being grounded in civil life and the laws thereof. But he who is regenerating, is by degrees introduced, from this more remote life, or from moral life, into a life nearer to Divine Doctrinals, that is, into spiritual life. When this is the case, he then begins to wonder why such commandments or precepts were sent down from heaven in so miraculous a manner, and written on tables by the finger of God, when yet they are known to every people, and written in their laws, although they never knew or heard any thing out of the Word. When he comes into this state of thought, if he be amongst those who are capable of being regenerated, he is led of the Lord into a still interior state, namely, into this, to think that deeper things lie concealed therein, with which as yet he is unacquainted ; and when he reads the Word in this state, he then finds every where throughout the prophets, and especially throughout the evangelists, that all of these precepts contain in them things more celestial ; as in respect to the honouring parents, he now sees, that when men are born anew, that is, when they are regenerated, they receive another father, and in this case become His sons, and that He it is Who is to be honoured, thus that this is the sense which lies hid interiorly in that precept. By degrees also he learns who this new father is, namely, that He is the Lord, and at length how He is to be honoured, namely, by being worshipped, and that He is worshipped when He is loved. When the regenerate person is in this truth, he is then in a Divine Doctrinal, and in this case he is in an angelic state, and thence looks at those things, which he before knew, as at things in an orderly succession, and as flowing from the Divine Being as it were like the steps of a ladder, above which Jehovah or the

Lord is, and on the steps thereof His angels, who ascend and descend; thus he sees those things, with which he had been before delighted, more remote from him according to degrees. The case is similar with respect to the other precepts of the decalogue, see n. 2609. Hence then it may appear, what is meant by life more remote from Divine Doctrinals, which is here signified by Jacob going out from Beersheba.

3691. "And went to Haran"—that hereby is signified to good and truth of that degree, appears from the signification of Haran, as denoting external good and truth, for by Haran is signified what is external, and by Laban who dwelt there is signified good and truth, thus by Haran is here denoted external good and truth; that this is signified by Haran, may be seen, n. 1430, 3612. Hence it is manifest, that by Jacob going forth from Beersheba and going to Haran, in the internal sense is signified, that he betook himself further from Divine Doctrinals, thus to external good and truth. The reason why it is said, the good and truth of that degree, is, because goods and truths are altogether distinct from each other according to degrees; interior goods and truths are in a superior degree, and exterior in an inferior degree; in a superior degree are the goods and truths appertaining to the rational principle, and in an inferior degree are the goods and truths of the natural principle, and in the lowest are sensual goods and truths which are of the body. Interior goods and truths, or those which are in a superior degree, flow into exterior goods and truths, or those which are in an inferior degree, and exhibit therein an image of themselves, almost as man's interior affections exhibit themselves in the countenance and the changes thereof. Hence it is manifest, that interior goods and truths are altogether separate from exterior goods and truths, or what is the same thing, that those which are in a superior degree are altogether separate from those in an inferior, and so separate, that the interior, or those which are in a superior degree, may exist without the exterior or those which are in an inferior degree. He who has not a distinct notion of degrees, cannot have a distinct notion of interior and exterior goods, nor how the case is with respect to man's soul, or with respect to his spirit and body, nor how the case is with respect to the heavens in another life. That there are three heavens is a known thing, and that one heaven is more interior than another, and that the third heaven is inmost. These heavens are most distinct from each other according to degrees; they who are in the inmost, or third heaven, are nearest to the Lord; they who are in the interior, or second heaven, are more remote; and they who are in the exterior, or first heaven, are still more remote. Communication between these heavens cannot have place in any other manner, than as the communication of man's inmost prin-

ciples with his exterior principles, for man, who is principled
in love to the Lord, and in charity towards his neighbour, is a
kind of little heaven, corresponding in image to the three heavens; he has also influx of good and truth out of the three
heavens from the Lord according to like degrees. The nature
and quality of these degrees with respect to each other, may
appear from those two cases adduced above, n. 3688, 3690.
They who are principled in real love to the Lord, so as to have
a perception of that love, are in a superior degree of good
and truth, and in the inmost and third heaven, consequently
nearer to the Lord, and are called celestial angels. They
who are principled in charity towards their neighbour, so as to
have a perception of charity, and not so much a perception of
love to the Lord, are in an inferior degree of good and truth,
and in the interior or second heaven, and thus more remote
from the Lord, and are called spiritual angels. But they who
are principled in charity towards their neighbour merely from
an affection of truth, so as not to have a perception of real
charity towards their neighbour, except from the truth with
which they are affected, are in a still inferior degree of good
and truth, and in the exterior or first heaven, and thereby still
more remote from the Lord, and are called good spirits. Hence
it may in some measure appear how the case is in respect to
degrees, namely, that those things or principles, which are in a
superior degree, exhibit themselves in an image in those which
are in an inferior degree; in love to the Lord there is a proximate image of the Lord, which is called a likeness, wherefore
they who are principled in real love to the Lord, are called His
likenesses; in charity there is also an image of the Lord, but
more remote, for in real charity the Lord is present, wherefore
they who are principled therein are called His images, see n. 50,
51, 1013; whereas they who are in the affection of truth, and
thence in a certain species of charity towards their neighbour,
are also images of the Lord, but more remotely. The three
heavens are distinguished into these three degrees, and according to these three degrees the Lord flows-in with Divine Good
and Truth, thus with wisdom and intelligence, and with heavenly joy and felicity.

3692. "And he lighted upon a place"—that hereby is signified a state, appears from the signification of place, as denoting state, see n. 1273, 1274, 1275, 1377, 2625, 2837, 3356, 3387.

3693. "And passed the night there because the sun was
set"—that hereby is signified life in an obscure principle, appears from the signification of night, as denoting a state of
shade, see n. 1712; thus to pass the night is to live in that
state; and from the signification of the sun being set, as denoting the being in an obscure principle, for then it is evening,
and that evening signifies an obscure principle, may be seen, n

3056. By an obscure principle is here meant obscurity of in
telligence as to truth, and obscurity of wisdom as to good, for
the light, which the angels have from the Lord, has in it intelligence and wisdom, and is also thence derived, see n. 1521,
1524, 1529, 1530, 3138, 3167, 3195, 3339, 3341, 3636, 3637,
3643. Wherefore so far as they are in light, so far also they
are in intelligence and wisdom, but so far as they are not in
light, thus so far as they are in shade, so far they are not in
intelligence and wisdom, see n. 2776, 3190, 3337. It is from
this ground that, in common discourse, light is predicated of
things appertaining to the understanding; man knows not that
it is from this ground, wherefore he believes that it is so predicated only in the way of comparison. But besides this, there
are also instances of other modes of speaking arising from a
perception of such things as exist in another life, in which man
is as to his spirit, which are generally received, as being interiorly acknowledged, but obliterated by things corporeal, which
are of such a nature as to extinguish the things of perception
in which his interior man is. That sun-set in the Word signifies the false and evil principle, in which they are who have no
charity and faith, thus that it signifies also the last time of the
Church, may be seen n. 1837; and also that it signifies an
obscure principle as to those things which appertain to good
and truth, such as has place with those who are in a degree
more remote from Divine doctrinals, may be seen n. 3691.
That sun-set, or the setting of the sun, has these significations,
may appear from the following passages in the Word, " Ye have
night instead of vision, and ye have darkness instead of divina-
tion; *and the sun will set upon the prophets*, and the day will
grow black upon them," Micah iii. 6; where the sun's setting
upon the prophets denotes that they have no longer any truth
and understanding of truth; prophets denote those who teach
truths of doctrine, see n. 2534. So in Amos, " It shall come to
pass in that day, *I will cause the sun to set at mid-day*, and
I will darken the earth in the day of light, and I will turn your
feasts into mourning, and all your songs into lamentation,"
viii. 9, 10. To cause the sun to set at mid-day denotes an
obscure principle as to truth with those who are in the know
ledges of good and truth; that mid-day is a state of light, or
of the knowledges of truth, see n. 1458, 3195. So in Isaiah,
" *Thy sun shall no more set*, neither shall thy moon be gathered,
because Jehovah shall be to thee for the light of eternity," lx.
20; speaking of the Lord's kingdom, where, by the sun no
more setting, is signified that they should be preserved in the
life of good and in wisdom, because in the celestial love and
light of the Lord; by the moon's not being gathered, is signified, that they should be preserved in the life of truth, and in
intelligence, because in the spiritual love and light of the Lord

That in another life the Lord is a sun to the celestial angels, and a moon to the spiritual, and that hence they have wisdom and intelligence, see n. 1053, 1521, 1529, 1530, 1531, 2441, 2495, 3636, 3643. Hence it may appear what is meant in the internal sense of the Word by sun-rise and sun-set. So in David, " Jehovah, my God, Thou art exceeding great, Thou hast put on glory and honour ; Who covereth Himself with light as with a garment ; he stretcheth out the heavens as a curtain ; He hath made the moon for stated feasts, *the sun knoweth his setting*, Thou disposest the darkness that it may become night," Psalm civ. 1, 2, 19, 20 ; where in like manner the moon denotes intelligence, and the sun wisdom from the Lord ; the setting of the sun denotes the obscurity of each principle. To dispose darkness that it may become night denotes the moderating a state of obscurity ; for that the angels have changes of state between the highest degree of light and a less degree, or between the highest degree of wisdom and a less degree, and that these changes of state are as the morning when the sun rises, and as mid-day when he is in his meridian height, and as the evening when he sets, and afterwards as morning again, by the Divine mercy of the Lord, will be shown elsewhere. So in Joshua, " From the wilderness and Lebanon even to the great river, the river Euphrates, the whole land of the Hittites, and even to the great sea, *the setting of the sun* shall be your border," i. 4 ; where is described the extension of the land of Canaan, by which is signified in the internal sense the Lord's kingdom, see n. 1607, 3038, 3481. That the river Euphrates is one border (or term), namely of things spiritual and celestial, see n. 1866, and that the great sea and setting of the sun is another, by which is represented the ultimate principle, which is respectively obscure ; that all the borders and all the places in that land are representative, see n. 1585. So in Moses, " If in taking a pledge thou shalt take for a pledge thy companion's garment, *before the sun set* thou shalt restore it to him, because it is his only covering, this his garment is for a skin, in which he shall lie down," Exod. xxii. 25, 26. And in another place, " If a poor man, thou shalt not lie down upon his pledge, restoring thou shalt restore to him the pledge, *before the sun set*, and he shall bless thee, and it shall be to thee righteousness before Jehovah thy God," Deut. xxiv. 12, 13. That in this law, as in all the rest, there is a representative and significative of the Divine law, which is that of good and truth in the Lord's kingdom, from whence those things are derived, is evident from the particulars thereof. That it contains, and is grounded in this law, that a man's companions ought not to be deprived of external truths, which are the doctrinals according to which they live, and their rituals, and that such truths are signified by garments, may be seen, n. 297, 1073, 2576. Restoring the pledge before the sun set denotes before truth perished with him, and because that truth is external, it is said that the garment is for a skin in which he shall lie down.   Again, "The soul which hath touched what is unclean, shall be unclean until the evening, and shall not eat of holy things, but when he shall have washed his flesh in waters, *and the sun hath set*, he shall be clean, and afterwards he shall eat of holy things," Levit. xxii 6, 7.   And in another place, " He that is not clean, towards evening shall wash himself with waters, *and when the sun shall set*, he shall enter into the midst of the camp," Deut. xxiii 11, 12.   That this law also derives its origin from the laws of good and truth, or the laws of order, which have place in the Lord's kingdom, may be very manifest, otherwise it would never have been commanded, that the unclean person should be unclean until the evening, and should then wash himself with waters, and after the sun was set, should be clean.   The law of order in the Lord's kingdom, in which the above law originates, is this, that good and angelic spirits, when they fell aside into a state of self-love, and thereby into a state of false principles, are in this case a little remitted into their natural or inferior state, and therein imbibe knowledges of good and truth as to that thing, which is signified by washing themselves with waters in the evening.   That to wash with waters signifies to be purified from false principles, may be seen, n. 3147, 3148 ; and that waters are the knowledges of truth, n. 28, 680, 739, 2702, 3058. And after that they have been in that obscure state, which is signified by the setting of the sun, they return into their former state, which is signified by their being clean, and entering into the midst of the camp ; on which subject, by the Divine mercy of the Lord, we shall speak elsewhere from experience.   From what has been said then it is evident, that sun-set in the Word signifies an obscure state as to truth with the good, and a state of what is false with the wicked.

3694. " And he took of the stones of the place"—that hereby are signified the truths of that state, appears from the signification of stones, as denoting inferior truths, such as are those of the natural man, see n. 643, 1298.

3695. " And placed them for his pillows"—that hereby is signified communication of a most common [or general] nature with the Divine [principle], appears from the signification of pillows, or bolsters [things of the head or neck], as denoting communication with things external, or communication of a most common [or general] nature ; for that the back of the head or neck denotes communication of interior things with exterior, or, what is the same, of superior things with inferior, and thereby conjunction, may be seen, n. 3542, 3603.   Hence those things which are under the back of the head or neck, that is, pillows or bolsters, signify here communication of inmost or

Divine things with outermost, which communication is also of a most common [or general] nature; for what is external is respectively common [or general], and what is outermost is most common [or general]; for the singulars of things interior appear as one, thus as a common [or general] principle, in things exterior. This also is what is represented and signified by the ladder set on the earth, whose top reached to heaven, and the angels of God ascended and descended upon it, of which we shall speak presently.

3696. "And he lay down in that place"—that hereby is signified tranquillity of state, appears from the signification of lying down, as denoting to be in a state of tranquillity; for lying down and sleeping has no other signification. That this is the signification of lying down, in the internal sense of the Word, may appear also from other passages of the Word, as will be seen beneath. With those who are about to be regenerated, who are here treated of in the internal representative sense, the case is this: that first of all they are in a state of tranquillity, or in a state of external peace; for external peace, or peace in externals, is called tranquillity: it is also produced from a Divine state of peace, which is intimately within it, and exists in externals by the removal of lusts and falsities, for these are what cause all restlessness. Every man also is in a state of tranquillity in the beginning of his life or in infancy, but in proportion as he advances in life, or grows up to manhood, in the same proportion he removes himself from that state, because he gives himself up to worldly cares, and thence to anxieties, by the lusts of self-love and the love of the world, and by the falsities therein originating. Nearly similar to this is the case with the new life of a regenerate man; in the beginning he is in a state of tranquillity, but as he passes into a new life, he also passes at the same time into an untranquil state; for the evil and false principles, which he had before imbibed, emerge and come forth, and disturb him, and this to such a degree at length, that he is immersed in temptations and vexations arising from the diabolical crew, who are continually striving to destroy the state of his new life. Nevertheless in the inmost ground of his spirit he is in a state of peace, for unless he was in such a state in his inmost principles, he would not engage in combat, inasmuch as he has continual respect to that state, as an end, in the combats wherein he is engaged, and unless he had such an end, he would in no wise have power and strength to engage in combat; hence also it is that he overcomes; and inasmuch as this state of peace is the end regarded, he also comes into this state after combats or temptations; it is as a state of spring, which succeeds a state of autumn and winter; or as a state of day-dawn, which succeeds evening and night. That a state of peace in things spiritual is like spring and day-dawn in things natural, may be seen, n. 1726, 2780 ; and that peace is from good and truth, and restlessness from what is evil and false, n. 3170. That to lie down in the Word signifies a state of tranquillity, may appear from the following passages : "If ye shall walk in My statutes, and shall observe My precepts, and shall do them, *I will give peace in the earth, and ye shall lie down*, and none shall make you afraid ; and I will cause to cease the evil beast from the land, and the sword shall not pass through your land," Levit. xxvi. 3, 6; where to lie down is manifestly predicated of a state of peace and tranquillity ; evil beast denotes the lusts of evil, see n. 45, 46, 908, which shall cease ; sword denotes the false principle combating against truth, n. 2799, which shall not pass through ; hence also it is evident, that peace and tranquillity of peace is from good and truth, and that the destruction thereof is from the evil and false principle. So in Isaiah, " The wolf shall tarry together with the lamb, and the leopard *shall lie down* with the kid, and the calf and the young lion together, and a little child shall lead them ; and the cow and the bear shall feed, *their young shall lie down together*," xi. 5, 6, 7 ; speaking of the Lord, and of the state of peace in His kingdom ; their lying down together denotes that they could not be infested by any evil and false principle. So in Hosea, " I will establish for them a covenant in that day with the beast of the field, and with the fowl of the heavens, and with the creeping thing of the earth ; and the bow, and the sword, and the battle will I break from off the earth, *and I will cause them to lie down confidently*," ii. 18 ; where in like manner to lie down denotes a state of tranquillity on the removal of false and evil principles, which occasion restlessness. So in David, " *I will lie down and sleep*, and rise up again, because Jehovah supporteth me ; I will not be afraid of myriads of the people who set themselves against me round about," Psalm iii. 6, 7 ; to lie down and sleep denotes a state of tranquillity and security. Again, " *I will lay me down in peace and sleep ;* because Thou, Jehovah, alone causest me to dwell confidently," Psalm iv. 9. And again, " *He will cause me to lie down in pastures of herb*, he will lead me to waters of rest ; he will refresh my soul," Psalm xxiii. 2, 3. From which passages it is evident, that a state of peace and tranquillity is signified by lying down ; and that by lying down in the present passage is signified tranquillity of state, for place in the internal sense is state, see n. 3692.

3697. Verses 12, 13, 14, 15. *And he dreamed, and behold a ladder set on the earth, and its head reaching to heaven, and behold the angels of God ascending and descending upon it And behold Jehovah standing above it, and He said, I am Jehovah, God of thy father Abraham, and God of Isaac. The land on which thou liest, to thee will I give it, and to thy seed.*

And thy seed shall be as the dust of the earth, and thou shalt break forth to the sea, and to the east, and to the north, and to the south; and in thee and in thy seed shall all the families of the ground be blessed. And behold I am with thee, and will keep thee in all whither thou goest, and will bring thee back to this ground, because I will not leave thee until I have done what I have spoken to thee. He dreamed, signifies foresight: and behold a ladder set on the earth, signifies communication of lowest truth and good thence derived: and its head reaching to heaven, signifies with the Divine [principle]: and behold the angels of God ascending and descending upon it, signifies infinite and eternal communication, and thence conjunction; and that from the lowest principle there is as it were ascent, and afterwards, when the order is inverted, descent: and behold Jehovah standing above it, signifies the Lord in the supreme: and He said, I am Jehovah, God of thy father Abraham, signifies the Lord in whom that good originates: and God of Isaac, signifies the Lord as to the Divine Human [principle]: the land on which thou liest, to thee will I give it, signifies the good in which He was principled, that it was from His own proprium: and to thy seed, signifies that also the truth: and thy seed shall be as the dust of the earth, signifies that Divine natural truth would be as natural good: and thou shalt break forth to the sea, and to the east, signifies the infinite extension of good: and to the north, and to the south, signifies the infinite extension of truth; thus all states of good and truth: and in thee shall all the families of the ground be blessed, signifies that all truths of good of doctrine will be conjoined to good: and in thy seed, signifies and to truth: and behold I am with thee, signifies the Divine [principle]: and will keep thee in all whither thou goest, signifies Divine Providence: and will bring thee back to this ground, signifies conjunction with Divine Doctrine: because I will not leave thee until I have done what I have spoken to thee, signifies that nothing would be wanting, but all would have effect.

3698. "He dreamed"—that hereby is signified foresight, appears from the signification of dreaming, as denoting in the internal sense to foretel things future, for prophetic dreams, which were Divine, were predictions of things to come, as may appear from those spoken of in the Word, see n. 1975, 1976; such being the signification of dreams and dreaming in the internal sense, therefore in the supreme sense, in which the Lord is treated of, they signify foresight; for predictions are from the Divine foresight of the Lord. That this is the only ground of predictions concerning events, which do not flow according to the common order of nature, and cannot be thence foreseen, may appear from the Word, also from this passage in Moses, "When a prophet shall speak in the name of Jehovah, but the word doth not come to pass, and that word doth not happen,. Jehovah hath not spoken, the prophet hath spoken it in arrogancy," Deut. xviii. 22. And although predictions of things which came to pass, they might be from the wicked and worshippers of another god, as appears from this passage, "If there arise in the midst of thee a prophet or a dreamer of dreams, and he give thee a sign or a wonder, and the sign or the wonder come to pass which he spake to thee, saying, Let us go after other gods whom thou hast not known, and let us serve them, thou shalt not obey the words of that prophet, or the dreamer of that dream, because Jehovah tempteth you," Deut. xiii. 2, 3, 4; from which passage it is evident that the prediction itself was from the Divine [principle], but the persuasion to worship other gods was from the proprium (or selfish principle) of the prophet, to whom it was permitted for the sake of tempting (or trying), as it is said. Hence also it is, and from other causes, that on several occasions in old times, they who worshipped Baalim and other gods, also prophesied, saw visions and dreamed dreams, and likewise that the things which were spoken by them came to pass, whereby many were seduced concerning whom, see Jeremiah, chap. xxiii.; besides others who were called diviners, soothsayers, jugglers, and pythons, who were such as studied natural magic, whereby nothing of what was Divine could be foretold, but only what was contrary to the Divine [principle], that is, contrary to the Lord, and contrary to the good of love and the truth of faith in Him; this is magic, whatsoever it may appear in its external form.

3699. "And behold a ladder set on the earth"—that hereby is signified communication of lowest truth and good thence derived, appears from the signification of ladder as denoting communication, of which we shall speak presently; and from the signification of earth, as denoting what is lowest, for it is said immediately afterwards, that its head reached unto heaven, which is highest. Hence it is evident, that the ladder set between earth and heaven, or between lowest and highest, denotes communication; that it is communication of lowest truth and of good thence derived, which is here signified by the ladder set on the earth, is manifest from this consideration, that the subject here treated of, in the internal sense, is concerning truth and its derivative good of that degree which is here represented by Jacob. In the original tongue, the term ladder is derived from an expression which signifies a path or way, and that path or way is predicated of truth, may be seen, n. 627, 2333; when the angels also hold discourse together concerning truth, it is exhibited representatively in the world of spirits by ways, see n. 189, 3477. Hence it is evident what is signified by a ladder, one extremity whereof is set on the earth, and the other reaches to heaven, namely, the communi-

cation of truth which is in the lowest place with truth which
is in the highest, which communication is treated of presently.
That there are truths and goods of the lowest order, and also
truths and goods of the highest order, and steps between them
as of a ladder, may be seen, n. 3691.

3700. "And its head reaching unto heaven"—that hereby
is signified with the Divine [principle], namely, that there was
communication therewith, appears from the signification of the
head or highest top of a ladder, as denoting what is supreme;
and from the signification of heaven, as denoting the Divine
[principle]; for heaven, in the supreme sense wherein the Lord
is treated of, denotes the essential Divine [principle], but in the
representative sense, wherein the regenerate man is treated of,
it denotes the inmost principle of good and derivative truth
which is from the Lord, such as exists in heaven, and from the
quality of which heaven is heaven. This is also called Divine,
as being from the Lord; for the Lord, or, what is the same
thing, the Divine [principle] which is from the Lord alone, is
all in all of heaven; whatever is not from the Divine [principle]
is not of heaven. Hence it is that it has been occasionally
said above, that the Lord is heaven itself, and that all who are
in heaven are in the Lord.

3701. "And behold the angels of God ascending and descending upon it"—that hereby is signified infinite and eternal
communication and thence conjunction; and that from the
lowest principle there is as it were an ascent, and afterwards,
when the order is inverted, a descent, appears from the signification of angels, as denoting somewhat Divine of the Lord,
which is understood by them when they are mentioned in the
Word, see n. 1925, 2319, 2821, 3039. That in the present case
they denote Divine truth, is manifest from this consideration,
that they are called the angels of God, for the term God is
applied whensoever in the internal sense truth is the subject
treated of, whereas the term Jehovah is applied in treating of
good, see n. 2586, 2769, 2807, 2822. Hence it is, that although
Jehovah is named presently, and it is said, Jehovah was standing above it, still they are here called angels of God, inasmuch
as the subject treated of is concerning truth from which good
is derived, which is here represented by Jacob, as has been
frequently said above. That by ascending and descending
on the ladder is signified, in the supreme sense, infinite and
eternal communication and thence conjunction, may appear
without further explication; communication and thence conjunction cannot be predicated of the Lord's essential Divine
[principle], and of His Divine Human [principle], unless at
the same time it be said to be infinite and eternal, for in the
Lord all is infinite and eternal, infinite in respect to esse, and
eternal in respect to existere. From what has been hitherto

said it is evident, that by the ladder set on the earth, and its head reaching to heaven, and behold the angels of God ascending and descending upon it, is signified in sum as it were an ascent from the lowest principle, and afterwards, when the order is inverted, a descent. How the case is with this ascent and descent, may appear from what has been said and shown above, n. 3539, 3548, 3556, 3563, 3570, 3576, 3603, 3607, 3610, 3665, 3690. But whereas this order, which is that of the regeneration of man, and which is described in this and the following verses in the internal sense, is altogether unknown in the Church, it may be expedient to illustrate further its nature and quality. It is a known thing, that man is born into the nature of his parents, and of his grandfathers, and also of his great grandfathers, in a long succession of ages, consequently he is born into the hereditary evil of them all successively accumulated, insomuch that as to what is from himself he is nothing but evil. Hence has come this further consequence, that both as to understanding and as to will he is altogether ruined, and of himself wills nothing of good, and thence understands nothing of truth, consequently, that what he calls good, yea believes to be good, is evil, and what he calls truth, yea believes to be truth, is false; as for example, to love himself better than others, to be better disposed towards himself than towards others, to desire what belongs to another, and to be concerned and studious about himself, and not about others except for the sake of himself, inasmuch as of himself he is inclined to these things, therefore he calls them good, and also true; and further, if any one injures, or endeavours to injure him, as to these goods and truths, as he calls them, he hates such a person, and also burns with revenge towards him, desiring and likewise meditating his ruin, wherein he perceives delight, and this in proportion as he actually confirms himself in the above dispositions, that is, in proportion as he more frequently brings them into exercise by act. Such an one, when he comes into another life, has the same desires, the essential nature remaining, which he has contracted in the world by actual life, and the essential delight thereof being manifestly perceived; wherefore he cannot be in any heavenly society, in which every one wishes better to others than to himself, but in some infernal society, which enjoys the same delight as himself. This nature is what ought to be extirpated during man's life in the world, which can be effected only by regeneration from the Lord, that is, by receiving altogether another will, and thence another understanding; or, in other words, by being made new as to both of these faculties. But, for this purpose, he must needs first of all be re-born as an infant, and learn what is evil and false, and also what is good and true, for without science or knowledge he cannot imbibe any good, inasmuch as

of himself he acknowledges nothing to be good but what is evil,
and nothing to be true but what is false; with this view, such
knowledges are insinuated into him, as are not altogether contrary to those which he before had, as that all love begins from
self, that self is first to be regarded and then others, that good
is to be done to such as appear poor and miserable in an external form, whatsoever may be their inward qualities; in like
manner, that widows and orphans, on account of their name
only, are objects of charity; and lastly, that enemies in general,
whosoever they be, are like objects; and by doing good to such,
man may merit heaven.   These, and similar knowledges, are
those of the infancy of his new life, and are such as, deriving
somewhat from his former life or the nature of his former life,
derive somewhat also from his new life, into which he is thus
introduced; and hence they are such as to admit in them whatsoever things are conducive towards forming the new will and
the new understanding.   These are the lowest goods and truths,
from which the regenerate life commences, and inasmuch as
they are admissive of interior truths, or such as are nearer to
Divine, false principles may be thereby extirpated, which
fore had been believed to be true.   Nevertheless, they who are
regenerated do not learn such truths barely as sciences, but as
life, for they practise those truths; the reason, however, and
ground of such practice is from the principle of the new will,
which the Lord insinuates whilst they are altogether ignorant
of it, and in proportion also as they receive of that new will, in
the same proportion also they receive of those knowledges, and
bring them into act, and believe; but in proportion as they do
not receive of the new will, so far they are capable indeed of
learning the above truths, but are incapable of bringing them
into act, because they regard only science, and not life.   This
is the state of infancy and childhood as to the new life, which
is about to succeed in place of the former life; but the state of
its youth and further growth is, when regard is no longer had
to any one's person, such as he appears in his external form,
but to his quality as to good, first in civil life, next in moral
life, and lastly in spiritual life, and good in this case is what a
man begins to give priority to, and to love, and from good the
person; and at length, when he is still further perfected, he
studies to do good to those who are principled in good, and this
according to the quality of the good in which they are principled, till he finally perceives a delight in such acts of bene-
ficence, and inasmuch as he perceives a delight in good, he
perceives also a pleasantness in whatsoever things confirm
good; these confirming principles he acknowledges for truths,
and they are also the truths of his new understanding, which
flow from the goods appertaining to his new will.   In the same
degree in which he perceives delight in this good, and pleas-

antness in these truths, he is made sensible also of what is undelightful in the evils of his former life, and of what is unpleasant in the false principles thereof; hence then a separation takes place of the things appertaining to the former will and the former understanding, from the things appertaining to the new will and the new understanding, and this, not according to the affection of knowing such things, but according to the affection of doing them. Consequently in this case he sees, that the truths of his infancy were respectively inverted, and that the same by degrees were reduced into another order, namely, to be mutually subordinate to each other, so that those which at first were in the prior place, are now in a posterior place; thus that by those truths which were the truths of his infancy and childhood, the angels of God as by a ladder ascended from earth to heaven, but afterwards, by the truths appertaining to his adult age, the angels of God as by a ladder descend from heaven to earth.

3702. " And behold Jehovah standing above it"—that hereby is signified the Lord in the supreme, may appear from this consideration, that in the Word of the Old Testament Jehovah is so often called Lord, see n. 1736, 3023, 3035; and that in the Word of the New Testament He is no where called Jehovah, but instead of Jehovah, the Lord, see n. 2921. That to stand above it denotes to be in the supreme (or highest principle), appears without explication. The arcanum, which lies concealed in the internal sense of these words, is, that all goods and truths descend from the Lord, and ascend to Him, that is, that He is the first and the last; for man is so created, that the Divine things of the Lord may descend through Him into the ultimate things of nature, and from the ultimate things of nature may ascend to Him; so that man might be a medium of union between the Divine [principle] and the world of nature, and thus by man, as by an uniting medium, the very ultimate principle of nature might have life from the Divine [principle], which would have been the case, if man had lived according to Divine order. That man is so created, is manifest from this consideration, that as to his body he is a little world, all the arcana of the world of nature being therein reposited, for every hidden property there is in the ether and its modifications, is reposited in the eye, and every property in the air is reposited in the ear; and whatever invisible thing floats and acts in the air, this is in the organ of smell where it is perceived, and whatever invisible thing floats and acts in the waters and other fluids, this is in the organ of taste; also the very changes of state are in the sense of touch throughout; besides that things still more hidden would be perceived in his interior organs, if his life was according to order. Hence it is evident, that descent of the Divine [principle] would have place through man into the ultimate of nature, and from the ultimate of nature there would be ascent to the Divine [principle], if man only acknowledged the Lord as his first and last end with faith of heart, that is, with love. In such a state were the most ancient people, who were celestial men, for whatever they apprehended by any sense, was to them a medium of thinking concerning the things of the Lord, thus concerning the Lord and His kingdom, and hence was the delight which they derived from things worldly and terrestrial, see n. 1409, 2896, 2897, 2995. Yea further, when they thus contemplated the inferior and ultimate things of nature, the objects of their contemplation appeared to them as if they were alive, for the life, from which they descended, was in their internal sight and perception, and the objects presented before their eyes were as images of that life, which images, although inanimate, were nevertheless thus animated in their sight; such perception the celestial angels have respecting all things which exist in the world, as has been often given me to perceive, and hence also infants have such perception, see n. 2297, 2298. Hence it is evident, what is the nature and quality of those, through whom the Divine things of the Lord descend even to the ultimates of nature, and from the ultimates of nature ascend to Him, and represent the Divine communication and thence conjunction, which in the supreme sense is signified by the angels ascending and descending on the ladder set on the earth, whose head reached unto heaven, and above which Jehovah stood.

3703. "And He said, I am Jehovah, God of thy father Abraham"—that hereby is signified the Lord, in that all good is from Him, may appear from this consideration, that Jehovah is the Lord's very Divine Esse, who is called the God of Abraham, by virtue of Divine Good. That Abraham represents the Lord as to Divine Good, may be seen, n. 2172, 2198. And whereas the Divine Good is that from which all celestial and spiritual goods are derived, and thence also all truths; therefore the expression, "father Abraham," is here used, and indeed "thy father," that is, the father of Jacob, when yet Isaac was his father. The ground and reason why father in the internal sense denotes good, is, because it is good from which all and singular things are, and truth by which all and singular things exist, thus all and singular things are and exist from the marriage of good and truth. Heaven itself, which consists of nothing else but the Divine marriage of good and truth, has its being from the Divine marriage of good and truth and of truth and good in the Lord. All and singular things also in universal nature have relation to good and truth; for in nature are represented the celestial and spiritual goods and truths which are of heaven, and in heaven are represented the Divine Goods and Truths which are of the Lord. Hence it may ap-

pear, that good is as a father, and truth is as a mother, and
that therefore by father, in the internal sense of the Word, is
signified good, and by mother, truth; and indeed the good and
truth from which inferior or derivative truths and goods have
birth, which respectively are as daughters and sons, and thence
likewise are called daughters and sons in the Word, see n. 489,
490, 491, 2362; and they are also respectively as brethren and
sisters, as grandchildren and great grandchildren, as sons-in-
law and daughters-in-law, in a word, as consanguinities and
affinities in every degree, and this from the marriage of good,
which is the father, with truth, which is the mother. That all
and singular things in the heavens are according to consanguinities of love and faith in the Lord, or, what is the same thing,
of good and truth, may be seen, n. 685, 917, 2739, 3612; and
that on this account the most ancient people compared all and
singular things to marriages, n. 54, 55; see also n. 718, 747,
1432, 2508, 2516, 2524, 2556.   That father in the internal
sense of the Word denotes good, may appear from several passages, as from the following, "Attend to me, ye that regard
justice, ye that seek Jehovah, look unto the rock whence ye
were hewn, and to the hole of the pit whence ye were digged;
look unto *Abraham your father*, and unto Sarah who bare you,
for I have called him alone, and have blessed him, and will
multiply him; for Jehovah will comfort Zion, he will comfort
all her wastes, and will place her wilderness like Eden, and her
desert as the garden of Jehovah," Isaiah li. 1, 2, 3; speaking
of the Lord, and of His coming, as is manifest from each particular, Who, as to Divine Truth, is called a rock and a pit, and
as to Divine Good, Abraham the father.   And whereas the
Divine marriage of good and truth is represented by Abraham
and Sarah, see n. 1468, 1901, 1965, 1989, 2011, 2063, 2065,
2172, 2173, 2198, 2507, 2833, 2836, 2904, 3245, 3251, 3305;
therefore it is said, Abraham your father and Sarah who bare
you.   Hence it is that it is said, that they should look unto the
rock and unto the pit, and also to Abraham their father and
Sarah.   And hence it is, that it immediately follows, that Jehovah will comfort Zion, whereby is meant the Church celestial, see n. 2362; and that He will comfort her wastes, and
place her wilderness like Eden, and her desert like the garden
of Jehovah.   The like is signified by Abraham in other passages in the Word, where he is called father, as in John, "Jesus
said, I speak what I have seen with My Father, and ye do
what ye have seen with your father; they answered and said
unto him, *Abraham is our father*; Jesus said unto them, *If ye
were the sons of Abraham, ye would do the works of Abraham*,
ye do the works of your father," viii. 38, 39.   And in Matthew,
"Presume not to say within yourselves, *We have Abraham for
a father*, for I say unto you, that God is able of these stones to

raise up children unto Abraham': behold the axe lieth at the root of the tree; every tree that beareth not good fruit shall be cut down and cast into the fire," iii. 9, 10. And in Luke, " When poor Lazarus died, he was carried by the angels into *Abraham's bosom ;* the rich man also died and was buried, and being in hell he lifted up his eyes, and saw *Abraham* afar off, and Lazarus in his bosom; and he cried and said, *Father Abraham*, have mercy on me; I beseech thee, *Father*, that thou wouldst send him to my father's house," xvi. 19 to the end. In these passages it is evident that Abraham is not meant, but the Lord as to Divine Good ; that Abraham is unknown in heaven, and that when mention is made of him in the Word, the Lord is understood, may be seen, n. 1834, 1876, 1989, 3305. That father in the internal sense denotes good, may appear from the following passages, " Honour *thy father and mother*, that thy days may be prolonged upon the land which Jehovah thy God giveth thee," Exod. xx. 12; Deut. v. 16. That this precept, like the other precepts of the decalogue, is true in each sense, and that in the internal sense to honour father and mother is to love what is good and true, and therein the Lord, may be seen, n. 2609, 3690. That days upon the land are states of good thence derived in the Lord's kingdom, appears from the signification of days, as denoting states, n. 23, 487, 488, 493, 893, 2788 ; and from the signification of Canaan, which here is the land, as denoting the Lord's kingdom, see n. 1607, 3038, 3481 ; and that to be prolonged is predicated of good, n. 1613. It was in consequence of this signification of father and mother, that in the representative Jewish Church several laws were enacted concerning parents and sons, in all which in the internal sense is signified good and truth, and in the supreme sense the Lord as to Divine Good and Divine Truth, as in Moses, " Whoever shall smite *his father* and *his mother*, dying he shall die; if any one shall curse *his father* or *his mother*, dying he shall die," Exod. xxi. 15, 17. Again, " Whatever man shall curse *his father*, or *his mother*, by killing shall be killed ; whoever shall curse *his father* or *his mother*, his bloods shall be upon him," Levit. xx. 9. And again, " Cursed is he who setteth light by *his father* and *his mother*, and all the people shall say, Amen," Deut. xxvii. 16. So in Ezekiel, " Behold the princes of Israel every man according to his arm, were in thee to shed blood, they have set light by *father* and *mother* in thee," xxii. 6, 7. And in Moses, " When a man hath a refractory and rebellious son, *in no wise obedient to the voice of his father*, or *to the voice of his mother*, and although they have chastised him, yet he hath not obeyed them, *his father* and *his mother* shall lay hold upon him, and shall bring him forth to the elders of the city, and to the gate of his place, and all the men of his city shall stone him with stones that he die," Deut. xxi. 18, 19,

21. In all these passages, by father and mother in the sense of the letter is meant father and mother, but in the internal sense is meant good and truth, and in the supreme sense the Lord as to Divine Good and Divine Truth; as the Lord Himself also teaches in Matthew, where it is written, "Jesus stretching out His hand over His disciples, said, Behold *My mother*, and My brethren: whosoever shall do the will of My Father Who is in the heavens, he is My brother and sister and *mother*," xii. 59. And again, "Be not willing to be called master, for one is your master, even Christ, but all ye are brethren; and *call ye not your father on earth*, for one is *your Father*, who is in the heavens," xxiii. 8, 9. To be called master, and to be called father on earth, is not here forbidden, but to acknowledge in heart any other father than the Lord, that is, when mention is made of master and father, it is requisite that the Lord be understood, Who in the supreme sense is represented by them, agreeable to what was said above, n. 3702, concerning the most ancient people, who were celestial men; that whatsoever they perceived on earth was to them a medium (or means) of thinking concerning the Lord. The same is implied in what the Lord spake to one of His disciples, who said, "Lord, suffer me first to go and *bury my father;* Jesus said unto him, Follow Me, and let the dead bury the dead," Matt. viii. 21, 22. For a father on earth in respect to the father in heaven, or to the Lord, is as a dead person to a living one; thus the law itself concerning honouring parents is as it were dead, unless in it there be honour, worship, and love to the Lord, for that law descends from this Divine Law, and hence is derived the essential living principle which is in that law; wherefore the Lord said, " Follow Me, let the dead bury the dead." The same is also signified by what Elijah said to Elisha, " Elijah passed by Elisha, and cast his garment over him, who left the oxen, and ran to Elijah, and said, *Let me kiss*, I pray, *my father and mother*, afterwards I will follow thee; he said therefore unto him, Depart, return, *for what have I done to thee?*" 1 Kings xix. 19, 20. That by Elijah was represented the Lord, may be seen, Preface to chap. xviii. and n. 2762. So in Malachi, " Behold, I send unto you Elijah the prophet, before the great and terrible day of Jehovah cometh, and *he shall turn the heart of the fathers to the sons, and the heart of the sons to their fathers*, lest I come and smite the earth with a curse," iv. 5, 6. And in Luke, speaking of John, " He shall go before the Lord in the spirit and virtue of Elijah, *to turn the hearts of the fathers to the sons*," i. 17; where it is evident, that by fathers and sons are not meant fathers and sons, but the goods and truths of the Church, which the Lord was about to restore. Again in Malachi, " Jehovah will be magnified from over the border of Israel, *the son shall honour the father*, and the servant the lord :

if then *I be a father*, where is my honour? if I be a Lord, where
is my fear?" i. 6; where father denotes those who are principled in the good of the Church, and Lord denotes those who
are principled in the truth of the Church; Father manifestly
denoting the Lord as to Divine Good, and Lord denoting Him
as to Divine Truth. So in David, "*My father and my mother*
have forsaken me, and Jehovah gathereth me," Psalm xxvii. 10;
where father and mother denote good and truth, which are
said to have forsaken, when man observes that of himself he is
not able to do any thing good, or to know any thing true; that
it is not to be understood as if David was forsaken by his
father and mother, is manifest. Again, "Thou art far more
beautiful than the sons of men, the *king's daughter* is wholly
glorious, her garment inwardly is of wrought gold; *instead of*
thy fathers shall be thy sons, thou shalt make them for princes
in the whole earth," Psalm xlv. 3, 14, 16; speaking of the
Lord, where instead of fathers shall be thy sons, denotes that
Divine Truths should be as Divine Goods; the king's daughter
denotes the love of truth; the garment of wrought gold denotes the quality of that truth derived from good. Inasmuch
as the subject treated of is concerning the Lord and His Divine
Human [principle], as is evident from the whole psalm and the
particulars contained in it, it may hence appear that all and
singular things therein are in a like predication, consequently,
that by the king's daughter is not meant king's daughter, nor
that her garment was of wrought gold, nor that instead of
fathers should be sons, nor that these should be princes in the
whole earth, but that Divine celestial and spiritual things are
what are signified by each expression. That daughter denotes
affection or love, may be seen, n. 490, 491, 2362; that king
denotes Divine Truth, n. 1728, 2015, 2069, 3009; that gold
denotes good, n. 113, 1551, 1552; that wrought (intwined or
intwisted) is predicated of the natural scientific principle, n.
2831, here therefore of Divine natural truth; that garment
denotes such truths as clothe good, n. 297, 2576; that sons
who are instead of fathers denote truths of good, in this case
Divine Truths as Divine Goods, n. 264, 489, 491, 533, 1147,
1729, 1733, 2159, 2623, 2803, 2813; that princes in the whole
earth denote the primary things of the Lord's kingdom and
Church, that princes are primary things, n. 1482, 2089; that
earth is the Lord's kingdom and Church, n. 1413, 1607, 1733,
1850, 2117, 2118, 3355. So in Moses, "Jehovah was delighted
with *thy fathers,* to love them, and He chose their seed after
them, you out of all people, according to this day, wherefore
circumcise the foreskin of your heart, and no longer harden
your neck," Deut. x. 15, 16; where fathers in the internal sense
denote the ancient and most ancient Church, who were so called
from the love of good and truth in which they were principled,

from the love of good the most ancient who were celestial men, and from the love of truth the ancient who were spiritual men. Their goods and truths in the Church are what are called the seed which God chose. That Abraham, Isaac, and Jacob, and his twelve sons, are not the fathers here meant, and that the Israelitish and Jewish people are not meant by the seed, is very manifest ; but these words are spoken of them and to them, in order that the internal sense may have somewhat external and thereby intelligible to man. So in Isaiah, "They shall lift up themselves, a child against an old man, and a vile person against an honourable, because a man shall lay hold of his brother in the *house of his father*, saying, Thou hast raiment, thou shalt be a prince unto us ; he shall say, There is no bread nor raiment in my house, make me not a prince of the people," iii. 7. The subject here treated of in the internal sense is concerning the perverted state of the Church, when truth is no longer acknow-ledged to be truth, nor is it known what good is ; a man's taking hold of his brother in the house of his father, denotes the acknowledging every thing whatever to be good ; raiment denotes truth, see n. 1073, 2576 ; prince denotes the primary principle of doctrine thence derived, n. 1482, 2089 ; there is no bread nor raiment in my house, denotes that there was neither good nor truth ; that bread is good, see n. 276, 680, 3478 ; that raiment is truth, n. 297, 2576. In the representative Churches there were several laws, grounded in the representa-tives of good and truth by father and mother, and also by daughters and sons, which laws derived thence their Divine [principle] ; such are these which follow : that the *daughter of a priest*, if she profaned herself by committing whoredom, profaning *her father*, should be burned with fire, Levit. xxi. 9 ; where the daughter of a priest denotes the affection of good, father denotes the good whence that affection is derived ; to commit whoredom, denotes to profane good ; what is meant by committing whoredom, may be seen, n. 2466, 2729, 3399 ; and what by profaning, n. 1008, 1010, 1059, 2051, 3398, 3399. Also, that if the daughter of a priest be a widow, or divorced, and she has no seed, she shall return to the *house of her father*, according to her youth, and *shall eat of the bread of her father*, there shall no stranger eat thereof, Levit. xxii. 13. Likewise this law, " If thou shalt see in captivity a wife of beautiful form, and shalt desire her, to take her to thyself for a woman, thou shalt bring her into the midst of thine house, and she shall shave her head, and shall make her nails, and shall put off the raiment of her captivity from off her, and shall sit in thy house, and *shall bemoan her father and her mother* a month of days, and afterwards thou shalt enter in unto her, and shalt know her, and she shall be to thee for a woman," Deut. xxi. 11, 12, 13. In this law, all and singular its contents are representative of natural truth, in that after it is purified from false principles it is adopted of good; such truth is signified by a wife in captivity, beautiful in form; purification from false principles is signified by bringing her into the midst of the house, shaving her head, making her nails, putting off the raiment of her captivity, and bemoaning her father and mother; adoption is signified by afterwards entering in unto her, knowing her, and taking her for a woman. The *laws of marriages*, in regard to their being contracted within each tribe and family, and also the *laws of inheritances*, in regard to their not passing from tribe to tribe, spoken of in the Word, derived hence also their origin, namely, from the celestial and spiritual marriage in the Lord's kingdom, or from the marriage of good and truth, which are signified by father and mother; in like manner the *laws* which were enacted concerning *degrees allowed and forbidden*: each law on these subjects, as mentioned in the Word, has reference inwardly to the law of consociation and conjunction of good and truth in heaven, and to the consociations of what is evil and false in hell, which are separate from them. Concerning degrees allowed and forbidden, see Levit. xx.; concerning inheritances that they should not pass from tribe to tribe, and concerning marriages that they should be contracted within each tribe, see Numb. xxvii. 7, 8, 9, and in other places. That in the heavens all and singular things are circumstanced according to consanguinities and affinities of good and truth, see n. 685, 917, 2739, 3612. Inasmuch as the Israelitish people represented the Lord's kingdom in the heavens, and thus the heavenly order therein prevailing, therefore it was commanded, that they should be distinguished according to *tribes*, and according to *families*, and according to the *houses of their fathers*, see Numb. xxvi. 1 to the end; and also that according to this order they should measure out the camp around the tent of the congregation, and likewise that they should journey according to the same order, as it is thus written in Moses, "Each man under his standard, in their ensigns *according to the house of their fathers* shall the sons of Israel measure out the camp, over against around the tent of the congregation; and thus also they were to set forward on their journey," Numb. ii. 2, 34; wherefore when Balaam saw Israel dwelling according to their tribes, the spirit of God came upon him, and he uttered an enunciation (*edidit enuntiatum*), saying, "How good are thy tabernacles, O Jacob, thy habitations, O Israel; as a valley are they planted, as gardens near a river," &c., Numb. xxiv. 2, 5, 6, and the following verses; in which prophecy, that neither Jacob nor Israel are meant, but the Lord's kingdom in the heavens, and His Church in the earths, which were represented by that order in which he then saw them, is evident from all the words in which it is expressed. From these considerations it may also be

known, what is signified in the internal sense of the Word by
orphans, that is, by those who are without a father, namely, those
who are in a state of innocence and charity, and desire to know
and to do what is good, and are not able; in such a state are
they especially who are out of the Church, of whom the Lord
takes care, and adopts them as sons in another life; and inasmuch as these are signified by orphans, therefore when they
are mentioned in the Word in several passages are also mentioned sojourners and widows: for by sojourners are signified
those who are instructed in goods and truths, see n. 1463; and
by widows those who are in a state of good and not so much
in truth, and who are in a state of truth and not so much in
good, and yet are desirous to be therein. Inasmuch as by these
three, namely, orphans, sojourners, and widows, somewhat
similar is signified in a series, therefore in several passages, as
was observed, they are named together, see Deut. xiv. 29;
chap. xvi. 14; chap. xxiv. 17, 19; Jer. vii. 6; chap. xxii. 3;
Ezek. xxii. 6, 7; Zech. vii. 10; Psalm xciv. 6; Psalm cxlvi. 9.
From what has been said then it may appear, what is signified
by father in the genuine sense, namely, good, and that in the
supreme sense it signifies the Lord. But whereas several expressions in the Word have also an opposite sense, so also has
the word father, and in this sense it signifies evil; and in like
manner mother, which in the genuine sense signifies truth, in
the opposite sense signifies the false principle. That this is the
case, may appear from the following passages: " The *iniquity
of his fathers* shall be recalled to memory with Jehovah, and
the *sin of his mother* shall not be blotted out," Psalm cix. 14.
Again, " They have receded, and done treacherously, *as their
fathers*, they have turned away like a bow of fraud," Psalm
lxxviii. 57. So in Moses, " Until the residue amongst you pine
away in their iniquity, in the lands of their enemies, and also in
the iniquities of their fathers, they shall pine away with them,"
Levit. xxvi. 39. And in Isaiah, " Prepare ye slaughter for his
sons, by reason of the *iniquity of their fathers*, and let them not
rise and possess the land, nor fill the faces of the earth with
cities," xiv. 21. Again, " I will recompense your iniquities, and
the iniquities of your fathers together," lxv. 7. So in Jeremiah,
" The houses of Israel were ashamed, they, their kings, their
princes, and their priests, and their prophets, saving to the
wood, *Thou art my father*, and to the stone, *Thou hast begotten
me*, because they have turned to me the back of the head, and
not the face," ii. 26, 27. Again, " I give before this people
stumbling-blocks (matters of offence), and they shall offend
therein the fathers and the sons together, the neighbour and his
companion, and shall perish," vi. 21. Again, " The *sons* gather
wood, and the *fathers* kindle a fire, and the women knead dough
to make cakes," vii. 18. And in Ezekiel, " I will do in thee

what I have not done, and whereunto I will not do any more the like, by reason of thine abominations, therefore the *fathers shall eat their sons, and the sons shall eat their fathers*, and I will do in thee judgments, and will disperse all thy remains to every wind," v. 9, 10 ; speaking of the profanation of what is holy. Again, " Thus saith the Lord Jehovah to Jerusalem, Thy tradings and thy generations were from the land of Canaan, *thy father* was an Amorite, and *thy mother* an Hittite," xvi. 3. So in Matthew, " The brother shall deliver up the brother to death, and the *father the son*, and *the children* shall rise up against *the parents*, and shall give them to death ; and so ye shall be hated of all for My name's sake. I am come to set a man at variance *against his father*, and *the son against his mother*, and the daughter-in-law against her mother-in-law ; and a man's foes shall be those of his own house. Whoever loveth *father and mother* above Me, is not worthy of Me, and whosoever loveth son and daughter above Me, is not worthy of Me," x. 21, 22, 35, 36, 37 ; Luke xii. 49, 52, 53. Again, " Every one who hath left houses, or brethren, or sisters, or *father* or *mother*, or wife, or children, or lands, for My name's sake, shall receive an hundredfold, and shall inherit eternal life," Matt. xix. 29 ; Luke xviii. 29, 30 ; Mark x. 29, 30. And in Luke, " If any one cometh to Me, and *hateth not his father* and *his mother*, and wife, and children, and brethren, and sisters, yea, and his own soul also, he cannot be My disciple," xiv. 26. And in Mark, " The brother shall deliver the brother to death, and the *father the children*, and *the children shall rise up against the parents*, and shall kill them, because ye shall be hated of all for My name's sake," xiii. 12, 13 ; Luke xxi. 16, 17 ; speaking of the consummation of the age, and describing the state of the Church perverted as to good and truth, namely, that evil will rise up against truth, and the false principle against good. That by father, in the opposite sense, is signified evil, is evident from the passages already adduced, and also from this in John, " Jesus said, If God was *your father*, ye would love Me, for I came forth and come from God. Ye are of your *father the devil*, and *the desire of your father* ye are willing to do ; he was a murderer from the beginning, and stood not in the truth, because the truth is not in him ; when he speaketh a lie, he speaketh from his own, because he is a liar, and the *father of it*," viii. 38, 39, 41, 42, 44.

3704. " And the God of Isaac"—that hereby is signified the Lord as to the Divine Human [principle], appears from the representation of Isaac, as denoting the Lord's Divine Rational principle ; and whereas the rational principle is that in which the human principle commences, see n. 2194, and thus from which and by which the human principle is, therefore here by the God of Isaac is signified ⬛ Lord's Divine Human [principle]. Inasmuch as all and ⬛ngular things in heaven, and all

and singular things appertaining to man, yea, in universal nature, have relation to good and truth, therefore also the Lord's
Divine [principle] is distinguished into Divine Good and Divine
Truth, and the Divine Good of the Lord is called Father, and
the Divine Truth Son ; nevertheless the Lord's Divine [principle]
is nothing else but good, yea, essential good, and the Divine
Truth is the Lord's Divine Good so appearing in heaven, or
before the angels. The case herein is like that of the sun : the
sun itself in its essence is nothing else but fire, and the light
which thence appears is not in the sun, but from the sun. That
the Lord as to Divine Good is represented by a sun, and also,
in another life, is a sun to the universal heaven, may be
seen, n. 1053, 1521, 1529, 1530, 1531, 2495, 3636, 3643 ;
and that the Lord as to Divine Truth is represented by light,
and also is light in another life to the universal heaven, see n.
1053, 1521, 1529, 1530, 2776, 3138, 3195, 3222, 3223, 3339,
3341, 3636, 3643. Thus the Lord in His essence is nothing else
but Divine Good, and this as to each principle, namely, as to
the essential Divine principle and the Divine Human : whereas
Divine Truth is not in Divine Good, but from Divine Good, for
so the Divine Good appears in heaven, as was said above ; and
since Divine Good appears as Divine Truth, therefore for the
sake of man's apprehension, the Lord's Divine [principle] is
distinguished into Divine Good and Divine Truth, and Divine
Good is what in the Word is called Father, and Divine Truth
is what is called Son. This is the arcanum which lies hid in
this circumstance, that the Lord so often speaks of His Father
as if He was distinct, and as it were another from Himself, and
yet in other places asserts that He is one with Himself. That
Father, in the internal sense, is good, and, in the supreme sense,
the Lord as to Divine Good, was shown above, n. 3703 ; and
that Son denotes truth, and the Son of God and the Son of Man
denote the Lord as to Divine Truth, was shown, n. 1729, 1730,
2159, 2803, 2813. And the same is manifest from all those passages where the Lord makes mention of His Father, and calls
Himself Son. That in the Word of the Old Testament it is the
Lord who is called Jehovah, may be seen, n. 1343, 1736, 2921 ;
and that He is there also called Father, is evident from these
passages, " Unto us a child is born, unto us a son is given, and
the government shall be upon his shoulder, and His name shall
be called Wonderful, Counsellor, God, Hero, *the Father of
eternity*, the Prince of Peace," Isaiah ix. 6 ; where it is very
manifest that the child born to us, and the son given to us, is
the Lord, consequently it is the Lord Who is called Father of
eternity. So in Jeremiah, " I will be for *a Father to Israel*
and Ephraim is My first-born," xxxi. 9 ; speaking of the Lord,
Who is the God of Israel, and the Holy One of Israel, as may
be seen, n. 3305, in the present case a Father to Israel. So in

Malachi, " Have not we all *one father?* hath not one God created us?" ii. 10 ; where to create, in the internal sense, denotes
to regenerate, as also in other passages of the Word, see n. 16,
88, 472 ; and whereas the Lord is the only Regenerator and Redeemer, it is He Who is here called Father and God ; as also
in Isaiah, " Thou art *our Father,* because Abraham doth not
know us, and Israel doth not acknowledge us ; *Thou Jehovah
art our Father, our Redeemer,* Thy name is from eternity,"
lxiii. 16.   Again, " I will clothe Him with thy coat, and will
strengthen Him with thy girdle, and I will give thy dominion
into His hand, *that He may be for a Father to the inhabitant
of Jerusalem, and to the house of Judah,* and I will give the
key of the house of David upon His shoulder ; and He shall
open and none shall shut, and He shall shut and none shall
open ; and I will fix him a nail in a faithful place, that He may
be for a throne of glory of his Father, upon Whom they may
hang *all the glory of his Father's house,* of sons and grandsons,
all vessels of a small (size or measure), from the vessels of cups
even to all vessels of psalteries," xxii. 21, 22, 23, 24.   That it
is the Lord Who is here represented and signified, and is called
a Father to the inhabitant of Jerusalem and to the house of
Judah, is very manifest ; for it is He, upon Whose shoulder is
the key of the house of David, Who openeth and none shutteth
and Who shutteth and none openeth, see preface to chap. xxii.,
and He hath the throne of His Father's glory, and upon Him
and from Him are all holy things, which are here called vessels,
celestial things vessels of cups, and holy spiritual things vessels
of psalteries.   Inasmuch as kings and priests represented the
Lord, kings, by the principle of royalty, the Lord as to Divine
Truth, and priests the Lord as to Divine Good, see n. 3670,
therefore priests were called fathers, as may appear in the book
of Judges, " Micah said to the Levite, Abide with me, and be
unto me for *a father and a priest,*" xvii. 10.   In like manner
said the sons of Dan, " Hold thy peace, put thy hand upon thy
mouth, and go with us, and be to us for *a father and a priest,*"
xviii. 19.   That kings themselves also so called them, appears
in the second book of the Kings, " The king of Israel said to
Elisha, Shall I smite, *O my father?* he said, Thou shalt not
smite," vi. 21, 22 ; and on the death of Elisha it is written of
Joash the king, that " He wept before his faces, and said, *My
father, my father,* the chariot of Israel and the horsemen
thereof," xiii. 14.   The reason why kings so called them was,
because they represented the Lord as to Divine Truth, and
priests represented Him as to Divine Good, and because truth
in respect to good is as a son to a father, for truth is from good.
This is perfectly well known in another life, and in consequence
thereof they call no other a father in heaven, nor have any
perception of any other father in the Word of the evangelists,

but the Lord, see n. 15, 1729. All infants are there taught, when they are initiated into the good of love and the truth thereof, to acknowledge the Lord alone for Father; yea, novitiates also, who come into heaven, are taught with anxious care, that there is one God; and they who have been born within the Church are taught, that the whole Trinity (*omne Trinum*) is in the Lord; for almost all who come from the Christian world, bring with them an idea of three Gods, although with their lips they had said that there is but one God; for to think of one, when the idea of three has before entered, and each of these is named God, and also is distinguished from the other as to attributes and offices, and likewise is separately worshipped, is a thing altogether impossible; hence it is that the worship of three Gods is in the heart, whereas the worship of one only is in the mouth. That the whole Trinity (*omne Trinum*) is in the Lord, is known in the Christian world, nevertheless in another life the Lord is little thought of, yea, also His Human [principle] is a scandal to many, because they distinguish the Human [principle] from the Divine, neither do they believe it to be Divine. Man says that himself is justified, and is thus made pure and almost holy, but he does not think that the Lord was glorified, that is, that His Human [principle] was made Divine, when yet He was conceived of Jehovah himself; and moreover no one can be justified, much less sanctified, except from the Divine [principle], and indeed from the Lord's Divine Human [principle], which is represented and signified in the sacred supper, where it is expressly said, that the bread is His body, and the wine His blood. That the Lord is one with the Father, and that He is from eternity, and that He rules the universe, consequently that He is essential Divine Good and Divine Truth, is very manifest from the Word. That He is one with the Father, appears from these words in John, "No one hath seen God at any time, the only-begotten Son, *Who is in the bosom of the Father*," &c., i. 18. Again, "The Jews sought to kill Jesus, because He had said that God was His Father, *making Himself equal with God*. Jesus answered and said, Verily, verily, I say unto you, the Son cannot do any thing of Himself, except what He seeth the Father doing, for the things which He doeth, those also the Son doeth in like manner. As the Father raiseth up the dead and vivifies them, so also the Son vivifies whom He will; neither doth the Father judge any one, but hath given all judgment to the Son, that all may honour the Son as they honour the Father; *as the Father hath life in Himself, so also hath He given to the Son to have life in Himself*. The Father Who hath sent Me, hath Himself witnessed of Me; ye have neither heard His voice at any time, nor seen His appearance. Search the scriptures, for they are what testify of Me," v. 1 to the end. By Father is here meant, as was said, the Divine Good; and by Son, the Divine Truth, each in the Lord. From the Divine Good, which is the Father, nothing can proceed or come forth but what is Divine, and this which proceeds or comes forth is Divine Truth, or the Son. So again, "*Every one who hath heard and learned of the Father, cometh to Me;* not that any one hath seen the Father, except he who is with the Father, he hath seen the Father," vi. 44 to 48. Again, "They said, Where is thy Father? Jesus answered, Ye have neither known Me, nor My Father; *if ye had known Me ye would have known My Father also,*" viii. 18, 19. Again, "*I and My Father are one:* if ye do not believe Me, believe the works, *that ye may know and believe, that the Father is in Me, and I in the Father,*" x. 30, 38. Again, "Jesus said, He that believeth on Me, believeth not on Me, but on Him Who sent Me, and *he who seeth Me, seeth Him Who sent Me;* I am come a light into the world, that every one who believeth on Me, may not abide in darkness," xii. 44, 45, 46. By the Father *sending* Him, is signified, in the internal sense, that He proceeds from the Father; and so also in other passages where the Lord says that the Father sent Him; that light is Divine Truth, may be seen above. Again, "I am the way, and the truth, and the life; no one cometh to the Father but by Me; *if ye have known Me, ye have known My Father also,* and from henceforth ye have known Him, *and have seen Him.* Philip saith, Lord, show us the Father; Jesus said, Am I so long time with you, and hast thou not known Me, Philip? *he who seeth Me, seeth the Father;* how then sayest thou, Show us the Father; *believest thou not that I am in the Father, and the Father in Me?* The words which I speak unto you, I speak not from Myself; the Father who dwelleth in Me, He doeth the works. Believe Me, *that I am in the Father, and the Father in Me.* Whatsoever ye shall ask in My name, I will do it, that the Father may be glorified in the Son," xiv. 6 to 11. Again, in the same evangelist, "He that hath My precepts, and doeth them, he it is who loveth Me, and he who loveth Me shall be loved of My Father, and I will love him, and will manifest Myself to him. If any one love Me, he will keep My Word, and My Father will love him, and we will come to him, and make our abode with him," xiv. 21, 23. They who are in Divine Truth, are they who have His precepts and do them, and they who are in Divine Good, are they who love, hence it is said, that he shall be loved of the Father, and we will come to him and make our abode with him, namely, Divine Good and Divine Truth; wherefore it is said in the same evangelist, "In that day ye shall know *that I am in My Father,* and ye in Me," xiv. 20; and in another place, "Holy Father, keep them in Thy name, that they may be one as we are," xvii. 11. From these passages it is evident, that the Lord uses the term Father as ex pressive of the Divine Good appertaining to Himself, and the term Son as expressive of the Divine Truth, which is from the Divine Good, thus that they are not two, but one. The reason why the Lord so spake was, that the Word might be received as well in earth as in heaven, and also because, before He was glorified, He was Divine Truth derived from Divine Good, but when He was glorified, He was essential Divine Good as to each essence, from Whom is all Divine Good and Divine Truth. THAT HE WAS FROM ETERNITY, may appear from this consideration, that it is the Lord who spake by the prophets, and that from this circumstance, and also because from Him was Divine Truth, He was called the Word, concerning which it is thus written in John, "*In the beginning was the Word, and the Word was with God, and God was the Word; this was in the beginning with God;* all things were made by Him, and without Him was nothing made which was made; in Him was life, and the life was the light of men. And the Word was made flesh, and dwelt in us, and we saw His glory, the glory as of the only-begotten of the Father," i. 1, 2, 3, 4, 14. The Word denotes all truth in the heavens and in the earths which is from the Divine [principle]. That he was from eternity, is also elsewhere manifestly taught in John, "John said, This was He, who, coming after me, *was before me, because He was before me.* There stands one in the midst of you, whom ye know not; He it is who, coming after me, was *before me,*" i. 15, 27, 30. Again, in the same evangelist, "If ye shall see the Son of Man ascending where He was before," vi. 62. Again, "Jesus said, Verily, verily, I say unto you, *before Abraham was, I am,*" viii. 58. Again, "He knew that *He came forth from God,* and went to God," xiii. 3. Again, "The Father Himself loveth you, because ye have loved Me, and have believed that *I came forth from God: I came forth from the Father and came into the world,* again I leave the world, and go to the Father." xvi. 27, 28. Again, "I have glorified Thee on earth, I have finished the work which Thou hast given Me to do; now therefore glorify Me, O Father, with Thine own self, with the glory *which I had with Thee before the world was:* that they may see My glory which Thou hast given Me, because Thou hast loved Me *before the foundation of the world,*" xvii. 5, 24. So in Isaiah, "Unto us a Child is born, unto us a Son is given, and His name shall be called Wonderful, Counsellor, God, Hero, *the Father of Eternity*, the Prince of Peace," ix. 6. THAT THE LORD RULES THE UNIVERSE, is evident from these words in Matthew, "All things are delivered unto Me of My Father," xi. 27. Again, "Jesus said to His disciples, All power is given to Me in heaven and in earth," xxviii. 18. And in John, "The Father hath given all things into the hand of the Son; he that believeth on the

Son hath eternal life," iii. 35, 36. "The Father judgeth not any one, but hath given all judgment to the Son," v. 22. Again, "Jesus knew that the Father had given all things into his hands," xiii. 3. Again, "All things that the Father hath are Mine," xvi. 15. Again, "Jesus said, Glorify Thy Son, that Thy Son also may glorify Thee, as Thou hast given Him power over all flesh," xvii. 1, 2. Again, "All Mine are Thine, and Thine Mine, but I am glorified in them; I am no longer in the world, for I come to Thee," xvii. 10, 11. And in Luke, "All things are delivered to Me of My Father," x. 22. From the above passages then it may appear, that the Divine Good is what is called Father, and the Divine Truth, what is called Son; and that the Lord from Divine Good by Divine Truth rules all and singular things in the universe. This being the case, and it being so evident from the Word, it is surprising that they do not, in the Christian world, as in heaven, acknowledge and adore the Lord alone, and thereby one God; for they know and teach, that the whole Trinity is in the Lord. That the Holy Spirit, Who also is worshipped as a God distinct from the Son and the Father, is the holy of the spirit, or the holy principle which by spirits or angels proceeds from the Lord, that is, from His Divine Good by Divine Truth, will be shown elsewhere by the Lord's Divine Mercy.

3705. "The land (or earth) on which thou liest, to thee will I give it"—that hereby is signified the good in which he was principled, that it was from his own proprium (or proper self), appears from the signification of earth (or land), as here denoting the good of the natural principle, of which we shall speak presently; and from the signification of giving it to thee, as denoting to be from his own proprium, of which also we shall speak presently. That land (or earth) signifies the good of the natural principle, is on this account, because by the land of Canaan is signified the Lord's kingdom, see n. 1413, 1437, 1585, 1607, 1866; and inasmuch as it signifies the Lord's kingdom, it also in the supreme sense signifies the Lord, n. 3038, for the Lord is all in all of His kingdom, insomuch that whatever is not from Him, and does not respect Him, is not of His kingdom; the Lord's kingdom also is signified in the Word by heaven and earth, see n. 1733, 1850, 2117, 2118; but in this case the interior principle thereof is signified by heaven, and the exterior by earth, n. 82, 1411, 1733, 3355; consequently in the supreme sense heaven signifies the Lord as to His Divine rational principle, and earth as to His Divine natural principle; in the present case therefore, the earth on which thou liest, signifies the good of the natural principle, in which he was, which was to be represented by Jacob. That Jacob is the Lord, as to the Divine natural principle, has been frequently said above; moreover, that the signification of earth (or land) is various, see n. 620

636, 1067, 2571, 3368, 3379.   And this by reason that Canaan, which is called the holy land (or earth), signifies the Lord's k ngdom in general; and when mention is made of heaven together with it, in such case, as was said, heaven signifies what is interior, and earth what is exterior ; and consequently, it also signifies the Lord's kingdom in the earths, that is, the Church, and this being the case, it also signifies the man who is the Lord's kingdom, or who is the Church.   Thus with such a man heaven denotes what is interior, and earth what is exterior, or, what is the same thing, heaven denotes the rational principle, and earth the natural, for the rational principle is interior with man, and the natural exterior; and inasmuch as earth has these significations, it also signifies that which makes man to be a kingdom of the Lord, namely, the good of love which is from the Divine [principle] ; hence it is evident how various the signification of earth is in the Word.   That by the expression, " I will give to thee," is signified that it was from His own proprium, may appear from the signification of giving in the Word, when it is predicated of the Lord ; for the Lord, as was shown above, is Divine Good and also Divine Truth, and the former is what is called Father, and the latter Son ; and whereas Divine Good is His (or of Himself), consequently His own proprium, it follows, that by giving to thee, when it is said as from Jehovah, and is predicated of the Lord, is signified that it is from His own proprium.   Hence it is manifest what is signified, in the internal sense, by what the Lord so often said, that the Father gave to Him, namely, that He gave to Himself; as in John, " Father, glorify Thy Son, that Thy Son also may glorify Thee, as *Thou hast given Him* power over all flesh, that He may give eternal life to all *which Thou hast given Him.*   I have glorified Thee upon earth, I have finished the work which *Thou hast given Me* to do.   I have manifested Thy name to the men, whom *Thou hast given Me* out of the world ; Thine they were, and *Thou hast given them to Me.*   Now they have known that all things *which Thou hast given Me,* are from Thee ; because the words *which Thou hast given Me,* I have given them. I pray for them *whom Thou hast given Me,* because they were Thine, *for all Mine are Thine, and Thine Mine,*" xvii. 1, 2, 4, 6 to 10 ; in which passages by the Father having given, is signified that they were from the Divine Good which was His own, thus from His own proprium.   Hence it may appear what a deep and secret sense lies concealed in all and singular the words which the Lord spake ; also how much the sense of the letter differs from the internal sense, and especially from the supreme sense.   The reason why the Lord so spake was, that man, who at that time was in total ignorance of all Divine Truth, might still in his manner and measure apprehend the Word, and thereby receive it ; and the angels in their manner and measure, for these latter knew that Jehovah and He were One, and that the Father was the Divine Good, hence also they knew, that when He said that the Father gave to Him, it was to denote that He Himself gave to Himself, and that thus it was from His own proprium.

3706. " And to thy seed "—that hereby is signified truth also, appears from the signification of seed, as denoting the truth of faith, see n. 255, 880, 1025, 1447, 1610, 2848, 3038, 3310, 3373.

3707. " And thy seed shall be as the dust of the earth"— that hereby is signified that Divine Truth natural would be as good natural, appears from the signification of seed, as denoting truth, see above, n. 3706, hence thy seed, or the seed of Jacob, is Divine Truth natural, for by Jacob is represented the Lord's Divine natural principle, as was shown above; and from the signification of dust of the earth, as denoting good, see n. 1610; hence, "Thy seed shall be as the dust of the earth," denotes, in the internal sense, that Divine Truth natural should be as Divine Good natural. The ground and reason why dust of the earth signifies good is, because by earth is signified the Lord's kingdom, consequently good, as was shown above, n. 3705; dust of that earth therefore denotes good, but good natural, because by earth, as was also shown n. 3705, is signified that which is exterior in the Lord's kingdom, thus the natural principle, heaven denoting, when it also is named, that which is interior, or the rational principle. Hence it is, that fructification of good and multiplication of truth is expressed in the Word throughout by seed being as the stars of the heavens and as the dust of the earth; by the stars of the heavens in this case are signified things rational, and by the dust of the earth things natural, which thus increase. What is meant by truth natural becoming as good natural, by the Divine Mercy of the Lord, will be explained in what follows.

3708. " And thou shalt break forth to the sea and to the east"—that hereby is signified the infinite extension of good, and that by breaking forth to the north and to the south is signified the infinite extension of truth, thus all states of good and truth, appears from the signification of breaking forth, as denoting extension, in the present case infinite extension because it is predicated of the Lord; and from the signification of sea or the west, as denoting good as yet obscure, thus in its commencement; and from the signification of east, as denoting good which is lucid and thus perfect; and from the signification of north, as denoting truth as yet in obscurity; and from the signification of south, as denoting truth in the light. In many passages in the Word mention is made of the sea or the west, of the east, of the north, and of the south; but inasmuch as it has not heretofore been known to any one, that these expres-

sions, like all and singular expressions in the Word, had an internal sense, in which sense they did not signify worldly things
according to the sense of the letter, but things spiritual and
celestial and in a supreme sense the Divine things of the Lord
Himself, therefore man could know no other but that by west,
east, north, and south, were meant only the quarters of the
world, and that by breaking forth to those quarters is meant
multiplication. But that by the above expressions are not signified such quarters, nor the multiplication of any people, but
states of good and truth, and the extension thereof, may appear
from all the passages in the Word, especially in the prophets,
where they are mentioned; for what is west, east, north, and
south, is altogether unknown in heaven, inasmuch as the sun
there, which is the Lord, is not like the sun of the world, which
rises and sets, and by its greatest altitude causes mid-day, and
by its least causes night, but it constantly appears, yet according to the states of those who receive light thence, for the light
thence derived has in it wisdom and intelligence, see n. 1619 to
1632, 2776, 3138, 3167, 3190, 3195, 3222, 3223, 3339, 3341
3485, 3636, 3643; wherefore it appears according to the state
of every one's wisdom and intelligence; with those who are
principled in good and truth, it appears in heat and light, but
celestial and spiritual, as the sun when it is in its rising and at
mid-day, whereas with those who are not principled in good
and truth, it appears as the sun when it is setting and at night.
Hence it is evident, that by the east, the south, the west, and
the north, in the internal sense of the Word, are signified states
of good and truth. It is to be observed, that states of good
and truth are described in the Word, not only by the quarters
of which we have been speaking, but also by times or states of
the year, namely, by spring, summer, autumn, and winter, as
also by times or states of the day, namely, by morning, mid-
day, evening, and night, and this for a similar reason; but in
treating of the extension of good and truth, it is described by
the quarters of the world. What is specifically signified by each
quarter, may appear from the passages in the Word where they
are mentioned. That the east is the Lord, and the good of love
and charity which is from the Lord, was shown above, n. 101,
1250, 3249; and that the south denotes truth in the light, was
shown, n. 1458, 3195; but what is signified by the west and what
by the north, in the genuine sense, and what in the opposite sense,
may appear from the following passages: "Fear not, because I
am with thee; I will bring thy seed from the *east*, and from the
west will I gather; I will say to the *north*, Give, and to the *south*,
Hinder not; bring My sons from far, and My daughters from
the extremity of the earth," Isaiah xliii. 5, 6; speaking of a
new spiritual Church, which is there called Jacob and Israel.
To bring seed from the east, and to gather from the west, denotes

those who are principled in good; to say to the north, Give, and
to the south, Do not hinder, denotes those who are principled in
truth.   So in David, "The redeemed of Jehovah shall say,
whom He hath redeemed from the hand of the enemy, and
gathered them from the lands, from the *east*, and from the *west*,
from the *north*, and from the *sea;* they wandered in the wilderness, in a desert of a way, they found not a city of habitation,"
Psalm cvii. 2, 3, 4; speaking of those who are in ignorance of
good and truth.   From the east and from the west denotes those
who are in ignorance of good; from the north and from the
sea denotes those who are in ignorance of truth; of those who
are in ignorance of good it is said, that they wandered in a wilderness, and of those who are in ignorance of truth, that they
wandered in a desert of a way, and concerning the ignorance of
both it is said, that they found not a city of habitation.   That
city denotes doctrine of truth, may be seen, n. 402, 2449, 2943,
3216; and that habitation is predicated of good, see n. 2268,
2451, 2712.   Again, in Isaiah, "Lo, these shall come from
far, and lo, these from the *north*, and from the *west*, and these
from the land of Sinim," xlix. 12; where the north denotes those
who are in obscurity as to truth, and the west, those who are
in obscurity as to good, who are said to come from far, because
remote from the light which is from the Lord.   So in Amos,
"Behold the days are about to come, in which I will send a
famine on the earth, and they shall wander *from sea to sea*,
and shall run to and fro from *the north even to the east*, to
seek the Word of Jehovah, and they shall not find it," viii. 11,
12; where famine denotes a scarcity and defect of knowledges,
see n. 1460, 3364; wandering from sea to sea denotes to inquire
where knowledges are; that seas denote knowledges in general,
see n. 28, 2850; to run to and fro from the north even to the
east, denotes from those knowledges which are in obscurity to
those which are in light.   That knowledges are here meant, is
evident, for it is said, to seek the Word of Jehovah, and they
shall not find it.   So in Jeremiah, "Proclaim these words
towards the *north*, and say, Return, thou backsliding Israel,
I will not cause My faces to fall upon you, inasmuch as I am
merciful: in those days the house of Judah shall go to the
house of Israel, and they shall come together from *the land of
the north* upon the land which I have caused your fathers to
inherit," iii. 12, 18; speaking of the restoration of the Church
amongst the Gentiles.   The north denotes those who are in
ignorance of truth, and yet in the life of good.   That in this
passage is not meant the north, nor the land of the north, is
evident, for Israel was no longer.   Again, in the same prophet,
"Jehovah is alive, who caused the sons of Israel to ascend out
of *the land of the north*," xvi. 15; where the north in like
manner denotes ignorance of truth.   Again, "Behold, I bring

them from *the land of the north*, and I will gather them from
the sides of the earth, the blind and the lame amongst them,"
xxxi. 8. The land of the north denotes ignorance of good,
because of truth: and whereas the land of Canaan represented
the Lord's kingdom, and thence also good, see n. 3705 ; and
whereas what was in the midst thereof, as Zion and Jerusalem,
represented the inmost principle of good to which truth was
adjoined, hence the parts which were distant therefrom represented obscurity as to good and truth ; all this which is in
obscurity is called the land of the north, and also the sides of
the earth ; moreover, inasmuch as all good, which flows-in with
light from the Lord, terminates in man's obscure principles, the
north is also called an assembly or congregation (*conventus*).
as in Isaiah, "Thou hast said in thine heart, I will ascend the
heavens, I will exalt my throne above the stars of God, and
I will sit in the *mount of the congregation*, in *the sides of the
north*," xiv. 13. Again, "Howl, O gate ; cry, O city ; thou,
whole Palestine, art dissolved : because a smoke cometh *from
the north*, solitary in *the congregations*," xiv. 31. So in David,
"Great is Jehovah, and exceedingly praised in the city of our
God, the mountain of His holiness, the joy of the whole earth,
the mount of Zion, *the sides of the north*, the city of the great
king," Psalm xlviii. 2, 3. And again, "The heavens are Thine,
the earth also is Thine ; Thou hast founded the world, and the
fulness thereof ; Thou hast created *the north* and the right
hand," lxxxix. 12, 13 ; where the north denotes those who are
more remote from the light of good and truth, and the right
hand those who are nearer thereto. That these are at the Lord's
right hand, see n. 1274, 1276. So in Zechariah, "I saw four
chariots coming forth between two mountains of brass, with
red, black, white, and strong grizzled horses ; the angel said,
These are the four winds of the heavens going forth from standing near the Lord of the whole earth ; the black horses going forth
into *the land of the north*, and the white went forth after them,
and the grizzled went forth into *the land of the south :* they that
went forth into *the land of the north* cause my spirit to rest in
the land of the north," vi. 1 to 8. Chariots going forth between
two mountains of brass, denote doctrinals of good. That chariots denote doctrinals, will be made apparent elsewhere : that
mountain denotes love, may be seen, n. 795, 1430, 2722 ; hence
two mountains denote two loves ; celestial love, which is love
to the Lord, and spiritual love, which is love towards our neighbour; that brass denotes the good thence derived, which is in the
natural principle, see n. 425, 1551 ; that horses denote things
intellectual, thus the understanding of the doctrinals of good,
see n. 2760, 2761, 2762, 3217 ; the land of the south denotes
those who are in the knowledges of good and truth, see n. 1458,
3195 ; the land of the north denotes those who are in ignorance

of good and truth, but in the life of good, in which are the upright Gentiles, amongst whom when the Church is established, the spirit of God is said to rest therein. So in Jeremiah, " Jehovah, who caused to ascend, and who brought back the seed of the house of Israel out of *the land of the north*, and out of all the lands whither I have driven them, to dwell upon their own land," xxiii. 8 ; where out of the land of the north denotes the obscurity of ignorance respecting what is good and true.   Again, " Shall iron be broken, iron *from the north*, and brass ?" xv. 12 ; iron denotes natural truth, see n. 425, 426 ; brass denotes natural good, n. 425, 1551. These are said to be from the north, because from the natural principle, where there is obscurity respectively, and a term or limit. That this prophetic declaration does not signify that iron and brass are from the north, is manifest without explication, for what of any Divine principle, yea, what of coherence could there be with what goes before and what follows after, if it was meant that iron and brass were from thence ? So in Matthew, " I say unto you, that many shall come *from the east and from the west*, and shall lie down with Abraham, Isaac, and Jacob," viii. 11 ; Luke xiii 29 ; where many from the east and from the west denote those who are in the knowledges and the life of good, and those who are in obscurity and ignorance, thus those who are within the Church and those who are without ; for that states of good are signified by east and west, was said above. That to lie down with Abraham, Isaac, and Jacob, is to be with the Lord, may be seen, n. 3305. That in like manner they will come from the east and from the west, who shall be with the Lord in His kingdom or in His Church, is said in the prophets, as in Isaiah, " I will bring thy seed *from the east*, and *from the west* will I gather thee," xliii. 5. And again, " They shall fear the name of Jehovah *from the west*, and *from the east* His glory," lix. 19. Again, " They shall know *from the rising of the sun, and from the setting*, that there is none beside Me ; I am Jehovah, and there is none besides," xlv. 6. Again, " I will raise up *from the north*, and he shall come ; *from the rising of the sun* he shall call upon My name," xli. 25. Moreover, that such is the signification of the east, the west, the south, and the north, may appear manifestly from the construction of the tabernacle ; from the encamping and journeying of the sons of Israel ; from the description of the land of Canaan ; also from the description of the new temple, of the new Jerusalem, and of the new earth : I. From the construction of the tabernacle, in that all things appertaining thereto were arranged according to the quarters of the world, see Exod. xxxviii. What was to be at the east and west angle, and what at the south and north angle, may be seen, Exod. xxvi. 18, 20, 22, 27 ; chap. xxvii. 9, 12, 14 ; and that the candlestick over against the table was to be on the side of the tabernacle *towards the south*, but the table on the *north side*, Exod. xxvi. 35; chap. xl. 22. II. FROM THE ENCAMPING AND JOURNEYING OF THE SONS OF ISRAEL, also according to quarters, in that they were to encamp around the tent of the congregation, the tribe of Judah, the tribe of Issachar, the tribe of Zebulon, *towards the east;* the tribe of Reuben, of Simeon, and of Gad, *towards the south;* the tribe of Ephraim, of Manasseh, and of Benjamin, *towards the west;* the tribe of Dan, of Asher, and of Naphtali, *towards the north*, Numb. ii. 1 to the end. Also that of the Levites, the Gershonites were to be *towards the west*, the Kohathites *towards the south*, the Merarites *towards the north*, and that Moses, Aaron, and his sons, should be before the tabernacle *towards the east*, see Numb. iii. 23 to 38, whereby was represented the celestial order, which in the Lord's kingdom is according to states of good and truth; and that *towards the south* they should sound [the trumpets] with proclamation for their journeys, see Numb. x. 6; and that as they encamped, so also they journeyed. Numb. ii. 34. III. FROM THE DESCRIPTION OF THE LAND OF CANAAN, which was first described by Moses as to the borders round about, and this at the *south angle*, at the *west angle*, the *north angle*, and the *east angle*, see Numb. xxxiv. 2 to 12; afterwards when it was given by lot to the tribes, see Joshua xv., xvi., xvii., xviii., xix.; hence, and also from the most ancient people who dwelt in the land of Canaan, all the places therein became representative and significative, according to their situation, distance, and borders [or boundaries], as to quarters, see n. 1607, 1866. IV. FROM THE DESCRIPTION OF THE NEW TEMPLE, OF THE NEW JERUSALEM, AND OF THE NEW EARTH, also according to the quarters of the world, in Ezekiel; as, that the building of the city was *on the south;* concerning the gate of the building, the faces whereof were *towards the east, towards the north, and towards the south*, xl. 2, 6, 19, 20 to 46: concerning the measure of the temple, and its door *towards the north* and *towards the south*, xli. 11: concerning the court *towards the north, the east, the south*, and *the west*, xliii. 1, 4, 10, 11, 17, 18, 19, 20: and that the glory of Jehovah, God of Israel, entered from *the way of the east*, xliii. 1, 2, 4: concerning the gates of the outer court, xli. 1, 2, 4: concerning the borders of the holy land, chap. xlvii.: towards *the north*, verses 15, 16, 17: towards *the east*, verse 18: towards *the south*, verse 19: towards *the west*, verse 20: and concerning the inheritances according to the quarters for each tribe, chap. xlviii.: and concerning the gates of the holy Jerusalem, on *the east, the north, the south, and the west*, Apoc. xxi. 13. From these circumstances it appears evident, that the four quarters of the world, according to which the above holy things or representatives of what is holy were arranged, in the internal sense do not signify such quarters, but states of good and truth in the Lord's kingdom. That the north and the west, in an opposite sense, signify what is false and evil, may appear from the following passages, "The Word of Jehovah came to me a second time, saying, What seest thou? I said, I see an open pot, and *the face thereof is towards the north;* and Jehovah said, *From the north shall evil be opened* upon all the inhabitants of the earth. Behold I call all the families of *the north* that they may come," Jer. i. 13, 14, 15. Again, "Set up a sign towards Zion, assemble together, stay not, because *I bring evil from the north,* and a great breaking," iv. 6. Again, "Behold the voice of a noise cometh, and a great tumult *from the land of the north,* to make the cities of Judah a waste," x. 22. Again, "Blow the trumpet in Tekoa, because *evil appeareth out of the north,* and a great breaking. Behold a people cometh *from the land of the north,* and a great nation shall be stirred up from *the sides of the earth,*" vi. 1, 22. Again, "I have received the cup from the hand of Jehovah, and I caused all nations to drink, Jerusalem and the cities of Judah, and the kings thereof, Pharaoh king of Egypt, and *all the western crowd,* all the kings of Arabia, and *all the kings of the west* dwelling in the wilderness, and *all the kings of the north,* near and afar off," xxv. 17 to 26. Again, "The swift one shall not escape, neither shall the strong one deliver himself; they have stumbled and fallen *towards the north,* near to the shore of the river Euphrates. Who is this that cometh up as a stream? Egypt riseth up as a stream, for he said, I will come up, I will cover the earth, I will destroy the city and them that dwell therein; but this is the day of the Lord Jehovih Zebaoth, a day of vengeance, because the Lord Jehovih hath a sacrifice in *the land of the north* near the river Euphrates. Egypt is a very beautiful heifer, *destruction cometh from the north,* the daughter of Egypt is ashamed, she is delivered into the *hand of the people of the north,*" xlvi. 6, 7, 8, 10, 20, 24. Again, "Thus saith Jehovah, Behold *waters coming up from the north,* which, as an overflowing stream, shall overflow the earth and the fulness thereof, the city and them that dwell therein," xlvii. 2. Again, "Jehovah spake against Babel, *a nation from the north* shall come up against her, which shall make her land a desolation that none shall dwell therein," l. 1, 3. Again, "Behold I stir up and cause to ascend against Babel a congregation of great nations from *the land of the north,* and they shall set themselves in array against her; from thence she shall be taken; behold *a people cometh from the north,* and a great nation, and many kings shall be stirred up from *the sides of the earth,*" l. 9, 41. Again, "Then shall the heavens and the earth, and all that is in them, sing over Babel, because wasters shall come to her *from the north,*" li. 48. So in Ezekiel, "Say unto Gog, Thou shalt come out of thy place *from the sides of the north,* and many people with thee, thou shalt come up against my people Israel, as a cloud to cover the earth," xxxviii. 14, 15, 16. Again, " Behold I am against thee, O Gog, the prince, I will cause thee to return, and leave but the sixth of thee, and will cause thee to descend *from the sides of the north,* and will bring thee upon the mountains of Israel; thou shalt fall upon the mountains of Israel, upon the faces of the field thou shalt fall,' xxxix. 1, 2, 4, 5. So in Zechariah, " Ho, ho, flee from the *land of the north,* saith Jehovah, for I will spread you abroad as the four winds of the heavens; O Zion, deliver thyself, who dwell est with the daughter of Babel," ii. 10, 11. Hence it is mani- fest, what is signified by the north in the opposite sense, namely, the false principle from which evil is derived and the false principle which is derived from evil. The false principle from which evil is derived, inasmuch as it originates in ratiocination concerning Divine things and against Divine things grounded in scientifics appertaining to the natural man, is called the peo ple of the north out of Egypt; that Egypt is such scientific prin- ciple, may be seen, n. 1164, 1165, 2588. The false principle which is derived from evil, inasmuch as it originates in external worship apparently holy, whose interiors are profane, is called the nation out of the north out of Babel; that Babel is such exter- nal worship, may be seen, n. 1182, 1283, 1295, 1304, 1306, 1307, 1308, 1321, 1322, 1326; that it is Babel also which causes vasta- tion, see n. 1327. Each, namely, the false principle from which evil is derived, and the false principle which is derived from evil, is predicated of Gog, for Gog is worship in externals with- out an internal principle, and thence denotes idolatrous wor- ship, such as was that of the Jews at all times; that Gog is such worship, see n. 1151. From the obscure principle which appertains to the natural man, there arises both what is true and what is false; when man suffers himself to be illuminated by the Word from the Lord, in such case his obscure principle becomes lucid, for there is opened an internal way, whereby influx and communication is effected through heaven from the Lord; but when he does not suffer himself to be illuminated by the Word from the Lord, but by his own intelligence, in such case his obscure principle becomes dark, and thus false, for the internal way is closed, and there is no influx and com- munication effected through heaven from the Lord, only of such a sort that he can appear as a man in external form, whilst his thoughts, and also his words, are grounded in what is evil and false. Hence it is, that with the former the north signifies what is true, but with the latter what is false; for the former ascend from the obscure principle, that is, are elevated to the light, whereas the latter descend from the obscure principle, that is, remove themselves from the light; thus the former are

carried to the south, but the latter to the shades of darkness.
That north denotes the darkness of false principle, and south
the light of truth, is very evident from Daniel, speaking of the
ram and the he-goat, and also of the king of the south and the
king of the north.   Of the ram and the he-goat, in that "The
ram pushed with his horn *towards the west*, and *towards the
north*, and *towards the south*, so that none of the beasts could
stand before him ; and that the he-goat came *from the west* over
all the faces of the earth ; and that from one of his horns there
came forth a horn, which grew exceedingly *towards the south*,
and *towards the east*, and towards honourableness," viii. 4, 5, 9.
Concerning the king of the south and the king of the north, the
king of the south signifying those who are principled in knowledges of truth, and the king of the north those who are principled in what is false, it is thus written: " At the end of years
they shall consociate with each other, so that the daughter of
the king of the south shall come to *the king of the north* to do
what is right, but her arm shall not obtain strength.   There
shall arise out of a stem he who shall come into the fortress of
the king of the north, and shall prevail ; and shall lead away
captivity *into Egypt*.   He shall come into the kingdom of the
king of the south, and shall fight with the *king of the north*.
The *king of the north* shall return, and shall present a greater
multitude than heretofore.   Many shall stand against *the king
of the south*.   *The king of the north* shall come, and shall take
the city of fortifications, and shall destroy many things.   *The
king of the south* shall mix himself in war with a great army,
but shall not stand, because they shall think thoughts against
him.   Afterwards he shall return, but shall not be as before.
The people of them that know their God shall confirm themselves.   At length, in the end of time, the *king of the south*
shall strive with him, therefore as a storm shall *the king of the
north* rush upon him with chariot and horses ; many shall fall
together in the land of honourableness.   But rumours shall ter-
rify him from *the east* and from *the north*, so that he shall go
forth with great anger ; he shall come to his end, nor shall there
be any to help him," chap. xi. 1, to the end.   That the king of
the south denotes those who are in the light of truth, and the
king of the north those who are in shade at first, and afterwards in the darkness of what is false, may appear from all the
particulars above mentioned ; and that thus the state of the
Church is described, how it is successively perverted.   They
are called kings of the south and of the north, because by kings,
in the internal sense of the Word, are signified truths, and, in
the opposite sense, falses, see n. 1672, 2015, 2069 ; and by kingdoms, the things appertaining to truth, and, in the opposite
sense, the things appertaining to what is false, see n. 1672,
2547.

3709. "And in thee shall all the families of the ground be blessed"—that hereby is signified that all the truths of the good of doctrine should be conjoined with good, appears from the signification of being blessed, as denoting to be conjoined, see n. 3504, 3514, 3530, 3565, 3584; and from the signification of families, as denoting goods, and also truths of good, see n. 1159, 1261; and from the signification of ground, as denoting what is of the Church, consequently the doctrine of good and truth in the natural or external man, which man is here represented by Jacob, see n. 268, 566, 990, 3671. Hence it is evident, that by these words, "In thee shall all the families of the ground be blessed," is signified, that all the truths of the good of doctrine should be conjoined with good. Truths of the good of doctrine are the doctrinals of love to the Lord and of charity towards our neighbour, which are said to be conjoined with good in the natural man, when it is pleasant and delightful to know them for the sake of doing them.

3710. "And in thy seed"—that hereby is signified with truth also, namely, that they would be conjoined therewith, appears from the signification of seed, as denoting truth, see n. 29, 1025, 1447, 1610, 2848, 3373.

3711. "Behold I am with thee"—that hereby is signified what is Divine; and that "I will keep thee in all whither thou goest" signifies the Divine Providence, appears from this consideration, that I is Jehovah, thus the Divine [principle] of the Lord; and from the signification of keeping in all whither thou goest, as denoting providence from the Divine [principle], that is, Divine Providence, inasmuch as the subject treated of is concerning the Lord. By the Divine [principle] and the Divine Providence is here meant, that the Lord also made His natural principle Divine.

3712. "And will bring thee back to this ground"—that hereby is signified conjunction with Divine Doctrine, appears from the signification of bringing back, as denoting to join together again; and from the signification of ground, as denoting the doctrine of good and truth in the natural man, see n. 268, 566, 990, in the present case Divine Doctrine, because by the sojourning of Jacob with Laban are represented the interceding means or media, by which the Lord made His natural principle Divine, and by the bringing back of Jacob, or his return to the land of Canaan, is represented the end of the interceding means or media, namely, that He made the natural principle Divine; thus by these words, "I will bring thee back to this ground," is signified conjunction with Divine Doctrine. Divine Doctrine is Divine Truth, and Divine Truth is all the Word of the Lord; essential Divine Doctrine is the Word in the supreme sense, in which the Lord alone is treated of; hence Divine Doctrine is the Word in the internal sense, in which the Lord's kingdom in the heavens and in the earths is treated of. Divine Doctrine is also the Word in the literal sense, in which the things that are in the world and upon the earths are treated of. And whereas the literal sense contains in it the internal sense, and this the supreme sense, and altogether corresponds thereto by representatives and significatives, therefore doctrine thence derived is also Divine. Inasmuch as Jacob represents the Lord's Divine Natural principle, he represents also the Word as to the literal sense, for that the Lord is the Word, that is, all Divine Truth, is a known thing. The case is the same in regard to the natural principle of the Word as in regard to its natural sense, this being respectively as a cloud, see the preface to chap. xviii., whereas its rational principle, or the interior spiritual principle of the Word, is as the internal sense, and since the Lord is the Word, it may be said that the internal sense is represented by Isaac, but the supreme sense by Abraham. Hence it is evident what is meant by conjunction with Divine Doctrine, when it is predicated of the Lord's Divine Natural principle, which is represented by Jacob. Nevertheless these things are not so in the Lord, for all in Him is Divine Good, and not Divine Truth, and still less Divine natural truth; but Divine Truth is the Divine Good appearing in heaven before the angels, and on earth before men, and although it is appearing, still it is Divine Truth, because it is from the Divine Good as light is the sun's because proceeding from the sun, see n 3704.

3713. "Because I will not leave thee until I shall have done what I have spoken to thee"—that hereby is signified that nothing would be wanting, but all would have effect, may appear without explication.

3714. Verses 16, 17. *And Jacob awoke out of his sleep, and said, Surely Jehovah is in this place, and I knew not. And he feared, and said, How terrible is this place; this is none other but the house of God, and this is the gate of heaven.* Jacob awoke out of his sleep, signifies illustration: and said, Surely Jehovah is in this place, signifies the Divine [principle] in this state: and I knew not, signifies in an obscure principle: and he feared, signifies an holy alteration: and he said, How terrible is this place, signifies sanctity of state: this is none other but the house of God, signifies the Lord's kingdom in the ultimate principle of order: and this is the gate of heaven, signifies the ultimate principle in which order closes, through which ultimate principle there is apparently an entrance out of nature.

3715. "Jacob awoke out of his sleep"—that hereby is signified illustration, appears from the signification of sleep, as denoting an obscure state in respect to waking, which is a bright or lucid state; hence to awake out of sleep, in a spiritual sense, is to be illustrated.

3716. " And said, Surely Jehovah is in this place"—that hereby is signified the Divine [principle] in this state, appears from the signification of saying in the historical parts of the Word, as denoting to perceive, of which frequent mention has been made above ; and from the signification of place, as denoting state, see n. 1273, 1274, 1275, 1377, 2625, 2837, 3356, 3387 ; that Jehovah is the Divine [principle], is manifest ; hence it is evident, that by saying surely Jehovah is in this' place, is signified a perception that the Divine [principle] was in this state.

3717. " And I knew not"—that hereby is signified in an obscure principle, may appear without explication ; for not to know, or to be ignorant, denotes what is obscure in respect to things appertaining to intellectual sight. From not knowing or being ignorant, as denoting what is obscure, as also from awaking out of sleep, as denoting to be illustrated, it is manifest what is the nature and quality of the internal sense of the Word, namely, that the things appertaining to the literal sense are such as they appear before the external sight or some other of the senses, and also are apprehended according to those senses, whereas the things appertaining to the internal sense are such as they appear before the internal sight or any of the internal senses. The things therefore which are contained in the literal sense, and which are apprehended by man according to the external senses, that is, according to things which are in the world, or according to the ideas thence derived, the same are perceived by angels according to the internal senses, that is, according to those things which are in heaven, or according to ideas thence derived. With regard to the former and the latter things, the case is similar as in regard to things which are in the light of the world compared with things which are in the light of heaven ; for the things which are in the light of the world are comparatively dead in respect to the things which are in the light of heaven ; for in the light of heaven there is wisdom and intelligence from the Lord, see n. 3636, 3643 ; wherefore when those things, which appertain to the light of the world, are obliterated or wiped away, there remain the things appertaining to the light of heaven ; thus instead of terrestrial there remain celestial things, and instead of natural, spiritual. As in the case above, not to know or to be ignorant denotes an obscure state concerning good and truth, and to awake out of sleep denotes to be illustrated ; and so in other cases.

3718. " And he feared "—that hereby is signified an holy alteration, appears from the signification of fear, as denoting an holy alteration, as is evident from what immediately follows, for he says, " How terrible is this place ; this is none other but the house of God, and this is the gate of heaven," in which

words, that an holy alteration is contained, may be very manifest. What fear is in the internal sense, may be seen, n. 2826.
It is in general two-fold, fear in a principle not holy, and fear
in an holy principle; fear in a principle not holy is a fear in
which the wicked are, but fear in an holy principle is a fear in
which the good are. This latter fear, namely, in which the
good are, is called holy fear, being grounded in admiration respecting what is divine, and also in love. Love without holy
fear is like somewhat unsavoury, or like meat unseasoned with
salt, and consequently insipid; but love with fear is like salted
meat which yet does not taste of salt. The fear of love is, lest
in any manner the Lord should suffer hurt, or a neighbour; thus
lest in any manner good and truth should suffer hurt, consequently the holy principle of love and faith, and thence of worship; but this fear is various, and not alike with one person as
with another. In general according to the proportion of good
and truth in which any one is principled, the same is the proportion of his fear lest good and truth should suffer hurt, nevertheless in the same proportion it does not appear as fear; but
in proportion as the love of good and truth is small in any one,
in the same proportion he has less of fear concerning good and
truth, and in the same proportion it appears not as love, but as
fear, and hence such have fear respecting hell. But where there
is nothing of the love of good and truth, there is nothing of
holy fear, but only fear for the loss of honour, of gain, of reputation on account of good and truth, also of punishments and
death, which fear is external, and especially affects the body
and natural man, and the thoughts thereof; whereas the former
fear, namely, holy fear, especially affects the spirit or internal
man, and the conscience thereof.

3719. "And he said, How terrible is this place"—that
hereby is signified sanctity of state, appears from the signification of fear, as denoting an holy alteration, see just above, n.
3718; and inasmuch as the word terrible, in the original tongue,
is derived from the same expression as fear, it is sanctity (or
holiness) which is signified thereby; and whereas fear in the
internal sense signifies what is holy, as was just now said
above, by the same expression in the original tongue is signified veneration and reverence, which likewise is holy fear;
and from the signification of place, as denoting state, see above,
n. 3716.

3720. "This is none else but the house of God"—that
hereby is signified the Lord's kingdom in the ultimate principle
of order; appears from the signification of the house of God.
Mention is made of the house of God in many passages of the
Word, and in the external sense, or according to the letter, it
signifies a consecrated building in which holy worship is performed, but in the internal sense it signifies the Church, and

in a more universal sense, heaven, and in the most universal sense, the universal kingdom of the Lord ; but in the supreme sense, it signifies the Lord Himself as to the Divine Human [principle] ; in the Word however it is sometimes called the house of God, sometimes the temple, each having a like signification, but with this difference, that it is called the house of God in treating of good, but the temple in treating of truth. Hence it is evident, that by the house of God is signified the Lord's celestial Church, and in a more universal sense the heaven of the celestial angels, and in the most universal sense the Lord's celestial kingdom, and in the supreme sense the Lord as to Divine Good ; and that by temple is signified the Lord's spiritual Church, and in a more universal sense the heaven of the spiritual angels, and in the most universal sense the Lord's spiritual kingdom, and in the supreme sense the Lord as to Divine Truth, see n. 2048. The ground and reason why the house of God signifies the celestial principle appertaining to good, and why the temple signifies the spiritual principle appertaining to truth, is, because house in the Word signifies good, see n. 710, 2233, 2234, 2559, 3128, 3652 ; and because with the most ancient people it was constructed of wood, by reason that wood signifies good, see n. 643, 1110, 2784, 2812 ; whereas temple signifies truth, because it was constructed of stones ; and that stones are truths, may be seen, n. 643, 1296, 1298. That wood and stone have such signification, is not only manifest from the Word where they are mentioned, but also from representatives in another life ; for they who place merit in good works, appear to themselves to cut wood ; and they who place merit in truths, namely, in that they believed they were better acquainted with truths than others, and yet lived bad lives, appear to themselves to cut stones ; of which circumstances I have been an eye-witness. Hence it was made manifest to me what is the signification of wood and stone, namely, that wood signifies good, and stone truth ; the same was evidenced from this circumstance, that when a wooden house was seen by me, there was instantly presented an idea of good, but when a house of stone was seen, there was presented an idea of truth ; concerning which circumstance I was also instructed by the angels. Hence it is, that when mention is made of the house of God in the Word, there is presented to the angels an idea of good, and of good of such a quality as is treated of in the series ; and when mention is made of temple, there is presented an idea of truth, and of truth of such a quality as is also treated of in the series. Hence likewise it may be concluded, how deep and altogether hidden are the heavenly arcana contained in the Word. The ground and reason why by the house of God is here signified the Lord's kingdom in the ultimate principle of order, is, because the subject treated of is concerning Jacob, by whom is represented the Lord's Divine natural principle, as has been frequently shown above. The natural principle is in the ultimate of order, for in it are terminated all interior principles, and they are together therein, and being together, and thus things innumerable being viewed together as one, there is a respective obscurity in that principle; concerning this obscurity, we have taken occasion to speak elsewhere.

3721. "And this is the gate of heaven"—that hereby is signified the ultimate principle wherein order closes, and through which ultimate principle there is apparently as it were an entrance out of nature [into interior principles], appears from the signification of gate, as denoting that through which there is egress and ingress (going out and coming in). The ground and reason why this is the ultimate principle in which order closes, is, because the subject treated of is concerning the natural principle which is represented by Jacob; what is meant by gate, is manifest from what was said and shown, n. 2851, 3187, and that the natural principle is the ultimate of order, appear from what was adduced, n. 775, 2181, 2987 to 3002, 3020, 3147 3167, 3483, 3489, 3513, 3570, 3576, 3671. The reason why through this ultimate principle there is apparently thus as it were an entrance out of nature [into interior principles], is, because it is the natural mind with man, through which the things of heaven, that is, of the Lord, flow and descend into nature and through the same mind the things of nature ascend, see n. 3702; but that the entrance is only apparently from nature through the natural mind into things interior, may appear from what has been abundantly said and shown above. It appears to man that worldly objects enter through his bodily or external senses, and affect the interior principles, and thus that there is an entrance from the ultimate principle of order to the principles within; but that this is a mere appearance and fallacy, is evident from the general rule (or law), that posterior principles cannot flow into prior principles, or, what is the same thing, inferior principles into superior; or, what is the same thing, exterior principles into interior; or, what is still the same thing, worldly and natural principles into heavenly and spiritual; for the former are of a grosser nature, and the latter purer, and those grosser principles which appertain to the external or natural man, exist and subsist from those which appertain to the internal and rational man, and they cannot affect the purer principles, but are affected by and from them. How the case is in respect to this influx, inasmuch as appearance and fallacy lead to a total denial of it, by the Divine Mercy of the Lord will be shown elsewhere, when we come to treat on the subject of influx. This then is the ground and reason why it is said, that through the ultimate principle, in which order closes, there is apparently as it were an entrance out of nature [into interior principles].

3722. Verses 18, 19. *And in the morning Jacob arose early, and took the stone, which he had placed for his pillows, and set it for a statue, and poured oil upon the head of it. And he called the name of that place Bethel; but the name of the city was Luz at the first.* In the morning Jacob arose early, signifies a state of illustration: and took the stone, signifies truth: which he had placed for his pillows, signifies with which there was communication with the Divine [principle]: and set it for a statue, signifies an holy border (or boundary): and poured oil upon the head of it, signifies the holy good from which it was derived: and he called the name of that place Bethel, signifies the quality of the state: but the name of the city was Luz at the first, signifies the quality of the former state.

3723. "In the morning Jacob arose early"—that hereby is signified a state of illustration, appears from the signification of rising in the morning early, as denoting a state of illustration, see n. 3458; for when mention is made of arising in the Word, it implies somewhat of elevation, see n. 2401, 2785, 2912, 2927, 3171; and morning signifies the coming of heavenly light, thus in the present case it denotes elevation from obscurity into light, consequently a state of illustration.

3724. "And took the stone"—that hereby is signified truth, appears from the signification of stone, as denoting truth, see n. 1296, 1298, 3720.

3725. "Which he had placed for his pillows"—that hereby is signified with which there was communication with the Divine [principle], appears from the signification of pillows, or bolsters, as denoting communication of a most general kind, see above, n. 3695.

3726. "And set it for a statue"—that hereby is signified an holy border [or boundary], appears from the signification of statue, of which we shall speak presently. How the case herein is, may appear from what goes before, where the subject treated of is concerning the order by which the Lord made His natural principle Divine, and, in a representative sense, how the Lord makes new or regenerates the natural principle of man. The nature of this order has been abundantly shown above, in that it is inverted during man's regeneration, whilst truth is regarded in the first place, and that it is restored when man is regenerated, and good is set in the first place, and truth in the last, on which subject, see n. 3325, 3330, 3332, 3336, 3539, 3548, 3556, 3563, 3570, 3576, 3603, 3688. This was represented by the ladder, by which the angels ascended and descended, where it is first said that they ascended, and afterwards that they descended, see n. 3701. The subject now treated of is concerning the ascent, as being from the ultimate principle of order, concerning which, see above, n. 3720, 3721. In the present verse that it is truth which is the ultimate principle of order; it is this ultimate principle which is called an holy border or boundary, and is signified by the stone which Jacob took, and set for a statue. That truth is the ultimate principle of order, may appear from this consideration, that good cannot terminate in good, but in truth, for truth is the recipient of good, see n. 2261, 2434, 3049, 3068, 3180, 3318, 3387, 3470, 3570. Good appertaining to man without truth, or without conjunction with truth, is such good as appertains to infants, who as yet have nothing of wisdom, because they have nothing of intelligence; but so far as an infant in his advancement to adult age, receives truth from good, or so far as truth with him is conjoined to good, so far he becomes a man. Hence it is evident, that good is the first principle of order, and truth the last; and hence it is, that man ought to begin from scientifics, which are the truths of the natural man, and afterwards from doctrinals, which are the truths of the spiritual man in his natural man, in order to be initiated into intelligence of wisdom, that is, to enter into spiritual life, whereby man becomes man, see n. 3504. For example, in order that man, as a spiritual man, may love his neighbour, he ought first to learn what spiritual love or charity is, and who is his neighbour; before he knows this, he may indeed love his neighbour, but as a natural, not as a spiritual man, that is, from a principle of natural good, not from a principle of spiritual good, see n. 3470, 3471; whereas when he has attained this knowledge, then spiritual good from the Lord may be implanted therein; and this is the case in all other instances of what are called knowledges or doctrinals, or in general truths. It is said that good from the Lord may be implanted in knowledges, also that truth is the recipient of good. They who have no other idea of knowledges, and also of truths, than that they are abstract things, which is the idea generally entertained concerning thoughts, can in no wise conceive what is meant by good being implanted in knowledges, and by truth being the recipient of good. But it is to be observed, that knowledges and truths are things no more abstracted from the very pure substances appertaining to the interior man or the spirit, than vision is abstracted from its organ the eye, or than hearing is abstracted from its organ the ear. There are purer substances, and those real, from which knowledges and thoughts exist, whose variations of form being animated and modified by an influx of life from the Lord, present them to the mind, whilst their agreeableness and harmonies, in succession or simultaneously, affect the mind, and constitute what is called beautiful, pleasant, and delightful. Spirits themselves are forms, that is, consist of continued forms, just as men do, but of a purer nature, and not visible to the bodily sight. And whereas these forms or substances are not to be seen by the corporeal eye, man at this day conceives no other than that knowledges and thoughts are abstract things; hence also comes the folly of mankind in the present age, in that they do not believe that they have a spirit within them which is to live after the death of the body, when yet this spirit is a substance much more real than the substance of the material body: yea, if you are disposed to believe it, the spirit, after being freed from corporeal principles, is that very body purified, which the generality of mankind say they are to have at the day of judgment, when they believe that they shall first rise again. That spirits, or what is the same thing, souls, have a body, see each other as in clear day, discourse together, hear each other, and enjoy a much more exquisite sensation than whilst they were in the body or the world, may appear manifestly from what has been above so abundantly related concerning them from experience.

3727. In regard to the signification of statue, as denoting an holy border, thus the ultimate principle of order, it has its ground in this circumstance, that in the most ancient times, stones were placed at their borders, which marked the possession or inheritance of one from that of another and were for a sign or for a witness that the borders or boundaries were at that place. The most ancient people who in every particular object, and in every particular statue, were led to think of somewhat celestial and spiritual see n. 1977, 2995, from these stones also which they set up were led to think concerning the ultimate principles in man, consequently concerning the ultimate principle of order, which is truth in the natural man. The ancients, who were after the flood, received this from the most ancient people who were before the flood, see n. 920, 1409, 2179, 2896, 2897, and began to account those stones holy which were set up in the borders, because, as was said, they signified holy truth which is in the ultimate of order. They also called those stones, statues, and hence it came to pass that statues were used in worship, and that they erected such in the places where they had their groves, and afterwards where they had their temples, and also that they anointed them with oil, of which we shall speak presently; for the worship of the ancient Church consisted of the perceptives and significatives of the most ancient people who were before the flood, as is evident from the passages above referred to. The most ancient people, inasmuch as they discoursed with angels, and were together with them whilst they were on earth, were instructed from heaven that stones signified truth, and that wood signified good, see above, n. 3720 Hence then it is that statues signify a holy boundary, thus truth, which is the ultimate principle of order in man, fo

the good, which fl ws-in through the internal man from the
Lord, terminates in the external man, and in the truth that is
therein. Man's th ught, speech, and action, which are the
ultimates of order, are nothing else but truths grounded in
good, being the images or forms of good, for they belong to
man's intellectual part, whereas the good which is in them, and
from which they are derived, belongs to his voluntary part.
That statues were erected for a sign, and for a witness, and also
for worship, and that in the internal sense they signify a holy
border, or truth in man's natural principle, which is the ultimate
of order, may appear from other passages of the Word, as from
the following, speaking of the covenant between Laban and
Jacob : " Now go, let us make a covenant, I and thou, and let
it be for *a witness* between me and thee ; and Jacob took *a
stone, and set it up for a statue :* Laban said to Jacob, Behold
this heap, and *behold the statue* which I have set up between
me and thee ; this heap is *witness*, and this *statue is witness*, that
I will not pass over to thy heap, and that thou shalt not pass
over to me, this heap, and this *statue*, for evil," Gen. xxxi.
44, 45, 51, 52. That statue in this passage signifies truth,
will be seen in the explication of it. So in Isaiah, " In that
day shall there be five cities in the land of Egypt speaking with
the lips of Canaan, and swearing to Jehovah of Zebaoth : in
that day shall there be an *altar to Jehovah* in the midst of the
land of Egypt, and *a statue at the border thereof* to Jehovah ;
which shall be *for a sign* and *for a witness* to Jehovah of
Zebaoth in the land of Egypt," xix. 18, 19, 20. Egypt in
this passage denotes the scientifics appertaining to the natural
man ; altar denotes Divine Worship in general, for the altar
was made the primary representative of worship in the second
ancient Church which commenced from Eber, see n. 921, 1343,
2777, 2811 ; the midst of the land of Egypt denotes the primary and inmost principle of worship, see n. 2940, 2973, 3436;
statue denotes truth which is the ultimate of order in the
natural principle. That it is in the border, for a sign and for
a witness, is manifest. So in Moses, " Moses wrote all the
words of Jehovah, and arose in the morning, and built an *altar*
near Mount Sinai, and *twelve statues* for the twelve tribes of
Israel," Exod. xxiv. 4 ; where altar in like manner was representative of all worship, and indeed representative of good in
worship. That twelve denote all things of truth in one complex,
may be seen, n. 577, 2089, 2129, 2130, 3272 ; that the twelve
tribes in like manner denote all things appertaining to the truth
of the Church, will be shown, by the Divine Mercy of the Lord,
in the following chapter. Inasmuch as altars were representative of all the good of worship, and the Jewish Church was instituted that it might represent the celestial Church, which acknowledged no other truth than what was grounded in good.

which is called celestial truth (for it was not willing in the least
to separate truth from good, insomuch that it was not willing
to name any thing of faith or truth, unless it thought concerning good, and this by virtue of good, see n. 202, 337, 2069,
2715, 2718, 3246), therefore truth was represented by the
stones of the altar, and it was forbidden to represent it by
statues, lest thereby truth should be separated from good, and
should be representatively worshipped instead of good; wherefore
it is thus written in Moses, "Thou shalt not plant to thyself a
grove of any kind of tree near *the altar of Jehovah* thy God,
which thou shalt make to thyself, and *thou shalt not erect to
thyself a statue*, which Jehovah thy God hateth," Deut. xvi.
21, 22; for to worship truth separate from good, or faith separate from charity, is contrary to the Divine [principle], because
contrary to order, and this is signified by the prohibition, "Thou
shalt not erect to thyself a statue, which Jehovah thy God
hateth."   Nevertheless, that they did erect statues, and thereby
represented those things which are contrary to order, is manifest
from these words in Hosea, " Israel *multiplies altars* according
to the multiplying of his fruit, *they make goodly statues* according to the good of their land, but he will overturn *their altars;*
he will lay waste *their statues*," x. 1, 2.   So in the first book of
Kings, " Judah did evil in the eyes of Jehovah, and they built
to themselves high places, and *statues*, and groves, upon every
high hill, and under every green tree," xiv. 23.   And in the
second book of Kings, "The sons of Israel *set up for themselves
statues*, and groves, upon every high hill, and under every green
tree," xvii. 10.   Again, in the same book, " Hezekiah removed
the high places, and *brake the statues*, and cut down the groves,
and brake in pieces the brazen serpent which Moses had made,
because they burned incense to it," xviii. 4.   Inasmuch as the
Gentiles had a tradition amongst them, that the holy principle
of worship was represented by altars and by statues, and yet
they were in what was evil and false, therefore their altars signified evils of worship, and statues the false principles thereof, for
which reason, it was commanded that they should be destroyed,
as in Moses, " *Ye shall overthrow the altars of the nations, and
shall break in pieces their statues*, and shall cut down their groves,"
Exod. xxxiv. 13; Deut. vii. 5; chap. xii. 3.   Again, " Thou
shalt not bow thyself to the gods of the nations, and worship
them, neither shalt thou do according to their works, because
destroying thou shalt destroy them, and breaking in pieces
thou shalt break in pieces their statues," Exod. xxiii. 24.   The
gods of the nations denote false principles, their works denote
evils; to break in pieces their statues, is to destroy worship
grounded in what is false.   So in Jeremiah, " Nebuchadnezzar
king of Babylon *shall break in pieces the statues of the house
of the sun* in the land of Egypt, and shall burn with fire the

houses of the gods of Egypt," xliii. 13. And in Ezekiel,
" Nebuchadnezzar king of Babylon, by the hoofs of his horses,
shall tread down all thy streets, shall slay the people with the
sword, and shall cause *the statues of thy strength* to come down
to the earth," xxvi. 11 ; speaking of Tyre. Nebuchadnezzar
king of Babylon, denotes what causes vastation, see n. 1327 ;
the hoofs of the horses denote the lowest intellectual principle,
such as are scientifics grounded merely in the things of sense ;
that hoofs denote the lowest principles, by the Divine Mercy of
the Lord, will be confirmed elsewhere ; horses denote intellectual principles, see n. 2760, 2761, 2762 ; streets denote
truths, and in an opposite sense false principles, n. 2336 ; which
to tread down, is to destroy the knowledges of truth, which
are signified by Tyre ; that Tyre, which is the subject here
treated of, denotes the knowledges of truth, may be seen, n.
1201 ; to slay the people with the sword, denotes to destroy
truths by what is false. That people is predicated of truths,
may be seen, n. 1259, 1260, 3295, 3581, and that sword denotes
the false combating, n. 2779. Hence it is evident, what is meant
by causing the statues of strength to come down to the earth
that strength is predicated of what is true and of what is false
is also manifest from the Word.

3728. " And he poured oil upon the head of it"—that hereby
is signified holy good, appears from the signification of oil, as
denoting the celestial principle of love or good, see n. 886,
3009 ; and from the signification of head, as denoting that
which is superior, or, what is the same thing, that which is
interior. That good is a superior or interior principle, and
truth inferior or exterior, has been shown above in many places.
Hence it is evident what was signified by the ancient rite of
pouring oil on the head of a statue, namely, that truth should
not be without good, but grounded in good, thus, that good
should have dominion, as the head over the body ; for truth
without good is not truth, but is a mere sound void of life, and
such that it is self-dissipated. In another life also it is dissipated with those, who have been distinguished above others
for their knowledge of truth or of the doctrinals of faith, and
even of the doctrinals of love, if they have not lived in good,
and thus if they have not retained truth grounded in good.
Hence the Church is not a Church by virtue of truth separate
from good, consequently not a Church by virtue of faith separate from charity, but by virtue of truth which is grounded in
good, or by virtue of faith which is grounded in charity. The
like is also signified by what the Lord said to Jacob, " I am
the God of Bethel, where thou *anointedst a statue*, where thou
didst vow to Me a vow," Gen. xxxi. 13 ; and by Jacob again
" *setting up a statue, a statue of stone*, and offering a libation
upon it, and *pouring oil upon it*," Gen. xxxv. 14. By offering a

libation on a statue, is signified the Divine Good of faith, and by pouring oil upon it, the Divine Good of love. Every one may see, that to pour oil upon a stone, without a signification of somewhat celestial and spiritual, would be ridiculous and idolatrous.

3729. " And he called the name of the place Bethel"—that hereby is signified quality of state, appears from the signification of name and of calling a name, as denoting quality, see n. 144, 145, 1754, 1896, 2009, 2724, 3006, 3421 ; and from the signification of place, as denoting state, see n. 2625, 2837, 3356, 3387. The quality of the state is what is signified by Bethel. Bethel, in the original tongue, signifies the house of God, and that the house of God is good in the ultimate principle of order, may be seen, n. 3720.

3730. " But the name of the city was Luz at the first"— that hereby is signified the quality of the former state, appears from the signification of name, as denoting quality, see immediately above, n. 3729 ; and from the signification of city, as denoting a doctrinal of truth, see n. 402, 2268, 2449, 2712. 2943, 3216. Luz, in the original tongue, signifies recession, thus disjunction, which has place when doctrinals of truth, or truth itself, are exalted to pre-eminence, and good is neglected. thus when truth alone is in the ultimate of order. But when truth is together with good in the ultimate of order, in this case there is no recession or disjunction, but accession or conjunction ; this is the quality of state which is signified by Luz.

3731. Verses 20, 21, 22. *And Jacob vowed a vow, saying, If God shall be with me, and shall keep me in this way wherein I walk, and shall give me bread to eat and raiment to put on, and I shall return in peace to the house of my father, and Jehovah shall be to me for a God ; and this stone, which I have set for a statue, shall be the house of God ; and all that Thou shalt give me, I will in tithing tithe it to Thee.* Jacob vowed a vow, signifies a state of providence : If God shall be with me, and shall keep me in this way wherein I walk, signifies the Divine [principle] continual : and shall give me bread to eat, signifies even to conjunction with Divine Good : and raiment to put on, signifies conjunction with Divine Truth : and I shall return in peace to the house of my father, signifies even to perfect union : and Jehovah shall be to me for a God, signifies that the Divine natural principle should also be Jehovah : and this stone which I have set for a statue, signifies truth which is the ultimate principle : shall be the house of God, signifies here, as before, the Lord's kingdom in the ultimate of order, in which superior principles are as in their house : and all that Thou shalt give me, I will in tithing tithe it to Thee, signifies that He made all and singular things Divine by His own proper power.

3732. " Jacob vowed a vow"—that hereby is signified a state of providence, appears from the signification of vowing a vow, as denoting, in the internal sense, to will that the Lord may provide; hence, in the supreme sense, in which the Lord is treated of, denoting a state of providence. The reason why vowing a vow, in the internal sense, denotes to will that the Lord may provide, is grounded in this, that in vows there is a desire and affection, that what is willed may come to pass, thus that the Lord may provide. Somewhat also of stipulation is implied, and at the same time somewhat of debt on the part of man, which he engages to discharge in case he comes to possess the object of his wish, as in the present instance respecting Jacob, who vows that Jehovah should be to him for a God, and the stone which he set for a statue should be the house of God, and that he would tithe all that was given him, if Jehovah would keep him in the way, and would give him bread to eat, and raiment to put on, and if he should return in peace to the house of his father. Hence it is manifest, that vows at that time were their several obligations, particularly to acknowledge God to be their God, in case He should provide for them what they desired, and also to repay Him by some gift or present, if He so provided. From these considerations it is very evident, what was the real character or quality of the fathers of the Jewish nation, as here in respect to Jacob, that as yet he did not acknowledge Jehovah, and that as yet he was undetermined in his choice, whether he should acknowledge Him or another for his God. This was peculiar respecting that nation, even from the time of their fathers, that every one was desirous to have his own God, and if any worshipped Jehovah, it was only on account of his being called Jehovah, and thus being distinguished by name from the gods of other nations; thus their worship, even in this respect, was idolatrous, for the worship of a name alone, supposing it even to be the name of Jehovah, is nothing else but mere idolatry, see n. 1094. The case is the same with those who call themselves Christians, and say they worship Christ, and yet do not live according to His precepts. All such worship Him with idolatrous worship, because they worship His name alone, for it is a false Christ whom they worship, concerning which false Christ, see Matt. xxiv. 23, 24, n. 3010.

3733. "If God shall be with me, and shall keep me in the way wherein I walk"—that hereby is signified the Divine [principle] continual, appears from the signification of God being with any one, and keeping him in the way wherein he walks, as denoting the Divine [principle] continual; for it is predicated of the Lord, who as to the very essence of life was Jehovah; hence His whole life, from the first of infancy to the last, was the Divine [principle] continual, and this even to the perfect union of the human essence with the Divine.

3734. "And shall give me bread to eat"—that hereby is

signified even to conjunction with Divine Good, appears from the signification of bread, as denoting all celestial and spiritual good which is from the Lord, and in the supreme sense the Lord Himself as to Divine Good, see n. 276, 680, 1798, 2165, 2177, 3464, 3478; and from the signification of eating, as denoting to be communicated, appropriated, and conjoined, see n. 2187, 2343, 3168, 3513, 3596.

3735. "And raiment to put on"—that hereby is signified conjunction with Divine Truth, appears from the signification of raiment, as denoting truth, see n. 1073, 2576, in the present case Divine Truth, because the Lord is treated of; and from the signification of putting on, as denoting to be appropriated and conjoined. The nature and quality of the internal sense of the Word may appear from these and other particulars, in that whilst bread and raiment are treated of in the sense of the letter, and whilst it is expressed historically, as in the present case, "If God shall give me bread to eat, and raiment to put on," the angels attendant on man think not at all of bread, but of the good of love, and, in the supreme sense, of the Divine Good of the Lord; neither do they at all think of raiment, but of truth, and, in the supreme sense, of the Divine Truth of the Lord. The things appertaining to the literal sense are to them only objects of thinking concerning things heavenly and Divine; for such things are the vessels which are in the ultimate principle of order. Thus when man thinks, whilst he is under holy influence, concerning bread, as concerning the bread in the sacred supper, or concerning the daily bread spoken of in the Lord's prayer, in such case the thought which man has concerning bread, serves the attendant angels as an object of thinking concerning the good of love which is from the Lord; for the angels do not at all comprehend man's thought concerning bread, but instead thereof have thought concerning good, such being the correspondence; in like manner, when man under holy influence thinks about raiment, the thought of the angels is about truth; and so it is in all other instances which occur in the Word. Hence it may appear what is the nature and quality of the conjunction of heaven and earth effected by the Word, namely, that a man who reads the Word under holy influence, by such correspondences is conjoined closely with heaven, and by heaven with the Lord, although man thinks only of those things in the Word which appertain to its literal sense. The essentially holy principle which influences man on such occasion, is derived from an influx of celestial and spiritual thoughts and affections, such as exist with the angels. To the intent that such influx might have place, and thereby man might have conjunction with the Lord, the Holy Supper was instituted by the Lord, where it is said expressly that the bread and wine is the Lord, for the body of the Lord signifies His

Divine Love, and reciprocal love with man, such as exists with the celestial angels, and the blood in like manner signifies His Divine Love and reciprocal love with man, but such as exists with the spiritual angels. Hence it is manifest, how much of Divine principle there is in every particular of the Word, notwithstanding man's ignorance of its nature and quality. Nevertheless, such as have been principled in the life of good during their abode in the world, come into the knowledges and perception of all those particulars after death, when they put off terrestrial and worldly things, and put on celestial and spiritual, and in like manner are in a spiritual and celestial idea like the angels.

3736. "And I shall return in peace to the house of my father"—that hereby is signified even to perfect union, may appear from this consideration, that the house of my father, when it is predicated of the Lord, is the essential Divine [principle] in which the Lord was from conception, and to return to that house, is to return to the essential Divine Good, which is called Father: that this good is the Father, may be seen, n. 3704. Hence it may appear, that by returning to that house, is signified to be united to the Divine Good. The same was meant by the Lord when He said, that He came forth from the Father, and was come into the world, and that again He went to the Father; by coming forth from the Father is to be understood, that the essential Divine [principle] assumed the human [principle]; by coming into the world is to be understood, that He was as a man; and by going again to the Father, that He united the human essence to the Divine Essence. This was also meant by these words of the Lord in John, "If ye shall see the Son of Man ascending where He was before," vi. 62. And again, "Jesus knew that the Father had given Him all things into His hands, and that He came forth from God, and went to God," xiii. 3. Again, "Yet a little time I am with you; whither I go, ye cannot come," xiii. 33. Again, "Now I go away to Him who sent me, and none of you asketh Me, Whither goest Thou? It is profitable for you that I go away, for if I go not away, the Comforter will not come unto you; but if I go away, I will send Him unto you. A little while and ye shall not see Me, and again a little while and ye shall see Me, and because I go to the Father," xvi. 5, 7, 16, 17. Again, "I came forth from the Father, and am come into the world; again I leave the world, and go to the Father," xvi. 28. In these passages, to go to the Father is to unite the human essence to the Divine Essence.

3737. "And Jehovah shall be to me for a God"—that here is signified that the Divine natural [principle] was also Jehovah, may appear from the series of things treated of in the supreme internal sense, which respects the unition of the Lord's

Human [principle] with His Divine; but in order that this sense may appear, the thought must be abstracted from the historical relation concerning Jacob, and kept fixed in the Lord's Divine Human [principle], and in the present case in His Divine Natural [principle], which is represented by Jacob. The essential human [principle], as has been before observed, consists of the rational principle, which is the same as the internal man, and of the natural principle, which is the same as the external man, and also of the body, which serves the natural principle as a means or outermost organ of living in the world, and by the natural serves the rational principle, and moreover by the rational the Divine. Inasmuch as the Lord came into the world, that He might make the whole human [principle] in Himself Divine, and this according to Divine Order, and by Jacob is represented the Lord's natural principle, and by the life of His sojourning, in the supreme sense, how the Lord made His natural principle Divine, therefore here, where it is said, "If I shall return in peace to the house of my father, Jehovah shall be to me for a God," is signified the unition of the Lord's Human [principle] with His Divine, and that as to the Divine natural principle, He should also be Jehovah, by the unition of the Divine Essence with the human, and of the human with the Divine. This unition is not to be understood, as of two who are distinct from each other, and only conjoined by love, as a father with a son, when the father loves the son, and the son the father, or as when a brother loves a brother, or a friend a friend, but it is a real unition into one, so that they are not two but one, as the Lord also teaches in several places, and because they are one, therefore also the whole human [principle] of the Lord is the Divine Esse or Jehovah, see n. 1343, 1736, 2156, 2329, 2447, 2921, 3023, 3035.

3738. "And this stone which I have set for a statue"—that hereby is signified that truth which is the ultimate, appears from what was said above, n. 3724, 3726, where the same words occur.

3739. "Shall be the house of God"—that hereby is signified the Lord's kingdom in the ultimate of order, in which superior principles are as in their house, appears also from what was said above, n. 3720, where the same words also occur, and further from what was said, n. 3721. In respect to this particular, that superior principles are in the ultimate of order as in their house, the case is this: such an order has been instituted by the Lord, that superior principles flow into inferior, and therein present an image of themselves in general, consequently they are together therein in a certain general form, and thus in order from the Supreme, that is, from the Lord; hence it is, that the proximate image of the Lord is in the inmost heaven, which is the heaven of innocence and peace, where the celestial dwell ; this heaven, as being the nearest to the Lord, is called His likeness. The next heaven, namely, that which succeeds, and is in an inferior degree, is an image of the Lord, because in this heaven, as in a certain general principle, are together exhibited the things which are in the superior heaven. The last heaven, which succeeds this again, is similarly circumstanced, inasmuch as the particulars and singulars of the next superior heaven flow into this heaven, and therein are represented and exhibited in common, in a correspondent form. The case is similar in regard to man, for he was created and formed to be an effigy of the three heavens; the principle in him, which is inmost, flows in like manner into that which is inferior, and this in like manner into that which is lowest or last. The natural or corporeal principle consists of such influx and concourse of superior principles in those which are beneath, and finally in those which are last. Hence comes the connection of last principles with the first principle, without which connection that which is last in order would not subsist a single moment. From these considerations it is manifest what is meant by this proposition, that superior principles are in the ultimate principle of order as in their house. Whether we speak of superior and inferior principles, or of interior and exterior, it is the same thing, for to man's view interior principles appear to be superior, and for this reason man in his idea places heaven on high, or in that which is above, when nevertheless it is within, or in that which is internal.

3740. "And all that Thou shalt give me I will in tithing tithe it to Thee"—that hereby is signified that He made all and singular things Divine by His own proper power, appears from the signification of giving, when it is predicated of the Lord, as denoting that He gave to Himself, see n. 3705, thus that it was by His own proper power ; and from the signification of tithing, and of tithes, as denoting goods and truths, which are stored up from the Lord in man's interiors, which goods are called remains, see n. 576, 1738, 2280. When these are predicated of the Lord, they denote the Divine Goods and Divine Truths, which the Lord procured to Himself by His own proper power, see n. 1738, 1906.

A CONTINUATION OF THE SUBJECT CONCERNING THE GRAND MAN
AND CORRESPONDENCE THEREWITH.

3741. *THE kingdom of heaven resembles one man, because all and singular the things therein correspond to the only Lord, Who alone is Man, that is, to His Divine Human [principle], see n.* 49, 288, 565, 1894. *By virtue of such correspondence with the Lord, and by being an image and likeness of Him, heaven is called the* GRAND MAN. *From the Lord's Divine [principle] are derived all the celestial things which belong to good, and all the spiritual things which belong to truth, in heaven. All the angels are forms, or substances formed according to the reception of the Divine principles which come from the Lord. The Divine principles of the Lord received by the angels are what are called celestial and spiritual, wherein the Divine Life and the Divine Light thence derived exists and is modified, as in its recipients. Hence it is, that the forms and material substances appertaining to man are also of such a nature, but in an inferior degree, as being grosser and more composite. That these also are forms recipient of celestial and spiritual things, is very manifest from signs absolutely visible, as from thought, which flows into the organic forms of the tongue, and produces speech; from the affections of the mind, which present themselves visible in the face; and from the will, which by the muscular forms flows into actions, &c. Thought and will, which produce such effects, are spiritual and celestial principles, whereas the forms or substances which receive them, and put them into act, are material; that these latter were formed altogether for the reception of the former, is evident. Hence it is plain, that the latter are derived from the former, and that unless they were so derived, they could not possibly exist such as they are.*

3742. *That there is only one principle of life, and that it is from the Lord alone, and that angels, spirits, and men, are only recipients of life, has been made known to me by experience so manifold, as to leave not a shadow of a doubt concerning it. All heaven is in a perception that this is the case, insomuch that the angels manifestly perceive the influx, and also how it flows in, and likewise the quantity and quality of their reception. When they are in a fuller state of reception, they are then in their peace and felicity, otherwise they are in a state of restlessness and of some anxiety. Nevertheless life is appropriated to them from the Lord, so that they perceive that they live as it were of themselves, but yet know that it is not of themselves. The appropriation of the Lord's life is an effect of His mercy and love towards the universal human race, in that He is willing to give Himself, and what is His, to every one, and that He actually gives, so far as they receive; that is, so far as they are in the life of good and in the life of truth, as likenesses and images of Him. And whereas such a Divine effort proceeds continually from the Lord, therefore His life, as was said, is appropriated.*

3743. *But they who are not principled in love to the Lord, and in charity towards their neighbour, consequently who are not*

*in the life of good and of truth, cannot acknowledge that there
is only one principle of influent life, and still less that this life
is from the Lord. All such are indignant, yea, express their
aversion at hearing it said, that they do not live from themselves. It is self-love which causes such indignation and aversion; and what is wonderful, although it is shown them by
living experience in another life, that they do not live from
themselves, and although at the time they are convinced that
this is the case, yet afterwards they relapse into their former
opinions, and imagine, that if they lived from another, and not
from themselves, all the delight of their life would perish, not
being aware that the truth is directly the reverse. Hence it is,
that the wicked appropriate evil to themselves, because they do
not believe that evils are from hell, and that good cannot be appropriated to them, because they believe that good is from themselves, and not from the Lord. Nevertheless, the wicked, and
also those in hell, are forms recipient of life from the Lord, but
such forms, that they either reject, or suffocate, or pervert good
and truth; and thus goods and truths, which are derived from
the life of the Lord, become with them evils and falses. The
case herein is like that of the sun's light, which, although white
itself and the one only principle of light, is nevertheless varied
as it passes through, or flows into, various forms, and thence
produces all the varieties of colours, beautiful and delightful, as
well as those which are not beautiful and not delightful.*

*3744. Hence then it may appear what the nature and qua-
lity of heaven is, and from what ground it is that heaven is
called the* Grand Man. *The varieties, as to the life of good
and truth therein, are innumerable, and are according to the
reception of life from the Lord. These varieties have a relation
to each other, altogether similar to what subsists between the organs, members, and viscera in man; all which are forms in a
perpetual variety recipient of life from their soul, or rather by
their soul from the Lord, and yet notwithstanding such their
variety, they together constitute one man.*

*3745. How great the variety is in the life of good and truth,
and what is its nature and quality, may appear from the variety in the human body. It is a well known fact, that no two
organs and members are alike; for instance, that the organ of
sight is not like the organ of hearing; the same is true of the
organ of smelling, the organ of taste, and also the organ of
touch, which last is diffused throughout the whole body. So also
of the members; the arms, the hands, the loins, the feet, and the
soles of the feet. And so likewise of the viscera which lie hid
within, as those of the head, namely, the cerebrum, the cerebellum, the medulla oblongata, and the medulla spinalis, with all
the minute organs, viscera, vessels, and fibres of which they are
composed; also those appertaining to the body beneath the head.*

as the heart, the lungs, the stomach, the liver, the pancreas, the spleen, the intestines, the mesentery, and the kidneys; and likewise those which are appropriated to generation in both sexes. All and each of these, it is well known, are dissimilar in form and in function, and so much so as to constitute entire difference. In like manner, there are forms within forms, which also are of such variety, that no one form, nor even one particle thereof, is altogether like another, that is, so like, that it may be substituted in place of the other, without some, though, it may be, a very small alteration. These things all and each correspond to the heavens, but in such a manner, that the things in man which are corporeal and material, in heaven are celestial and spiritual; and they so correspond, that the material exist and subsist from the spiritual.

3746. In general all these varieties have reference to those things which belong to the head, to those which belong to the thorax, to those which belong to the abdomen, and to those which belong to the members of generation; in like manner to those things which are interior and which are exterior in each.

3747. I have occasionally discoursed with the spirits of the learned of the present age on this subject, observing to them that the distinction of man into internal and external is the only distinction they have any knowledge of, and that they know this, not from any reflection on the interior principles of thought and affection in themselves, but from the Word of the Lord; and that still they are ignorant what the internal man is, and that several even have doubts whether such a man exists, and also deny his existence, because they do not live the life of the internal man, but of the external; and that they are much seduced by the appearance respecting brute animals, in that they seem to have the same organs, viscera, senses, appetites, and affections as man. I observed further to them, that the learned know less of such subjects than the simple, and that still they seem to themselves to know much more; for they debate and dispute about the commerce of soul and body, yea, about the nature of the soul, what it is, when yet the simple know that the soul is the internal man, and that it is the spirit which is to live after the death of the body; also that it is the real man which is in the body. Moreover, that the learned, more than the simple, liken themselves to the brutes, and ascribe all things to nature, and scarce any thing to the Divine Being; and further, that they do not reflect that man, in distinction from other animals, has a capacity of thinking about heaven, and about God, and thereby of being elevated above himself, consequently of being joined to the Lord by love, and thus of necessarily living after death for ever. And that they are especially ignorant of the fact, that all and singular the things belonging to man depend on the Lord through heaven, and that heaven is the GRAND MAN, to

*which all and singular the things in man correspond, as do all
and singular the things in nature. And possibly, that when
they shall hear and read these observations, they will seem to
them like paradoxes, and unless established by experience, will
be rejected by them as visionary and fanciful. In like manner,
when they shall hear that there are three degrees of life in man,
as there are three degrees of life in the heavens, that is, three
heavens ; and that man so corresponds to the three heavens, as
to be himself, in image, a little heaven, when he is principled in
the life of good and truth, and by that life is an image of the
Lord. I have been instructed concerning these degrees of life,
that it is the last degree of life which is called the external or
natural man, by which degree man is like the animals as to concupiscences and phantasies. And that the next degree of life
is what is called the internal and rational man, by which man
is superior to the animals, for by virtue thereof he can think
and will what is good and true, and have dominion over the
natural man, by restraining and also rejecting its concupiscences, and the phantasies thence derived ; and moreover, by
reflecting within himself concerning heaven, yea, concerning the
Divine Being, which the brute animals are altogether incapable
of doing. And that the third degree of life is what is most unknown to man, although it is that through which the Lord flows
into the rational mind, thus giving man a faculty of thinking
as a man, and also conscience, and perception of what is good
and true, and elevation from the Lord towards Himself. But
these things are remote from the ideas of the learned of our age,
who only debate and dispute whether such things be ; and who,
so long as they do this, are incapable of knowing that they do
exist, and still less of knowing what they are.*

*3748. There was a certain spirit, who, during his abode in
the world, had gained great reputation amongst the vulgar for
his learning, being of a subtle genius in confirming false principles, but very dense and stupid in the confirmation of what is
good and true. This spirit imagined, as heretofore in the world,
that he knew every thing, for such spirits believe themselves to
be most wise, and that nothing is hid from their knowledge, and
such as they have been in the life of the body, such they remain
in another life ; for all things which belong to the life of any
one, that is, to his love and affection, follow him into another
world, and are in him as the soul is in the body, because he has
formed his soul, as regards its quality, from such things or principles. This spirit, I say, imagining himself to be possessed of
all knowledge, came to me and discoursed with me, and as I
was acquainted with his nature and quality, I asked him, Who
is most intelligent, a person who is acquainted with many false
principles, or a person who is acquainted with a small degree
of truth ? He replied, He who is acquainted with a small de-*

gree of truth. The reason of his giving this answer was, because he imagined that the false principles, with which he himself was acquainted, were truths, and that in consequence of them he was wise. He was afterwards desirous of reasoning about the GRAND MAN, and about the influx from it into all and singular the things of men on earth, but as he understood nothing about the matter, I asked him, how he conceived that thought, which is a spritual principle, moves the whole face, and exhibits therein its own expression or countenance; and also moves all the organs of speech, and this distinctly to the spiritual perception of such thought; and that the will moves the muscles of the whole body, and the thousands of fibres which are dispersed throughout it, to one action, when nevertheless the moving principle is spiritual, and that which is moved is corporeal? But he knew not what answer to give. I discoursed further with him concerning the nature of endeavour, asking him whether he knew that endeavour produces actions and motions, and that all action and motion contains endeavour, in order to its existence and subsistence? He replied, That he did not know this. Wherefore, he was then asked, How he could be desirous to reason, when he was not acquainted even with first principles, in which case reasoning must needs be like scattered dust with no coherence, which false principles dissipate in such a manner, that at length nothing is known, and consequently nothing believed.

3749. A certain spirit came to me unawares, and entered by influx into the head. Spirits are distinguished according to the parts of the body into which their influx is. I wondered who and whence he was, but after he had been silent for some time, the attendant angels said, that he was taken from the spirits attendant upon a certain learned person still living in the world, who had gained extraordinary reputation for his learning. Communication was instantly given by this intermediate spirit with the thought of that person. I asked the spirit, What idea this great scholar was enabled to form concerning the GRAND MAN, and concerning its influx and consequent correspondence? He said, That he could form no idea. He was next asked, What idea he had of heaven? He said, None at all. except a blasphemous one, in supposing that the inhabitants are always playing on musical instruments, such as the country people are wont to make a jingle with. Nevertheless, this person stands high in reputation, and it is believed that he knows the nature of the influx of the soul, and of its commerce with the body; possibly it is also believed, that he knows better than other men the nature of heaven. Hence it may appear, what sort of persons at this day teach others; those, namely, who, from mere scandals, oppose the goods and truths of faith, although they publish the contrary.

3750. What kind of idea of heaven they also have, who are

*believed to have more than ordinary communication therewith,
and influx thence, was also shown me to the life. They who
appear above the head, are those who in the world were desirous
to be worshipped as gods, and with whom self-love was exalted
to the utmost height, by degrees of power, and by a consequent
imaginary liberty ; they are also deceitful under an appearance
of innocence and love to the Lord. They appear on high above
the head from a phantasy of height, but still they are beneath
the feet in hell. One of these spirits let himself down to me ;
and it was told me by others, that in the world he had been a
pope. He discoursed with me in a mild engaging manner, and
first concerning Peter and his keys, which he imagined he himself was in possession of. When he was questioned concerning
the power of admitting into heaven whomever he pleased, he had
so gross an idea of heaven, that he represented a kind of a door
which gave entrance ; and he said, that he opened that door to
the poor gratis, but that the rich paid for admission according
to their ability, and that what they paid was holy. Being
asked, Whether he believed that the persons thus let into heaven
remained there ? he said, that he did not know ; only this, that
if they did not remain there, they went out again. It was
further told him, that he could not possibly know their inte
riors, whether they were worthy of heaven, and that he might
perhaps admit robbers, who ought to be in hell. To this he an
swered, That it was no concern of his whether they were worthy
or not, and that if they were not worthy, they might be let out
again. But he was instructed what is meant by Peter's keys,
to wit, faith grounded in love and charity ; and inasmuch as
the Lord alone gives such faith, therefore it is the Lord alone
who lets into heaven, and that Peter does not appear to any
one, he being a simple spirit, who has no more power than any
other person. His opinion respecting the Lord was this, that
He ought to be worshipped, so far as He gives such power, but in
case He does not give it, it was evident that he thought Him no
longer an object of worship. Moreover, in discoursing with
him concerning the internal man, he appeared to have filthy
ideas on the subject. What a liberty, fulness, and delight of
respiration he enjoyed, when he sat upon his throne in the Con-
sistory, and believed that he spake from the Holy Ghost, was
shown me to the life. He was let into a state similar to what
he had been in on such occasions (for in another life every one
may easily be let into the state of life which he had enjoyed
during his abode in the world, since the state of his life remains
with every one after death) ; and a respiration was communicated to me, such as he had at those times. It was free, and
attended with delight, slow, regular, deep, filling the breast, but
when he was contradicted, there was somewhat as it were rolling itself and creeping in the abdomen, arising from the con*

*tinuation of the respiration ; and when he imagined that what
he pronounced was Divine, he had a perception thereof from
the respiration being more tacit and as it were in agreement
therewith. It was afterwards shown me by whom such popes
are governed on these occasions, namely, by a crowd of sirens
who are above the head, who had contracted a nature and life
of insinuating themselves into all kinds of affections, with a
design of acquiring rule, and of subjecting others to themselves,
and of destroying whoever they can for the sake of themselves,
whilst holiness and innocence were used as means to effect their
purposes. They are afraid for themselves, and act cautiously,
but when occasion offers, and it will turn to their own account,
they are guilty of the most cruel and merciless atrocities*

GENESIS.

CHAPTER THE TWENTY-NINTH.

3751. BEFORE the preceding chapter, were explained the
things which the Lord predicted concerning the last time of the
Church, in Matthew, chap. xxiv. 15, 16, 17, 18. Following the
order of such explication, we shall now proceed to unfold before this chapter, the things which succeed in verses 19, 20, 21,
22, as expressed in these words: "*But wo unto them that are
with child, and to them that give suck in those days. And pray
ye that your flight be not in the winter, neither on the sabbath.
For then shall be great affliction, such as was not from the beginning of the world even until now, neither shall be. And
except those days should be shortened, no one would be saved ;
but for the elect's sake those days shall be shortened.*"

3752. What these words signify, it is impossible for any
one to comprehend, unless he be enlightened by the internal
sense. That they do not relate to the destruction of Jerusalem,
is manifest from several particulars in this chapter, as from
these words, "Except those days should be shortened, no flesh
would be saved, but for the elect's sake those days shall be
shortened ;" and from the following, "After the affliction of
those days the sun shall be darkened, and the moon shall not
give her light, and the stars shall fall from heaven, and the
virtues of the heavens shall be moved ; and then shall appear
the sign of the Son of Man, and they shall see the Son of Man
coming in the clouds of heaven with virtue and glory ;" the

same is manifest also from other passages. That neither do they relate to the destruction of the world, is also evident from several passages in the same chapter, as from that above explained, where it is said, " He that is on the house-top, let him not come down to take away any thing out of his house, and he who is in the field, let him not return back to take his garments ;" and also from this, " Pray ye that your flight be not in the winter, neither on the sabbath ;" and from the following, "Then two shall be in the field, the one shall be taken, the other left ; two shall be grinding at the mill, the one shall be taken, the other left." But it is evident that they relate to the last time of the Church, that is, to its vastation, which is then said to have place, when there is no longer any charity.

3753. Every one who thinks holily of the Lord, and who believes that the Divine was in Him, and that He spake from the Divine, may know and believe, that the above words, like the rest which the Lord taught and spake, were not spoken of one nation only, but of the universal human race ; and not of their worldly, but of their spiritual state ; and also, that the Lord's words comprehended the things belonging to His kingdom and to the Church, these being Divine and eternal. Whoever believes in this manner, must needs conclude that these words, " Wo to them that are with child, and to them that give suck in those days," do not signify those that are with child and give suck ; and that these words, " Pray ye that your flight be not in the winter, neither on the sabbath," do not signify any flight on account of worldly enemies ; and so in relation to the other passages.

3754. The subject treated of in the preceding verses was concerning three states of perversion of good and truth in the Church ; in the verses before us a fourth state is treated of, which is also the last. Concerning the first state, it has been already shown to consist in this, that the men of the Church began no longer to know what was good and true, but disputed with each other concerning good and truth, whence came falsities, see n. 3354. Concerning the second state, it was shown to consist in this, that they began to despise good and truth, and to hold them in aversion, and thus that faith in the Lord was about to expire, according to the degrees in which charity was about to cease, see n. 3487, 3488. Concerning the third state, it was shown to be a state of desolation in the Church as to good and truth, see n. 3651, 3652. The fourth state is now treated of, which is that of the profanation of good and truth. That this state is here described, may appear from all the particulars of the above passage in the internal sense, which sense is as follows.

3755. *But wo to them that are with child, and to them that give suck in those days,* signifies those who have imbibed the good of love to the Lord and the good of innocence. Wo is a form of expression signifying the danger of eternal damnation; *to be with child* is to conceive the good of heavenly love; *to give suck* denotes also a state of innocence; *those days* signify the states in which the Church then is. *But pray ye that your flight be not in the winter, neither on the sabbath,* signifies removal from those things, that it be not done precipitately in a state of too much cold, or in a state of too much heat. *Flight* denotes removal from a state of the good of love and innocence, just now spoken of; *flight in the winter,* denotes removal thence in a state of too much cold; cold signifies when there is aversion to those things occasioned by self-love; *flight on the sab bath,* denotes removal from them in a state of too much heat; heat signifies an external sanctity, when self-love and the love of the world are within. *For then shall be great affliction, such as was not from the beginning of the world even until now, neither shall be,* signifies the highest degree of perversion and vastation of the Church as to good and truth, which is profanation; for profanation of what is holy occasions death eternal and much more grievous than any other states of evil, and so much the more grievous, as the goods and truths profaned are of an interior kind; and as such interior goods and truths are open and known in the Christian Church, and are profaned, therefore it is said, that then shall be great affliction, such as was not from the beginning of the world even until now, neither shall be. *And except those days should be shortened, no flesh would be preserved; but for the elect's sake those days shall be shortened,* signifies the removal of those who are of the Church from interior goods and truths to exterior, so that they may still be saved who are in the life of good and truth; by the days being shortened, is signified a state of removal; by no flesh being preserved, is signified that otherwise none could be saved; by the elect, are signified those who are in the life of good and truth.

3756. That this is the internal sense of the above words, might be fully shown, for instance, that those who are with child signify those who first imbibe good; and those who give suck, signify those who imbibe innocence; and that flight denotes removal from good and innocence; flight in the winter, aversion to such goods by self-love possessing the interiors; and flight on the sabbath, profanation, which has place when there is holiness in externals, and self-love and the love of the world within. But as the same and similar expressions occur throughout in what follows, therefore, by the Divine Mercy of the Lord, their signification shall be shown to be such as is here pointed out, when we come to explain those expressions.

3757. But what is meant by the profanation of what is holy, **is** known to few; nevertheless it is apparent from what has been said and shown on the subject above, namely, that they may profane holy things, who know, and acknowledge, and imbibe good and truth, but not they who do not acknowledge, and still less they who do not know, see n. 593, 1008, 1010, 1059, 3398 ; consequently, that they who are within the Church may profane holy things, but not they who are without, n. 2051. That they who are of the celestial Church may profane holy goods, and that they who are of the spiritual Church may profane holy truths, n. 3399. That therefore interior truths were not discovered to the Jews, lest they should profane them, n. 3398. That the gentiles, of all other people, are least capable of profanation, n. 2051. That profanation is a commixture and conjunction of good and evil, also of truth and the false principle, n. 1001, 1003, 2426. That this was signified by the eating of blood, which was so severely prohibited in the Jewish Church, n. 1003. That therefore men are withheld, as far as is possible, from the acknowledgment and belief of good and truth, if they cannot continue therein, n. 3398, 3402 ; and that on this account they are kept in ignorance, n. 301, 302, 303 ; and that on this account also worship becomes external, n. 1327, 1328. That internal truths are not revealed before the Church is vastated, because in this case good and truth can no longer be profaned, n. 3398, 3399. That the Lord therefore first came into the world when this was the case, n. 3398. Concerning the great danger arising from the profanation of what is holy and of the Word, n. 551, 582.

CHAPTER XXIX.

1. AND Jacob lifted up his feet, and went to the land of the sons of the east.

2. And he saw, and behold a well in a field, and behold there three droves of a flock lying near it, because out of that well they made the droves drink ; and a great stone was on the mouth of the well.

3. And all the droves were gathered together thither, and they rolled away the stone from over the well's mouth, and made the flock drink, and they brought back the stone over the mouth of the well to its place.

4. And Jacob said to them, My brethren, whence are ye? and they said, We are from Haran.

5. And he said to them, Know ye Laban, the son of Nahor? and they said, We know.

6. And he said to them, Hath he peace? and they said, Peace, and behold, Rachel his daughter cometh with the flock.

7. And he said, Behold as yet the day is great, it is not time for the cattle to be gathered together : make the flock drink, and go ye, feed.

8. And they said, We cannot until all the droves are gathered together, and they roll away the stone from over the well's mouth, and we shall make the flock drink.

9. As yet he was speaking with them, and Rachel came with the flock, which was her father's, because she was a shepherdess.

10. And it came to pass, that Jacob saw Rachel the daughter of Laban, his mother's brother, and the flock of Laban his mother's brother, and Jacob came near, and rolled away the stone from over the well's mouth, and made the flock of Laban his mother's brother drink.

11. And Jacob kissed Rachel, and lifted up his voice, and wept.

12. And Jacob told Rachel, that he was her father's brother, and that he was the son of Rebecca ; and she ran, and told her father.

13. And it came to pass, as Laban heard the report of Jacob his sister's son, he ran to meet him, and embraced him, and kissed him, and brought him to his house, and he told to Laban all those words.

14. And Laban said unto him, Surely thou art my bone and my flesh, and he dwelt with him a month of days.

15. And Laban said to Jacob, Because thou art my brother shouldest thou therefore serve me for nought? tell me, what shall be thy reward?

16. And Laban had two daughters, the name of the elder was Leah, and the name of the younger Rachel.

17. And Leah's eyes were weak, and Rachel was beautiful in form, and beautiful in aspect.

18. And Jacob loved Rachel, and said, I will serve thee seven years for Rachel thy younger daughter.

19. And Laban said, It is better that I should give her to thee, than give her to another man ; abide with me.

20. And Jacob served for Rachel seven years, and they were in his eyes as some days in his loving her.

21. And Jacob said to Laban, Give my woman, because the days are fulfilled, and I will come to her.

22. And Laban gathered together all the men of the place, and made a feast.

23. And it was in the evening, and he took Leah his daughter, and brought her to him, and he came to her.

24. And Laban gave her Zilpah, his handmaid, an handmaid to his daughter Leah.

25. And it was in the morning, and behold it was Leah ; and he said to Laban. What is this that thou hast done to me ?

Did I not serve with thee for Rachel? and why hast thou defrauded me?

26. And Laban said, It is not so done in our place, to give the younger in birth before the first-born.

27. Fulfil this week, and we will give thee her also, for the service which thou shalt serve with me as yet seven other years.

28. And Jacob did so, and fulfilled this week, and he gave him Rachel his daughter for a woman to him.

29. And Laban gave to Rachel his daughter Bilhah his handmaid to be to her for an handmaid.

30. And he came also to Rachel, and he loved also Rachel better than Leah, and served with him as yet seven other years.

31. And Jehovah saw that Leah was hated, and He opened her womb, and Rachel was barren.

32. And Leah conceived, and brought forth a son, and called his name Reuben, for she said, Jehovah hath seen my affliction, because now my man [vir] will love me.

33. And she conceived as yet, and brought forth a son, and said, Because Jehovah hath heard that I was hated, and hath given me this also, and she called his name Simeon.

34. And she conceived as yet, and brought forth a son, and said, Now this time my man [vir] will adhere to me, because I have borne him three sons, therefore she called his name Levi.

35. And she conceived as yet, and brought forth a son, and said, This time I will confess Jehovah, therefore she called his name Judah, and she stood still from bringing forth.

THE CONTENTS.

3758. THE subject treated of in this chapter is concerning the Lord's natural principle, represented by Jacob, how the good of truth was therein conjoined with kindred good from a Divine origin, which good is Laban; at first by the affection of external truth, which is Leah, and next by the affection of internal truth, which is Rachel.

3759. Afterwards by the birth of the four sons of Jacob from Leah is described, in the supreme sense, the ascent from external truth to internal good; but in the representative sense is described the state of the Church, which is such, that it does not acknowledge and receive internal truths, which are in the Word, but external truths; and this being the case, that it ascends to interior things according to this order, namely, its first principle is truth which is said to be of faith; next, exercise according to such truth; afterwards charity derived from that truth; and lastly celestial love. These four degrees are signified by the four sons of Jacob born of Leah, namely, by Reuben, Simeon, Levi, and Judah.

THE INTERNAL SENSE.

3760. VERSE 1. *AND Jacob lifted up his feet, and went to the land of the sons of the east.* Jacob lifted up his feet, signifies elevation of the natural principle: and went to the land of the sons of the east, signifies to truths of love.

3761. "Jacob lifted up his feet"—that hereby is signified elevation of the natural principle, appears from the significa tion of lifting up, as denoting elevation; and from the significa tion of feet, as denoting the natural principle, of which we shall speak presently. The elevation, which is here signified, is that treated of in this chapter, which is from external truth to inter nal good; in the supreme sense, how the Lord elevated His natural principle even to the Divine, according to order, ascending from external truth by degrees to internal good; and in the representative sense, how the Lord makes new man's natural principle, in the course of regeneration, according to a similar order. That the man, who in adult age is regenerated, advances according to the order described in this and the following chapters in the internal sense, is known to few; the reason is, because few reflect upon it, and also because few at this day can be regenerated, for these are the last times of the Church, when there is no longer any charity, consequently no longer any faith, and this being the case, it is not known what faith is, although every one says that man is saved by faith; hence it is still less known what charity is, and since these two principles are known only by name, and unknown as to essence, it is on this account said, that few reflect upon the order according to which man is made new, or is regenerated, and also that few at this day can be regenerated. The subject here treated of being concerning the natural principle, and this being represented by Jacob, it is not said that *he arose,* and went to the land of the sons of the east, but that he lifted up his feet; each expression signifies elevation. That to arise has this signification, may be seen, n. 2401, 2785, 2912, 2927, 3171. The reason why mention is here made of lifting up the feet, is, because it has respect to the natural principle, for feet signify the natural principle, see n. 2162, 3147. The reason why feet signify the natural principle, or natural principles, is from correspondence with the GRAND MAN, of which some account has been given at the close of the preceding chapters, in which GRAND MAN, they who appertain to the province of the feet, are such as are in natural light, and but little in spiritual; from the same ground also it is, that the parts under the feet, as the soles and the heels, signify the lowest natural principle, see n. 259; and hence the shoe, which is also occasionally mentioned in the Word, signifies the natural corporeal principle, which is the ultimate, see n. 1748.

3762. "And went to the land of the sons of the east"— that hereby is signified to truths of love, namely, elevation thereto, appears from the signification of the sons of the east. That Aram, or Syria, was called the land of the sons of the east, is manifest, because thither Jacob betook himself, see n. 3249. That by Syria in general are signified the knowledges of good, was shown, n. 1232, 1234, but specifically by Aram Naharaim, or Syria of rivers, are signified the knowledges of truth, n. 3051, 3664; but here it is not said that he went to Aram, or Syria, but to the land of the sons of the east, in order to signify what is treated of in this chapter throughout, namely, ascent to the truths of love. Those are called truths of love which were elsewhere termed celestial truths, being knowledges respecting charity towards our neighbour and love to the Lord; in the supreme sense, in which the Lord is treated of, they are truths of Divine Love. Those truths, namely, which respect charity towards our neighbour, and love to the Lord, must be learned, before man can be regenerated, and must also be acknowledged and believed, and so far as they are acknowledged, believed, and imbibed in the life, so far also man is regenerated, and in such case they are so far implanted in man's natural principle as in their proper ground. They are implanted in this ground first by instruction from parents and masters, next by the Word of the Lord, afterwards by man's own reflection about them, but hereby they are only stored up in the natural memory, and have their place therein amongst other knowledges; nevertheless, they are not acknowledged, believed, and imbibed, unless the life be formed according to them, for in this case man comes into the affection thereof, and so far as he comes into the affection thereof grounded in the life, so far they are implanted in his natural principle as in their proper ground. The truths, which are not thus implanted, are indeed with man, but only in his memory, as somewhat of mere knowledge, or as historical facts, which conduce to no other end than to talk about, and thereby acquire reputation, and by such reputation to be advanced to wealth and dignity; but in this case they are not implanted. That the land of the sons of the east signifies the truths of love, thus the knowledges of truth which tend to good, may appear from the signification of sons, as denoting tr ths, see n. 489, 491, 533, 1147, 2623 ; and from the signification of east as denoting love, see n. 101, 1250, 3249. Their land denotes the ground in which they are. That the sons of the east denote those who are principled in the knowledges of truth and good, consequently who are principled in truths of love, may appear also from other passages in the Word, as in the first book of Kings, "The wisdom of Solomon was multiplied *more than the wisdom of all the sons of the east*, and than all the wisdom of the Egyptians," v. 10 ; where the wisdom of the sons of the east signifies interior knowledges of truth and good, thus those who are principled therein ; but the wisdom of the Egyptians signifies the science of the same knowledges, which is in an inferior degree. That Egyptians signify scientifics in general, may be seen, n. 1164, 1165, 1462. So in Jeremiah, "Thus saith Jehovah, Arise ye, go up against Kedar, lay waste *the sons of the east*, let them take their tents and their flocks, also their curtains and all their vessels, and let them take their camels," xlix. 28. That the sons of the east here mean those who are in the knowledges of good and truth, is manifest from this consideration, that they were to take their tents and flocks, also their curtains and all their vessels, and likewise their camels, for tents signify the holy things of good, see n. 414, 1102, 2145, 2152, 3312 ; flocks, the goods of charity, n. 343, 2566 ; curtains, holy truths, n. 2576, 3478 ; vessels, truths of faith and scientifics, n. 3068, 3079 ; camels, scientifics in general, n. 3048, 3071, 3143, 3145. Thus sons of the east signify those who are in these things, that is, who are in the knowledges of good and truth. That the wise men from the east, who came to Jesus at His birth, were of those who were called the sons of the east, may appear from the fact, that they had the knowledge that the Lord was about to be born, and that they were acquainted with His coming by a star, which appeared to them in the east, concerning whom it is thus written in Matthew, "When Jesus was born in Bethlehem of Judea, behold *wise men from the east* came to Jerusalem, saying, Where is He that is born King of the Jews ? for we have seen His star in the east, and are come to worship Him," ii. 1, 2. That amongst the sons of the east, who were of Syria, such prophetic knowledge had existed from ancient times, is manifest from Balaam's prophecy concerning the Lord's coming, as it is thus written, "I see Him, and not now ; I behold Him, and not nigh ; *a star shall arise* out of Jacob, and a sceptre shall rise up out of Israel," Numb. xxiv. 17. That Balaam was from the land of the sons of the east, or from Syria, is plain from these words, "Balaam uttered his enunciation, and said, Balak hath brought me from *Syria, out of the mountains of the east*," Numb. xxiii. 7. Those wise men, who came to Jesus at

His birth, are called magi, but so were wise men called at that
time, as is evident from several passages, as Gen. xli. 8; Exod.
vii. 11; Dan. ii. 27; iv. 3, 4; 1 Kings v. 10; and from the prophets
throughout. That sons of the east, in an opposite sense, signify
the knowledges of what is evil and false, thus those who are
principled therein, appears from Isaiah, "The rivalship of
Ephraim shall depart, and the enemies of Judah shall be cut
off; they shall fly on the shoulders of the Philistines toward
the sea, and at the same time shall plunder *the sons of the
east*," xi. 14. So in Ezekiel, "Against the sons of Ammon,
behold I have delivered thee up to *the sons of the east* for an
inheritance, and they shall place thy ordinances in thee," xxv.
4, 10. And in the book of Judges, "When Israel sowed, and
Midian, and Amalek, and *the sons of the east* came up, and ascended over him," vi. 3; where Midian denotes those who are
principled in what is false, because not in good of life, see n
3242; Amalek denotes those who are in false principles, which
are opposed by truths, n. 1679; the sons of the east denote
those who are in the knowledges of what is false.

3763. Verses 2, 3. *And he saw, and behold a well in a
field, and behold there three droves of a flock lying down near
it, because out of that well they made the droves drink, and a
great stone was on the mouth of the well. And all the droves
were gathered together thither, and they rolled away the stone
from over the well's mouth, and made the flock drink, and they
brought back the stone over the mouth of the well to its place.*
He saw, signifies perception: behold a well, signifies the Word
in a field, signifies the Churches : and behold there three droves
of a flock lying down near it, signifies the holy things of
Churches and of doctrinals : because out of that well they
made the droves drink, signifies that thence was science : and
a great stone was on the mouth of the well, signifies that it
was closed : and all the droves were gathered together thither,
signifies that all Churches and their doctrinals were thence
derived : and they rolled away the stone from over the well's
mouth, signifies that they unclosed it : and made the flock
drink, signifies that thence was doctrine : and they brought
back the stone over the mouth of the well to its place, signifies
that meanwhile it was closed.

3764. "He saw"—that hereby is signified perception, appears
from the signification of seeing, as denoting to perceive, concerning which, more will be said in what follows in this chapter, verse 32, treating of Reuben, who was so named from seeing.

3765. "Behold a well"—that hereby is signified the Word,
appears from the signification of well, as denoting the Word,
and also doctrine derived from the Word, see n. 2702, 3096,
3424. The Word is here called a well, because the subject
treated of is concerning the natural principle, which considered

in itself apprehends the Word only as to the literal sense; whereas the Word is called a fountain when the rational principle is treated of, by which the Word may be perceived according to the internal sense.

3766. "In a field"—that hereby is signified for the Churches, appears from the signification of field, as denoting the Church in respect to good, see n. 2971. The Church, in the Word, is signified by land, by ground, and by field, but with a difference.' The reason why field denotes the Church, is, because the Church as a field receives the seeds of good and truth, for the Church is in possession of the Word, from whence those seeds are received; hence also it is, that whatever is in a field signifies also somewhat appertaining to the Church, as sowing, reaping, ripe corn, wheat, barley, &c., and this also with a difference.

3767. "And behold there three droves of a flock lying down near it"—that hereby are signified the holy things of Churches and doctrinals, appears from the signification of three, as denoting what is holy, see n. 720, 901; and from the signification of droves of a flock, as denoting those things which appertain to the Church, thus denoting doctrinals; specifically, flock signifies those who are within the Church, and learn and imbibe the good things of charity and the truths of faith, and in this case a shepherd signifies one who teaches such things; but in general, flock signifies all those who are principled in good, thus who belong to the Lord's Church in the universal orb of earths; and inasmuch as all these are by doctrinals introduced into good and truth, therefore also by flock are signified doctrinals; for the things which form man to such and such principles, and the man himself who is formed to such and such principles, are understood, in the internal sense, by the same expression; for the subject, which is man, is understood from that principle by virtue whereof he is man; hence it is, that it has been occasionally observed, that names signify things, and also signify those to whom such things appertain; as for instance, Tyre and Zidon signify the knowledges of good and truth, and they also signify those who are principled in such knowledges; in like manner Egypt signifies science, and Ashur reasoning, but at the same time they are applied to denote those who are principled in science and reasoning, and so in other cases. Speech therefore in heaven amongst the angels is expressed by things without an idea of persons, thus by universals, and this by reason that thus they comprehend things innumerable, but especially by reason of their attributing all good and truth to the Lord, and to themselves nothing, in consequence whereof the ideas of their speech are not determinate but to the Lord alone. From these considerations then it is evident, from what ground it is that flock is said to signify Churches, and also doctrinals. Droves of a flock are said to lie down near the

well, because doctrinals are derived from the Word. That
well denotes the Word, was said just above, n. 3765.

3768. "Because out of that well they made the droves
drink"—that hereby is signified that thence, namely, from the
Word, was science, appears from the signification of well, as
denoting the Word, see just above, n. 3765; and from the
signification of making to drink, as denoting to be instructed,
see n. 3069; and from the signification of droves, as denoting
the science of doctrinals, see also above, n. 3767. Hence it is
evident, that by making the droves drink out of the well, is
signified, that the science of the doctrinals of good and truth
is derived from the Word. In what now follows concerning
Jacob, in the supreme sense, the Lord is treated of, how He
made His natural principle Divine, and in this chapter is described the initiation; and in the internal representative sense
the regenerate are treated of, how the Lord renews their natural
man, and in this chapter is described the initiation into such
renewal; therefore the subject here treated of is concerning
the Word, and concerning doctrine thence derived, for by doctrine derived from the Word is effected such initiation and regeneration. And inasmuch as these things are signified by a
well and by three droves of a flock, therefore a well and three
droves of a flock are mentioned historically, which would have
been too trifling to have been mentioned in the Divine Word,
unless they had signified such things. What is implied herein,
may be very evident, namely, that all science and doctrine of
good and truth is derived from the Word. The natural man
indeed may know, and also perceive, what is good and true,
but only natural and civil good and truth, but he cannot know
what spiritual good and truth is, for the knowledge of this can
only come from revelation, or from the Word. For example,
a man may know by virtue of the rational principle common
to all, that his neighbour ought to be loved, and that God ought
to be worshipped; but how his neighbour is to be loved, and
how God is to be worshipped, can be known only from the
Word, thus what is spiritually good and true can only be
known thence; as for instance, that God Himself is man's
Neighbour, consequently they who are principled in good, and
this according to the good in which they are principled; and
that good is man's neighbour on this account, because that in
good the Lord is, and thus in the love of good the Lord is
loved. In like manner, they who have not the Word, cannot
know that all good is from the Lord, and that it enters into
man by influx, and causes the affection of good, and that this
affection is called charity; neither can it be known, without
the Word, who is the God of the universe, and that the Lord
is that God must be concealed from those who have not the
Word, when yet the inmost principle of affection or charity,

consequently the inmost of good, ought to have respect to Him. Hence it is evident, what spiritual good is, and that it can be known only from the Word. With regard to the Gentiles, so long as they are in the world they do not indeed know this, but still, whilst they live in mutual charity with each other, they acquire thereby the faculty of knowing, so that in another life they are capable of being instructed on such subjects, and also of easily receiving and imbibing instruction, see n. 2589 to 2604.

3769. "And a great stone was over the well's mouth"—that hereby is signified that it was closed, namely, the Word, may appear without explication. The Word is said to be closed, when it is understood only as in the sense of the letter, and when all is assumed for doctrine which is contained in the letter. And it is still more closed, when those things are acknowledged as doctrinals, which favour the lusts of self-love and the love of the world, for these especially roll a great stone over the mouth of the well, that is, close up the Word; and in this case, as mankind do not know, so neither are they desirous to know, that any interior sense is contained in the Word, when nevertheless they may see this from several passages, where the sense of the letter is unfolded according to the interior sense; and also from the doctrinals received in the Church, to which by various explications they refer all the sense of the letter of the Word. What is meant by the Word being closed, is especially apparent from the Jews, who explain all and singular things therein according to the letter, and thence believe that they are the elect in preference to all nations on the face of the earth, and that the Messiah will come to introduce them into the land of Canaan, and exalt them above all nations and peoples of the earth; for they are immersed in terrestrial corporeal loves, which are of such a nature as altogether to close up the Word as to things interior. Therefore also they do not as yet know whether there be any heavenly kingdom, whether they shall live after death, what the internal man is, nor even that there is any such thing as a spiritual principle; still less do they know that the Messiah came to save souls. That the Word is closed up in regard to them, is abundantly apparent also from this consideration, that although they live amongst Christians, still they do not at all receive their doctrinals; according to what is written in Isaiah, " Say to this people, Hearing, hear ye, and do not understand; and seeing, see ye, and do not know. Make the heart of this people fat, and their ears heavy, and besmear their eyes. And I said, Lord, how long? And He said, Until the cities are wasted, until there be no inhabitant, and the house until there be no man, and the ground be wasted to a desert," vi. 9, 10, 11; Matt. xiii. 14, 15; John xii 40, 41. So far as man is immersed in self-love and the love of the world, and in the lusts

thereof, so far the Word is closed up to him, for those loves
have self for an end, which end kindles a natural lumen, but
extinguishes heavenly light, so that men in such case see acutely
the things which are of self and the world, and not at all the
things which are of the Lord and His kingdom; and when this
is the case, they may indeed read the Word, but then it is with
a view to gain honour and wealth, or for appearance sake, or
from custom, and a habit of reading thence acquired, or from
a principle of piety, and still not with a view to amend the life.
To such persons the Word is closed in different manners; to
some so far that they have no desire at all to know any thing
but what their doctrinals dictate, of whatever kind they be.
For example: should any one assert, that the power of opening
and shutting heaven was not given to Peter, but that it was
given to faith originating in love, which faith is signified by
Peter's keys, inasmuch as self-love and the love of the world
oppose such an assertion, they in no wise acknowledge it to be
true. And should any one assert, that saints ought not to be
worshipped, but the Lord alone, neither do they receive this. Or
should any one assert, that the bread and wine in the Holy
Supper means the Lord's love towards the universal human race
and the reciprocal love of man to the Lord, this they do not
believe. Or further, should any one assert, that faith is of no
avail, unless it be the good of faith, that is, charity; this they
explain inversely, and so in other cases. They who are such,
cannot at all see, nor be willing to see the truth which is in the
Word, but abide obstinately in their particular tenets; and are
not even willing to hear that there is an internal sense, wherein
the sanctity and glory of the Word consist; yea, when they
are told that it is so, they nauseate the bare mention of it from
the aversion they have to hear it. Thus the Word is closed up,
when yet it is such in its own nature as to be open into heaven,
and through heaven to the Lord, and is only closed up in respect
to man, so far as he is immersed in evils of self-love and the
love of the world as to the ends of this life, and in false principles thence derived. Hence it is apparent what a great stone
being over the well's mouth means.

3770. "And thither all the droves were gathered together"
—that hereby is signified that all Churches and their doctrinals
are thence derived, appears from the signification of droves, as
denoting Churches, and also the doctrinals which are of the
Churches, see above, n. 3767, 3768. That these are from the
Word, is signified by being gathered together thither.

3771. "And they rolled away the stone from over the well's
mouth"—that hereby is signified that they unclosed it, appears
from what was said above, n. 3769, concerning the signification
of a great stone over the well's mouth, as denoting that the
Word was closed up. Hence it is evident, that their rolling

away the stone from over the well's mouth, signifies that they unclosed it.

3772. " And made the flock drink"—that hereby is signified that doctrine was thence, appears from the signification of making to drink, as denoting to instruct, see n. 3069, 3768; and from the signification of flock, as denoting those who are principled in the goods and truths of faith, see n. 343, 3767. Thus to make the flock drink, is to instruct out of the Word, consequently it is doctrine.

3773. "And they brought back the stone over the mouth of the well to its place"—that hereby is signified that meanwhile it was closed up, appears from what has been said, n. 3769, 3771, concerning the stone over the well's mouth. In respect to this circumstance, that the Word is unclosed to the Churches, and afterwards that it is closed up, the case is this. In the beginning, when any Church is established, the Word is at first closed to the men thereof, and afterwards unclosed, the Lord so providing, and hence they learn, that all doctrine is founded on these two precepts, that the Lord is to be loved above all things, and their neighbour as themselves. When these two precepts are regarded as the end, then the Word is unclosed, for all the law and the prophets, that is, the whole Word, depend on them, insomuch that all things are therein grounded, and have reference thereto. And whereas in this case the men of the Church are in the principles of truth and good, they are enlightened in all and singular the things which they see in the Word, for the Lord by His angels is in such case present with them, and teaches them, although they do not know it, and also leads them into the life of truth and good. This may also appear from the examples of all Churches, in that they were such in their infancy, that they worshipped the Lord from a principle of love, and loved their neighbour from the heart. But in process of time, Churches remove themselves from these two precepts, and turn aside from the good of love and charity to those things which are said to be of faith, thus from life to doctrine, and so far as they do this, so far the Word is closed. This is what is signified in the internal sense by these words, " Behold a well in a field, and behold there three droves of a flock lying down near it, because out of that well they made the droves drink, and a great stone was upon the mouth of the well ; and thither all the droves were gathered together, and they rolled away the stone from over the well's mouth, and made the flock drink, and they brought back the stone over the well's mouth to its place."

3774. Verses 4, 5, 6. *And Jacob said unto them, My brethren, whence are ye ? And they said, We are from Haran. And he said unto them, Know ye Laban the son of Nahor? And they said, We know. And he said unto them, Hath he peace? And they said, Peace, and behold, Rachel his daughter cometh with the flock.* Jacob said unto them, signifies truth of good: My brethren, whence are ye? signifies charity there from what origin? and they said, We are from Haran, signifies from good of a common stock: and he said unto them, Know ye Laban the son of Nahor? signifies whether or no they have good of his stock: and they said, We know, signifies affirmation: and he said unto them, Hath he peace? signifies is not that from the Lord's kingdom: and they said, Peace, signifies affirmation: and behold, Rachel his daughter, signifies the affection of interior truth: cometh with the flock, signifies interior doctrinals.

3775. "Jacob said unto them"—that hereby is signified the truth of good, appears from the representation of Jacob, as denoting the Lord's Divine natural principle, concerning which see above. Inasmuch as all and singular things, wherever they be, have relation to good and truth, see n. 3166, 3513, 3519, so also have those which are in the natural principle; and whereas good and truth in the natural principle, during man's regeneration, is in a different state in the beginning from what it is in the progress and the end, therefore Jacob represents the natural principle as to good and truth according to the state, in the present case, as to truth of good. But to explain minutely these various things in every case, would be only to render them more obscure, especially with those who have not a distinct idea respecting truth and good, and still less respecting truth as productive of, and as produced from, good.

3776. "My brethren, whence are ye?"—that hereby is signified charity there, from what origin? appears from the signification of brethren, as denoting those who are principled in good, and thence denoting good itself, consequently charity, see n. 367, 2360, 3303, 3459; and from the signification of the word, "whence are ye?" as denoting from what origin? From this case it is also evident, that what in the sense of the letter implies inquiry, and is determined to persons, in the internal sense falls into an idea undetermined to any person; for the historicals of the letter become annulled in heaven with the angels, when they leave man and enter heaven. Hence it may appear how the case is in regard to Jacob's question to the men of Haran, "My brethren, whence are ye?" as signifying charity there, from what origin? The case herein is this. Charity, which appears as charity in its external form, is not always charity in its internal form. Its quality and its origin is known from its end. Charity, which comes from a selfish or worldly end, is not charity in its internal form, neither ought it to be called charity; but charity, which regards for its end the neighbour, the general good, the Lord's kingdom, and thus the Lord Himself, is essential charity, and has in it an affection of doing good from the heart, and thence a delight of life, which in another life becomes eternal blessedness. It is of the utmost importance to know this, in order that man may know what the Lord's kingdom in Himself is. Inquiry respecting this charity, or, what is the same thing, respecting this good, is the subject now treated of in these verses; and here it is first inquired, from what origin was charity there, which is signified by these words, " My brethren, whence are ye?"

3777. " And they said, We are from Haran"—that hereby is signified from good of a common stock, appears from the signification of Haran as denoting collateral good of a common stock, see n. 3612.

3778. " And he said unto them, Know ye Laban the son of Nahor?"—that hereby is signified whether they had the good of his stock, appears from the representation of Laban, as denoting collateral good of a common stock, see n. 3612, 3665; and from the representation of Nahor, as denoting that common stock, from which the good represented by Laban was derived; that to know, in the internal sense, denotes to be from thence, is manifest from the series. How the case is in respect to the representation of collateral good by Nahor, Bethuel, and Laban, it may be expedient briefly to explain. Terah, who was the father of three sons, namely, of Abram, Nahor, and Haran, see Gen. xi. 27, represents the common stock from which the Churches were derived; Terah himself indeed was an idolater, but representatives regard only things and not persons, see n. 1361. Now whereas the representative Jewish Church commenced in Abraham, and was renewed amongst his posterity descended from Jacob, therefore Terah and his three sons put on a representation of Churches. Abram put on a representation of a genuine Church, such as exists amongst those who have the Word; whereas Nahor his brother put on a representation of a Church such as exists amongst the Gentiles who have not the Word. That the Lord's Church is spread throughout the globe, and exists also amongst the Gentiles who live in charity, is manifest from what has been shown throughout respecting the Gentiles. Hence then it is, that Nahor, his son Bethuel, and Bethuel's son Laban, represented collateral good of a common stock, that is, good in which they are, who belong to the Lord's Church amongst the Gentiles. This good differs in this respect from good of a common stock, derived in a right line of descent, that they who are in it have no genuine truths to conjoin with it, but that most of the conjoined truths are the external appearances, which are called the fallacies of the senses, for these persons are not in possession of the Word whereby they may be enlightened. Good indeed in its essence is simply one, but receiving its quality from the truths implanted in it, it thereby becomes various. The truths, which appear as truths to the

Gentiles, are in general such as teach the worship of one God, and that He is to be looked to as the giver of good, and all good attributed to Him, and so long as they live in the world, they do not know that this God is the Lord. Their apparent truths also teach them to adore their God under images, which they account holy; with many particulars besides. Nevertheless, these apparent truths are no hindrance to their being saved like Christians, provided they live in love to their God, and in love towards their neighbour; for hereby they have the faculty of receiving interior truths in another life, see n. 932, 1032, 1059, 2049, 2051, 2284, 2589 to 2604, 2861, 2863, 3263. Hence it is evident what is meant by collateral good of a common stock. That Nahor represents those out of the Church, who are in a brotherhood by virtue of good, may be seen, n. 2863, 2864, 2868; that Bethuel represents good of the Gentiles of the first class, n. 2865, 3665; and that Laban represents the affection of external or corporeal good, and properly collateral good of a common stock, see n. 3612, 3665. With respect to this good the case is, that first of all it is serviceable to man for procuring to himself spiritual good, it being external-corporeal, and grounded in external appearances, which in reality are fallacies of the senses. In childhood, man acknowledges no other good to be true and good, and although he is taught what internal good and truth is, still he has no idea thereof but what is corporeal; and inasmuch as his first idea thereof is such, therefore such good and truth is the first whereby interior truths and goods are introduced. This is the arcanum which is here represented by Jacob and Laban.

3779. "And they said, We know"—that hereby is signified affirmation, may appear without explication.

3780. "And he said unto them, Hath he peace?"—that hereby is signified is not that good derived from the Lord's kingdom, appears from the signification of peace, of which we shall speak presently. In the historical sense, inquiry is made concerning Laban, whether he has peace, but in the internal sense, it is concerning the good which is represented by Laban. That Laban denotes collateral good of a common stock, that is, such good as exists amongst the Gentiles, who are in the general Church, that is, in the Lord's kingdom, may be seen just above, n. 3778. Hence it is evident what is signified by the words, is it not of the Lord's kingdom? In regard to peace, it signifies, in the supreme sense, the Lord Himself, and thence, in the internal sense, His kingdom, and is the Lord's Divine [principle] inmostly affecting the good in which they of His kingdom are principled. That this is the signification of peace in the Word, may appear from several passages, as in Isaiah, " Unto us a child is born, unto us a Son is given, upon Whose shoulder is the government; and His name shall be called

Wonderful, Counsellor, God, Hero, the Father of Eternity, *the Prince of Peace.* To Him that multiplieth government and *peace* there shall be no end upon the throne of David, and upon his kingdom," ix. 5, 6 ; where Prince of Peace manifestly means the Lord, and He that multiplieth government and peace denotes the things which are in His kingdom, thus His kingdom itself. Again, " The work of righteousness shall be *peace,* and the labour of righteousness *rest* and *security* for ever ; and My people shall dwell *in an habitation of peace,*" xxxii. 17, 18 ; speaking of the Lord's kingdom, where peace, rest, and security succeed each other ; an habitation of peace denotes heaven. Again, " *The angels of peace* weep bitterly ; the paths are laid waste, he that passeth the way hath ceased," xxxiii. 7, 8. Angels of peace denote those who are in the Lord's kingdom, thus the kingdom itself, and, in the supreme sense, the Lord ; the paths being laid waste, and he that passeth the way ceasing, signifies, that there is no longer any truth in any place. That paths and ways denote truths, see n. 627, 2333. Again, " How delightful upon the mountains are the feet of Him that preaches good tidings, *that causeth to hear peace,* that saith to Zion, Thy King reigneth," lii. 7 ; where he that preaches good tidings, and causeth to hear peace, denotes the Lord's kingdom. Again, "The mountains shall recede, and the hills shall be removed, but My mercy shall not recede from being with thee, *and the covenant of My peace* shall not be removed," liv. 10. Again, " *The way of peace* have they not known, neither is there judgment in their goings," lix. 8. So in Jeremiah, " I will take away my peace from this people, saith Jehovah, even loving kindness and mercy," xvi. 5. Again, " *The folds of peace* are wasted because of the burning of Jehovah," xxv. 37. Again, " The prophet who *prophesieth concerning peace,* when the Word of Jehovah cometh the prophet shall be known, that Jehovah hath sent him," xxviii. 9. Again, " I know the thoughts which I think over you, saith Jehovah, *thoughts of peace,*" xxix. 11. So in Haggai, " The glory of this latter house shall be greater than of the former, for in this place *I will give peace,*" ii. 9. And in Zechariah, " They shall be *a seed of peace,* the vine shall give its fruit, and the earth shall give its produce, and the heavens shall give their dew," viii. 12. So in David, " Keep integrity, and see what is right, because *at last man hath peace,*" xxxvii. 37. And in Luke, " Jesus saith to His disciples, Whatsoever house ye enter, first say, *Peace be to this house ;* and if the *son of peace* be there, *your peace* shall rest upon it ; but if not, it shall return upon you," x. 5, 6. And in John, "*Peace* I leave with you, *My peace* I give unto you ; not as the world giveth, give I unto you," xiv. 27. Again, "Jesus said, These things have I spoken unto you, that *in Me ye may have peace,*" xvi. 33. In all these passages, peace, in the supreme sense, signifies the Lord; and in the representative sense it signifies His kingdom, and good from the Lord therein, thus the Divine principle which flows into good or the affection of good, which also causes joys and happiness from the inmost. Hence it is manifest what these words of the benediction mean: "Jehovah shall lift up His faces to thee, and *shall set peace for thee*," Numb. vi. 26; and what the salutation used of old, *Peace be unto you;* and the same salutation addressed by the Lord to the Apostles, John xx. 19, 21, 26. See also what is said concerning peace, n. 92, 93, 1726, 2780, 3170, 3696.

3781. "And they said, Peace"—that hereby is signified affirmation, may appear without explication, for it is an affirmative reply.

3782. "And behold, Rachel his daughter"—that hereby is signified the affection of interior truth, appears from the representation of Rachel, as denoting the affection of interior truth; and of Leah, as denoting the affection of exterior truth, of which we shall speak presently.

3783. "Cometh with a flock"—that hereby are signified interior doctrinals, appears from the signification of flock, as denoting the Church and also doctrinals, see n. 3767, 3768, 3772, in the present case interior doctrinals, because it is said of Rachel, that she came with a flock.

3784. Verses 7, 8. *And he said, Behold, as yet the day is great, it is not time for the cattle to be gathered together: make ye the flock drink, and go ye, feed. And they said, We cannot until all the droves are gathered together, and they roll away the stone from over the well's mouth, and we shall make the flock drink.* He said, Behold, as yet the day is great, signifies that now the state was advancing: it is not time for the cattle to be gathered together, signifies that the goods and truths of the churches and of doctrinals could not as yet be gathered into one: make ye the flock drink, and go ye, feed, signifies instruction nevertheless thence derived to a few: and they said, We cannot until all the droves be gathered together, signifies that they ought to be together: and they roll away the stone from over the well's mouth, signifies that thus the things of the Word are discovered: and we shall make the flock drink, signifies that in this case they are instructed.

3785. "He said, Behold, as yet the day is great"—that hereby is signified that the state was now advancing, appears from the signification of day, as denoting state, see n. 23, 487, 488, 493, 893, 2788, 3462. That *Behold it is yet great*, denotes advancing, is evident from the series.

3786. "It is not time for the cattle to be gathered together" —that hereby is signified that the goods and truths of the Churches and of doctrinals could not yet be gathered into one, appears from the signification of time, as denoting state in

general, see n. 2625, 2788, 2837, 3254, 3356; and from the signification of being gathered together, as denoting to be in one;
and from the signification of cattle, as denoting in general the
goods and truths of Churches and of doctrinals.　The ground
and reason why cattle in general have this signification, is, because animals in the rituals of the representative Church, and
in the Word, denote the affections of good or truth, as may
appear from what has been shown above, n. 45, 46, 142, 143,
246, 714, 715, 2679, 2697, 2979, 3203, 3502, 3508, 3510, 3665,
3699, 3701.　The case is the same in general with the Church
at its establishment; the doctrinals of good and truth must first
be collected into one, for these are the things on which it is
built.　Doctrinals have also a connection with, and mutual
respect to, each other, and therefore unless they are first collected into one, there will be a defect, which defect must be
supplied by man's rational principle, and how blind and fanciful this is, in things spiritual and divine, whilst its conclusions
are from itself, has been abundantly shown above.　On this
account the Word, which contains all the doctrinals of good
and truth, was given to the Church.　In this the Church in
general is circumstanced as the Church in particular with the
regenerate man, for such a man is a Church in particular.
That the doctrinals of good and truth, which belong to the
Church, must needs first be together in man before he is regenerated, has been shown above.　This then is what is signified
in the internal sense by these words, " Behold, as yet the day
is great, it is not time for the cattle to be gathered together."

3787. " Make ye the flock drink, and go ye, feed"—that
hereby is signified instruction nevertheless thence derived to a
few, appears from the signification of making the flock drink.
as denoting to instruct out of the Word, see n. 3772; and from
the signification of the words, " Go ye, feed," as denoting life
and doctrine thence derived.　That going denotes life, see n.
3335, 3690; and that feeding denotes doctrine, see n. 343, and
what follows.　The arcanum which here lies hid, is, that there
are few who ever arrive at a full state (concerning which state
see n. 2636), and thus who can be regenerated.

3788. " And they said, We cannot, until all the droves are
gathered together"—that hereby is signified that they ought to
be together, appears from the signification of gathering, as denoting to be made into one, or to be together, as above, n.
3786; and from the signification of droves, as denoting doctrinals, see n. 3767, 3768.　What these words imply, may appear
from what was said above, n. 3786, 3787.

3789. " And they rolled away the stone from over the well's
mouth"—that hereby is signified that thus the things appertaining to the Word are discovered, appears from the signification
of rolling away the stone, as denoting to be discovered, see n.

3769, 3771, 3773 ; and from the signification of well, as denoting the Word, see n. 3424, 3765.

3790. "And we shall make the flock drink"—that hereby is signified that in this case they are instructed, appears from the signification of making the flock drink, as denoting to instruct, see n. 3772, 3787. This is also evident from what goes before.

3791. Verses 9, 10, 11. *As yet he was speaking with them, and Rachel came with the flock, which was her father's, because she was a shepherdess. And it came to pass that Jacob saw Rachel the daughter of Laban his mother's brother, and the flock of Laban his mother's brother, and Jacob came near, and rolled away the stone from over the well's mouth, and made the flock of Laban his mother's brother drink. And Jacob kissed Rachel, and lifted up his voice, and wept.* As yet he was speaking with them, signifies thought on the occasion: and Rachel came with the flock, signifies the affection of interior truth appertaining to the Church and doctrine : which was her father's, signifies from good as to origin : because she was a shepherdess, signifies that the affection of interior truth teaches what is in the Word : and it came to pass that Jacob saw Rachel the daughter of Laban his mother's brother, signifies the acknowledgment of the affection of that truth from what origin it was : and the flock of Laban his mother's brother, signifies the Church and doctrine thence derived : and Jacob came near, and rolled away the stone from over the well's mouth, signifies that the Lord from natural good has opened the Word as to its interior contents : and he made the flock of Laban his mother's brother drink, signifies instruction : and Jacob kissed Rachel, signifies love towards interior truths : and lifted up his voice and wept, signifies the ardor of love.

3792. "As yet he was speaking with them"—that hereby is signified thought on the occasion, appears from the signification of speaking in the historical parts of the Word, as denoting to think, see n. 2271, 2287, 2619. That it was thought on that occasion, is evident, because at the very time when he was speaking with them, or, what is the same thing, whilst he was yet speaking with them, Rachel came.

3793. "And Rachel came with a flock"—that hereby is signified the affection of interior truth appertaining to the Church and doctrine, appears from the representation of Rachel, as denoting the affection of interior truth ; and from the signification of flock, as denoting the Church and also doctrine, see n. 3767, 3768, 3783. For the better comprehending the case of the representation of Rachel, as denoting the affection of interior truth, and of Leah, as denoting the affection of exterior truth, it may be expedient to make a few observations on the subject. The natural principle, which is represented by

Jacob, consists of good and truth, and in this principle, as in all and singular the things in man, yea in universal nature, there ought to be a marriage of good and truth. Without the marriage of good and truth nothing is produced, all production and all effect being thence derived. In the natural principle in man at his birth, the marriage of good and truth does not exist, because man alone is not born into Divine order; there is indeed the good of innocence and charity, which in first infancy flows in from the Lord, but there is no truth with which that good may be connected. As he advances in years, this good, which in infancy was insinuated into him from the Lord, is drawn in towards the interiors, and is there kept by the Lord, as a means whereby the states of life, which he afterwards puts on, may be tempered. Hence it is, that man, without the good of his infancy and of his first childhood, would be worse and more fierce than any wild beast. When this good of infancy is drawn in, then evil succeeds and enters into man's natural principle, with which evil the false principle connects itself, occasioning a conjunction, and, as it were, a marriage in him of evil and the false. In order, therefore, that man may be saved, he must be regenerated, and evil must be removed, and good from the Lord insinuated, and according to the good which he receives, truth is insinuated into him, for the purpose of effecting the coupling, or, as it were, the marriage of good and truth. These are the things which are represented by Jacob, and by his two wives Rachel and Leah. Jacob therefore now puts on the representation of natural good, and Rachel the representation of truth; but whereas all conjunction of truth with good is wrought by affection, it is the affection of truth about to be connected with good which Rachel represents. Moreover, in the natural principle, as in the rational, there is an interior and exterior principle; Rachel represents the affection of interior truth, and Leah the affection of exterior truth. Laban, who is their father, represents good of a common stock, but collateral good, as was said, which good is that which in a collateral line corresponds to the truth of the rational principle, which is Rebecca, see n. 3012, 3013, 3077. Hence the daughters of that good represent the affections in the natural principle, for these are like daughters of that good as a father. And as these affections are to enter into connection with natural good, they represent the affections of truth; one the affection of interior truth, and the other the affection of exterior truth. With respect to the regeneration of man as to his natural principle, the case is altogether the same as with Jacob and the two daughters of Laban, Rachel and Leah. Whoever, therefore, is able to see and apprehend the Word here according to its internal sense, sees this arcanum discovered to him. No one, however, can see this, but he who is in good and truth. Whatever perception others may have of the things relating to moral and civil life, and however intelligent they may thus appear, they can still see nothing of this sort so as to acknowledge it, for they do not know what good and truth is, imagining evil to be good, and what is false to be truth, wherefore the very instant good is mentioned, an idea of evil is presented to them, and the very instant truth is mentioned, there is presented an idea of what is false; hence it is, that they perceive nothing of what is contained in the internal sense of the Word, but on the first hearing a darkness arises, which extinguishes the light.

3794. "Which was her father's"—that hereby is signified from good as to origin, appears from the representation of Laban, who is the father, as denoting collateral good of a common stock, see n. 3612, 3665, 3778; and also from the signification of father, as denoting good, see n. 3703.

3795. "Because she was a shepherdess," or one that feedeth --that hereby is signified that the affection of interior truth teaches what is in the Word, appears from the signification of shepherd, or one that feedeth, as denoting one who leads and teaches, see n. 343; and from the representation of Rachel, who in the present case is *she*, as denoting the affection of interior truth, see above, n. 3793. The reason why it is said, *in the Word*, is, because she came to the well with the flock; and that the well denotes the Word, may be seen, n. 3765. Moreover, it is the affection of interior truth which teaches; for by virtue of that affection, a Church is a Church, and a shepherd a shepherd. The ground and reason why shepherd, or one that feeds, in the Word, signifies those who lead and teach, is, because flock signifies those who are led and taught, consequently it signifies Churches, and also doctrines of the Church, see n. 3767, 3768, 3783. That shepherd and flock have such a signification, is well known in the Christian world, for so they who teach and learn are named, and therefore it is needless to prove this from the Word.

3796. "And it came to pass, that Jacob saw Rachel, the daughter of Laban his mother's brother"—that hereby is signified the acknowledgment of the affection of that truth from what origin it was, appears from the signification of seeing, as here denoting to acknowledge, as is evident from the series; and from the representation of Rachel, as denoting the affection of interior truth, see above, n. 3793. The daughter of Laban his mother's brother, implies its origin, namely, that it was from collateral good, which was joined in brotherhood with rational truth represented by Rebecca, the mother of Jacob. With respect to the affections of truth and good, the case is this: genuine affections of truth and good, which are perceived by man, are all from a Divine origin, because from the Lord, but in the way, as they descend, they part into various and diverse streams, and there form to themselves new sources, for as they flow into affections not genuine and spurious, and into affections of what is evil and false in man, they receive this variation. In the external form, these various and diverse affections resemble such as are genuine, but in the internal form it is otherwise. The single character, by which they are distinguished, is from their end; if they have their end in self or the world, then those affections are not genuine, but if they have their end in neighbourly good, in the good of societies, in the good of country, and especially in the good of the Church, and the good of the Lord's kingdom, in this case they are genuine, for they have a view to the Lord, inasmuch as the Lord is in those goods. It is therefore the part of a wise man to know the ends by which he is governed. Sometimes it appears as if his ends were selfish, when yet they are not so; for man is of such a nature, that in all and singular things he reflects upon himself, and this from custom and habit: but if any one is desirous to know the ends by which he is influenced, let him attend only to the delight which he perceives in himself as arising from praise and self-glory, and to the delight which he perceives as arising from use separate from self; if he perceives this latter delight, he is then in genuine affection. He should also attend to the various states in which he is, for states themselves for the most part vary the perception. These things man may examine in himself, but in others he cannot, for the ends of every one's affection are known to the Lord alone. Hence it is that the Lord said, " Judge not, lest ye be judged; condemn not, lest ye be condemned," Luke vi. 37; for a thousand persons may appear to be in a like affection as to truth and good, and yet each may be in a different affection as to origin, that is, as to end. The ground and reason why the nature and quality of affection is to be determined by the end, and why it is accordingly either genuine, or spurious, or false, is, because man's ruling end is his essential life, for man respects as an end what belongs to his life, or, what is the same thing, to his love. When the good of his neighbour, the general good, the good of the Church, and of the Lord's kingdom, is the end regarded, in this case man, as to his soul, is in the Lord's kingdom, for the Lord's kingdom is nothing else but a kingdom of ends and uses respecting the good of the human race, see n. 3645. The very angels attendant on man have their abode solely in his ends of life. So far as man has respect to an end of the same kind as influences the Lord's kingdom, so far the angels are delighted with him, and join themselves to him as a brother; but so far as man is influenced by selfish ends, so far the angels recede and evil spirits from hell accede, for in hell none but selfish ends have rule. From these considerations it may appear how important it is for every one to examine and know the source of his affection, which can only be known from its end.

3797. "And the flock of Laban his mother's brother"—that hereby is signified the Church, and doctrine thence derived, appears from the signification of flock, as denoting the Church and doctrine, see n. 3767, 3768, 3783. The reason why here also Laban is called his mother's brother, is, because thereby is likewise signified acknowledgment in respect to origin, as just above.

3798. "And Jacob came near and rolled away the stone from over the well's mouth"—that hereby is signified that the Lord by virtue of natural good has uncovered the Word as to things interior, appears from the representation of Jacob, as denoting the Lord's Divine Natural, in the present case denoting the good therein ; and from the signification of rolling away the stone from over the well's mouth, as denoting to uncover the Word as to its interior contents, see n. 3769, 3771, 3773, 3789. The reason why the supreme internal sense here is, that the Lord by virtue of natural good uncovered the Word as to things interior, is, because Jacob here represents good in the natural principle, for Jacob puts on the representation of good, inasmuch as now truth was to be adjoined thereto by the affection which Rachel represents, see above, n. 3775, 3793, and because by virtue of good the Word is uncovered as to its interiors, see n. 3773. That the Word is uncovered by virtue of good, is very manifest; since every one, by virtue of the love in which he is, sees the things of that love, and what he sees he calls truths, because they are agreeable to that love. There is in every one's love the light of his life, for love is like a flame from which light issues ; such therefore as the love or flame is, such is its light of truth. They who are in the love of good are enabled to see the things of that love, consequently the truths which are in the Word, and this according to the measure and quality of their love of good; for in this case, light or intelligence flows from heaven, that is, through heaven from the Lord. Hence it is that, as was said above, no one can see and acknowledge the interior things of the Word, unless he be in good as to life.

3799. "And he made the flock of Laban his mother's brother drink"—that hereby is signified instruction, appears from the signification of making the flock drink, as denoting instruction, concerning which see n. 3772. The reason why Laban is here a third time called his mother's brother, is, because it points out the origin from which was derived the flock and Rachel, that is, the doctrine and affection of interior truth.

3800. "And Jacob kissed Rachel"—that hereby is signified love towards interior truths, appears from the signification of kissing, as denoting unition and conjunction from affection, concerning which see n. 3573, 3574, consequently denoting love, because love considered in itself is unition and conjunction from affection ; and from the representation of Rachel, as denoting the affection of interior truth, see n. 3793. Hence it is manifest, that Jacob kissing Rachel signifies love towards interior truths.

3801. "And lifted up his voice and wept"—that hereby is signified the ardor of love, appears from the signification of lifting up the voice and weeping, as denoting the ardor of love; for weeping has relation both to sorrow and to love, and denotes the highest degree of each.

3802. Verses 12, 13. *And Jacob told Rachel that he was her father's brother, and that he was the son of Rebecca ; and she ran and told her father. And it came to pass, as Laban heard the report of Jacob his sister's son, he ran to meet him, and embraced him, and kissed him, and brought him to his house, and he told to Laban all those words.* And Jacob told Rachel that he was her father's brother, signifies the affinity of the good which is Jacob, and of the good which is Laban : and that he was the son of Rebecca, signifies conjunction of affinities : and she ran and told her father, signifies acknowledgment by interior truths : and it came to pass, as Laban heard the report of Jacob his sister's son, signifies the acknowledgment of good which had affinity : he ran to meet him, signifies agreement : and embraced him, signifies affection : and kissed him, signifies initiation : and brought him to his house, signifies conjunction : and he told to Laban all those words, signifies from truths.

3803. "And Jacob told Rachel that he was her father's brother"—that hereby is signified the affinity of the good which is Jacob, and of the good which is Laban, appears from the signification of telling, as denoting to make known; and from the representation of Jacob, as denoting good, concerning which see above; and from the represenation of Rachel, to whom it was made known, as denoting the affection of interior truth, see n. 3793 ; and from the signification of brother, who is here Jacob, as denoting good, see n. 367, 2360, 3303, 3459 ; and from the signification of father, who is here Laban, as also denoting good, see n. 3703. Hence, and from the series, it is evident, that Jacob telling Rachel that he was her father's brother signifies the affinity of the good which is Jacob, and of the good which is Laban. But to explain the affinity itself, and thence the conjunction of each by the affection of interior truth, which is Rachel, would be to make the thing more obscure, since few know what the good of the natural principle is, and that this good is distinct from the good of the rational principle, and what the collateral good of a common stock is, and also what the affection of interior truth is. He who has not acquired to himself some idea concerning these several principles by his own investigation, receives but a faint, if any, idea from a description; for a man receives only so much from others, as he either has of his own, or acquires to himself by the examination of a thing in himself: the overplus passes away. It is enough to know, that there are innumerable affinities of good and truth, and that the heavenly societies are arranged according to them, see n. 685, 917, 2739, 3612. The reason why Jacob calls himself the brother of Laban, when yet he was his sister's son, is, because all are brethren by virtue of good; hence also it is, that Laban in his turn calls Jacob brother, verse 15. It is good which constitutes the principle of consanguinity, and which effects conjunction; for good is of love, and love is spiritual conjunction. It was from this ground that in the ancient Churches all they, who were in good, were called brethren, and so even in the Jewish Church; but inasmuch as the men of this latter Church esteemed all others vile in comparison with themselves, and conceived themselves alone to be the elect, they therefore called only those brethren who were born Jews, and all others they distinguished by the name of companions or strangers. The primitive Christian Church also called all brethren who were in good, but afterwards only those who were within the pale of their own congregation. Nevertheless, the name of brother at length was lost amongst Christians together with good, and when truth succeeded in the place of good, or faith in the place of charity, then they were not capable any longer of calling each other brethren from a principle of good, but they adopted the term neighbour. It is also a sure effect of the doctrine of faith without charity, that with those who are therein, brotherhood with one lower than themselves seems to be beneath them; for brotherhood with them does not derive its origin from the Lord, nor consequently from good, but from themselves, and consequently from honour and gain.

3803½. "And that he was the son of Rebecca"—that hereby is signified conjunction of affinities, may appear without explication; for it was Rebecca, who was the mother of Jacob, and the sister of Laban, from whom the conjunction was derived.

3804. "And she ran and told her father"—that hereby is signified acknowledgment by interior truths, appears from the signification of running and telling, as denoting the affection of making known, in the present case from acknowledgment; and from the signification of her father, as denoting the good which is Laban. That the acknowledgment was by interior truths, is represented by Rachel, who is the affection of interior truth Hence it comes that these words signify acknowledgment by interior truths. The case herein is this : the good which Jacob represents, which is the good of the natural prin ciple, like all good in general, is known and acknowledged as to its existence, but not as to its quality, except by truths ; for good receives its quality from truths, and thus by truths is known and acknowledged. Good does not become the good which is called the good of charity, until truths are implanted in it, and it receives a quality according to the quality of the implanted truths. Hence it is, that the good of one person, although it appears exactly like that of another, in reality is not so, for from this ground, the good of all and singular the persons in the universe must necessarily differ. The case here- in is the same as that of human faces, wherein the affections for the most part are portrayed, in that no two are exactly alike throughout the whole human race. Essential truths con- stitute as it were the face of good, the beauty of which is from the form of truth, but what affects is good. Such are all angel- ical forms, and such would man be, if from interior life he were in love to the Lord, and in charity towards his neighbour. He was created into such forms, because he was created into the likeness and image of God ; and such forms are they who are regenerated, as to their spirits, however they appear as to the body. Hence it may be evident what is meant by good being acknowledged by interior truths.

3805. "And it came to pass as Laban heard the report of Jacob his sister's son"—that hereby is signified the acknow- ledgment of good which had affinity, appears in like manner from what results from the signification of these words in the internal sense ; it is reciprocal acknowledgment which is thus described. The subject here treated of, as is evident, is con- cerning the election of good, which election precedes the mar- riage of good and truth.

3806. "And ran to meet him"—that hereby is signified agreement, appears from the signification of running to meet, as denoting agreement, for it has respect to the conjunction which is next treated of. Agreement or similitude, as is well known, conjoins.

3807. "And embraced him"—that hereby is signified affec- tion, appears from the signification of embracing, as denoting affection ; for interior affection falls into that gesture, every affection having gestures in the body corresponding to it. That affection in general is attended with embracing, is a well known fact.

3808. "And kissed him"—that hereby is signified initiation, appears from the signification of kissing, as denoting conjunc- tion from affection, see n. 3573, 3574, 3800 ; in the present case, denoting initiation into that conjunction, for initiation is pre- ceding conjunction.

3809. " And brought him to his house"—that hereby is signified to conjunction, appears from the signification of bringing to a house as denoting to himself, for man himself, in the internal sense, is called a house, see n. 3128, 3142, 3538 ; and this from the principle of good, which properly is a house, see n. 2233, 2234, 3652, 3720 ; in the present case therefore to the good which is represented by Laban ; wherefore by bringing to his house is here signified conjunction.   In this passage, in the internal sense, is fully described the process of the conjunction of natural good which is Jacob, with collateral good which is Laban.   The five particulars which constitute this process, are mutual acknowledgment, agreement, affection, initiation, and conjunction.   Mutual acknowledgment was signified by Rachel's running and telling her father, and by Laban's hearing the report of Jacob his sister's son, see n. 3804, 3805 ; agreement was signified by Laban's running to meet him, see n. 3806 ; affection by Laban's embracing him, n. 3807 ; initiation by kissing him, n. 3808 ; and conjunction by bringing him to his house, which is the subject here treated of.

3810. " And he told to Laban all these words"—that hereby is signified from truths, namely, that acknowledgment, agreement, affection, initiation, and conjunction were grounded therein, appears from the series of things treated of, and also from the words explained according to the internal sense whereof this is the closing period.   See what was said above, n. 3804.

3811. Verses 14, 15. *And Laban said unto him, Surely thou art my bone and my flesh.   And he dwelt with him a month of days.   And Laban said unto Jacob, Because thou art my brother, shouldest thou therefore serve me for nought ? tell me what shall be thy reward.*   Laban said unto him, Surely thou art my bone and my flesh, signifies conjoined as to truths and as to goods : and he dwelt with him a month of days, signifies a new state of life : and Laban said unto Jacob, Because thou art my brother, signifies because they have consanguinity grounded in good : shouldest thou serve me for nought ? tell me what shall be thy reward, signifies that there should be a means (or medium) of conjunction.

3812. " Laban said unto him, Surely thou art my bone and my flesh"—that hereby is signified conjoined as to truths and as to goods, appears from the signification of the words, "Thou art my bone and my flesh," as denoting conjunction.   The ancients applied this form of speaking to those who were of one house, or of one family, or in some relationship, my bone and my flesh, see n. 157.   Hence it is that these words signify conjunction.   The reason why it is as to truths and as to goods, is, because all spiritual conjunction is effected by those principles, and all natural conjunction has relation to the same.   Moreover, bone and flesh signify man's proprium; bone, his intellectual proprium, and flesh, his will proprium; thus bone, proprium as to truth, for this is of the intellect; and flesh, proprium as to good, for this is of the will, see n. 148, 149. As concerns proprium in general, it is two-fold, the one infernal, the other celestial. Man receives the infernal proprium from hell, and the celestial proprium from heaven, that is, through heaven from the Lord; for all evil, and every false principle thence derived, flows-in from hell; and all good, and truth thence derived, flows-in from the Lord. That this is the case, is known to man from the doctrine of faith, but scarce one in ten thousand believes it. Hence it comes, that man appropriates to himself, or makes his own, the evil which flows-in from hell, and that the good, which flows-in from the Lord, does not affect him, consequently is not imputed to him. The reason why man does not believe that evil flows-in from hell, and good from the Lord, is, because he is in self-love, which love is attended with this principle of unbelief, insomuch that it is exceedingly indignant when it hears it asserted, that every thing is the effect of influx. Hence then it is, that all man's proprium is nothing but evil, see n. 210, 215, 694, 731, 874, 875, 876, 987, 1023, 1044, 1047. But the reason why man believes that evil is from hell, and good from the Lord, is, because he is not in self-love, but in love towards his neighbour, and towards the Lord, for this love is ever attended with this principle of belief. Hence it is, that man receives from the Lord a heavenly proprium, concerning which see n. 155, 164, 731, 1023, 1044, 1937, 1947, 2882, 2883, 2891. This proprium in each sense is signified by bone and flesh; and this is the reason why bones in the Word signify truth, and, in an opposite sense, the false principle; and flesh, good, and, in an opposite sense, evil. That such is the signification of bones, may appear from the following passages, "Jehovah shall lead thee continually, and shall satisfy thy soul in droughts, and *shall render thy bones alert*, that thou mayest be as a watered garden," Isaiah lviii. 11; where rendering the bones alert denotes to vivify the intellectual proprium, that is, to enlighten with intelligence, whence it is said, "that thou mayest be as a watered garden." That garden denotes intelligence, may be seen, n. 100, 108, 1588. Again, in the same prophet, "Then ye shall see, and your heart shall rejoice, and *your bones shall bud forth like the herb*," lxvi. 14; where by bones budding forth as the herb, the same is signified as above. So in Jeremiah, " Her Nazarites were whiter than snow, they were fairer than milk, *their bones were more ruddy than gems*, a sapphire was their polishing; their form is more obscure than blackness, they are not known in the streets, *their skin cleaveth to their bone*, it is withered, it is become like wood," Lam. iv. 7, 8. Nazarite denotes the celestial man, see

n. 3301; whiter than snow and fairer than milk, denotes that
they were principled in celestial truth, and as this truth is
grounded in the love of good, it is therefore said, that their
bones were more ruddy than gems; whiteness and fairness are
predicated of truth, see n. 3301; ruddiness (or redness) is predicated of good, n. 3300; gems are predicated of truths
grounded in good, n. 114; by their skin cleaving to their bone
is described a change of state as to the celestial things of love,
namely, that there was no flesh on the bone, that is, no longer
any good; for in such case all truth becomes like skin which
cleaves to the bone; it is withered, and becomes as wood. So
in Ezekiel, "Parabolize a parable against the house of rebellion,
and say unto them, Thus saith the Lord Jehovih, set on a pot,
set it on, and also pour waters into it, gathering the *pieces
thereof* into it, every *good piece*, the thigh and the shoulder,
fill it with the choice of bones, taking from the choice of the
flock, and let there be also *a fire of bones* under it, let the
bones also be boiled in the midst of it," xxiv. 3, 4, 5, 10. In
this passage, pot denotes violence offered to good and truth,
whence that city is called a city of bloods, verse 6. The pieces,
the good piece, the thigh and the shoulder gathered into it, are
flesh, which are goods; the choice of bones, with which the pot
was filled, denotes truths; a fire of bones denotes the affection
of truth; the bones being boiled in the midst of it, denotes
violence offered to truths. That this parable conceals Divine
arcana, every one may see, and also that these arcana can in
no wise be known, unless it be known what is signified in the
internal sense by pot, by pieces, by thigh and shoulder, by
choice of bones, by a fire of bones, and by boiling. So in
Micah, "Is it not for you to know judgment, who hate the
good and love the evil, who pluck their skin from off them, and
their flesh from off *their bones*, who have eaten the *flesh of My
people*, and have withdrawn the skin thereof from off them,
and *have broken their bones*, and have divided them as into a
pot, and as flesh into the midst of a cauldron?" iii. 2, 3; where
the signification is the same. So in Ezekiel, "He brought me
forth in the spirit of Jehovah, and set me in the midst of a valley which was *full of bones*, and said unto me, Shall *these bones*
live? He said unto me, Prophesy *upon these bones*, and say unto
them, O, dry bones, hear the Word of Jehovah; thus saith the
Lord Jehovih to *these bones*, Behold I bring spirits into you, that
ye may live, I will give nerves upon you, and will cause flesh
to come up upon you, and will cover you over with skin, and
will give spirit in you that ye may live. I prophesied, and *the
bones came together, bone to its bone*, and I saw when behold
nerves came upon them, and *flesh* came up, and they were
covered over with skin above, and there was no spirit in them,
and spirit came into them, and they revived, and stood upon

their feet," xxxvii. 1 and the following verses. The subject here treated of, in a general view, is concerning the establishment of the Church amongst the Gentiles; and, in a particular view, concerning the regeneration of an individual man; dry bones denote the intellectual proprium, which is inanimate till it receives life from the Lord, but which is thereby animated or made alive; the flesh, which the Lord causes to come up upon the bones, is the will proprium, which is called the celestial proprium, consequently it is good; spirit is the Lord's life, which, in flowing into man's good that from proprium seems to itself to will and to act, vivifies that good, and the truth grounded therein, so that from dry bones there is made a man. So in David, "*All My bones* are dissolved; My heart is become like wax; I can number *all My bones;* they have divided to themselves My garments, and upon My vesture they have cast a lot," Psalm xxii. 15, 18, 19; speaking of the Lord's temptations as to Divine Truths, which were the Lord's proprium, and hence are called My bones, and as to Divine Good, which was the Lord's proprium, and hence is called My heart (that heart denotes good, see n. 3313, 3635); and as bones signify these truths, numbering which, is desiring to dissipate them by reasonings and false principles, therefore also it immediately follows, that they divided His garments, and cast a lot upon His vesture, for garments also denote truths, but of an exterior order, see n. 297, 1073, 2576. Dividing those garments, and casting a lot upon His vesture, signifies the same in Matthew xxvii. 35. So again, " My soul exulteth in Jehovah, it shall be glad in His salvation, *all my bones shall say*, Who is like unto Thee ?" Psalm xxxv. 9, 10; where it is manifest that bones in the spiritual sense denote the intellectual proprium. Again, "Thou shalt cause me to hear joy and gladness, *the bones* which Thou hast bruised shall exult," Psalm li. 10; where the bones which were bruised exulting, signifies recreation by truths after temptations. As bone signified the intellectual proprium, or proprium as to truth, and in a supreme sense the Divine Truth which was the Lord's Proprium, it was hence ordained as a statute respecting the passover, that they should not break a bone of the paschal lamb, which is thus expressed in Moses, " In one house it shall be eaten; thou shalt not bring of the flesh abroad out of the house, and *ye shall not break a bone in it*," Exod. xii. 46. And in another place, "They shall not leave of it until the morning, and *they shall not break a bone of it*," Numb. ix. 12; where not to break a bone, in a supreme sense, denotes not to violate Truth Divine, and in a representative sense, not to violate the truth of any good whatever, for the quality of good and the form of good are derived from truths, and truth is the support of good, as bones are of flesh. That the Word, which is Divine Truth itself, vivifies the dead, was represented by the man reviving, and rising upon his feet, who, when cast into the sepulchre of Elisha, *touched his bones*, 2 Kings xiii. 21 : that Elisha represented the Lord as to Truth Divine, or the Word, may be seen, n. 2762. That bones in an opposite sense signify the false principle which is from proprium, appears from the following passages : " In that tim ‚they shall draw forth *the bones of the kings of Judah*, and *th₋ bones of his princes*, and *the bones of the priests*, and *the bones of the prophets*, and *the bones of the inhabitants of Jerusalem*, from their sepulchres ; and shall spread them forth to the sun, and to the moon, and to all the host of heaven, which they had loved, and which they had served," Jer. viii. 1, 2. And in Ezekiel, " I will give the carcases of the sons of Israel before their idols, and I *will scatter your bones* around your altars," vi. 5. And in Moses, " God who brought him forth out of Egypt, he hath as it were the strength of an unicorn, he shall devour the nations his enemies, and shall *break their bones*, and shall bruise their weapons." Numb. xxiv. 8. And in the second book of the Kings, " Josias the king brake the statues, and cut down the groves, and filled their place with the *bones of men ;* he took the bones out of the sepulchres, and burnt them upon the altar, that he might render it unclean ; he sacrificed all the priests of the high places, who were therein, upon the altars, and *burned the bones of men upon them*," xxiii. 14, 16, 20. Again in Moses, " The soul which hath touched on the surface of a field one slain with the sword, or one dead, or *the bone of a man*, or a sepulchre, shall be unclean seven days," Numb. xix. 16, 18. Since bones signify falses, and sepulchres the evils in which they are, and since hypocrisy is evil having the outward appearance of good, but inwardly defiled with false and profane principles, therefore the Lord says in Matthew, " Wo unto you scribes and Pharisees, *hypocrites ;* because ye make yourselves like unto *whited sepulchres*, which outwardly indeed appear beautiful, but within are *full of the bones of the dead*, and of all uncleanness ; so also ye outwardly appear unto men to be just, but inwardly ye are full of hypocrisy and iniquity," xxiii. 27, 28. From these passages then it is evident, that bones signify the intellectual proprium, both as to what is true and what is false.

3813. In regard to flesh, it signifies in a supreme sense the proprium of the Lord's Divine Human, which is Divine Good, and in a respective sense the will-proprium of man, vivified by the proprium of the Lord's Divine Human, that is, by His Divine Good. This proprium is what is called the celestial pro- prium, which in itself is the Lord alone, but appropriated to those who are in good, and thence in truth. Such a proprium belongs to the angels who are in the heavens, and to the men who, as to their interiors or their spirit, are in the Lord's king- dom. But in an opposite sense, flesh signifies the will-proprium of man, which in itself is nothing but evil, and not being vivified by the Lord is called dead, from which the man himself is said to be dead. That flesh, in a supreme sense, is the proprium of the Lord's Divine Human, thus His Divine Good, is manifest from the Lord's words in John : "Jesus said, I am the living bread which came down from heaven ; if any one eat of this bread, he shall live for ever : the bread which I shall give *is My flesh*, which I shall give for the life of the world. The Jews strove amongst themselves, saying, How can He give flesh to eat? Jesus therefore said unto them, Verily, verily, I say unto you, except ye shall eat *the flesh of the Son of Man*, and shall drink His blood, ye shall not have life in yourselves : whoso eateth *My flesh*, and drinketh My blood, hath eternal life, and I will raise him up at the last day ; *for My flesh is truly meat*, and My blood is truly drink : whoso eateth *My flesh*, and drinketh My blood, abideth in Me, and I in him : this is the bread which came down from heaven," vi. 51 to 58. That the flesh here spoken of is the proprium of the Lord's Divine Human, thus the Divine Good, is very evident, and this is what in the holy supper is called body. That body in the holy supper, or flesh, is the Divine Good, and blood the Divine Truth, may be seen, n. 1798, 2165, 2177, 3464, 3735 ; and whereas bread and wine signify the same thing as flesh and blood, namely, bread, the Lord's Divine Good, and wine, His Divine Truth, therefore the former were enjoined instead of the latter. Hence it is that the Lord said, I am the living bread ; the bread which I shall give is My flesh ; whoso eateth My flesh, and drinketh My blood, abideth in Me, and I in him ; this is the bread which came down from heaven. That to eat denotes to be communicated, to be conjoined, and to be appropriated, see n. 2187, 2343, 3168, 3513, 3596. The same was represented in the Jewish Church by this circumstance, that Aaron, his sons, and they who sacrified, and others who were clean, might eat the flesh of the sacrifices, and this was holy, see Exod. xii. 7, 8, 9 ; chap. xxix. 30 to 34 ; Levit. vii. 15 to 21 ; chap. viii. 31 ; Deut. xii. 27 ; chap. xvi. 4. On this account, if an unclean person ate of that flesh, he was to be cut off from his people, Levit. vii. 21. That these sacrifices were called bread, may be seen, n. 2165 : that that flesh was called the flesh of holiness, see Jer. xi. 15 ; Hagg. ii. 12 ; and the flesh of the offering which was on the tables in the Lord's kingdom, Ezek. xl. 43 ; speaking of the new temple ; by which the worship of the Lord in His kingdom is manifestly signified. That flesh in a respective sense denotes the will-proprium of man vivified by the Lord's Divine Good, is manifest also from the following passages : "I will give them one heart, and will give a new spirit in the midst of you, and will remove the heart of stone *out of their flesh*, and will give them a *heart of flesh*," Ezek. xi. 19 ; chap. xxxvi. 26 ; where heart of stone out of their flesh denotes the

will-principle and proprium not vivified, and heart of flesh de
notes the will-principle and proprium vivified. That the heart
represents the good of the will-principle, may be seen, n. 2930,
3313, 3635. So in David, "O God, Thou art my God; in the
morning I seek Thee: my soul thirsteth for Thee, *my flesh*
desireth Thee in the land of drought, and I am weary without
waters," Psalm lxiii. 2. Again, "My soul hath a desire towards the courts of Jehovah; my heart and my flesh are jubi
lant towards the living God," Psalm lxxxiv. 3. So in Job
"I have known my Redeemer, he liveth, and at last shall rise
upon the dust; and afterwards these things shall be encompassed with my skin, and from *my flesh I shall see God*, whom
I shall see for myself, and mine eyes shall see, and not another,"
xix. 25, 26, 27. To be encompassed with skin, denotes the
natural principle, such as man has with him after death, see n.
3539; from the flesh to see God, denotes proprium vivified,
therefore he says, whom I shall see for myself, and mine eyes
shall see, and not another. Inasmuch as it was known to the
Churches that flesh signified proprium, and the book of Job is
a book of the ancient Church, see n. 3540, therefore it spoke
thus from what was significative in this case, as in many others,
according to the custom of that time; consequently, those who
deduce from this passage, that the dead body itself shall be
collected from the four winds, and shall rise again, do not know
the internal sense of the Word. They who do know the internal
sense, know also that they shall come hereafter into another
life with a body, but of a nature more pure than the present
body, for that in the other life there are bodies of a purer
order, since they see each other, discourse together, and enjoy
every sense as in the present body, but in a more exquisite
degree. The body which man carries about with him here on
earth, is designed for uses on earth, and therefore consists of
bones and flesh; and the body which the spirit carries about
with it in another life, is designed for uses in that life, and does
not consist of bones and flesh, but of things which correspond
to them, see n. 3726. That flesh in an opposite sense signifies
man's will-proprium, which in itself is nothing but evil, appears
from the following passages: "They shall eat every man the
flesh of his own arm," Isaiah ix. 19. Again, in the same prophet, "I will feed their oppressors with *their own flesh*, and they
shall be made drunken with their blood as with new wine,"
xlix. 26. So in Jeremiah, "I will feed them with *the flesh
of their sons*, and with *the flesh of their daughters*, and they
shall eat every man *the flesh of his companion*," xix. 9. And in
Zechariah, "The remnant shall eat every one the *flesh of another*," xi. 9. And in Moses, "I will chastise you sixfold by
reason of your sins; and ye shall eat *the flesh of your sons*, and
the flesh of your daughters shall ye eat," Levit. xxvi. 28, 29.

The will-proprium or nature of man is thus described, for it is nothing else than evil and its false, or hatred against truths and goods, which things are signified by eating the flesh of his arm, the flesh of sons and daughters, and the flesh of another. So in John, "I saw one angel standing in the sun, who cried with a great voice, saying to all the birds flying in the midst of heaven, Come and be ye gathered together to the supper of the great God, that ye may eat the *flesh of kings*, and the *flesh of captains over a thousand*, and the *flesh of the strong*, and the *flesh of horses* and of those that sit upon them, and the *flesh of all freemen* and servants, and of the small and great," Apoc. xix. 17, 18 ; Ezek. xxxix. 17, 18, 19, 20. That the flesh of kings, of captains over a thousand, of the strong, of horses and those that sit upon them, of freemen and servants, do not signify such things, may appear to every one ; consequently, that flesh signifies something else, which has heretofore been unknown. That it denotes evils which come from falses, and the evils from which falses come, both from man's will-proprium, is evident from each expression. Since the false which results from man's intellectual proprium, in the internal sense, is blood, and the evil which results from his will-proprium is flesh, therefore the Lord thus speaks of the man about to be regenerated, " As many as received, to them gave He power to become the sons of God, believing in His name, who were born, *not of bloods, nor of the will of the flesh,* nor of the will of man, but of God," John i. 12, 13. Hence it is, that flesh, in general, means every man, see n. 574, 1050, for whether we say man, or man's proprium, it is the same thing. That flesh, in the supreme sense, signifies the Lord's Divine Human, appears from the passage above quoted, and also from this in John, " *The Word was made flesh.* and dwelt in us, and we saw His glory, the glory as of the only begotten of the Father," i. 14. By this flesh all flesh is vivified, that is, by the Lord's Divine Human every man is vivified, by the appropriation of His love, which appropriation is signified by eating the flesh of the Son of Man, John vi. 51 to 58, and by eating the bread in the holy supper ; for the bread is the body or flesh, Matt. xxvi. 26, 27.

3814. "And dwelt with him a month of days"—that this signifies a new state of life, appears from the signification of dwelling, as being life, see n. 1293, 3384, 3613 ; and from the signification of month of days, as being a new state. That all times denote states, see n. 1274, 1382, 2625, 2788, 2837, 3254, 3356, 3404. Thus years, months, and days, denote states, but the quality of the state appears from the numbers affixed to them. When, however, a year, a month, or a day, is mentioned in the singular number, it signifies an entire state, or the end of a preceding and the beginning of a subsequent state, as has been shown above throughout the explications. Here therefore a month signifies the end of a preceding and the beginning of a subsequent state, thus, a new state. This is also signified by month in other parts of the Word, as in Isaiah, "At length it shall come to pass *from month to its month*, and from sabbath to sabbath, all flesh shall come to bow down themselves to Me, saith Jehovah," lxvi. 23. And in the Apocalypse, "He showed me a pure river of water of life, clear as crystal, coming forth from the throne of God and the Lamb. In the midst of the street thereof, and of the river, on this side and that, was the tree of life bearing twelve fruits, *yielding its fruit every month*," xxii. 1, 2. Yielding its fruit every month, signifies a state ever new, according to the reception and consequent exercise of good. So in Moses, "Number the sons of Levi, according to the house of their father, from *the son of a month*, and upwards, thou shalt number them. Number every firstborn, a male of the sons of Israel, from *the son of a month*, and upwards, and take the number of their names," Numb. iii. 15, 40. Since a month signifies the end of a preceding, and the beginning of a subsequent state, or a new state, therefore it was commanded that their numbering should be from the son of a month and upwards. Again, "If thou shalt see in captivity a woman beautiful in form, and shalt desire her, that thou mayest take her to thee for a wife, she shall remove the garment of her captivity from off her, and shall sit in thy house, and shall bewail her father and her mother *a month of days;* afterwards thou shalt enter in to her, and shalt know her, and she shall be unto thee for a wife," Deut. xxi. 11, 13; where month of days evidently denotes the end of a preceding, and the beginning of a subsequent or new state.

3815. "And Laban said unto Jacob, Because thou art my brother"—that this signifies because they were from consanguineous good, appears from the representation of Laban, as being collateral good of a common stock; and from the representation of Jacob, as being good of the natural principle, concerning which see above; and from the signification of brother, as being good, see n. 3803, in the present case, consanguineous good; for it is said by Laban to Jacob, consequently by good to good. All relationship derives its origin from good, for good is of love. The first degree of love in the descending line is called consanguineous, and is meant in a proper sense by brother. That in the spiritual world, or in heaven, no other consanguinities and affinities exist, but those of love to the Lord and neighbourly love, or, what is the same thing, of good, was made manifest to me from the fact, that all the societies which constitute heaven, and which are innumerable, are most distinct from each other, according to the degrees and differences of love, and faith thence derived, see n. 685, 917, 2739, 3612. Also from this, that they mutually know each other, not from any affinity which had existed in the life of the body, but solely from a principle of good, and truth thence derived. A father does not know a son or a daughter, nor a brother, a brother or sister, nor indeed a husband, a wife, unless they have been in similar good. They meet indeed on their first coming into another life, but they are soon dissociated, for essential good, or love and charity, determines every one to his particular society, and enrolls him in it. In the society in which every one is enrolled, consanguinity commences, and thence the affinities proceed, all the way to the circumferences.

3616. "Shouldest thou therefore serve me for nought? tell me what shall be thy reward"—that this signifies that there should be a medium of conjunction, appears from the signification of serving for nought, as being without a principle of obligation; and from the signification of reward, as being a medium of conjunction. Reward is occasionally mentioned in the Word, and signifies nothing else in the internal sense than a means of conjunction. The reason is, because the angels are altogether unwilling to hear any thing about reward, as paid for what appertains to themselves; indeed, they are altogether averse to the idea of reward for any good, or for any good deed, knowing that proprium, or what comes from self, is nothing but mere evil with every one, and that this being the case, whatever they do from proprium, or self, would be attended with the opposite to reward, and that all good is from the Lord, and enters by influx, and this solely out of mercy, thus not from themselves, and it is with a view to this good that they think of reward In fact, good itself becomes not good when recompense is thought of as the reward of good, for in such case a selfish end instantly adjoins itself, and so far as this is the case, it induces a negation that good is from the Lord, and from mercy, consequently so far it removes influx, and of course removes heaven and blessedness, which are in good and its affection. The affection of good, or love to the Lord and neighbourly love, has in it a principle of blessedness and happiness, and this is in the affection and love itself. To do any thing from affection and its blessedness, and at the same time with a view to reward, is to act from principles quite opposite to each other. Hence then it is, that the angels, when mention is made of reward in the Word, do not perceive any thing of reward, but that which is given them *gratis* and of mercy by the Lord. Nevertheless, reward serves as a medium of conjunction with those who are not yet initiated, for they who are not yet initiated in good and its affection, that is, who are not yet fully regenerated, cannot do otherwise than think also of reward, because in doing good they do it not from the affection of good, but from the affection of somewhat blessed and happy in regard to themselves, and at the same time from fear of hell. But when man is regen-

erated, this is inverted, and becomes the affection of good, and
then he no longer expects reward. This may be illustrated by
what passes in civil life, as in the case of a person who loves
his country, and has such an affection towards it, as to find a
pleasure in promoting its good from good-will. Such a person would lament the want of opportunity of doing his country
good, and would make it a matter of supplication that such
opportunity might be granted, this being the object of his affection, consequently the source of his pleasure and blessedness.
Such an one also is honoured and exalted to posts of dignity,
for these, to him, are means of serving his country, although
they are called rewards. But those who have no affection for
their country, but only for themselves and the world, are moved
to action by motives of honour and wealth, which also they regard as ends of life. Such persons prefer themselves to their
country, or their own to the general good, and are respectively
sordid and mean; and yet still they are above all others desirous
to make it appear, that they act in all cases from a sincere love.
Nevertheless when they think privately about it, they insist
that no one does so act, and wonder that any one can. They
who are such in the life of the body, with regard to their
country, or the public good, are such also in another life with
regard to the Lord's kingdom, for every one's affection or love
follows him after death, affection or love being the life of
every one.

3817. Verses 16, 17. *And Laban had two daughters, the
name of the elder was Leah, and the name of the younger
Rachel, and Leah's eyes were weak, and Rachel was beautiful
in form, and beautiful in aspect.* Laban had two daughters,
signifies the affections of truth grounded in good which is from
a common stock: the name of the elder was Leah, signifies the
affection of external truth with its quality: and the name of the
younger Rachel, signifies the affection of internal truth with its
quality: and the eyes of Leah were weak, signifies the affection
of external truth as being such in regard to understanding: and
Rachel was beautiful in form and beautiful in aspect, signifies
the affection of internal truth as being such in regard to what
is spiritual.

3818. "Laban had two daughters"—that this signifies the
affections grounded in good which is from a common stock,
appears from the representation of Laban, as being good of a
common stock, but laterally descended, see n. 3612, 3665, 3778;
and from the signification of daughters, as being affections, see
n. 2362, in the present case affections of truth from the good
which is Laban, see n. 3793.

3819. "The name of the elder was Leah"—that this signifies the affection of external truth with its quality, and that the
name of the younger, Rachel, signifies the affection of internal

truth with its quality, appears from the representation of Leah, as being the affection of external truth, and from the representation of Rachel, as being the affection of internal truth, see n. 3793 ; and from the signification of name, as being quality, see n. 144, 145, 1754, 1896, 2009, 2724, 3006. Leah is called the elder, because external truth is first learnt, and Rachel is called the younger, because internal truth is learnt afterwards ; or what is the same thing, man is first affected with external truths, and afterwards with internal, for external truths are the planes of internal ones, being general principles into which particular ones are insinuated ; for a man, without a general idea of a thing, comprehends nothing particular. Hence it is, that the literal sense of the Word contains general, but the internal sense, particular truths. The former are what are called external, but the latter internal ; and whereas truths without affection are not truths, from not being connected with life, therefore, when mention is made of external and internal truths, the affections thereof are understood.

3820. "And the eyes of Leah were weak"—that this signifies the affection of external truth as being such in regard to its understanding, appears from the representation of Leah, as being the affection of external truth, see n. 3793 ; and from the signification of eyes, as being the understanding, see n. 2701 ; and from the signification of weak, as being so respectively. That the affections of external truth are weak as to understanding, or what is the same thing, that they who are in those affections are weak, may appear manifest from external, that is, general ideas, which are not as yet illustrated by particulars, in that they are infirm and wavering, and are as it were carried away by every breath of wind, or in other words, suffer themselves to be drawn over to every opinion ; whereas, when they are illustrated by particulars, they become firm and steadfast, deriving from those particulars the essential and formal principles, which are signified by the beautiful form and aspect of Rachel, who represents the affections of interior truth. What is meant by external truths and the affections thereof, and by internal truths and their affections, and that the former are respectively weak-eyed, and the latter beautiful in form and aspect, may be illustrated by the following example. They who are in external truths know only this general truth in respect to charity, *That the poor ought to be relieved*, having no discernment by which to discover who are truly poor, and still less to discover that poor, in the Word, means those who are spiritually poor. In consequence of this, they do good alike to the evil and the good, not being aware, that doing good to the evil is doing evil to the good, since the evil are thus supplied with the means of doing evil to the good ; wherefore they, who are in such simplicity of zeal, are subject to the greatest infestations from the cunning and deceitful. They, on the contrary, who are in internal truths, know who are truly poor, and discern the peculiar quality of each, and do good to every one according to his quality. To take another example: they who are in external truths know only this general truth, *That they ought to love their neighbour*, and believe that every one is a neighbour in the same degree, and thus, that every one is to be embraced with the same love, and so they suffer themselves to be seduced. But they who are in internal truths know in what degree every one is a neighbour, and that the degree differs in all. Hence, they are acquainted with innumerable things of which the others are ignorant, and consequently, they do not suffer themselves to be led away by the mere name of neighbour, nor to do evil from the persuasion of good which the name induces. To take yet another example: they who are only in external truths suppose *That the learned shall shine like stars in another life*, and that all who have laboured in the Lord's vineyard will receive a larger reward than others. But they who are in internal truths know that the learned, the wise, and the intelligent, signify those who are in good, whether they be in any human wisdom and intelligence or not, and that these shall shine as the stars; and that they who labour in the Lord's vineyard receive each a reward according to the affection of good and truth from which they labour; and that they who labour for the sake of themselves and the world, that is, for the sake of self-exaltation and opulence, have their reward in the life of the body, but in another life have their lot with the wicked, see Matt. vii. 22, 23. Hence it is manifest how weak in understanding they are who are only in external truths, and that internal truths are what give them essence and form, and also qualify the good which belongs to them. Nevertheless, they who are in external truth, and at the same time in simple good, during their life in the world, in another life receive internal truths, and the wisdom thence derived, for simple good places them in a state and faculty for reception.

3821. "And Rachel was beautiful in form, and beautiful in aspect"—that this signifies the affection of interior truth as being such in regard to what is spiritual, appears from what has been just now said above. Form signifies essence, and aspect the beauty thence derived.

3822. Verses 18, 19, 20. *And Jacob loved Rachel, and said, I will serve thee seven years for Rachel thy younger daughter. And Laban said, It is better that I should give her to thee than give her to another man ; abide with me. And Jacob served for Rachel seven years, and they were in his eyes as some days in his loving her.* Jacob loved Rachel, signifies the love of good towards internal truth : and said, I will serve thee seven years for Rachel thy younger daughter, signifies studious application, and in such case a holy state in order to be conjoined with internal truth : and Laban said, It is better that I should give her to thee than give her to another man, abide with me, signifies a means of conjunction by interior truth with that good : and Jacob served for Rachel seven years, signifies effect : and they were in his eyes as some days in his loving her, signifies a state of love.

3823. " Jacob loved Rachel "—that this signifies the love of good towards internal truth, appears from the representation of Jacob, as being good of the natural principle, see n. 3599, 3659, 3775 ; and from the representation of Rachel, as being the affection of internal truth, see n. 3793, 3819, in the present case internal truth about to be conjoined to good of the natural principle, with a view to which conjunction there was love.

3824. " And said, I will serve thee seven years for Rachel thy younger daughter"—that this signifies studious application, and in such case a holy state, in order to be conjoined with internal truth, appears from the signification of serving, as being studious application; and from the signification of seven, as being what is holy, see n. 395, 433, 716, 881; and from the signification of years, as being states, see n. 487, 488, 493, 893; that it was in order to conjunction is evident. Hence it is manifest, that serving thee seven years for Rachel thy younger daughter, signifies studious application, and in such case a holy state in order to be conjoined with internal truth. Internal truths are said to be conjoined to the natural principle, when they are learnt, acknowledged, and believed. Man's natural principle, or its memory, contains truths both external and internal, and in the form of scientific doctrinals; but they are not conjoined until man is affected with them for the sake of use respecting life, or until they are loved for the sake of life. In this case good is coupled with them, whereby they are conjoined with the rational principle, consequently with the internal man. By this way an influx of life into them from the Lord is opened.

3825. " And Laban said, It is better that I should give her to thee than give her to another man, abide with me"—that this signifies a means of conjunction by interior truth with that good, appears from the signification of reward (in regard to which a reply and affirmation is here made), as being a means of conjunction, see n. 3816. That Rachel, who is here meant by *her*, denotes interior truth, and that Jacob, who is here meant by *thee*, denotes good, has been shown above. In regard to the conjunction of the good, which is Jacob, with the good, which is Laban, by means of interior truth, which is Rachel, it is an arcanum which cannot easily be rendered comprehensible, it being necessary that a clear idea be first had of each good, and also of the affection of interior truth. The understanding of every subject is according to the ideas; none if there be no idea, obscure if the idea be obscure, perverted if the idea be perverted, and clear if the idea be clear. It is also according to the affections, by which the idea, although clear, is also varied. It may, however, be expedient to observe briefly, that in every man who is regenerated, the good of his natural principle, such as is here represented by Jacob, is conjoined first with the good, such as is here represented by Laban, by the affection of interior truth, which is here represented by Rachel, and afterwards with the good of the rational principle and the truth thereof, which are Isaac and Rebecca. By that first conjunction, man is in a state of receiving internal or spiritual truths, which are the means of conjunction of the natural principle with the rational, or of the external man with the internal.

3826. "And Jacob served for Rachel seven years"—that this signifies effect, appears from the signification of these words, as being studious application, and in such case, a holy state in order to be conjoined with internal truth, see n. 3824. That in the present case they denote the effect of this thing, is evident.

3822. "And they were in his eyes as some days in his loving her"—that this signifies a state of love, in that it was without irksomeness, appears from the signification of being in his eyes, as being to appear so; and from the signification of days, as being states, see n. 893, 2788, 3462, 3785. Hence, as some days in his loving her, denotes a state of love. When man is in a state of love, or of heavenly affection, he is then in an angelic state, namely, in a state as it were out of time, provided there be no impatience in the affection, for impatience is a corporeal affection, and so far as man is in it, so far he is in time; but so far as man is not in impatience whilst he is in heavenly affection, so far he is not in time. This is manifest in a sort of image from all the joy and gladness belonging to affection or love, in that, during their presence with man, time does not appear to him, for he is then in the internal man. The affection of genuine love withdraws man from corporeal and worldly objects, for it elevates his mind towards heaven, and thus withdraws it from the things of time. The reason time appears to be something, is owing to the mind's reflecting on those things which are not objects of affection or love, consequently which are irksome. Hence it is evident, what these words signify, that "the seven years were in his eyes as some days in his loving her."

3828. Verses 21, 22, 23, 24. *And Jacob said unto Laban, Give my woman, because my days are fulfilled, and I will come to her. And Laban gathered together all the men of the place, and made a feast. And it was in the evening, and he took Leah his daughter, and brought her to him, and he came to her. And*

Laban gave her Zilpah his handmaid, an handmaid to his daughter Leah. Jacob said unto Laban, Give my woman, signifies that from common good there was now conjunction with the affection of interior truth : because my days are fulfilled, that I may come to her, signifies that now there was a state : and Laban gathered together all the men of the place, signifies all the truths of that state: and made a feast, signifies initiation : and it was in the evening, signifies a state as yet obscure : and he took Leah his daughter, and brought her to him, and he came to her, signifies that as yet there was conjunction only with the affection of external truth : and Laban gave her Zilpah his handmaid, an handmaid to his daughter Leah, signifies external affections or external bonds, which are subservient means.

3829. " Jacob said unto Laban, Give my woman"—that this signifies that there was conjunction from common good with the affection of interior truth, appears from the representation of Jacob, as being the good of the natural principle (concerning which, see above), in the present case common good, because the things of the natural principle are respectively common, there being innumerable things which flow from the internal man into the natural or external man, which appear in this latter as one common principle, and still more so before the particulars of common principles are received, as in the present case. Hence it is, that the good, which is represented by Jacob, is now called common good. That conjunction with the affection of interior truth is signified, is evident, for Rachel, who is here called my woman, represents the affection of interior truth, as has been shown above.

3830. " Because my days are fulfilled, that I may come to her"—that this signifies that now there was a state, appears from the signification of days, as being states, see n. 23, 487, 488, 493, 893, 2788, 3462, 3785. That my days are fulfilled, that I may come to her, signifies that that state now existed, is apparent without explication.

3831. "And Laban gathered together all the men of the place"—that this signifies all the truths of that state, appears from the signification of men, as being truths, see n. 3134; and from the signification of place, as being state, see n. 2625, 2837, 3356, 3387.

3832. " And made a feast"—that this signifies initiation, appears from the signification of feast, as being appropriation and conjunction, see n. 3596, in the present case initiation, because initiation precedes conjunction, and likewise insures and testifies it. The feasts which were made in old time, amongst those who were in significa ives and representatives, signified nothing else than initiation into the mutual love which is of charity. The nuptial feasts, too, signified initiation into conjugial love, and the holy feasts, initiation into spiritual and celestial love, and this because feasting, or eating and drinking, signified appropriation and conjunction, as was shown above, n. 3734. In consequence of this signification, the Lord also said, " Many shall come from the east and from the west, and shall *recline* with Abraham, Isaac, and Jacob, in the kingdom of heaven," Matt. viii. 11. And in another place, to His disciples, " *That ye may eat and drink on My table* in My kingdom," Luke xxii. 30. And when He instituted the holy supper, He said, " I say unto you, that *I will not drink* from henceforth of this fruit of the vine until that day, *when I shall drink it new with you in the kingdom of My Father*," Matt. xxvi. 29, Every one may see, that reclining, eating, and drinking, in the Lord's kingdom, do not signify to recline, to eat, and to drink, but to do something which has respect to that kingdom, namely, to appropriate the good of love and the truth of faith, or to partake of what is called spiritual and celestial food. It is also manifest from the above words, that there is an internal sense in all that the Lord spake, and that without the understanding of this sense it cannot be known what is meant by reclining with Abraham, Isaac, and Jacob, what by eating and drinking in the Lord's kingdom on His table, and what by His drinking with them of the fruit of the vine in the kingdom of His Father; neither can it be known what is meant by eating bread and drinking wine in the holy supper.

3833. " And it was in the evening"—that this signifies a state as yet obscure, appears from the signification of evening, as being an obscure state, see n. 3056. Feasts which were made in the evening, or suppers, amongst the ancients who were in congruous rituals, signified nothing else than the state of initiation which precedes conjunction, which state is obscure with respect to conjunction; for, during man's initiation into truth, and thence into good, all that he learns is obscure to him; but when good is conjoined thereto, and he thence respects truth, in this case all is clear to him, and this successively more and more, for now he is no longer in doubt whether a thing be, or whether it be so, but he knows that it is, and that it is so. When man is in this state, he then begins to know innumerable things, for he now proceeds from the good and truth which he believes and perceives, as from a centre to the circumferences, and in proportion as he proceeds, in the same proportion he sees the things which are round about, and successively extends his views, by a continual removal and dilatation of their boundaries. Thenceforth, also, he commences from every object in the space within those boundaries, and hence, as from new centres, he produces new circumferences, and so forth. By this means, the light of truth derived from good increases immensely, and becomes a continuous lucidity, for he

is in the light of heaven which is from the Lord. But with
those who are in doubt, and in disquisition whether a thing be,
and whether it be so, these innumerable, yea, indefinite things
do not at all appear. All and singular things are to them
obscure, and are scarce respected as one really existing thing,
but rather as one thing whose existence is doubtful. In such
a state is human wisdom and intelligence at this day, when he
is deemed wise who can reason with ingenuity whether a thing
exists, and he is deemed still wiser who can reason in proof of
its non-existence. For example: in respect to this question,
Whether there is that internal sense of the Word which is
called mystical? Until this is believed, it is impossible for any
one to attain the least knowledge of those innumerable things
which are in the internal sense, and which are so many as to
fill the universal heaven with an infinite variety. So also in
regard to the Divine Providence; he who reasons concerning
it, whether it be only universal, and not extended to particular
things, cannot possibly become acquainted with the innumerable arcana respecting Providence, which are as many in number as the contingencies of every one's life, from first to last,
and from the creation of the world to its end, yea, to eternity.
Again, he who reasons whether it be possible for any one to
be in good, because the will of man is radically depraved, cannot possibly know all the arcana relating to regeneration, nor
even that a new will is implanted by the Lord, together with
the arcana of such implantation; and so in all other cases.
Hence it may be clearly seen in what obscurity such persons
are, and that they do not even see, much less touch, the first
threshold of wisdom.

3834. "And he took Leah his daughter, and brought her to
him, and he came to her"—that this signifies that as yet there
was conjunction only with the affection of external truth, appears from the representation of Leah, as being the affection
of external truth, see n. 3793, 3819. That bringing her to him,
and his coming to her, signifies conjunction of a conjugial
kind, is evident. The case herein is this: he who is in the
affection of internal truth, that is, in a desire of knowing the
interior arcana of the Lord's kingdom, has not at first those
arcana conjoined to him, although he is acquainted with them,
and although he at times acknowledges, and as it were believes
them, for as yet there are present with him worldly and corporeal affections, which cause him indeed to receive and as it
were to believe those arcana, but so far as these affections are
present, so far those interior truths cannot be conjoined. The
affection of truth grounded in good, and the affection of good,
applies those arcana to itself, and so far as man is in these affections, so far interior truths are conjoined to him, truths being
the vessels recipient of good. The Lord's Providence operates

in this to prevent celestial and spiritual truths, such as all interior truths are, being conjoined with any other than genuine affections. Hence it is, that the common affection of truth grounded in good, precedes, and the truths which are insinuated therein, are nothing but common truths. States of truth are altogether according to states of good, or states of faith according to states of charity. For example: it is possible even for the wicked to know that the Lord rules the universal heaven, and also that heaven consists in mutual love and love to the Lord, and further, that by such love the inhabitants of heaven have conjunction with the Lord, and wisdom, and likewise happiness. Nay, it is possible for them to be in the persuasion that it is so, and yet the truth of faith, and still less the good of love, may not be conjoined to them. The life shows whether such conjunction has place or not, just as a tree is known from its fruit. The case in this respect is like that of grapes in which there are no stones, and which, when sown in earth however fruitful, rot and become mere dung; or like an ignis fatuus in the night, which is dissipated as soon as the sun arises. But by the Divine mercy of the Lord, more will be said on this subject in the following pages.

3835. "And Laban gave her Zilpah his handmaid, a handmaid to his daughter Leah"—that this signifies external affections, or external bonds, which are subservient means, appears from the signification of handmaid, as being external affections, see n. 1895, 2567. Laban's giving her, signifies that they come from collateral good of a common stock, for this is the origin of such affections. They are called external bonds, because all affections are bonds, see n. 1077, 1080, 1835, 1944, for nothing holds man in bonds but his affection. The affection of each man does not indeed appear to him as a bond, yet still it is so called, because it rules him, and keeps him bound to it. The internal affections are called internal bonds, as the affections of truth and good are the bonds of conscience. To these correspond external bonds or external affections, for every internal has a corresponding external. Since every man who is regenerated, is introduced to internal things by external, and this state of introduction is the subject here treated of, therefore it is here said, that Laban's handmaid was given to his daughter Leah for a handmaid, which signifies that those affections were given which serve for means of introduction. That these affections were the most external, such as those which are called the affections of the body, is evident from the fact, that Leah represents the affections of external truth. But on this subject also, by the Divine mercy of the Lord, more will be said elsewhere.

3836. Verses 25, 26. *And it was in the morning, and behold it was Leah, and he said unto Laban, What is this that thou*

*hast done to me?   Did not I serve with thee for Rachel ?   And
why hast thou defrauded me ?   And Laban said, It is not so
done in our place, to give the younger before the first-born.*   It
was in the morning, signifies illustration in that state : and
behold it was Leah, signifies that there was conjunction with
external truth : and he said unto Laban, What is this that thou
hast done ? signifies indignation : did not I serve with thee for
Rachel ? signifies that there was studious application for the
affection of internal truth : and why hast thou defrauded me ?
signifies greater indignation : and Laban said, It is not so
done in our place, signifies that the state is not such : to
give the younger before the first-born, signifies that the affection of interior truth should precede the affection of external
truth.

3837. "It was in the morning"—that this signifies illustration in that state, appears from the signification of morning,
as being illustration, see n. 3458, 3723 ; and as all time signifies state, see n. 2625, 2788, 2837, 3356, so also does morning
tide or morning.   Illustration has respect to what presently
follows, namely, that he acknowledged that there was conjunction only with external truth.

3838. "And behold it was Leah"—that this signifies that
there was conjunction with external truth, appears from the
representation of Leah, as being the affection of external truth,
see n. 3793, 3819.   That it signifies conjunction with this affection, is plain, because it was Leah who was given for a woman
instead of Rachel.   What this implies, appears from what has
been already said of conjunction with external truths previous
to conjunction with internal truths, n. 3834, and from what
will be said presently, n. 3843.

3839. "And he said unto Laban, What is this that thou
hast done?"—that this signifies indignation, appears from the
affection contained in these words, and in those which follow.
That it is an affection of indignation, is evident.   This affection
according to the historical series falls into these words.   There
are two principles which constitute the internal sense of the
Word, namely, affections and things ; the affections which are
concealed in the expressions of the Word, are not apparent to
man, but are stored up in its inmost recesses ; nor can they
appear, for man, during his life in the body, is in worldly and
corporeal affections, which have nothing in common with the
affections which are contained in the internal sense of the
Word, these latter being affections of spiritual and celestial love,
which man is the less capable of perceiving, because few are
in them, and those few are for the most part persons of simplicity of character, who cannot reflect upon their affections.
The rest of mankind do not even know what genuine affection
is.   These spiritual and celestial affections are contained in

charity towards our neighbour, and in love towards God. Persons not in them, believe them to have nothing of substance or reality in them, when yet they fill the universal heaven, and this with ineffable variety. Such affections, with their varieties, are what are stored up in the internal sense of the Word, and lie concealed therein, not only in each series, but in each expression, yea, in each jot or tittle, and shine brightly before the angels, when the Word is read by those who are at once in simple good and in innocence, and this, as was observed, with indefinite variety. There are principally two kinds of affections, which shine forth in brightness from the Word before the angels, namely, the affections of truth and the affections of good; the affections of truth before the spiritual, and the affections of good before the celestial angels. The affections of good, which are affections of love to the Lord, are altogether ineffable in respect to man, and hence are also incomprehensible; but the affections of truth, which are affections of mutual love, may in some measure be comprehended in their most general principles, yet only by those who are principled in genuine mutual love, and this not from any internal perception but such as is obscure. For example, in regard to the affection of indignation, which is the subject here treated of, whoever does not know what the affection of charity is, in consequence of not being in it, cannot possibly have any idea of the affection of indignation, but as of such indignation as man has when any thing evil befalls him, which is the indignation of anger. But no such indignation prevails with the angels, but an indignation altogether different, which is not of anger, but of zeal, in which there is nothing of evil, and which is as far removed from hatred or revenge, or from the spirit of returning evil for evil, as heaven is from hell, for it originates in good. Its nature, however, as was observed before, cannot be expressed by any words. The case is similar in regard to the other affections which are from good and truth, and which are their affections. This is evident also from the fact, that the angels are only in the ends regarded, and in the uses of the ends, see n. 1317, 1645, 3645. Ends regarded, are nothing else but loves or affections, see n. 1317, 1568, 1571, 1909, 3425, 3796, for what a man loves, he regards as an end. And this being the case, they are in the affections of the things which are contained in the Word, and this with all variety, according to the kinds of affections in which they are. Hence it is evident, how holy the Word is, for in the Divine Love, or in the love which is from the Divine, there is holiness, and hence in the things contained in the Word.

3840. "Did not I serve with thee for Rachel?"—that this signifies that there was study for the affection of internal truth, appears from the representation of Rachel, as being the affection of internal truth, see n. 3758, 3782 3793, 3819; and from the signification of serving, as being study, see n. 3824.

3841. "And why hast thou defrauded me?"—that this signifies greater indignation, appears from what was just now said above, n. 3839.

3842. "And Laban said, It is not so done in our place"—that this signifies that the state is not such, appears from the signification of place, as being state, see n. 1273, 1274, 1275, 1377, 2025, 2837, 3356, 3387. Hence it is evident, that the expression, "It is not so done in our place," signifies that the state is not such.

3843. "To give the younger before the first-born"—that this signifies that the affection of interior truth should precede the affection of external truth, appears from the representation of Rachel, who is here the younger, as being the affection of interior truth, see n. 3758, 3782, 3793, 3819; and from the representation of Leah, who is here the first-born, as being the affection of external truth, see n. 3793, 3819. Hence it is evident, that giving the younger before the first-born, signifies that the affection of interior truth should precede the affection of external truth. How the case herein is, was briefly explained above, n. 3834, and may further appear from the following observations. He who knows not the state of man, may be led to believe that he has conjunction with truths, not only external, but also internal, when he is acquainted with them, or has them in his memory. Nevertheless, no conjunction is effected with truths, until man lives according to them, for life is the evidence of conjunction. Truth, in this respect, is like every thing else which is implanted in man from childhood, namely, that it does not become properly his, until he acts according to it, and this from affection, in which case, it influences his will, and is no longer brought into act from knowledge or doctrine, but from a certain unknown delight, and, as it were, from the particular bent of his inclination or nature; for every one acquires to himself such a particular bent of inclination by frequent use or habit, and this from the things which he learns. Conjunction with truths therefore cannot take place with man, until those principles, which he has imbibed by doctrines, are insinuated from the external man into the interior. When they are in the interior man, he then no longer acts from the memory, but from the bent of his inclination, till at length the principles insinuated flow spontaneously into act, being inscribed on the interior memory, and what is thus produced appears as if it was innate. This is manifest from the languages, which a man has learnt in childhood, and also from the faculty of reasoning, and likewise from conscience. Hence it is evident, that truths of doctrine, even such as are of an interior nature, are not conjoined to man, until they are formed into life. But on this subject, by the Divine Mercy of the Lord, more will be said elsewhere.

3844. Verses 27, 28, 29, 30. *Fulfil this week, and we will give thee her also for the service which thou shalt serve with me as yet seven other years. And Jacob did so, and fulfilled this week, and he gave him Rachel his daughter for a woman to him. And Laban gave to Rachel his daughter Bilhah, his handmaid, to be to her for a handmaid. And he came also to Rachel, and he loved also Rachel better than Leah, and served with him as yet seven other years.* Fulfil this week, signifies succession of study: and we will give thee her also for the services which thou shalt serve with me as yet seven other years, signifies that in such case there would be a full state of study: and Jacob did so, and fulfilled this week, signifies the effect thereof: and he gave him Rachel his daughter for a woman to him, signifies conjunction of good in this case with the affection of interior truth: and Laban gave unto Rachel his daughter Bilhah, his handmaid, to be to her for a handmaid, signifies exterior affections which are bonds or subservient means: and he came also to Rachel, signifies conjunction with the affection of internal truth: and he loved also Rachel more than Leah, signifies the love of internal truth more than of external truth: and he served with him as yet seven other years, signifies holy study.

3845. "Fulfil this week"—that this signifies succession of further study, appears from the signification of fulfilling, as being to serve, or to fulfil by serving, thus, as being studious application, see n. 3824; and from the signification of week. as being a state and also an entire period, see n. 728, 2044, in the present case, therefore, a subsequent state and period, consequently, what is successive. In regard to the signification of a week, the case is the same as with the signification of a month, see n. 3814, namely, that when it is mentioned in the singular number, it is the end of a former and the beginning of a subsequent state, or a new state, to fulfil which, is to proceed from the beginning to the end. The reason why a week, like all portions of time in particular, is a state and also a period, is, because all states have also their periods, that is, their beginning, successive progress, and end, but these periods are not perceived as times in another life, but as states and their revolutions. It here is manifest what the ancients meant by a week, namely, in a proper sense, every period distinguished into seven, whether it was of days, or of years, or of ages; or whether it was great or small. That in the present case it denotes a period of seven years, is evident; and as seven with them signified what is holy, see n. 84 to 87, 395, 433, 716, 881, hence a week signified a holy period, and also the holiness of a period.

3846. "And we will give thee her also for the service which thou shalt serve with me as yet seven other years"—that this signifies that in such case there would be a full state of studious application, appears from the signification of service and serving, as being studious application, see n. 3824; and from the signification of seven years, as being the same as week, namely, a state and entire period, as above, n. 3845, thus, a full state, which is also holy, see n. 3824. This expression, we will give thee her also, signifies that in such case there would be conjunction with the affection of internal truth. The reason why serving is study in the internal sense, is, because the labour of the external man is study in the internal man. Hence study is called a labour of the mind.

3847. "And Jacob did so, and fulfilled this week"—that this signifies their effect, appears from the signification of fulfilling a week, as being a succession of study, see above, n. 3845 : that the effect of it is here meant, is evident.

3848. "And he gave him Rachel his daughter for a woman to him"—that this signifies the conjunction of good afterwards with the affection of interior truth, appears from the representation of Jacob, as being the good of the natural principle (see above); and from the representation of Rachel, as being the affection of interior truth (see also above) : that giving her for a woman denotes conjunction, is evident. Since all conjunction of good with truth at first apparently proceeds from the exteriors to the interiors in order, and at length to the inmost, therefore here it is said the affection of interior truth, for the very affection itself, which is of truth, flows from good. The conjunction of good with the affection of internal truth for the first time takes place, when the good of the natural principle is conjoined to rational truth, and thereby to rational good. This conjunction is represented by Jacob after the birth of his twelve sons, when he returned to the house of his mother and father, of which we shall treat elsewhere.

3849. "And Laban gave to Rachel his daughter his handmaid Bilhah, to be to her for a handmaid"—that this signifies exterior affections, which are bonds or subservient means, appears from what was said above, n. 3835. The reason why Bilhah, the handmaid of Rachel, signifies exterior affections, and Zilpah, the handmaid of Leah, external affections, is, because Rachel represents the affection of internal truth, and Leah, the affection of external truth. Exterior affections are the natural affections which are subservient to internal ones. The reason why these exterior affections are means serviceable to the conjunction of truth with good, is, because nothing of doctrine, nor even any thing of science, can have admission into man, save by means of affections ; for affections have life in them, but not so the truths of doctrine and of science with out affections. That this is the case, is very evident, for a man cannot even think, nor so much as utter a single syllable without affection. Every one who attends, will perceive, that a voice without affection is like the voice of an automaton, and thus is but a lifeless sound, and that therefore in proportion to the quantity and quality of affection in any expression, in the same proportion is the quantity and quality of life in it. Hence it is evident of what nature truths are without good, and that affection is in truths by virtue of good. He may also know, from the nature of the human understanding, that it is no understanding unless the will be in it, the life of the understanding being derived from the will. Hence also it is evident what is the nature of truths without good, namely, that they are no truths, and that truths derive their life from good, for truths belong to man's intellectual part, and good to his voluntary part. Hence every one may judge what is the nature of faith, which relates to truth, without charity, which relates to good, and that the truths of faith without the good of charity are dead, for, as was observed, the quantity and quality of affection in truths, determines the quantity and quality of life in them. That truths still appear animated, although unattended with the good of charity, is owing to the affections of self-love and the love of the world, which have no life but what in a spiritual sense is called death, that is, an infernal life. I use the term affection, meaning by it the continuity of love. From these considerations then it may appear, that affections are means subservient to the conjunction of truth with good; and that affections are what introduce truths, and also arrange them in order, genuine affections (which are those of love to the Lord and of neighbourly love) into a heavenly, but evil affections (which are those of self-love and the love of the world) into an infernal, or into the opposite to a heavenly arrangement. The most external affections are those of the body, which are called the appetites and pleasures; the next interior are those of the animal mind, and are called natural affections; but the internal are those of the rational mind, and are called spiritual affections. To these last, or spiritual affections of the mind, doctrinal truths are introduced by the exterior and most external or the natural and corporeal affections. Hence these affections are subservient means, and are signified by the handmaids given by Laban to Rachel and to Leah. Their being called Laban's handmaids, signifies that they derived their origin from the good which Laban represents, concerning which see above. The truths, which are first learnt, cannot be insinuated by other affections at first; genuine affections come in process of time, but not until man acts from love of good.

3850. "And he came also to Rachel"—that this signifies conjunction with the affection of internal truth, appears from the signification of coming to, as being to be conjoined; and from the representation of Rachel, as being the affection of internal truth, concerning which, see above.

3851. "And he loved Rachel better than Leah"—that this signifies the love of internal truth more than external truth, appears from the representation of Rachel and of Leah ; Rachel being internal truth, and Leah, external truth. What is meant by internal truth, and what by external, may be seen, n. 3820.

3852. "And he served with him yet seven other years"— that this signifies holy study, appears from the signification of serving, as being study, see n. 3824, 3846; and from the signification of seven, as being what is holy, see n. 395, 433, 716, 881, 3824. Holy study is that which conjoins internal truths to good, for all internal truths have respect to the Lord, and love conjoins them to Him ; this love being the essential principle of holiness.

3853. Verse 31. *And Jehovah saw that Leah was hated and He opened her womb, and Rachel was barren.* Jehovah saw, signifies the Lord's foresight (*prœvidentia*) and providence : that Leah was hated, signifies that the affection of external truth was not so dear because it was further from the Divine : and He opened her womb, signifies that thence came doctrines of Churches : and Rachel was barren, signifies that interior truths were not received.

3854. "Jehovah saw"—that this signifies the Lord's foresight and providence, appears from the signification of seeing, when it is predicated of the Lord, as being foresight and providence, concerning which we shall speak in the following verse, when we come to treat of Reuben, whose name was given from seeing. That Jehovah is the Lord, may be seen, n. 1343, 1736, 1793, 2156, 2329, 2921, 3023, 3035. As regards foresight and providence in general, it is to be observed, that foresight has respect to man, and providence to the Lord. The Lord foresaw from eternity what the human race would be, and what would be the peculiar quality of each member of it, and that evil would continually increase, till at length man would of himself rush headlong into hell. On this account, the Lord has not only provided means, by which man may be turned from hell and led to heaven, but also by His providence He continually turns and leads him. The Lord also foresaw, that it would be impossible for any good to be rooted in man, except in his free-will, since whatever is not rooted in the free-will, is dissipated on the first approach of evil and temptation. This the Lord foresaw, and also that man of himself, or of his free-will, would thus incline towards the deepest hell, on which account the Lord provides, that in case a man should not suffer himself to be led in freedom to heaven, he may still be turned towards a milder hell, but in case he suffer himself to be led in freedom to what

is good, he may be led to heaven.   Hence it is manifest what
foresight means, and what providence, and that the things
which are foreseen are thus provided for.   And hence it may
appear, how great an error it is to believe, that the Lord has
not foreseen, and does not see, the most individual things in
man, and that He does not foresee and lead in them, when the
truth really is, that the Lord's foresight and providence is in
the very minutest of all these most individual things, and in
things so very minute, that it is impossible by any stretch of
thought to comprehend a thousand thousandth part of them.
Every smallest moment of man's life contains in it a series of
consequences extending to eternity, for each moment is a new
beginning of subsequent ones, and this is the case with all and
singular the moments of his life both in regard to his understanding and will.   And as the Lord foresaw from eternity what
would be man's peculiar quality, and what it would be to
eternity, it is manifest that the Divine Providence is operative
in the most particular and individual things respecting him,
governing and inclining him, as was said, to such a quality, and
this by a continual management of his free-will.   But on this
subject, by the Divine Mercy of the Lord, more will be said in
the following pages.

3855. "That Leah was hated"—that this signifies that the
affection of external truth was not so dear because it was further from the Divine, appears from the signification of hated,
as being what is not dear; and from the representation of Leah,
as being the affection of external truth (concerning which, see
above).   That external truths are more remote from the Divine
than internal truths, may appear from the fact, that external
things exist from internal, for external things are images and
forms compounded of myriads of internal things, which appear
as one; and this being the nature of external things, they are
further from the Divine, for the Divine is above the inmost of
man, or in the supreme.   The Lord flows from the supreme into
the inmost of man, and through these into his interiors, and
through these again into the external, and thus mediately as
well as immediately.   Since the externals are further from the
Divine, they are also on this account respectively inordinate,
nor do they suffer themselves to be reduced to order like the
internals.   This case is like that of seeds, which are more perfect within than without, and within are so perfect, as to be
able thence to produce a whole plant, or a whole tree, in its
order, with leaves and fruits, whose external forms may easily
suffer injury from several causes, but not so, the internal or inmost forms of the seeds, which are in an inner and more perfect nature.   The case is similar with the internals and externals of man, wherefore also, in the process of his regeneration,
he is regenerated as to the rational principle before he is regen-

erated as to the natural, see n. 3493 ; and the regeneration of
the natural principle is both later and more difficult, in consequence of the many inordinate things contained in it, and of
its being exposed to injuries from the body and the world ; and
this being the case, it is here said that these inordinate things
are not so dear. But so far as they agree with internal things
and so far as they conduce to the life and to the sight of inter
nal things in themselves, and to man's regeneration, so far even
they are dear.

3856. "And He opened her womb"—that this signifies that
thence came the doctrines of Churches, appears from the signification of opening the womb, or of conceiving and bringing
forth, as denoting to become a Church ; and as this is effected
by doctrinals, therefore, opening the womb signifies the doctrines of Churches. That conceptions and births, in the Word,
signify spiritual conceptions and births, such as exist when man
is born anew, may be seen, n. 1145, 1255, 1330, 2584. How
the case is, will appear from what presently follows.

3857. "And Rachel was barren"—that this signifies that interior truths were not received, appears from the representation
of Rachel, as being the affection of interior truth (concerning
which, see above); and from the signification of barren, as
being that thence there were no doctrines, consequently, no
Churches ; for this expression is opposed to what is said of
Leah, namely, that Jehovah opened her womb, which signifies
that thence came doctrines of Churches. The reason why interior truths were not received, is, because interior truths are
such as transcend man's faith, for they do not fall into his ideas,
neither are they according to the external appearances or fallacies of the senses, by which every man suffers himself to be led,
so as not to believe what does not in some measure coincide
with them. As for example : it is an interior truth, that times
and spaces do not exist in the other life, but states instead of
them ; but man, who is in time and space during his life in the
world, derives all his ideas from them, insomuch, that without
them he cannot think at all, see n. 3404. Consequently, unless
the states which exist in the other life, were described to man
by times and spaces, or by such objects as derive thence their
forms, he would perceive nothing, thus he would believe nothing, and so there would be no reception, and thus the doctrine would be barren, and the Church annulled. To take
another example : unless celestial and spiritual affections were
described by those things which belong to worldly and corporeal affections, man would not perceive any thing, for he
is in these latter, and thence is capable of forming notions
concerning celestial and spiritual affections, when nevertheless
they are as different, or as distinct from each other, as heaven
is from earth, see n. 3839. For instance : in regard to the

glory of heaven, or of the angels in heaven, unless man formed
to himself an idea of the glory of heaven, according to the
idea of glory which prevails in the world, he would not be
able to comprehend, consequently neither to acknowledge it;
and so in all other cases. It was on this account that the
Lord spake in the Word according to man's apprehension, and
according to its appearances. The literal sense of the Word is
of this nature, but still it is such as to contain in it an internal
sense, which is the repository of interior truths. Hence then it
is, that it is said of Leah, that Jehovah opened her womb, and
of Rachel, that she was barren; for Leah represents the affection of exterior truth, and Rachel, the affection of interior
truth, as was said above. But inasmuch as exterior truths are
the first truths which man learns, it is provided by the Lord,
that by them he may be introduced to interior truths, and this
is what is signified by God at length remembering Rachel, and
hearkening to her, and opening her womb, Gen. xxx. 22. The
truth of the above observations may appear from the Churches
which existed of old, and from their doctrinals, in that their
doctrinals were formed from external truths; as in the case of
the ancient Church which was after the flood, its doctrinals
were for the most part external representatives and significatives,
in which internal truths were stored up and concealed. The
greatest part of the members of this Church believed holy
worship to consist in those external representatives and significatives, and had any one told them in the beginning, that these
things were not the essentials of Divine worship, but that the
essentials were the spiritual and celestial things represented and
signified thereby, they would altogether have rejected such doctrine, and thus no Church would have been established. This
was still more particularly the case with the Jewish Church, so
that had any one told the Jews, that their rituals derived their
sanctity from the Divine things of the Lord which were in them,
they would not have acknowledged it at all. Such also was the
nature of man when the Lord came into the world, and still
more corporeal was he become, especially they who belonged to
the Church. This is plain from the disciples themselves, who
were continually attendant on the Lord, and heard so many
things concerning His kingdom, and who nevertheless could
not yet perceive interior truths, not being able to form any other
notion of the Lord, than what the Jews at this day entertain
of the Messiah whom they expect, namely, that He would exalt
them to dominion and glory above all the nations in the universe
And even after they had heard so many things from the Lord
respecting His kingdom, still they could not but think that the
kingdom of heaven was like an earthly kingdom, and that God
the Father was supreme therein, and the Son next to him in
supremacy, and afterwards they twelve, and thus that they were

to reign in order; wherefore also James and John requested that they might sit, the one on His right hand, the other on His left, Mark x. 35, 36, 37; and the rest of the disciples were angry at their desiring to be greater than the rest, Mark x. 41; Matt. xx. 24.   For the same reason, the Lord also, after He had taught them what it was to be greatest in heaven (Matt. xx. 25, 26, 27, 28; Mark x. 42, 43, 44, 45), still spoke according to their apprehension, saying, that they should sit on twelve. thrones, and judge the twelve tribes of Israel, Luke xxii. 24, 30; Matt. xix. 28.   If they had been told, that disciples did not mean themselves, but all who are in the good of love and faith, n. 3354, 3488; also, that in the Lord's kingdom there are neither thrones, nor principalities, nor governments, as in the world, and that they could not even judge the very smallest thing in a single man, n. 2129, 2553, they would have rejected the Word, and leaving the Lord, would have returned every one to his own occupation.   The reason why the Lord so spake was, that they might receive external truths, and thereby be introduced to internal ones, for in those external truths which the Lord spake, internal truths were concealed, and in process of time these latter are made manifest, and when this is the case, those external truths are dissipated, and serve only as objects or means of thinking about internal ones.   Hence it may be known what is meant by the circumstance, that Jehovah first opened Leah's womb, and she bare sons to Jacob, and that Rachel bare sons afterwards.

3858. Since the subject now to be treated of is concerning the twelve sons of Jacob, and from them, as fathers, the twelve tribes of Israel were named, it may be expedient to premise what the tribes signify, and why there were twelve.   No one has yet known the arcanum which lies herein, because it has been believed that the historical parts of the Word were barely historical, and that there was no more of a Divine principle therein, than makes them serviceable as instances, when holy things are treated of.   Hence also it has been believed, that the twelve tribes signify nothing but partitions of the Israelitish people into so many distinct nations or common families, when yet they involve Divine things, namely, so many universal partitions of faith and love, consequently, things relating to the Lord's kingdom in the heavens and on the earth, each tribe involving some distinct universal; but what each involves and signifies, will appear from what presently follows, when we come to treat of the sons of Jacob, from whom those tribes were named.   In general, the twelve tribes signified all things appertaining to the doctrine of truth and good, or of faith and love; for these things, namely, truth and good, or faith and love, constitute the Lord's kingdom, for the things of truth or faith are the all of thought therein, and the things of good or love are

the all of affection; and the Jewish Church was instituted, that
it might represent tne Lord's kingdom; and therefore the parti-
tion of that people into twelve tribes had this signification. This
is the arcanum which has never hitherto been discovered. That
twelve signify *all things* in general, was shown, n. 577, 2089,
2129, 2130, 3272; but that tribes signify the things of truth
and good, or of faith and love, and that consequently, the
twelve tribes signify the all of those things, it may be expedient
to prove from the Word, before I treat particularly of the signification of each tribe. The passages in proof of this are as
follow: "The holy city New Jerusalem hath *twelve* gates, and
above the gates *twelve* angels, and names written which are of
the *twelve tribes of the sons of Israel;* and in them the names
of the *twelve apostles of the Lamb.* He measured the city with
a reed, *twelve thousand* furlongs, and he measured the wall
thereof, a *hundred forty and four* cubits, which is the measure
of a man, that is, of an angel; the *twelve* gates were *twelve*
pearls," Apoc. xxi. 12, 14, 16, 17, 21. That the holy city, or
New Jerusalem, is the Lord's New Church, is manifest from
all the particulars contained in the Apocalypse. In some of the
foregoing chapters, the subject treated of is concerning the state
of the Church, what it would be before its end. This chapter
treats of the New Church, and this being the case, the gates,
wall, and foundations of the city are nothing else but things of
the Church, or of charity and faith, for these constitute the
Church. Hence it may be seen by every one, that the twelve
so often mentioned in the above passage, also the tribes, and
likewise the apostles, do not mean twelve, nor tribes, nor apostles, but that twelve mean all in one complex, as may be seen,
n. 577, 2089, 2129, 2130, 3272; in like manner, a hundred
forty and four, which is twelve times twelve. And as twelve
signifies all, it is evident, that the twelve tribes signify all
things of the Church, which, as was said above, are truth and
good, or faith and love. So likewise the twelve apostles, who
also represented all things of the Church, that is, all things of
faith and love, as may be seen, n. 2129, 3354, 3488, 3857.
Hence then this number is called the measure of a man, that
is, of an angel, which means a state of truth and good; that
measure denotes state, see n. 3104, that man is that which appertains to the Church, is plain from what was said concerning
the signification of man, n. 478, 479, 565, 768, 1871, 1894, and
also from this, that the Lord's kingdom is called the GRAND
MAN, and this by virtue of the good and truth which come
from the Lord; on which subject see the close of the chapters, n. 3624 to 3649, 3741 to 3751. That angel denotes the
same, may be seen, n. 1705, 1754, 1925, 2821, 3039. As the
New Jerusalem is treated of in the Apocalypse, so is it also in
the prophets in the Old Testament, and there in like manner it

signifies the Lord's New Church, as in Isaiah, chap. lxv. 18, 19, and following verses; in Zechariah. chap. xiv.; especially in Ezekiel, chap. xl. xli. xlii. xliii. xliv. xlv. xlvi. xlvii. xlviii.; where the New Jerusalem, the new temple, and the new earth, describe, in an internal sense, the Lord's kingdom in the heavens, and His kingdom on the earth, which is the Church. From what is said in those passages in Ezekiel, it is more manifest than from any others, what is signified by *earth*, by *Jerusalem*, by *temple*, and by all things therein, and also what by the *twelve tribes*, for the subject treated of is concerning the division of the earth, and *its inheritance according to tribes*, and also concerning the *city*, its *walls*, *foundations*, and *gates*, and all things belonging to the temple therein. From these passages I shall here quote only those which speak of the tribes. "The Lord Jehovih said, This is the boundary into which ye shall divide the *earth*, according to the *twelve tribes of Israel*, ye shall divide this *earth* according to the *tribes of Israel;* but it shall be ye shall divide it by lot for an inheritance, and to the sojourners who sojourn in the midst of you, they shall cast lot with you for an inheritance in the *midst of the tribes of Israel*," Ezekiel xlvii. 13, 21, 22, 23. "As for the *earth*, it shall be to the prince for a possession in Israel, and the princes shall no more afflict My people, and they shall *give the earth* to the house of Israel *according to their tribes*," xlv. 8. Concerning the inheritances, how they were assigned to *each particular tribe*, which is also mentioned by name, see chap. xlviii. 1, and following verses. And concerning the *gates* of the city, according to the *names of the tribes of Israel*, see the same chapter, verses 31 to 34. That tribes do not mean tribes, is evident, for ten tribes were already at that time dispersed through the whole earth, neither did they afterwards return, nor can they ever return, for they are become Gentiles, and yet mention is made of each, how they should inherit the earth, and what should be the boundaries to each, namely, what boundary to the tribe of Dan, verse 2; what boundary to the tribe of Asher, verse 3; what to Naphtali, Manasseh, Ephraim, Reuben, Judah: and of the inheritance of the Levites, what should be the boundary of Benjamin, what of Simeon, what of Issachar, of Zebulon, and of Gad, verse 4 to 29 of the same chapter. Also that the city should have twelve gates according to the names of the tribes of Israel; that three should be towards the north, namely, Reuben's, Judah's, and Levi's; three towards the east, namely, Joseph's, Benjamin's, and Dan's; three towards the south, namely, Simeon's, Issachar's, and Zebulon's; and three towards the west, namely, Gad's, Asher's, and Naphtali's, verses 31, 32, 33, 34, of the same chapter. Hence it is evident, that the twelve tribes signify all things of the Lord's kingdom, or all things of faith and love,

for these constitute the Lord's kingdom, as was said above. As
the twelve tribes signified all things of the Lord's kingdom,
therefore their encampments, and also their journeyings, represented the Lord's kingdom. Of these encampments and journeyings, it is thus written in Moses, " *That they should encamp
according to the tribes around the tent of the assembly,* towards
the east, Judah, Issachar, and Zebulon; towards the south,
Reuben, Simeon, and Gad; towards the west, Ephraim, Manasseh, and Benjamin ; and towards the north, Dan, Asher, and
Naphtali ; and that as they encamped, so they journeyed,"
Numb. ii. 1 to the end. That in this they represented the
Lord's kingdom, is evident from the prophecy of Balaam :
" When Balaam lifted up his eyes, and saw Israel *dwelling
according to the tribes,* the spirit of God came upon him, and
he uttered his enunciation, and said, How good are thy tabernacles, O Jacob, thy habitations, O Israel ; as valleys are they
planted, as gardens near a river, as lign-aloes which Jehovah
hath planted, as cedars near the waters," Numb. xxiv. 2, 3, 5, 6
That Balaam spake these words from Jehovah, is expressly said
in chap. xxii. 8, 18, 19, 35, 38 ; chap. xxiii. 5, 12, 16, 26 ; chap
xxiv. 2, 13.   Hence it is also evident what was represented by
the inheritances of the land of Canaan according to the tribes,
concerning which it is written in Moses, " That He should take
the sum of the company of the sons of Israel according to the
house of their fathers, from a son of twenty years, *every one
that went forth into the army of Israel;* and that the land
should be distributed by lot, *according to the names of the tribes
of their fathers they should receive inheritance,*" Numb. xxvi.
7 to 56 ; chap. xxxiii. 54; chap. xxxiv. 19 to 29: and that the
land was divided by Joshua, " by lot according to the tribes,"
Joshua xiii. xv. xvi. xvii. xviii. xix.   That this represented the
Lord's kingdom, as was said, is evident from all the particulars
contained in the account, for the land of Canaan signifies the
Lord's kingdom, see n. 1585, 1607, 3038, 3481, 3705.   The reason why the sons of Israel are called armies, and why it is said
that they should encamp according to their armies, and should
journey according to their armies, Numb. ii. 4, 6, 8, 11, 13,
15, 19, 21, 22, 23, 26, 28, 30, is, because army signifies the
same thing, namely, truths and goods, see n. 3448 ; and the
Lord is called Jehovah Zebaoth, or Jehovah of armies, n. 3448.
Hence they were called the armies of Jehovah when they went
forth out of Egypt, as in Moses, " It came to pass at the end of
thirty years and four hundred years, it came to pass in that very
day, that *all the armies of Jehovah went forth* from the land of
Egypt," Exod. xii. 41.   Every one may know, that a nation of
the kind the Israelites were in Egypt, and afterwards in the
wilderness, were only called the armies of Jehovah representatively, for they were in no good or truth, being the very worst

of all nations. Hence also it is manifest what the names of the twelve tribes in Aaron's breast-plate, which was called urim and thummim, signify; of which it is thus written in Moses, "There shall be therein four rows, twelve stones, and these stones shall be according to *the names of the sons of Israel,* twelve according to their names; the engravings of a signet shall be to each over its name for the *twelve tribes,*" Exod. xxviii. 21; chap. xxxix. 14; for Aaron represented the Lord's Divine Priesthood, on which account, all the things with which he was invested signified Divine celestial and spiritual things. But what they signified, will appear, by the Divine Mercy of the Lord, when we come to treat more particularly concerning them. In the breast-plate itself, inasmuch as it was most holy, there were representations of all things appertaining to love and faith in the Lord, which are the urim and thummim. The reason why the names were engraven on precious stones was, because stones in general signify truths, see n. 1298, 3720, and precious stones, truths which are pellucid from good, n. 114; and as the name of each particular tribe signified its quality, therefore a particular kind of stone was assigned, to mark each particular tribe, see Exod. xxviii. 17, 18, 19, 20; chap. xxxix. 8, 10, 11, 12, 13; which stone by its colour and pellucidity expressed the quality which was signified by the tribe; hence it was that Jehovah or the Lord gave answers by the urim and thummim. The two onyx stones, which were on the two shoulders of the ephod, represented the same, but in a lesser degree, as the twelve stones on the breast-plate, for shoulders signify all power, thus the Lord's omnipotence, see n. 1085; but the breast, or the heart and lungs, signified Divine celestial and spiritual love; the heart, Divine celestial love, and the lungs, Divine spiritual love; see n. 3635, and the end of this chapter, where I shall treat of the GRAND MAN, and of the correspondence thereof with the province of the heart, and with that of the lungs. Of the two stones on the shoulder of the ephod, it is thus written in Moses, "Thou shalt take two onyx stones, and shalt engrave on them the *names of the sons of Israel,* six of the names on one stone, and the remaining six names on the other stone, according to their generations; thou shalt place the two stones on the shoulders of the ephod, stones of remembrance of the *sons of Israel,*" Exod. xxviii. 9, 10, 11, 12; chap. xxxix. 6, 7. As tribes signified the things of truth and good, or of faith and love, and each tribe signified some universal principle thereof, and the tribe of Levi signified love (as will appear from the explication of verse 34 of this chapter), it may hence be known what was signified by placing rods, one for each tribe, in the tent of assembly, and by Levi's rod alone flourishing with almonds; of which it is thus written in Moses, "Let every one take a rod for the head of the house of their fathers, *twelve rods,* and let them be left in the tent of assembly, and thou shalt write Aaron's name upon the *rod of Levi,* and the rod of Aaron shall be set in the midst of the rods.   On the day following, lo! the *rod of Aaron* flourished for the *tribe of Levi,* brought forth flower, so that the flower flowered, and bare almonds," Numb. xvii. 17 to 23.   This signified that love was the essential and the principal of all things in the Lord's kingdom, and that from it came all fructification.   The reason why Aaron's name was upon it, was, because Aaron represented the Lord as to his Divine Priesthood.   That the Lord's priesthood signifies the Divine Good, which is of His love and mercy, and the Lord's royalty, the Divine Truth, which is from the Divine Good, may be seen, n. 1728, 2015, 3670.   From the cases above adduced it may appear plain, what tribes, and twelve tribes, signify in the following passages: "I heard the number of the sealed, *a hundred forty four thousand* out of *all the tribes of Israel;* of the *tribe of Judah* were sealed *twelve* thousand; of the *tribe of Reuben* were sealed *twelve* thousand; of the *tribe of Gad* were sealed *twelve* thousand; of the *tribe of Asher* were sealed *twelve* thousand; of the *tribe of Naphtali* were sealed *twelve* thousand; of the *tribe of Manasseh* were sealed *twelve* thousand; of the *tribe of Simeon* were sealed *twelve* thousand; of the *tribe of Levi* were sealed *twelve* thousand; of the *tribe of Issachar* were sealed *twelve* thousand; of the *tribe of Zebulon* were sealed *twelve* thousand; of the *tribe of Joseph* were sealed *twelve* thousand; of the *tribe of Benjamin* were sealed *twelve* thousand," Apoc. vii. 4, 5, 6, 7, 8.   And in Moses, "Remember the days of eternity, understand the years of generation and generation, when the Most High gave inheritance to the nations, when He separated the sons of man, appointed the boundaries of the people *according to the number of the sons of Israel,*" Deut. xxxii. 7, 8.   And in David, "Jerusalem is built as a city, which coheres together, thither the *tribes* go up, the *tribes of Jah,* a testimony to Israel, to confess to the name of Jehovah," Psalm cxxii. 3, 4.   And in Joshua, "Behold the ark of the covenant of the Lord of the whole earth passeth before you into Jordan; take ye *twelve men out of the tribes of Israel,* one man *out of a tribe;* and it shall come to pass when the soles of the feet of the priests, who carry the ark of Jehovah, the Lord of the whole earth, shall rest in the waters of Jordan, the waters of Jordan shall be cut off, they shall stand together in one heap," iii. 11 to 17.   Again, "Take up out of the midst of Jordan, out of the place where the feet of the priests stood tor preparation, *twelve stones,* which ye shall carry over with you, every man one stone upon his shoulder, *according to the number of the tribes of Israel,* that it may be for a sign that the waters of Jordan were cut off.   Moreover, Joshua set up *twelve stones* in the midst of Jordan, in the place where the feet of the priests

stood who carried the ark of the covenant," Joshua iv. 1 to 9.
Again, "Elijah took *twelve stones, according to the number of the
tribes of the sons of Jacob*, unto whom the Word of Jehovah came,
saying, Israel shall be thy name, and he built an altar to the name
of Jehovah," 1 Kings xviii. 31, 32. That tribes denote the goods
of love and the truths of faith, is evident also from the Lord's
words in Matthew, "Then shall appear the sign of the Son of
Man, and *then shall all the tribes of the earth wail*, and they
shall see the Son of Man coming in the clouds of heaven with
virtue and glory," xxiv. 30; where by all the tribes of the
earth wailing, is signified that there would no longer be any
acknowledgment of truth and life of good, for the subject treated
of in this chapter of Matthew is concerning the consummation of the age. In like manner in the Apocalypse, "Behold,
He shall come with clouds, and every eye shall see Him, and
they also who pierced Him, and *all the tribes of the earth* shall
mourn over Him," i. 7. What is meant by coming in the clouds
may be seen in the preface to chap. xviii. of Genesis; see fur
ther what was shown me by experience concerning twelve, n
2129, 2130. The reason why all things of faith and love are
called tribes, is, because the same expression in the original
tongue signifies also a sceptre and a staff. That a sceptre and
likewise a staff denotes power, by the Divine Mercy of the Lord
will be shown elsewhere. Hence the name tribe involves in it
this circumstance, that goods and truths have in them all power
from the Lord. On this account, the angels are called powers,
and likewise principalities, for princes signify the primary things
of charity and faith, as in the case of the twelve princes descended from Ishmael, Gen. xxv. 16, see n. 2089, 3272; and
also of the princes who presided over the tribes, Numb. vii. 1
to the end; chap. xiii. 4 to 16. From what has been above
said of the twelve tribes, it may be known why the disciples of
the Lord, who were afterwards called apostles, were twelve in
number, and that they represented the Church of the Lord as
to goods and truths in like manner as the tribes, n. 2129, 3354,
3488, 3857. That Peter represented faith, James charity, and
John the works of charity, may be seen in the preface to chap.
xviii. and to chap. xxii. of Genesis, also n. 3750. This likewise is plain from what the Lord said of them and with them.

3859. Verse 32. *And Leah conceived and bare a son, and
called his name Reuben, because she said, Jehovah hath seen
mine affliction, inasmuch as now my man will love me.* Leah
conceived and bare a son, signifies spiritual conception and
birth from what is external to what is internal: and called his
name Reuben, signifies the quality thereof, which is described:
because she said, Jehovah hath seen, signifies in a supreme
sense foresight; in an internal sense faith; in an interior sense
understanding; in an external sense sight; in the present case,

faith from the Lord : mine affliction, signifies a state of arriving at good : inasmuch as now my man will love me, signifies that hence would come the good of truth.

3860. "Leah conceived and bare a son"—that this signifies spiritual conception and birth from what is external to what is internal, appears from the signification of conceiving and bearing, as being, in the internal sense, to be regenerated ; for a man, who is regenerated, is conceived and born anew, wherefore regeneration is called a new, but spiritual birth. Man indeed is born as a man of his parents, but he is not made a man until he is re-born of the Lord. Spiritual and celestial life is what makes a man, for it distinguishes him from brutes. This spiritual conception and birth is signified in the Word by the conceptions and births mentioned therein, and by what is here said, that Leah conceived and bare a son. That generations and nativities have relation to faith and love, which they signify, see n. 613, 1145, 1255, 2020, 2584, 3856. That these conceptions and births are from what is external to what is internal, is signified by Leah's conceiving and bearing, for Leah represents the affection of external truth, see n. 3793, 3819, and Reuben, the truth of faith, which is the beginning of regeneration, and the external principle from which regeneration commences. How the case herein is, will appear evident from what follows concerning the children of Jacob by Leah and by Rachel.

3861. "And called his name Reuben"—that this signifies the quality of Reuben, which is described, appears from the signification of name and of calling a name, as being quality, see n. 144, 145, 1754, 1896, 2009, 2724, 3006, 3421. The quality itself is described by these words, *Jehovah hath seen mine affliction, and now my man will love me*, which are Reuben. That all the names in the Word signify things, has been often shown above, see n. 1224, 1264, 1876, 1888 ; and that the ancients gave names significative of states, n. 340, 1946, 2643, 3422. That the names of all the sons of Jacob here signify universals of the Church, will be seen presently. The universal itself is also inherent in the name of each ; but what universal, it is impossible for any one to know, unless he first knows what is involved in the internal sense of each expression which gives occasion to the name of each. For instance, what was involved in the internal sense of the expression, *He hath seen*, which gave occasion to the name Reuben ; what, also, in the internal sense of the expression, *He hath heard*, which gave occasion to the name Simeon ; what in the internal sense of *He hath adhered to*, which gave occasion to the name Levi ; and what in the internal sense of *Confessing*, which gave occasion to the name Judah ; and so of the rest.

3862. It was shown above, n. 3858, that the twelve tribes

signified all the principles of truth and good, or of faith and love, and since the subject now treated of is concerning the sons of Jacob, one by one, from whom the tribes were named, therefore it is right here to unfold another arcanum, namely, what is involved in them. That all celestial and spiritual heat, or love and charity, is perceived in an external form in heaven as flame from the sun, and that all celestial and spiritual light, or faith, appears in an external form in heaven as light from the sun; also, that this celestial and spiritual heat has in it wisdom, and that the light thence proceeding has in it intelligence, and this because they are from the Lord, Who, in heaven, is like a sun, may be seen, n. 1053, 1521 to 1533, 1619 to 1632, 2441, 2495, 2776, 3138, 3167, 3190, 3195, 3222, 3223, 3338, 3339, 3341, 3413, 3485, 3636, 3643. Hence it is evident, that all good is from the heat which flows from the Lord as a sun, and that all truth is from the light thence derived; and further, that all affections, which are of love or good, are variations of that celestial and spiritual heat which is from the Lord, and that thence come changes of state; and that all thoughts, which are of faith or truth, are variegations of that celestial and spiritual light which is from the Lord, and that thence comes intelligence. In this heat and light are all the angels who are in heaven, and their affections and thoughts are from no other source, and are nothing else than such variations and variegations. This is plain from their discourses, which, in consequence of this, their origin, are variegations or modifications of heavenly light containing heavenly heat, making them ineffable, and so various and full, as to be incomprehensible, see n. 3342, 3344, 3345. In order that these things might be exhibited representatively in the world, names were given to each of the sons of Jacob, which were significative of the universals of good and truth, or of love and faith, or of universals in regard to the variations of celestial and spiritual heat, and the variegations of light thence proceeding. The essential order of these universals is what determines the flame and consequent splendour. When the order commences from love, every thing, which follows thence in genuine order, appears flaming, but when the order commences from faith, every thing, which follows in genuine order, appears lucid or bright, but with all difference according to the things which follow. On the contrary, if the order be not genuine, every thing appears obscure, but with all difference. Of this order and the difference thence arising, by the Divine Mercy of the Lord, more will be said in the following pages. Hence then it is, that the Lord gave answers by the urim and thummim; and that according to the state of the case they received answers, by lights, and by the resplendence thereof from precious and transparent stones, on which were inscribed the names of the

twelve tribes, for, as was observed, on the names were inscribed
the universals of love and faith which are in the Lord's kingdom, consequently the universals of flame and light, whereby
the things of love and faith are represented in heaven. It may
be expedient therefore first to prove from the Word, that the
order of names, in which the tribes are named, is various in the
Word, and this according to the state of the thing treated of ;
and that thence it may be known, that the answers from the
Lord, given by the urim and thummim, were resplendencies
of light according to the state of the thing in question, grounded
in order ; for all the light of heaven varies according to the
states of a thing, and the states of the thing vary according to
the order of good and truth. But what principle of truth and
good each son of Jacob signifies, will appear from the explication, namely, that Reuben signifies *faith from the Lord;*
Simeon, *faith of the will* which is from the Lord ; Levi, *spiritual love* or charity ; Judah, the *Divine Principle of love* and
the Lord's celestial kingdom. What the eight remaining sons
signify, will be seen in the following chapter. Their order
according to nativity is what is here described, which stands
thus : *Reuben, Simeon, Levi, Judah, Dan, Naphtali, Gad,
Asher, Issachar, Zebulon, Joseph, Benjamin,* see verses 32, 33,
34, 35, of this chapter ; and verses 6, 8, 11, 13, 18, 20, 24, of
chap. xxx. ; and verse 18 of chap. xxxv. This order is according to the state of the thing here treated of, namely, the regeneration of man, for on this occasion the commencement is from
the truth of faith, which is Reuben, and the progression thence
is to the willing what is true, which is Simeon ; thence to
charity, which is Levi ; thus to the Lord, Who, in a supreme
sense, is Judah. That spiritual conception and birth, or regeneration, goes from what is external to what is internal, was
shown above, n. 3860, that is, from the truth of faith to the
good of love. Previous to Jacob's coming to his father Isaac
in Mamre Kirjath Arba, they are named in this order, *Reuben, Simeon, Levi, Judah, Issachar, Zebulon, Joseph, Benjamin, Dan, Naphtali, Gad, Asher,* Gen. xxxv. 23, 24, 25, 26 ;
where the sons born of Leah and Rachel are first named, and
afterwards those born of the handmaids, and this according to
the state of the thing there treated of. They are enumerated
in a still different order, when they journeyed and came to
Egypt, see Gen. xlvi. 9 to 19 ; and in another order, when they
were blessed by Jacob, at that time Israel, before his death,
Gen. xlix. 3 to 27 ; and in another, when they were blessed by
Moses, Deut. xxxiii. 6 to 24. They were in this latter order
when they encamped around the tent of assembly, to the east,
Judah, Issachar, Zebulon; to the south, *Reuben, Simeon, Gad;*
to the west, *Ephraim, Manasseh, Benjamin;* to the north, *Dan,
Asher, Naphtali,* Numb. ii. 1 to the end. And in this order

they stood to bless the people on Mount Gerizim, and to curse on Mount Ebal, see Deut. xxvii. 12, 13. When the princes chosen from each tribe were sent to explore the land, they are enumerated in this order, *Reuben, Simeon, Judah, Issachar, Ephraim, Benjamin, Zebulon, Joseph* or *Manasseh, Dan, Asher, Naphtali, Gad,* Numb. xiii. 4 to 16. But the princes who were to give the land for inheritance, are enumerated in another order, Numb. xxxiv. 19 to 29. In what order the lot was cast and came forth, when the land was given for inheritance, see Joshua, chap. xiii. to xix. In speaking of the boundaries of the new or holy land, in Ezekiel, which the tribes were to inherit, they are mentioned in this order, *Dan, Asher, Naphtali, Manasseh, Ephraim, Reuben, Judah, Benjamin, Simeon, Issachar, Zebulon, Gad,* all from the corner eastward to the corner of the sea or west, except Gad, who was at the corner of the south towards the south, xlviii. 2 to 8, 23 to 26; and in speaking of the gates of the new or holy city, they are mentioned in this order: towards the north three gates, of *Reuben,* of *Judah,* of *Levi;* towards the east three gates, of *Joseph,* of *Benjamin,* of *Dan;* towards the south three gates, of *Simeon,* of *Issachar,* of *Zebulon;* towards the west three gates, of *Gad,* of *Asher,* of *Naphtali,* Ezek. xlviii. 31 to 34. The order of those who were sealed, twelve thousand out of every tribe, may be seen, Apoc. vii. 5 to 8. In all these passages the enumeration of tribes is altogether according to the state of the thing treated of, to which the order corresponds. The real state of the thing appears from what precedes, and from what follows in the above passages. The order of the precious stones in the urim and thummim, is mentioned and described in the Word, but to what tribe each stone corresponded, is not mentioned, for they represented all the principles of light from celestial flame, that is, all the principles of truth from good, or all the principles of faith from love, and as they had this representation, therefore celestial light itself was miraculously translucent according to the thing in question, to which answer was given, being refulgent and resplendent for the affirmative of good and truth. Not to mention variegations of colours according to the differences of the state of good and truth; as in heaven, where all celestial and spiritual things are expressed by lights and their distinctions, and this in a manner ineffable and altogether incomprehensible to man; for, as has been occasionally shown, in heavenly light there is life from the Lord, consequently wisdom and intelligence. Hence, in the distinctions of light there is every thing which belongs to life, that is, to wisdom and intelligence, and in those of flame, of radiance, and of splendour, there is every thing which belongs to the life of good, and of truth from good, or to love towards the Lord and faith derived from it. This then was the urim and thummim, which was on the breast-plate of the ephod, and on the heart of Aaron. This is evident also from the fact, that the urim and thummim signify lights and perfections, and that the breast-plate, on which it was placed, was called the breast-plate of judgment, because judgment is intelligence and wisdom, see n. 2235. The reason why it was on Aaron's heart, was, because heart signifies the Divine Love, see n. 3635, and at the end of this chapter. Hence those precious stones were set in bottoms of gold, for gold. in the internal sense, is the good which is of love, see n. 113, 1551, 1552, and precious stone is the truth which is pellucid from good, n. 114. The urim and thummim it is thus written of in Moses, "Thou shalt make the *breast-plate of judgment*, a work of consideration, as the work of the ephod shalt thou make it, of gold, of blue, and of purple, and of scarlet double-dyed, and of fine twined linen thou shalt make it : the square shall be doubled, and thou shalt fill in it fillings of stone, there shall be four orders of stone ; *bottoms of gold* shall be in their fillings ; and *the stones shall be according to the names of the sons of Israel ;* engravings of a signet each according to its name shall be for the *twelve tribes,*" Exod. xxviii. 15 to 21 ; chap. xxxix. 8 to 14. The same passage points out the stones which were to be in each row. And further, "The breast-plate shall not depart from off the ephod ; and Aaron shall carry the *names of the sons of Israel* in the *breast-plate upon his heart,* in his entering in to the holy [place], for a memorial before Jehovah continually ; and thou shalt give to the *breast-plate of judgment, urim and thummim,* and they shall be upon the *heart of Aaron,* in his entering in before Jehovah ; and Aaron shall carry the *judgment of the sons of Israel upon his heart* before Jehovah continually," Exod. xxviii. 28, 29, 30 ; Levit. viii. 7, 8. That Jehovah or the Lord was inquired of by the urim, and gave answers, Moses thus declares, "Jehovah said to Moses, Take Joshua the son of Nun, thou shalt give of thy glory upon him, that all the congregation of the sons of Israel may obey : he shall stand before Eleazer the priest, and he *shall inquire of him in the judgment of urim before Jehovah,*" Numb. xxvii. 18, 20, 21. And in Samuel, "Saul inquired of Jehovah, and Jehovah did not answer him either by dreams, or by *urim,* or by the prophets," 1 Sam. xxviii. 6.

3863. " Because she said, that Jehovah hath seen"—that this signifies, in a supreme sense, foresight ; in an internal sense, faith ; in an interior sense, understanding ; and in an external sense, sight ; in the present case, faith from the Lord, appears from the signification of seeing, of which we shall speak presently. From what has been said above, it is very evident, that the twelve tribes, which had their names from the twelve sons of Jacob, signified all the principles of truth and good, or of faith and love, or all the principles of the Church, and that each tribe signified some universal; thus the twelve tribes, the twelve universals, which comprehend and include in them all and singular the things which belong to the Church, and in an universal sense, all things belonging to the Lord's kingdom. The universal which Reuben signifies, is faith. The reason why faith is the first universal, is, because in order to man's being regenerated, or being made a Church, he must first learn and imbibe the things belonging to faith, that is, to spiritual truth, for the doctrine of faith or of truth introduced him. The nature of man is such, that of himself he does not know what heavenly good is, but must be taught it by the doctrine, which is called the doctrine of faith. Every doctrine of faith has respect to life as an end, and therefore to good, for good is life. It was a controverted point amongst the ancients, which was the first-begotten of the Church, the truth of faith, or the good of love. They who maintained that truth was the first begotten, argued from external appearance, and concluded accordingly, because truth is and ought to be first learnt, and introduces man to good. But they knew not that good is essentially the first-begotten, and that it is insinuated from the Lord through the internal man, in order that it may adopt and receive the truth which is introduced by the external man, and that in good there is life from the Lord, and that in truth there is no life but what it receives by good, insomuch that good is the soul of truth, and appropriates to itself and puts on truth as the soul does its body. Hence it is manifest, that according to external appearance, truth is in the first place, and as it were the first-begotten, in the process of man's regeneration, when nevertheless good essentially is in the first place and the first-begotten, and so becomes when man is regenerated. That this is the case, see n. 3539, 3548, 3556, 3563, 3570, 3576, 3603, 3701. As the subject treated of in this chapter, and in the foregoing, is the regeneration of the natural principle, and here concerning its first state, which is that of introduction by truth to good, therefore the first son of Jacob, or Reuben, was named from *Jehovah seeing*, which, in the internal sense, signifies faith from the Lord. Faith considered in itself, is faith in the understanding and faith in the will; to know and to understand the truth of faith is called faith in the understanding, but to will the truth of faith is called faith in the will. Faith in the understanding is signified by Reuben, but faith in the will, by Simeon. That faith in the understanding, or the understanding of truth, precedes faith in the will, or the willing of truth, may be manifest to every one; for when any thing is unknown to man, as heavenly good is, he must necessarily first know that it exists, and understand its nature, before he can will it. That to see, in the external sense, signifies sight, is evident without

explication; that to see, in the interior sense, signifies understanding, is also manifest; for the sight of the internal man is
nothing else but the understanding, on which account the understanding, in common discourse, is called the internal sight,
and light is predicated of it, as of external, and is called intellectual light. That to see, in the internal sense, is faith from
the Lord, is evident from the fact, that the interior understanding has no other objects than the things belonging to truth and
good, for these are the things of faith. This interior understanding, or internal sight, which has for its objects the truths
of faith, does not manifest itself so much as the understanding
which has for its objects the truths of civil and moral life, for
it is within the latter, and in the light of heaven, and this light
is in obscurity so long as man is in the light of the world.
Nevertheless, to those who are regenerated, it reveals itself,
especially by conscience. That to see, in a supreme sense, is
foresight, may be evident, for the intelligence, which is predicated of the Lord, is infinite intelligence, which is nothing else
but foresight. That *seeing*, whence Reuben had his name, in
the internal sense, signifies faith from the Lord, is manifest
from numberless passages in the Word, of which we shall adduce the following: " Jehovah said to Moses, Make thee a serpent, and set it on wood, and it shall come to pass that every
one who hath been bitten, and *shall see it*, shall live. Moses
made a serpent of brass, and set it upon wood, and it came to
pass, if a serpent bit a man, and he *looked upon* the serpent of
brass, he revived," Numb. xxi. 8, 9. That the brazen serpent
represented the Lord as to the external sensual or natural principle, may be seen, n. 197; that brass denotes the natural
principle, n. 425, 1551. That faith in Him was represented by
the revival of those who saw, or looked upon it, the Lord Himself teaches in John, "As Moses lifted up the serpent in the
wilderness, so must the Son of Man be lifted up, *that whosoever
believeth on Him* should not perish, but should have eternal
life," iii. 14, 15. And in Isaiah, "The Lord said, Go and say
unto this people, Hearing hear ye, but do not understand, and
seeing see ye, and do not know; make fat the heart of this people, and make their ears heavy, and *besmear their eyes, lest they
should see with their eyes*, and hear with their ears, and their
heart should understand," vi. 9, 10. That seeing and not
knowing, signifies to understand what is true and still not to
acknowledge it, is evident; and that besmearing the eyes, lest
they should see with their eyes, signifies to deprive them of the
understanding of truth, and that seeing here signifies faith in
the Lord, is plain from the Lord's words in Matthew, chap. xiii.
13, 14; and in John, chap. xii. 36, 37, 39, 40. So in Ezekiel,
" Son of man, thou dwellest in the midst of a house of rebellion, *who have eyes to see*, but *do not see*, who have ears to hear,

and do not hear," xii. 2. Having eyes to see but not seeing,
signifies that they were able to understand the truths of faith,
but were not willing, and this by reason of evils, which are
the house of rebellion, inducing a deceitful light on falses, and
darkness on truths, according to these words in Isaiah, "This is
a people of rebellion, lying sons, sons not willing to hear the
law of Jehovah, who have said to them that see, See not, and
to them that have vision, *See not for us right things*, speak
to us smooth things, *see illusions*," xxx. 9, 10. Again, in the
same prophet, "The people that walked in darkness *have seen a
great light*, they who dwelt in the land of the shadow of death,
on them hath the light shined," ix. 1; where to see a great light
denotes to receive and believe the truths which are of faith.
On those who are in faith, heavenly light is said to shine forth,
for the light, which is in heaven, is Divine Truth derived from
Divine Good. Again, "Jehovah hath poured forth upon you
the spirit of drowsiness, and hath *closed your eyes*, the prophets
and your heads, *the seers* hath He covered," xxix. 10; where
closing the eyes denotes the understanding of truth. That eye
denotes understanding, see n. 2701. To cover the seers, denotes
those who know and teach the truths of faith. Seers were formerly called prophets, and that prophets signify those who teach,
and also truths of doctrine, may be seen, n. 2534. Again, "The
priest and the prophet err through strong drink, they err *amongst
the seers*, they stagger in judgment," xxviii. 7; where the sense
is the same; the judgment, wherein they stagger, is the truth of
faith, see n. 2235. Again, " *The eyes of them that see* shall not
wink, and the ears of them that hear shall hearken," xxxii. 3.
Again, " *Thine eyes shall behold* the king in his beauty, *they
shall see* the land of far distances," xxxiii. 17. To behold the
king in beauty denotes the truths of faith, which are called
beautiful from good; to see the land of far distances denotes
the good of love. That king denotes the truth of faith, see n.
1672, 2015, 2069, 3009, 3670; that beautiful is predicated as
derived from good, see n. 553, 3080, 3821; that land denotes
the good of love, see n. 620, 636, 3368, 3379. So in Matthew,
"Blessed are the pure in heart, for they *shall see God*," v. 8;
where it is evident, that seeing God means believing in Him,
or seeing Him by faith, for they who are in faith, by faith see
God, for God is in faith, and in that which constitutes true
faith. Again, in the same evangelist, "If *thine eye* offend
thee, pluck it out; for it is better for thee to enter into life *with
one eye*, than *having two eyes* to be cast into hell-fire," xviii. 9.
That eye in this passage does not mean eye, and that it is not
to be plucked out, is evident, for the bodily eye does not offend,
but the understanding of truth, which is meant by eye in the
case, see n. 2701. That it is better not to know and apprehend
the truths of faith, than to know and apprehend them, and still

live a life of evil, is signified by its being better to enter into
life with one eye, than having two eyes to be cast into hell-fire.
Again, " Blessed are your *eyes*, because *they see*, and your ears,
because they hear : Verily I say unto you, that many prophets
and righteous men have desired to *see the things which ye see*,
but *have not seen them*," xiii. 13 to 17 ; John xii. 40. To see
denotes to know and understand the things relating to faith in
the Lord, consequently it denotes faith ; for they were not
blessed in consequence of seeing the Lord, and His miracles,
but in consequence of believing, as may appear from these
words in John, " I said unto you, that ye also *have seen Me,
and believe not :* This is the will of Him Who sent Me, that
every one who *seeth the Son, and believeth on Him*, should have
eternal life ; not that any one *hath seen* the Father, except He
Who is with the Father, He *hath seen* the Father ; verily, verily,
I say unto you, whosoever believeth on Me hath eternal life," vi.
36, 40, 46, 47. To see and not to believe denotes to know the
truths of faith and not to receive them ; to see and to believe
denotes to know and to receive ; no one having seen the Father
except He Who is with the Father, denotes that Divine Good
cannot be acknowledged except by Divine Truth. That the
Father is Divine Good, and the Son Divine Truth, may be
seen, n. 3704. Hence the internal sense is, that no one can
have heavenly good, unless he acknowledge the Lord. In like
manner in the same evangelist, " *No one hath seen God a*
any time the only-begotten Son, Who is in the bosom of the
Father, He hath made Him manifest," i. 18. And again, " Jesus said, *Whoso seeth Me, seeth Him* Who sent Me ; I am come
a light into the world, that *whosoever believeth on Me* should
not abide in darkness," xii. 45, 46 ; where it is said plainly,
that to see is to believe or to have faith. Again, " Jesus
said, If ye have known Me, ye have known My Father also,
and from henceforth ye have known Him and *have seen Him ;
whoso believeth on Me, hath seen the Father*," xiv. 7, 9. Again,
" The world cannot receive the Spirit *of Truth*, because it *seeth
Him not*, neither knoweth Him : I will not leave you orphans,
I come to you ; yet a little while and the *world shall see me no
more, but ye shall see Me*, because I live ye shall live also," xiv.
17, 18, 19 ; where to see denotes to have faith, for the Lord is
seen only by faith, for faith is the eye of love, the Lord being
seen of love by faith, and love is the life of faith, wherefore it
is said, Ye shall see Me ; because I live, ye shall live also.
Again, " Jesus said, For judgment am I come into this world,
that *they who see not may see*, but that *they who see may be made
blind ;* the Pharisees said, Are we *blind* also ? Jesus said unto
them, If ye were *blind*, ye would not have sin, but now ye say,
We see, therefore your sin remaineth," ix. 39, 40, 41. Here,
they who see denote those who imagine themselves to be more

intelligent than all others; of these it is said, that they should be made blind, that is, should not receive faith. That not to see, or to be blind, is predicated of those who are in falses, and also of those who are in ignorance, may be seen, n. 2383. So in Luke, "To you it is given to know the mysteries of the kingdom of God, but to others in parables, that *seeing they may not see*, and hearing they may not hear," viii. 10. Again, "I say unto you, there are some of those standing here, who shall not taste death, *until they shall see the kingdom of God*," ix. 27; Mark ix. 1: to see the kingdom of God denotes to believe. Again, "Jesus said unto His disciples, The day shall come, when ye shall desire *to see one of the days of the Son of Man*, but shall not *see*, xvii. 22; speaking of the consummation of the age, or of the last time of the Church, when there is no longer any faith. Again, "It came to pass when Jesus reclined with them, He took bread and blessed it, and breaking, gave it to them, and *their eyes were opened*, and they knew Him," xxiv. 30, 31; which signifies that the Lord appears by good, but not by truth without good, for bread is the good of love, see n. 276, 680, 2165, 2177, 3478, 3735, 3813. From these and several other passages it is evident, that to see, in the internal sense, denotes faith from the Lord, for there is no other faith, which is real, but what comes from the Lord: this also enables man to see, that is, to believe; but self-derived faith, or faith grounded in man's proprium, is not faith, for it causes him to see falses as truths, and truths as falses, and if he sees truths as truths, still he does not see, because he does not believe, for he sees himself in them, and not the Lord. That to see denotes to have faith in the Lord, may appear from what has been frequently said above concerning the light of heaven, namely, that being from the Lord, it has with it intelligence and wisdom, consequently faith in Him, for faith in the Lord is contained in intelligence and wisdom, wherefore to see from that light, as the angels do, can signify nothing else but faith in the Lord. The Lord Himself also is in that light, because it proceeds from Him. It is this light also which shines bright in the consciences of those who have faith in the Lord, although man is ignorant of it during his life in the body, for the light of the world then obscures the light of heaven.

3864. "Mine affliction"—that this signifies a state of arriving at good, appears from the signification of affliction, as being temptation, concerning which, see n. 1846; and as this is the means of arriving at good, mine affliction here signifies a state of coming from truth, which is an external principle, and of arriving at good, which is an internal principle.

3865. "Because now my man will love me"—that this signifies that hence would come the good of truth, appears from the signification of *will love*, as being good thence derived, **for**

all good is of love, wherefore loving here signifies good ; and
from the signification of man, as being truth, concerning which,
see n. 3134.   What the good of truth means has been often explained above, namely, that it is the affection of truth for the
sake of life, for life is the good which is respected in truth by
those who are afterwards regenerated.   Without a life accord
ing to truth, no conjunction of truth with good is effected, con
sequently there is no appropriation.   Every one may see this,
from attending to those who live ill, and to those who live well.
They who live ill, although they have been instructed during
childhood and youth in the doctrines of the Church, like other
people, are still found on examination to believe nothing at all
concerning the Lord, or faith in Him and the truths of the
Church; while they who live well, have faith in the truths
which they believe to be truths.   But they who teach truths,
as the rulers of the Church do, and live ill, may indeed profess
to believe, yet still in heart they do not believe.   With some
of them, what they call faith is a mere persuasion which has
the semblance of faith, amounting to no more than mere knowledge confirmed, not because it is truth, but because it is expedient to make profession of it for reasons of office, of honour,
and of gain.   This penetrates no deeper than through the ears
into the memory, and from the memory it makes a way out to
the lips, but does not enter into the heart, and so come into confession.   Hence it is evident, that the life teaches the quality
of the acknowledgment of truth, that is, the quality of faith ;
and that faith separate from the good of life, declares, that however a man lives, he may still be saved through grace ; and
that it argues against the doctrine, that every one's life remains
with him after death.

3866. From the internal sense of the words, which Leah
spake concerning Reuben at his birth, " Jehovah hath seen
mine affliction, because now my man will love me," it is plain
what principle of the Church Reuben signifies, or the tribe
which took its name from Reuben, namely, that which is the
first of regeneration, or which is the first on man's being made
a Church, and that this is truth of doctrine whereby he may
attain to good of life.

3867. Verse 33. *And she conceived as yet, and bare a son,
and said, Because Jehovah hath heard that I was hated, and
hath given me also this, and she called his name Simeon.*   She
conceived as yet, and bare a son, signifies, as before, spiritual
conception and birth from an external towards more interior
principles : Because Jehovah hath heard, signifies in a supreme
sense providence ; in an internal sense, the will of faith ; in an
interior sense, obedience : in an external sense, hearing ; in the
present case, faith in the will, which comes from the Lord alone :
that I was hated, signifies a state of faith if the will be not

correspondent to it: and hath given me also this, signifies what is successive: and she called his name Simeon, signifies his quality.

3868. "She conceived as yet, and bare a son"—that this signifies spiritual conception and birth from an external towards more interior principles, appears from what was said above, n. 3860, where the same words occur. Advancement is said to be made from an external towards more interior principles when it is made from the knowledge, which is of the understanding, to the will; or, to speak spiritually, when it is made from truth, which is of faith, to charity. For the understanding proceeds from the will, and manifests the will in a sort of visible form; in like manner, faith proceeds from charity, and manifests charity in a sort of form. Hence it is evident, that the understanding is the external of the will, and that faith is the external of charity, or, what is the same thing, that the will is the internal of the understanding, and charity the internal of faith. Thus, to advance from an external to more interior principles, is to advance from faith in the understanding to faith in the will, or from faith to charity, which is represented by Levi, who is treated of in what presently follows. It is to be observed that faith, when distinguished from charity, means truth, such as the truth of doctrine, or such as there is in the confession called the Apostles' Creed; and this is agreeable to the general apprehension of the Word as received in the Church, for to have faith in truths is believed to be the faith which ensures salvation. There are few who know that faith is trust and confidence, and among those few, still fewer who know that trust or confidence comes from charity, and cannot exist in any one who has not lived the life of charity.

3869. "Because Jehovah hath heard"—that this signifies in a supreme sense providence; in an internal sense, the will of faith; in an interior sense, obedience; in an external sense, hearing; in the present case, faith in the will, which comes from the Lord alone, appears from the signification of hearing. That hearing has relation to the sense of hearing, it is needless to explain; but that hearing, in an interior sense, is obedience, and in an internal sense, faith in the will, appears from several passages in the Word, as will be seen presently; and also from the quality of hearing in respect to that of sight. That the sight, in the interior sense, is the understanding, and in the internal sense, faith in the understanding, may be seen, n. 3863, and this because things appear to the internal sight according to their quality, and thus are apprehended by a kind of faith, but of an intellectual kind. So too when the things which are heard penetrate to the interiors of man, they also are changed into something like sight, for what was heard is seen interiorly, and therefore hearing signifies what seeing does, to wit, what relates to the understanding, and also to faith. Hearing, however, at the same time persuades that a thing is so, and affects not only the intellectual part of man, but also his voluntary part, causing him to will what he sees. Hence it is, that hearing signifies the understanding of a thing, and at the same time obedience, and in a spiritual sense, faith in the voluntary part. Since all this is concealed in hearing, to wit, obedience and faith in the will, therefore this, too, is signified by *hearing, hearkening* and *attending*, in common discourse, for to hear, and hearken to any one, means to be obedient. The reason why the interiors of a thing are sometimes contained in the expressions of man's discourse, is, because it is the spirit of man which thinks and perceives the meaning of the expressions in speech, and it is in a kind of communion with spirits and angels, who are in the principles of words. Moreover, such is the circle of things in man, that whatever enters by the ear and eye, or the hearing and sight, passes into his understanding, and through the understanding into the will, and from the will into act. This is the case also with the truth of faith : it first becomes the truth of faith in knowledge, afterwards, the truth of faith in will, and lastly, the truth of faith in act, or charity. Faith in knowledge, or in the understanding, is Reuben, as has been already shown ; faith in the will is Simeon, and faith in the will, when it becomes charity, is Levi. That hearing, in a supreme sense, is providence, may appear from what was said above, n. 3863, concerning seeing, as being, in a supreme sense, foresight ; for the Lord's foresight is the seeing from eternity to eternity that so a thing is ; but the Lord's providence, the ruling that a thing may be so, and the bending man's free-will to good, so far as He foresees that man suffers himself to be bended in freedom, see n. 3854. That Jehovah hearing, whence Simeon had his name, in an interior sense, signifies obedience, and in an internal sense, faith in the will from the Lord alone, is evident from numberless passages in the Word, as from the following, "Lo! a voice out of the cloud, saying, This is My beloved Son, in whom I am well pleased, *hear ye Him*," Matt. xvii. 5 ; where to hear Him, denotes to have faith in Him, and to obey His precepts, or to have faith in the will. So in John, "Verily, verily, I say unto you, that the hour shall come, when the dead *shall hear the voice of the Son of God*, and *they who hear shall live ;* marvel not at this, because the hour cometh in which all who are in the graves *shall hear His voice*," v. 25, 28 ; where to hear the voice of the Son of God denotes to have faith in the Lord's words, and to will them. They who have faith in the will, receive life, wherefore it is said, they who hear shall live. Again, "He who entereth in by the door is the shepherd of the sheep, to Him the porter openeth, and *the sheep hear His voice*. And other sheep I have, which are not of this sheepfold, them also must I bring, and *they shall hear My voice*, and shall become one flock, and one shepherd; My sheep *hear My voice*, and I know them, and they follow Me," x. 2, 3, 16, 27; where to hear a voice manifestly denotes to obey from faith in the will. Again, "Every one who is of the truth *heareth My voice*," xviii. 37; where the same thing is meant. So in Luke, "Abraham said unto him, They have Moses and the prophets, *let them hear them;* if they *hear not* Moses and the prophets, neither will they be persuaded if one rose from the dead," xvi. 29, 31; where hearing Moses and the prophets denotes to know the things contained in the Word, and to have faith in the Word, thus also to will them, for to have faith and not to will is to see and not to hear, but to have faith and to will is both to see and to hear; wherefore, seeing and hearing are mentioned together in the Word throughout, and seeing signifies the same as Reuben, and hearing, the same as Simeon, for they are joined together as brother is to brother. That seeing and hearing are mentioned conjointly, appears from the following passages: "Therefore speak I to them by parables, *because seeing they see not, and hearing they hear not*, neither understand; and in them is fulfilled the prophecy of Isaiah, which saith, *By hearing ye shall hear*, and shall not understand, and *seeing ye shall see*, and shall not perceive; for the heart of this people is made gross, *and their ears are dull of hearing*, and *their eyes have they closed*, lest at any time they *should see with their eyes*, and *hear with their ears*, and understand with the heart. But blessed are your *eyes, for they see, and your ears, for they hear*. Verily I say unto you, that many prophets and just men have desired *to see the things which ye see*, but have not seen them, and *to hear the things which ye hear*, and have not heard them," Matt. xiii. 13 to 17; John xii. 40; Isaiah vi. 9. So in Mark, "Jesus said to the disciples, Why dispute ye because ye have no bread? Are not ye as yet intelligent, neither do ye understand? Have ye your heart yet hardened? *Having eyes see ye not, and having ears hear ye not?*" viii. 17, 18. And in Luke, "To you it is given to know the mysteries of the kingdom of God, but to others in parables, that *seeing they may not see, and hearing they may not hear*," viii. 10. And in Isaiah, "*The eyes of the blind* shall be opened, and *the ears of the deaf* shall be opened," xxxv. 5. Again, "Then shall *the deaf hear* in that day the words of the book, and *the eyes of the blind shall see* out of thick darkness, and out of darkness," xxix. 18. "*Hear, ye deaf*, and *look, ye blind, that ye may see*," xlii. 18 "Bring forth the *blind* people which will have *eyes*, and the deaf which will have ears," xliii. 8. Again, "*The eyes of them that see* shall not wink, and *the ears of them that hear* shall hearken," xxxii. 3. Again, "*Let thine eyes respect* thy teachers, and *thine ears hear* the Word," xxx. 20, 21. Again,

" Who stoppeth *his ear lest he should hear* bloods, and shutteth
his eyes lest they should see evil, He shall dwell in high (places),"
xxxiii. 15, 16. And in Ezekiel, "Son of man, thou dwellest in
the midst of the house of rebellion, who have *eyes to see but see
not, who have ears to hear and hear not,*" xii. 2. In these passages, mention is made both of seeing and hearing, because the
one follows the other, namely, faith in the understanding, which
is seeing, and faith in the will, which is hearing, otherwise 'it
would have been sufficient to have mentioned one only. Hence
it is manifest, why one son of Jacob was named from seeing,
and another from hearing. That seeing signifies faith in knowledge or in the understanding, and hearing faith in obedience
or in the will, is from correspondences in the other life, and
significatives thence derived. Those spirits who are intellectual, and thence in faith, belong to the province of the eye,
and those who are obedient, and thence in faith, belong to the
province of the ear. That it is so, will be seen, by the Divine
Mercy of the Lord, at the close of the chapters, where the
GRAND MAN, and the correspondence of all things in the human
body therewith, will be treated of. Hence then it is, that *the
eye,* in an internal sense, denotes understanding, see n. 2701,
and *the ear,* obedience, and in a spiritual sense, faith thence derived, or faith in the will, as appears also from the following
passages : " Yea, *thou hast not heard,* yea, thou hast not known,
yea, from that time *thine ear was not opened,*" Isaiah xlviii. 8.
Again, "The Lord Jehovih will stir up *mine ear to hear,* like
the learned, the Lord Jehovih *hath opened mine ear,* and I was
not rebellious," l. 4, 5. Again, "In attending attend to Me
and eat good, that your soul may be delighted in fatness ; *incline your ear,* and go to Me, *hear* that your soul may live," lv
2, 3. And in Jeremiah, "To whom shall I speak and testify,
that they may hear ? behold *their ear is uncircumcised,* an
they cannot hearken," vi. 10. Again, "This I have commanded
them, saying, *Hear My voice,* then will I be to you a God, and
ye shall be to me a people ; and *they heard not, neither inclined
their ear,*" vii. 23, 24, 26. Again, "*Hear ye* women the Word
of Jehovah, and let *your ear* receive the Word of His mouth,"
ix. 19. Again, "Ye have not inclined *your ear,* and *have not
obeyed Me,*" xxxv. 15. And in Ezekiel, "Son of man, all My
words, which I have spoken with thee, *receive into thine heart,
and hear with thine ears,*" iii. 10. Again, "I will give My
zeal against thee, and they shall deal with thee in anger, they
shall remove thy nose and *thine ears,*" xxiii. 25 ; to remove
the nose and the ears denotes the perception of truth and good,
and the obedience of faith. So in Zechariah, "They have re-
fused to attend, and have given a refractory shoulder, and *their
ears have they made heavy, that they may not hear,* and their
heart have they set as adamant, *that they might not hear the*

law," vii. 11, 12. And in Amos, " Thus saith Jehovah, As the
shepherd hath snatched from the mouth of the lion two legs, or
a small part of an ear, so shall the sons of Israel be snatched
away in Samaria, in the corner of a bed, and in the extreme
part of a couch," iii. 12; where two legs denote the will of
good, and a small piece of an ear the will of truth. That a
small piece of an ear means this, can only appear, as was said,
from the correspondences and significatives thence derived in
another life, according to which the internal sense of the Word,
and also the rituals in the Israelitish and Jewish Church, must
be understood. Hence it was, that when Aaron and his sons
were inaugurated into the ministry, it was commanded amongst
other things, that Moses should take of the blood of a "ram,
and should put it on the *auricle of Aaron's ear*, and *upon the
auricle of the ear of his sons;* and upon the thumb of their
right hand, and upon the thumb of their right foot," Exod.
xxix. 20. This ritual represented the will of faith, into which
the priest also was, as it were, to be initiated; that this ritual
was holy, may be obvious to every one from the fact, that it
was enjoined to Moses by Jehovah, thus also it may be obvious
that to put blood on the auricle of the ear was holy. But what
particular holy thing this signified, can only be known from
the internal sense of the Word, which sense here is, that the
holiness of faith from the will should be secured. That ear
signifies obedience, and, in an internal sense, the faith thence
derived, appears even more plainly from the ritual respecting
a servant, who was not willing to depart from service; of whom
it is thus written in Moses, "If a man-servant or maid-servant
shall not be willing to depart from service, his lord shall bring
him unto God, and shall bring him to the door, or to the door
post, and *his lord shall bore his ear through with an awl*, and
he shall serve him for ever," Exod. xxi. 6; Deut. xv. 17. To
bore the ear through with an awl at the door-post denotes to
serve or obey perpetually; in a spiritual sense not to be willing
to understand truth, but to will truth from obedience, which is
respectively not freedom. Since the ears mean, in the internal
sense, the obedience of faith, and hearing, obedience, it is manifest what these words of the Lord, which He so often spake,
signify, " *He who hath an ear to hear, let him hear*," Matt. xiii.
9, 43; Mark iv. 9, 23; chap. vii. 16; Luke viii. 8; chap. xiv.
35; Apoc. ii. 7, 11, 29; chap. iii. 14, 22. That to hear in a
supreme sense denotes providence, and to see, foresight, appears
from the passages in the Word where eyes and ears are predicated of Jehovah, or the Lord, as in Isaiah, " O Jehovah, *incline thine ears, and hear, open thine eyes, and see*, O Jehovah,"
xxxvii. 17. And in Daniel, " Incline, O my God, *thine ear,
and hear;* open, O Jehovah, *thine eyes*, and see our waste-
nesses," ix. 18. And in David, " O God, incline *thine ear* unto

me, and *hear* my discourse," Psalm xvii. 6.   Again, "Incline *thine ear* unto me, and preserve me," Psalm lxxi. 3.   Again, "*Turn an ear* to my prayers, because of Thy truth; answer me, because of Thy justice," Psalm cxliii. 1.   And in Jeremiah, " O Jehovah, Thou hast heard my voice ; hide not *Thine ear* at my sighing, at my cry," Lam. iii. 56.   Again in David, " O Jehovah, hide not Thy faces from me, in the day when I have straitness ; incline *Thine ear* to me, in the day I cry, answer me," Psalm cii. 3.   That Jehovah has neither ears nor eyes, like a man, is a well known truth, but ear and eye signify an attribute predicable of His Divine Being, namely, infinite will, and infinite intelligence.   Infinite will is providence, and infinite intelligence is foresight ; this is what ear and eye mean, in the supreme sense, when attributed to Jehovah.   From these considerations then, it is evident what, in every sense, the expression, " Jehovah hath heard," whence Simeon had his name, signifies.

3870. "That I was hated "—that this signifies a state of faith, if the will be not correspondent thereto, appears from the signification of being hated, as being not loved, for such is the state of faith if the will does not correspond to it.   The subject treated of in the internal sense is the progress of man's regeneration from the external to the internal, that is, from the truth of faith to the good of charity.   The truth of faith is external, and the good of charity is internal.   In order that the truth of faith may live, it must be introduced into the will, and receive life there, for truth does not live from knowing, but from willing, inasmuch as life flows in from the Lord through the new will which He creates in man.   The first life manifests itself by obedience, which is the beginning of will ; the second, by the affection of doing the truth, which is a progression of the will, and which exists when delight and blessedness are perceived in doing the truth.   Unless the progress of faith be such, truth does not become truth, but something separate from life, sometimes confirmative of the false, and sometimes persuasive of it, thus something defiled, for it attaches itself to man's evil affection, or his lust, that is, to his own will, which is contrary to charity.   Such is the nature of this, which many at this day believe to be the true faith, and to have a saving power alone without the works of charity.   But this faith, which is separate from, and therefore contrary to charity, is represented in what follows by Reuben, in that he lay with Bilhah his father's concubine, Gen. xxxv. 22, and which Jacob expresses his detestation of in these words, " Reuben, my first-born, thou art my strength, and the beginning of my virtue; thou art light as water, lest thou shouldest excel, because thou hast gone up to thy father's bed, then defiledst thou my couch," Gen. xlix. 3, 4. The will and affection of this faith, as contrary to charity, is also described in the same chapter by Simeon and Levi in these words, "Simeon and Levi are brethren, arms of violence are their daggers; let not my soul come into their secret, in their assembly let not my glory unite itself, because in their fury they slew a man, and in their will they unstrung an ox. Cursed is their fury because vehement, and their anger because griev-ous; I will divide them in Jacob, and disperse them in Israel,' verses 5, 6, 7. That faith separate from charity is here de-scribed by Simeon and Levi, will be shown, by the Divine Mercy of the Lord, in what follows.

3871. "And hath given me also this"—that this signifies a successive, namely, faith in obedience or the will, as succeed-ing faith in knowledge or the understanding, was shown above. This is what the words, "He hath given me also this," signify.

3872. "And she called his name Simeon"—that this signifies his quality, appears from the signification of name, and of call-ing a name, as being quality, see n. 144, 145, 1754, 1896, 2009, 2724, 3006, 3421. The quality itself is contained in the inter-nal sense of the words which Leah spake, "Jehovah hath heard that I was hated, and hath given me also this." This quality is what is signified by Simeon, and also by the tribe which was named from him; and this is another universal of the Church, or principle in man's regeneration when he is made a Church, namely, obedience, or the willingness to do the truth of faith, into which obedience, and in which will, charity is implanted, which next succeeds, and is signified by Levi.

3873. Verse 34. *And she conceived as yet, and bare a son, and said, Now this time my man will adhere to me, because I have borne him three sons, and she called his name Levi.* She conceived as yet, and bare a son, signifies, as before, spiritual conception and birth from an external to a principle still more internal : and said, Now this time my man will adhere to me, signifies, in a supreme sense, love and mercy ; in an internal sense, charity; in an external sense, conjunction; in the present case, spiritual love : because I have borne him three sons, sig-nifies what is successive : therefore she called his name Levi, signifies his quality.

3874. "She conceived as yet, and bare a son"—that this signifies spiritual conception, and birth from an external to a principle still more internal, appears from what was said above, n. 3860, 3868, where the same words occur.

3875. "And said, Now this time my man will adhere to me" —that this signifies, in a supreme sense, love and mercy : in an internal sense, charity ; in an external sense, conjunction ; and in the present case, spiritual love, appears from the significa-tion of adhering. That to adhere, in an external, or proximately interior sense, is conjunction, may appear without explication. That to adhere, in an internal sense, denotes charity, is evident

from the fact, that charity, or what is the same thing, mutual
love, is spiritual conjunction, for it is a conjunction of the will-
affections, and a consequent agreement of the thoughts of the
understanding, thus it is a conjunction of minds in both their
principles. That to adhere, in a supreme sense, is love and
mercy, is hence manifest, for the infinite and eternal, which is
predicated of charity or spiritual love, is mercy, which is the
Divine Love towards the human race, sunk, as it is, into such
great miseries ; for since man of himself is nothing but evil,
and what is in him, so far as it is from himself, is nothing but
what is infernal, and since he is looked upon by the Lord from
Divine Love, his elevation in this case out of the hell, in which
he is of himself, and his deliverance is called mercy. Hence,
since mercy is from the Divine Love, therefore adhering, in a
supreme sense, signifies both love and mercy. That to adhere,
in an internal sense, signifies spiritual love, or what is the same
thing, charity towards our neighbour, may appear also from other
passages in the Word, as in Isaiah, "Let not the son of the
stranger say, *who hath adhered to Jehovah*, saying, Jehovah by
separating separates me from His people ; the sons of the stranger, *who adhere to Jehovah*, to minister unto Him, and to *love*
the name of Jehovah, shall be to Him for servants," lvi. 3, 6 ;
where to adhere to Jehovah denotes to observe the commandments, which is an effect of spiritual love, for no one observes
the commandments of God from the heart but he who is in the
good of charity towards his neighbour. So in Jeremiah, "In
those days the sons of Israel shall come, they and the sons of
Judah, going and weeping shall they go, and shall seek Jehovah their God, they shall ask Zion concerning the way, thither
shall their faces be; come ye and *let us adhere to* Jehovah with
the covenant of an age, it is not given to oblivion," l. 4, 5 ;
where to adhere to Jehovah denotes in like manner to observe
the commandments from the heart, that is, from the good of
charity. So in Zechariah, "*Many nations shall adhere to Jehovah* in that day, and shall be to Me for a people," ii. 15 ;
where the sense is the same. Again, in Isaiah, "Jehovah will
have mercy on Jacob, and will again choose Israel, and will
place them on their land, and *the sojourner shall adhere to them*,
and they shall join themselves to the house of Jacob," xiv. 1.
The sojourner adhering to them denotes being in a similar ob-
servance of the law; to adjoin themselves to the house of Jacob
denotes to be in the good of charity, in which they are, who
are signified by the house of Jacob. So in Matthew, "No one
can serve two masters, for he will either hate the one and love
the other, or *he will adhere to the one* and despise the other,"
vi. 24. Here loving denotes the celestial principle of love, and
adhering, its spiritual principle ; each is mentioned as being
distinct from the other, otherwise it would have been sufficient

to mention one. They who are in spiritual love are therefore called the sons of Levi, as in Malachi, "Who can endure the day of His coming, and who shall stand when He shall appear? He shall sit melting and purifying silver, and He shall purify *the sons of Levi*, and purge them as gold and silver," iii. 2, 3. That in a supreme sense the Lord is Levi, from His Divine Love and Mercy towards those who are in spiritual love, the same prophet thus declares, "That ye may know that I have sent this commandment to you, to be *My covenant with Levi*, saith Jehovah Zebaoth, My covenant shall be with him of life and peace. Ye have departed out of the way, ye have caused many to stumble at the law, ye have corrupted *the covenant of Levi*, therefore I have given you to be despised," ii. 4, 5, 8, 9. And since Levi, in a supreme sense, is the Divine Love or Mercy of the Lord, and, in an internal sense, spiritual love, therefore the tribe of Levi was made the priesthood, for the priesthood, in the internal sense of the Word, is nothing else than the holiness of love, while royalty is the holiness of faith, see n. 1728, 2015.

3670. Since the word *adhere*, from which Levi was named, sig-nifies spiritual love, which is the same as mutual love, the same word in the original tongue signifies mutual giving and receiving and mutual giving and receiving in the Jewish Church repre-sented mutual love, on which subject, by the Divine Mercy of the Lord, we shall speak elsewhere. Mutual love differs from friendship in this, that mutual love regards the good which is in a man, and being directed to good, it is directed to him who is in good; but friendship regards the man, and it also becomes mutual love, when it respects the man from good, or for the sake of good; but when it does not respect him from good, or for the sake of good, but for the sake of self which it calls good, then friendship is not mutual love, but approaches to self-love, and so far as it approaches this, so far it is opposite to mutual love. Mutual love, in itself, is nothing else than charity towards the neighbour, for neighbour, in the internal sense, is nothing else than good, and, in a supreme sense, the Lord, since all good is from Him, and He is good itself, see n. 2425, 3419. This mutual love or cha-rity is what is meant by spiritual love, and what is signified by Levi. Celestial love also, and conjugial love, are expressed in the literal sense of the Word by *adhering*, but then it is derived from a word in the original tongue different from that from which Levi comes. This expression signifies a still closer con-junction, as in the following passages, "Thou shalt fear Jeho-vah thy God, thou shalt serve Him, and *shalt adhere to Him*," Deut. x. 20. "Ye shall go after Jehovah your God, and shall fear Him, and shall keep His precepts, and shall hear His voice, and shall serve Him, and *shall adhere to Him*," Deut. xiii. 5. "*To love Jehovah your God*, and to go in all His ways, and *to adhere to Him*," Deut. xi. 22. "*To love Jehovah thy*

God, to obey His voice, and *to adhere to Him,* because He is
thy life," Deut. xxx. 20.   And in Joshua, "Study exceedingly
to do the precept and the law, which Moses the servant of
Jehovah commanded you, *to love* Jehovah your God, and to
walk in all His ways, and to keep His precepts, and *to adhere
to Him,* and to serve Him in all your heart, and in all your
soul," xxii. 5.   And in the second book of the Kings, "King
Hezekiah trusted in Jehovah the God of Israel, *he adhered to
Jehovah,* he did not depart from after Him, and he kept His
commandments, which Jehovah commanded Moses," xviii. 5,
6.   And in Jeremiah, "*As a girdle adhereth to the loins of a
man,* so have I *caused to adhere to Me* the whole house of
Israel, and the whole house of Judah, to be to Me for a people,
and for a name, and for a praise, and for a renown, and they
have not obeyed," xiii. 11.   That conjugial love is also expressed by adhering, is evident from the following passages :
"Therefore shall a man leave his father and his mother, and
shall adhere unto his wife, and they shall be one flesh," Gen. ii.
24.   "Because of your hardness of heart, Moses wrote this
commandment, but from the beginning of creation God made
them male and female ; for this shall a man leave his father
and mother, and *shall adhere to his wife,* and they shall be one
flesh ; what therefore God hath *joined together,* man shall not
put asunder," Mark x. 5 to 9 ; Matt. xix. 5.   "*The soul of
Shechem adhered to Dinah* the daughter of Jacob ; *he loved* the
damsel, and spake to the heart of the damsel," Gen. xxxiv. 3.
"Solomon loved many foreign women, *Solomon adhered to them
to love* them," 1 Kings xi. 1, 2.   Hence then it is evident, that
to adhere is an expression of love, received into use by the
Churches in ancient times, which were in significatives ; and
that it means nothing else in the internal sense than spiritual
conjunction, which is charity and love.

3876. "Because I have borne him three sons"—that this
signifies a successive, appears from what was said above, n.
3871. The successive, which the three sons here signify, is,
that charity now arrives ; for during the process of man's regeneration, that is, of his being made a Church, he must first
know and understand what the truth of faith is ; secondly, he
must will and do it ; and thirdly, he must be affected with it :
and when a man is affected with truth, that is, when he perceives delight and blessedness in doing according to truth, he
is then in charity and mutual love.   Thus, successivity is what
is here meant by the words, "I have borne him three sons."

3877. "Therefore she called his name Levi"—that this signifies his quality, appears from the signification of name, and
of calling a name, as being quality, see above, n. 3872.   The
quality is what is contained in these words, "Now this time
my man will adhere to me, because I have borne him three

sons," concerning which words see above, n. 3875, 3876. This quality is signified by Levi, and also by the tribe named from him: and this is the third universal of the Church, or the third thing in the process of man's regeneration, or of being made a Church, and is charity. The case with respect to charity is, that it contains in itself the will of truth, and thereby the understanding of truth, for whoever is in charity has both those principles; but before man comes to charity, he must first be in the external, or in the understanding of truth, next in the will of truth, and lastly in the capacity of being affected by truth, which is charity; and when he is in charity, he has respect to the Lord, Whom, in a supreme sense, Judah, the fourth son of Jacob, signifies.

3878. Verse 35. *And she conceived as yet, and bare a son, and said, This time I will confess Jehovah, therefore she called his name Judah, and she stood still from bringing forth.* She conceived as yet, and bare a son, signifies, as before, spiritual conception and birth from an external principle to a principle still more internal: and said, This time I will confess Jehovah, signifies, in a supreme sense, the Lord; in an internal sense, the Word; in an external sense, doctrine thence derived; in the present case, the Divine principle of love, and the Lord's celestial kingdom: therefore she called his name Judah, signifies his quality: and she stood still from bringing forth, signifies ascent by a scale from the earth to Jehovah, or the Lord.

3879. "She conceived as yet, and bare a son"—that this signifies spiritual conception and birth from an external to a still more internal principle, appears from what was said above, n. 3860, 3868, where similar words occur.

3880. "And she said, This time I will confess Jehovah"—that this signifies, in a supreme sense, the Lord; in an internal sense, the Word; in an external sense, doctrine thence derived; in the present case, the Divine principle of love, and the Lord's celestial kingdom, appears from the signification of confessing. That to confess, in an external or proximately interior sense, signifies doctrine derived from the Word, is evident, for confession is nothing else, even as the word is applied in common discourse, than a man's declaration of his faith before the Lord; thus it comprehends in it whatever the man believes, consequently, whatever constitutes the doctrine which he maintains. That to confess, in an internal sense, denotes the Word, follows hence, for all the doctrine of faith and charity ought to be derived from the Word; for, as man of himself knows nothing or things celestial and spiritual, of course he can only know them by Divine Revelation, which is the Word. The reason why to confess, in a supreme sense, denotes the Lord, is, because the Lord is the Word, consequently doctrine derived from the Word, and because the Word in its internal sense respects the Lord alone, and treats of His kingdom, see n. 1871, 2859, 2894, 3245, 3305, 3393, 3432, 3439, 3454. Hence it is, that confessing Jehovah signifies the Divine principle of love and His celestial kingdom, for the Lord is Divine Love itself, and the influx of this constitutes His kingdom, and this, by means of the Word which is from Him. That Judah, who was named from confessing Jehovah, signifies the Divine principle of love, and the Lord's celestial kingdom, may be seen above, n. 3654; hence it is that it is said, that confessing in the present case has this signification. But what confessing and confession mean, may appear from those passages in the Word in which they occur, as in Isaiah, "Thou shalt say in that day, *I will confess to Thee, O Jehovah*, because Thou wast angry with me, Thine anger is turned away, and Thou hast comforted me : and ye shall say in that day, *Confess to Jehovah*, call upon His name, make known in the people His works, make mention that His name is exalted," xii. 1, 4. And in David, "*We confess to Thee, O God, we confess*, that Thy name is near, Thy wonderful works declare," Psalm lxxv. 2. Again, "A psalm *for confession*, make jubilee to Jehovah all the earth, He hath made us, and not we ourselves, His people and the flock of His pasture ; enter in by His gates *in confession*, His courts in praise, *confess ye to Him*, bless ye His name, because Jehovah is good, His mercy is to eternity, and His truth even to generation and generation," Psalm c. 1 to 5. Here it is manifest that confessing and confession mean the acknowledgment of Jehovah or the Lord, and the things which are from Him. That this acknowledgment is doctrine and the Word, is evident. Again, in Isaiah, "Jehovah will comfort Zion, He will comfort all her wastes, joy and gladness shall be found therein, *confession* and the voice of singing," li. 3. And in Jeremiah, "Thus saith Jehovah, Behold I bring back again the captivity of the tents of Jacob, and I will have mercy on his dwellings, and the city shall be built on its heap, and the palace shall be inhabited according to its custom, and there shall come forth from them *confession* and the voice of them who sport," xxx. 18, 19. And in David, "*I will confess to Jehovah* according to His justice, and I will sing the name of Jehovah Most High," Psalm vii. 17. Again, "When I shall pass to the house of God with the voice of singing and *of confession*, with the multitude that keep a feast," Psalm xlii. 4. Again, "*I will confess to Thee* amongst the nations, O Lord, I will sound an instrument to Thee amongst the people, because Thy mercy is great even to heaven," lvii. 9, 10. From these passages, it is evident, that confession has reference to the celestial principle of love, and is distinguished from what relates to the spiritual principle of love, for it is said confession and the voice of singing, confession and the voice of them who sport. I will confess to Thee amongst the nations, and I will sound an instrument to Thee amongst the people; in which expressions, confession and confessing denote what is celestial, and the voice of singing, the voice of those who sport, and sounding an instrument, denote what is spiritual. It is also said, to confess amongst the nations, and to sound an instrument amongst the people, because nations signify those who are in good, and people, those who are in truth, see n. 1416, 1849, 2928, that is, those who are in celestial love, and those who are in spiritual love. In the Word, two expressions for the most part occur, one having reference to the celestial principle or good, and the other to the spiritual principle or truth, in order that there may be a Divine Marriage in every part of the Word, or a marriage of good and truth, see n. 683, 793, 801, 2173, 2516, 2712, 3132. Hence also it is evident, that confession involves the celestial principle of love, and that genuine confession, or that which comes from the heart, can only be made from good, the confession which is from truth being called the voice of singing, the voice of them who sport, and playing on an instrument. So also in these passages, "I will praise the name of God with a song, and I will make Him great with *confession*," Psalm lxix. 30. Again, "*I will confess to Thee*, with an instrument of psaltery, Thy truth, my God, I will sing to Thee on the harp, O Holy of Israel," Psalm lxxi. 22. That singing on the harp and other stringed instruments signify spiritual things, may be seen, n. 418, 419, 420. Again, "Enter His gates *in confession*, His courts in praise, *confess to Him*, bless His name," Psalm c. 4; where confession and confessing proceed from the love of good, but praise and blessing, from the love of truth. Again, "Answer Jehovah *by confession*, play on the harp to our God," Psalm cxlvii. 7. Again, "*I will confess to Thee* in the great congregation, in a numerous people will I praise Thee," Psalm xxxv. 18. Again, "*I will confess to Jehovah* with my mouth, and in the midst of many will I praise Him," Psalm cix. 30. Again, "We are Thy people, the flock of Thy pasture, *we will confess to Thee*, to eternity, to generation and generation will we recount Thy praise," Psalm lxxix. 13. Again, "*Let them confess to Jehovah*, His mercy, and His wonderful works to the sons of man, *let them sacrifice the sacrifices of confession*, and announce His works with singing," Psalm cvii. 21, 22. That these passages contain two expressions for one thing, is manifest. These would appear like vain repetitions, unless one involved the celestial principle, or good, and the other, the spiritual principle, or truth; consequently, the Divine Marriage, the Lord's kingdom itself being such a marriage. This arcanum pervades the Word throughout, but it cannot in any wise be discovered except by the internal sense, and by knowledge therefrom of the class, celestial or spiritual, to which each expression belongs. But, in general, it must be known what is

meant by celestial, and what by spiritual, they having been
often treated of above. Real confession of the heart, as it is
from celestial love, is, in a genuine sense, confession. The
man who is in this confession acknowledges that all good is
from the Lord, and that all evil is from himself, and when he
is in this acknowledgment, he is in a state of humiliation, for
he then acknowledges that the Lord is the all in him, and that
he himself is respectively nothing, and when confession is made
from this state, it is from celestial love. But the sacrifices of
confession, which were offered in the Jewish Church, were
thanksgivings, and were called, in an universal sense, eucharistic and retributory sacrifices, which were of a twofold kind,
namely, confessional and votive. That the sacrifices of confession involved the celestial principle of love, may appear from
their institution, of which it is thus written in Moses, "This is the
law of the eucharistic sacrifice, which shall be offered to Jehovah; if *he shall offer it for confession*, then he shall offer, be
sides the sacrifice *of confession*, unleavened cakes mixed with
oil, and unleavened wafers anointed with oil, and fine flour,
he shall offer his offering cakes mixed with oil upon unleavened
cakes of bread, *besides the sacrifice of confession*," Levit. vii. 11,
12, 13, 14. All the things here mentioned,—the unleavened
cakes mixed with oil, the unleavened wafers anointed with oil,
the fine flour garnished, and the leavened cakes of bread, signify the celestial things of love and faith, and confessions
thence derived, and that these should be made in humiliation.
That fine flour, and cakes thereof, denote the celestial principle
of love and the spiritual principle of faith from love, which is
charity, may be seen, n. 2177. That what is unleavened denotes purification from evils and falses, see n. 2342; that oil
denotes the celestial principle of love, see n. 886, 3728; that
bread denotes the same, n. 2165, 2177, 3464, 3478, 3735. But
the votive sacrifices, which were another kind of eucharistics,
in an external sense, signify retribution; in an internal sense,
the will that the Lord would provide; and in a supreme sense,
a state of providence, see n. 3732. Hence it is, that mention is
made of each in the Word throughout, as in David, "*Sacrifice
to God confession, and pay thy vows unto the Highest; he who
sacrificeth confession*, honoureth Me, and he who ordereth his
way, to him will I show the salvation of God," Psalm l. 14, 23.
Again, "*Thy vows* are upon me, O God, *I will repay confessions
to Thee*," Psalm lvi. 13. Again, "*I will sacrifice to Thee the
sacrifice of confession*, and will call upon the name of Jehovah;
I will pay to Jehovah my vows," Psalm cxvi. 17, 18. And in
Jonah, "*I will sacrifice to Thee with the voice of confession,
I will pay* what I have vowed," ii. 9. From these considerations then it is manifest what is meant by the confession from
which Judah was named, namely, that in a supreme sense, it

denotes the Lord, and the Divine principle of love; in an internal sense, the Word, and also the Lord's celestial kingdom; and in an exterior sense, doctrine from the Word, which is the doctrine of the Church celestial. That these things are signified by Judah in the Word, may appear from what now follows.

3881. "Therefore she called his name Judah"—that this signifies his quality, appears from the signification of name, and of calling a name, as being quality, see n. 144, 145, 1754, 1896, 2009, 2724, 3006, 3421. The quality itself is contained in the internal sense of the words which Leah spake, "This time I will confess Jehovah," concerning which sense see above, n. 3880; where it is shown to involve, in a supreme sense, the Lord, and the Divine principle of His love; in an internal sense, the Word, and also the Lord's celestial kingdom; and in an exterior sense, doctrine derived from the Word, which is the doctrine of the Church celestial. That these things are signified in the Word by Judah, wherever the name occurs, is yet scarce known to any one, because the historical parts of the Word are believed to be merely historical, and the prophetical to be in a measure obliterated, except in some particular passages from which doctrinal tenets may be derived. That there is a spiritual sense in them, is not believed, because at this day it is not known what the spiritual sense of the Word is, nor what a spiritual principle is. The principal reason of this is, that men live a natural life, and the natural life is such, that when it is regarded as an end, or loved above all other things, it obliterates both knowledges and faith; insomuch, that when spiritual life and the spiritual sense of the Word are mentioned, they appear like something unreal, or like something unpleasant and sad, which excites loathing, because it is in disagreement with the natural life. As mankind, at this day, are in such a state, they do not apprehend, nor are they willing to apprehend any thing else to be meant by names in the Word, but the things themselves which are named, such as nations, people, persons, countries, cities, mountains, rivers, when yet names, in the spiritual sense, signify things. That Judah, in an internal sense, signifies the Lord's celestial Church, and in a universal sense, His celestial kingdom, and in a supreme sense, the Lord Himself, may appear from several passages in the Old Testament, where Judah is mentioned, as from the following: "Thou art *Judah*, thy brethren shall praise thee, thy hand shall be in the neck of thine enemies, thy father's sons shall bow down themselves to thee. Judah is a lion's whelp; thou hast come up, my son, from the prey. He hath bended himself, he hath couched as a lion, and as an old lion, who shall stir him up? The sceptre shall not depart from Judah, nor a lawgiver from between his feet, until Shiloh come, and to him shall be the gathering together of the people; binding his ass's foal unto the

vine, and the son of his she-ass to the noble vine. He shall
wash his garment in wine, and his covering in the blood of
grapes. His eye is red with wine, and his teeth are white with
milk," Gen. xlix. 8 to 12. This prophecy of Jacob (at that time
Israel), concerning Judah, cannot possibly be understood by any
one, not even a single word of it, save from the internal sense.
For instance, it cannot be known what is meant by his brethren
praising him, and by his father's sons bowing down themselves
to him, by his going up from the prey like a lion's whelp, and
bending himself and couching as a lion; or what by Shiloh, by
binding his ass's foal to a vine, and the son of his she-ass to a
noble vine, by washing his garment in wine, and his covering
in the blood of grapes, by his eyes being red with wine, and his
teeth white with milk. It is impossible, as was said, for any
one to understand what these expressions mean, save from the
internal sense, when yet, all and singular, they involve the celestial things of the Lord's kingdom, and things Divine; and
hereby it is predicted, that the Lord's celestial kingdom, and in
a supreme sense, the Lord Himself, should be represented by
Judah. But of all these expressions, by the Divine Mercy of
the Lord, I shall speak more particularly when I come to the
explication of that chapter. The case is the same in other parts
of the Word, especially in the prophets, where mention is made
of Judah; as in Ezekiel, "Thou son of man, take to thee one
piece of wood, and write upon it for Judah and his sons, Israel
his companions, and take one piece of wood, and write upon it
for Joseph, the wood of Ephraim and of all the house of Israel
his companions, and join them together, the one to the other
for thyself into one wood, and they shall be for one in My
hand. I will make them into one nation in the land in the
mountains of Israel; and they shall all have one king for a
king. My servant David shall be a king over them, and they
shall all have one shepherd, and they shall walk in My judgments, and shall keep My statutes, and do them, and shall
dwell upon the land which I have given to My servant Jacob,
in which their fathers have dwelt, they and their sons shall
dwell upon it, and their sons' sons even to eternity, and My
servant David shall be their prince to eternity, and I will establish with them a covenant of peace. It shall be to them a
covenant of eternity. I will give to them and will multiply them,
and will give My sanctuary in the midst of them to eternity;
thus shall My habitation be with them, and I will be to them
for a God, and they shall be to Me for a people," xxxvii. 16 to
28. Whoever supposes that Judah here means Judah, Israel,
Israel, Joseph, Joseph, Ephraim, Ephraim, and David, David,
will believe that all these things are to come to pass as they
are described in the sense of the letter, namely, that Israel shall
be again consociated with Judah, as well as the tribe of Ephraim:

likewise that David shall rule over them, and that they shall thus dwell upon the land given unto Jacob for ever; and that a covenant of eternity will in this case be established with them, and a sanctuary in the midst of them to eternity. But all these particulars have not the least reference to the Jewish nation, but to the Lord's celestial kingdom, which is Judah, and to His spiritual kingdom, which is Israel, and to the Lord himself Who is David. Hence it is plain, that names do not mean persons, but things, celestial and Divine. The case is similar in regard to the following words in Zechariah, "Many peoples and numerous nations shall come to seek Jehovah Zebaoth: in those days, ten men (*viri*) shall take hold of, out of all tongues of nations, even shall take hold of the wing of a man of Judah, saying, We will go with you, because we have heard that God is with you," viii. 23. They who apprehend these words according to the letter, will say, as the Jewish nation to this day believe, that as this prophecy has not yet been fulfilled, it assuredly will be, and thus that the Jews will return to the land of Canaan, and many will follow them out of every nation and tongue, and will lay hold of the wing of a man of Judah, and will pray for leave to follow them; and that then God, namely, the Messiah, whom Christians call the Lord, will be with them, and that to Him they must first be converted. This would be the interpretation of the words, if a man of Judah meant a Jew. But the subject treated of here, in the internal sense, is a new spiritual Church among the Gentiles, and a man of Judah signifies the saving faith which comes from love to the Lord. That Judah does not mean Judah, but, as was observed, in an internal sense, the Lord's celestial kingdom, which was represented in the Church established with Judah or the Jews, may also appear from the following passages: "When the Lord shall lift up a sign to the nations, shall gather together the expelled of Israel, and shall collect the dispersed of Judah from the four wings of the earth, then shall the emulation of Ephraim depart, and the enemies of Judah shall be cut off; Ephraim shall not have emulation with Judah, and Judah shall not straiten Ephraim," Isaiah xi. 12, 13. And in Jeremiah, "Behold, the days are coming, saith Jehovah, and I will raise up to David a righteous branch, who shall reign as a king, and shall prosper, and shall do judgment and justice in the earth: in His days Judah shall be saved, and Israel shall dwell securely; and this is His name which they shall call Him, Jehovah our Justice," xxiii. 5, 6. And in Joel, "Then ye shall know that I am Jehovah your God, dwelling in Zion the mountain of My holiness, and Jerusalem shall be holiness: and it shall come to pass in that day, the mountains shall drop new wine, and the hills shall flow with milk, and all the rivers of Judah shall flow with waters, and a fountain shall come forth from the house of Jehovah, and shall water the stream of

Shittim: Judah shall sit to eternity, and Jerusalem to generation and generation," iii. 17, 18, 19. And in Zechariah, "In that day I will smite every horse with stupor, and his rider with madness, and upon the house of Judah will I open Mine eyes, and every horse of the peoples will I smite with blindness. And the leaders of Judah shall say in their heart, I will confirm to myself the inhabitants of Jerusalem in Jehovah Zebaoth their God. In that day I will set the leaders of Judah as an hearth of fire in the wood, and as a torch of fire in a sheaf, and they shall devour to the right and to the left all the people round about; and Jerusalem shall yet be inhabited beneath itself in Jerusalem; and Jehovah shall save the tents of Judah first, that the glory of the house of David, and the glory of the inhabitant of Jerusalem, may not exalt itself above Judah. In that day Jehovah will protect the inhabitant of Jerusalem; and the house of David shall be as God, as the angel of Jehovah before them; and I will pour forth upon the house of David, and upon the inhabitant of Jerusalem, the spirit of grace," xii. 4 to 10. The subject here treated of is the Lord's celestial kingdom, that truth should not have dominion therein over good, but that truth should be subordinate to good. Truth is signified by the house of David and the inhabitant of Jerusalem, and good, by Judah. Hence it is evident why it is first said, that the glory of the house of David, and the glory of the inhabitant of Jerusalem, shall not exalt itself above Judah, and next, that the house of David shall be as God, and as the angel of Jehovah, and that the spirit of grace shall be poured forth upon it, and upon the inhabitant of Jerusalem, for such is the state, when truth is subordinate to good, or faith to love. The horse which shall be smitten with stupor, and the horse of the people with blindness, denotes self-intelligence, see n. 2761, 2762, 3217. Again, in the same prophet, "In that day shall there be upon the bells of the horses, holiness to Jehovah; and the pots in the house of Jehovah shall be as bowls before the altar; and every pot in Jerusalem and in Judah shall be holiness to Jehovah Zebaoth," xiv. 20, 21; speaking of the Lord's kingdom. So in Malachi, "Behold, I send My angel, who shall prepare the way before Me; and the Lord Whom ye seek shall suddenly come to His temple, and the angel of the covenant, Whom ye desire; behold He cometh, but who abideth the day of His coming? Then shall the meat-offering of Judah and of Jerusalem be sweet to Jehovah, according to the days of an age and according to former years," iii. 1, 2, 4; speaking manifestly of the Lord's coming. It is well known that the meat-offering of Judah and Jerusalem was not then sweet, but that worship from love, which is the meat-offering of Judah, and the worship from faith derived from love, which is the meat-offering of Jerusalem, were so. So in Jeremiah, "Thus saith

Jehovah Zebaoth, Yet shall they say this word in the land of Judah, and in the cities thereof, in turning their captivity, Jehovah bless thee, O habitation of justice, O mountain of holiness, and in it shall dwell Judah and all the cities thereof together. Behold the days come, saith Jehovah, in which I will establish a new covenant with the house of Israel, and with the house of Judah, not like the covenant which I established with their fathers," xxxi. 23, 24, 31, 32. And in David, "The Lord hath chosen the tribe of Judah, the mountain of Zion which He loved, and hath built as heights His sanctuary, as the earth hath He founded it for ever," Psalm lxxviii. 68, 69. From these and many other passages, which it would be tedious to mention, it may appear what is signified in the Word by Judah, and that thereby is not meant the Jewish nation, since this was very far from being a celestial Church, or the Lord's celestial kingdom, being the worst of all nations in regard to love to the Lord, and charity towards their neighbour, and in regard also to faith, and this from the days of their first fathers, namely, the sons of Jacob, even down to the present time. That such persons, however, were still capable of representing the celestial and spiritual things of the Lord's kingdom, may be seen, n. 3479, 3480, 3481, since in representations the person is not reflected upon, but only the thing which is represented, see n. 665, 1097, 1361, 3147, 3670. When, however, they did not remain in the rituals ordained by Jehovah or the Lord, but turned away from them to idolatries, they then no longer represented celestial and spiritual things, but the opposite, namely, infernal and diabolical things, according to the Lord's words in John, "Ye are of your father the devil, and the desires of your father ye are willing to do; he was a murderer from the beginning, and stood not in the truth," viii. 44. That such an infernal and diabolical principle is signified by Judah in an opposite sense, may appear from these words in Isaiah, "Jerusalem hath stumbled, and Judah is fallen, because their tongue and their works are against Jehovah, to rebel against the eyes of His glory," iii. 8. And in Malachi, "Judah hath acted treacherously, and is become an abomination in Israel and in Jerusalem, and Judah hath profaned the holiness of Jehovah, because he hath loved and betrothed to himself the daughter of a strange god," ii. 11. And also in the following passages: Isaiah iii. 1, and the subsequent verses; chap. viii. 7, 8; Jer. ii. 28; chap. iii. 7 to 11; chap. ix. 26; chap. xi. 9, 10, 12; chap. xiii. 9; chap. xiv. 2; chap. xvii. 1; chap. xviii. 12, 13; chap. xix. 7; chap. xxxii. 35; chap. xxxvi. 31; chap. xliv. 12, 14, 26, 28; Hosea v. 5; chap. viii. 14; Amos ii. 4, 5; Zeph. i. 4; and in many other places.

3882. "And she stood still from bearing"—that this signifies ascent by a scale from the earth to Jehovah or the Lord, appears from the signification of bearing or of birth, as being truth and good, these being births in a spiritual sense, for man is regenerated or born anew by truth and good. These also are what are signified by the four births of Leah, namely, Reuben, Simeon, Levi, and Judah. Reuben signifies the truth which is the first thing in regeneration or the new birth, but this is only as to knowledge, or as to knowing truth. Simeon signifies the truth which is the second thing in regeneration or the new birth; this truth is as to the will, or as to willing what is true. Levi signifies the truth which is the third thing in regeneration or the new birth; this truth is as to the affection, or being affected with truth, which is the same thing as charity. But Judah signifies good, which is the fourth thing in regeneration or the new birth, and this is the celestial principle of love. When the regenerate man, or he who is born anew, arrives at this stage, the Lord appears to him, for he has then ascended from the lowest step, as by a ladder, up to the step where the Lord is. This also is the ascent, which was signified by the ladder seen by Jacob in the dream, whose top reached to heaven, and on which the angels of God ascended and descended, and above which stood Jehovah or the Lord; see the foregoing chapter, verse 12. Hence it is evident, that this is what is signified by standing still from bearing. That the con ceiving and bearing, four times mentioned, signifies advancement from an external to an internal principle, or from truth to good, that is, from earth to heaven, may be seen, n. 3860, 3868, 3874, 3879. Descent follows afterwards, for man cannot descend unless he has first ascended. Descent is nothing else than looking at truth from good, as a man from a mountain, upon which he has climbed, views the things which lie beneath. That then the view comprehends at one glance innumerable things which cannot be comprehended by those who stand beneath, or in the valley, is plain to every one. The case is exactly similar in regard to those who are in good, that is, in love to the Lord and in charity towards their neighbour, compared with those who are only in truth, that is, in faith alone.

A CONTINUATION OF THE SUBJECT CONCERNING THE GRAND MAN, AND CONCERNING CORRESPONDENCE, IN THE PRESENT CASE, CONCERNING CORRESPONDENCE WITH THE HEART AND LUNGS.

3883. *It has been already shown what the* GRAND MAN *is, and what is meant by correspondence therewith, namely, that the* GRAND MAN *is the universal heaven, which, in the general,* is a likeness and image of the Lord, and that correspondence is that of the Lord's Divine principle with the celestial and spiritual things therein, and of the celestial and spiritual things therein with the natural things which exist in the world, and principally with those which exist in man. Thus, there is a correspondence of the Lord's Divine principle, through heaven, or the GRAND MAN, with man, and with all the parts of man, insomuch that man exists, that is, subsists from thence.

3884. Since it is altogether unknown in the world, that there is a correspondence of heaven, or the GRAND MAN, with all things of man, and that man exists and subsists from thence, and as what is said on the subject may seem paradoxical and incredible, it is expedient to relate those facts which experience has enabled me to know with certainty. Once, when the interior heaven was opened to me, and I was discoursing therein with the angels, it was allowed me to make the following observations. Let it be previously noted, that although I was in heaven, still I was not out of myself, but in the body, for heaven is in man, in whatever place he be, and thus, when it pleases the Lord, a man may be in heaven and yet not be withdrawn from the body. Hence it was given me to perceive the general operations of heaven as manifestly as any object is perceived by any of the senses. There were four operations, which on this occasion I perceived. The first was into the brain at the left temple, and was a general one as to the organs of reason, for the left part of the brain corresponds to things rational or intellectual, but the right, to affections or things voluntary. The second general operation which I perceived, was into the respiration of the lungs, which led my respiration gently, but from within, so that I had no need to draw breath, or respire, by any exertion of my will. The real respiration of heaven was then manifestly perceived by me. It is internal, and on that account imperceptible to man; but by a wonderful correspondence it flows into man's respiration, which is external, that is, belongs to the body, and if man was deprived of this influx, he would instantly drop down dead. The third operation which I perceived was into the systole and diastole of the heart, which had, on the occasion, more of softness with me than I had ever experienced at any other time. The times of the pulse were regular, about three within each turn of respiration; yet such as to close in the pulmonary principles, and thereby to rule them. How the alternate pulses of the heart insinuated themselves into the alternate respirations of the lungs, at the close of each respiration, I was in some measure enabled to observe. The alternations of the pulse were so observable, that I was able to count them; they were distinct and soft. The fourth general operation was upon the kidneys, which also it was given me to perceive, but only obscurely. From these observations it was made manifest that heaven, or the GRAND MAN, has cardiac pulses, and that it has respirations; and that the cardiac pulses of heaven, or the GRAND MAN, have correspondence with the heart, and with its systolic and diastolic motions, and that the respirations of heaven, or the GRAND MAN, have correspondence with the lungs, and their respirations; but that they are both unobservable to man, being imperceptible, because internal.

3885. Once also, when I was withdrawn from the ideas originating in the sensualities of the body, a heavenly light appeared to me, which withdrew me further from them, for the light of heaven contains spiritual life, see n. 1524, 2776, 3167, 3195, 3339, 3636, 3643. When I was in this light, corporeal and worldly things appeared as beneath me, and nevertheless I still perceived them, but as being more remote from me, and not belonging to me. I then seemed to myself to be in heaven with my head, but not with my body. In this state, also, it was given me to observe the general respiration of heaven, and what its nature was; it was interior, easy, spontaneous, and corresponding to my respiration as three to one. It was also given me to observe the reciprocations of the pulses of the heart; and then I was informed by the angels that all and singular the creatures on the earth derive thence their pulses and their respirations, and that the reason why they do not take place at the same instant in all, is, because both the cardiac pulse and the pulmonary respiration which exist in the heavens, pass off into a sort of continuity, and thus into effort, which is of such a nature as to excite those motions variously according to the state of every subject.

3886. It is, however, to be observed, that the variations as to pulses and as to respiration in the heavens, are manifold, being equal in number to the societies therein, for they are according to the states of thought and affection with the angels, which states are according to their states of faith and love; but with respect to the general pulse and respiration, the case is as above described. Once, also, it was given me to observe the cardiac pulses of those who were of the province of the hinder part of the head, and to note separately the pulses of the celestial, and the pulses of the spiritual, in that province. The pulses of the celestial were tacit and gentle, but those of the spiritual were strong and vibratory. The momenta of the pulse of the celestial were to those of the spiritual as five to two; for the pulse of the celestial flows into the pulse of the spiritual, and thus goes forth and passes into nature. And what is wonderful, the discourse of the celestial angels is not heard by the spiritual angels, but is perceived under a species of pulse of the heart, and this, because the discourse of the celestial angels is not intelligible to the spiritual angels, for it is produced by the love-affections, whereas that of the spiritual is produced by intellect *ual ideas, see n.* 1647, 1759, 2157, 3343 ; *and the love-affections belong to the province of the heart, but the intellectual ideas, to the province of the lungs.*

3887. *In heaven, or the* GRAND MAN, *there are two kingdoms, one of which is called celestial, the other, spiritual. The celestial kingdom consists of angels who are called celestial, and these are they who have been principled in love to the Lord, and thence in all wisdom, for they are in the Lord, and are thereby in a state of peace and innocence superior to others. They appear to others like infants, for a state of peace and innocence presents such an appearance. Every thing in their kingdom is as it were alive before them, for whatever comes immediately from the Lord is alive. Such is the celestial kingdom. The other kingdom is called spiritual. It consists of angels who are called spiritual, and who have been in the good of charity towards their neighbour. They place the delight of their life in this, that they can do good to others without recompense, it being their recompense to be allowed to do good to others. The more they will and desire this, so much the greater is their intelligence and felicity, for in another life every one is gifted with intelligence and felicity from the Lord, according to the use which he yields from the will-affection. Such is the spiritual kingdom. They who are in the Lord's celestial kingdom belong all to the province of the heart, and they who are in the spiritual kingdom belong all to the province of the lungs. The influx from the celestial kingdom into the spiritual is similar to the influx of the heart into the lungs, and also of all things which belong to the heart into all which belong to the lungs ; for the heart rules in the whole of the body and in all its parts, by the blood-vessels, as the lungs rule by respiration. Hence there is an influx in every part of the body, as of the heart into the lungs, but according to the form and state of each part. Hence too comes all the sensation, as well as all the action, which are proper to the body ; as may appear from fœtuses and new-born infants, which are not capable of any bodily sensation, nor of any voluntary action, until their lungs are opened, and thereby an influx given of the one into the other. The case is similar in the spiritual world, only with this difference, that the spiritual world does not contain things corporeal and natural, but things celestial and spiritual, which are the good of love and the truth of faith. Hence the cardiac motions, with the inhabitants of the spiritual world, are according to states of love, and the respiratory motions, according to states of faith ; the influx of the one into the other causing in them spiritual sensation and spiritual action. These things will necessarily appear to man to be paradoxical, from his having no idea of the good of love and the truth of faith, but as abstract things which have no power of effecting any thing, when yet the contrary is true, namely, that all perception and sensation, and all energy and action, even in man, are derived from them.*

3888. *These two kingdoms have their manifestations and fixedness in man by means of the two kingdoms in him, namely, the kingdom of the will and the kingdom of the understanding, which two kingdoms constitute the mind of man, yea, the man himself. The will is that to which the pulse of the heart corresponds, and the understanding is that to which the respiration of the lungs corresponds. Hence also it is, that in the body of man there are likewise two kingdoms, namely, of the heart and of the lungs. He who is acquainted with this arcanum may also know how the case is in respect to the influx of the will into the understanding, and of the understanding into the will, consequently, in respect to the influx of the good of love into the truth of faith, and vice versa; thus how the case is in regard to the regeneration of man. But they who are only in corporeal ideas, that is, who are in the will of what is evil, and the understanding of what is false, cannot possibly comprehend these things, for they must necessarily think in a sensual and corporeal way of things spiritual and celestial, consequently, they must think from darkness of the things of heavenly light, or of the truth of faith, and from coldness of the things of heavenly flame, or of the good of love. This darkness and cold so extinguish things celestial and spiritual, that they appear to such persons to have no existence.*

3889. *In order that I might know, not only that there is a correspondence of the celestial things of love with the motions of the heart, and of the spiritual things of faith from love with the motions of the lungs, but also the manner of its existence, it was given me for a considerable space of time to be with the angels, who showed it me to the life. By a wonderful fluxion, which no words can describe, into circular gyrations, they formed the resemblance of a heart and the resemblance of lungs, with all their interior and exterior contextures. They then traced the flux of heaven as it flowed spontaneously, for heaven is in the effort into such a form, by virtue of the influx of love from the Lord. Thus they exhibited the several parts which there are in the heart, and afterwards the union between the heart and the lungs, which also they represented by the marriage of good and truth. From this it was manifest that the heart corresponds to the celestial principle of good, and the lungs to the spiritual principle of truth; and that the conjunction of both, in a material form, resembles the conjunction of the heart and the lungs. I was also told that the case is similar in the body throughout, namely, in its several members, organs, and viscera, in that there is a conjunction in each between those things therein which belong to the heart, and those which belong to the lungs; for where both do not act, and each distinctly takes its turn, it is impossible there should exist any motion of life from any voluntary principle, or any sense of life from any intellectual principle.*

3890. *It has been occasionally observed above, that heaven, or the* GRAND MAN, *is distinguished into innumerable societies, and in general into as many as there are organs and viscera in the human body, and that each particular society belongs to one of those organs and viscera, see n. 3745. Also, that the societies, although innumerable and various, still act in unity ; as all things in the body, although various, are one. The societies therein, which belong to the province of the heart, are celestial societies, and are in the midst, or in the inmost principles : but those which appertain to the province of the lungs are spiritual societies, encompassing the celestial, and being in exterior principles. The influx from the Lord is through the celestial into the spiritual, or through the centre into the circumferences, that is, through inmost into exterior principles. The reason of this is, because the Lord flows in by love or mercy, whence comes all that is celestial in His kingdom ; and through love or mercy He flows into the good of faith, whence comes all that is spiritual in His kingdom, and this with ineffable variety ; yet the variety does not arise from the influx, but from the reception.*

3891. *That not only the universal heaven respires as one man, but also the individual societies in concert, and even every single angel and spirit, has been evidenced to me by such repeated experience as not to leave the least doubt on the subject. Spirits are surprised that any one should doubt about it ; but as there are few who have any other idea of angels and spirits than as of somewhat immaterial, and consequently as of mere thoughts nearly void of substance, and still fewer who conceive them to enjoy, like men, the senses of seeing, of hearing, and of touching ; and fewer still who believe them to have respiration, and thence to have life, like men, but of an interior kind, such as is the life of a spirit in respect to that of a man, therefore it may be expedient to adduce yet further experience on the subject. On a time it was foretold me, before I went to sleep, that there were several who were conspiring together against me, with intent to kill me by suffocation, but I did not at all attend to their threats, being secure under the Lord's protection, and therefore I fell asleep without apprehension ; but awaking at midnight, I was made very sensible that I did not respire from myself, but from heaven, for the respiration was not my own, yet still I respired. On other occasions repeatedly it has been given me to be sensible of the breathing or respiration of spirits, and also of angels, by the fact that they respired in me, and that my own respiration had place still at the same time, but distinct from theirs. Howbeit, no one can be made sensible of this,*

unless his interiors be opened, and he be thus brought into com
munication with heaven.

3892. *I have been informed by the most ancient people, who
were celestial men, and who were eminently principled in love
to the Lord, that they had no external respiration, like their posterity, but internal, and that they respired with the angels, with
whom they were in consort, because they were in celestial love.
I was further informed, that their states of respiration were
altogether according to their states of love and consequent faith.
(See what has been related above on this subject, n. 608, 805,
1118, 1119, 1120.)*

3893. *On one occasion there were angelic choirs, who were
celebrating the Lord together, and this from gladness of heart.
Their celebration was heard at intervals, as consisting of sweet
singing, for spirits and angels have amongst each other a sono-
rous voice, and are heard by each other as a man is heard by a
man ; but human singing, as to sweetness and harmony, which
is celestial, is not to be compared to it. From the variety of the
sound, I perceived that there were several choirs, and I was
instructed by the angels who attended me, that they belonged to
the province of the lungs and to the functions thereof, for their
province is singing ; and that this is the office of the lungs, it
was also given me to know from experience. It was allowed
them to rule my respiration, which they did so gently and
sweetly, and also interiorly, that I was scarce sensible of any
respiration of my own. I was further instructed, that they who
are allotted to involuntary respiration, and they who are allotted
to voluntary respiration, are distinct from each other ; and it
was told me, that they who are allotted to involuntary respiration are present with man during sleep, for as soon as he sleeps
the voluntary principle of his respiration ceases, and he receives
an involuntary principle of respiration.*

3894. *It was said above, n. 3892, that the respirations of
angels and spirits are altogether according to the states of their
love and consequent faith ; and it is from this ground that one
society does not respire in the same manner as another ; also
that the wicked, who are in self-love and the love of the world,
and thereby in what is false, cannot abide in consort with the
good, but when they come near them, seem to themselves unable
to respire, and appear as it were to be suffocated ; in consequence
whereof, like persons half dead, or like stones, they fall down
into hell, where they again receive the respiration which they
have in common with the infernal inhabitants. Hence it may
appear, that they who are in what is evil and false cannot be in
the* GRAND MAN, *or in heaven ; for when their respiration begins to cease in consequence of approximation thereto, instantly
all their apperception and thought also ceases, and likewise all*

*their energy to do what is evil and to persuade what is false,
and with their energy all action and vital motion perishes, and
thus they can do no other than cast themselves down headlong
thence.*

3894½. *This being the case, and well-disposed spirits, on
their entrance into another life, being at first remitted into the
life which they had in the world. n. 2119, thus also into the
loves and pleasures of that life, it is impossible for them as yet,
before they are prepared, to be in consort with the angels, even
as to respiration. For this reason, in the course of their preparation, they are first inaugurated into angelic life by concordant respirations, and then they come at the same time into interior perceptions and celestial freedom. This is effected in the
society of several, or in choirs, in which one respires in like
manner as another, and also perceives in like manner, and in
the same manner acts from freedom; how this is effected was
also exhibited to the life.*

3895. *The principle persuasive of what is evil and false,
and also the principle persuasive of truth when man is in the
life of evil, is of such a nature in another life that it as it were
suffocates others, and even suffocates well-disposed spirits, until
they are inaugurated into angelic respiration. They, therefore,
who are in such persuasive principle, are removed by the Lord,
and kept down in hell, where one cannot hurt another, for there
the persuasive principle of one is nearly like that of another,
and hence their respirations are concordant. Certain spirits,
who were in such persuasive principle, came to me with intent
to suffocate me, and even occasioned somewhat of suffocation,
but I was delivered by the Lord. An infant was then sent by
the Lord, at whose presence they were so tortured that they could
scarce respire, in which state they were kept till they made supplication, and thus were put down into hell. The principle
persuasive of truth, when man is in the life of evil, is such,
that he persuades himself that truth is truth, not for the sake
of good as an end, but for the sake of evil as an end, namely,
that he may gain honours, reputation, and wealth thereby. The
very worst of men may be in such a persuasive principle, and
also in an apparent zeal, to such a degree as to condemn to hell
all who are not in the truth, however they may be in good.
(Concerning this persuasive principle, see n. 2689, 3865.) Such
persons, when they first come into the other life, believe themselves angels, but they cannot come near any angelic society,
being as it were suffocated on their approach by their own persuasive principle. These are they of whom the Lord spake in
Matthew, "Many shall say to Me in that day, Lord, Lord, have
we not prophesied by Thy name, and by Thy name cast out
demons, and in Thy name done many virtues? But then will*

I confess to them, I know you not, depart from Me, ye workers of iniquity."

3896. *The subject concerning the* GRAND MAN, *and correspondence, will be continued at the end of the next chapter.*

GENESIS.

CHAPTER THE THIRTIETH.

3897. BY way of preface to this chapter, according to the plan proposed, those things which the Lord taught concerning the last judgment, or the last times of the Church (in Matthew, chap. xxiv.), shall now be unfolded. The preceding chapter was prefaced by an explication of what is contained from verse 19 to 22 ; what now follows is from verse 23 to 29, namely, " *Then if any one shall say to you, Lo! here is Christ, or there, believe not: for there shall arise false Christs and false prophets, and they shall give great signs and prodigies, to seduce, if possible, even the elect. Behold, I have told you before : wherefore, if they shall say to you, Behold, he is in the wilderness, go not forth ; Behold, he is in the secret chambers, believe not. For as the lightning goeth forth from the east, and appeareth even to the west, so shall also the coming of the Son of Man be. For wheresoever the carcase shall be, thither will also the eagles be gathered together.*"

3898. What these words involve can be known to no one but from the internal sense, for instance, what is signified by false Christs arising who should give signs and prodigies ; what, by their saying, that Christ is in the wilderness, and that in this case they should not go forth, or, that if they should say, he is in the secret chambers, they should not believe ; what, by the coming of the Son of Man being as lightning, which goes forth from the east and appears even to the west; also what by the eagles gathering together where the carcase is. These things, like those which precede and follow in the same chapter, seem, in the sense of the letter, to be in no series, when yet in the internal sense they are in a series the most beautiful, which first becomes apparent when it is understood what is signified by the false Christs, the signs and prodigies, the wilderness and secret chambers, also by the coming of the Son of Man, and lastly, by the carcase and the eagles. The reason why the Lord spake in this manner was, that they might not understand the Word, lest they should profane it ; for when the Church was vastated, as it was at that time amongst the Jews, if they had understood, they would have profaned ; and for the very same reason the Lord spake by parables, as He Himself teaches in Matthew, chap. xiii. 13, 14, 15 ; and in Mark iv. 11 ; and in Luke viii. 10. For the Word cannot be profaned by those who do not know its mysteries, but by those who do know them, see n. 301, 302, 303, 593, 1008, 1010, 1059, 1327, 1328, 2051, 3398, 3402, and more by those who appear to themselves learned, than by those who appear to themselves unlearned. But the reason why the interior contents of the Word are now opened, is, because the Church at this day is vastated to such a degree, that is, is so void of faith and love, that although men know and understand, still they do not acknowledge, and still less believe, see n. 3398, 3399, except the few, who are in the life of good, and are called the elect, who now may be instructed, and amongst whom a New Church is about to be established. Where such persons are, the Lord alone knows ; there will be few within the Church ; the New Churches established in former times have been established amongst the Gentiles, see n. 2986.

3899. The subject treated of in the preceding verses of this chapter in Matthew, is the successive vastation of the Church, namely, that first they began no longer to know what was good and true, but disputed about good and truth. Next, that they despised them. Thirdly, that they did not acknowledge them. Fourthly, that they profaned them, see n. 3754. The subject now treated of, is the state of the Church, what it then is as to doctrine in general, and amongst those in particular who are in holy external worship, but in profane internal worship, that is, who in tongue profess the Lord with holy veneration, but worship themselves and the world at heart, the worship of the Lord being thus employed by them as the means of obtaining honours and wealth. So far as such persons have acknowledged the Lord, and heavenly life and faith, so far they profane them when they become of such a nature. This state of the Church is now treated of, as may appear from the internal sense of the Lord's words above quoted, which is as follows.

3900. *Then if any one shall say to you, Lo ! here is Christ, or there, believe not*, signifies an admonition to take heed to themselves respecting their doctrine. Christ is the Lord as to Divine Truth, consequently, as to the Word and as to doctrine from the Word. That in the present case the contrary is signified, namely, the Divine Truth falsified, or the doctrine of what is false, is manifest. That Jesus is Divine Good, and Christ Divine Truth, may be seen, n. 3004, 3005, 3008, 3009. *For there shall arise false Christs and false prophets*, signifies the falses of that doctrine. That false Christs denote doctrinals derived from the Word and falsified, or truths not Divine, is evident from what was just now said, see also n. 3010, 3732 ; and that false prophets denote those who teach such falses, may be seen, n. 2534. They who teach falses are those espe- cially in the Christian world, who regard their own exaltation, and also worldly opulence, as ends of life, for such pervert the truths of the Word in favour of themselves, it being the very nature of self-love, and the love of the world, when respected as ends, to think of nothing else but self-gratification ; these are false Christs and false prophets. *And shall give great signs and prodigies*, signifies confirming and persuading principles, from external appearances and fallacies, whereby the simple suffer themselves to be seduced ; that this is signified by giving great signs and prodigies, by the Divine Mercy of the Lord, will be shown elsewhere. *To seduce, if possible, even the elect*, signifies those who are in the life of good and truth, and thereby belong with the Lord ; these are they who in the Word are called the elect. They seldom appear in the company of those who veil profane worship under what is holy, or if they appear they are not known, for the Lord hides and thus protects them ; for until they are established in their principles, they suffer themselves easily to be led away by external sanctities, but when they are established, they continue steadfast, being kept by the Lord in consort with the angels, which they themselves are ignorant of ; in which case it is impossible for them to be seduced by that wicked crew. *Behold I have told you before*, signifies an exhortation to prudence, namely, to take heed to themselves, as being among false prophets, who appear in sheep's clothing, but inwardly are ravenous wolves, Matthew viii. 25 These false prophets are the sons of the age, who are more prudent, that is, more cunning than the sons of the light in their generation, concerning whom see Luke, chap. xvi. 8. Wherefore the Lord exhorts them in these words, " Behold I send you as sheep into the midst of wolves, be ye therefore prudent as serpents, and simple as doves," Matt. x. 16. *If therefore they shall say to you, Behold he is in the wilderness, go not forth ; Behold he is in the secret chambers, believe not*, signifies that they are not to be believed in what they say of truth, nor in what they say of good, with other things besides. That this is what these words signify, can be known only to those who are acquainted with the internal sense. That an arcanum is contained in them, may appear from the fact, that the Lord spake them, and that without some other sense, which lies interiorly concealed in them, the literal sense is no sense at all : for what could be the use of the exhortation, not to go forth, if they should say that Christ was in the wilder- ness, and not to believe, if they should say that He was in the

secret chambers? But truth vastated is what is signified by
wilderness, and good vastated, by secret or inner chambers.
The reason why truth vastated is signified by wilderness, is,
because when the Church is vastated, that is, when it has no
longer any Divine Truth, because it has no longer any good
or love to the Lord and neighbourly love, it is called a wilderness, or said to be in a wilderness, for wilderness means whatever
is not cultivated or inhabited, see n. 2708, and also whatever
has little life in it, n. 1927, as is then the case with truth in the
Church.   Hence it is evident that wilderness here denotes the
Church which has no truth.   But secret or inner chambers, in
the internal sense, signify the church as to good, and also simply
good.   The Church which is in good is called the house of God,
the secret or inner chambers of which, and the things which
are in the house, are goods.   That the house of God is Divine
Good, and that house in general denotes the good which is of
love and charity, may be seen, n. 2233, 2234, 2559, 3142, 3652,
3720.   The reason why they are not to be believed in what they
say of truth, and in what they say of good, is, because they call
what is false true, and what is evil good, for they who regard
themselves and the world as the ends of life, mean nothing else
by truth and good, but that they themselves are to be adored,
and to be benefited; and if they inspire piety, it is that they
may appear in sheep's clothing.   Moreover, since the Word
which the Lord spake contains in it things innumerable, and
wilderness is an expression of large signification, for every thing
is called a wilderness which is not cultivated and inhabited,
and all interior things are called secret or inner chambers,
therefore wilderness signifies the Word of the Old Testament,
this being supposed to be abrogated, and secret chambers, the
Word of the New Testament, as teaching interior things, or
things relating to the internal man.   So, too, the whole Word
is called a wilderness, when it is no longer serviceable for
doctrinals; and human institutions are called secret or inner
chambers, which, as they depart from the precepts and insti-
tutes of the Word, cause the Word to be a wilderness.   This
also is known in the Christian world, for they who are in holy
external worship, and in profane internal worship, for the sake
of innovations which respect self-exaltation and opulence as
the ends of life, abrogate the Word, and this to such a degree,
that they do not even permit it to be read by others.   And
they who are not in such profane worship, although they
account the Word holy, and permit it to be read by the
vulgar, still bend and explain all things in it to favour their
own doctrinals, whereby they render the Word a wilderness as
to the rest of its contents, which are not according to their doctrinals.   This is plain enough to be seen from those who make
salvation depend on faith alone, and despise the works of cha-

rity, thus making all that a wilderness which the Lord Himself
spake in the New Testament, and so often in the Old, concerning love and charity.   Hence it is manifest what is signified by
the words, " If they shall say to you, Behold he is in the wilderness, go not forth ; Behold he is in the secret chambers, be-
,lieve not." *For as the lightning comes forth from the east, and
appears even to the west, so shall also the coming of the Son of
Man be,* signifies that it was thus with the internal worship of
the Lord, as with lightning, which is instantly dissipated ; for
lightning signifies what is of heavenly light, thus what is predicated of love and faith, for these principles are of heavenly
light.   The east, in a supreme sense, is the Lord, and, in an internal sense, it is the good of love, of charity and faith from
the Lord, see n. 101, 1250, 3249.   The west, in an internal sense,
is what has set or ceased to be, thus it is non-acknowledgment
of the Lord, or of the good of love, of charity, and of faith.
Consequently, the lightning which goeth forth from the east
and appears even to the west, denotes dissipation [or dispersion].
The coming of the Lord is not according to the letter, that He
will appear again in the world in person, but is His presence in
every one, which happens as often as the gospel is preached,
and any thing holy is thought of.   *For wheresoever the carcase
shall be, thither shall the eagles be gathered together*, signifies
that confirmations of what is false, by means of reasonings,
will be multiplied in the vastated Church.   The Church, when
it is void of good, and thereby of the truth of faith, or when it
is vastated, is said to be dead, for its life is derived from good
and truth.   Hence, when dead, it is compared to a carcase.
Reasonings concerning goods and truths, that they only exist
so far as they are comprehended, and confirmations of what is
evil and false by such reasonings, are eagles, as may appear
from what will be said presently.   That carcase in this passage
is a Church without the life of charity and faith, is manifest
from the Lord's words in Luke, speaking of the consummation
of the age, " The disciples said, Where, Lord ? (namely, where
would be the consummation of the age or the last judgment ?)
Jesus said unto them, *Where the body is, there will the eagles
be gathered together*," chap. xvii. 37.   It is here called body instead of carcase, for it is a dead body which is here meant, and
it signifies the Church, since it is evident from the Word throughout, that judgment must first begin at the house of God or at
the Church.   These are the things signified by the Lord's words
here quoted and explained ; and that they follow each other in
a most beautiful series, although it does not appear so in the
sense of the letter, may be manifest to every one who contem-
plates them in their connection according to the explication.

3901. The ground and reason why the last state of the
Church is compared to eagles gathered together to a carcase or

body, is, because eagles signify man's rational principles, which, when predicated of the good, are true rational principles, but when predicated of the wicked, are false rational principles, or principles of mere ratiocination. Birds in general signify man's knowledges, in both a good and a bad sense, see n. 40, 745, 776, 866, 991, 3219; and each species signifies some particular species of knowledge. Eagles, as flying aloft, and being sharp-sighted, signify rational principles. That this is the case, may appear from several passages in the Word, of which I adduce the following as proofs. First, where eagles signify true rational principles, as in Moses, " Jehovah found His people in the land of wilderness, and in emptiness, howling, and desert, He instructed them, He guarded them as the pupil of an eye, *as an eagle stirreth up its nest*, fluttereth over its young, spreadeth out its wings, taketh him, and carrieth him upon his wing," Deut. xxxii. 10, 11. Instruction in the truths and goods of faith is what is here described, and compared to an eagle. The description and comparison contains the whole process of instruction, until man is made rational and spiritual. All comparisons in the Word are made by significatives, and hence, in the present case, by an eagle denoting the rational principle. So again, "Jehovah said to Moses, Ye have seen what things I have done to the Egyptians, and *have carried you on the wings of eagles*, that I might bring you to Myself," Exod. xix. 3, 4; where the signification is the same. And in Isaiah, " They who wait on Jehovah shall be renewed in strength, *they shall ascend with strong wing like eagles*, they shall run and shall not be weary, they shall walk and shall not be faint," xl. 31. To be renewed in strength is to grow in a will to what is good; to ascend with a strong wing like eagles is to grow in the understanding of truth, thus as to the rational principle. The subject in this, as in other passages, is expounded by two expressions, one of which has reference to good, which is of the will, and the other to truth, which is of the understanding. This is the case in respect to running and not being weary, and to walking and not being faint. So in Ezekiel, " Parabolize a parable concerning the house of Israel, and say, Thus saith the Lord Jehovih, *A great eagle, long winged, full of feathers*, which had embroidering, came upon Lebanon, and took a small branch of a cedar, carried it into a land of commerce, and placed it in a city of dealers in spices, where it budded and became a luxuriant vine. There was *another great eagle, great in feathers*, to which behold this vine applied its roots, and put forth its young shoots thereto, to water it from the little beds of its plantations in a good land, beside many waters, but it shall come to devastation. He sent His ambassadors into Egypt to give him horses and much people," xvii. 2 to 9, 15. In this passage the eagle first mentioned denotes the rational principle receiving illustration from the Divine, and the eagle mentioned in the second place denotes the rational principle receiving illustration from the proprium, by reasonings from things sensual and scientific; it next denotes the rational principle become perverted. Egypt denotes scientifics, see n. 1164, 1165, 1186, 1462. Horses denote the intellectual principle thence derived, see n. 2761, 2762, 3217. So in Daniel, " The vision of Daniel; four beasts came up out of the sea, diverse the one from the other, the first like a lion, *but he had the wings of an eagle;* I saw until his wings were plucked away, and he was taken up from the earth, and stood erect upon his feet as a man, and a man's heart was given him," vii. 3, 4. The first state of the Church is what is here described by a lion which had eagle's wings, and eagle's wings signify things rational from the proprium, which being taken away, there were given things rational and voluntary from the Divine, signified by the beast being taken up from the earth, and standing erect on his feet as a man, and having a man's heart given him. Again in Ezekiel, " The likeness of the faces of the four animals or cherubs, they four had the face of a man, and the face of a lion to the right, and they four had the face of an ox to the left, and they four had *the face of an eagle,*" i. 10 " Their wheels were called galgal, and each had four faces; the face of the first was the face of a cherub, and the face of the second was the face of a man, and of the third the face of a lion, and of the fourth *the face of an eagle,*" x. 13, 14. And in the Apocalypse, " Around the throne were four animals full of eyes before and behind; the first animal was like a lion, the second animal like a calf, the third animal had a face as a man, the fourth animal was *like a flying eagle,*" iv. 7. That the animals here seen signify divine arcana, is manifest, consequently that the likeness of their faces has a similar signification. The arcana themselves cannot however be known, unless it be first known what a lion, a calf, a man, and an eagle, signify in the internal sense. That the face of an eagle denotes circumspection and thereby providence, is manifest, for the cherubs, which were represented by the animals in Ezekiel, signify the providence of the Lord to prevent man entering of himself, and by virtue of his own rational principle, into the mysteries of faith, see n. 308. Hence also it is evident, that eagle, when predicated of man, in the internal sense denotes the rational principle, and this because an eagle flies aloft, and then takes an extensive view of things beneath. So in Job, " By thy intelligence doth the hawk fly, and spread its wings towards the south; according to thy mouth doth *the eagle lift herself up,* and exalt her nest," xxxix. 26, 27. That eagle here denotes reason, which is of intelligence, is manifest. Such was the signification of eagle in the ancient Church, and the book of

Job is a book of the ancient Church, see n. 3570 ; for books at that time were all written by significatives, but the significatives in process of time were so obliterated, that it is not even known at this day that birds, in general, are thoughts, although they are so frequently mentioned in the Word, where they plainly can have no other signification. That eagle, in an opposite sense, signifies rational principles not true, consequently false, is evident from the following passages : " Jehovah shall raise up over thee a nation from afar, from the furthest part of the earth, *as an eagle flies*, a nation whose tongue thou hearest not, a nation hard of faces," Deut. xxviii. 49, 50. And in Jeremiah, " Behold, a cloud cometh up, and as a storm his chariot, *his horses are swifter than eagles;* wo unto us because we are vastated," iv. 13. Again, " Thy boasting hath deceived thee, the pride of thine heart dwelling in holes of the rock, occupying the height of the hill, because *thou exaltest as an eagle thy nest*, thence I will cast thee down. Behold, *as an eagle ascendeth and flieth*, and stretcheth her wings over Bozrah, in that day the heart of the mighty ones of Edom shall be as the heart of a woman who is in straitness," xlix. 16, 17, 22. Again, " They who pursued us were *swifter than eagles*, they pursued us on the mountains, they have laid snares for us in the wilderness," Lam. iv. 19. And in Micah, " Make thee bald, and shave thyself upon the sons of thy delights, dilate thy baldness *as an eagle*, because they have removed from thee," i. 16. And in Obadiah, " *If thou exaltest thyself as an eagle*, and if thou settest thy nest amongst the stars, thence will I pull thee down," verse 4. And in Habakkuk, " Lo, I raise up the Chaldeans, a nation bitter and hasty, marching into the breadths of the earth, to inherit habitations not their own, *whose horses are lighter than eagles*, their horsemen shall come from far, they shall fly *as an eagle hastening to devour*," i. 6, 8. In these passages, eagle signifies the false induced by reasonings from the fallacies of the senses and external appearances. That in the prophet last cited, Chaldeans signify those who are in external sanctity, but interiorly in the false, may be seen, n. 1368. That these, like Babel, are they who vastate the Church, see n. 1327. That the breadths of the earth denote truths, n. 3433, 3434. Vastation is signified by marching into the breadths of the earth. That horses denote the intellectual principles of such persons, which are of similar quality, n. 2761, 2762, 3217. Hence it is evident, what is meant by an eagle hastening to devour, namely, to desolate man as to truths, for the subject here treated of is the desolation of the Church. Comparison is made in the above passages with eagles, but comparisons, in the Word, as was observed, are from significatives. Hence then it is manifest, what the comparison with the eagles, which should be gathered together to the carcase, signifies.

CHAPTER XXX.

1. AND Rachel saw that she did not bring forth unto
Jacob, and Rachel was jealous towards her sister, and said
unto Jacob, Give me sons, or else I die.

2. And Jacob was inflamed with anger towards Rachel, and
said, Am I in God's stead? Who withholdeth from thee the
fruit of the womb?

3. And she said, Behold my maid-servant Bilhah, come to
her, and let her bear upon my knees, and I shall also be builded
up by her.

4. And she gave him Bilhah her servant for a woman, and
Jacob came to her.

5. And Bilhah conceived, and bare Jacob a son.

6. And Rachel said, God hath judged me, and hath also
heard my voice, and hath given me a son, therefore she called
his name Dan.

7. And she conceived as yet, and Bilhah, Rachel's handmaid, bare a second son to Jacob.

8. And Rachel said, With the strugglings of God have I
struggled with my sister, and have also prevailed, and she
called his name Naphtali.

9. And Leah saw that she stood still from bearing, and she
took Zilpah her handmaid, and gave her unto Jacob for a
woman.

10. And Zilpah, Leah's handmaid, bare a son to Jacob.

11. And Leah said, There cometh a troop, and she called
his name Gad.

12. And Zilpah, Leah's handmaid, bare a second son to
Jacob.

13. And Leah said, In my blessedness, because the daugh
ters will make me blessed, and she called his name Asher.

14. And Reuben went in the days of wheat-harvest, and
found mandrakes (*dudaim*) in the field, and brought them unto
Leah his mother, and Rachel said to Leah, Give me I pray of
thy son's mandrakes.

15. And she said unto her, Is it a small thing that thou hast
taken my man, and wilt thou take also my son's mandrakes?
And Rachel said, Therefore he shall lie with thee this night
for thy son's mandrakes.

16. And Jacob came from the field in the evening, and
Leah went forth to meet him, and said, Thou shalt come to me,
because by hiring I have hired thee in my son's mandrakes;
and he lay with her that night.

17. And God hearkened to Leah, and she conceived, and
bare a fifth son unto Jacob.

18. And Leah said, God hath given my reward, in that I

have given my handmaid to my man, and she called his name Issachar.

19. And Leah conceived as yet, and bare a sixth son unto Jacob.

20. And Leah said, GOD had endowed me with a good dowry, this time my man will cohabit with me, because I have borne him six sons, and she called his name Zebulon.

21. And afterwards she bare a daughter, and called her. name Dinah.

22. And GOD remembered Rachel, and GOD hearkened to her, and opened her womb.

23. And she conceived and bare a son, and said, GOD hath gathered together my reproach.

24. And she called his name Joseph, saying, Let JEHOVAH add to me another son.

　　　*　*　*　*　*　*　*

25. And it came to pass, when Rachel had borne Joseph. that Jacob said unto Laban, Send me, and I will go to my place and to my land.

26. Give me my women, and my sons, because I have served thee for them, and I will go, because thou hast known my service with which I have served thee.

27. And Laban said unto him, If, I pray, I have found grace in thine eyes, I have experienced, and JEHOVAH hath blessed me for thy sake.

28. And he said, Appoint thy reward upon me, and I will give it.

29. And he said unto him, Thou hast known in what quality I have served thee, and in what quality thine acquisition was with me.

30. Because it was little which thou hadst before me, and it is broke forth into a multitude, and JEHOVAH hath blessed thee at my foot, and now when shall I do also for mine own house?

31. And he said, What shall I give thee? And Jacob said, thou shalt not give me any thing, if thou wilt do for me this word, I will return, will feed, will guard thy flock.

32. I will pass through all thy flock to-day, removing thence all the cattle speckled and spotted, and all the black cattle in. the lambs, and the spotted and speckled in the she-goats, and it shall be my hire.

33. And my justice shall answer for me on the morrow, because thou comest upon my hire before thee, every one which is not speckled and spotted in the she-goats, and black in the lambs, that was stolen with me.

34. And Laban said, Behold let it be according to thy word.

35. And he removed in that day the he-goats variegated and spotted, and the she goats speckled and spotted, every

thing that had white in it, and every thing black in the lambs, and gave them into the hands of his sons.

36. And he set a way of three days between himself and between Jacob, and Jacob fed the rest of Laban's flocks.

37. And Jacob took to himself a fresh rod of poplar, and hazle, and plane-tree, and pilled in them white pillings, making bare the white which was on the rods.

38. And he set the rods which he had pilled in gutters, in the drinking-troughs of water, whither the flocks came to drink, over against the flocks, and they grew warm in coming to drink.

39. And the flocks grew warm at the rods, and the flocks brought forth variegated, speckled, and spotted.

40. And Jacob separated the lambs, and gave the faces of the flock to the variegated, and all the black in the flock of Laban, and he set for himself droves for himself alone, and did not set them to the flock of Laban.

41. And it came to pass, as every one of the flock of the first in coition grew warm, that Jacob set the rods at the eyes of the flock in the gutters, to cause them to grow warm at the rods.

42. And to the flock next in coition he did not set them, and of the next in coition was Laban's, and of the first in coition was Jacob's.

43. And the man spread himself abroad exceedingly exceedingly, and he had many flocks, and maid-servants, and camels, and asses.

THE CONTENTS.

3902. IN the foregoing chapter, by the four sons of Jacob born of Leah, the state of the Church was treated of, or the state of man who is made a Church, as to the ascent from the truth which is of faith to the good which is of love. In this chapter, by the sons of Jacob, born of Rachel's and Leah's handmaids, and of Leah, and lastly of Rachel, the subject treated of is the conjunction of natural truth with spiritual good by media; and this, in the order in which it is effected in every man who is regenerated.

3903. After this conjunction, a description is given of the fructification and multiplication of truth and good, which is signified by the flock which Jacob procured to himself by the flock of Laban.

THE INTERNAL SENSE.

3904. VERSES 1, 2. *AND Rachel saw that she did not bring forth unto Jacob, and Rachel was jealous towards her sister, and said unto Jacob, Give me sons, or else I die. And Jacob was inflamed with anger towards Rachel, and said, Am I in God's stead? Who withholdeth from thee the fruit of the womb?* Rachel saw that she did not bring forth unto Jacob, signifies that interior truth was not yet acknowledged: and Rachel was jealous (or zealous) towards her sister, signifies indignation, in that it was not acknowledged like external truth: and she said unto Jacob, Give me sons, signifies that from the good of natural truth she was desirous to have interior truths: or else I die, signifies that thus she would not rise again: and Jacob was inflamed with anger towards Rachel, signifies indignation on the part of natural good: and said, Am I in God's stead? signifies that it was impossible for him: who withholdeth from thee the fruit of the womb? signifies that this must be effected from an internal principle.

3905. "Rachel saw that she did not bring forth unto Jacob" —that this signifies that interior truth was not yet acknowledged, appears from the representation of Rachel, as being the affection of interior truth, or interior truth, see n. 3758, 3782, 3793, 3819; and from the signification of bringing forth, as being to acknowledge in faith and also in act, of which we shall speak presently; and from the representation of Jacob, as being the good of natural truth, see n. 3669, 3677, 3829, and in the preceding chapter throughout. The reason why to bring forth denotes to acknowledge in faith and also in act, is, because births in the Word signify spiritual births, see n. 1145, 1255, 3860, 3868. Spiritual birth is the acknowledgment of, and faith in, truth and good; in the present case acknowledgment in faith and also in act, namely, of the interior truth represented by Rachel. Since nothing is acknowledged in faith, until the life is formed accordingly, therefore it is said, acknowledgment in faith, and also in act. The truths of faith, which are not learnt for the sake of acting, but only for the sake of knowing, adjoin themselves to the affections of what is evil and false, wherefore they are not truths of faith with him who learnt them, but interiorly are contrary to faith.

3906. "And Rachel was jealous (or zealous) towards her sister"—that this signifies indignation because the interior truth was not acknowledged as the external was, appears from the signification of being jealous, as being somewhat of indignation, and this because she did not bring forth like Leah; and from the representation of Rachel, as being interior truth (concerning which, see n. 3905); and from the signification of sister, who here is Leah, as being external truth; that Leah is external truth, may be seen, n. 3793, 3819. With those who are regen erated, the case is this: they learn what internal truth is, but in the beginning they do not acknowledge it with such a degree of faith, as to live according to it; for internal truths are con-joined to spiritual affection, which cannot flow-in, until external truths are adapted to correspondence with internal. For ex-ample, in respect to this internal truth, that all good is from the Lord, and that what is from man's proprium is not good; this may be known in the beginning of regeneration, but still not be acknowledged in faith and act, for to acknowledge it in faith and act, is to have a perception that it is so, and an affec-tion to will it to be so, and this in every act of good; also a perception that good from the proprium will necessarily have respect to self, or to preference of self before others, and thus as to contempt of others, and moreover to merit in the good which it does. All these things have place in external truth until internal truth is joined to it, and they cannot be joined until self-regard begins to cease, and neighbourly regard begins to be felt. Hence it may be evident, what is meant by the in-dignation, because internal truth was not yet acknowledged like external.

3907. "And she said unto Jacob, Give me sons"—that this signifies that from the good of natural truth, she desired to have interior truths, appears from the representation of Jacob, as being the good of natural truth, see n. 3905; and from the signification of sons, as being truths, see n. 489, 491, 533, 1147, 2623, in the present case interior truths, because from Rachel, who represents interior truth, see n. 3758, 3782, 3793, 3819.

3908. "Or else I die"—that this signifies that thus she would not rise again, appears from the signification of dying, as being not to rise again into life. In ancient times, wives called themselves dead, when they did not bring forth a son or a daughter, and also believed themselves to be as it were dead, because no remembrance of them, or as it were life, would be left to posterity; but their calling and believing themselves dead arose from worldly causes. Nevertheless, as every cause exists from a prior cause, and the all of every cause in the nat ural world, from a cause in the spiritual world, so it was in the present instance; the cause in the spiritual world originated in the marriage of good and truth, from which the births are no other than the truths of faith and the goods of charity. These spiritual things in that world are sons and daughters, and are also signified by sons and daughters in the Word. Whoever is without these births, namely, the truths of faith and the goods of charity, is as it were dead, that is, amongst the dead who do not rise again to life or heaven. Hence it may appear what is meant by the words of Rachel, " or else I die."

3909. " And Jacob was inflamed with anger against Rachel "
—that this signifies indignation on the part of natural good,
appears from the signification of being inflamed with anger, as
being to be indignant, of which we shall speak presently ; and
from the representation of Jacob, as being good of the natural
principle (concerning which see above); it is said towards
Rachel, because interior truth, represented by Rachel, could
not yet be acknowledged in faith and act, by the good of the
natural principle which is represented by Jacob. The reason
why being inflamed with anger, in the internal sense, is to be
indignant, is, because every natural affection, when it ascends
towards the interiors, or towards heaven, becomes milder, and
at length is changed into a heavenly affection ; for the things
which are extant in the sense of the letter, as, in the present
case, Jacob's being inflamed with anger, are respectively harsh,
because they are natural and corporeal, but they become mild
and gentle in proportion as they are elevated out of the natural
and corporeal man into the internal or spiritual man. Hence it
is, that the sense of the letter is such, because it is accommo ·
dated to the apprehension of the natural man, and the internal
sense is not such, because it is accommodated to the apprehen
sion of the spiritual man. From these considerations it is evi
dent, that being inflamed with anger signifies to be indignant.
True spiritual indignation does not take any tincture of anger
from the natural man, and still less does celestial indignation ;
but it takes its tincture from the interior essence of zeal, which
zeal, in the external form, appears like anger, but in its internal
form is not anger, nor even the indignation of anger, but is
somewhat of sadness attended with a wish that what caused it
might not be so, and in a still interior form, it is a mere obscu
rity, arising from what is not good and true in another, which
intercepts heavenly delight.

3910. "And he said, Am I in God's stead?"—that this sig
nifies that it was impossible for him, appears from the signifi
cation of not being in God's stead, as being what is impossible,
for God, so called in the Word, is from ability or potency, but
the term Jehovah from esse or essence, see n. 300. Hence it is,
that the term God is used in speaking of truth, and Jehovah, in
speaking of good, n. 2769, 2807, 2822, for ability is predicated
of truth when esse is predicated of good, since good has power
by truth, for by truth good produces whatever exists. Hence
it may appear, that these words, "Am I in God's stead?" sig
nify that it was impossible for him.

3911. "Who withholdeth from thee the fruit of the womb?"
—that this signifies that this must be effected from the internal,
appears from the sense which results from the internal sense
of the words, for the fruit of the womb, in the internal sense,
signifies the same as birth, namely, the acknowledgment of

truth and good in faith and act, see n. 3905, and still more, namely, the conjunction of truth and good thence derived That acknowledgment and this conjunction cannot exist from the external man, but from the internal; for all good flows in from the Lord through the internal man into the external, and adopts the truths which are insinuated through the sensual principles of the external man, and causes man to acknowledge those truths in faith and act, and that they may be adjoined, and thereby appropriated to man. That all good flows in from the Lord, through the internal man, into the truths which are collected in the memory of the external man, has been frequently shown above. This is what is meant by the explication of these words, that this must be effected from the internal.

2912. Verses 3, 4, 5. *And she said, Behold my maid-servant Bilhah; come to her, and let her bear upon my knees, and I also shall be builded up by her. And she gave him Bilhah her handmaid for a woman, and Jacob came to her, and Bilhah conceived, and bare a son unto Jacob.* She said, Behold my maid-servant Bilhah, signifies the affirming medium which exists between natural truth and interior truth: come to her, signifies that with that medium there was a faculty of conjunction: and let her bear upon my knees, signifies acknowledgment by the affection of interior truth, from which conjunction comes: and I also shall be builded up by her, signifies that thus she would have life: and she gave him Bilhah her handmaid for a woman, signifies the affirmative medium adjoined: and Jacob came to her, signifies that it was conjoined: and Bilhah conceived, and bare a son unto Jacob, signifies reception and acknowledgment.

3913. "She said, Behold my maid-servant Bilhah"—that this signifies the affirming medium which exists between natural truth and interior truth, appears from the signification of maid-servant and of handmaid, as being the affection of the knowledges which belong to the exterior man, see n. 1895, 2567, 3835, 3849; and as this affection is the medium of conjoining interior truths with natural or external ones, therefore, in the present case, maid-servant signifies the affirming medium between those truths; and from the representation of Bilhah, as being the quality of that medium. The handmaids given to Jacob for women by Rachel and Leah, that they might produce offspring, represented and signified, in the internal sense, nothing else than such a subservient principle, in the present case subservient as a medium of conjunction of interior truth with external; for Rachel signifies interior truth, and Leah, external, see n. 3793, 3819. The subject here treated of by the twelve sons of Jacob, is the twelve general or cardinal things, by which man is initiated into things spiritual and celestial, during the

process of regeneration, or of being made a Church. Whilst
man is being regenerated, or made a Church, that is, whilst
from being dead he is made alive, or from corporeal, celestial,
he is led by the Lord through several states. The general
states are those which are denoted by these twelve sons, and
afterwards by the twelve tribes, and therefore the twelve tribes
signify all things relating to faith and love, as may be seen
above, n. 3858; for things general involve all things particular
and singular, and the latter have relation to the former. In the
process of man's regeneration, the internal man is to be conjoined with the external, consequently the goods and truths of
the internal man are to be conjoined to the goods and truths
of the external, for man is man from goods and truths. These
cannot be conjoined without media. Media are those things
which derive something from the one part, and something from
the other, and which have this effect, that in proportion as man
approaches to the one, the other becomes subordinate. These
media are the things which are signified by the handmaids here
spoken of; the media on the part of the internal man, by the
handmaids of Rachel, and the media on the part of the external
man, by the handmaids of Leah. That media of conjunction
are necessary, may appear from the fact, that the natural man
of himself is in no agreement with the spiritual man, but in
such a state of disagreement, as to be altogether opposite; for
the natural man regards and loves himself and the world,
whereas the spiritual man does not regard himself and the
world, except in so far as is conducive to promote uses in the
spiritual world, thus he regards its service, and loves it from
its use and end. The natural man seems to himself to have
life, when he is exalted to dignities, and so to super-eminence
over others, but the spiritual seems to himself to have life in
humiliation, and in being the least; not that he despises dignities, if by them, as media, he can be serviceable to his neighbour, to society in general, and to the Church; nor does he
reflect upon the dignities to which he is advanced, for the sake
of himself, but of those uses which he regards as ends. The
natural man is in his blessedness, when he is richer than others,
and in possession of the world's wealth, but the spiritual is in
his blessedness, when he is in the knowledges of truth and
good, which are his riches, and still more, when he is in the
exercise of good according to truths; still he does not despise
riches, because thereby he may be active, and in the world.
From these few considerations it may appear, that the state of
the natural man and of the spiritual are opposed to each other
by the ends which they regard, but that still they may be conjoined, and that such conjunction has place, when the things
of the external man are made subordinate and subservient to
the ends regarded by the internal man. In order, then, that

man may become spiritual, it is necessary that the things of
the external man be reduced to compliance, and that thus selfish and worldly ends of life be put off, and ends regarding the
neighbour and the Lord's kingdom be put on. The former
ends can in no wise be put off, and the latter put on, thus they
cannot be conjoined, except by media. These media are what
are signified by the handmaids, and specifically, by the four
sons born of the handmaids. The first medium is affirming or
affirmative of internal truth, namely, that so it is ; when this
affirmative exists, man is in the beginning of regeneration, and
good operates from the internal man, and causes affirmation.
This good cannot flow into a negative principle, nor even into
a doubting one, nor until the affirmative has place. This good
afterwards manifests itself by affection, namely, by this, that
man is affected with truth, or begins to be delighted with it, at
first, in that he knows it, and next, in that he acts according to
it. For example : in regard to this truth, that the Lord is salvation to the human race. Unless man makes this affirmative,
it is impossible for all those things which he has learnt from
the Word, or in the Church, concerning the Lord, and has
stored up amongst scientifics in his natural memory, to be conjoined with his internal man, that is, with the things therein
which may be things of faith. Thus no affection can flow in,
not even into the general principles of what is conducive to
salvation. When, however, it becomes affirmative, there is an
accession of things innumerable, and they are filled with the
good which flows in : for good is continually flowing in from
the Lord ; but where there is no affirmative, it is not received.
An affirmative, therefore, is the first medium, and as it were
the first habitation of good flowing in from the Lord. The case
is similar in regard to all the other truths which are called the
truths of faith.

3914. " Come to her "—that this signifies that with that
medium there was a faculty of conjunction, appears from the
signification of coming or entering in to any one, when matrimonial connection is spoken of, as being conjunction, in the
present case, the faculty of conjunction with the affirmative,
for the first conjunction must be with the affirmation, that a
thing is so.

3915. " And let her bear upon my knees "—that this signifies acknowledgment by the affection of interior truth, from
which conjunction comes, appears from the signification of
bearing, as being to acknowledge in faith and act (concerning
which see above, n. 3905) ; and from the signification of knees
or thighs, as being the things which belong to conjugial love,
see n. 3021, thus to the conjunction of the truth of faith, and
of the good of love, this conjunction being the very essential
conjugial principle in the Lord's kingdom. Thus bearing upon

my knees signifies an acknowledgment of the interior truth which is represented by Rachel. The custom which prevailed amongst the ancients, of acknowledging sons and daughters to be legitimate, who were born of handmaids by consent of the wife, and of their bearing upon their knees in order that they might be acknowledged, was derived from the ancient Church, the worship of which consisted in rituals, which were representative and significative of things celestial and spiritual. In that Church, since bearing signified the acknowledgment of truth, and the knees, conjugial love, or the conjunction of truth and good from affection, such a ritual was received, in case the wife was barren, lest she should represent the dead who do not rise again to life, according to what was said above, n. 3908. These words, in the internal sense, signify the second degree of affirmation or acknowledgment, which is grounded in affection, for there must be affection in acknowledgment or affirmation, to produce conjunction, all conjunction being produced by affection, since without affection truths are lifeless. For example: to know these truths, that a man ought to love his neighbour, and that charity consists in doing so, and in charity, spiritual life, is mere science unless attended with affection, that is, unless it is willed from the heart. Without affection these truths are not alive, and however the man knows them, still he does not love his neighbour, but himself in preference to his neighbour, and is in natural life, and not in spiritual. Natural affection then has dominion over spiritual affection, and so long as this is the case, man is called dead, for he has a life contrary to heavenly life, and heavenly life is the real and essential one.

3916. "And I also shall be builded up by her"—that this signifies that thus she would have life, appears from the signification of being builded up, as not to die, see n. 3908, consequently, being to rise again or live.

3917. "And she gave him Bilhah her handmaid for a woman"—that this signifies the affirmative medium adjoined, appears from the representation of Bilhah, and from the signification of handmaid, as being an affirmative medium, see n. 3913; and from the signification of giving for a woman, as being to adjoin.

3918. "And Jacob came to her"—that this signifies that it was conjoined, appears from the signification of coming or entering in to any one, when predicated of matrimonial connection, as being conjunction, see above, n. 3914.

3919. "And Bilhah conceived and bare Jacob a son"—that this signifies reception and acknowledgment, appears from the signification of conceiving, as being reception; and from the signification of bearing, as being acknowledgment, see n. 3860, 3868, 3905, 3911. Conceptions and births in a spiritual sense are receptions of truth from good, and consequent ac-knowledgments.

3920. Verse 6. *And Rachel said, God hath judged me, and hath also heard my voice, and hath given me a son, there-fore she called his name Dan.* Rachel said, God hath judged me, and hath also heard my voice, signifies, in a supreme sense, justice and mercy; in an internal sense, the holy principle of faith; and in an external sense, good of life: and hath given me a son, signifies this truth acknowledged: therefore she called his name, signifies his quality.

3921. "Rachel said, God hath judged me, and hath also heard my voice"—that this signifies, in a supreme sense, jus-tice and mercy, in an internal sense, the holy principle of faith, and in an external sense, good of life, appears from the signi-fication of God judging me, and from the signification of hearing my voice. That God judging me denotes the justice of the Lord, may appear without explication, as also that hearing my voice denotes mercy: for the Lord judges all from justice, and hears all from mercy. He judges from justice, because from Divine Truth, and He hears from mercy, because from Divine Good; from justice, those who do not receive Divine Good, and from mercy, those who do receive. Never-theless, when He judges from justice, He judges also at the same time from mercy, for in all Divine Justice there is mercy as in all Divine Truth there is Divine Good. But this subject being too mysterious to admit of a brief explication, by the Divine Mercy of the Lord, will be more fully expounded else where. The reason why God judging me, and also hearing my voice, denotes the holiness of faith, is, because the faith which is predicated of truth, corresponds to the Divine Justice, and the holiness, which is good, corresponds to the Divine Mercy of the Lord. Moreover, judging or judgment is predicated of the truth of faith, see n. 2235; and whereas it is said of God that He judged, it is good or holy. Hence it is evident, that the holy principle of faith, is at once signified by both expres-sions; and as one principle is at the same time signified by both, they are both joined together by the particles *and also.* The reason why in an external sense it denotes the good of life, is also from correspondence, for the good of life corresponds to the holiness of faith. That the meaning of this expression, God hath judged me, and hath also heard, cannot be known with-out the internal sense, is evident from the fact, that in the sense of the letter the words do not so cohere as to present one idea to the understanding. The reason why in this verse, and in those which follow, even to the birth of Joseph, the expres-sion God is used, whereas, in the verses immediately preceding, He is called Jehovah, is, because the subject here treated of is the regeneration of the spiritual man, and in the preceding

verses the regeneration of the celestial man, for the name God
is used in treating of the good of faith, which is proper to the
spiritual man, but the name Jehovah, in treating of the good
of love, which is proper to the celestial man, see n. 2586, 2769,
2807, 2822; for Judah, to whom the subject was continued in
the foregoing chapter, represented the celestial man, see n. 3881,
but Joseph, to whom it is continued in this chapter, represented the spiritual man, concerning whom see the subsequent
verses 23 and 24. That the name Jehovah was used in con-
tinuing the subject to Judah, may be seen in the preceding
chapter, verses 32, 33, 35; that the name God is used in con-
tinuing it to Joseph, may be seen in this chapter, verses 6, 8,
17, 18, 20, 22, 23, and afterwards again the name Jehovah,
because it proceeds from the spiritual man to the celestial. This
is the arcanum which lies concealed in these chapters, which
no one can know but from the internal sense, and unless he
knows also what the celestial man is, and what the spiritual.

3922. "And hath given me a son"—that this signifies truth
acknowledged, appears from the signification of son, as being
truth, see n. 489, 491, 533, 1147; and from the signification of
giving a son, as being to give this truth, which is the same thing
as to acknowledge, for every truth, which is acknowledged, is
given by the Lord. To give a son, implies the same as to bear,
or bring forth, and that to bring forth is to acknowledge, may
be seen, n. 3905, 3915, 3919.

3923. "Therefore she called his name Dan"—that this signifies his quality, appears from the signification of name and
of calling a name, as being quality, see n. 144, 145, 1754,
1896, 2009, 2724, 3421; the quality itself is in the name of
Dan, for he was so called from *judging*, but although the name
was given him from judging, still it involves those things which
are signified by all these words of Rachel, "God hath judged
me, and hath also heard my voice," that is, good of life, and
the holiness of faith, also, in a supreme sense, the Lord's justice
and mercy. This is the general principle of the Church, which
Dan signifies, and which the tribe named from Dan represents.
This general principle is the first which is to be affirmed or acknowledged, before man can be regenerated or be made a Church.
Unless it be affirmed and acknowledged, the other things relating
to faith and life cannot possibly be received, consequently,
cannot be affirmed, and still less acknowledged; for he who only
affirms faith as belonging to himself, and not the holy principle
of faith, that is, charity (for this is the holy principle of faith),
and does not affirm this by the good of life, that is, by the
works of charity, cannot any longer relish the essence of faith,
for he rejects it. Affirmation and acknowledgment is the first
general principle with the man who is in the process of regeneration, but it is the last with the man who is regenerated:

thus Dan is the first principle with the man about to be regenerated, and Joseph is the last, for Joseph is the spiritual man
himself. Joseph, however, is the first principle with the man
who is regenerated, and Dan is the last, because the man about
to be regenerated commences his process from the affirmation
that it is, namely, the holy principle of faith, and the good of
life, whereas the regenerated man, who is spiritual, is in spiritual good itself, and thence regards such affirmation as the last
principle, for the holy things of faith and the goods of life are
established in him. That Dan is the affirmative principle,
which must be the first in the process of man's regeneration,
may also appear from other passages in the Word where Dan
is mentioned, as from the prophecy of Jacob, at that time
Israel, concerning his sons, "*Dan* shall judge his people, as
one of the tribes of Israel. *Dan* will be a serpent upon the
way, an adder upon the path, biting the heels of the horse, and
his rider falleth backward; I wait for Thy salvation, Jehovah,"
Gen. xlix. 16, 17, 18. Dan, in this passage, is the affirmative
principle of truth, of which it is said, that it will be a serpent
upon the way, and an adder upon the path, when it reasons
concerning truth from the things of sense; biting the heels of
the horse, when it consults the lowest intellectual or scientific
things, and forms conclusions thence; and that it is then drawn
away from truth, is signified by his rider falling backward,
wherefore it is said, I wait for Thy salvation, Jehovah. That he
is a serpent who reasons on Divine mysteries from the things
of sense and science, may be seen, n. 195, 196, 197; that way
and path denotes truth, n. 627, 2333; that the heels of a horse
denote the lowest intellectual or scientific things, n. 259; for a
horse denotes the intellectual principle, n. 2761, 2762, the lowest of which is the heel. So in the prophecy of Moses concerning the twelve tribes, "To *Dan* he said, *Dan* is a lion's whelp,
he leapeth forth from Bashan," Deut. xxxiii. 22. A lion, in
the internal sense of the Word, signifies the truth of the Church,
from its strength, for it is truth which fights and conquers.
Hence a lion's whelp denotes the beginning of truth, which is
affirmation and acknowledgment; it is said to leap from Bashan,
because from good of the natural principle. So in Jeremiah,
"Wash thine heart from wickedness, O Jerusalem, to the end
that thou mayest be saved; how long dost thou cause the
thoughts of thine iniquity to tarry in the midst of thee? because the voice of one declaring *from Dan*, and causing to
hear iniquity from Mount Ephraim," iv. 14, 15. From Dan,
denotes from truth which is to be affirmed; from Mount Ephraim,
denotes from the affection thereof. Again, "We wait for peace,
but there is no good; for a time of healing, and behold terror.
From Dan was heard the snorting of his horses, at the voice
of the neighings of his strong ones the whole land trembled,

and they came and consumed the land and the fulness thereof,
the city and those who dwell therein; for behold I send unto
you serpents, cockatrices, which have no incantation, and they
shall bite you," viii. 15, 16, 17.   The snorting of horses heard
from Dan, denotes reasoning concerning truth from a principle
not affirmative; the land which trembled, and the fulness of
which they consumed, denote the Church and all things belonging to it; for they who reason concerning truth from a
principle not affirmative, or from a negative principle, destroy
all things of faith; serpents and cockatrices denote reasonings
as above.   So in Ezekiel, "*Dan* and Javan coming to thy fairs
brought smooth iron, cassia and calamus were in thy market,"
xxvii. 19; speaking of Tyre, which signifies the knowledges of
truth and good, see n. 1201.   Dan denotes the first truths which
are affirmed; fairs and markets denote the acquisitions of truth
and good, n. 2967; smooth iron denotes natural truth, which
is the first, n. 425, 426; cassia and calamus in like manner denote natural truth, but from which good comes.   So in Amos,
"In that day the beautiful virgins and youths shall faint with
thirst; they who sware to the guilt of Samaria, and said, Thy
God liveth, *O Dan*, and the way of Beersheba liveth, shall fall
and not rise again," viii. 13, 14.   Thy God liveth, O Dan, and
the way of Beersheba liveth, denotes that they were in a negative as to all things relating to faith and the doctrine thereof.
That way denotes truth, see n. 627, 2333; that Beersheba denotes doctrine, see n. 2723, 2858, 2859, 3466.   The reason why
a negative is hereby denoted in regard to all things of faith, is,
because Dan was the last boundary of the land of Canaan, and
Beersheba the first, or the midst or inmost of the land; for the
land of Canaan represented and signified the Lord's kingdom,
and thus the Church, see n. 1607, 3038, 3481, consequently all
things of love and faith, for these belong to the Lord's kingdom
and Church.   Hence all things in the land of Canaan were
representative according to distances, situations, and boundaries, see n. 1585, 1866, 3686.   The first boundary, or the midst
or inmost of the land, was Beersheba, before the building of
Jerusalem, because Abraham was there, and also Isaac, but the
last or outmost boundary was Dan.   Hence, when all things
were to be signified in one complex, it was said, "From Dan
even to Beersheba," as in the second book of Samuel, "To
transfer the kingdom from the house of Saul, and to erect the
throne of David, over Israel and over Judah, *from Dan even
to Beersheba*," iii. 10.   Again, "All Israel was gathered together *from Dan even to Beersheba*," xvii. 11.   Again, "David
said to Joab, Wander through all the tribes of Israel, *from Dan
even to Beersheba*," xxiv. 2, 15.   And in the first book of the
Kings, "Judah and Israel dwelt in security, every one under
his vine, and under his fig-tree, *from Dan and even to Beer-*

sheba," iv. 25. This expression, in the historical sense, meant
all things of the land of Canaan, but in the internal sense, all
things of the Lord's kingdom, and also all things of the Church.
The reason why Dan is the first boundary, as here described,
and also the last, as was said above, is, because the affirmative
of truth and good is the first of all at the commencement of
faith and charity in man, and is the last when man is in charity
and thence in faith. Hence it was, that the last lot fell for
Dan when the land of Canaan was divided for inheritance,
Joshua xix. 40 ; for the lot was cast before Jehovah, Josh.
xviii. 6. Hence it fell out according to the representation of
each tribe ; and whereas the lot did not fall to Dan amongst the
inheritances of the rest of the tribes, but beyond their borders,
Judges xviii. 1, therefore that tribe was passed over and not
mentioned in the Apocalypse, chap. vii. 5 to 8, in speaking of
the twelve thousand which were sealed. For they who are
only in the affirmative principle respecting truth and also good,
and go no further, are not in the Lord's kingdom, that is, among
the sealed ; the very worst of men may know truths and goods
and also affirm them, but the quality of such affirmation is de
termined by the life. Dan is likewise mentioned as a boundary
(Gen. xiv. 14), speaking of Abraham, in that he pursued his
enemies thitherto, and Dan has a similar signification in that
passage. The city called Dan was not indeed at that time built
by the posterity of Dan, but afterwards (see Joshua xix. 47 ;
Judges xviii. 29). But this was the name given even at that
time to the first boundary, in respect to the entrance into the
land of Canaan, or to the last boundary, in respect to the going
out, the inmost of which land was Hebron, and afterwards
Beersheba, where Abraham and Isaac dwelt.

3924. Verses 7, 8. *And she conceived as yet, and Bilhah,
Rachel's handmaid, bare a second son unto Jacob. And Rachel
said, With the strugglings of God have I struggled with my
sister, and have also prevailed, and she called his name Naphtali.* She conceived as yet, and Bilhah, Rachel's handmaid,
bare, signifies here, as before, reception and acknowledgment :
a second son unto Jacob, signifies another general truth : and
Rachel said, With the strugglings of God have I struggled
with my sister, and have also prevailed, signifies, in a supreme
sense, proper ability ; in an internal sense, temptation in which
there is victory ; and in an external sense, resistance arising
from the natural man : and she called his name Naphtali, signifies his quality.

3925. " She conceived as yet, and Bilhah, Rachel's handmaid, bare"—that this signifies reception and acknowledgment,
appears from the signification of conceiving, being reception,
and from the signification of bearing, being acknowledgment,
see above, n. 3919 ; also from the signification of handmaid,

being a subservient medium, see n. 3913, 3917, for the subject here treated of is another general medium which serves for the conjunction of the internal man with the external.

3926. " A second son unto Jacob"—that this signifies another general truth, appears from the signification of son, as being truth, see n. 489, 491, 533, 1147. That it here signifies a general truth, is evident from what was said and shown above concerning the twelve sons of Jacob, and the twelve tribes named from them, as denoting the general principles of the Church, consequently the general principles of faith and love, or of truth and good, which are signified and represented by them. That in an opposite sense, they also denote general principles of no faith and love, or all the principles of what is false and evil, will appear from the following pages.

3927. "And Rachel said, With the strugglings of God have I struggled with my sister, and have also prevailed"—that this signifies, in a supreme sense, proper ability; in an internal sense, temptation in which is victory; and in an external sense, resistance arising from the natural man, appears from the signification of the strugglings of God, and of struggling, being tempt ations; for temptations are nothing else but strugglings of the internal man with the external, or of the spiritual man with the natural, inasmuch as each is willing to have dominion, and when dominion is disputed, the combat ensues, which is here called struggling. That to prevail is to overcome, is apparent without explication. The reason why these words, in a supreme sense, signify proper ability, is, because the Lord, whilst He was in the world, and in His Human in the world, from His own proper ability, sustained and overcame all temptations, differing in this from every man, who in no case sustains and overcomes any temptation from his own proper ability, but from that of the Lord in him. See what was said and shown above on this subject, namely, that the Lord endured the most grievous temptations, and such as no others ever endured, n. 1663, 1668, 1690, 1737, 1787, 1789, 1812, 1813, 1815, 1820, 2776, 2786, 2795, 2813, 2816, 3318. That the Lord fought and conquered from His own proper ability, n. 1616, 1692, 1813, 3381; and that the Lord alone fights in man, n. 1692. That in an internal sense, the strugglings of God, and prevailing, denote temptations in which man conquers, is evident from what has been just now said above. The reason why, in an external sense, is denoted resistance arising from the natural man, is, because all temptation is nothing else than such resistance; for in spiritual temptations, as was said, there is a dispute concerning the dominion, or as to which shall have the supremacy, the internal man or the external, or what is the same thing, the spiritual man or the natural, they being altogether opposite to each other, see n. 3913. When man is in temptations, his internal or spiritual man is under the Lord's rule by means of angels, but his external or natural man is under the rule of infernal spirits, and the combat between them is what is perceived in man as temptation. When man is such in faith and life as to be capable of being regenerated, he will then conquer in temptations, but when he is such as to be incapable of being regenerated, he then falls in temptations. That resistance arises from the natural man, is signified by the words, "I have struggled with my sister," for Leah, who here is the sister, signifies the affection of the external man, but Rachel, the affection of the internal, see n. 3793, 3819.

3928. "And she called his name Naphtali"—that this signifies the quality thereof, namely, of the temptation in which man overcomes, and also of the resistance which arises from the natural man, appears from the signification of name and of calling a name, being quality, see n. 144, 145, 1754, 1896, 2009, 2724, 3421. The quality itself is what is signified by Naphtali, for Naphtali was named from strugglings. Hence also Naphtali represents this other general truth of the Church, for temptation is the means of the conjunction of the internal man with the external, inasmuch as they are at disagreement with each other, but are reduced to agreement and correspondence by temptations. The external man is such, that of himself he lusts after mere corporeal and worldly things alone, these being the delights of his life; but the internal man, when he is open towards heaven, and desires the things of heaven, as is the case with those who are capable of being regenerated, finds his delight in heavenly things, and the combat is between these two opposite delights, whilst man is in temptations. Man, at the time, is ignorant of this, because he does not know what heavenly delight is, and what infernal delight is, still less that they are thus opposite to each other. But the celestial angels can in no wise be with man in his corporeal and worldly delight, until it be reduced to compliance, that is, until it be no longer regarded as an end, but as a means subservient to heavenly delight (according to what was shown above, n. 3913); when this is the case, the angels can be with man in each delight, but then delight becomes blessedness, and at length happiness in the other life. He who believes that the delight of the natural man before regeneration is not infernal, and that it is not possessed by diabolical spirits, is much deceived, and knows not how it is with man in this respect, to wit, that before re generation he is possessed, as to his natural man, by genii and infernal spirits, however he may appear to himself to be like another, and also notwithstanding his associating with others in holy things, and his reasoning about the truths and goods of faith, yea, and believing himself established in them. If he does not perceive in himself somewhat of affection in favour of

what is just and equitable in his function, and in favour of what
is true and good in society and in life, let him know that he is
in the same delight as the infernals, for in his delight there is
no other love but that of self and the world, and when such
love constitutes the delight, there is nothing in it either of
charity or of faith.   Where this delight has become dominant,
it cannot be checked and dissipated by any other medium than
an affirmation and acknowledgment of the holy principle of
faith and good of life, which is the first medium signified by
Dan, as was shown above ; and next by temptation, which is a
second medium, and is signified by Naphtali ; for this medium
follows the other, inasmuch as they who do not affirm and acknowledge good and truth, which are of faith and charity, cannot come into any temptation-combat, because there is nothing
inwardly repugnant to what is evil and false, the suggestions
whereof are favoured by natural delight.   In other parts of
the Word, where Naphtali is mentioned, the state of man after
temptations is signified thereby, as in the prophecy of Jacob,
at that time Israel, "*Naphtali* is a hind let loose, giving say
ings of elegance," Gen. xlix. 21 ; where hind let loose denotes
the affection of natural truth in the free state, which comes
after temptation ; which state also is the quality which exists in
the temptations that are signified by Naphtali, for in temptations
the combat is concerning freedom.   So, too, in the prophecy of
Moses, "To *Naphtali* he said, *Naphtali* satisfied with the good
pleasure, and full of the blessing of Jehovah, shall possess the
west and the south," Deut. xxxiii. 23 ; for the representations of
the sons of Jacob, and of the tribes, are according to the order
in which they are recounted, see n. 3862.   So also in the
prophecy of Deborah and Barak, "Zebulon was a people who
devoted the soul to die, and *Naphtali* on the heights of the
field," Judges v. 18 ; speaking also in the internal sense concerning temptation-combats, where Naphtali denotes those who
fear nothing of evil, because they are in truths and goods, which
is being on the heights of the field.

3929. Verses 9, 10, 11. *And Leah saw that she had stood
still from bearing, and she took Zilpah her handmaid, and
gave her to Jacob for a woman. And Zilpah, Leah's handmaid, bare a son unto Jacob. And Leah said, There cometh a
troop, and she called his name Gad.* Leah saw that she had
stood still from bearing, signifies that no other external truths
were acknowledged : and she took Zilpah her handmaid, signifies an affirmative conjoining medium : and gave her to Jacob
for a woman, signifies that it is conjoined : and Zilpah, Leah's
handmaid, bare a son unto Jacob, signifies acknowledgment :
and Leah said, There cometh a troop, signifies, in a supreme
sense, omnipotence and omniscience, in an internal sense, the

good of faith, and in an external sense, works: and she called his name Gad, signifies the quality thereof.

3930. "Leah saw that she stood still from bearing"—that this signifies that no other external truths were acknowledged appears from the representation of Leah, as being externa ,truth, see n. 3793, 3819; and from the signification of bearing, as being to acknowledge in faith and act, see n. 3905, 3915, 3919. Hence, Leah's standing still from bearing, denotes, in the internal sense, that no other external truths were acknowledged.

3931. "And she took Zilpah her handmaid"—that this signifies an affirmative-medium conjoined, appears from the signification of handmaid, as being an affirmative medium serviceable for the conjunction of the external man with the internal, see n. 3913, 3917.

3932. "And gave her to Jacob for a woman"—that this signifies that it is conjoined, appears from the signification of giving for a woman, as being to conjoin, as above, n. 3915, 3917.

3933. "And Zilpah, Leah's handmaid, bare a son unto Jacob"—that this signifies acknowledgment, namely, of externa. truth, appears from the signification of bearing, as being acknowledgment; and from the signification of handmaid, as being an affirmative conjoining medium; and from the signification of son, as being truth, see n. 489, 491, 533, 1147.

3934. "And Leah said, There cometh a troop"—that this signifies, in a supreme sense, omnipotence and omniscience, in an internal sense, the good of faith, and in an external sense, works, appears from the signification of troop in this passage. The reason why troop, in a supreme sense, denotes omnipotence and omniscience, is, because troop in the present case is a multitude, and when multitude is predicated of the Lord's Divine [principle], it is an infinite multitude, which is nothing else than omnipotence and omniscience. Omnipotence is predicated of quantity in relation to magnitude, and omniscience, of quantity in relation to multitude. Omnipotence also is predicated of infinite good, or what is the same thing, of the Divine Love, or of the Divine Will, but omniscience of infinite truth, or what is the same thing, of the Divine Intelligence. That troop in an internal sense denotes the good of faith, is from correspondence, for the good, which is of charity, corresponds to the Lord's Divine Omnipotence, and the truth, which is of faith, to His omniscience. The reason why troop, in an external sense, denotes works, is, because these correspond to the good of faith. The good of faith produces works, since the good of faith cannot exist without them, just as thinking good, and willing good, cannot exist without doing good, the former being the internal, and the latter the corresponding external. Moreover, in regard to works, unless they correspond to the good of faith, they are not works of charity, nor works of faith, for they do not proceed from their internal, but are dead works, in which there is neither good nor truth. But when they do correspond, they are then works either of charity or of faith. The works of charity are what flow from charity as their soul, but the works of faith are what flow from faith. The works of charity have place with the regenerate man, but the works of faith with the man who is not yet regenerate, but who is in the process of regeneration. Just as it is with the two affections, namely, the affection of good and the affection of truth. The regenerate man does good from the affection of good, thus from the will to good, but the man who is in the process of regeneration, does good from the affection of truth, thus from a knowledge of what is good. The difference between these two affections has been often shown above. Hence it is evident what constitutes good works. Moreover, the good of faith, in respect to works, is comparatively like man's will and derivative thought in respect to his face, which it is well known is an image of the mind, that is, of the man's will and derivative thought. If the will and thought be not exhibited in the face, as their image, in this case it is not will and thought, but it is either hypocrisy or deceit, for a face is exhibited which differs from what the man wills and thinks. The case is similar with every act of the body in respect to the interiors which belong to the thought and will. Man's internal lives in his external by act or by acting, and in case such act or acting is not according to his internal, it is a plain proof, that either it is not the internal, but some customary and habitual motion, which produces the act, or that it is somewhat feigned and pretended, as is the case in hypocrisy and deceit. Hence again it is evident what constitutes works. From these considerations it follows, that whoever professes faith, and especially whoever professes the good of faith, and denies works, is without faith, and still more without charity, particularly if he reject works. Inasmuch as this is the case respecting the works of charity and of faith, and it is absolutely impossible for a man to be in charity and faith, unless he be in works, therefore in the Word such frequent mention is made of works, as may appear from the following passages: "Thine eyes are open upon all the ways of the sons of man, to give to every one according to his ways, and *according to the fruit of his works*," Jer. xxxii. 19. Again, in the same prophet, "Turn ye every one from his evil way, *and make your works good*," xxxv. 15. Again, "I will render to them according *to their work*, and according *to the work of their hands*," xxv. 14. And in Hosea, "I will visit upon him his ways, and *will render to him his works*." iv. 9.

And in Micah, "The land shall be for a desolation upon the inhabitants thereof, *by reason of the fruit of their works*," vii. 13. And in Zechariah, "Thus saith Jehovah Zebaoth, Turn ye from your evil ways, and *your evil works;* Jehovah Zebaoth hath thought to do unto us according to our ways, and *according to our works,* so hath He done unto us," i. 4, 6. And in the Apocalypse, " Blessed are the dead who henceforth die in the Lord, yea, saith the spirit, that they may rest from their labours, *their works follow them,*" xiv. 13. Again, " I saw the dead small and great standing before God, and the books were opened : and another book was opened, which is of life, and the *dead were judged* according to those things which were written in the books, *according to their works.* The sea gave up those who were therein dead, and death and hell gave up those who were therein dead ; *therefore they were judged every one according to their works,*" xx. 12, 13. Again, " Behold I come quickly, my reward is with me, *to give to every one according to his work,*" Apoc. xxii. 12. And in John, "This is the judgment, that light is come into the world, but men loved darkness rather than light, *because their works were evil;* every one who *doeth evil* hateth the light, neither cometh to the light, lest *his works* should be reproved ; but he who doeth truth, cometh to the light, that *his works may be made manifest,* because they are wrought in God," iii. 19, 20, 21. Again, "The world can not hate you, but Me it hateth, because I testify concerning it, *that their works are evil,*" vii. 7. Again, " Jesus said to the Jews, If ye were Abraham's sons, *ye would do the works of Abraham; ye do the works of your father,*" viii. 39, 41. Again "If ye know these things, blessed are ye *if ye do them,*" xiii 17. And in Matthew, " Let your light shine before men, that they may see *your good works.* Whoso *doeth* and teacheth, shall be called great in the kingdom of the heavens," v. 16, 19. Again, " Not every one who saith unto Me, Lord, Lord, shal enter into the kingdom of the heavens, but he who *doeth the will of My Father* who is in the heavens. Many will say to Me in that day, Lord, Lord, have we not prophesied by Thy name, and by Thy name cast out demons, and in Thy name done many virtues? But then will I confess unto them, I know ye not, depart from Me *ye workers of iniquity,*" vii. 21, 22, 23. And in Luke, "The master of the house shall say unto them, I know you not whence ye are ; then shall ye begin to say, We have eaten in Thy presence, and drunk, and Thou hast taught in our streets ; but He will say, I tell you, I know you not whence ye are, depart from Me all *ye workers of iniquity,*" xiii. 25, 26, 27. Again, in Matthew, " Every one who heareth My words, and *doeth them,* I will compare to a prudent man ; but every one who heareth my words, and *doeth them not,* shall be compared to a foolish man," vii. 24, 26. Again, in the same evangelist, "*The Son of Man shall come in the glory of His Father, with His angels, and then shall He render to every one according to his works,*" xvi. 27. From these passages it is manifest, that works are what save or condemn a man, that is, that good works save him, and that evil works condemn him; for works contain the principle of man's will. He who wills good, does good; but he who does not do good, however he may profess to will good, still does not will it when he does not do it. In this case it is as though he should say, I will it, but I do not will it. Now since the will itself is in the works, and charity belongs to the will, and faith to charity, it is evident what of will, or of charity and faith, belongs to man, when he does not good works, and especially when he does the contrary, or evil works. It is moreover to be noted, that the Lord's kingdom commences in man from the life which is of works, for he is then in the beginning of regeneration; but when the Lord's kingdom is established in man, it terminates in works, and then the man is regenerated. The internal man is now in the external correspondently, and works belong to the external man, as charity and its derivative faith do to the internal, so that works are then charity. As the life of the internal man thus exists in the works of the external, therefore the Lord, in speaking of the last judgment, in Matt. xxv. 32 to 46, recounts nothing but works, declaring that those shall enter into eternal life who have done good works, and those into damnation who have done evil works. From what has been said it may also be seen what is signified by that which is said of John, that he lay at the breast and in the bosom of Jesus, and that Jesus loved him above the rest of the disciples, John xiii. 23, 25; chap. xxi. 20; for John represented good works (see preface to chap. xviii. and to chap. xxi. of Genesis). The nature of the works of faith, which also from appearance may be called its fruits, and of the works of charity, by the Divine Mercy of the Lord, will be more fully shown elsewhere.

3935. "And she called his name Gad"—that this signifies the quality thereof, appears from the signification of name and of calling a name, as being quality, concerning which see above; Gad signifies the quality itself, namely, the quality of the good of faith, and of works. Quality signifies whatever is in a thing as its inward principle; here, whatever is in the good of faith and in works. The inward principles thus influencing are innumerable, for the quality is various in every particular person; and there is also a contrary principle influencing those who are not in the good of faith, and thus not in good works, and this quality also is signified by Gad, when he is named in an opposite sense. The good of faith, which is of the internal man, and the good works, which are of the external, in case they correspond, as was shown above, is a third general medium necessary to be acknowledged in faith and act, before man can enter into the Lord's kingdom, that is, by regeneration become a Church.

3936. Verses 12, 13. *And Zilpah, Leah's handmaid, bare a second son unto Jacob. And Leah said, In my blessedness, because the daughters will make me blessed, and she called his name Asher.* Zilpah, Leah's handmaid, bare a second son unto Jacob, signifies the acknowledgment of another principle : and Leah said, In my blessedness, because the daughters will make me blessed, signifies, in a supreme sense, eternity ; in an internal sense, the happiness of eternal life ; and in an external sense, delight of the affections: and she called his name Asher, signifies quality.

3937. " Zilpah, Leah's handmaid, bare a second son unto Jacob"—that this signifies the acknowledgment of another principle, appears from the signification of bearing, being acknowledgment, see n. 3911, 3915, 3919 ; and from the signification of handmaid, as being an affirmative medium serviceable for the conjunction of the external man with the internal, see n. 3913, 3917 ; and from the signification of son, as being truth, in the present case, a general truth, see above, n. 3926 ; and from the representation of Jacob, and also of Leah and of Zilpah, concerning which see above. Hence it is manifest what the internal sense of these words is, namely, an acknowledgment of another general truth to serve as a medium of conjoining the external man with the internal.

3938. "And Leah said, In my blessedness, because the daughters will make me blessed"—that this signifies, in a supreme sense, eternity, in an internal sense, the happiness of eternal life, and in an external sense, the delight of the affections, appears from the signification of blessedness, and from the signification of " the daughters will make me blessed." That blessedness, in a supreme sense, denotes eternity, can only be made apparent from correspondence with things in man ; for things Divine, or such as are infinite, can only be apprehended from the finite things, of which man is capable of forming an idea. Without this idea derived from things finite, and especially from the things of space and time, it is impossible for man to comprehend the least of things Divine, and still less of what is infinite. Man cannot even think at all without an idea of space and time, see n. 3404, for he is in space and time as to the body, consequently as to the thoughts which come from the external things of the senses. The angels, however, not being in time and space, have ideas of state, and hence it is, that spaces and times in the Word signify states, see n. 1274, 1382, 2625, 2788, 2837, 3254, 3356, 3827. There are two states, namely, a state which corresponds to space, and a state which corresponds to time. The state which corresponds

to space is state as to esse, and the state which corresponds to
time is state as to existere, see n. 2625.   There are two principles which constitute man, namely, esse and existere.   The
esse of man is nothing but a recipient of the eternal principle
which proceeds from the Lord, for men, spirits, and angels are
merely recipients, or forms receptive of life from the Lord; it
is the reception of life of which existere is predicated.   Man
believes *that he is*, and this of himself, when yet he *is* not of
himself, but exists so, as was said.   Esse is in the Lord alone,
and it is called Jehovah.   From the Esse which is Jehovah,
come all the things which appear *as if they are*.   But the Lord's
Esse, or Jehovah, can in no wise be communicated to any one
only to the Lord's Human.   This was made the Divine Esse,
that is, Jehovah.   That the Lord as to each essence is Jehovah,
may be seen, n. 1736, 2004, 2005, 2018, 2025, 2156, 2329, 2921,
3023, 3035.   Existere is predicated also of the Lord, but only
during His abode in the world, where He put on the Divine
Esse; but when He was made the Divine Esse, existere could
no longer be predicated of Him, otherwise than as something
proceeding from Him.   What proceeds from Him is what
appears as an existere in Him, whereas it is not in Him, but is
from Him and causes men, spirits, and angels to exist. that is,
to live.   Existere with man, spirit, and angel, is living, and
living is eternal happiness.   The happiness of eternal life is
what eternity corresponds to in a supreme sense, this being
eternity from the Lord's Divine Esse.   That the happiness of
eternal life is what blessedness, in an internal sense, signifies,
is evident; also that it signifies the delight of the affections, in
an external sense, and thus there is no need of any further explication of the subject.   It is the delight of the affections of
truth and good corresponding to the happiness of eternal life,
which is signified.   All affections have their delights, but such
as the affections are, such are the delights.   The affections of
evil and the false have also their delights, and until man is
regenerated, and receives from the Lord the affections of truth
and good, it appears to him as if there were no other delights
but those arising from the affections of evil and the false; consequently that if he should be deprived of these delights, he
must necessarily perish.   But they, however, who receive from
the Lord the delights of the affections of truth and good, by
degrees see and perceive the nature of the delights of the life
of evil and the false, which they once believed to be the only
delights existing, and that they are respectively vile and filthy.
And the more advancement they make in the delights of the
affections of truth and good, the more vile do the delights of
evil and the false appear, till at length they hold them in aversion.   I have occasionally discoursed with those in another life
who have been in the delights of evil and the false, and it was

given me to tell them, that they have no life until they are
deprived of their delights.   They replied (as people of similar
principles in the world do), that if they were deprived of those
delights, there would be nothing of life remaining with them.
But it was given me to answer, that life then first commences,
and is attended with such happiness as is enjoyed in heaven,
which is respectively ineffable.   This, however, they were not
able to comprehend, because what is unknown is believed to
be nothing.   The case is similar with all those in the world
who are in selfish and worldly loves, and, consequently, are
void of charity.   They know the delight of the former loves,
but not the delight of charity, and thus they are quite ignorant
what charity is, and especially, that there is any delight in
charity, when yet the delight of charity is what fills the universal heaven, and constitutes the blessedness and happiness
therein, and if you are disposed to credit it, constitutes also the
intelligence and wisdom and their delights, for the Lord flows
into the delights of charity with the light of truth and the flame
of good, and hence with intelligence and wisdom.   But falses
and evils reject, suffocate, and pervert those delights, and hence
comes folly and insanity.   From these facts it may be seen
what the delight of the affections is, and what its quality, in
that it corresponds to the happiness of eternal life.   The man
of modern times believes, that if at the hour of death he has
but the confidence of faith, he may come into heaven, without
any regard to the affections in which he has lived through the
whole course of his life.   I have also occasionally discoursed
with those who have lived and believed in this manner.   When
they come into another life, they at first entertain no other
thought than that they can enter into heaven, not attending to
their past life, namely, that thereby they have put on the
delight of the affection of evil and the false, originating in self-
love and the love of the world, which loves they had regarded
as ends of life.   It has been given me to tell them, that every
one may be admitted into heaven, because heaven is denied by
the Lord to no one, but whether or no they are capable of
living therein, they may discover in case they are admitted.
Some, who firmly believed this, were also admitted.   But as it
is the life of love to the Lord and of neighbourly love, which
in heaven constitutes all the sphere and happiness of life, when
they came thither, they began to be tortured, not being able to
respire in such a sphere, and at the same instant they were
made sensible of the filthiness of their affections, and thus of
infernal torment, in consequence whereof they cast themselves
down headlong thence, saying, that they wished to remove
themselves afar off, wondering that this should be heaven,
which to them was hell.   Hence it is evident what is the nature
of the one delight, and what of the other, and that they who are

in the delight of the affection of evil and the false, cannot possibly abide with those who are in the delight of the affection of good and truth, and that they are opposites, like heaven and hell, see n. 537, 538, 539, 541, 547, 1397, 1398, 2130, 2401. Moreover, in regard to the happiness of eternal life, it is not perceivable by the man who is in the affection of good and truth, during his abode in the world, but instead thereof a certain delight is perceivable. The reason is, because in the body he is engaged in worldly cares, and thence in anxieties, which cause, that the happiness of eternal life, which is inwardly in him, cannot be manifested otherwise at this time, for flowing from within into cares and anxieties, which are attendant on man without, it is lost as it were amongst those cares and anxieties, and becomes a kind of obscure delight; yet still it is a delight containing in it a principle of blessedness, and therein of happiness. To be content in God is such a delight. When, however, man puts off the body, and worldly cares and anxieties with it, then the happiness which before lay concealed in obscurity in his interior man, comes forth into full manifestation. Since such frequent mention has been made of affection, it may be expedient to say what is meant by affection. Affection is nothing else than love, but the continuity of love, for man is affected either by what is evil and false, or by what is good and true, from the love-principle. This love-principle, as it is present and exerts its influence in all and singular the things which belong to man, is not perceived as love, but is varied according to things, and according to states and the changes thereof, and this continually in all things which man wills, thinks, and acts. This continuity of love is called affection, and it is this which rules in the life of man, and constitutes all his delight, and consequently, his very life, for the life of man is nothing but the delight of his affection, thus, it is nothing but the affection of his love. Love is man's willing, and hence, his thinking, and thus, his acting.

3939. " And she called his name Asher"—that this signifies quality, appears from calling a name signifying quality, see above; the quality itself is represented by Asher. Asher, in the original tongue, signifies blessedness, but it involves all those things which are signified by the words of Leah his mother, *In my blessedness, because the daughters will make me blessed;* namely, delight of the affections corresponding to the happiness of eternal life. This is the fourth general principle which unites the external man with the internal; for when a man begins to perceive in himself this corresponding delight, then his external man begins to be united with his internal. The delights of the affections of truth and good are what conjoin, for without the delights of the affections there is no conjunction, the life of man being in those delights. That all conjunction is wrought by affections may be seen, n. 3024, 3066, 3336, 3849, 3909. The daughters who shall make blessed, signify Churches. That daughters in the internal sense of the Word denote Churches, may be seen, n. 2362. This then was said by Leah, because the births of the handmaids signify general truths, which are media serviceable for conjunction, that the Church may exist with man, for when man perceives the above delight or affection, he then begins to be a Church, and on this account this is said of the fourth or last son born of the handmaids. In the Word throughout, mention is made of Asher, but wherever he is named, he, as well as the rest of Jacob's sons, signifies the quality treated of in that place, that is, what their quality is in the state to which the subject treated of has reference. Their quality also is according to the order in which they are named; thus, one quality is intended to be expressed when the order commences with Reuben or faith, and another quality, when it commences with Judah or celestial love, and another, when it commences with Joseph or spiritual love, for the essence and quality of the beginning of the order is derived and passes into the subsequent terms. Hence, their significations are various in the passages where they are named. In the present case, where their nativity is treated of, they signify general principles of the Church, consequently, all things of faith and love which constitute the Church; and this because in what precedes, the subject treated of is the regeneration of man, or the states of man before he becomes a Church, and in a supreme sense, the Lord, how He made His Human Divine, thus, of ascent by the ladder, which was seen by Jacob in Bethel, even to Jehovah.

3940. Verses 14, 15, 16. *And Reuben went in the days of wheat-harvest, and found mandrakes [dudaim] in the field, and brought them to Leah his mother, and Rachel said to Leah, Give me, I pray, of thy son's mandrakes. And she said to her, Is it a small thing that thou hast taken my man, and wilt thou take also my son's mandrakes? And Rachel said, Therefore he shall lie with thee this night for thy son's mandrakes. And Jacob came from the field in the evening, and Leah went forth to meet him, and said, Thou shalt come to me, because hiring I have hired thee in my son's mandrakes; and he lay with her in that night.* Reuben went in the days of wheat-harvest, signifies faith as to its state of love and charity: and found mandrakes in the field, signifies those things which are of conjugial love in the truth and good of charity and love: and brought them to Leah his mother, signifies application to the affection of external truth: and Rachel said to Leah, signifies the perception of affection, and the desire of interior truth: Give me, I pray, of thy son's mandrakes, signifies of those things which belong to conjugial love, with which mutual and reciprocal conjunction might be effected: and she said to her, Is it a small thing that thou hast taken my man? signifies that there is conjugial desire: and wilt thou take also my son's mandrakes? signifies that thus the conjugial principle of natural good with external truth would be withdrawn: and Rachel said, signifies consent: Therefore he shall lie with thee this night for thy son's mandrakes, signifies that there should be conjunction: and Jacob came from the field in the evening, signifies the good of truth in a state of good, but in an obscure state, such as is proper to the natural principle: and Leah went forth to meet him, signifies desire on the part of the affection of external truth: and said, Thou shalt come to me, signifies that there would be conjunction therewith: because hiring I have hired thee in my son's mandrakes, signifies that thus it was stipulated from what was provided: and he lay with her in that night, signifies conjunction.

3941. "Reuben went in the days of wheat-harvest"—that this signifies faith as to its state of love and charity, appears from Reuben representing faith, which is the first principle of regeneration, see n. 3861, 3866; and from days, as being states, see n. 23, 487, 488, 493, 893, 2788, 3462, 3785; and from wheat, denoting love and charity, of which we shall speak presently. Hence, wheat-harvest denotes an advancing state of love and charity. The subject treated of by the four sons of Jacob born of the handmaids, was, the media of the conjunction of the external man with the internal. The subject now treated of is the conjunction of good and truth by the remaining sons, wherefore, in the first place, mandrakes are spoken of, signifying this conjunction or conjugial principle. The reason why wheat-harvest denotes an advancing state of love and charity, is, because a field signifies the Church, or the things belonging to the Church; and the seeds which are sown in a field signify the things which are of good and truth; and the produce of those seeds, as wheat, barley, and other produce, denote the things which are of love and charity, and also of faith. The states of the Church as to these things are therefore compared to seed-time and harvest, and are also called seed-time and harvest, as in Gen. chap. viii. verse 22; n. 932. That wheat denotes the things which are of love and charity, may also appear from the following passages: "Jehovah maketh him to ride upon the high places of the earth, and feedeth him with the produce of fields. He maketh him to suck honey out of the rock, and oil out of the flinty rock, butter of the herd and milk of the flock, with the fat of lambs and of rams, the sons of Bashan, and of goats, with *the fat of the kidneys of wheat*, and thou drinkest the blood of the grape, pure wine," Deut. xxxii. 13, 14. This passage, in the internal sense, treats of the ancient Church, and its state at its establishment, and all the things relating to love and charity, and to faith, as existing in that church, are here described by significatives. The fat of the kidneys of wheat denotes the celestial principle of love and charity; and inasmuch as fat or fatness signifies the celestial principle, n. 353, and wheat signifies love, therefore they are frequently joined together in the Word, as in David, "I wish that my people was obedient to Me, that Israel would walk in My ways; *He would feed them with the fat of wheat*, and with honey out of the stony rock will I satisfy them," Psalm lxxxi. 14, 16. Again, "Jehovah, Who maketh thy border peace, *will satisfy thee with the fat of wheat*," Psalm cxlvii. 14. That wheat denotes love and charity is manifest from these words in Jeremiah, " Many pastors have destroyed My vineyard, they have trodden down the portion of My field, they have reduced the portion of My field to a desert wilderness. The wasters have come upon all the hills in the wilderness, because the sword of Jehovah devoureth from the end of the earth even to the end of the earth, there is no peace for any flesh, *they have sown wheat*, and have reaped thorns," xii. 10, 12, 13. Vineyard and field denote the church; desert wilderness, its vastation; the devouring sword, the vastation of truth; no peace denotes no affecting good; to sow wheat denotes the goods which are of love and charity; to reap thorns, the evils and falses which are of self-love and the love of the world. That vineyard denotes the spiritual Church, may be seen, n. 1069; that field denotes the Church as to good, n. 2971; that wilderness denotes vastation, n. 1927, 2708; that devouring sword denotes the vastation of truth, n. 2799; that peace denotes good affecting, n. 3780. So in Joel, "The field is wasted, the ground mourneth, because the corn is wasted, the new wine is dried up, the oil languisheth, the husbandmen are ashamed, the vine-dressers howl, *over the wheat and over the barley, because the harvest of the field* is perished. Gird yourselves and lament ye priests, howl ye ministers of the altar," i. 11, 13. That a state of the Church vastated is what is here described, is obvious to every one; thus that field and ground denote the Church, corn, its good, and new wine, its truth, see n. 3580; and that wheat denotes celestial love, and barley spiritual love; and whereas a state of the Church is treated of, it is said, Gird ye and lament ye priests, and howl ye ministers of the altar. So in Ezekiel, "The spirit of Jehovah to the prophet; *Take to thyself wheat*, and barley, and beans, and lentiles and 'millet, and vetches, and put them into one vessel, and make them into bread for thyself; with the dung of man thou shalt make for thyself a cake before their eyes; thus the sons of Israel shall eat their bread ··nclean," iv. 9, 12; speaking of the profanation of good and truth. Wheat, barley, beans, lentiles, millet and vetches denote various kinds of good and its derivative truth; bread or a cake made thereof with human dung denotes the profanation of them all. So in the Apocalypse, "I saw when behold a black horse, and he who sat upon him had a pair of balances in his hand; and I heard a voice out of the midst of the four animals, saying, *A measure of wheat for a penny,* and three measures of· barley for a penny; but hurt not the oil and the wine," vi. 5, 6; speaking also of the vastation of good and truth; a measure of wheat for a penny denotes the scarcity of love, and three measures of barley for a penny denotes the scarcity of charity. So in Ezekiel, "Judah and the land of Israel were thy merchants, *in wheat of minnith and pannay,* and honey and oil, and balsam, they traded," xxvii. 17; speaking of Tyre, which signifies the knowledges of good and truth. Wheat of minnith and pannay, honey, oil, and balsam denote the good things of love and charity, and the happiness thereof; Judah denotes the celestial Church, and the land of Israel, the spiritual Church, from which those good things come; trading denotes acquisition. So in Moses, "*A land of wheat and barley,* and of the vine, and the fig-tree, and the pomegranate, a land of the olive, of oil, and of honey," Deut. viii. 8; describing the land of Canaan, which, in the internal sense, is the Lord's kingdom, see n. 1413, 1437, 1585, 1607, 3038, 3705; wheat and barley denote the good things of love and charity, the vine and fig-tree denote the good things of faith. So in Matthew, "Whose fan is in His hand, and He will thoroughly purge His floor, and *will gather His wheat into the barn,* but He will burn the chaff with unquenchable fire," iii. 12; speaking of the Lord, where wheat denotes the good things of love and charity, and chaff, the things in which there is nothing of good. Again, "Suffer both to grow together to the harvest, and in the time of harvest I will say to the reapers, Gather together first the tares, and bind them in bundles to burn them, *but gather the wheat into My barn,*" Matt. xiii. 30. Tares denote evils and falses, and wheat, goods. They are comparisons, but all comparisons in the Word are made by significatives.

3942. "And found mandrakes in the field"—that this signifies the things which are of conjugial love, in the truth and good of charity and love, appears from mandrakes, signifying the things which are of conjugial love, of which we shall speak presently; and from field, signifying the Church, consequently, the truth of faith and the good of charity, for these constitute the Church, see n. 368, 2971, 3196, 3310, 3500, 3503, 3766. What mandrakes (*dudaim*) are, is not known to interpreters. It is supposed that they were fruits or flowers, which are variously named according to various opinions; but what particular kinds of fruits or flowers they were, is of little concern to know; only that among the ancients who were of the Church, all fruits and flowers were significative; for they knew that universal nature was a theatre representative of the Lord's kingdom, see n. 3483, and that all and singular the things in its three kingdoms, and consequently every fruit and flower, represented some particular in the spiritual world. That mandrakes signify the conjugial principle of good and truth, may appear from the series of the things treated of in the internal sense; and also from the derivation of that word in the original tongue, for it is derived from the word *dudim*, which signifies loves, and by loves, conjunction. That dudaim is thence derived, and that it signifies the conjugial principle, is manifest from the following passage, "In the morning we will rise to the vineyards, we will see whether the vine flourisheth, and putteth forth grapes, whether the pomegranates put forth blossoms, there I will give my loves (*dudim*) to thee; *the mandrakes* (dudaim) *have given a smell*," Can. vii. 12, 13. Hence it is evident what mandrakes denote. In regard to the book which contains what is called the Canticles or Solomon's Songs, it is not among the books which are called Moses and the Prophets, because it has not an internal sense; but it is written in the ancient style, and is full of significatives collected from the books of the ancient Church, and of several particulars which in the ancient Church signified celestial and spiritual love, and especially conjugial love. That this is the nature of the book, appears from the fact, that many indecent things occur in the sense of the letter, which is not the case in the books which are called Moses and the Prophets; but as it contains significatives of celestial and conjugial love, it appears as if it contained something mystical. From the signification of mandrakes then it may appear, that Reuben's finding them in the field, signifies the conjugial principle which is in the truth and good of love and charity, that is, which is capable of being conjoined; for the conjugial principle is nothing else, in the spiritual sense, than that truth which is capable of being conjoined with good, and that good which is capable of being conjoined with truth; hence comes all conjugial love, see n. 2728, 2729, 3132. On this account, genuine conjugial love does not exist, unless the parties are in good and truth, and thus are together in the heavenly marriage.

3943. "And brought them to Leah his mother"—that this signifies application to the affection of external truth, appears from bringing to, here signifying application; and from Leah, representing the affection of external truth, see n. 3793, 3819.

3944. "And Rachel said to Leah"—that this signifies the perception of affection, and the desire of interior truth, appears from saying, signifying to perceive, see n. 1898, 1919, 2080, 2619, 2862, 3395, 3509; and from Rachel, representing the affection of interior truth, see n. 3758, 3782, 3793, 3819. That it denotes the affection and desire of that truth, is also evident from what presently follows, for Rachel says, " G. ve me, I pray, of thy son's mandrakes."

3945. " Give me, I pray, of thy son's mandrakes"—that this signifies the affection and desire of those things which belong to conjugial love, with which mutual and reciprocal conjunction might be effected, appears from mandrakes, signifying the things which belong to conjugial love, see above, n. 3942. That affection and desire are denoted, is manifest, see n. 3944 ; that conjugial love is mutual and reciprocal conjunction, see n. 2731.

3946. " And she said to her, Is it a small thing that thou hast taken my man?"—that this signifies that there is conjugial desire, appears from the signification of taking a man who is also another's, as in the present instance Jacob, who is also Leah's, in that it implies mutual love amongst them. Hence it is that these words, " Is it a small thing that thou hast taken my man?" signify conjugial desire.

3947. " And wilt thou take also my son's mandrakes ?"— that this signifies that thus the conjugial principle of natural good with external truth would be withdrawn, appears from taking, signifying, in the present case, to withdraw ; and from mandrakes, signifying the conjugial principle, see n. 3942 ; and from son, signifying truth, see n. 489, 491, 533, 1147 ; in the present case, external truth, because it is Leah who speaks, and that Leah denotes external truth, has been shown above.

3948. " And Rachel said, Therefore he shall lie with thee this night for thy son's mandrakes"—that this signifies consent that there should be conjunction, is apparent without explication.

3949. "And Jacob came from the field in the evening"— that this signifies the good of truth in a state of good, but in an obscure state such as is proper to the natural principle, appears from Jacob, representing the good of the truth of the natural principle, see n. 3669, 3677, 3775, 3829 ; and from field, signifying the Church in respect to good, see n. 2971, thus signifying good ; and from evening, signifying what is obscure, see n. 3056, 3833.

3950. " And Leah went forth to meet him, and said, Thou shalt come to me"—that this signifies desire on the part of the affection of external truth, that it might be conjoined thereto, may appear from the representation of Leah, as being the affection of external truth, concerning which see above. That it denotes desire to be conjoined, is evident without explication.

3951. " Because hiring I have hired thee in my son's mandrakes"—that this signifies that thus it was stipulated from what was provided, appears from the signification of hiring, as being what is stipulated, which is also evident from what goes before.

The reason why it was from what was provided, is, because all conjunction of truth with good, and of good with truth, as taking place in man, is from what was provided, that is, of the Lord's providence.   The subject here treated of is the conjunction of good with truth and of truth with good, thus concerning the good which is appropriated to man; for good is not good with man until it is conjoined with truth; and whereas all good comes from the Lord, that is, all appropriation of good by its conjunction with truth, therefore it is here said from what was provided.   The providence of the Lord is principally employed about this conjunction.   By this conjunction man becomes man, and is distinguihed from the brute animals, and he becomes man in proportion as he receives of that conjunction, that is, as he suffers the Lord to effect it.   This then is the good which belongs to man, and there is no other good which is spiritual, and abides to eternity.   Moreover, the goods of the external man, which are the delights of life during man's abode in the world, are only good in proportion as they have the above good in them.   In the case of the good of riches for example : so far as riches have spiritual good in them, that is, have for an end the good of man's neighbour, the good of his country or the public good, and the good of the Church, so far they are good.   They, however, who hence conclude, that the spiritual good of which I have been speaking cannot have place in worldly opulence, and therefore persuade themselves that they ought to renounce the use of riches, in order to be more at leisure to think of heaven, are much deceived.   For if they renounce the use of riches, or deprive themselves thereof, they cannot afterwards do good to any one, neither can they themselves live in the world except in a state of wretchedness, and thus they cannot any longer have for an end the good of their neighbour, or the good of their country, or even the good of the Church, but only themselves, that they may be saved, and become greater than others in the heavens.   Besides, in renouncing the use of worldly things, they also expose themselves to contempt, which renders them vile in the sight of others, and consequently, unfits them for the discharge of the duties which might make them useful. But when men regard the good of their neighbour, of their country, and of the Church, as an end of life, they then also have for an end, or for a means, the state of life requisite to enable them to accomplish their end. Just as in the case of bodily nourishment, the end of which is, that there be a sound mind in a sound body.   If a man deprives the body of its proper nourishment, he deprives himself also of the state of life necessary for the accomplishment of this end ; wherefore, the spiritual man does not despise bodily nourishment, nor yet the pleasures attending it, but then he does not regard these things as an end of life, but only as means subservient to an end. This example may be applied to all the other cases of a similar nature.

3952. "And lay with her in that night"—that this signifies conjunction, may appear also without explication. The reason why the foregoing passages for the most part are explained only as to the significations of the expressions in the internal sense, is, because they are of such a nature, that they cannot be apprehended unless they are expounded in one series; for the subject treated of, is the conjunction of truth with good and of good with truth, which conjunction is the conjugial principle understood in the spiritual sense, that is, it constitutes with man and in the Church the heavenly marriage. The arcana of this heavenly marriage are described and revealed in the above passages, and they are as follows. The heavenly marriage, as was said, is that of good with truth and of truth with good, yet not between good and truth of one and the same degree, but between good and truth of an inferior degree and of a superior, that is, not between the good of the external man and the truth of the same, but between the good of the external man and the truth of the internal, or, what is the same thing, not between the good of the natural man and the truth thereof, but between the good of the natural man and the truth of the spiritual man; it is this conjunction which constitutes a marriage. The case is similar in regard to the internal or spiritual man; between the good and truth in the spiritual man there subsists no heavenly marriage, but between the good of the spiritual man and the truth of the celestial man, for the celestial man is respectively in a superior degree. Neither does the heavenly marriage subsist between good and truth in the celestial man, but between good of the celestial man and Truth Divine which proceeds from the Lord. Hence also it is manifest, that the essential Divine Marriage of the Lord does not subsist between Good Divine and Truth Divine in His Divine Human, but between the good of the Divine Human and the Essential Divine, that is, between the Son and the Father, for the good of the Lord's Divine Human is what is called in the Word the Son of God, and the Essential Divine is called the Father. These are the arcana which are contained in the internal sense in what is said concerning mandrakes. Every one may see that some arcanum must necessarily be contained therein, for to mention that Reuben found mandrakes in the field, and that Rachel desired them, and that to procure them she engaged that Jacob should lie with Leah, and that Leah went to meet Jacob when he came from the field in the evening, and said, that she had hired him for mandrakes—these are circumstances too trifling to constitute any historical part of the Word, unless something Divine were hidden in them. What this Divine somewhat is, cannot, however, be known to any one unless he knows what is signified by the sons of Jacob, and by the tribes named from them ; and unless he further knows the series of the subject treated of in the internal sense, and still further, what the heavenly marriage is, for this is treated of, namely, that it is the conjunction of the good of the external man with the affection of truth of the internal man. But in order to render this arcanum more clear to the apprehension, it may be expedient to give a further illustration of it. The truths of the external man are those scientifics and doctrinals which he first learnt from his parents, and also from his masters, and next from books, and lastly by his own study. The good of the external man is the pleasure and delight which he perceives in those truths. Scientifics, which are truths, and delights, which are good, are conjoined, but they do not constitute in him the heavenly marriage, for with those who are in self-love and the love of the world, and thence in evil and the false, even scientifics, yea doctrinals, are conjoined to delights, but they are the delights of those loves, with which even truths may be conjoined. Nevertheless such persons are out of the heavenly marriage. But when the pleasure or delight, which is the good of the external or natural man, is from spiritual love, that is, from love towards our neighbour, our country or the public, towards the Church, and the Lord's kingdom, and especially when it is from celestial love, which is love to the Lord, and these things flow-in from the internal or spiritual man into the delight of the external or natural man, and constitute that delight, in this case the above conjunction with the scientifics and doctrinals of the external or natural man constitutes with him the heavenly marriage. This cannot have place with the wicked, but with the good, namely, with such as regard these principles of spiritual and celestial love as ends of life ; but the manner of the influx of the internal or spiritual man into the external or natural man, may be seen above, n. 3286, 3288, 3314, 3321. When these things are previously known, it may then be known also what is signified by the above particulars, which are explained only according to the internal sense of the expressions ; as that Reuben, who denotes the truth of faith which is the first of regeneration, found mandrakes ; that he brought them to Leah his mother, who denotes the affection of external truth ; that Rachel, who denotes the affection of interior truth, desired them, and that they were also given to her ; that Leah on this account lay with her man Jacob, who denotes the good of truth in the natural man ; also in what follows, that of Leah there were born unto Jacob sons, Issachar and Zebulon, who signify and represent the things of conjugial love, thus of the heavenly marriage, and afterwards Joseph, who signifies and represents the Lord's spiritual kingdom, which is the essential marriage treated of.

3953. Verses 17, 18. *And God hea kened to Leah, and she conceived, and bare unto Jacob a fifth son. And Leah said, God hath given my reward, in that I have given my handmaid to my man, and she called his name Issachar.* God hearkened to Leah, signifies Love Divine : and she conceived and bare unto Jacob a fifth son, signifies reception and acknowledgment : and Leah said, God hath given my reward in that I have given my handmaid to my man, signifies, in a supreme sense, the Divine Good of truth and. the truth of good, in an internal sense, conjugial celestial love, and in an external sense, mutual love : and she called his name Issachar, signifies quality.

3954. "And God hearkened to Leah"—that this signifies Love Divine, appears from the signification of hearkening to any one, when it is predicated of God or the Lord, as being Love Divine ; for to hearken to any one is to do what he prays for and wishes ; and as this is from Divine Good, and Divine Good comes from Divine Love, therefore hearkening to any one, in a supreme sense, denotes Love Divine, which is here signified. With respect to the internal sense of the Word, the case is this, that when the sense of the letter ascends towards heaven, and there enters into the sphere where the thoughts are employed under the Lord's influence, and concerning the Lord, and things which relate to the Lord, it is at length so perceived by the angels. The internal sense of the Word is for the angels, and to this sense the sense of the letter serves as a plane or means of thinking ; but the sense of the letter cannot come to the angels, because in several passages it treats of worldly, terrestrial, and corporeal things, about which the angels cannot think, because they are in spiritual and celestial things, and thereby far above the former. On this account the Word was given, which may be serviceable to man, and at the same time to angels, and in this the Word differs from all other writing.

3955. "And she conceived and bare unto Jacob a fifth son"—that this signifies reception and acknowledgment, appears from the signification of conceiving, as being reception, and of bearing, as being acknowledgment, see n. 3860, 3868, 3905, 3911, 3919.

3956. "And Leah said, God hath given my reward, in that I have given my handmaid to my man"—that this signifies, in a supreme sense, the Divine Good of truth and truth of good, in an internal sense, conjugial celestial love, and in an external sense, mutual love, may appear from the signification of reward. Frequent mention is made in the Word of reward, but few know the meaning of the expression as there applied. It is known in the Church, that man cannot merit any thing by the goods he does, for they are not his, but the Lord's ; also, that meriting or merit has respect to man, and so is joined to self-love, and to an idea of self-pre-eminence, consequently to contempt of others. Works, therefore, which are done for the sake of reward, are not good in themselves, since they do not flow from a genuine fountain, namely, from charity towards the neighbour. Such charity has in it this principle, that it wills good to its neighbour as well as to itself, and with the angels, that it wills better to its neighbour than to itself. Such also is the affection of charity; and therefore it likewise is averse to all merit, and consequently to every good deed which respects reward. The reward which they who are in charity enjoy, is, that they are able to do good, and allowed to do good, and that the good deed is accepted; this being the essential delight, yea the blessedness, which they enjoy who are in the affection of charity. Hence it may appear what the reward is which is mentioned in the Word, namely, that it is the delight and blessedness of the affection of charity, or, what is the same thing, the delight and blessedness of mutual love, see n. 3816, for the affection of charity and mutual love are the same thing; see what was said above on this subject, n. 1110, 1111, 1774, 1835, 1877, 2027, 2273, 2340, 2373, 2400. From these considerations it is evident, that reward, in an external sense, here signifies mutual love. That reward, in a still higher, or in an internal sense, signifies conjugial celestial love, may appear from what was said above concerning the heavenly marriage, n. 2618, 2739, 2741, 2803, 3024, 3132, 3952, namely, that it is the conjunction of good and truth, and that mutual love is derived from that conjunction, or from that marriage, see n. 2737, 2738. Hence it may appear that reward, in an internal sense, denotes conjugial celestial love. That reward, in a supreme sense, denotes the Divine Good of truth and truth of good, appears from the fact, that thence comes the heavenly marriage; for that union is in the Lord, and proceeds from Him, and when it flows into heaven, it constitutes the conjugial principle of good and truth, and by this principle, mutual love. What has been said, and what goes before, show the signification, in the internal sense, of these words of Leah, " God hath given my reward, in that I have given my handmaid to my man," for handmaid signifies an affirmative medium, serviceable for the conjunction of the external and internal man, see n. 3913, 3917, 3931. Thus until the things signified by the sons of the handmaids are affirmed and acknowledged, there cannot exist any conjunction of good and truth, nor consequently any mutual love; for those affirmations must needs precede : this is what is meant by the above words.

3957. "And called his name Issachar"—that this signifies quality, appears from the signification of calling a name, being quality, see above, n. 3923, 3935 ; for he was named Issachar from reward, and hence the name involves those things which

were said above concerning reward, and at the same time those
things which are signified by the rest of the words of Leah.
Since Issachar signifies reward, and reward, in an external
sense, denotes mutual love, and in an internal sense, the conjunction of good and truth, it may be expedient to observe,
that very few at this day in Christendom know that reward has
such signification, and this because they do not know what
mutual love is, and still less, that good must be conjoined to
truth, in order that man may be in the heavenly marriage.   It
has been granted me to discourse on this subject with several
who have come from Christendom into another life, and also
with some of the more learned, but what is surprising. scarcely
any one of those, with whom it was granted me to discourse,
knew any thing at all about the subject, when nevertheless they
might have known much from themselves, if only they had
been willing to use their reason; but whereas they were not
solicitous about a life after death, but merely about their life in
the world, they had therefore no concern about such subjects.
The things they might have known from themselves, if only, as
was said, they had been willing to use their reason, are the
following : FIRSTLY, that when man is divested of the body,
he enjoys much greater powers of understanding than during
his life in the body, since whilst he is in the body, corporeal
and worldly things engage his thoughts, and induce obscurity;
whereas when he is divested of the body, such things do not
interrupt, but he is like those persons who are in interior thought
by an abstraction of the mind from the outward things of sense.
Hence they might know, that the state after death is much
clearer and brighter than the state before death, and that when
a man dies, he passes comparatively from shade into light,
since he passes from the things of the world to the things of
heaven, and from the things of the body to the things of the
spirit; but, what is surprising, although they can understand
these things, still they think the contrary, namely, that the
state of life in the body is comparatively clear, and the state of
life, when the body is put off, is obscure.   SECONDLY, they may
know, if they would but use their reason, that the life which
man has habitually formed to himself in the world, follows him,
in other words, that he has a life of the same nature after death;
for they may know, that no one can put off the life which he
has habitually formed to himself from infancy, unless he dies
absolutely, and that this life cannot be instantaneously trans-
muted into another, still less into an opposite life.   For example : he who has habitually formed to himself a life of deceit,
and has found in deceit the delight of his life, cannot put off
the life of deceit, but is also in that life after death.   So, too,
they who have lived in self-love, and thereby in hatred and
revenge against those who have not submitted to them, or in

other similar evils, cont'nue in the same after the life of the
body, for those evils are the things which they love, and which
constitute the delights of their life, consequently the very life
itself; and so in other cases. THIRDLY, a man may know from
himself, that when he passes into another life, he leaves several
things behind, such as cares respecting food, clothing, habitation, and the acquirement of money and wealth, for in another
life there are no such cares; also cares respecting promotion to
dignities, which so much engage man's thoughts during his life
in the body; and that these are succeeded by other things,
which have no relation to the kingdom of this world.   Hence,
FOURTHLY, it may be known, that he whose thoughts have been
employed solely about such earthly things, so as to be totally
occupied therein, and to make such things alone the delight of
his life, is not fit to be among those whose delight it is to think
of heavenly things, or things relating to heaven.   Hence also
it may be known, FIFTHLY, that when these external things of
the body and the world are removed, man is such as he was
inwardly, namely, thinks and wills such things.   In this case,
if the thoughts inwardly had been deceitful, engaged in artful
machinations, aspiring to dignities, to gain, to reputation for
the sake of worldly and corporeal things, or if they had been
influenced by hatred, revenge, and other similar evils, he will
necessarily after death think the same things, consequently he
will think infernal things, however with a view to the above
ends he might have concealed his thoughts before men, and in
an external form have appeared upright, and induced others to
believe that the above evils had never engaged his attention.
That these external appearances, or pretences of uprightness,
are also taken away in another life, may likewise be known
from the fact, that external things are put off with the body,
and are no more of any use; hence every one may conclude
from himself, how man will then appear in the sight of angels.
The SIXTH THING which may also be known, is, that heaven, or
the Lord by and through heaven, is continually operating, and
flowing in with good and truth, and that if there be not in men
some recipient of good and truth, as a ground or plane, in the
interior man which lives after the death of the body, the influent good and truth cannot be received, and that man on this
account, during his life in the world, ought to be solicitous to
procure to himself interiorly such a plane.   This cannot be
procured but by thinking what is good in regard to his neighbour, and by willing what is good for him, and thence doing
good to him, and thereby acquiring to himself a life-delight
in such things.   This plane is acquired by charity towards
man's neighbour, that is, by mutual love, and it is this plane
which is called conscience.   Into this plane good and truth
from the Lord can flow, and be received therein, but not

where there is no charity, and conseq ently no conscience. In this latter case the influent good and truth is transfluent, and is changed into what is evil and false. The SEVENTH THING which man may know from himself, is, that love to God and love towards his neighbour are what make man to be man, distinct from brute animals, and that those loves constitute heavenly life or heaven, and their opposites, infernal life or hell. But the reason why man does not know the above things is, because he is not willing to know them, for he lives an opposite life ; also, because he does not believe that there is a life after death ; and further, because he has received principles of faith, and none of charity, and hence believes according to the doctrinals which generally prevail, that in case there is a life after death, he may be saved by virtue of faith, without any regard to his manner of life, and this, if he should receive faith even at his dying hour.

3958. Verses 19, 20. *And Leah conceived as yet, and bare a sixth son unto Jacob. And Leah said, God hath endowed me with a good dowry, this time my man will cohabit with me, because I have borne him six sons, and she called his name Zebulon.* Leah conceived as yet, and bare a sixth son unto Jacob, signifies reception and acknowledgment : and Leah said, God hath endowed me with a good dowry, this time my man will cohabit with me, because I have borne him six sons, signifies, in a supreme sense, the Lord's essential Divine, and his Divine Human, in an internal sense, the heavenly marriage, and in an external sense, conjugial love : and she called his name Zebulon, signifies quality.

3959. "Leah conceived as yet, and bare a sixth son unto Jacob"—that this signifies reception and acknowledgment, namely, of truth, appears from the signification of conceiving, as being to receive, and of bearing, as being to acknowledge, see n. 3955 ; and from the signification of son, as being truth, see n. 489, 491, 533, 1147, 2623, 3373.

3960. "And Leah said, God hath endowed me with a good dowry, this time my man will cohabit with me, because I have borne him six sons"—that this signifies, in a supreme sense, the Lord's essential Divine and His Divine Human, in an internal sense, the heavenly marriage, and in an external sense, conjugial love, appears from the signification of cohabiting, and also from the rest of the words which Leah spoke on the occasion. The reason why to cohabit or cohabitation denotes, in a supreme sense, the Lord's essential Divine and His Divine Human, is, because the essential Divine, which is called the Father, is in the Divine Human, which is called the Son of God, mutually and reciprocally, according to the words of the Lord Himself in John, " Whoso seeth Me, seeth the Father ; believe Me that I am in the Father, and the Father in Me,"

xiv. 9, 10, 11 ; chap. x. 38 ; that this union is the essential Divine Marriage, may be seen, n. 3211, 3952. This union is not cohabitation, but is expressed by cohabitation in the sense of the letter ; for principles which are one, are exhibited as two in the sense of the letter, as in the case of the Father and the Son, yea, as three, as in the case of Father, Son, and Holy Spirit, and this for several reasons, of which, by the Divine Mercy of the Lord, we shall speak elsewhere. It is from this ground that to cohabit, or cohabitation, in an internal sense, denotes the heavenly marriage, for from the Divine Marriage, which is the union of the Father and the Son, or of the Lord's essential Divine with His Divine Human, the heavenly marriage exists. The heavenly marriage is called the Lord's kingdom, and also heaven, and inasmuch as this exists from the Divine Marriage, which is the Lord, therefore this is signified in an internal sense by cohabition. Hence, heaven is called the habitation of God, as in Isaiah, " Look from the heavens, and see *from the habitation of thy holiness, and of thine honourableness ;* where have thy zeal, and thy virtues, the moving of thy bowels, and thy mercies to me, contained themselves," lxiii. 15. The habitation of holiness denotes the celestial, and the habitation of honourableness, the spiritual kingdom ; habitation in this passage is derived from the same expression as cohabiting and Zebulon are derived from in the passage under consideration. The reason why to cohabit, or cohabitation, denotes, in an external sense, conjugial love, is, because all genuine conjugial love exists from no other source than from the heavenly marriage, which is that of good and truth, and this from the Divine Marriage, which is the Lord as to His essential Divine and His Divine Human. See what was said above on this subject, namely, that the heavenly marriage is from the Divine Good which is in the Lord, and from the Divine Truth which is from Him, n. 2508, 2618, 2803, 3132 ; that hence is derived conjugial love, n. 2728, 2729 ; that they who are in genuine conjugial love cohabit together in the inmost principles of life, n. 2732, thus in the love of good and truth, for these are the inmost principles of life ; that conjugial love is the fundamental love of all loves, n. 2737, 2738, 2739 ; that the marriage of good and truth is in heaven, in the Church, and with every individual therein, in each particular principle of nature, n. 718, 747, 917, 1432, 2173, 2516, 2712, 2758 ; that the same exists in each particular of the Word, n. 683, 793, 801, 2516, 2712, thus, in a supreme sence, the Lord Himself is therein ; that Jesus Christ signifies the Divine Marriage, n. 3004. These are the things which are signified, not only by cohabiting, or by these words, "This time my man will cohabit with me," but also by the preceding words, "God hath endowed me with a good dowry :" but the former words signify the truth of good, whereas the latter signify the good of truth, for each constitutes the heavenly marriage; and inasmuch as this is the conclusion, it is said, "because I have borne him six sons;" for six here signify the same as twelve, namely, all things of faith and love, the half and the double number having the same signification in the Word, when the same subject is treated of.

3961. "And called his name Zebulon"—that this signifies quality, appears from the signification of calling a name, as being quality, see above; he was named Zebulon from cohabiting, and hence the name involves the things which were said above (n. 3960), concerning cohabitation, and at the same time the things which are signified by the rest of Leah's words.

3962. Verse 21. *And afterwards she bare a daughter, and called her name Dinah.* Afterwards she bare a daughter, signifies the affection of all (namely, general truths), and likewise the Church of faith in which is good: and called her name Dinah, signifies quality.

3963. "Afterwards she bare a daughter"—that this signifies the affection of all (namely, general truths), and also the Church of faith in which is good, appears from daughter signifying affection, and also the Church, see n. 2362, but affection of what object, and a Church of what quality, is discoverable from what is added, as the Church celestial from the addition of Zion, which is called the daughter of Zion, and the Church spiritual from the addition of Jerusalem, which is called the daughter of Jerusalem, and so forth. In the present case, where nothing is added, daughter signifies a Church of faith in which is good; for the subject hitherto treated of is concerning general truths of faith wherein is good, and concerning their reception and acknowledgment; those truths are signified, as has been shown, by the ten sons of Jacob above spoken of; and whereas, after them, immediate mention is made of a daughter being born, it is evident from the series, that she denotes the Church in which are all those general truths. Whether we speak of a Church of faith in which is good, or of a spiritual Church, it is the same thing, and also whether we speak of the affections of all general truths; for the Church is a Church by virtue of the affection of truth in which is good, and of good in which is truth; but not by virtue of the affection of truth in which is not good, nor by virtue of the affection of good in which there is not truth. They who say they are of the Church, who are in the affection of truth and not in the good of truth, that is, who do not live according to truth, are much deceived; they are out of the Church, notwithstanding their admission into the congregation of the Church, for they are in the affection of evil, with which truth cannot be conjoined. Their affection of truth is not from the Lord, but from themselves, for they have respect to themselves, that by the knowledges of truth they may gain reputation, and thereby honours and riches, but they have no respect to the Church, or to the Lord's kingdom, and still less to the Lord Himself. Neither are they of the Church, notwithstanding their being admitted into the congregation of the Church, who are in the affection of good from which no truth springs, for such are in natural and not spiritual good, and suffer themselves to be led away into every evil, and also into every false principle, if so be the evil is only covered with an appearance of good, and the false principle with an appearance of truth, see n. 3470, 3471, 3518.

3964. "And called her name Dinah"—that this signifies quality, appears from name and calling a name, signifying quality, concerning which see above. The quality which Dinah represents and signifies, is every thing appertaining to a Church of faith in which is good, whereof we have just been speaking. This is also evident from the derivation of her name, for in the original tongue Dinah signifies judgment; that judgment in the Word is predicated of the truth of faith, may be seen, n. 2235 ; and that to judge in the internal sense denotes the holy principle of faith, and in an external sense, good of life, n. 3921 ; these are the principles of the Church.

3965. Verses 22, 23, 24. *And God remembered Rachel, and God hearkened to her, and opened her womb. And she conceived, and bare a son, and said, God hath gathered together my reproach. And she called his name Joseph, saying, Let Jehovah add to me another son.* God remembered Rachel, and God hearkened to her, signifies foresight and providence : and opened her womb, signifies the faculty of receiving and acknowledging : and she conceived and bare a son, signifies reception and acknowledgment : and said, God hath gathered together my reproach, and she called his name Joseph, saying, Let Jehovah add to me another son, signifies, in a supreme sense, the Lord as to the Divine Spiritual [principle] ; in an internal sense, the spiritual kingdom of good of faith; and in an external sense, salvation, also fructification and multiplication.

3966. "God remembered Rachel, and God hearkened to her"—that this signifies foresight and providence, appears from the signification of remembering, when it is predicated of God, as in the present case, as being foresight, for to remember any one is to see to him, and to see, in a supreme sense, is foresight, as may be seen, n. 3863 ; and from the signification of hearkening to any one, when it is predicated of God, as being providence, see n. 3869.

3967. "And opened her womb"—that this signifies the faculty of receiving and acknowledging, appears from opening the womb, signifying to give the faculty of conceiving and bringing forth, thus, in an internal sense, the faculty of receiving and acknowledging, namely, the goods of truth, and the truths of good. That to conceive and to bring forth denote reception and acknowledgment, has been abundantly shown above.

3968. "And she conceived and bare a son"—that this signifies reception and acknowledgment, as above, see n. 3919, 3925, 3955, 3959.

3969. "And said, God hath gathered together my reproach, and she called his name Joseph, saying, Let Jehovah add to me another son"—that this signifies, in a supreme sense, the Lord as to the Divine Spiritual [principle]; in an internal sense, the spiritual kingdom, or good of faith; and in an external sense, salvation, also fructification and multiplication, appears from the representation of Joseph in the Word, of which we shall speak presently; also from the signification of the words, "God hath gathered together my reproach," and likewise of these, "Let Jehovah add to me another son," for he was named Joseph from gathering together and adding. God hath gathered together my reproach, signifies that Rachel was now no longer barren, thus was not dead, as she said of herself, verse 1 of this chapter, n. 3908; for Rachel represents the affection of interior truth, or the interior man as to truth, see n. 3758, 3782, 3793, 3819: the interior man as to truth and good is as it were dead, if the exterior or natural man does not correspond thereto as to goods and truths, see n. 3493, 3620, 3623. They must be conjoined together on both sides, until they are no longer two, but together one man. This conjunction cannot exist, until the natural or external man is prepared, that is, until he has received and acknowledged the general truths, which are signified by the ten sons of Jacob born of Leah and the handmaids, and until the good of the natural man is conjoined with truths therein, which conjunction is signified by the last son of Jacob born of Leah, namely, by Zebulon, who was so named from cohabitation, see n. 3960, 3961. After this conjunction is effected, then the interior man and the exterior enter into the heavenly marriage, concerning which, see n. 3952. The reason why this marriage is not entered into before, is most mysterious, for it is the good of the interior man which conjoins itself with the good of the exterior, and by this with the truth of the exterior, and also the good of the interior man by the affection of truth therein with the good of the exterior man, and also with truth therein, thus immediately and mediately, concerning which immediate and mediate conjunction, see n. 3314, 3573, 3616. Whereas in this case, and not before, the interior man is conjoined with the exterior, and until this conjunction is effected, the interior man is as it were no man, and thus as it were dead, as was said above, therefore it is said, God hath gathered together my reproach; this then it is which is signified by reproach. which God is said to have gathered, that is, to have taken away, or to have delivered from.   But the words which follow, namely, 'Let Jehovah add to me another son," from which words the name Joseph was derived, signify another arcanum, which is this : Joseph represents the Lord's spiritual kingdom, thus the spiritual man, for in every spiritual man there is that kingdom.   There are two principles which constitute the spiritual man, namely, charity and faith, or what is the same thing, good and truth ; charity from which faith is derived, or good from which truth is derived, is represented by Joseph ; and faith in which there is charity, or truth in which there is good, is signified by another son, and is represented by Benjamin, concerning whom, see Gen. xxxv. 16, 17, 18.   Thus Joseph is the celestial-spiritual man, and Benjamin the spiritual-celestial.   The nature of the difference between them may appear from what has been so frequently said above concerning good from which truth is derived, and concerning truth in which there is good.   This then is what is signified by the other words of Rachel, " Let Jehovah add to me another son."   These arcana, however, cannot be seen except by those who are in the charity of faith, for they, as to their interiors, are in the light of heaven, in which light there is intelligence ; but not by those who are only in the light of the world, for in this light there is not intelligence, only so far as it has in it the light of heaven.   By the angels who are in the light of heaven, these arcana are reckoned amongst the most common or least mysterious.   From these considerations then it may appear, that these words, "God hath gathered together my reproach, and let Jehovah add to me another son," in a supreme sense, signify the Lord as to the Divine spiritual [principle] ; and in an internal sense, the Lord's spiritual kingdom, or the good of faith, for this is the spiritual principle which prevails in that kingdom. The reason why, in an external sense, those words signify salvation, also fructification and multiplication, is, because these things follow of consequence, see n. 3971.   What the Lord's spiritual kingdom is, may appear from what has been so often said and shown above concerning that kingdom, namely, that it consists of those who are in charity and thence in faith. This kingdom is distinguished from the Lord's celestial kingdom, for in the celestial kingdom are they who are in love to the Lord, and thence in charity ; these constitute the third or inmost heaven, whereas the spiritual constitute the second or interior heaven.   The reason why the name God is first applied, as where it is said, "God hath gathered together my reproach," and afterwards the name Jehovah, as in these words, " Let Jehovah add unto me another son," is, because the former expression respects the ascent from truth to good, whereas the latter respects the descent from good to truth.   The spiritual man is in the good of faith, that is, in good from which truth is derived, but before he becomes spiritual, he is in the truth of faith, that is, in truth wherein good is; and the name God is used in treating of truth, but Jehovah in treating of good, see n. 2586, 2807, 2822, 3921. That Joseph represents the Lord's spiritual kingdom, or the spiritual man, thus the good of faith, may also appear from those passages in the Word where he is mentioned, as in the prophecy of Jacob, at that time Israel, "*Joseph* is the son of a fruitful one, the son of a fruitful one near a fountain, of a daughter, he marcheth upon a wall, and the archers shall bitterly grieve him, and shall cast darts, and shall hate him; and he shall sit in the firmness of his bow, and the arms of his hands shall be made strong, from the hands of the mighty one of Jacob; hence the shepherd, the stone of Israel. From the God of thy father, and He shall help thee, and with Schaddai, and He shall bless thee with the blessings of heaven from above, with the blessings of the abyss which lieth beneath, with the blessings of the paps and of the womb. The blessings of thy father shall prevail over the blessings of thy progenitors even to the desire of the hills of an age, they shall be for the head of *Joseph*, and for the crown of the Nazarite of his brethren," Gen. xlix. 22 to 26. These prophetic words contain, in a supreme sense, a description of the Lord's Divine spiritual [principle], and in an internal sense, of His spiritual kingdom; what each particular expression involves, will be shown, by the Divine mercy of the Lord, in the explication of that chapter. In like manner in the prophecy of Moses, "Unto *Joseph* he said, Blessed of Jehovah is his land, concerning the precious things of heaven, concerning the dew, concerning the abyss also lying beneath; and concerning the precious things of the produce of the sun, and concerning the precious things of the putting forth of months; and concerning the precious things of the mountains of the east, and concerning the precious things of the hills of an age; and concerning the precious things of the earth and its fulness; and the good pleasure of Him who dwelleth in the bush; they shall come to the head of *Joseph*, and to the crown of the Nazarite of his brethren," Deut. xxxiii. 13 to 17. Since Israel represents the Lord's spiritual Church, n. 3305, 3654, therefore Jacob, at that time Israel, before his death, said unto Joseph, "Thy two sons, who were born unto thee in the land of Egypt, before I came to thee into Egypt, shall be mine, *Ephraim* and *Manasseh*, as Reuben and Simeon. The angel, who hath redeemed me from all evil, bless the lads, that my name may be called in them, and the name of my fathers Abraham and Isaac, and they may increase into a multitude in the midst of the earth," Gen. xlviii 5, 16: for there are two principles which constitute the spiritual Church, the intellectual and voluntary, the intellectual being represented by Ephraim, and the voluntary by Manasseh; hence it is evident why the two sons of Joseph were adopted by Jacob, at that time Israel, and acknowledged as his own. Ephraim also is frequently mentioned in the Word, especially in the prophetic Word, and he there signifies the intellectual principle of truth and good, which belongs to the spiritual Church. So in Ezekiel, " Jehovah said, Son of man, take unto thee one [piece of] wood, and *write upon it for Judah*, and for the sons of Israel his companions; and take one [piece of] wood, and *write upon it for Joseph*, the wood of Ephraim, and of all the house of Israel his companions; and join them together, one to the other for thyself into one [piece of] wood, that they may both be one in thy hand; thus saith the Lord Jehovih, I, behold I do take the *wood of Joseph*, which is in the hand of Ephraim and of the tribes of Israel his companions, and will add them upon the *wood of Judah*, and will make them into one wood, and they shall be one in My hand; and I will make them into one natior in the earth, in the mountains of Israel; and they shall all have one king for a king, and they shall be no longer two nations and they shall no more be divided again into two kingdoms,' xxxvii. 16, 17, 19, 22. The subject here treated of is the Lord's celestial and spiritual kingdoms; the celestial kingdom is Ju dah, see n. 3654, 3881, 3921, and the spiritual, Joseph, and that these kingdoms should not be two but one; they were also made into one by the coming of the Lord into the world. That by the Lord's coming the spiritual were saved, may be seen, n. 2661, 2716, 2833, 2834. These are they of whom the Lord speaks in John, "And other sheep I have which are not of this fold; them also I must bring, and they shall hear my voice, and there shall be one flock and one shepherd," x. 16. This is what is signified by the two [pieces of] wood, namely, of Judah and Joseph, which were to be joined together into one, and should be one in the Lord's hand. For the celestial constitute the third heaven, which is the inmost; but the spiritual, the second heaven, which is the interior; and there they are one, because the one flows into the other, namely, the celestial into the spiritual, the spiritual kingdom being as a plane to the celestial, and thus they are co-established. The Divine Celes tial in the third or inmost heaven is love to the Lord, and the celestial-spiritual in this heaven is charity. This charity is principal in the second or interior heaven, where the spiritual are, and hence it is manifest what is the nature of influx of one into the other. and also what is the nature of their co-establish-ment by influx. Wood signifies good, as well the good of love to the Lord, as the good of charity towards our neighbour, see n. 2784, 2812, 3720; therefore it was commanded to write Ju dah and Joseph upon the [pieces of] wood, which were to be made one. So in Zechariah, " I will make *the house of Judah*

powerful, and I will save *the house of Joseph*, and I will cause
them to dwell, because I have mercy on them, and they shall
be as if I had not left them, because I Jehovah am their God,
and I will answer them," x. 6.   Speaking also of the two kingdoms, the celestial and spiritual: the celestial kingdom is Judah, and the spiritual is Joseph; and concerning the salvation
of the spiritual.   So in Amos, "Thus saith Jehovah to the house
of Israel, Seek Me and ye shall live, seek Jehovah and ye shall
live; lest as it were fire invade *the house of Joseph*, and devour,
and there be none to extinguish; hate what is evil, and love
what is good, and establish judgment in the gate, perhaps Jehovah God will have mercy on *the remains of Joseph*," v. 4, 6, 17.
In this passage also the spiritual are signified by Joseph; the
house of Israel is the spiritual Church, see n. 3305, 3654; Joseph
is the good of that Church, wherefore it is said, "Jehovah said
to the house of Israel, Seek Me and ye shall live, lest as it were
fire invade the house of Joseph."   So in David, "Shepherd of
Israel, turn thy ear, thou who *leadest Joseph as a flock*, who
sittest on the cherubim, shine forth before *Ephraim*, and *Benjamin*, and *Manasseh*, stir up thy strength, and go for salvation
to us," Psalm lxxx. 1, 2.   In this passage also, Joseph is the
spiritual man; and Ephraim, Benjamin, and Manasseh are the
three principles proper to the spiritual Church.   Again, "Exalt
the song, and give the timbrel, the pleasant harp with the psaltery, sound with the trumpet in the month, in the holy day, on
the day of our festival, for this is a statute for Israel, a judgment
for the God of Jacob, He hath appointed it a *testimony for Joseph* in his going forth against the land of Egypt; I heard a
'ip which I knew not," Psalm lxxxi. 2, 3, 4, 5.   That Joseph
in this passage is the spiritual Church, or the spiritual man, is
evident from the particular words and expressions contained in
it, for there are expressions in the Word which express spiritual things, and others which express celestial things, and this
regularly throughout the Word.   The expressions used in this
passage are expressive of spiritual things, as song, timbrel, the
harp with the psaltery, sounding with the trumpet, in the month,
in the holy day, on the day of our festival; hence also it is manifest that the subject treated of is the spiritual Church, which is
Joseph.   So in Ezekiel, "Thus saith the Lord Jehovih, This is
the boundary to which ye shall inherit the land, according to
the twelve tribes of Israel, *the ropes* (or cords) *to Joseph*," xlvii.
13; speaking of the Lord's spiritual kingdom, wherefore it is
said, the ropes to Joseph.   The Lord's Divine spiritual [prin-
ciple] is what is also called His regal [principle], for the Lord's
regal [principle] is the Divine Truth, whereas His sacerdotal
or priestly [principle] is the Divine Good, see n. 2015, 3009,
3670.   The essential regal [principle] of the Lord is represented
by Joseph, in that he was made king in the land of Egypt, of

which representation, by the Divine Mercy of the Lord, we shall speak elsewhere. As regards the Lord's Divine spiritual [principle], or the Divine Truth, which is represented by Joseph in a supreme sense, it is not in the Lord, but from the Lord, for the Lord is nothing else but Divine Good, yet from Divine Good proceeds Divine Truth. The case herein is comparatively like that of the sun and its light, light is not in the sun, but proceeds from the sun; or like that of fire and its luminous principle, the luminous principle not being in the fire, but proceeding from it. The essential Divine Good is also in the Word compared to the sun, and likewise to fire, and is moreover called the sun and fire. The Lord's celestial kingdom lives from the good which proceeds from the Lord, but the spiritual kingdom lives from the truth thence derived, wherefore the Lord, in another life, appears to the celestial as a sun, but to the spiritual as a moon, see n. 1053, 1521, 1529, 1530, 1531, 3636, 3643. There is heat and there is light which proceed from the sun; the heat comparatively is the good of love, which is also called celestial and spiritual heat; the light comparatively is the truth thence derived, which is also called spiritual light, see n. 3636, 3643. In the celestial heat and spiritual light, however, which proceed from the Lord as from a sun in another life, there is the good of love and the truth of faith, thus wisdom and intelligence, see n. 1521, 1522, 1523, 1542, 1619 to 1632, 2776, 3138, 3190, 3195, 3222, 3223, 3339, 3485, 3636, 3643, 3862; for the principles which proceed from the Lord are living. Hence it may appear what the Divine spiritual is, and whence the spiritual kingdom and the celestial kingdom, and that the spiritual kingdom is the good of faith, that is, charity, which flows-in from the Lord immediately, and also mediately through the celestial. The Divine spiritual which proceeds from the Lord is called in the Word the spirit of truth, and is holy truth, and is not of any spirit, but is of the Lord by the spirit sent from the Lord, as may appear from the words of the Lord Himself in John, "When He the spirit of truth shall come, He will lead you into all truth, for He shall not speak from Himself, but whatsoever He shall hear that shall He speak, He shall also announce to you things to come. He shall glorify Me, because He shall take of Mine, and shall announce it unto you," xvi. 13, 14.

* * * * * * *

3970. Verses 25, 26. *And it came to pass, when Rachel had borne Joseph, that Jacob said unto Laban, Send me, and I will go to my place, and to my land. Give my women, and my sons, in that I have served thee for them, and I will go, because thou hast known my service which I have served for thee.* It came to pass when Rachel had borne Joseph, signifies the acknowledgment of the spiritual principle represented by Joseph:

Jacob said to Laban, signifies the good of natural truth to collateral good from a Divine origin, by which there was conjunction of interior principles: Send me, and I will go to my place, and to my land, signifies that in this case there was a desire of the natural principle represented by Jacob for a state of conjunction with the Divine of the rational principle : give my women, signifies that the affections of truth were his : and my sons, signifies the truths also thence derived : in that I have' served thee for them, signifies by virtue of his own proper ability : and I will go, signifies conjunction with the Divine of the rational principle : because thou hast known my service with which I have served thee, signifies labour and study by virtue of his own proper ability.

3971. " It came to pass when Rachel had borne Joseph"— that this signifies acknowledgment of the spiritual principle represented by Joseph, appears from the signification of bearing, as being to acknowledge, see n. 3905, 3911, 3915. 3919; and from the representation of Rachel, as being the affection of interior truth, see n. 3758, 3782, 3793, 3819; and from the representation of Joseph, as being the spiritual kingdom. thus the spiritual man, see n. 3969, consequently the spiritual principle; for the spiritual principle, inasmuch as it is from the Lord, constitutes the spiritual man and the spiritual kingdom. The subject treated of above in what relates to the sons of Jacob born of the handmaids and of Leah, is, the reception and acknowledgment of general truths, and finally, the conjunction thereof with the interior man, thus the regeneration of man until he is made spiritual, the spiritual man being Joseph. The subject treated of in what now immediately follows, is the fructification and multiplication of truth and good, which are signified by the flock, which Jacob procured to himself by the flock of Laban. When conjunction is effected of the interior man with the external, or of the spiritual with the natural, there is a fructification of good, and a multiplication of truth, for that conjunction is the heavenly marriage with man, and those effects are the fruits of this marriage. Hence also it is, that Joseph, in an external sense, signifies fructification and multiplication, see n. 3965, 3969; fructification is predicated of good, and multiplication of truth, see n. 43, 55. 913, 983. 2846, 2847.

3972. " And Jacob said to Laban"—that this signifies the good of natural truth to collateral good from a Divine origin, whereby there is conjunction of the interiors, appears from the representation of Jacob, being the good of natural truth, see n. 3659, 3669, 3677, 3775, 3829; and from the representation of Laban, as being collateral good from a Divine origin, see n. 3612, 3665, 3778; that the conjunction of the interiors is effected by that good, has been occasionally explained above, see n. 3665, 3690, and elsewhere. This good is signified by the flock of Laban, by which Jacob procured to himself his flock, as it is described in the subsequent verses.

3973. "Send me, and I will go to my place and to my land," —that this signifies that on this occasion there was a desire of the natural principle represented by Jacob for a state of conjunction with the Divine of the rational, appears from the representation of Jacob, who speaks these words, as being the good of natural truth, see immediately above, n. 3972; and from the signification of place, as being state, see n. 2625, 2837, 3356, 3387; and from the signification of land in this case, as denoting the Divine of the rational principle, for my land means his father Isaac, and his mother Rebecca, for to them he was disposed to be sent and to go. That Isaac denotes the Divine Rational as to good, see n. 2083, 2630, 3012, 3194, 3210; and that Rebecca denotes Truth Divine conjoined to Good Divine of the rational principle, see n. 3012, 3013, 3077; that a desire of conjunction is understood, appears from the affection contained in the words.

3974. "Give my women"—that this signifies that the affections of truth were his; and that "my sons" signify also the truths thence derived, appears from the signification of women, as being the affections of truth, his woman Leah, the affection of external truth, and Rachel, the affection of interior truth, concerning which see above; and from the signification of sons, as being truths thence derived, for sons signify truths, see n. 489, 491, 533, 1147, 2623, 3373. It was a statute amongst the ancients, that the women, who were given as servants, should be the property of the master with whom they served, and also the sons who were born of them, as may appear from the following passage in Moses, "If thou shalt buy an Hebrew servant, he shall serve six years, and in the seventh he shall go away free; if his lord shall give him a woman, and she shall bear him sons or daughters, the woman and the sons born of her shall be his lord's, and shall go forth with his body," Exod. xxi. 2, 4. As this statute was also in the ancient Church, and was thence known to Laban, therefore he claimed to himself both the women and sons of Jacob, as appears in the following chapter, xxxi.: "Laban said unto Jacob, The daughters are my daughters, and the sons my sons, and the flock my flock, and all which thou seest, this and that is mine," verse 43; it was in consequence of Jacob knowing this, that he said to Laban, Give my women and my sons. But the above statute (concerning which, see the passage at large in the book of Moses) represented the right of the internal or rational principle of man to the goods and truths of the external or natural principle, which it has procured to itself; for servant represented the truth of the natural principle, such as it is in the beginning, before genuine truths are insinuated. The truth which is in the beginning is not truth, but appears like truth, nevertheless it is serviceable as a means of introducing genuine truths and goods, according to what was shown above. When, therefore, goods and truths are insinuated by it or by its service, in this case it is dismissed, and the genuine goods and truths so procured are retained; it was on account of this representation that the above law concerning servants was enacted. But with regard to Jacob, he was not a bought servant, but of a family more illustrious than Laban; he, namely, Jacob, bought for himself Laban's daughters, and also the sons who were born of them, by his service, for they were his as a reward, wherefore Laban did not entertain proper sentiments on this occasion. Moreover an Hebrew servant signified the truth which serves to introduce genuine goods and truths, and the woman of such a servant signified the affection of natural good; but it was otherwise in the case of Jacob, since he represents the good of natural truth, and his women, the affections of truth. Neither is that principle represented by Laban which is represented by lord in the passage above quoted concerning the Hebrew servant, that is, the rational principle, but collateral good, see n. 3612, 3665, 3778, which is of such a quality, that it is not genuine good, but appearing as genuine, and is serviceable for the introduction of truths, see n. 3665, 3690, which thereby were Jacob's. The particulars above adduced are indeed such that very few will be capable of apprehending them, because very few know what is meant by the truth and the good of the natural principle, and that these are distinct from the truth and good of the rational principle; still less is it known that the goods and truths which are not genuine, and yet appear to be so, are serviceable for introducing genuine truths and goods, especially in the beginning of regeneration. Nevertheless, since these are the particulars contained in the internal sense of the words, and also in the internal sense of what follows concerning the flock of Laban, from which Jacob procured to himself a flock, it was expedient to mention them. Possibly some may comprehend them; they who have a desire to know such things, that is, who are in the affection of spiritual good and truth, receive illustration concerning them.

3975. "In that I have served thee for them"—that this signifies by virtue of his own proper ability, appears from the signification of serving, as being labour and study, see n. 3824, 3846, which, when predicated of the Lord, denotes own proper ability; for the Lord, by virtue of His own proper ability, procured to Himself Divine Goods and Divine Truths, and made His Human Divine; see n. 1616, 1749, 1755, 1921, 2025, 2026, 2083, 2500, 2523, 2632, 2816, 3382.

3976. "And I will go"—that this signifies conjunction with

the Divine Rational, appears from the signification of going, namely, to his place and to his land, as above, n. 3973, which signifies a desire of conjunction with the Divine of the rational principle.

3977. " Because thou hast known my service with which I have served thee"—that this signifies labour and study from his own proper ability, may appear from what was said and adduced above, n. 3975, thus without further explication. The meaning of these words is also evident from what was said above, n. 3974, and also from what follows.

3978. Verses 27, 28, 29, 30. *And Laban said unto him, If, I pray, I have found grace in thine eyes, I have experienced, and Jehovah hath blessed me for thy sake. And he said, Appoint thy reward upon me, and I will give it. And he said unto him, Thou hast known in what quality I have served thee, and in what quality thine acquisition was with me. Because it was little which thou hadst before me, and it hath broke forth into a multitude, and Jehovah hath blessed thee at my foot; and now when shall I do also for mine own house?* Laban said unto him, signifies perception from that good which is signified by Laban · If, I pray, I have found grace in thine eyes, signifies propensity : I have experienced, and Jehovah hath blessed me for thy sake, signifies from the Divine, for the sake of the good of the natural principle which he was to serve : and he said, Appoint thy reward upon me, and I will give it, signifies that of himself he would give what he willed : and he said unto him, Thou hast known in what quality I have served thee, signifies that he knew his mind and ability : and what was the quality of thine acquisition with me, signifies also that it was from the Divine : because it was little which thou hadst before me, signifies that his good is barren before it be conjoined : and it hath broke forth to a multitude, signifies fruitfulness afterwards : and Jehovah hath blessed thee at my foot, signifies that it was from the Divine which the natural had : and now when shall I do also for mine own house? signifies that now his own good shall thence be made fruitful.

3979. " Laban said to him"—that this signifies perception from the good which is signified by Laban, appears from the signification of saying, as being perception, see n. 1898, 1919, 2080, 2619, 2862, 3395, 3509 ; and from the representation of Laban, as being collateral good derived from the Divine, see n. 3612, 3665, 3778. The reason why perception from that good is denoted (which perception is signified by the words, " Laban said to him"), is, because persons in the Word signify nothing else but things, in a supreme sense, Divine things in the Lord, and in an internal sense, such things in man as are treated of. Thus, two persons signify two things appertaining to the same man.

3980. " If, I pray, I have found grace in thine eyes"—that this signifies propensity, appears from the signification of finding grace in the eyes of any one, as being propensity. Propensity is predicated of the good which is signified by Laban, when it wills to be present. Whoever reflects, or is capable of reflecting upon the affections of good and truth in himself, and also on what is delightful and pleasant, will observe the propensity of one more than of another; but these and similar things do not appear without reflection.

3981. " I have experienced, and Jehovah hath blessed me for thy sake"—that this signifies that it was from the Divine for the sake of the good of the natural principle which was to be served, appears from the signification of experiencing that Jehovah had blessed, as being to know for certain that it was from the Divine. That it was for the sake of the good of the natural principle, which was to be served, is signified by the words, " for thy sake ;" for Jacob is the good of natural truth, see n. 3659, 3669, 3677, 3775, 3829, and Laban is the collateral good which serves, as has been abundantly shown above · see also below, n. 3982, 3986.

3982. " And he said, Appoint thy reward upon me, and I will give it"—that this signifies that of himself he would give what he willed, may appear without explication. What has been said hitherto of Laban and Jacob is of such a nature, as not to admit of being explained with clearness to the understanding, as well because the mind is incapable of being instantaneously bended from historical things to the spiritual ones, which are treated of in the internal sense (for the historical relation always adheres to and fills the idea, and yet it ought to be as nothing in order that the things not historical may be comprehended in their series), as because a clear notion ought first to be had of those goods which are represented by each, namely, by Laban and Jacob, and that the good represented by Laban is such, that it is merely a useful good, useful to introduce genuine truths and goods, and when it has answered this purpose, it is afterwards left. The nature of this good has been treated of above. It is like the immature principle in unripe fruits, by which juice is introduced, which, when it has served this purpose, afterwards withers away, and the fruits ripen by means of other fibres, and at length by the fibres of genuine juice. It is a known thing, that man in infancy and childhood learns several things for this useful purpose only, that by them as by means he may learn things more useful, and successively, by these, things more useful still, until at length he learns such things as regard eternal life, in which case the former things are almost obliterated. So during the process of man's being born anew of the Lord, he is led by several affections of good and truth, which are not affections of genuine good and truth,

but only useful to apprehend, and afterwards to imbibe such
good and truth, and when this purpose is effected, then the
former things are forgotten and left, because they had only
served as means. This is the case with the collateral good
which is signified by Laban, in respect to the good of truth
which is signified by Jacob, and also by the flock of each,
whereof we shall speak further in what follows. These are the
arcana contained in this and in the subsequent relation, but
historically delivered, in order that the Word may be read with
delight, even by children and the simple, to the intent, that
whilst they are in holy delight arising from the historical sense,
their attendant angels may be in the sanctity of the internal
sense, which internal sense is adequate to angelic intelligence,
whilst the external sense is adequate to human intelligence.
Hence arises the consociation of man with the angels, which
man is altogether ignorant of, only perceiving thence a certain
delight, wherein is holiness.

3983. "And he said unto him, Thou hast known in what
quality I have served thee"—that this signifies that he knew
his mind and ability, may appear from the series of things in
the internal sense. That to know a person's quality is to know
his mind, is evident; and that to know his quality in service,
is to know his ability, may appear from the signification of
serving in the present case, as denoting proper ability, see n.
3975, 3977; for Jacob represents the Divine of the Lord's natural principle as to good and truth, which has ability. Hence
it follows, that the subsequent words, "what was the quality
of thine acquisition with me," signify also that it was from the
Divine.

3984. "Because it was little which thou hadst before me"—
that this signifies that his good is barren unless it be conjoined,
may also appear from the series of things in the internal sense;
for the subject treated of is the quality of the good represented
by Laban, before it was conjoined with the good of truth, which
is Jacob, that it was of little use, that is, barren: how the case
is, will appear from what now follows.

3985. "And hath broke forth to a multitude"—that this
signifies fruitfulness afterwards, appears from the signification
of breaking forth to a multitude, as denoting fruitfulness,
namely, after it was conjoined.

3986. "And Jehovah hath blessed thee at my foot"—that
this signifies from the Divine which the natural had, appears
from the signification of Jehovah blessing, as being to be gifted
with good, see n. 3406, and as being conjunction, see n. 3504,
3514, 3530, 3565, 3584, thus it is to be gifted with good by
conjunction, in the present case with the good of the natural
principle which is represented by Jacob. The natural principle
is what is signified by foot. That foot denotes the natural prin

ciple, may be seen, n. 2162, 3147, 3761, and will further appear
from the correspondence of the Grand Man with singular the
things of man, as pointed out at the close of each chapter.
Hence it is evident, that these words, " Jehovah hath blessed
thee at my foot," signify that it was from the Divine which the
natural had.   The arcanum which lies concealed in this passage, and in those which immediately precede, is known to few.
if to any one, and therefore it is expedient that it should be
revealed.   The goods in men, as well within the Church as
without, are altogether various, and so much so, that the good
of one man is never in all respects like that of another.   The
varieties derive their existence from the truths with which the
goods are conjoined, for every good takes its quality from truths,
and truths their essential from goods.   Varieties also derive
their existence from the affections of every one's love, which
are rooted in and appropriated to man by his life.   Few genuine
truths appertain to man even within the Church, and still fewer
to man without the Church, and hence the affections of genuine
truth are rarely found.   Nevertheless, they who are in the good
of life, or who live in love to God and charity towards their
neighbour, are saved.   Their capacity to be saved is hence,
that the Lord's Divine is in the good of love to God and in the
good of charity towards the neighbour, and where the Divine
is within, there all things are disposed into such an order, as to
be capable of being conjoined with the genuine goods and
genuine truths which exist in the heavens.   That this is the
case, may appear from the societies which constitute heaven,
and which are innumerable, all and singular whereof are various as to good and truth, and yet taken together form one
heaven.   They are in this respect like the members and organs
of the human body, which, although various throughout, still
constitute one man.   One is never constituted with several of
the same identical units, or of such as are altogether similar,
but of various units conjoined harmonically, and these various
units so conjoined constitute every one.   The case is similar
with respect to goods and truths in the spiritual world, which,
although various, so as not to be altogether alike in one man
as in another, still make one from the Divine by love and
charity, for love and charity is spiritual conjunction, and their
variety is heavenly harmony, which makes such concord, that
they are one in the Divine, that is, in the Lord.   Moreover, the
good of love to God, and the good of charity towards the neighbour, however truths may be various, and the affections of
truth various, are still receptive of genuine truth and good, for
they are not hard and resisting, if we may use the expressions,
but as it were soft and yielding, and suffer themselves to be
led of the Lord, and thus to be bended to good, and by good
to Him.   It is otherwise with those persons who are in self-love

and the love of the world. They do not suffer themselves to be led and bended by the Lord and to the Lord, but resist with hardness, for they desire to lead themselves, and their resistance is still greater when false principles are confirmed in them. So long as this is the case, they do not admit the Divine. From these considerations then it may appear what is signified in the internal sense by the above words which Jacob spake to Laban; for Laban signifies such good as is not genuine, because genuine truths have not been implanted in it, but which still is such that they may be conjoined to it, and is capable of admitting into it the Divine. Such good as this is usually found to prevail with young people before they have received genuine truths, and also with the simple within the Church, who are acquainted with few truths of faith, but yet live in charity, and also with well-disposed Gentiles, who are in the holy worship of their gods. By such good it is possible that genuine truths and goods may be introduced, as may appear from what was said, n. 3690, of infants and the simple within the Church, and of well-disposed Gentiles out of the Church, n. 2598, 2599, 2600, 2601, 2602, 2603.

3987. "And now when shall I do also for mine own house?" —that this signifies that now his own good shall thence be made fruitful, appears from the signification of house, as being good, see n. 2233, 2234, 3128, 3652, in the present case mine own house, being the good which Jacob signifies. That to do for this house denotes the fructification of good thence, is evident from the fact, that the fructification of good and the multiplication of truth is now treated of ; for by Joseph who was last born this fructification is signified, see n. 3965, 3969, 3971, and by the flock which Jacob procured to himself by the flock of Laban, this signification is described. That good is not fructified, neither truth multiplied, until the conjunction of the external man with the internal is effected, may appear from this, that it is the part of the interior man to will good to another, and thence to think good, and of the external man to do good, and thence to teach good. Unless doing good is conjoined with willing good, and teaching good with thinking good, the man is not in possession of good, for the wicked can will evil and do good, and also think evil and teach good, as may be known to every one. Hypocrites and profane persons are distinguished by their study and art in this respect, insomuch that they can feign themselves angels of light, being devils inwardly. Hence it may appear that good cannot be made fruitful with any one, unless doing good is conjoined with willing good, and teaching good with thinking good, that is, unless the external man be conjoined with the internal.

3988. Verses 31, 32, 33. *And he said, What shall I give thee ? And Jacob said, Thou shalt not give me any thing, if*

*thou wilt do for me this word, I will return, will feed, will
guard thy flock. I will pass through all thy flock to-day, removing thence all the cattle speckled and spotted, and all the
black cattle in the lambs, and the spotted and speckled in the
she-goats, and it shall be my hire. And my justice shall answer
for me on the morrow, because thou comest upon my hire before
thee, every one which is not speckled and spotted in the she-
goats, and black in the lambs, that was stolen with me.* He said,
What shall I give thee? signifies knowledge: and Jacob said,
signifies reply: Thou shalt not give me any thing, if thou wilt
do for me this word, signifies that it shall be brought on the
part of good which is from truth: I will return, will feed, will
guard thy flock, signifies that the good signified by Laban was
to be applied to use: I will pass through all thy flock to-day,
signifies that he perceives every good as to its quality: removing thence all the cattle speckled and spotted, signifies that
every good of his shall be separated, wherewith evil is mixed,
which is the speckled, and wherewith the false is mixed, which
is the spotted: and all the black cattle in the lambs, signifies
the proprium of innocence, which is of the good signified by
Laban: and the spotted and speckled in the she-goats, signifies
that afterwards every good of truth shall be his, in which the
false and evil is mixed: and it shall be my hire, signifies that
it should be] from himself: and my justice shall answer for
me, signifies the Divine sanctity appertaining to himself: on
the morrow, signifies to eternity: because thou comest upon
my hire before thee, signifies his proprium: every one which
is not speckled and spotted in the she-goats, signifies what is
derived from the good understood by Laban, and is not mixed
with evil and false in the goods of truth: and black in the
lambs, signifies the first state of innocence: that was stolen
with me, signifies that it was not his.

3989. "He said, What shall I give thee?"—that this signifies knowledge, may appear from its being a solicitation and
interrogation to know what and how much of hire he was willing to have. "And Jacob said"—that this signifies reply,
appears without explication.

3990. "Thou shalt not give me any thing, if thou wilt do
for me this word"—that this signifies that it shall be brought
on the part of good which is derived from truth, appears from
the signification of not giving any thing, as being not to be
brought from the good which is represented by Laban, but
from the good which is represented by Jacob, which is the good
of truth, see n. 3669, 3677, 3829. What was to be brought, is
described in what follows.

3991. "I will return, will feed, will guard thy flock"—that
this signifies that the good represented by Laban was to be applied to use, namely, to the use of introducing genuine goods

and truths, as was shown above, appears from the signification of flock, in this case Laban's, as being the good represented by him.   To return, to feed, and to guard his flock, is to apply to use, as is also manifest from what follows, since Jacob by that flock procured to himself his own flock, for it served him for a means, thus for use.

3992. " I will pass through all thy flock to-day"—that this signifies that he perceives every good as to its quality, appear from the signification of flock, as being good, see n. 343, 3518; and from the signification of passing through it all, as being to know and perceive what its quality is.

3993. " Removing thence all the cattle speckled and spotted" —that this signifies that every good of his shall be separated, wherewith evil is mixed, which is the speckled, and wherewith the false is mixed, which is the spotted, appears from the signification of removing, as being to separate ; and from the signification of cattle, which in the present case are goats and lambs as being goods and truths, see n. 1824, 3519.   That these and the subsequent verses of this chapter contain arcana, may be seen from the fact, that there are several circumstances recorded therein, which would not have been worthy of being recorded in the Divine Word, unless they had contained greater arcana than appear in the letter, as that Jacob should ask for his hire the speckled and spotted cattle in the she-goats, and the black in the lambs ; that afterwards he placed in the gutters rods of hazel and plane-tree peeled to the white before the flocks of Laban when they grew warm, and as to the lambs that he gave the faces of the flock to the variegated and black in the flock of Laban ; and that thus he became rich not by good, but by evil artifice.   In these circumstances there does not appear to be any thing Divine, when yet the Word is Divine in all and singular things, and as to the smallest iota.   Moreover, to know these circumstances is of no profit, and does not in the least conduce to salvation, when nevertheless the Word, as being Divine, contains in it only such things as conduce to salvation and eternal life.   From these and similar circumstances which occur elsewhere, every one may conclude, that there is some arcanum contained therein, and that they all, notwithstanding their expression in the sense of the letter, are inwardly replete with things Divine.   But what their inward contents are, cannot in any wise appear except from the internal sense, that is, unless it be known how these things are perceived by the angels, for the angels are in the spiritual sense, whilst man is in the natural historical sense ; and how far these two senses appear removed from each other, although they are most closely conjoined, may be very manifest from the above and other passages. The real arcanum, which is contained in these and the following verses of this chapter, may indeed in some measure be known

from what has been said above of Laban and Jacob, namely,
that Laban denotes a good, whereby genuine goods and truths
may be introduced, and that Jacob denotes the good of truth.
But as few know that there is a natural principle corresponding
to spiritual good, and fewer what spiritual good is, and that
there ought to be a correspondence, and still fewer that a kind
of good appearing as good is the medium of introducing genuine goods and truths, therefore the arcana treating on these
subjects cannot easily be explained to the apprehension, because they fall into the shade of the understanding, and it is
like a person speaking in a foreign language, in which case,
however clearly he may expound his subject, still the hearer
does not understand it. Nevertheless, since the contents of the
internal sense of the Word are now laid open, it is expedient
to say somewhat on the above subject. In a supreme sense the
Lord is here treated of, how He made His natural principle
Divine; and in a representative sense the natural principle in
man, how the Lord regenerates it, and reduces it to correspondence with the man of his interior, that is, with the man
which is to live after the decease of the body, and is then called
the spirit of man, which, when it is loose from the body, has
with it all things of the external man, except bones and flesh.
Unless the correspondence of the internal man with the external
be effected in time, or in the life of the body, it is not effected
afterwards. The subject here treated of, in the internal sense,
is the conjunction of each by regeneration from the Lord.
The subject treated of heretofore was concerning the general
truths which man ought to receive before he can be regenerated.
Those truths were signified by the ten sons of Jacob born of
Leah and the handmaids. After he has received and acknowledged those truths, the conjunction of the external man with
the interior was treated of, or of the natural man with the
spiritual, which was signified by Joseph. The subject now
treated of according to order is the fructification of good and
the multiplication of truth, which then first has place, when
conjunction has been effected, and this in a degree according
to the conjunction. This fructification and multiplication is
what is signified by the flock which Jacob procured to himself
by the flock of Laban. Flock here signifies good and truth, as
in many other parts of the Word; the flock of Laban the good
which is represented by Laban, the quality of which has been
above described, and the flock of Jacob genuine good and
truth which is procured by the former. But how genuine
goods and truths are procured, is here described. Howbeit,
this can in no wise be comprehended, unless it be known what
is signified in the internal sense by the speckled, what by the
spotted, what by the black, and what by the white, wherefore
't may be expedient first to treat on this subject. The speckled

and spotted is what is derived from black and white. Black in general signifies evil, in particular man's **proprium,** because this is nothing but evil; but darkish signifies in general the false, and in particular the principles of the false. White, in the internal sense, signifies truth, properly the Lord's justice and merit, and hence the Lord's justice and merit in man. This white is called bright, being resplendent by virtue of the light proceeding from the Lord. White, in an opposite sense, signifies man's own justice or own merit, for truth without good has in it such merit; for when any one does good, not from the good of truth, in such case he is always desirous to be recompensed, for he does it for the sake of himself; but when he does truth from a principle of good, the truth is illustrated by light proceeding from the Lord. Hence it is manifest what is meant by spotted, namely, truth which is mixed with the false; and what is meant by speckled, namely, good which is mixed with evil. In another life there actually appear colours, beautiful and splendid beyond description, see n. 1053, 1624. They arise from the variegations of light and shade in white and black. Light, however, in another life, although it appears like light before the eyes, is nevertheless not like light in the world. Light in heaven has in it intelligence and wisdom, for Divine intelligence and wisdom from the Lord is there presented as light, and also illuminates the universal heaven, see n. 2776, 3138, 3167, 3190, 3195, 3222, 3223, 3225, 3339, 3340, 3341, 3485, 3636, 3643, 3862. Shade also in another life, although it appears like shade, is still not like shade in the world, for shade in another life is the absence of light, consequently the want of intelligence and wisdom. Hence then come white and black, and as they exist, the one in another life from light wherein is intelligence and wisdom, and the other from shade which is the want of intelligence and wisdom, it is evident they signify the things which are mentioned above. Hence also come colours, which are modifications of light and shade in black and white, as in planes. The variegations thence are what are called colours, see n. 1042, 1043, 1053. From these considerations now it may appear that speckled, or what is marked and distinguished with points, that is, with black and white, denotes good mixed with evil, and that spotted denotes truth mixed with falsity. These are the things which are taken from the good of Laban, being to serve for the introduction of genuine goods and truths. But in what manner these things can so serve, is an arcanum which may indeed be exhibited clearly to view with those who are in the light of heaven, because in such light, as was said, there is intelligence, but not so with those who are in the light of the world, unless the light of the world with them be illustrated by the light of heaven, as it is with those who are regenerated; for every regenerate person

sees goods and truths in his natural lumen by virtue of the
light of heaven, for the light of heaven constitutes his intel
lectual sight, and the lumen of the world his natural sight.
But how the case herein is, it may be expedient briefly to explain. Pure good, that is, good unmixed with evil, does not
exist in man, nor pure truth, unmixed with falsity; for the will-
principle of man is nothing but mere evil, and from it there
continually flows what is false into his intellectual principle;
for it is a known thing that man hereditarily brings with him
evil successively accumulated from his parents, and from this
evil he actually himself produces evil, and makes it his own,
and still superadds evil from himself. Evils, however, with
man are of various kinds; there are evils wherewith good cannot be mixed, and there are evils wherewith goods can be
mixed. The case is the same with falses, and unless it was so,
it would be impossible for any man to be regenerated. The
evils and falses wherewith goods and truths cannot be mixed,
are such as are contrary to love to God and to love towards
our neighbour, hatreds, revenges, cruelties, and consequent
contempt of others in comparison with ourselves, also the persuasions of what is false thence derived; but the evils and
falses wherewith goods and truths can be mixed, are such as
are not contrary to love to God and to love towards our neighbour. For example, if any one loves himself in preference to
others, and under the influence of that love studies to excel
others in moral and civil life, in scientifics and doctrinals, and
to be exalted to dignities and likewise to opulence above others,
and yet acknowledges and adores God, performs from his heart
duties towards his neighbour, and does from conscience what is
just and equitable, the evil of that self-love is such as to admit
good and truth to be mixed with it; for it is the evil which is
proper to man, and is hereditarily born with him, and suddenly
to take it away from him would be to extinguish the fire of his
first life. But if any love himself in preference to others, and
under the influence of that love despises others in comparison
with himself, hates those who do not honour, and as it were
adore him, and therefrom feels the delight of hatred in revenge
and cruelty, the evil of his love is such as not to admit of good
and truth being mixed with it, for they are contraries. Again,
if any one believe himself to be pure from sins, and cleansed
like a person cleansed of filth by washing in water, when he
has once done the work of repentance, and discharged the
duties which he had imposed upon himself by repentance, or
after confession has been told by his confessor that he is so
cleansed, or after he has been partaker of the Holy Supper, in
case such an one lives a new life, in the affection of what is
good and true, this false principle is such as to admit of good
being mixed with it; but in case he lives a worldly and carnal

life, as heretofore, the false is then such as not to admit of good
being mixed with it. So again, he who believes that man is
saved by virtue of believing what is good, and not by virtue of
willing what is good, and nevertheless wills what is good, and in
consequence thereof does what is good, this false principle is
such as to admit of good and truth being adjoined to it; but not
so in case he does not will and thence do what is good. Again,
if any one be ignorant that man rises again after death, and in
consequence thereof does not believe a resurrection, or if he be
acquainted with a resurrection, and still doubts and almost
denies it, and yet lives in truth and good, this false principle
also is such as to be admissive of good and truth to be mixed
with it; but if such a person live in what is false and evil, the
false in this case is admissive of no such mixture, because of
contrariety, and the false destroys the true, and the evil the
good. Further, pretence and cunning, which have good for
their end, whether it be the good of the neighbour, or of a
man's country, or of the Church, are prudence, and the evils
thereto admixed may be mixed with good, from and for the
sake of the end proposed; but pretence and cunning, which
have evil for their end, are not prudence, but are artifice and
deceit, wherewith good can in no wise be conjoined, for deceit,
which has evil for its end, induces an infernal principle in all
and singular the things in man, and places evil in the midst,
and rejects good to the circumference, which order is essentially
infernal. The case is similar in numberless other instances.
That there are evils and falses to which goods and truths can
be adjoined, may appear from the fact, that there are so many
diverse dogmas and doctrinals, several of which are altogether
heretical, and yet in every one of them salvation is attainable;
and also from this, that among the Gentiles who are out of the
Church, there is likewise a Church of the Lord, and that although they are in false principles, still such as live a life of
charity are saved, see n. 2589 to 2604, which could not possibly
be the case, unless there were evils which can be mixed with
goods, and falses which can be mixed with truths. Evils which
are mixed with goods, and falses with truths, are wonderfully
arranged in order by the Lord, for they are not conjoined,
still less are they united, but they are adjoined and applied,
and this in such a sort, that goods with truths are in the midst,
as in a centre, whilst such evils and falses are by gradations
as the circuits or circumferences, in consequence whereof the
latter are illustrated by the former, and are variegated like
white and black by the light proceeding from the midst or
centre. This is a heavenly order. These then are the things
signified in the internal sense by speckled and spotted.

3994. "And all the black cattle in the lambs"—that this
signifies the proprium of innocence, which is of the good sig

nified by Laban, appears from the signification of black, as
being proprium, see immediately above, n. 3993; and from the
signification of lamb, as being innocence, of which we shall
speak presently. With respect to the proprium of innocence,
which is signified by the black in the lambs, the case is this: in
all good there must be innocence, to make it good; charity
without innocence is not charity, still less is it love to the
Lord; consequently, innocence is the very essential of love and
charity, and thus of good. The proprium of innocence consists in knowing, acknowledging, and believing, not with the
mouth but with the heart, that nothing but evil comes from
self, and that all good is from the Lord; consequently that
man's proprium is nothing but black, namely, both the will-
proprium which is evil, and the intellectual proprium which is
false. When man is in this confession and faith from the heart,
then the Lord flows in with good and truth, and insinuates into
him a celestial proprium, which is bright and shining. It is
impossible for any one to be in true humiliation, unless he be
in this acknowledgment and faith from the heart, for in this
case he is in self-annihilation, yea, in self-aversion, and thereby
in absence from himself, and thus in a state of receiving the
Divine [principle] of the Lord. Hence it is, that the Lord flows
with good into an humble and contrite heart. Such is the proprium of innocence, which is here signified by the black in the
lambs, which Jacob chose to himself, whereas the white in the
lambs is merit which is placed in goods. That white denotes
merit, was said above, n. 3993. This Jacob did not choose,
because it is contrary to innocence, for he who places merit in
goods, acknowledges and believes that all good is from himself,
for in the goods which he does he has respect unto himself, not
unto the Lord, and hence he demands recompense from merit.
Wherefore such a person also despises others in comparison
with himself, yea, he even condemns them, consequently in so
far recedes from heavenly order, that is, from good and truth.
Hence it may appear, that charity towards the neighbour and
love to the Lord cannot possibly exist, unless innocence be in
them; consequently, that no one can come into heaven unless
he has somewhat of innocence, according to the Lord's words,
"Verily I say unto you, whosoever shall not receive the kingdom of God as an infant, he shall not enter therein," Mark x.
15; Luke xviii. 17. Infants in this and other passages in the
Word signify innocence; see what was said above on this subject, namely, that infancy is not innocence, but that innocence
dwells in wisdom, n. 2305, 3494. The quality of the innocence
of infancy, and the quality of the innocence of wisdom, may
be seen, n. 2306, 3183; also the quality of proprium when vivified by innocence and charity from the Lord, n, 154; that innocence makes good to be good, n. 2526, 2780. That lambs

signify innocence, may appear from several passages in the Word, of which the following may serve to put the matter out of all doubt: " *The wolf* shall dwell *with the lamb*, and the leopard shall lie down with the kid, and the calf and the young lion, and the ox together, and a little child shall lead them," Isaiah xi. 6; speaking of the Lord's kingdom, and of the state of peace and innocence therein. The wolf denotes those who are against innocence, the lamb those who are in innocence. Again, in the same prophet, " *The wolf and the lamb shall feea together*, and the lion shall eat straw like the ox, and dust shall be the serpent's bread; they shall not do evil, and they shall not destroy in the whole mountain of My holiness," lxv. 25; where wolf, as above, denotes those who are against innocence, and lamb, those who are in innocence. The wolf and the lamb being opposites, the Lord also said to the seventy whom He sent forth, " Behold, I send you as *lambs into the midst of wolves*," Luke x. 3. So in Moses, " He causeth him to suck honey out of the rock, and oil out of the flinty rock, butter of the herd, and milk of the flock, with *fat of lambs* and rams, the sons of Bashan," Deut. xxxii. 13, 14; speaking, in the internal sense, concerning the celestial things of the ancient Church, where fat of lambs denotes the charity of innocence. Lambs in the original tongue are expressed by various names, and thereby are signified different degrees of innocence, for, as was said, in all good there must be innocence to make it good, and hence also in truth. They are here expressed by a word whereby sheep also are expressed, as Levit. i. 10; chap. iii. 7; chap. v. 6; chap. xvii. 3; chap. xxii. 19; Numb. xviii. 17; and it is the innocence of the faith of charity which is signified. They are expressed by different words in other places, as in Isaiah, "Send ye *the lamb* of the ruler of the earth from the rock towards the wilderness to the mountain of the daughter of Zion," xvi. 1 And still by another expression in the same prophet, "The Lord Jehovih cometh in strength, and His arm shall rule for Him; as a shepherd He shall feed His flock, *He shall gather the lambs into His arm*, and shall carry them in His bosom, He shall lead the sucklings," xl. 9, 10; where to gather the lambs into His arm, and to carry them in His bosom, denotes those who are in charity wherein is innocence. So in John, " Jesus being manifested to Peter, said, Simon Jonah, lovest thou Me more than these? He saith unto Him, Yea, Lord, Thou knowest that I love Thee: He saith unto Him, *Feed My lambs*. He saith unto him again, Simon Jonah, lovest thou Me? He saith unto him, Yea, Lord, Thou knowest that I love Thee: He saith unto him, *Feed My sheep*," xxi. 15, 16. Peter in this and other passages signifies faith; see the preface to chap. xviii. and the preface to chap. xxii. of Genesis, and n. 3750; and as faith is not faith unless it be from charity towards the neighbour, and so from love to the Lord, and as there is no charity and love unless from innocence, hence the Lord first asks Peter whether he loves Him, that is, whether there be love in faith, and afterwards saith, Feed My lambs, that is, those who are in innocence ; and lastly, after asking the same question, saith, Feed My sheep, that is, those who are in charity. Since the Lord is the essential innocence which is in His kingdom, for from Him is the all of innocence, therefore He is called the Lamb, as in John, " The day following John the Baptist seeth Jesus coming to Him, and saith, Behold *the Lamb of God*, Who taketh away the sin of the world," i. 29, 36. And in the Apocalypse, " They shall fight *with the Lamb*, but the *Lamb shall overcome them*, because He is the Lord of lords, and King of kings, and they who are with Him are called and chosen," xvii. 14 ; and in other passages in the Apocalypse, as chap. v. 6 ; chap. vi. 1, 16 ; chap. vii. 9, 14, 17 ; chap. xii. 11 ; chap. xiii. 8 ; chap. xiv. 1, 4 ; chap. xix. 7, 9 ; chap. xxi. 22, 23, 27 ; chap. xxii. 1, 3. That the paschal lamb is the Lord in a supreme sense, is a known thing, for the passover signifies the Lord's glorification, that is, the putting on of the Divine as to the Human, and in a representative sense, the regeneration of man ; and the paschal lamb that which is the essential of regeneration, namely, innocence ; for no one can be regenerated except by charity in which is innocence. Since innocence is primary in the Lord's kingdom, and is the very celestial principle therein, and since sacrifices and burnt-offerings represented the spiritual and celestial things of the Lord's kingdom, therefore the very essential of His kingdom, which is innocence, was represented by lambs ; wherefore the continual or daily burnt-offering was made of lambs, of one in the morning, and another between the evenings, Exod. xxix. 38, 39, 40 ; Numb. xxviii. 3, 4 ; and of two on the sabbath days, Numb. xxviii. 9, 10 ; and by more lambs still on stated festivals, Levit. xxiii. 12 ; Numb. xxviii. 11, 19, 27 ; chap. xxix. 1 to the end. The reason why a woman at her delivery, when the days of cleansing were accomplished, was to offer a lamb for a burnt-offering, or a young dove, or a turtle, Levit. xii. 6, was, that the effect of conjugial love might be signified ; (that this love is innocence, may be seen, n. 2736 ;) and because infants signify innocence.

3995 " And the spotted and speckled in the she-goats"-- that this signifies that afterwards every good of truth shall be his in which the false and evil is mixed, appears from the signification of spotted, as being what is false, and of speckled, as being what is evil, concerning which see above, n. 3993 ; and from the signification of she-goats, as being good of truth, or charity of faith, see n. 3519. That all this should be his, is signified also by what follows, " And it shall be my hire."— What is meant by the good of truth, or the charity of faith, shall be briefly explained. During the process of man's regeneration, the truth which is of faith apparently precedes, and the good which is of charity apparently follows. When man, however, is regenerated, then the good which is of charity manifestly precedes, and the truth which is of faith manifestly follows; but that in the former case it is only an appearance, whereas in the latter it is essentially so, may be seen, n. 3539, 3548, 3556, 3563, 3570, 3576, 3603, 3616, 3701. For when man is regenerated, he does good from the truth which he has learnt, since from truth he learns what is good, but still it is good within which operates this. Good flows-in from the Lord by an internal way, or by the way of the soul, and truth, by an external way, or by the way of the senses which is that of the body. The truth which enters by this latter way, is adopted by the good which is within, and is conjoined thereto, and this with a continuance until man is regenerated. When this is the case, there is a turning, and truth is brought into act from good. Hence it is manifest what is meant by the good of truth, and what by the truth of good; and hence it is that so many say at this day, that the goods of charity are fruits of faith, for so it appears in the beginning of regeneration, and from this appearance they make this conclusion, nor do they know otherwise, inasmuch as there are few who are regenerated, and no one can know this but he who is regenerated, that is, who is in the affection of good, or in charity; from the affection of good or from charity, this may be clearly seen, and also be perceived. They, however, who are not regenerated, do not even know what the affection of good, or what charity is, but reason on the subject, as on a thing foreign to, or out of them; wherefore they call charity the fruit of faith, when yet faith is from charity. Nevertheless, it is not of so much concern for the simple to know what is prior and what is posterior, if they live in charity, for charity is the life of faith. Cattle here signify both lambs and sheep, kids, she-goats, rams, and he-goats, but only lambs and she-goats are mentioned, and this because lambs signify innocence, and she-goats, the charity of faith, for these things are here treated of in the internal sense. Hence it is, that spotted in the original tongue is expressed by a word which also signifies lambs, as Isaiah xl. 11; and speckled, by a word which also signifies a dealer in cattle, as 2 Kings iii. 4; Amos i. 1.

3996. "And it shall be my hire"—that this signifies what was from himself, appears from the signification of hire, as being what was Jacob's, on account of his service; and that this was of his own ability, or what is the same thing, from himself, may be seen above, n. 3975, 3977, 3982.

3997. "And my justice shall answer for me"—that this signifies the Divine Holiness which appertained to himself, appears from the signification of justice, in that it is predicated of good (concerning which see n. 612, 2235); but when it is said of the Lord, as in the present case, it is the Divine Holiness, for every spiritual and celestial good proceeds from the Lord's Divine Holiness.

3998. "On the morrow"—that this signifies to eternity, appears from the signification of morrow. When mention is made in the Word of yesterday, to-day, or to-morrow, in a supreme sense eternity is signified, yesterday signifying from eternity, to-day, eternity, and to-morrow, to eternity. That to-day denotes eternity, may be seen, n. 2838; for times in the Word, as ages, years, months, weeks, days, and hours, signify states, according to what has been often shown. Nevertheless, in the Lord there are no states, but all is eternal and infinite. Hence it is evident that to-morrow signifies to eternity.

3999. "Because thou comest upon my hire before thee"— that this signifies his proprium, appears from the signification of hire, when it is predicated of the Lord, as being proprium, namely, what was acquired from his own proper ability, see above, n. 3975, 3977, 3982, 3996.

4000. "All that is not speckled and spotted in the she-goats"- --that this signifies what is derived from the good understood by Laban, and is not mixed with what is evil and false in the goods of truth, appears from what was said above, n. 3993, 3995, where similar words occur.

4001. "And black in the lambs"—that this signifies the first state of innocence, appears from the signification of black, as being proprium, and from the signification of lamb, as being innocence, see above, n. 3994. The reason why black in the lambs is here the first state of innocence, is, because the proprium of the man who is regenerated at first has rule, for he thinks from proprium to do good, and also must do it as from proprium, in order that he may be gifted with celestial proprium, see n. 1712, 1937, 1947, 2882, 2883, 2891. Hence it is that black in the lambs here signifies the first state of innocence.

4002. "That was stolen with me"—that this signifies that it was not his, may appear without explication. This indeed sounds rather harsh in the sense of the letter, but when the expression passes towards heaven, the harshness is removed, and it becomes gentle and mild. As also in Matthew, "Watch ye, because ye know not in what hour your Lord cometh; this know ye, if the father of the family knew *in what hour the thief would come*, he would watch, and would not suffer his house to be dug through," xxiv. 42, 43. And in the Apocalypse, "Unless thou watchest, *I will come upon thee as a thief*, and thou shalt not know in what hour I will come upon thee", iii. 3 Again, "*Behold I come as a thief* blessed is he who

watcheth and keepeth his garments," xvi. 15; speaking of the
Lord, where as a thief signifies nothing else but unawares and
unexpectedly. To steal, in the internal sense, is to claim to
oneself that which is the Lord's, namely, good and truth, and
whereas all do this in the beginning of regeneration, and that
is the first state of innocence (see just above, n. 4001), therefore
the expression is milder than it sounds in the letter: consequently, that was stolen with me, signifies that it was not his.

4003. Verses 34, 35, 36. *And Laban said, Behold let it be
according to thy word. And he removed in that day the he-
goats variegated and spotted, and all the she-goats speckled and
spotted, every thing that had white in it, and every thing black
in the lambs, and gave them into the hand of his sons. And
he set a way of three days between himself and between Jacob ;
and Jacob fed the rest of Laban's flocks.* Laban said, Behold
let it be according to thy word, signifies consent: and he removed in that day the he-goats variegated and spotted, signifies
that those truths of good were separated which were sprinkled
and mixed with the evils and falses, which were proper to the
good signified by Laban : and all the she-goats speckled and
spotted, signifies the goods thereof wherein evils and falses
were mixed : every thing which had white in it, signifies truth :
and every thing black in the lambs, signifies the proprium of
innocence : and gave them into the hand of his sons, signifies
that those things were given to truths : and he set a way of
three days between himself and between Jacob, signifies their
state altogether separated : and Jacob fed the rest of Laban's
flocks, signifies that from those which were left he took those
goods and truths which might be conjoined.

4004. "Laban said, Behold let it be according to thy word "
—that this signifies consent, appears without explication.

4005. "And he removed in that day the he-goats variegated and spotted"—that this signifies that those truths of good
were separated which were sprinkled and mixed with the evils
and falses, which were proper to the good signified by Laban,
appears from the signification of removing, as being to separate ; and from the signification of he-goats, as being truths of
good, of which we shall speak presently ; and from the signification of variegated, as being what is sprinkled and mixed
with evils, of which also we shall speak presently ; and from
the signification of spotted, as being what is sprinkled and
mixed with falses, concerning which see above. Mention is
here made of he-goats, and afterwards of she-goats, for he-
goats signify truths of good, and she-goats, goods of truth, the
difference between which may be seen, n. 3995. In the Word,
an accurate distinction is made between males and females, as
is evident from the sacrifices and burnt-offerings, in which it
was specifically commanded what should be offered, whether a

he-lamb or a she-lamb, whether a he-goat or a she-goat, whether
a sheep or a ram, and so in other cases. From this it may be
manifest, that a male signifies one thing, and a female another.
Male, in general, signifies truth, and female, good; in the present case, therefore, he-goats signify the truths of good, and
she-goats, which are presently mentioned, the goods which are
adjoined thereto; and as a difference of this sort exists between
them, it is also said, that he removed the variegated he-goats,
but not the speckled, as is said of she-goats; for variegated
signifies truth sprinkled and mixed with evils, whereas speckled
signifies good sprinkled and mixed with evils, see above, n.
3993. Truth mixed with evils is properly of the understanding, but good mixed with evils is properly of the will; this is
the difference. That these are from the good signified by Laban, is evident, because they are from the flock of Laban, for
flock, in the Word, signifies good and truth, or, what is the
same thing, they who are in good and truth, thus who are of
the Lord's Church. This arcanum cannot be explained further,
because it cannot be made manifest, unless to an apprehension
at once instructed and enlightened concerning truths and goods;
for it ought to be known what is meant by truths of good, and
what by goods thence derived, also, that from one good, which
is here represented by Laban, so many various goods can be
separated. They who have no knowledge respecting these
things, do not know that every good contains innumerable
goods, and indeed so many, that they can scarcely be arranged
into common genera by the most skilful person, for there are
goods procured by truths, and truths born thence, from which
again there are goods procured. There are truths born from
goods, and this also in a series. There are goods mixed with
evils, and truths mixed with falses, concerning which see above,
n. 3993; and the mixtures and temperatures of these are so
various and manifold, as to exceed myriads of myriads, and
they are also varied according to all the states of life, and the
states of life, in general, are according to ages, and, in particular, according to affections, of whatever kind they be. Hence
it may in some sort be apprehended, that so many various
goods could be separated from the good of Laban, of which
goods some were adjoined to the truths signified by the sons of
Jacob, some were left, and from these latter others were derived.
But these things are of such a nature, as was said, that they
cannot be received except by an understanding which is at once
instructed and enlightened.

4006. "And all the she-goats speckled and spotted"—that
this signifies the goods thereof wherein evils and falses were
mixed, appears from the signification of she-goats, as being
goods of truth, see n. 3995, in the present case goods which
were adjoined to the truths treated of just above, n. 4005; and

from the signification of speckled, as being goods mixed with
evils; and from the signification of spotted, as being truths
mixed with falses, concerning which see n. 3993, 3995.

4007. "Every thing which had white in it"—that this sig
nifies wherein was truth, appears from the signification of white,
as being truth, but properly the Lord's justice and merit, and
hence the Lord's justice and merit appertaining to man, see n.
3301, 3993. The reason why white has this signification, is,
because the light of heaven which is from the Lord, and produces brightness and whiteness, signifies truth. What, therefore, is illustrated by that light, and becomes bright and white,
is what is called the Lord's justice and merit in man. They
who acknowledge and from good receive the Lord's justice,
and reject their own justice, are they who are specifically signified by the just, of whom the Lord says in Matthew, "The
just shall shine as the sun in the kingdom of the Father," xiii.
43. That white, shining, or bright has this signification, is
evident also from other passages in the Word, as in Moses,
"His eyes were redder than wine, and his teeth *whiter* than
milk," Gen. xlix. 12; speaking of Judah, who represents the
Lord as to the Divine [principle] of His love, and, in the internal sense, the celestial kingdom, thus the celestial man, as
may be seen, n. 3881. His eyes being redder than wine, signifies Divine Wisdom; His teeth being whiter than milk, signifies justice. So in David, "Thou shalt purify me with hys-
sop, and I shall be made clean, Thou shalt wash me, and *I shall
be whiter than snow*," Psalm li. 7. To wash and to be made
whiter than snow, signifies to be purified from sins, by the reception and putting on of the Lord's justice. So in the Apocalypse, "In the midst of the seven candlesticks was one like
unto the Son of Man, His head and *hairs were white*, as *white
wool, like snow*, and His eyes as a flame of fire," i. 13, 14.
Again, "Thou hast a few names in Sardis, who have not polluted ther garments, and *they shall walk with Me in white*,
because they are worthy; he who overcometh shall be *clothed
in white raiment*," iii. 4, 5. Again, "I counsel thee that thou
buy of Me gold purified with fire, that thou mayest be rich,
and that thou put on *white raiment*," iii. 18. Again, "There
were given to every soul under the altar *white garments*," vi. 9,
11. Again, "I saw them standing before the throne and before
the Lamb *clothed in white garments;* one of the elders said
unto me, Who are these *clothed in white garments*, and whence
came they? to whom I said, Lord, Thou knowest; He said
unto me, These are they who come out of great affliction, and
have washed their garments, and *have made their garments
white in the blood of the Lamb*," vii. 9, 13, 14. Again, "The
angels *clothed with linen white and shining*, and girded about
the breasts with golden girdles," xv. 6. Again, "I saw, when

behold a *white horse*, and He who sat upon him had a bow, to whom was given a crown," vi. 2. And in another place, " I saw heaven open, when behold a *white horse ;* His armies in heaven followed Him upon *white horses, clothed in fine linen white* and clean," xix. 11, 14. In all these passages white sig nifies the truth of faith, white raiment and white garments being nothing else ; but the truth of faith does not appertain to those who believe they have faith from themselves, or that they are wise from themselves, but to those who believe from the Lord ; the latter have faith and wisdom given them, for they attribute nothing of truth and good to themselves, still less do they believe that they merit by the truths and goods in themselves, and still less that they are justified thereby, but only by attributing those things to the Lord, thus all to grace and mercy. This it is to be clothed in white raiment, and also to make it white in the blood of the Lamb. There are two things which are put off by all who enter into heaven, namely, proprium and the confidence thence derived, and self-merit or proper justice, and they put on heavenly proprium which is from the Lord, and the Lord's merit or justice, and so far as they put on these, so far do they enter interiorly into heaven. These are the things specifically signified by red and by white, by red, the good of love which they then have, and by white, the truth of faith.

4008 " And every thing black in the lambs"—that this signifies the proprium of innocence, appears from what was said above, n. 3994, where the same words occur.

4009. "And gave into the hand of his sons"—that this signifies that those things were given to truths, appears from the signification of *sons*, as being truths, see n. 489, 491, 433, 2623, 3373. To give into their hands is to give to their authority and disposal, for hand signifies ability, see n. 878, 3387. The truths, which are here signified by sons, are what are called sensual, as belonging to things of sense, and are the outermost of the natural mind ; for the natural part of man on one side communicates with the sensual things of the body, and on the other part, with the rational things of the rational mind ; by those intermediates there is effected a kind of ascent from things sensual which are of the body, and are open towards the world, to things rational which are of the rational mind, and are open towards heaven, thus also a descent from the latter, that is, from heaven to the world. This effect exists in man alone. It is this ascent and descent which is treated of in the internal sense of these chapters ; and in order that all and singular the things may be exhibited representatively, the rational is represented by Isaac and Rebecca, the natural by Jacob and his two women, and the sensual by their sons ; but whereas in the sensual, as the ultimate of order, prior principles co-exist, therefore every son represents some general principle in which those prior principles are, as has been shown above.

4010. "And he set a way of three days between himself and between Jacob"—that this signifies their state altogether separated, appears from the signification of setting a way, as being to be separated; and from the signification of three, as being the ultimate, the complete, or the end, see n. 1825, 2788, thus, what is altogether separated; and from the signification of days, as being states, see n. 23, 487, 488, 493, 893, 2788, 3462.

4011. "And Jacob fed the rest of Laban's flocks"—that this signifies that from those which were left he took those goods and truths which might be conjoined, appears from the signification of flocks, as being goods and truths, see n. 343, 2566, 3767, 3768, 3772, 3783. That to feed the rest of the flocks is to take from those that were left those goods and truths which might be conjoined, is evident from what follows, for in what follows this is the subject treated of.

4012. Verses 37, 38, 39, 40. *And Jacob took to himself a fresh rod of poplar, and hazel, and plane-tree, and peeled in them white peelings, making bare the white which was on the rods. And he set the rods which he peeled in gutters, in the drinking-troughs of water whither the flocks came to drink, over against the flocks, and they grew warm in coming to drink. And the flock grew warm at the rods, and the flocks brought forth variegated, speckled, and spotted. And Jacob separated the lambs, and gave the faces of the flock to the variegated, and all the black in the flock of Laban, and he set for himself droves for himself alone, and did not set them to the flock of Laban.* Jacob took to himself a fresh rod of poplar, signifies own proper ability of natural good: and hazel and plane-tree, signifies ability thence of natural truths: and peeled in them white peelings, making bare the white which was on the rods, signifies the arrangement of the ability of interior truth: and he set the rods which he peeled in gutters, signifies further preparation: in the drinking-troughs of water whither the flocks came to drink, signifies the affections of truth: over against the flocks, and they grew warm in their coming to drink, signifies even to ardour of affection, that they might be conjoined: and the flocks grew warm at the rods, signifies effect from own proper ability: and the flocks brought forth variegated, speckled, and spotted, signifies that hence natural good itself had such things by virtue of the middle good signified by Laban: and Jacob separated the lambs, signifies as to innocence: and gave the faces of the flock to the variegated, signifies to truth sprinkled with evils and falses: and all the black, signifies to such a state: in the flock of Laban, signifies in the good signified by Laban: and he set for himself droves for himself alone, signifies separation of goods and truths by virtue of own proper ability: and did not set them to the flock of Laban, signifies absolute separation from the good signified by Laban.

4013. "And Jacob took to himself a fresh rod of poplar"— that this signifies own proper ability of natural good, appears from the signification of rod, as being ability; and from the signification of poplar, as being good of the natural principle. of which we shall speak presently. Mention is made of rod in the Word throughout, and it every where signifies ability, as well from the fact of its being used by shepherds, for the sake of having power over their flocks, as from its serving for the support of the body, and as it were for a right hand, for hand signifies ability, see n. 878, 3387. But as this was the signification of rod, it was also used of old by kings; hence a staff and also a sceptre was a badge of royalty; nor was it used by kings only, but also by priests and prophets, that these latter also by a rod might signify the ability which they had, as in the case of Moses and Aaron, on which account Moses was so often commanded to stretch out his rod, and in some cases his rand, when miracles were to be wrought, and this because Divine Ability was signified by the rod, and by the hand. In consequence of the signification of rod being ability, the Egyptian magicians also used it, when they performed magical miracles. Hence at this day, magicians are represented by rods in the hand. From these facts it may appear, that rod signifies ability. In the original, however, the rods used by shepherds, and kings, and by priests and prophets, are expressed by a different expression; in the present case by an expression denoting the staff of travellers, and also of shepherds, as may appear from passages in other parts of the Word, as Gen. xxxii. 10; Exod. xii. 11; 1 Sam. xvii. 40, 43; Zech. xi. 7, 10. In the present case indeed rod is not mentioned as supporting the hand, but as a twig cut from a tree, namely, from a poplar, a hazel, and a plane-tree, to set in the watering-troughs before the faces of the flock, but still it signifies the same signification, for thereby in an internal sense is described the power of natural good, and thence of natural truths. In respect to poplar, of which the rod was made, it is to be observed, that trees in general signify perceptions and knowledges, perceptions when they are predicated of the celestial man, but knowledges when predicated of the spiritual man, see n. 103, 2163, 2682, 2722, 2972. Hence trees in particular signify goods and truths, for these are of perceptions and knowledges. Some species of trees signify interior goods and truths, which are of the spiritual man, as olives and vines, and some species exterior goods and truths which are of the natural man, as the poplar, the hazel, and the plane-tree. And as, in ancient times, every tree signified some species of good and truth, hence worship was performed in groves according to the species of trees, see n. 2722. The poplar which is here mentioned is the white poplar, so called from whiteness, whence its derivation. Hence it was, that poplar signified good which was from truth, or what is the same thing, good of truth, as also in Hosea, chap. iv. 13, but here falsified.

4014. "And hazel and plane-tree"—that this signifies the ability thence of natural truths, appears from the signification of hazel and plane-tree, as being natural truths. That this is the signification of those trees, cannot so well appear from other passages in the Word, because they are not mentioned elsewhere, except the plane-tree, in Ezekiel, "The cedars did not conceal him in the garden of God, the fir-trees were not equal to his branches, and the *plane-trees* were not as his branches, there was not any tree equal to him in its beauty," xxxi. 8; speaking of the scientific and rational principles in the man of the spiritual Church. The garden of God is the spiritual Church cedars are rational principles, fir-trees and plane-trees are natural principles, fir-trees natural principles as to good, and plane-trees, as to truth.

4015. "And peeled in them white peelings, making bare the white which was on the rods"—that this signifies the arrangement of the ability of interior truth, appears from the signification of peeling and of peelings, as being the removal of exterior things, in order that interior things may be manifested, thus the making bare; and from the signification of white, as being truth, see n. 3993, 4007; and from the signification of rod, as being ability, see n. 4013, in the present case interior ability, because upon the rods underneath the bark. The arrangement of the ability of interior truth is the ability of the interior man into the exterior, or of the spiritual man into the natural. All arrangement of good and truth in the natural man comes from the spiritual man, that is, through the spiritual man from the Lord, and indeed through the truth therein, for the Lord flows into the good of the spiritual or interior man, and through the truth there into the natural man, but not through the good immediately, until man is regenerated: wherefore all arrangement in the natural man is effected from the interior man. The natural principle or the natural man cannot possibly otherwise be arranged, that is, be regenerated. That it is effected from the interior man is manifest from the acknowledgment of truth, which is not acknowledgment unless it be from the interior man, also from conscience, which is acknowledgment of truth from an interior principle, and likewise from perception. Since arrangement from the interior man is effected by truth, therefore ability is predicated of truth, and also of rod which signifies ability, see n. 3091; as may be confirmed from several passages in the Word. Not that truth has in it any ability from itself, but from good, and thus there is ability in truth from good, that is, through good from the Lord. Hence it may in some measure appear what is meant by the arrangement of the ability of interior truth. In the supreme sense, wherein the Lord is treated of, it signifies own proper ability, for the Divine has own proper ability, because it comes from no other.

4016. " And he set the rods which he peeled in gutters"—that this signifies further preparation, appears from what follows, for the subject treated of is the effect of the interior power of truth in the natural principle, for rods signify power, see n. 4013, 4015 ; peeling, arrangement from the interior principle, n. 4015, and gutters, the good of truth in the natural principle, n. 3095.

4017. " In the drinking-troughs of water, whither the flocks came to drink"—that this signifies the affections of truth, appears from the signification of water, as being knowledges and scientifics, which are truths of the natural principle, see n. 28, 2702, 3058 ; and from the signification of drinking-troughs, which, as being continents of water, in the internal sense are goods of truth, for goods are the continents of truth, see n. 3095 ; and from the signification of coming to drink, as being the affection of truth. The reason why coming to drink denotes the affection of truth is, because it implies thirst, for thirst in the Word signifies appetite and desire, thus the affection of knowing and imbibing truth, and this because water signifies truth in general ; whereas hunger signifies the appetite, the desire, and thus the affection of imbibing good, and this because bread, which is taken for food in general (see n. 2165), signifies good. Hence it is evident that these words signify the affections of truth.

4018. " Over against the flocks, and they grew warm in coming to drink"—that this signifies even to ardour of affection that they might be conjoined, appears from the signification of growing warm in coming to drink, as denoting ardour of affection. That to grow warm denotes ardour, is evident, and that to come to drink denotes the affection of truth, see just above, n. 4017. The reason why over against the flocks denotes that truths and goods of the natural principle might be conjoined, is, because it implies intuition, and thence excited affection, for thus spiritual principles are conjoined. Moreover all implantation of truth and good, and also all conjunction, is wrought by affection. Truths and goods which are learnt, wherewith man is not affected, enter indeed into the memory, but adhere thereto as lightly as a feather to a wall, which is blown away by the slightest breath of wind. In respect to things which enter into the memory, the case is this : those which enter without affection fall into its shade, but those which enter with affection, into its light, and the things which are there in light are seen and appear clearly and livingly on every exciting of a similar thing, but not so the things which lie hid round about in the shade. This is a consequence of the affection which is of love. Hence it may appear, that all implantation of truth, and conjunction thereof with good, is wrought by affection, and the greater the affection, the stronger is the conjunction. Ardour of affection, in the present case, is inmost affection. Truths, however, cannot be implanted and conjoined with good, except by the affections of truth and good, which affections flow from charity towards the neighbour, and from love to the Lord, as from their proper fountains; but evils and falses are implanted and conjoined by affections of what is evil and false, which affections flow from self-love and the love of the world as their sources. This being the case, and the subject here treated of, in the internal sense, being the conjunction of good and truth in the natural man, therefore here, and in what follows, mention is made of the flock growing warm when they came to drink, whereby such things are signified.

4019. "And the flocks grew warm at the rods"—that this signifies effect from own proper ability, appears from the signification of growing warm in the present case, as being the effect, namely, of affection, see n. 4018; and from the signification of rods, as being own proper ability, see above, n. 4013, 4015.

4020. "And the flocks brought forth variegated, speckled, and spotted"—that this signifies that hence natural good had such things by virtue of the middle good signified by Laban, appears from the signification of bringing forth, as being acknowledgment and conjunction, see n. 3911, 3915; and from the signification of variegated, as being truths mixed with evils, see n. 4005; and from the signification of speckled, as being goods mixed with evils; and from the signification of spotted, as being truths mixed with falses, see n. 3993, 3995, 4005. Such are the things which are here signified, and which acceded to the good of natural truth represented by Jacob, from the good signified by Laban.

4021. "And Jacob separated the lambs"—that this signifies as to innocence, appears from the signification of lambs, as being innocence, see n. 3994. I use the words, as to innocence, because the subject treated of in what now follows is the arrangement of the good and truth of the natural principle to receive innocence, and to be fitted thereto.

4022. "And gave the faces of the flock to the variegated" —that this signifies to truths sprinkled with evils and falses, appears from the signification of variegated, as being truth sprinkled and mixed with evils, see n. 4005, 4020.

4023. "And all the black"—this signifies to such a state,

as is signified by black in the lambs, of which state, see n. 3994, 4001.

4024. "In the flock of Laban"—that this signifies in the good signified by Laban, appears from the signification of flock, and from the representation of Laban, as being good, namely, middle good, whereby the natural principle has goods and truths, of which see above.

4025. "And he set for himself droves for himself alone"—that this signifies separation of goods and truths from his own ability, appears from the signification of droves, or of the flock, as being goods and truths; and from the signification of setting for himself, for himself alone, as being to separate those things which were procured by his own ability. The subject here treated of, in the supreme sense, is how the Lord made His natural principle Divine, and this from His own ability, but still by means according to order. The goods and truths, which He made Divine in Himself, are here the droves which He set for Himself, for Himself alone.

4026. "And did not set them to the flock of Laban"—that this signifies separation absolute from the good signified by Laban, appears from what has been already said, thus without further explication; for goods and truths Divine are altogether separate from those goods and truths which partake at all of what is human, for they transcend, and become infinite.

4027. The things which have been here unfolded, in the internal sense, are too interior and too hidden to admit of being clearly explained to the understanding; for the subject treated of in the supreme sense, is how the Lord made His natural principle Divine; and in the representative sense, how the Lord makes man's natural principle new when He regenerates him; all these things are here fully exhibited in the internal sense. The things therein contained in the supreme sense concerning the Lord, how He made the natural in Himself Divine, are such as to exceed even angelic understanding. Something of them may be seen in the regeneration of man, because the regeneration of man is an image of the Lord's glorification, see n. 3138, 3212, 3296, 3490. Of regeneration man may have some idea, but not unless he be regenerated; nevertheless it will be but an obscure one so long as he lives in the body, for corporeal and worldly things, in which even the regenerate man is, continually pour forth clouds, and keep the mind in lower things. Those, however, who are not regenerated, cannot possibly have any conception on the subject, being out of the knowledges thereof because out of perceptions; yea, they are totally ignorant what regeneration is, nor do they believe that it can possibly exist. They do not even know the nature of the affection of charity whereby regeneration is effected, nor consequently of conscience, still less of the internal man, and still less of the correspondence of the internal man with the external; the words indeed they may know, and several do know them, but the thing they are ignorant of. And as the knowledge of these things is wanting, however clearly the arcana should be explained which are contained in the internal sense, still it would be like holding something before the sight in darkness, or saying something to the deaf. Moreover, the affections of selfish and worldly love which prevail with the unregenerate, do not allow them to know such things, nor even to hear, for they reject them instantly, yea, spew them back again. The case is otherwise with those who are in the affection of charity; they are delighted with such things, for their attendant angels are in their happiness when man is in them, because they are then in those things which treat of the Lord, in Whom they are, and which treat of their neighbour and of his regeneration. From the angels, that is, through the angels from the Lord, delight and blessedness flow into the man who is in the affection of charity, when he reads those things, and more so when he believes a holiness to be in them, and still more when he apprehends any thing which is contained in the internal sense. The subject treated of in what has been said hitherto, is the influx of the Lord into the good of the internal man, and indeed through the good into the truth; also the influx thence into the external or natural man; and the affection of good and truth into which the influx is made, and likewise the reception of truth, and the conjunction thereof with good there; moreover the good which serves as a medium, and which is here signified by Laban and his flock. On these subjects the angels who are in the internal sense of the Word, or to whom the internal sense is the Word, see and perceive innumerable things, whereof scarcely any one can come to the understanding of man, and what does come, falls into its obscurity, which is the reason why these things are not explained more particularly.

4028. Verses 41, 42. *And it came to pass as every one of the flock of the first in coition grew warm, that Jacob set the rods at the eyes of the flock in the gutters, to cause them to grow warm at the rods. And to the flock next to be in coition he did not set them, and of the next in coition was Laban's, and of the first in coition was Jacob's.* It came to pass as every one of the flock of the first in coition grew warm, signifies those things which were spontaneous: Jacob set the rods at the eyes of the flock in the gutters, to cause them to grow warm at the rods, signifies things called forth and conjoined from his own ability: and to the flock next to be in coition he did not set them, signifies things compelled: and of the next in coition was Laban's, signifies that those things were left: and of the first in coition was Jacob's, signifies that the spontaneous things, or those which were from his own freedom, were conjoined.

4029. "It came to pass as every one of the flock of the first in coition grew warm"—that this signifies those things which were spontaneous, appears from the signification of growing warm, as being the ardour and effect of affection (see above, n. 4018, 4019); and from the signification of flock, as being truth and good (of which see also above); and from the signification of the first in coition, as being things spontaneous. That the first in coition are things spontaneous, is evident from the connection of things in the internal sense, as well as from the fact, that whatever comes from affection is spontaneous, and especially from the ardour of affection, which is signified by growing warm, wherefore in this verse there is mention twice made of growing warm; as also from the derivation of this expression in the original tongue, as denoting conjunction by the inmost principle of love, and the subject here treated of is the conjunction of truth and good in the natural principle, which can only be wrought by what is spontaneous, that is, in freedom. Hence it may appear, that the words, "as every one of the flock of the first in coition grew warm," or in all the warmth of the first in coition of the flock, signify truths and goods which are spontaneous or from a freedom, or what is the same thing, from utmost affection. That every thing which is of love or affection is free, may be seen, n. 2870; that all conjunction of truth and good is wrought in freedom, and that there is no conjunction in what is compelled, see n. 2875, 3145, 3146, 3158; consequently that all reformation and regeneration is wrought by freedom, n. 1937, 1947, 2876, 2881, 2877, 2878, 2879, 2880; if it could be wrought by compulsion, that all would be saved, n. 2881.

4030. "And Jacob set the rods at the eyes of the flock in the gutters to cause them to grow warm at the rods"—that this signifies things called forth and conjoined from his own ability, appears from the signification of rods, as being ability, and when it is predicated of the Lord, His own ability, see n. 4013, 4015; and from the signification of setting at the eyes in the gutters to cause to grow warm, as being to call forth that they might be conjoined, as appears from what has been said above, n. 4018, and elsewhere, concerning the signification of those expressions.

4031. "And to the flock next to be in coition he did not set"—that this signifies things compelled, appears from the signification of next to be in coition. That being first in coition denotes what is spontaneous, or free, was shown above, n. 4029; hence, and also from the connection of things in the internal sense, it is evident that being next in coition denotes what is compelled or not free. The same appears also from the fact, that here it is not said, "to cause to grow warm," as was said of the first in coition, for causing to grow warm signifies affec-

tion, and in this case the ardour of affection ; whatever is not
of affection is from a want of spontaneousness or freedom, every
thing spontaneous or free being of affection or of love, see n.
2870.   The same appears also from the derivation of this expression in the original tongue, as denoting deficiency, for when
ardour of affection is deficient, then freedom ceases, and what
is wrought in such case is said to be not free, and at length
compelled.   That all conjunction of truth and good is effected
in freedom, or from what is spontaneous, consequently all reformation and regeneration, may appear from the passages
above cited, n. 4029. Of course in non-freedom, or compulsion,
no conjunction and no regeneration can be wrought.   What is
meant by freedom, and whence it is, may be seen, n. 2870 to
2893, where the freedom of man was treated of.   He who does
not know that no conjunction of good and truth, that is, appropriation, thus that no regeneration can be wrought except
in man's freedom, if he reasons concerning the Lord's providence, the salvation of man, and the damnation of several, will
cast himself into mere shades, and thence into grievous errors ;
for he supposes that the Lord, if He be willing, can save every
one, and this by innumerable means, as by miracles, by the
dead who shall rise again, by immediate revelations, by angels
who shall withhold from evils, and shall impel to good by a
manifestly strong force, and by several states, leading man to
do the work of repentance when they are induced, and by many
things besides.   But he does not know that all these means are
compulsory, and that man cannot be reformed by them, for
whatever compels man does not impart to him any affection
and if it be of such a nature as to impart, it ties itself to the
affection of evil ; for it appears as if it infused a sanctity, and
this indeed is the case, but still when the state is changed, the
man returns to his former affections, that is, to evils and falses
and he then conjoins that sanctity with what is evil and false,
and it becomes profane, and then is of such a nature as to lead
into the most grievous hell of all.   For he first acknowledges
and believes, and is also affected with what is holy, and afterwards he denies and even holds it in aversion. That they who
acknowledge in heart, and afterwards deny, are they who profane, but not so they who have not acknowledged in heart, may
be seen, n. 301, 302, 303, 571, 582, 593, 1001, 1008, 1010, 1059,
1327, 1328, 2051, 2426, 3398, 3399, 3402, 3898. Hence at this
day manifest miracles are not wrought, but unapparent or in
visible ones, which are such as not to infuse a holy principle,
nor take away man's freedom · and hence the dead do not rise
again, neither is man withheld from evils and led to good by
a manifestly strong force, either by immediate revelations or
by angels. It is man's freedom on which the Lord operates,
and by which He bends him ; for all freedom is of love or its

affection, consequently of the will thereof, see n. 3158. If he does not receive good and truth in freedom, it cannot be appropriated to him, or become his: that to which he is compelled is not his, but belongs to him who compels, since he does it not from himself, although it is done by himself. It appears sometimes as if man is compelled to good, as in temptations and spiritual combats, but that at such times he has a stronger freedom than at other times, may be seen, n. 1937, 1947, 2881. It appears also as if man were compelled to good, when he compels himself to it, but it is one thing for a man to compel himself, and another thing to be compelled; he who compels himself, does it from freedom within, whereas to be compelled is from non-freedom. This being the case, it may appear into what shades, and thence into what errors, those may cast themselves, who reason concerning the Lord's providence, the salvation of man, and the damnation of several, and do not know that freedom is the means by which the Lord operates, and in no wise compulsion, for compulsion in holy things is dangerous, unless it be received from freedom.

4033. "And of the next in coition was Laban's"—that this signifies that things compelled were left; and that "of the first in coition was Jacob's," signifies that things spontaneous, or those which were from his freedom, were conjoined, appears from what has been said just above, n. 4029, 4032. By things compelled are here signified things which were not conjoined, nor could be conjoined; and by things spontaneous, those which were conjoined and also were capable of being so. The reason why these latter things are signified, is, because things spontaneous are according to the affections and the quality thereof. After the good which is signified by Laban and his flock had served those uses which are spoken of above, it is then separated; the separation is treated of in the following chapter.

4034. Verse 43. *And the man spread himself abroad exceedingly exceedingly, and he had many flocks, and maidservants, and men-servants, and camels, and asses.* The man spread himself abroad exceedingly exceedingly, signifies multiplication: and he had many flocks, signifies interior goods and truths thence derived: and maid-servants and men-servants, signify middle goods and truths: and camels and asses, signify truths of good exterior and external.

4035. "And the man spread himself abroad exceedingly exceedingly"—that this signifies the multiplication of good and truth, appears from the signification of spreading himself abroad, as being to be multiplied; that it was to an immense degree, is signified by exceedingly exceedingly.

4036. "And he had many flocks"—that this signifies interior goods and truths thence derived, appears from the signification

₰f flocks, as being goods and truths, see n. 343; that they were interior, see n. 2566, 3783.

4037. "And maid-servants and men-servants"—that this signifies middle goods and truths, that is, natural goods and truths themselves, appears from the signification of maid-servants, as being the affections of the natural principle, consequently the goods therein, see n. 1895, 2567, 3835, 3849; and from the signification of men-servants, as being the scientifics which are the truths of the natural man, see n. 2567, 3019, 3020, 3409.

4038. "And camels and asses"—that this signifies truths of good exterior and external, appears from the signification of camels, as being the common scientifics of the natural man, see n. 3048, 3071, 3143, 3145; (common scientifics are the inferior or exterior truths of good;) and from the signification of asses, as being truths of good still inferior or external, see n. 2781. What is meant by interior goods and truths, also by middle, and likewise by exterior and external, may appear from what is said, n. 4009. There are three things in general in man, namely, the corporeal, the natural, and the rational. The corporeal principle is the outmost, the natural is the middle, the rational is the interior. So far as one prevails with man above the other, so far he is said to be either corporeal, or natural, or rational. These three parts of man wonderfully communicate, namely, the corporeal with the natural, and the natural with the rational. When man is first born, he is merely corporeal, but there is a faculty in him rendering him capable of being perfected. Afterwards he becomes natural, at length rational; and hence it may appear that there is a communication of one principle with the other. The corporeal communicates with the natural by the things of sense, and this distinctly by those things which pertain to the understanding, and which pertain to the will, for each is to be perfected in man, that he may be made and be a man. The sensual of the sight and hearing especially are what perfect his intellectual faculty, the three remaining sensuals have especial respect to the will. The corporeal principle of man, by means of those sensuals, communicates with his natural principle, which is the middle part, as was said; for those things which enter by the sensuals, repose themselves in the natural principle as in a sort of receptacle; this receptacle is the memory. The delight, pleasure, and cupidity therein pertain to the will, and are called natural goods, whereas the scientifics therein pertain to the understanding, and are called natural truths. The natural principle of man, by these things which are now spoken of, communicates with his rational principle, which is the interior part, as was said. The things which elevate themselves thence towards the rational principle, repose themselves in the rational principle also as in a sort of receptacle ; this receptacle is the interior memory, see n. 2469, 2470, 2471, 2472, 2473 to 2480. What is blessed and happy herein pertains to the will, and is of rational good, whereas interior views of things and perceptions pertain to the understanding, and all things relating thereto are called rational truths. These three things are what constitute man. There are communications between them : external sensuals are the things by which man's corporeal principle communicates with his natural, and interior sensuals are the things by which man's natural principle communicates with his rational. The things therefore in man's natural principle which are derived from external sensuals that are proper to the body, are what are called the truths of good exterior and external ; but what are derived from internal sensuals, which are proper to his spirit, and communicate with the rational principle, are what are called interior goods and truths. What are between these, and partake of each principle, are what are called middle goods and truths. These three are in order from the interiors, and they are signified, in the internal sense, by flocks, by maid-servants and men-servants, and by camels and asses.

A CONTINUATION OF THE SUBJECT CONCERNING THE GRAND MAN, AND CONCERNING CORRESPONDENCE WITH THE CEREBRUM AND THE CEREBELLUM.

4039. *THE correspondence of the heart and of the lungs with the* GRAND MAN, *or with heaven, was treated of at the end of the preceding chapter ; the subject now about to be treated of is the correspondence of the cerebrum and the cerebellum, and of the medullæ which are annexed thereto. But before treating of the correspondence, I must premise some particulars of the form of the brain in general, whence it is, and what it represents.*

4040. *When the brain is denuded of the skull and the teguments which encompass it, wonderful circumvolutions and gyres are brought into view, containing what are called the cortical substances. From these run the fibres which constitute the medulla part of the brain. These fibres then proceed by nerves into the body, and there perform functions according to the directions and sovereign disposals of the brain. All these things are altogether in a heavenly form ; such form being imprinted by the Lord on the heavens, and thence on those things which are in man, and especially on his cerebrum and cerebellum.*

4041. *The heavenly form is stupendous, and altogether ex-*

ceeds all human intelligence, for it is far above the ideas of the forms which man can in any wise conceive from worldly things, even by analytic means. All the heavenly societies are arranged in that form, and what is wonderful, there is a gyration along the forms, which angels and spirits are not sensible of. This is like the case of the flux of the earth about its axis daily, and about the sun yearly, which the inhabitants do not perceive. The quality of the heavenly form in the lowest sphere was shown me; it was like that of the circumvolutions which appear in the human brains, and it was given me perceptibly to see that flux or those gyrations. This continued for some days; and it enabled me to conclude that the brain is formed according to the form of the fluxion of heaven. The interior things, however, which are therein, and which do not appear to the eye, are according to the interior forms of heaven, which are quite incomprehensible; and it was said by the angels, that man is created according to the forms of the three heavens, and that thus there is impressed on him the image of heaven, so that man is, in the least form, a little heaven, and that hence comes his correspondence with the heavens.

4042. Hence then it is that through man alone there is a descent from the heavens into the world, and an ascent from the world into the heavens. The brain and its interiors are the means, by which the descent and ascent is effected, for there are the very principles, or the first and last ends, from which all and singular the things in the body flow forth and are derived; it is there also whence come the thoughts which are of the understanding, and the affections which are of the will.

4043. The reason why the forms still more interior, which also are more universal, are, as was said, not comprehensible, is, because when forms are named, they carry with them an idea of space and time, when yet, in the interiors, where heaven is, not any thing is perceived by spaces and by times, these being proper to nature, but by states and their variations and changes. But as variations and changes cannot be conceived by man without such things as relate to form, as was said before, and also to space and time, when yet such things do not exist in the heavens; it may hence appear how incomprehensible these things are, and also how ineffable. All the human words, moreover, by which they must be uttered and comprehended, inasmuch as they involve natural things, are inadequate to express them. In the heavens such things are exhibited by variations of heavenly light and of heavenly flame, which come from the Lord, and this in such and so great a fulness, that thousands and thousands of perceptions can scarce fall upon any thing perceptible with man. Still, however, the things which are doing in the heavens, are represented in the world of spirits by forms, to which the forms which appear in the world bear some similitude.

4042—4046.] GENESIS. 459

4044. *Representations are nothing but images of spiritual things in natural, and when the latter are rightly represented in the former, they then correspond. But he who does not know what the spiritual is, but only what the natural, would suppose that such representations and consequent correspondences were not possible, for he would say to himself, How can what is spiritual act upon what is material? But if he would reflect upon those things which are doing every moment in himself, he might be able to procure some idea thereof, namely, of how the will can act on the muscles of the body, and present real actions, and of how the thought can act on the organs of speech, by moving the lungs, the windpipe, the throat, the tongue, and the lips, and present speech; also of how the affections can act on the face, and there present images of themselves, so that hence what a person thinks and wills is often known to another. These cases may give some idea of representations and correspondences. Now as such things are exhibited in man, and as there is not any thing which can subsist from himself, but from another, and thus again from another, and finally from the First, and this by connection of correspondences; it may hence be concluded by those who have any extent of judgment, that there is a correspondence between man and heaven, and moreover, between heaven and the Lord, Who is the First.*

4045. *Since such a correspondence exists, and heaven is distinguished into numerous lesser heavens, and these into still lesser, and every where into societies, there are therein heavens which have reference to the cerebrum and the cerebellum in general, and in those heavens, such as have reference to the parts or members which exist in the brains; for instance, there are those which have reference to the dura mater, those which have reference to the pia mater, to the sinuses, and also to the bodies and cavities therein, as the corpus callosum, the corpora striata, the lesser glands, the ventricles, the infundibulum, and so forth. The nature of those which have such reference, has been discovered to me, as may appear from what follows.*

4046. *There appeared several spirits at a middle distance above the head, who acted in common by the manner of a pulse of the heart, but it was a kind of reciprocal undulation downwards and upwards, with a kind of cold breathing into my forehead. Hence I was enabled to conclude that they were of a middle sort, namely, that they belonged both to the province of the heart and to that of the lungs, and also that they were not interior spirits. They afterwards presented a flaming lumen, gross but still luminous, which first appeared under the left part of the chin, afterwards under the left eye, next above the eye, but it was obscure, yet still flaming, not bright. From these circumstances I was enabled to conclude as to their quality, for things luminous indicate affections as well as degrees of intelli jence. Afterwards, when I applied my hand to the left part of the skull or head, I was sensible of a pulse underneath the palm, undulating in like manner downwards and upwards, from which discovery I knew that they belonged to the brain. When I inquired who they were, they were unwilling to speak; it was said by others that they do not speak willingly. At length, being driven to speak, they said that thus it would be discovered what their quality was. I perceived that there were amongst them such as constitute the province of the dura mater, which is the common integument of the cerebrum or cerebellum. Afterwards it was discovered of what quality they were, for it was given me to know it from discourse with them. They were, as during their lives when men, such as thought nothing of spiritual and celestial things, nor spake about them, because they believed only in what was natural, and this because they could not penetrate further; nevertheless they did not confess this. Still, however, like others, they worshipped the Divine, had stated times of prayer, and were good citizens. There were afterwards others, who also flowed into the pulse, yet not by undulation downwards and upwards, but transversely; others again, who flowed in, not reciprocally, but more continuously; and also others, whose pulse beat with activity from one place to another. They said, that they had reference to the exterior thin plate of the dura mater; and that they were amongst those who thought about spiritual and celestial things only from such things as are objects of the external senses, having no other conception of interior things. Judging from what I heard, they seemed to be of the female sex. They who reason from external sensual, consequently from worldly and terrestrial things, of things which belong to heaven, that is, of the spiritualities of faith and love, in proportion as they unite and confound those things, go more exteriorly, even to the external skin of the head, which they represent; but still if they have lived a life of good, they are within the GRAND MAN, although in its extremes; for every one who is in the life of good from the affection of charity is saved.*

4047. There appeared also others above the head, whose common action flowing in above the head was fluent in a transverse direction from before backwards; and there appeared also others, whose influent action was from each temple towards the midst of the cerebrum. It was perceived that they were those who belonged to the province of the pia mater, which is another integument, investing more nearly the cerebrum and cerebellum, and communicating with them by emitted threads. It was given me to know their quality from their discourse, for they talked with me. They were as they had been in the world, not trusting much to their own thought, and thereby determining themselves to think any thing certain on holy things, but depending on the faith of others, and not canvassing any point to discover whether

*it was true. That this was their quality, was only shown me
by an influx of their perception into the Lord's prayer whilst I
was reading it; for all spirits and angels, whatever be their
number, may be known as to their quality from the Lord's
prayer, and this, by an influx of the ideas of thought and of
their affections into the contents of the prayer. Hence also it
was perceived that they were such in quality; and, moreover,
that they could serve the angels as media (there are spirits mediate between the heavens, by whom communication is effected);
for their ideas were not closed, but open, thus they suffered themselves to be acted upon, and easily admitted and received the
influx. Besides, they were modest and pacific, and said they
were in heaven.*

4048. *There was a certain spirit near at my head, who spake
with me; I perceived from the tone of his voice, that he was in
a state of tranquillity, as of a kind of peaceful sleep. He asked
this thing and that, but with such prudence, that a person awake
could not have asked more prudently. It was perceived tha
interior angels spake by him, and that he was in such a stat
as to perceive and produce what they spake. I asked concernin
that state, and told him that his state was such. He replied
that he spake nothing but what is good and true, and that h
apperceived whether any thing else flows in, and in case it did,
he did not admit or utter it. Of his state he said that it was
peaceful, and it was also given to perceive it by communication.
It was said that they who have reference to the sinuses or larger
blood-vessels in the cerebrum are of such a quality; and that
they who are like him, have reference to the longitudinal sinus,
which is between the two hemispheres of the brain, and are there
in a state of peace, however the brain on each side be in tumult.*

4049. *There were certain spirits above the head a little in
front, who spake with me. They discoursed pleasantly, and
their influx was tolerably gentle. They were distinguished from
others by this, that they had continually an eagerness and desire
to come into heaven. It was said that they who have reference
to the ventricles or larger cavities of the brain, and belong to
that province, are of this nature. The reason was also added,
that the better species of lymph which is therein, is of such a
nature, namely, as to return into the brain, and hence also has
such a tendency. The brain is heaven; the tendency is eagerness and desire: such are the correspondences.*

4050. *There first appeared to me a certain face over an
azure window, which face presently betook itself inwards. There
then appeared a little star about the region of the left eye; afterwards, several fiery stars which had a white glitter. Next appeared walls, but no roof, the walls only on the left side; lastly,
as it were the starry heaven: but whereas these things were seen
in a place where evil spirits were, I imagined that it was some*

*what hideous which was presented me to see. Presently, how-
ever, the wall and the heaven disappeared, and I saw a well,
out of which came forth as it were a bright mist or vapour; it
seemed also as if something was pumped out of the well. I inquired what these things signified and represented? I was answered, that it was a representation of the infundibulum in the
brain, over which was the brain which is signified by heaven,
and what was next seen was that vessel which is signified by a
well, and is called the infundibulum, and that the mist or
vapour which arose thence was the lymph which passes through,
and is pumped out thence; and that this lymph was of a two-
fold kind, namely, what is mixed with the animal spirits, which
is among the useful lymphs, and what is mixed with the serosi-
ties, which is among the excrementitious lymphs. It was afterwards shown me what those are who belong to this province, but
only those who were of the viler sort. They were also seen;
they run about hither and thither, apply themselves to those
whom they see, attend to every particular, and tell others what
they hear, prone to suspicion, impatient, restless, in imitation
of that lymph which is therein and is conveyed to and fro, their
reasonings are the fluids there which represent. These, however,
are of the middle sort; but they who have reference to the excrementitious lymphs therein, are such as draw down spiritual
truths to things terrestrial, and there defile them, as for example, when they hear any thing concerning conjugial love, apply
it to whoredoms and adulteries, and thus draw down to these
the things which belong to conjugial love, and so in other cases.
These appeared in front at some distance to the right. But
they who are of the good sort, are like those spoken of just above,
n. 4049.*

*4051. There are societies which have reference to that region
in the brain which is called the isthmus, and also to the little
knots of fibres in the brain, of a kind of glandular appearance,
from which fibres proceed for various functions, which fibres
act in unity in those principles or glands, but in different ways
in the extremes. One society of the spirits, to which such things
correspond, was presented to me, of which I observed the following particulars: the spirits came in front, and accosted me,
saying, that they were men; but it was given me to reply, that
they were not men endowed with bodies, but spirits, and thus
also men, inasmuch as every thing of spirit conspires to that
which is of man, even to a form similar to man endowed with
body, for the spirit is the internal man; also because men are
men from intelligence and wisdom, and not from form; consequently, that good spirits, and especially angels, are more eminently men than they who are in the body, because they are more
in the light of wisdom. After this reply they said, that there
were several in the society, in which there was not one like an*

other ; but as it seemed to me impossible that a society of dis-similars can exist in the other life, I spoke with them on this subject, and was at length instructed, that although dissimilar, still they are consociated as to end, which was one to them. They said further, that they are such that every one acts and speaks dissimilarly from every other, and that still they are similar in will and thought. This they illustrated by an exam-ple : as that when one in the society says of an angel, that he is the least in heaven, another says he is the greatest, and a third, that he is neither least nor greatest, and this with further variety ; and that still the thoughts act in unity, since he who wills to be least is the greatest, and is thence respectively the greatest, and that there is neither least nor greatest, because they do not think of super-eminence ; and so in other cases. Thus they are consociated in principles, but act differently in extremes. They applied themselves to my ear, and said, that they were good spirits, and that such was their manner of speaking. It was said of them, that it is not known whence they come, and that they are among wandering societies.

4052. Moreover, such is the correspondence of the brain with the GRAND MAN, *that they who are in the principles of good have reference to those things in the brain which are its princi-ples, and which are called glands or cortical substances ; whereas they who are in the principles of truth have reference to those things in the brain which proceed from those principles, and which are called fibres. There is, however, this distinction, that those who correspond to the right part of the brain, are in the will of good, and thence in the will of truth ; whereas those who correspond to the left of the brain, are in the understand-ing, and thence in the affection, of good and truth. The reason of this is, that those who are in heaven at the Lord's right hand, are in good from the will, but those who are at the Lord's left hand, are in good from the understanding. The former are called celestial, but the latter spiritual.*

4053. That there are such correspondences, has hitherto been known to no one, and I am aware that all who hear will won-der, and this because it is not known what the internal man is, and what the external, and that the internal man is in the spiritual world, and the external in the natural ; and that it is the internal man who lives in the external, and flows into and rules him. Hence, however, as well as from what was adduced above, n. 4044, it may be known that there is such a thing as influx and correspondence ; a fact which is most notorious in another life : also, that what is natural is nothing but a repre-sentation of things spiritual, from which it exists and subsists ; and that what is natural is representative in such a sort as it is correspondent.

4054. The brain, like heaven, is in a sphere of ends, **which** *are uses, for whatever flows from the Lord is an end having respect to the salvation of the human race. This is the end which rules in heaven, and which thence rules in the brain, for the brain, where the mind of man is, has respect to ends in the body, to wit, that the body may serve the soul, that the soul may be happy to eternity. But there are societies which have no end of use, only of enjoying the company of friends and mistresses, and the pleasures thence resulting, thus who live in self indulgence alone, and whose sole concern is a concubine, and whether a private or a public one, it is for the same end. The number of societies of such spirits at this day is incredible. As soon as they approach, their sphere operates, and extinguishes in others the affections of truth and good, and when these affections are extinguished, the spirits are in the pleasure of their friendship. They are obstipations of the brain, and induce in it stupidity. Several societies of such spirits have been with me, and their presence was perceptible from a dulness, languor, and privation of affection. Sometimes I have discoursed with them. They are pests and destructions, though in civil life, during their abode in the world, they appeared to be good, delightful, facetious, and ingenious, for they are skilled in grace and fashion, and in the art of insinuating themselves thereby, especially into friendship ; but they know not, nor are willing to know, what it is to be a friend to good, or what is the nature of the friendship of good. A sad and sorrowful lot awaits them : they live at length in filth, and in such stupidity that there is scarce any thing of humanity, as regards understanding, remaining in them. For the end makes the man, and such as the end is, such is the man, consequently, such his humanity after death.*

4055. A continuation of the subject concerning the Grand Man *and correspondence, may be seen at the close of the next chapter.*

GENESIS.

CHAPTER THE THIRTY-FIRST.

4056. AT the beginning of chapters xxvi. xxvii. xxviii. xxix. xxx. was explained what the Lord spoke and predicted in Matthew, chap. xxiv. from verse 3 to 28, of the consummation of the age or the last judgment ; the remaining verses in that chapter are now to be explained, and at present, the contents of verses 29, 30, 31, "*But immediately after the affliction of*

*those days, the sun shall be obscured, and the moon shall not
give her light, and the stars shall fall from heaven, and the
powers of the heavens shall be moved. And then shall appear
the sign of the Son of Man in heaven, and then shall all the
tribes of the earth mourn. And they shall see the Son of Man
coming in the clouds of heaven with power and much glory.
And He shall send forth His angels with a trumpet and a great
voice, and they shall gather together His elect from the four
winds, from the extreme of the heavens even to the extreme
thereof.*"

4057. What is meant by the consummation of the age or
the last judgment, was explained above, namely, the last time
of the Church; it is called its last time, when there is no longer
therein any charity and faith; and it was also shown that such
consummations or last times have occasionally existed. The
consummation of the first Church was described by the flood; the
consummation of the second Church, by the extirpation of the
nations in the land of Canaan, and also by several extirpations
and excisions mentioned in the prophets. The consummation
of the third Church is not described in the Word, but is predicted; it was the destruction of Jerusalem, and the dispersing
of the Jewish nation, with whom that Church existed, over the
face of the earth. The fourth consummation is that of the
present Christian Church, which consummation is predicted by
the Lord in the evangelists, and also in the Apocalypse, and
which is now at hand.

4058. The subject treated of in the preceding verses in this
chapter in Matthew, was the successive vastation of the Church,
namely, that first they began not to know what is good and
truth, but to dispute on the subject; secondly, that they despised good and truth; thirdly, that they did not acknowledge
them in heart; fourthly, that they profaned them. These are
the subjects treated of in that chapter from verse 3 to 22; and
whereas the truth of faith and the good of charity would still
remain in the midst, or with some who are called the elect,
therefore the state of the truth of faith is treated of as to its
quality on this occasion, from verse 23 to 28; and the state of
the good of love and charity is treated of in the verses which
are now adduced. The beginning of the new Church is also
treated of.

4059. From all the particulars declared in these verses, it
is very evident that they contain an internal sense, and that
unless this sense be understood, it cannot in any wise be known
what they involve; as, when it is said that the sun shall be
obscured, and also the moon, and that the stars shall fall from
heaven, and that the powers of the heavens shall be moved;
that the Lord is about to appear in the clouds of heaven, that
the angels shall sound with the trumpet, and thereby shall

gather together the elect. He who does no know the internal
sense of these words, will believe that such events will come to
pass; yea, that the world and all the visible objects in the universe are to perish; but that the last judgment does not mean
any destruction of the world, but only the consummation of the
Church, or its vastation as to charity and faith, may be seen,
n. 3353, and manifestly appears from the words which follow
in this same chapter in Matthew, "Then two shall be in the
field, one shall be taken, the other shall be left: Two (women)
shall be grinding at the mill, one shall be taken, the other shall
be left," verses 40, 41.

4060. That therefore the above words which were adduced
signify a state of the Church at that time as to good, that is, as
to charity towards the neighbour and love to the Lord, appears
from their internal sense, which is as follows. *But immediately
after the affliction of those days*, signifies a state of the Church
as to the truth of faith, which state is treated of in what precedes; desolation of truth in the Word throughout is called
affliction. That days denote states, may be seen, n. 23, 487,
488, 493, 893, 2788, 3462, 3785. Hence it is evident, that
these words signify that there will be no charity when there is
no longer any faith; for faith leads to charity, because it teaches
what charity is, and charity receives its quality from the truths
of faith, whereas the truths of faith receive their essence and
their life from charity, as has been abundantly shown in the
preceding volumes. *The sun shall be obscured, and the moon
shall not give her light*, signifies love to the Lord, which is the
sun, and charity towards the neighbour, which is the moon; to
be obscured and not to give light, signifies that they would not
appear, thus that they would vanish. That the sun is the celestial principle of love, and the moon the spiritual principle of
love, that is, that the sun is love to the Lord, and the moon
charity towards the neighbour, which charity comes by faith,
may be seen, n. 1053, 1529, 1530, 2120, 2441, 2495. The reason of this signification of the sun and moon is, because the
Lord in another life appears as a sun to those in heaven who
are in love to Him, who are called celestial, and as a moon to
those who are in charity towards the neighbour, who are called
spiritual, see n. 1053, 1521, 1529, 1530, 1531, 3636, 3643. The
sun and moon in the heavens, or the Lord, is in no case obscured, nor loses light, but shines perpetually, thus neither is
love to Him at any time obscured with the celestial, nor
charity towards the neighbour with the spiritual in the heavens,
nor on the earth with those on whom those angels are attendant,
that is, who are in love and charity; but with those who are in
no love and charity, but in self-love and the love of the world,
and thence in hatreds and revenges, these occasion the above
obscurity to themselves. The case herein is as with the sun of

the world, which shines perpetually, but when clouds interpose themselves, it does not appear, see n. 2441. *And the stars shall fall from heaven*, signifies that the knowledges of good and truth shall perish. Nothing else is signified in the Word by stars, whenever they are named, see n. 1808, 2849. *And the powers of the heavens shall be moved*, signifies the foundations of the Church, which are said to be moved and shaken, when the above principles perish; for the Church in the earths is the foundation of heaven, since the influx of good and truth through the heavens from the Lord ultimately terminates in the goods and truths of the man of the Church; thus when the man of the Church is in such a perverted state, as no longer to admit the influx of good and truth, then the powers of the heavens are said to be moved; on which account it is always provided by the Lord, that somewhat of a Church should remain, and when an old Church perishes, that a new one should be established. *And then shall appear the sign of the Son of Man in heaven*, signifies on this occasion the appearing of Truth Divine; sign denotes an appearing; the Son of Man, the Lord as to Truth Divine, see n. 2803, 2813, 3704. This appearing, or this sign, is what the disciples were inquiring about, when they said unto the Lord, "Tell us when shall these things come to pass, especially what is the sign of thy coming, and of the consummation of the age," verse 3 of this chapter; for they knew from the Word, that when the age was consummated, the Lord would come; and they knew from the Lord, that He would come again, and thereby they understood that the Lord would come again into the world, not as yet knowing, that as often as the Church has been vastated, so often has the Lord come. Not that He has come in person, as when He assumed the Human by nativity and made this Divine, but by appearings; either manifest, as when He appeared to Abraham in Mamre, to Moses in the bush, to the people of Israel on Mount Sinai, and to Joshua when he entered the land of Canaan; or not so manifest, as by the inspirations whereby the Word [was given], and afterwards by the Word; for in the Word the Lord is present, since all things of the Word are from Him and relate to Him, as may appear manifest from what has been so frequently observed before on the subject. This latter appearing is what is here signified by the sign of the Son of Man, and what is treated of in this verse. *And then shall all the tribes of the earth mourn*, signifies, that all shall be in grief who are in the good of love and in the truth of faith. That mourning has this signification, may be seen in Zechariah, chap. xii. verses 10, 11, 12, 13, 14; and that tribes signify all the principles of good and truth, or of love and faith, see n. 3858, 3926, consequently those who are in them; they are called tribes of the earth, because they are signified who are within the Church. That earth denotes the Church, may be seen, n. 662, 1066, 1067, 1262, 1733, 1850, 2117, 2928, 3355. *And they shall see the Son of Man coming in the clouds of the heavens with power and much glory*, signifies, that then the Word shall be revealed as to its internal sense, in which the Lord is. The Son of Man is Truth Divine which is therein, see n. 2803, 2813, 3704. Cloud is the literal sense: power is predicated of the good, and glory of the truth, which is in the Word. That these things are signified by seeing the Son of Man coming in the clouds of the heavens, see the preface to chap. xviii. of Genesis. This is the coming of the Lord which is here meant, but not that He will appear in the clouds according to the letter. The subject which next follows is the establishment of a New Church, which is effected on the vastation and rejection of the old. *He shall send forth His angels with a trumpet and a great voice*, signifies election, not that it is effected by visible angels, still less by trumpets, and by great voices, but by an influx of holy good and holy truth from the Lord by angels, wherefore angels in the Word signify somewhat of the Lord, see n. 1925, 2821, 3039, in the present case such principles as are from the Lord, and relate to the Lord Trumpet and a great voice signify evangelizing, as also in other passages in the Word. *And they shall gather together the elect from the four winds, from the extreme of the heavens even to the extreme thereof*, signifies the establishment of a New Church. The elect are they who are in the good of love and faith, see n. 3755, 3900; the four winds, from which they shall be gathered together, are all states of good and truth, see n. 3708; the extreme of the heavens to the extreme thereof, denotes the internal and external things of the Church. This then is what is signified by the above words of the Lord.

CHAPTER XXXI.

1. AND He heard the words of the sons of Laban, saying, Jacob hath taken all things which our father had; and from the things which our father had, hath made all this abundance.

2. And Jacob saw the faces of Laban, and behold, he was in no wise with him as yesterday.

3. And JEHOVAH said unto Jacob, Return to the land of thy fathers, and to thy nativity; and I will be with thee.

4. And Jacob sent and called Rachel and Leah the field to his flock,

5. And said unto them, I see the faces of your father, that

he is in no wise to me as yesterday : and the GOD of my father hath been with me.

6. And ye know that in all my strength I have served your father.

7. And your father hath deceived me, and hath changed my reward in ten manners (or modes); and GOD hath not given him to do evil with me.

8. If he said thus, The speckled shall be thy reward, and all the flocks brought forth speckled : and if he said thus, The variegated shall be thy reward, and all the flocks brought forth variegated.

9. And GOD hath snatched away the acquisition of your father, and hath given it to me.

10. And it came to pass in the time that the flock grew warm, that I lifted up mine eyes, and saw in a dream, and behold, the goats ascending upon the flock variegated, speckled, and grizzled.

11. And the angel of GOD said unto me in a dream, Jacob. and I said, Behold me.

12. And he said, Lift up I pray thine eyes, and see all the goats ascending upon the flock, variegated, speckled, and grizzled; because I have seen all that Laban doeth to thee.

13. I am the GOD of Bethel, where thou anointedst the statue, where thou vowedst a vow to Me : now arise, go forth from this land, and return to the land of thy nativity.

14. And Rachel and Leah answered, and said unto him, Have we any longer a portion and inheritance in the house of our father?

15. Are not we esteemed aliens to him? because he hath sold us, and hath devoured also by devouring our silver.

16. Because all the riches which GOD hath snatched away from our father, they are for us, and for our sons : and now all that GOD hath said unto thee, do.

17. And Jacob arose, and lifted up his sons and his women upon the camels,

18. And drew away all his acquisition, and all his substance which he had procured, the acquisition of his purchase, which he procured in Padan-Aram, to come to Isaac his father in the land of Canaan.

19. And Laban had gone to shear the flock : and Rachel stole the teraphim which her father had.

20. And Jacob stole the heart of Laban the Aramæan, whereby he did not tell him that he was flying.

21. And he fled, and all that he had; and arose, and passed the river, and set his faces to Mount Gilead.

22. And it was told Laban on the third day that Jacob fled.

23. And he took his brothers with him, and pursued after him a way of seven days, and joined him in Mount Gilead

24. And GOD came to Laban the Aramæan in a dream by night, and said unto him, Take heed to thyself lest haply thou speak with Jacob from good even to evil.

25. And Laban overtook Jacob: and Jacob fixed his tent in the mountain; and Laban fixed with his brethren in Mount Gilead.

26. And Laban said unto Jacob, What hast thou done? and thou hast stolen my heart, and hast withdrawn my daughters as captives for the sword.

27. Wherefore hast thou concealed thy flight, and hast robbed me, and hast not told me, and I would have sent thee in gladness and in songs, in the drum and in the harp?

28. And hast not permitted me to kiss my sons and my daughters? now thou hast acted foolishly in doing.

29. Let GOD have my hand to do with you evil; and the GOD of your father in the night past said unto me, saying, Take heed to thyself of speaking with Jacob from good even to evil.

30. And now going thou hast gone, because desiring thou hast desired to the house of thy father; wherefore hast thou stolen my gods?

31. And Jacob answered, and said unto Laban, Because I feared: because I said, Perchance thou wilt snatch away thy daughters from being with me.

32. With whom thou findest thy gods, he shall not live: before thy brethren search for thyself what is with me, and take to thyself: and Jacob knew not that Rachel had stolen them.

33. And Laban came into the tent of Jacob, and into the tent of Leah, and into the tent of both the handmaids, and he found not: and he went forth from the tent of Leah, and came into the tent of Rachel.

34. And Rachel took the teraphim, and placed them in the straw of the camel, and sat upon them: and Laban handled all the tent, and found not.

35. And she said to her father, Let there not be anger in the eyes of my lord that I cannot rise from before thee, because the way of woman is upon me: and he searched, and did not find the teraphim.

36. And Jacob was angry, and chode with Laban; and Jacob answered, and said unto Laban, What is my transgression? what is my sin, that thou hast pursued after me?

37. Whereas thou hast handled all my vessels, what hast thou found of all the vessels of thine house? set it here before my brethren and thy brethren, and let them judge between us both.

38. These twenty years have I been with thee; thy sheep and thy goats have not been abortive; and the rams of thy flock have I not eaten.

39. That which was torn have I not brought to thee : I have indemnified it; of my hand hast thou required it, what was stolen by night and stolen by day.

40. I have been, in the day the heat devoured me, and cold in the night; and my sleep was driven away from mine eyes.

41. These to me twenty years I have served thee in thy house; fourteen years in thy two daughters, and six years in thy flock; and thou hast changed my reward ten manners.

42. Unless the GOD of my father, the GOD of Abraham, and the dread of Isaac, had been with me, thou wouldst now have sent me away empty: my misery, and the weariness of my hands, GOD hath seen, and hath judged in the past night.

43. And Laban answered, and said unto Jacob, The daughters are my daughters, and the sons my sons, and the flock my flock; and all which thou seest is mine: and for my daughters, what shall I do for them to-day, or for their sons whom they have borne?

44. And now go, let us establish a covenant I and thou; and let it be for a witness between me and between thee.

45. And Jacob took a stone, and set it up for a statue.

46. And Jacob said unto his brethren, Gather together stones; and they took stones and made an heap; and did eat there upon the heap.

47. And Laban called it Jegar Sahadutha; and Jacob called it Galeed.

48. And Laban said, This heap is a witness between me and between thee to-day. Therefore he called the name thereof Galeed:

49. And Mizpah; because he said, Let JEHOVAH look between me and between thee, because we shall lie concealed a man from his companion.

50. If thou afflict my daughters, and if thou takest women over my daughters, no man is with us; see, GOD is a witness between me and between thee.

51. And Laban said to Jacob, Behold this heap, and behold the statue, which I have set up between me and between thee:

52. This heap is a witness, and the statue a witness, if I shall not pass this heap to thee, and if thou shalt not pass this heap to me, and this statue, for evil.

53. The GOD of Abraham and the GOD of Nahor judge between us, the GOD of their father: and Jacob sware into the dread of his father Isaac.

54. And Jacob sacrificed a sacrifice in the mountain, and called his brethren to eat bread; and they did eat bread, and spent the night in the mountain.

55. And in the morning Laban arose early, and kissed his sons and his daughters, and blessed them; and Laban went, and returned to his place.

THE CONTENTS.

4061. THE subject here treated of in the internal sense is the separation of the good and truth which are represented by Jacob and his women, from the good signified by Laban, in order that they might be conjoined with the Divine from a direct Divine stock; also, the state of each during separation.

THE INTERNAL SENSE.

4062. VERSES 1, 2, 3. *AND he heard the words of the sons of Laban, saying, Jacob hath taken all things which our father had; and from the things which our father had, hath made all this abundance. And Jacob saw the faces of Laban, and behold, he was in no wise with him as yesterday. And Jehovah said unto Jacob, Return to the land of thy fathers, and to thy nativity; and I will be with thee.* He heard the words of the sons of Laban, saying, signifies truths of the good signified by Laban, what their quality is in respect to the good acquired thence in the natural principle by the Lord: Jacob hath taken all things which our father had, signifies that all things of the good now meant by Jacob were given to him thence: and from the things which our father had, hath made all this abundance, signifies that he gave to himself: and Jacob saw the faces of Laban, signifies a change of state taking place with that good, when the good meant by Jacob receded: and behold he was in no wise with him as yesterday, signifies the state altogether changed towards the good signified by Jacob, from which however nothing was taken away, but it had its own things as hitherto, except a state as to conjunction: and Jehovah said unto Jacob, signifies the Lord's perception from the Divine: Return to the land of thy fathers, signifies that now he should betake himself nearer to good Divine: and to thy nativity, signifies that he should betake himself also to truth thence derived: and I will be with thee, signifies that it would then be Divine.

4063. "He heard the words of the sons of Laban, saying" —that this signifies truths of the good signified by Laban, what their quality was in respect to the good acquired thence in the natural principle by the Lord, appears from the signification of sons, as being truths, concerning which, see n. 489, 491, 533, 1147, 2623, 3337; and from the representation of Laban, as being collateral good of a common stock, see n. 3612, 3665, 3778, thus such a good as may serve for introducing goods and genuine truths, see n. 3974, 3982, 3986, in the present case what had served, for the subject treated of is its separation. That Jacob heard the words, involves, in the internal sense, what their quality was in respect to the good acquired in the natural principle by the Lord, as may appear from what now follows, for they were in indignation, and said that Jacob had taken all things which their father had, and Jacob saw the faces of Laban, that he was not as yesterday. That Jacob represents the Lord's natural principle, and in the preceding chapter the good of truth in that principle, may be seen, n. 3659, 3669, 3677, 3775, 3829, 4009. How the case is with the good signified by Laban in respect to the good of truth represented by Jacob, may appear from what was said and shown in the preceding chapter. This may be further illustrated by states of the regeneration of man, which also is here treated of in the representative sense. During the process of man's regeneration, he is kept by the Lord in a kind of mediatory good, which serves for introducing genuine goods and truths, but after these goods and truths are introduced, it is separated thence. Every one, who has any knowledge of regeneration and the new man, is capable of comprehending that the new man is altogether different from the old, for he is in the affection of spiritual and celestial things, these things constituting his delights and blessedness, whereas the old man is in the affection of worldly and terrestrial things, which constitute his delights and satisfactions. Thus the new man has respect to ends in heaven, but the old man, to ends in the world. Hence it is manifest that the new man is altogether other and different from the old. In order that man may be led from the state of the old man into the state of the new, the concupiscences of the world must be put off, and the affections of heaven must be put on. This is effected by innumerable means, which are known to the Lord alone, and of which several are known also to angels from the Lord, but few, if any, to man. Nevertheless, all and singular these means are manifested in the internal sense of the Word. While, therefore, man from the old man is made into the new, that is, while he is regenerating, this is not effected in a moment, as some suppose, but by a process of several years, yea, of a man's whole life even to its last period; for his concupiscences are to be extirpated, and heavenly affections to be insinuated, and he is to be gifted with a life which he had not before, yea, of which he before had scarce any notion. Since, therefore, the states of his life are to be so much changed, he must needs be kept for a considerable time in a sort of middle good, that is, in a good which partakes both of the affections of the world and of the affections of heaven, and unless he be kept in this middle good, he in no wise admits heavenly goods and truths. This middle good is what is sig

nified by Laban and his flock. Man, however, is kept in this
middle good no longer than until it has served the above use,
and when this is ended, it is then separated: this separation is
the subject treated of in this chapter. That there is a middle
good, and that when it has served for use, it is separated, may
be illustrated by the changes of state which every man under-
goes from infancy to old age. It is known, that the states of
man in infancy, in boyhood, in youth, in adult age, and in old
age, are different and distinct from each other. It is also known,
that man puts off the state of infancy with its playthings when
he passes into the state of boyhood, and that he puts off the
state of boyhood when he passes into the state of youth, and
this again when he passes into the state of adult age, and
lastly this when he passes into the state of old age. Now if he
weighs the matter well, it may also be known to him, that each
age has its delights, and that by these delights he is successively
introduced into the delights of the subsequent age, and that
these delights were serviceable in bringing him thither, and at
length to the delight of intelligence and wisdom in old age
Hence it is manifest that former things are always left, when a
new state of life is put on. This comparison, however, can
only serve to show, that delights are means, and that these are
left when man enters into a subsequent state, whereas, during
man's regeneration, his state becomes altogether other than, and
different from the foregoing, and he is led to it not in a natural
manner, but in a supernatural, by the Lord; neither does any
one arrive at this state except by the means of regeneration,
which are provided by the Lord alone, thus by the middle good
of which we have been speaking. When he is brought to such a
state, that he no longer regards worldly, terrestrial, and corporeal things as ends, but the things which are of heaven, then
this middle good is separated. To regard as an end is to love the
one in preference to the other.

4064. "Jacob hath taken all things which our father had"
—that this signifies that all things of the good meant by Jacob
were given to him thence, namely, from that middle good, may
appear without explication; but that they were not given to
him thence, will be evident from what follows. They are the
sons of Laban who said this.

4065. "And from the things which our father had, he hath
made all this abundance"—that this signifies that he gave to
himself, appears from the signification of making abundance,
as being to give to himself; for it is predicated of the Lord, in
the supreme sense, Who in no case took any thing of good
and truth from another, but from Himself. Other good, indeed,
had served Him as a means, which had relationship also with
what was maternal, for Laban, who signifies that good, was the
brother of Rebecca, who was the mother of Jacob; but by that

means He procured to Himself those things, whereby He made
His natural principle Divine by His own proper power. It is
one thing to procure somewhat *from* a means, and another
thing to procure it *by* a means. The Lord procured good to
Himself by a means, because He was born a man, and derived
from the mother an hereditary principle which was to be expelled; but He did not procure good from a means, because
He was conceived of Jehovah, from Whom He had the Divine,
wherefore He gave to Himself all the goods and truths which
He made Divine; for the essential Divine has no need of any,
not even of that middle good, only so far as He willed that all
things should be done according to order.

4066. "And Jacob saw the faces of Laban"—that this signifies a change of state with that good, when the good meant
by Jacob receded, appears from the representation of Jacob, as
being good of the natural principle, and from the representation
of Laban, as being a middle good, of which frequent mention has
been made above; and from the signification of faces, as being the
interiors, concerning which, see n. 358, 1999, 2434, 3527, 3573
in the present case changes of the interiors, or, what is the same
thing, changes of state; for it is said, he saw his faces, and behold
he was in no wise with him as yesterday. The reason why the
interiors are signified in the Word by faces, is, because the interiors shine forth from the face, and present themselves in
the face, as in a mirror or image whence, the face or countenance signifies states of the thoughts and states of the affections.

4067. "And behold he was in no wise with him as yesterday"—that this signifies the state altogether changed towards
the good signified by Jacob, from which however nothing was
taken away, but it had its own things as hitherto, except the
states as to conjunction, may appear from this, that his being in
no wise with him as yesterday, denotes a state altogether
changed towards Jacob, that is, towards the good signified by
Jacob; and from what precedes, in that nothing was taken
away from Laban, that is, from the good signified by Laban,
but it had its own things as hitherto. In order that it may be
comprehended how the case is in regard to the goods and truths
in man, it may be expedient to reveal what is known scarce to
any one. It is indeed known and acknowledged that all good
and all truth is from the Lord; and it is even acknowledged by
some that there is an influx, but of such a nature as to be
unknown to man. Yet as it is not known, at least not acknowledged in heart, that about man there are spirits and
angels, and that the internal man is in the midst of them, and
is thus ruled of the Lord, it is little believed, although it is
professed. There are innumerable societies in another life, which
are disposed and arranged by the Lord according to all the

genera of good and truth, and societies which are in the opposite, according to all the genera of evil and the false; insomuch that there is not any genus of good and truth, nor
any species of that genus, nor even any specific difference, but
what has such angelic societies, or to which angelic societies
do not correspond.   On the other hand, there is not any genus of
evil and the false, nor any species of that genus, nor even any
specific difference, which has not corresponding diabolical societies.   Every man is in society with these as to his interiors, that
is, as to his thoughts and affections, although he is ignorant
of it.   Hence comes all which man thinks and wills, insomuch
that if the societies of spirits and angels, in which he is, were
taken away, in that instant he would cease to have either thought
or will, yea, in that instant he would fall down absolutely dead.
Such is the state of man, although he believes that he has all
things from himself, and that there is neither hell nor heaven, or
that hell is far removed from him, and also heaven.   Moreover,
the good in man appears to him as somewhat simple or as
one; nevertheless, it is so manifold and consists of such various
things, that it can in no wise be explored even in its general
principles alone.   The case is the same with the evil in man.
Such as the good is in man, such is the society of angels with
which he is associated, and such as the evil is in man, such is
the society of evil spirits with which he is associated.   Man invites to himself such societies, or places himself in the society of
such, inasmuch as like associates with like.   For example: he
who is covetous invites to himself the societies of such as are in
a similar lust.   He who loves himself in preference to others, and
despises others, invites to himself similar spirits.   He who takes
delight in revenge, invites such as are in a similar delight; and
so in other cases.   Such spirits communicate with hell, and
man is in the midst of them, and is ruled altogether by them,
so that he is no longer under his own power and guidance, but
under theirs, although he supposes, from the delight and consequent liberty which he enjoys, that he rules himself.   He,
however, who is not covetous, or does not love himself in preference to others, and does not despise others, and who does not
take delight in revenge, is in the society of similar angels, and
by them is led by the Lord, and indeed by freedom, to every
good and truth to which he suffers himself to be led.   And as
he suffers himself to be led to an interior and more perfect good,
so he is led to interior and more perfect angelic societies.   The
changes of his state are nothing else but changes of societies.
That this is the case, is evidenced to me by continual experience which has now been enjoyed for several years, whereby
the circumstance is become as familiar to me as any thing which
a man has been accustomed to from his infancy.   From these
facts then it may appear, how the case is with the regeneration

of man, and with the middle delights and goods, whereby he is led by the Lord from a state of the old man to a state of the new, namely, that this is effected by angelic societies, and by the changes of them. Middle goods and delights are nothing else but such societies, which are applied to man by the Lord, to the intent that by them he may be introduced to spiritual and celestial goods and truths; and when he is brought to these goods and truths, then those societies are separated, and interior and more perfect societies are adjoined. Nothing else is meant by the middle good which is signified by Laban, and by the separation of that good, which is the subject treated of in this chapter.

4068. "And Jehovah said unto Jacob"—that this signifies the Lord's perception from the Divine, appears from the signification of saying in the historical parts of the Word, as being to perceive, see n. 1781, 1815, 1819, 1822, 1898, 1919, 2080, 2619, 2862, 3365, 3509. That Jehovah is the Lord, may be seen, n. 1343, 1736, 1793, 2921, 3023, 3035. Hence it is evident that, Jehovah said, signifies the Lord's perception from the Divine.

4069. "Return to the land of thy fathers"—that this signifies that now he should betake himself nearer to good Divine appears from the signification of the land of thy fathers, as here being good Divine, because it is predicated of the Lord, for the land, that is, Canaan, signifies the Lord's kingdom, see n. 1607, 3481, and, in a supreme sense, the Lord's Divine Human, since this flows into and constitutes His kingdom, see n. 3038, 3705; and that father denotes good, see n. 3703. And as now the goods and truths were procured, whereby the Lord might make His natural principle Divine, which goods and truths were represented by Jacob's tarrying with Laban, and by his acquisitions on the occasion, it hence follows, that returning to the land of his fathers denotes to betake himself nearer to good Divine.

4070. "And to thy nativity"—that this signifies that he should betake himself also to truth thence derived, appears from the signification of nativity, as being truth which is from good; for all truth is born of good, and has no other origin, it being called truth because it is of good, and confirms that from which it is, that is, good; hence comes the signification of nativity in this passage. That nativities denote the things of faith, may be seen, n. 1145, 1255; and that to bring forth denotes to acknowledge in faith and act, n. 3905, 3915.

4071. "And I will be with thee"—that this signifies that in such case the Divine, appears from this, that Jehovah spake, and Jehovah means the Lord, as above, n. 4068, thus the Divine. To be with Him, in Whom it is, or Who is it, denotes the Divine. The supreme sense, which treats of the Lord, is such as to appear divided in the sense of the letter, but it is one in the supreme internal sense.

4072. Verses 4 to 13. *And Jacob sent and called Rachel and Leah the field to his flock, and said unto them, I see the faces of your father, that he is in no wise to me as yesterday ; and the God of my father hath been with me. And ye know that in all my strength I have served your father. And your father hath deceived me, and hath changed my reward in ten manners (or modes), and God hath not given to him to do evil with me. If he said thus, The speckled shall be thy reward, and all the flocks brought forth speckled ; and if he said thus, The variegated shall be thy reward, and all the flocks brought forth variegated. And God hath snatched away the acquisition of your father, and hath given it to me. And it came to pass in the time that the flock grew warm, and I lifted up mine eyes, and saw in a dream, and behold the goats ascending upon the flock, variegated, and speckled, and grizzled. And the angel of God said unto me in a dream, Jacob : and I said, Behold me. And he said, Lift up I pray thine eyes, and see all the goats ascending upon the flock, variegated, speckled, and grizzled ; because I have seen all that Laban doeth to thee. I am the God of Bethel, where thou anointedst a statue, where thou vowedst a vow to me : now arise, go forth from this land, and return to the land of thy nativity.* Jacob sent and called Rachel and Leah the field to his flock, signifies adjunction of the affections of truth on the part of the good now meant by Jacob, and application then when he departed : and said unto them, I see the faces of your father, that he is in no wise to me as yesterday, signifies change of state in the good signified by Laban : and the God of my father hath been with me, signifies that all things which he had were from the Divine : and ye know that in all my strength I have served your father, signifies that it was from his own proper power : and your father hath deceived me, and hath changed my reward in ten manners (or modes), signifies a state of good to himself, when of himself he applied those things which are of that good, and its very great change : and God hath not given to him to do evil with me, signifies that still he could not hinder : if he said thus, The speckled shall be thy reward, and all the flocks brought forth speckled, signifies his freedom, and that in his freedom those things were taken of the Lord, in this case as to evils adjoined to goods : and if he said thus, The variegated shall be thy reward, and all the flocks brought forth variegated, signifies the same things as to falses adjoined : and God hath snatched away the acquisition of your father, and hath given it to me, signifies that those things were from the Divine : and it came to pass in the time that the flock grew warm, signifies ardour of affection that they might be conjoined : and I lifted up mine eyes, and saw in a dream, signifies the perception of natural good in obscurity : and behold the goats ascending upon the flock variegated, speckled, and grizzled, signifies the effect that natural good understood by Jacob should hence imbibe such things : and the angel of God said unto me in a dream, Jacob ; and I said, Behold me, signifies perception from the Divine, and presence in that obscure state : and he said, Lift up I pray thine eyes, signifies attention thereto from proprium: and see all the goats ascending upon the flock variegated, speckled, and grizzled, signifies that such things were introduced : because I have seen all that Laban doeth to thee, signifies the proprium of the good signified by Laban, that it is not such as to act of itself : I am the God of Bethel, signifies the Divine in the natural : where thou anointedst a statue, signifies where is the good of truth, and the boundary : where thou vowedst a vow, signifies what is holy : now arise, signifies elevation : go forth from this land, signifies separation from that good : and return to the land of thy nativity, signifies conjunction with the Divine Good of truth.

4073. "And Jacob sent and called Rachel and Leah, the held to his flock"—that this signifies adjunction of the affections of truth on the part of the good now meant by Jacob, and application when he departed, appears from the representation of Jacob, as being good of the natural principle, whereof frequent mention has been made above ; and from the representation of Rachel and Leah, as being affections of truth adjoined to that good, Rachel the affection of interior truth, and Leah the affection of external truth, concerning which, see n. 3758, 3782, 3793, 3819. That to send to these and call the field to his flock denotes to adjoin to himself, is manifest. Field signifies those things which are of good, and where good is, see n. 2971, 3196, 3310, 3317 ; and flock signifies the goods and truths themselves, which were now acquired, to which the affections of truth understood by Rachel and Leah were applied, when he departed. Jacob in this chapter represents the good of the natural principle, in that it acceded nearer to conjunction with the Divine, see n. 4069, because it was in readiness to separate itself, and was in separation, from the good signified by Laban, see n. 3775, concerning Jacob. For representations are according to changes of state as to good and truth, and changes of state are according to changes of the spirits and angels who are in such good and truth, agreeably to what was said above, n. 4067. When the societies of spirits and angels, which are in a middle good, recede, then new societies accede, which are in a more perfect good. The state of man is altogether according to the societies of the spirits and angels in the midst of whom he is ; such is his will and such is his thought. With respect, however, to the changes of his state, there is a differ ence, according as he invites those societies to himself, or himself adjoins them to himself, and according as those societies are adjoined to him of the Lord. When he himself adjoins himself to them, he is then in evil; but when they are adjoined to him by the Lord, he is then in good. When he is in good, such good flows in through those societies, as is serviceable for the reformation of his life. The things here said in the internal sense, of the good represented by Jacob, of the affections of truth, which are Rachel and Leah, and of the application of these when he departed from the good signified by Laban, are in every respect exhibited thus to the life in the case of societies and their changes. From these, the angels perceive the states of man, thus his goods and truths as to their quality; consequently innumerable things which scarce appear to man as one general thing. Hence the angels are in essential causes, for they see and perceive those societies, whereas man is in effects, and does not see them, but only is enabled to perceive them obscurely by some changes of state thence arising; nor does he see any thing as to good and truth, unless he receive illustration by angels from the Lord.

4074. "And he said unto them, I see the faces of your father, that he is in no wise to me as yesterday"—that this signifies a change of state in the good signified by Laban, appears from what was said above, n. 4067, where the same words occur.

4075. "And the God of my father hath been with me"—that this signifies that all things which he had were from the Divine, appears from this, that the God of a father, when it is predicated of the Lord, denotes the Divine which He had; and that the expression, hath been with me, denotes, that hence He derived all that He had. The Lord, when He made the Human in Himself Divine, had also about Him societies of spirits and angels, for He willed that all things should be done according to order; but He invited to Himself such as were serviceable, and changed them at His good pleasure. Nevertheless He did not take from them any thing of good and truth, but from the Divine. Thus also He reduced into order both heaven and hell, and this successively, until He fully glorified Himself. That societies of spirits and angels were capable of being serviceable for use, and that still He took nothing from them, may be illustrated by examples. The societies which are such as to believe that good is from themselves, and thereby place merit in goods, were serviceable to the Lord for this use, to introduce Himself to a knowledge of such good, and thence into wisdom concerning good without merit, such as the good is which comes from the Divine. This knowledge and consequent wisdom was not derived from those societies, but by them. So again, the societies which believe themselves to be very wise, and yet reason concerning good and truth, and the particulars thereof, as to whether or no a thing be so, which for the most part are societies of the spiritual, were serviceable to the Lord for this use, to introduce Himself into knowledge concerning them, and that He might know how much they are respectively in a shade, and that they would perish unless the Divine had mercy on them, and also in several points of knowledge which were from the Divine, and not from those societies, but by them. So again, the societies which are in love to God, and believe that, if they look upon an Infinite, and worship an hidden God, they may be in love to Him, when yet they are not, unless they make that Infinite finite by some idea, or present to themselves the hidden God as visible by finite intellectual ideas (for otherwise it would be like looking into darkness, and embracing with love that which is in darkness, whence many fanciful and groundless conceits would arise, according to the ideas of each individual); such societies were also serviceable for use, to introduce to a knowledge of the quality of their interiors, and also of the quality of their love, and likewise into commiseration, and that neither could they be saved, unless the human of the Lord was also made Divine, and thus rendered an object on which they might look. Nevertheless this wisdom was not from those societies, but by them, from the Divine. The case is similar in other instances. Hence it is manifest how the matter is in regard to this, that nothing was taken from the good signified by Laban, but that all things which the Lord had were from the Divine, that is, from Himself.

4076. "And ye know that in all my strength I have served your father"—that this signifies that it was from his own proper power, appears from the signification of serving, as being study see n. 3824, 3846; but when it is predicated of the Lord, proper power, see n. 3975, 3977, and still more when it is said, in all my strength.

4077. "And your father hath deceived me, and hath changed my reward in ten modes"—that this signifies a state of good to himself, when of himself he applied those things which are of that good, and a very great change, appears from the signification of father, in the present case Laban, as being a middle good (of which see above); and from the signification of reward, as being from himself, see n. 3996, 3999; and from the signification of ten modes, as being a very great change; ten denotes very much, see n. 1988, and modes denote change. The real state of that good, when the Lord of Himself applied those things which are of that good, is implied as being changed. If now instead of the good which is signified by Laban, such a society of spirits and angels be conceived as are in such good, it is manifest how the case is. The societies do not easily recede from the man with whom they are associated, but when he recedes, they are indignant, and behave in the same manner as Laban here did to Jacob : yea, likewise if they perceive that any good has come to him by them, they say that it has come from them ; for in indignation they speak from evil. The case in this respect is similar with every man who is regenerated, namely, that societies are applied to him by the Lord, which serve for introducing genuine goods and truths, not from them but by them ; and when he who is in the process of regeneration is transferred into other societies, then the societies are indignant which have been there before. These things do not appear to man, because he does not believe that he is in the society of spirits and angels, but they appear manifestly to the angels, and also to those to whom, by the Divine Mercy of the Lord, it is given to discourse with them, and to be present with them as one of them. Hence it has been given me to know hat the case is as above described. Spirits complain exceed-.ngly that man does not know this, not even that they are with .nan, and they complain still more, that many deny, not only heir presence, but also the existence of hell and heaven. This, .iowever, they ascribe to man's stupidity; when nevertheless rnan has not the least of thought, nor the least of will, but by influx through them from the Lord ; and that it is by them that the Lord mediately governs the human race, and every individual in particular.

4078. "And God hath not given to him to do evil with me" —that this signifies that he could not hinder, appears from the signification of not giving to do evil, when it is predicated of the Lord, as being not to be able to hinder ; for nothing can do evil to the Divine, but its influx may be hindered, and all evil has this effect. Hence it appears what is here signified by · doing evil.

4079. "If he said thus, The speckled shall be thy reward, and all the flocks brought forth speckled"—that this signifies his freedom, and that in his freedom those things were taken . of the Lord, in this case as to evils adjoined to goods, appears from the state of the thing in the internal sense, which is, that he had freedom to change the reward, and thus that in his freedom those things were taken. That these were as to evils adjoined to goods, appears from the signification of speckled, as denoting goods with which evils are mixed, see n. 3993, 3995, 4005.

4080. "And if he said thus, The variegated shall be thy reward, and all the flocks brought forth variegated"—that this signifies the same things as to falses adjoined, appears from what has been just said, and from the signification of variegated, as being truths sprinkled and mixed with evils, see n. 4005, consequently falses.

4081. "And God hath snatched away the acquisition of your father, and hath given it to me"—that this signifies that those things were from the Divine, appears from what was said and shown above, n. 4065, 4075.

4082. "And it came to pass in the time that the flock grew warm"—that this signifies ardour of affection that they might be conjoined, appears from the signification of growing warm, as being ardour of affection and its effect, see n. 4018, 4019; thus that they, namely, goods and truths, might be conjoined.

4083. "And I lifted up mine eyes and saw in a dream"— that this signifies the perception of natural good in obscurity, appears from the signification of lifting up the eyes, as being to think, and also to intend, see n. 2789, 2829, 3198, thus to perceive; and from the signification of in a dream, as being in obscurity, see n. 2514, 2528. The good of the natural principle is Jacob.

4084. "And behold the goats ascending upon the flock, ·ariegated, speckled, and grizzled"—that this signifies the ⸱ffect, that natural good understood by Jacob should hence ⸱nbibe such things, may appear from what was said in the ⸱receding chapter on this subject; for by the flock of Laban, ⸱he variegated, the speckled, and the grizzled, that is, such principles as are signified thereby, became the property of Jacob.

4085. "And the angel of God said unto me in a dream, Jacob: and I said, Behold me"—that this signifies perception from the Divine, and presence in obscurity, appears from the signification of saying in the historical parts of the Word, as ⸱eing to perceive, of which frequent mention has been made above; and from the signification of the angel of God, as being what is from the Divine, for angel in the Word, wherever it occurs, signifies somewhat of the Lord, that is, of the Divine (see n. 1925, 2319, 2821, 3039); because an angel does not speak from himself, but from the Lord, especially when in a dream, as in the present case to Jacob. The angels are such, as to be indignant if any thing of good and truth be attributed to them in what they speak, and so far as they are able, they remove such an idea in others, especially in man: for they know and perceive that they have from the Lord, thus from the Divine, every thing good and true which they think, will, and effect. Hence it may appear, that angels in the Word signify somewhat of the Lord, that is, of the Divine; and from the signification of in a dream, as denoting in obscurity, see n. 2514, 2528. Presence in the natural principle, and therein in obscurity, is signified by Jacob's answer.

4086. "And said, Lift up I pray thine eyes"—that this signifies attention thereto from proprium, appears from the signification of lifting up the eyes, as being to think and attend, see

n. 2789, 2829, thus to attend to.   That it was from proprium in the present case, is evident from the fact, that it is said, *Lift up* thine eyes and *see;* also from the series.

4087. " And see all the goats ascending upon the flock, variegated, speckled, and grizzled "—that this signifies that such things were introduced, thus that he imbibed such things, appears from what was said above, n. 4084, where similar words occur.

4088. " Because I have seen all that Laban doeth to thee " —that this signifies the proprium of the good signified by Laban, that it is not such as to act of itself, appears from the representation of Laban, as being a middle good, concerning which see above.   That the proprium of this good is not such as to act of itself, is signified by the words, " I have seen all that he doeth to thee."   That this is the signification is evident from an attention to the subject in the internal sense, and also from the societies which are in such good, for from these the quality of that good may be manifestly seen, they being socie-ties of spirits, which serve for media and for communication concerning which societies, see n. 4047.   They are not such as to do much of themselves or of proprium, but suffer themselves to be led by others, thus to good by the angels, and to evil by wicked spirits, which also is discoverable from the historical facts here recorded of Laban; especially from what follows. Hence it is evident what is signified by the proprium of the good signified by Laban, that it is not such as to act from itself. The internal contents of these verses, 6, 7, 8, 9, 10, 11, 12, are explained only in a summary way, because of their similarity to what was treated of in the preceding chapter, where a fuller explication is given of them.

4089. " I am the God of Bethel "—that this signifies the Divine in the natural, appears from the signification of Bethel. as being good in the ultimate of order, see n. 3729; conse-quently in the natural principle, this being the ultimate of order, inasmuch as celestial and spiritual principles terminate therein. Hence it is evident that the God of Bethel denotes the Divine in the natural.   Since Bethel signifies good in the natural prin-ciple, it also signifies the knowledges of things celestial therein, for these are of good.

4090. " Where thou anointedst a statue "—that this signifies where is the good of truth, and the boundary, appears from the signification of statue, as being a holy boundary, thus the ultimate of order, consequently truth, see n. 3727; and from the signification of anointing, or pouring oil upon the head of a statue, which was done by Jacob, as being to make truth good, see n. 3728.

4091. " Where thou vowedst a vow to me "—that this sig-nifies what is holy, appears from the signification of vowing a

vow, as being to be willing that the Lord may provide, see n.
3732, and as whatever the Lord provides proceeds from Him,
and whatever proceeds from Him is holy, therefore vowing a
vow here signifies what is holy. That to vow a vow denotes
that which proceeds from the Lord, consequently what is holy
appears at first sight a far-fetched signification, but the reason
of this is, because it is man who vows a vow, whereby he binds
himself to some obligation, or imposes somewhat on himself
respecting the Divine, in case he obtains his wish; but when it
is the Divine itself, or the Lord, of Whom this is predicated,
in this case it is not any vow, but it is to will and to provide, or
to do. What therefore the Divine, or the Lord, does, proceeds
from Him, and whatever proceeds from Him is holy.

4092. "Now arise"—that this signifies elevation, appears
from the signification of arising, as implying elevation, wherever the expression occurs, see n. 2401, 2785, 2912, 2927; and
what is meant by elevation, n. 3171.

4093. "Go forth from this land"—that this signifies separation from that good which is signified by Laban, appears
without explication.

4094. "And return to the land of thy nativity"—that this
signifies conjunction with the Divine Good of Truth, appears
from the signification of returning to the land, as being to betake himself nearer to Good Divine (of which, see n. 4069);
and from the signification of nativity, as being truth, see also
above, n. 4070. Hence it is manifest, that returning to the land
of nativity signifies a conjunction with the Divine Good of
Truth.

4095. Verses 14, 15, 16. *And Rachel and Leah answered
and said unto him, Have we any longer a portion and inheritance in the house of our father? Are not we esteemed aliens
to him? because he hath sold us and hath devoured also by
devouring our silver. Because all the riches which God hath
snatched away from our father, they are for us, and for our
sons: and now all that God hath said unto thee, do.* Rachel
and Leah answered, and said unto him, signifies the reciprocality
of the affections of truth: Have we any longer a portion and
inheritance in the house of our father? signifies the first state
of their separation from the good signified by Laban: are not
we esteemed aliens to him? because he hath sold us, signifies
that he had alienated them, so that they were no longer his:
and hath devoured also by devouring our silver, signifies the
truth of those affections which he would consume, if they were
not separated: because all the riches which God hath snatched
away from our father, they are for us, and for our sons, signifies
that all things were from own proper power, and nothing was
given by any one, inflowing from His Divine into that which

thence received it: ar l now all that God hath said unto thee, do, signifies the Lord's providence.

4096. " Rachel and Leah answered, and said unto him"— that this signifies the reciprocality of the affections of truth, appears from the signification of answering when assent is given, as being reciprocality, see n. 2919, and as being reception, n. 2941, 2957; and from the representation of Rachel, as being the affection of interior truth, and of Leah, as being the affection of external truth, see n. 3758, 3782, 3793, 3819. The subject treated of in what goes before, in the internal sense, was the good of the natural principle, signified by Jacob, when it was separated from the middle good, which is Laban, how the good of the natural principle adjoined to itself the affections of truth, which are signified by Rachel and Leah. The subject now treated of is the reciprocal application of the affections of truth to good. This application is contained in the internal sense of the words which Rachel and Leah now speak. These things, however, are such, that they do not fall into any but an understanding which is instructed, and perceives a delight in the knowledge of them, consequently which has for an end spiritual knowledges. Others have no concern about them and are not able to stretch the mind to the consideration of them, for they who have worldly and terrestrial things for an end, cannot withdraw the senses thence, and if they did withdraw them, they would perceive what is undelightful, for then they would depart and remove from those things which they have for an end, that is, which they love. Let every one, who is of such a quality, make the experiment for himself, whether he be willing to know how good adjoins itself to the affections of truth, and how the affections of truth apply themselves, and whether or no it is not irksome to him to know this, and he will say that such things are of no profit to him, and also that he apprehends nothing about them. But if such things be told him as relate to his business in the world, however deep and hidden they may be, and what is the quality of such and such a person as to his affections, also, how by those affections he may adjoin him to himself, by applying himself to his intentions and expressions, this he not only apprehends, but has also a perception of the interior things thereof. In like manner, he who studies from affection to investigate the abstruse principles of the sciences, loves to look into, and also does look into subjects of a more intricate nature than what are here treated of; but when spiritual good and truth are the subjects, he feels it irksome, and holds it in aversion. These observations are made in order to show the quality of the men of the Church at this day. But how the case is with good when it adjoins truths to itself by affections, and with truths when they apply them-

selves, cannot so well appear while the idea or thought is held
in good and truth, as while it is held in the societies of spirits
and angels through which they flow-in, for, as was said, n.
4067, man's willing and thinking is thence derived, or thence
inflows, and appears as in him.   To know from the societies of
spirits and angels how the case is, is to know from causes themselves, and to know from the heaven of angels, is to know from
ends of causes.   There are also historical things which adjoin
themselves and illustrate, and thus they appear more manifestly.
The subject treated of in the internal sense, is the adjunction of
good to truths, and the application of these latter in the natural
principle; for Jacob is the good therein, as has been often said,
and his women are the affections of truth.   The good, which
is of love and charity, inflows from the Lord, and indeed through
the angels attendant on man, and into no other than his knowledges; and as good is there fixed, the thought is kept in truths
which are of knowledges, and thence several things are excited
which have relationship and agreement, and this until the man
thinks that the thing is so, and wills it from affection because
it is so.   When this is the case, then good conjoins itself to
truths, and truths apply themselves, in freedom, for all affec
tion causes freedom, see n. 2870, 2875, 3158, 4031.   But when
this is the case, doubts, and sometimes negatives, are excited
even by the spirits who are adjoined to him, but so far as affection prevails, so far he is led to the affirmative, and then he is
at the same time confirmed in truths by the former principles.
When good thus inflows, it is not perceived that it is through
the angels, because it inflows interiorly, and into the obscurity
the man takes from things worldly and corporeal.   It is however
to be observed, that good does not inflow from the angels, but
through the angels from the Lord; this the angels confess, and
therefore they never claim to themselves any good, yea, they
are indignant when any one attributes it to them.   From these
facts then, as from essential causes, it may be seen how the case
is with the adjunction of good to truths, and with the application
of these latter, which is the subject here treated of in the internal sense.

4097. "Have we any longer a portion and inheritance in
the house of our father?"—that this signifies the first state of
their separation from the good signified by Laban, appears from
the signification of the words, "have we any longer a portion
and inheritance," as being, have we any longer any conjunction;
and from the signification of the house of our father, as being
the good represented by Laban.   The result of these significations is, that the above words signify the first state of their
separation from the good signified by Laban.   The first state is,
that the mind is kept in doubt; the second state is, that doubt
is dispelled by reasons; the third state is affirmation: the last

is act. Thus good with truths insinuates itself from the intellectual into the voluntary part, and is appropriated.

4098. "Are not we esteemed aliens to him? because he hath sold us"—that this signifies that he had alienated them, so that they were no longer his, appears from the signification of being ¡esteemed aliens, as being to be alienated; and from the signification of selling, as being so to alienate as to be no longer his.

4099. "And he hath devoured by devouring our silver"—that this signifies the truth of those affections which he would consume, if they were not separated, appears from the signification of devouring, as being to consume; and from the signification of silver, as being truth, see n. 1551, 2954. That our silver denotes the truth of those affections is evident, for Rachel and Leah represent the affections of truth, as has been everywhere shown above. What these words involve cannot be known, unless it be known how the case is with the goods and truths which are insinuated by a middle good, or unless it be known what is the nature of the societies of spirits which serve for a middle good. These societies are in worldly principles, whereas the societies of angels, which serve for introducing the affections of truth, are not in worldly but in heavenly principles. These two societies act in the man who is regenerating. So far as he is initiated into heavenly principles by the angels, so far the spirits who are in worldly ones are removed, and unless they are removed, truths are dissipated. Worldly and heavenly things are in concord in man, when heavenly things have dominion over worldly; but they are in discord, when worldly things have dominion over heavenly. When they are ¡n concord, then truths are multiplied in man's natural principle; but when they are in discord, then truths are diminished, yea, are consumed, because worldly things overshadow heavenly, consequently place them in doubt; whereas when heavenly things have dominion, they illustrate worldly things, and place them in clearness, and take away doubts. Those things which are most loved have dominion. From these considerations it may appear, what is meant by the truth of affections being consumed if they were not separated, which is signified by these words, he hath devoured by devouring our silver.

4100. "Because all the riches which God hath snatched from our father, are for us, and our sons"—that this signifies that all things were from His own proper power (and that nothing was given by any one), influent from His Divine into that which thence received it, appears from what was said and explained above, n. 4065, 4075, 4081.

4101. "And now all that God hath said unto thee, do"—that this signifies the Lord's providence, appears from the signification of the words, all that God hath said unto thee, as being to obey; and when it is predicated of the Lord, being to provide, for He does not from another, but from Himself, neither does God say to Him that He should do, but He Himself says, that is, does from Himself.

4102. Verses 17, 18. *And Jacob arose, and lifted up his sons and his women upon the camels, and brought away all his acquisition, and all his substance which he had procured, the acquisition of his purchase, which he procured in Padan-aram, to come to Isaac his father the land of Canaan.* Jacob arose, signifies elevation of the good meant by Jacob: and lifted up his sons and his women upon the camels, signifies elevation of truths and the affections thereof, and orderly arrangement in general principles: and brought away all his acquisition, and all his substance which he had procured, signifies the separation of truth and good from Laban's: the acquisition of his purchase, signifies the things procured from them elsewhere: which he procured in Padan-aram, signifies the knowledges of truth and good in the natural principle: to come to Isaac his father the land of Canaan, signifies to conjoin to Divine Good of the rational principle, that the Human might be made Divine.

4103. "Jacob arose"—that this signifies elevation of the good meant by Jacob, appears from the signification of arising, as being elevation, see n. 2401, 2785, 2912, 2927; and from the representation of Jacob, as being good of the natural principle, frequently spoken of above, in the present case good which accedes nearer to the Divine, because about to be separated from middle good, or from Laban, see n. 4073. Elevation, which is signified by arising, means nearer access to the Divine. In respect to man, he is said to be elevated when he accedes nearer to heavenly things, and this by reason that heaven is believed to be elevated, or to be on high, which is so said from appearance, for heaven, consequently the things of heaven, or things celestial and spiritual, are not on high, but in the internal, see n. 450, 1735, 2148. Wherefore man is in heaven as to his interiors, when he is in spiritual love and faith.

4104. "And lifted up his sons and his women upon the camels"—that this signifies elevation of truths and the affections thereof, and orderly arrangement in general principles, appears from the signification of sons, as being truths, see n. 489, 491, 533, 1147, 2623; and from the signification of women, in the present case Rachel and Leah, also the handmaids, as being the affections of truth, of knowledges, and of sciences, concerning which see above; and from the signification of camels, as being general scientifics in the natural principle, see n. 3048, 3071, 3143, 3145. He who does not know how the case is in regard to representations and correspondences, cannot believe that these words, "he lifted up his sons and his women upon the camels," signify such things, for they appear to him

too remote to involve and contain such a spiritual meaning, for
he thinks of sons, of women, and of camels. The angels, however, who see and perceive all such things spiritually, do not
think about sons, but when sons are named, they think of
truths; neither about women, but when women are named,
they think of the affections of truth, of knowledges, and of
sciences; nor about camels, but of generals in the natural principle. Such is correspondence, and such is angelic thought;
and what is wonderful, such is the thought of the internal of
the spiritual man, during his life in the body, although the
external is entirely ignorant of it. Wherefore the man who is
regenerated, when he dies comes into similar thought, and can
think and discourse with the angels, and this without instruction, which could in no wise be effected, unless his interior
thought had been such. The reason why it is such, is from the
correspondence of things natural and spiritual. Hence it may
appear, that although the literal sense of the Word is natural
still it contains in itself, and in each expression, spiritual things
that is, such things as are of interior thought and thence of interior speech, or of spiritual thought and speech, or such as is
proper to the angels. In regard to the elevation of truths and
the affections thereof, and their orderly arrangement in generals, the case is this. Truths and affections are elevated, when
preference is given to those things which relate to eternal life
and the Lord's kingdom, above those things which relate to the
bodily life and the kingdom of the world. When man acknowledges the former things to be principal and primary, and
the latter things to be instrumental and secondary, then truths
and the affections thereof are elevated with him, for he is so far
translated into the light of heaven, in which is intelligence and
wisdom, and so far the things which are of the light of the
world are to him images, and as it were mirrors, wherein he
sees the things of the Lord's kingdom. The contrary happens
when preference is given to those things which relate to the
bodily life and the kingdom of the world, above those things
which relate to eternal life and the Lord's kingdom, as, when
man believes that the latter things are not, because he has not
seen them, and because no one has come from the other world
and brought tidings of them; also when he believes that in case
such things are, it will fare with him as well as with others, and
confirms himself in the reality of the things of the bodily life,
and lives a life of the world, and altogether despises charity
and faith. With such a person, truths and their affections are
not elevated, but are either suffocated, or rejected, or perverted, for he is in natural light, into which there is no influx
of heavenly light. Hence it is evident what is meant by the
elevation of truths and the affections thereof. In respect to
their orderly arrangement in generals, it is a consequence   for

so far as man prefers eavenly to world.y things, so far the
things which are in his natural principle are arranged to the
state of heaven, so that they appear there, as was said, like
images and mirrors of heavenly things, for they are corresponding representatives.   The ends regarded are what cause
such arrangement, that is, the Lord by ends with man.   There
are three things which follow in order, namely, ends, causes,
and effects.   Ends produce causes, and by causes effects.   Such
therefore as the ends are, such are the causes which exist, and
such the effects thence produced.   Ends are the inmost things
in man, causes are the middle, and are called middle ends, and
effects are the ultimate, and are called ultimate ends, and effects
are also those things which are called general.   Hence it is evident what is meant by orderly arrangement in generals, namely,
that when those things which regard eternal life and the Lord's
kingdom are respected as an end, all middle ends or causes,
and all ultimate ends or effects, are arranged according to the
essential end, and this in the natural principle, because effects.
or, what is the same thing, generals, are therein.   Every man
in adult age, who has any strength of judgment, may know, if
he does but consider the matter, that he is in two kingdoms,
namely, in a spiritual and a natural kingdom, also, that the
spiritual kingdom is interior, and the natural kingdom exterioi,
and consequently that he can prefer the one to the other, or
regard one as an end in preference to the other, and hence,
that that kingdom has dominion in him which he regards as an
end, or to which he gives the preference.   If therefore he regard
the spiritual kingdom as an end, and gives it the preference.
that is, the things of that kingdom, he then acknowledges love
to the Lord and charity towards the neighbour, as principal
and primary; consequently, he acknowledges all things which
confirm such love and charity, which things are called the
things of faith, for these belong to that kingdom; and then all
things are disposed and arranged in his natural principle accord
ing to those things, that they may be subservient and obedient
But when he regards the natural kingdom as an end, and gives
it the preference, that is, the things of that kingdom, he then
extinguishes the things belonging to love to the Lord and
charity towards the neighbour, and to faith, insomuch that he
makes them of no account, but makes the love of the world
and self-love, and the things appertaining thereto, to be all and
every thing   When this is the case, all things in his natural
principle are arranged according to those ends, thus in utter
contrariety to the things of heaven; hence he makes in himself a hell.   To regard as an end is to love, for every end is of
the love, since whatever is loved is regarded as an end.

4105. "And brought away all his acquisition and all his
substance which he procured"—that this signifies tne sepa-

ration of truth and good which are from Laban's, appears from
the signification of bringing away, as being to separate; and
from the signification of acquisition, as being truth; and from
the signification of substance, as being good. Which he procured, has respect to Laban and his flock, whereby he acquired
those principles. The reason why acquisition denotes truth,
and substance good, is, because acquisition in the original
tongue is an expression which also signifies cattle in general,
which, in particular, signify truths, when flocks signify goods;
and substance signifies the faculties from which those truths
and goods are derived. For when in the Word two expressions
are used of nearly the same signification, the one is then predicated of truth, and the other of good, because of the heavenly
marriage, which is that of truth and good in the whole and
every part of the Word, see n. 683, 793, 801, 2173, 2516, 2712.

4106. "The acquisition of his purchase"—that this signifies
t.e things procured from them elsewhere, appears from the
signification of acquisition, as being truths, concerning which
see above; and from the signification of purchase, as being
those things which were procured elsewhere; for acquisitions
which were purchased, were elsewhere, but still from those
things which were procured by the flock of Laban.

4107. "Which he procured in Padan-aram"—that this signifies knowledges of good and truth in the natural principle,
appears from the signification of Padan-aram, as being knowledges of good and truth, see n. 3664, 3680.

4108. "To come to Isaac his father the land of Canaan"—
that this signifies to conjoin to Divine Good of the rational
principle, that the Human might be made Divine, appears from
the representation of Isaac, as being the Divine Rational, see
n. 1893, 2066, 2083, 2630, and in particular, the good of the
rational, see n. 3012, 3194, 3210; and from the signification of
the land of Canaan, as being the Lord's celestial kingdom, see
n. 1607, 3481, and, in the supreme sense, that is, when it is
predicated of the Lord, denoting His Divine Human, see n.
3038, 3705. Hence it is evident, that coming to Isaac his
father, the land of Canaan, signifies to conjoin to the Divine
Good of the rational principle, that the Human might be made
Divine. In regard to the conjunction of the rational and natural principles in man, it is to be observed, that the rational is
of the internal man, and the natural of the external man, and
that their conjunction constitutes humanity, and that the humanity is such as the conjunction is, and that conjunction has
place when they act in unity, and that they act in unity when
the natural ministers and is subservient to the rational. This
effect can in no wise exist in man except from the Lord; but
with the Lord it was effected from Himself.

4109. Verses 19, 20, 21. *And Laban had gone to shear his*

flock; and Rachel stole the teraphim which her father had. And Jacob stole the heart of Laban the Aramœan, whereby he did not tell him that he was flying. And he fled, and all that he had; and arose, and passed the river, and set his faces to Mount Gilead. Laban had gone to shear his flock, signifies a state of use, and of an end of good, which is the flock of Laban: and Rachel stole the teraphim which her father had, signifies a change of the state signified by Laban as to truth: and Jacob stole the heart of Laban the Aramæan, signifies a change of the state signified by Laban as to good; Laban the Aramæan is such a good wherein there is not Divine truth and good, as above: whereby he did not tell him that he was flying, signifies by separation: and he fled, and all that he had, signifies separation: and arose, signifies elevation: and passed the river, signifies a state where there was conjunction: and set his faces to Mount Gilead, signifies good in that state.

4110. " Laban had gone to shear his flock"—that this signi fies a state of use and of the end of good, which is the flock of Laban, appears from the signification of shearing, as being use, thus end, for use is end, of which we shall speak presently : and from the signification of flock, as being good, see n. 343, 2566. Hence it is evident that a state of use and of end is signified by going to shear. The subject now treated of is the separation of the middle good, which is Laban, from the good thence procured, which is Jacob. How the case is in respect to the separation, cannot be known but from the societies of spirits who are in that good, and from whom it inflows with man, on which subject it is permitted me from experience to relate the following particulars. There are good spirits, and there are spirits of a middle sort, and there are evil spirits, who are adjoined to man during his regeneration, to the end, that he may be introduced by them into genuine goods and truths, and this by means of angels from the Lord; but they are such spirits, or societies of spirits, as are not in agreement with the person about to be regenerated, except as to time; and therefore when they have fulfilled their use, they are separated. Their separation is effected in different ways, the separation of good spirits in one way, of spirits of a middle sort in another, and of evil spirits in a third. The separation of good spirits is effected when they do not know it, knowing that from the good pleasure of the Lord it is well with them wherever they are, or are translated by the Lord. The separation, however, of spirits of a middle sort is effected by several means, until they recede in freedom, for they are remitted into a state of their good, consequently, into a state of use and end thence derived, that they may perceive therein their delight and bless edness; but as they have had pleasure in their former consort, they are at times brought back, and at times remitted, until they are made sensible of an undelightfulness in tarrying longer, and thereby recede in freedom. Evil spirits are also indeed removed in freedom, yet in a freedom which appears to them as freedom. They are adjoined to the intent they may induce negative principles, by the discussion of which man may be more confirmed in truths and goods; and when he begins to be confirmed, they then perceive what is undelightful, and feel delight in separation, and thus are separated by the freedom of their delight. This is the case in regard to the separation of the spirits attendant upon man during regeneration; consequently, in regard to the changes of his state as to good and truth. That to shear the flock is to perform use, is evident from this, that shearing the flock, in the internal sense, is nothing else but use, for wool is the product of it. That shearing the flock denotes use, is manifest also from the following passage in Moses, "All the first-born which is born in thy herd, and in thy flock, thou shalt sanctify to Jehovah thy God; thou shalt not do work by the first-born of thine ox, and *thou shalt not shear the first-born of thy flock;* but thou shalt eat it every year before Jehovah thy God, in the place which Jehovah shall choose," Deut. xv. 19; where not shearing the first-born of the flock means not to perform thence domestic use. As shearing the flock signified use, therefore to shear the flock and to be present at shearing was in old time reputed an honourable office and employment, as may appear from what is said of Judah, that "*he sheared his flock,*" Gen. xxxviii. 12, 13; and from the sons of David in the second book of Samuel, "It came to pass after two years of days, that Absalom had *shearers* in Baalchazor, which is in Ephraim; and Absalom called all the king's sons, and Absalom came to the king, and said, *Behold, I pray, shearers for thy servant,* let the king go, I pray, and thy servants with thy servant," xiii. 23, 24.

4111. "And Rachel stole the teraphim which her father had"—that this signifies a change of the state signified by Laban as to truth, appears from the signification of stealing in the present case, as being to take away what is dear and holy, thus to change the state; and from the signification of teraphim, as being truths, of which we shall speak presently; and from the signification of father, in the present case Laban, as being the good signified by him, concerning which see above; father also signifies good, n. 3703. Hence it is evident that Rachel stealing the teraphim which her father had, signifies a change of the state signified by Laban as to truth. What these words involve, may also appear from the state of spirits when they are separating. The states of spirits as to good and truth are according to the societies in which they are, for all thought inflows through others, as has been shown above, and proximately through those with whom they are in society. When therefore they are removed from one society, and remitted to another, the states of their thoughts and affections are changed, consequently, their states as to truth and good. If, however, they are remitted into discordant societies, they then perceive what is undelightful, and from what is undelightful what is forced, and therefore they are thence separated, and are conveyed into concordant societies. Hence it is, that the evil cannot associate with, and dwell in, societies of the good, nor the good in societies of the evil, also, that all spirits and angels are distinctly arranged into societies according to the affections which are of the love; but every affection, which is of the love, contains in it manifold and various principles, see n. 3078, 3189, 4005, yet one is still the ruling principle; and thus every one may be in several societies, but still he has a particular tendency to that which is of the ruling affection, into which he is finally conveyed. In regard to the good which is signified by Laban, and to its change of state, so long as it was with the good which is represented by Jacob, it was nearer to the Divine, for Jacob is that good in the natural principle, and as being nearer to the Divine, it was also then in a more perfect state of truth and good. When, however, it was separated thence, it then came into another state as to truth and good; for changes of state in another life are nothing but approximations to, and removals from, the Divine. Hence then it is manifest what is meant by the change of state when the good signified by Laban was separated. The reason why Rachel stealing the teraphim which her father had, signifies a change of state as to truths, is, because teraphim signifies his gods, as is evident from what follows, for Laban says to Jacob, "Wherefore hast thou stolen *my gods?*" verse 30; and Jacob replies, "With whom thou findest *thy gods*, he shall not live before our brethren," verse 31; and gods, in the internal sense, signify truths, wherefore also in the Word mention is made of God when truth is treated of, see n. 2586, 2769, 2807, 2822. Teraphim were idols, which were applied to when they consulted or inquired of God, and because the answers which they received were to them Truths Divine, therefore truths are signified by them, as in Hosea, "Many days sat the sons of Israel, no king, and no prince, and no sacrifice, neither *ephod and teraphim*," iii. 4. Ephod and teraphim denote Truths Divine, which they received by answers, for when they inquired of God, they also put on the ephod, 1 Sam. xxiii. 9, 10, 11, 12. So in Zechariah, "*The teraphim speak iniquity*, and the diviners see a lie, and dreams speak vanity," x. 2; where also the teraphim denote answers, but in that state, iniquitous answers. And as such things were signified by teraphim, they were also with some, although prohibited, as with Micah in the book of Judges, "Micah had a house of God, and he made an ephod and tera phim, and filled the hand of one of his sons, that he might be to him for a priest; and some of the Danites said to their brethren, Know ye that in these houses there is an ephod and teraphim, and a graven and molten [image]. And when they had entered the house of Micah, they took the graven [image], the ephod and teraphim, and the molten [image]. And the heart of the priest was good, and he took the ephod and teraphim, and the graven [image]; and Micah pursued the sons of Dan, and said, Ye have taken my gods which I have made, and the priest, and have departed; what have I besides?" xvii. 5; chap. xviii. 14, 18, 24. Also with Michal, David's wife, of whom it is written in the first book of Samuel, "Michal, David's wife, took the teraphim, and set them in a bed, and covered them with a garment; the ambassadors of Saul came, but behold the teraphim in the bed," xix. 14, 16. That nevertheless they were idols, which were prohibited, is evident from what is said of them, 1 Sam. xv. 23; 2 Kings xxiii. 24; Ezek. xxi. 26

4112. "And Jacob stole the heart of Laban the Aramæan" —that this signifies a change of the state signified by Laban as to good, appears from the signification of stealing, as being to take away what is dear and holy, thus to change the state as just above, n. 4111; and from the signification of heart, as being that which proceeds from the will, and when the will is of good, as being good, see n. 2930, 3313, 3888, 3889; and from the representation of Laban, as being a middle good, which is now separated, and because it is separated, Laban is now called Aramæan, as also in verse 24 following, for Laban the Aramæan is such good, in which there is not Divine Good and Truth, as before. The reason of this signification is, because Aram or Syria was separated by a river, namely, the Euphrates, from the land of Canaan. Thus it is out of the land of Canaan, which signifies, in the internal sense, the Lord's kingdom, and, in the supreme sense, the Lord's Divine Human, see above, n. 4108. Aram and Syria specifically signify the knowledges of truth and good, see n. 1232, 1234, 3051, 3249, 3664, 3680, and this because the ancient Church was in Aram and Syria, and the remains of it continued there a long time, as appears from Balaam, who was from that country, and knew Jehovah, and also prophesied of the Lord. But after idolatry grew therein to a great height, and Abram was called forth thence, and a representative Church was instituted in the land of Canaan, then Aram or Syria put on the representation of a country out of the Church, or separate from the Church, consequently, removed from those things which are of the Lord's kingdom, the signification of the knowledges of good and truth being still retained. The reason why Jacob is said to have stolen the heart of Laban, whereby he did not tell him that he was flying, is, because a change of state as to *truth* was spoken of just above, here therefore a change of state as to *good* is spoken of, for in the Word wherever truth is treated of, there also good is treated of, because of the heavenly marriage, which is that of truth and good, in the whole and in every part of the Word, see n. 683, 793, 801, 2516, 2712.

4113. " Whereby he did not tell him that he was flying"— that this signifies by separation, may appear without explication. Jacob stealing the heart of Laban the Aramæan, whereby he did not tell him that he was flying, means, in the historical sense, that Jacob deprived Laban of the hope of possessing all things which were his, and reduced him to a state of straitness; for Laban believed, because Jacob served him, that all things which were Jacob's should be his, not only Jacob's women, his daughters, and their sons, but also his flocks, according to the law at that time also known, and likewise received, of which it is thus written in Moses, " If thou shalt buy an Hebrew servant, six years shall he serve, and in the seventh he shall go forth free : if his lord shall give unto him a woman, and she shall bring forth unto him sons and daughters; the woman and her sons shall be his lord's, and he shall go forth with his body,' Exod. xxi. 2, 4.   That Laban had this thought, is evident from Jacob's words in the following verse of this chapter, " Unless the God of my father, the God of Abraham, and the dread of Isaac, had been with me, thou wouldest now have sent me away empty," verse 42.   And from the words of Laban, " Laban answered, and said to Jacob, The daughters are my daughters, and the sons my sons, and the flock my flock; and all that thou seest, this is mine," verse 43.   Not considering, that Jacob was not a bought servant, nor even a servant, and that he was of a more noble family than himself; also, that he received for hire both the women and the flock, and thus that the above law had no respect to Jacob.   Now since Jacob by flying deprived Laban of this hope, and thereby reduced him to a state of straitness, it is said that he stole the heart of Laban the Aramæan, by this, that he did not tell him that he was flying; but in the internal sense these words signify a change of the state signified by Laban as to good by separation.   Concerning the change of state by separation, see what was said just above, n. 4111.

4114. " And he fled, and all that he had"—that this signifies separation, appears from what has been already said without further explication.

4115. " And arose"—that this signifies elevation, appears from what was said above of the signification of arising, n. 4103.

4116. " And passed the river"—that this signifies a state where there was conjunction, appears from the signification of river, in the present case Euphrates, as being conjunction with

the Divine. The reason why the river Euphrates has this signification, is, because it was the boundary of the land of Canaan
on that side, and all the boundaries of the land of Canaan represented and thence signified that which was last and first:
that which was last because it there closed, and that which was
first because it there commenced. All boundaries are such,
that they are the last to those who go out, and the first to those
who enter in. Now since Jacob was entering in, this river was
the first boundary, consequently conjunction with the Divine,
in the supreme sense; for the land of Canaan signifies, in the
internal sense, the Lord's celestial kingdom, see n. 1607, 3481;
and in the supreme sense, the Lord's Divine Human, 3038,
3705. Hence it is evident what is signified by passing the
river. That all things in the land of Canaan were representative according to distances, situations, and boundaries, may be
seen, n. 1585, 3686; thus that the terminating rivers were re-
resentative, as the river of Egypt, the Euphrates, and Jordan,
... 1866.

4117. "And set his faces to Mount Gilead"—that this signifies good in that state, appears from the signification of mountain, as being the celestial principle of love, that is, good, see
... 795, 1430, with which there was conjunction; Gilead signifies its quality. Since the river was the boundary, and in that
boundary was the first of conjunction, as was said, therefore
Mount Gilead, which was on this side of Jordan, signifies the
good with which that first of conjunction was effected. The
land Gilead, where the mount was, was within the limits of the
land of Canaan understood in an extended sense; it was on
this side Jordan, and fell as an inheritance to the Reubenites
and Gadites, and especially to the half tribe of Manasseh; and
as the inheritance extended thus far, it is said, that it was within the limits of the land of Canaan understood in an extended
sense. That it fell to them as an inheritance, appears in Moses,
Numb. xxxii. 1, 26 to 41; Deut. iii. 8, 10 to 16; Joshua xiii.
24 to 31. When, therefore, the land of Canaan was presented
in one complex, it was said from Gilead to Dan, and in another sense from Beersheba to Dan, for Dan also was a boundary, see n. 1710, 3923. That it was said from Beersheba to
Dan, may be seen, n. 2858, 2859. That it was said from Gilead
to Dan, appears from Moses, "Moses went up from the plains
of Moab upon Mount Nebo, the head of Pisgah, which is towards Jericho, where Jehovah showed him *the land of Gilead
even to Dan*," Deut. xxxiv. 1; and in the book of Judges,
"*Gilead* inhabiting in the passage of Jordan; and Dan, why
shall he fear ships?" v. 17. Gilead, as being a boundary, in a
spiritual sense signifies the first good, which is that of things
of the bodily senses, for it is the good or pleasurable enjoy-
ment of these into which the man who is regenerated is first

initiated. In this sense Gilead is taken in the prophets. as Jer.
viii. 22 ; chap. xxii. 6 ; chap. xlvi. 11 ; chap. l. 19 ; Ezek. xlvii.
18 ; Obadiah 19 ; Micah vii. 14 ; Zech. x. 10 ; Psalm lx. 7 ;
and in an opposite sense, Hosea vi. 8 ; chap. xii. 11.

4118. Verses 22, 23, 24,.25. *And it was told Laban on the
third day that Jacob fled. And he took his brothers with him,
and pursued after him a way of seven days, and joined him in
Mount Gilead. And God came to Laban the Aramœan in a
dream by night, and said unto him, Take heed to thyself lest
haply thou speak with Jacob from good even to evil. And Laban overtook Jacob : and Jacob fixed his tent in the mountain ;
and Laban fixed with his brethren in Mount Gilead.* It was
told Laban on the third day, signifies an end : that Jacob fled,
signifies separation : and he took his brothers with him, signifies goods in the place of those which he lost : and pursued
after him, signifies continued ardour of conjunction : a way of
seven days, signifies the holiness of truth : and joined him in
Mount Gilead, signifies by it somewhat of conjunction : and
God came to Laban the Aramæan in a dream by night, signifies
obscure perception of that good left to itself : and said unto
him, Take heed to thyself lest haply thou speak with Jacob
from good even to evil, signifies that there was no communication any longer : and Laban overtook Jacob, signifies somewhat
of conjunction : and Jacob fixed his tent in the mountain, signifies a state of love in which was the good now understood by
Jacob : and Laban fixed with his brethren in Mount Gilead,
signifies a state of good in the somewhat of that conjunction.

4119. "It was told Laban on the third day"—that this signifies an end, namely, of conjunction, appears from the signification of the third day, as being what is last, also what is complete, thus an end, see n. 1825, 2788, and also a beginning, n.
2788 ; for the end of a state of conjunction is the beginning of
a following state, which is that of separation, which state is
here signified by the third day.

4120. "That Jacob fled"—that this signifies separation,
appears from the signification of flying, as being to be separated, see n. 4113, 4114.

4121. "And he took his brothers with him"—that this signifies goods in the place of those which he lost, appears from
the signification of brethren, as being goods, see n. 2360, 3160,
3303, 3459, 3803, 3815. Brethren in the internal sense signify
those who are in similar good and truth, that is, in a similar
affection of good and truth ; for in another life, all are consociated according to affections, and they who are consociated constitute a brotherhood, not that they call themselves brethren,
but that they are brethren by conjunction. Essential good and
truth in another life make what is called on earth consanguinity
and relationship, wherefore they correspond : for goods and

truths considered in themselves do not acknowledge any other father but the Lord, for they are from Him alone. Hence, all are in brotherhood who are in goods and truths. Nevertheless there are degrees according to the quality of goods and truths. These degrees are signified in the Word by brethren, sisters, sons-in-law, daughters-in-law, grandsons, granddaughters, and by several names of families. On earth, however, they are so named in respect to common parents, however they differ in affections, but in another life such brotherhood and relationship is dissipated, and they all come into other brotherhoods, unless on earth they have been in similar good. At first, indeed, they generally meet, but in a short time are disjoined, for gain in that life does not consociate, but, as was said, affection, the quality of which then appears as in clear day, even that of the affection which one has had towards another; and this being the case, and affection drawing every one to his own society, therefore those who have been of different inclinations are dissociated Then also all brotherhood and all friendship, which was merely from the external man, is obliterated with both parties, and the brotherhood and friendship of the internal man alone remains The reason why taking his brethren with him signifies good in the place of those which he lost, is, because when one society is separated from another, as was said above, n. 4077, 4110, 4111, then it comes to another, consequently to other goods in the place of the former.

4122. "And pursued after him"—that this signifies continued ardour of conjunction, appears from the signification of pursuing him, as being continued ardour of conjunction. The subject here treated of in the internal sense is the separation of middle good from genuine good, after middle good has served its use. The process of separation is here fully described, but it is such, that it cannot even be perceived by man to exist, nevertheless it manifestly appears to the angels with innumerable various particulars, for thereby they see and perceive in the man who is regenerating, all the changes of that state, being present with him as ministers, and according to those changes, and by them, they lead him of the Lord to good, so far as man suffers himself to be led; and as this process is of so great a use in heaven, therefore it is here so abundantly treated of. Hence also it may appear what is the nature of the internal sense of the Word, namely, that it is the angelic Word.

4123. "A way of seven days"—that this signifies the holiness of truth, appears from the signification of way, as being truth, see n. 627, 2333; and from the signification of seven, as being what is holy, see n. 395 433, 716, 881, in the present case the ardour of conjunction, or of conjoining himself, with the holiness of truth.

4122—4129.] GENESIS. 501

4124. "And joined him in Mount Gilead"—that this signifies something of conjunction thereby, appears from the signification of joining, as being conjunction; and of Mount Gilead, as being the good which is the first of conjunction, see above, n. 4117. Thus, joining him in Mount Gilead signifies somewhat of conjunction.

4125. "And God came to Laban the Aramæan in a dream by night"—that this signifies the obscure perception of that good left to itself, appears from the representation of Laban, as being a middle good, spoken of above, who is called Aramæan when he is separated from the good represented by Jacob, n. 4112; and from the signification of a dream by night, as being what is obscure, see n. 2514, 2528. Perception in that obscure state is signified by God coming in a dream by night.

4126. "And said unto him, Take heed to thyself lest haply thou speak with Jacob from good even to evil"—that this signifies that there should be no communication any longer, appears from the signification of speaking from good even to evil, as being to speak good and think evil, and thence finally to speak evil and do evil; for he who thinks evil, at length speaks it and does it. Such a person is no longer conjoined with another, because it is thought and will which conjoin, but not words. In the world, indeed, words conjoin, but only when another believes that good is also thought and willed. In another life, however, all thought is manifest, for it is communicated by a certain sphere, which is a spiritual sphere, that proceeds from another, and manifests the quality of his intentions, that is, of his will and thought; wherefore conjunction is according thereto. Hence it is evident that these words, "Speak not from good even to evil," in the internal sense signify, that there should be no conjunction any longer.

4127. "And Laban overtook Jacob"—that this signifies something of conjunction, appears from what was said above, n. 4124.

4128. "And Jacob fixed his tent in the mountain"—that this signifies a state of love in which the good was, which is now understood by Jacob, appears from the signification of tent, as being the holiness of love, see n. 414, 1102, 2145, 2152, 3312, and of fixing a tent, as being a state of that love; and from the signification of mountain, as being good, as above, n. 4117, in the present case the good now understood by Jacob, of which see above, n. 4073.

4129 "And Laban fixed with his brethren in Mount Gilead" —that this signifies a state of good in something of that conjunction, appears from the representation of Laban, as being a good now separated from the good represented by Jacob; and from the signification of fixing, as being a state of that good; (it is not said, to fix a tent, because it was not a state of holy love except by something of that conjunction;) and from the signification of brethren, as being the goods wherewith the good signified by Laban was associated, see above, n. 4121; and from the signification of Mount Gilead, as being where was the first and last of conjunction, see above, n. 4117. Hence it is evident, that Laban fixing with his brethren in Mount Gilead, signifies a state of good in something of that conjunction. What these words, which have been now explained further involve, cannot be so well unfolded to the apprehension, except from what happens in another life, when societies of spirits and angels from the Lord are adjoined to man, and are separated from him, the process of their adjunction and separation being such, according to the order which there exists. The interesting particulars of that process are here fully described, but to explain them one by one, would be to speak mere arcana, for they are altogether unknown to man. Some particulars were mentioned on the subject above, in speaking of the conjunction and separation of societies with the man about to be regenerated : but it is enough to know, that the arcana of this process are here contained in the internal sense, and indeed are of such importance and of such a quality, that it is impossible they should be fully explained to the apprehension as to a thousandth part of them.

4130. Verses 26, 27, 28, 29, 30. *And Laban said unto Jacob, What hast thou done? and thou hast stolen my heart, and hast withdrawn my daughters as captives for the sword. Wherefore hast thou concealed thy flight, and hast robbed me, and hast not told me? and I would have sent thee in gladness, and in songs, in the drum and in the harp. And hast not permitted me to kiss my sons and my daughters? now thou hast acted foolishly in doing. Let God have my hand to do with you evil, and the God of your father in the night past said unto me, saying, Take heed to thyself of speaking with Jacob from good even to evil. And now going thou hast gone, because desiring thou hast desired to the house of thy father; wherefore hast thou stolen my gods?* Laban said unto Jacob, signifies a state of communication : what hast thou done? signifies indignation : and thou hast stolen my heart, signifies that he had no longer Divine Good as before : and hast withdrawn my daughters, signifies that neither had he the affections of truth as before : as captives for the sword, signifies that they were taken away from him : wherefore hast thou concealed thy flight, and hast robbed me, and hast not told me? signifies the state in case the separation had been from freedom on his part : and I would have sent thee in gladness and in songs, signifies a state in which he would then have believed from proprium that he had been as to truths : in the drum and in the harp, signifies as to spiritual good : and hast not permitted me to kiss my sons

and my daughters, signifies disjunction by virtue of a free
state according to the faith of that good : now thou hast acted
foolishly in doing, signifies indignation : let God have my
hand to do with you evil, signifies a state of indignation if he
had ability : and the God of your father in the night past said
unt' me, signifies that it was not permitted by the Divine :
saying, Take heed to thyself of speaking with Jacob from good
even to evil, signifies a forbidding of communication : and
now going thou hast gone, signifies that by virtue of proprium
he separated himself : because desiring thou hast desired to
the house of thy father, signifies a desire of conjunction with
the Divine Good flowing in directly : wherefore hast thou
stolen my gods? signifies indignation on account of a state of
lost truth.

4131. "Laban said unto Jacob"—that this signifies a state
of communication of that good which is now represented by
Laban, with that good which is now represented by Jacob, appears from the signification of saying, as here being communication, see n. 3060 ; because somewhat of conjunction was
effected, concerning which see just above, n. 4124, 4127, 4129,
and now it immediately follows, Laban said to Jacob, therefore
saying signifies communication.

4132. "What hast thou done?"—that this signifies indignation, appears from the affection which is in these and the following words of Laban, as being indignation.

4133. "And thou hast stolen my heart"—that this signifies
that he had no longer Divine Good as before, appears from the
signification of stealing the heart, as being to take away what
is dear and holy, see above, n. 4112 ; hence, that he had no
longer Divine Good as before, by separation.

4134. "And hast withdrawn my daughters"—that this signifies that neither had he affections of truth as before, appears
from the signification of daughters, here Rachel and Leah, as
being the affections of truth, see n. 3758, 3782, 3793, 3819.

4135. "As captives for the sword"—that this signifies that
the affections of truth were taken away from him, appears without explication.   They are called captives for the sword, because
sword is predicated of truth, see n. 2799.   How this is, has
been explained before.

4136. "Wherefore hast thou concealed thy flight, and hast
robbed me, and hast not told me?"—that this signifies the state
in case the separation had been from freedom on his part, appears from the signification of concealing flight, as being to
separate himself against the other's inclination ; (that to fly is
to be separated, may be seen, n. 4113, 4114, 4120 ;) and from
the signification of robbing me, as being to take away what is
dear and holy, see n. 4112, 4133 ; and from the signification
of not telling me, as being, here, by separation, see n. 4113

Hence it follows that these words signify that the separation was made against his inclination, when yet it ought to have been made from freedom. A state of freedom is signified and described by the words which now follow, " I would have sent thee in joy and in songs, in the drum and in the dance ;' but these are the words of Laban according to his faith at that time. How the separation of middle from genuine good is effected in those who are regenerated, namely, in freedom, may be seen above, n. 4110, 4111. That this is the case, does not appear to man, for he knows not how goods are varied in him, still less how the state of every good is changed ; not even how the good of infancy is varied and changed into the good of childhood, and this into the succeeding good of youth, after-wards into the good of adult age, and lastly into that of old age. With those who are not regenerated, goods are not the things changed, but affections and their delights : but with those who are regenerated, they are changes of the state of goods, and this from infancy to the close of life ; for it is fore-seen by the Lord what kind of life man is about to lead, and how he will suffer himself to be led by Him, and as all and singular things, yea, the most particular, are foreseen, they are also provided for ; but how the case then is with changes of the state of goods, man knows nothing, and this principally because he has no knowledges of such a thing, nor at this day desires to have ; and as the Lord does not flow immediately into man, and teach, but into his thoughts, thus mediately, therefore he cannot in any wise know the changes of the state of those goods : since man is such as to be without the knowledges on this subject, and moreover there are few at this day who suffer themselves to be regenerated, therefore if these things were explained more fully, they could not be comprehended. That few at this day know any thing of spiritual good, and also that few know any thing of freedom, has been made known to me by experience from those who come into another life out of the Christian world. It is permitted me to adduce one example only for the sake of illustration. There was a certain dignitary in the Church who believed himself more learned than others, and also while he lived was acknowledged by others to be learned, but as he had lived an evil life, he was in such stupid ignorance of good and freedom, and the delight and blessedness thence resulting, that he did not know the least difference between infernal delight and freedom, and heavenly delight and freedom, yea, he said that there was no difference. Now since such ignorance prevails even with those who are reputed to excel in learning, it may hence be concluded in to what shades, yea, into how great and wild fancies of the imagination those things would fall, which should here be said of good and free-dom, which are the subjects treated of in the internal sense;

when, nevertheless, there is not a single expression in the Word which does not involve a heavenly arcanum, although before man it appears of no moment, and this because of his defect of knowledges, or of his being ignorant at this day of heavenly things, and willing to continue ignorant.

4137. "And I would have sent thee in gladness and in songs"—that this signifies a state in which he would then have believed from proprium that he had been as to truths, appears from the signification of sending thee, as being that he should have separated himself by freedom free principle; but that he had not separated when he was in that state, appears from what was said above, n. 4113. Hence it is evident that these words were spoken by Laban in that state in which he then had believed from proprium that he had been, for to believe from proprium is to believe from what is not true, whereas to believe not from proprium, but from the Lord, is to believe from truth. That it is a state as to truths, is signified by sending in gladness and in songs, for gladness and songs are predicated of truths. In the Word throughout there is mention made of gladness and joy, and sometimes of both together, but gladness is mentioned when the subject treated of is truth and the affection thereof, and joy is mentioned in treating of good and its affection, as in Isaiah, " Behold *joy* and *gladness*, to kill the ox and to slaughter the cattle, to eat flesh and to drink wine," xxii. 13 ; where joy is predicated of good, and gladness of truth. Again, " A shout over wine in the streets, all *gladness* shall be desolated, and all *joy* shall be banished," xxiv. 11. Again, " The redeemed of Jehovah shall return, and shall come to Zion with *singing*, and the *joy* of eternity upon their head ; *joy* and *gladness* shall overtake them, and sadness and groaning shall flee away," xxxv. 10 ; chap. li. 11. Again, " Jehovah shall comfort Zion, *joy* and *gladness* shall be found therein, confession and the voice of singing," li. 3. So in Jeremiah, " I will cause to cease from the cities of Judah, and from the streets of Jerusalem, the *voice of joy* and *the voice of gladness*, the voice of the bridegroom and the voice of the bride, because the earth shall be for wasting," vii. 34 ; chap. xxv. 10. Again, " *The voice of joy and the voice of gladness*, and the voice of the bridegroom and the voice of the bride, the voice of them that say, Confess ye to Jehovah Zebaoth," xxxiii. 11. Again, " *Gladness* and *exultation* are gathered together from Carmel and from the land of Moab," xlviii. 33. So in Joel, " Is not food cut off before our eyes, *gladness* and *exultation* from the house of our God?" i. 16. And in Zechariah, " A fast shall be to the house of Judah for *joy* and for *gladness*, and for festive goods," viii. 19. He who does not know that in the whole and in every part of the Word there is a heavenly marriage, that is, a marriage of good and truth, would suppose that joy and gladness

were one, and that the expressions were used only for the sake
of giving greater emphasis to the subject; thus, that one is
superfluous. This, however, is not the case, for there is not the
least of an expression without a spiritual sense. In the passages
adduced, and also in others, joy is predicated of good, and gladness of truth, see also n. 3118. That songs are also predicated
of truths, appears from several passages in the Word where
mention is made of songs, as Isaiah v. 1; chap. xxiv. 9; chap.
xxvi. 1; chap. xxx. 29; chap. xlii. 10; Ezek. xxvi. 13; Amos
v. 23; and in other places. It is to be observed, that all things
in the Lord's kingdom have relation either to good or to truth,
that is, to those things which are of love, and of faith from
charity. Those things which have relation to good, or which
are of love, are called celestial; but those things which have
reference to truth, or which are of faith from charity, are called
spiritual. Now as the whole and every part of the Word treats
of the Lord's kingdom, and, in the supreme sense, of the Lord
and the Lord's kingdom is the marriage of good and truth, or
the heavenly marriage, and the Lord Himself is He in Whom
exists the Divine Marriage, and from Whom proceeds the heavenly marriage, therefore this marriage exists in the whole and
in every part of the Word, as is more especially manifest in the
prophets, where repetitions of one thing occur, the expressions
alone being changed. These expressions, however, are in no
case without meaning, but one expression signifies the celestial
that is, what relates to love or good, and the other the spiritual,
that is, what relates to faith from charity or to truth. Hence it
is evident, how the heavenly marriage, that is, the Lord's kingdom, is in the whole and in every part of the Word, and in a
supreme sense, the Divine Marriage itself, or the Lord.

4138. "In the drum and in the harp"—that this signifies as
to spiritual good, namely, a state in which on this occasion he
would have believed from proprium that he had been as to that
good, appears from this, that drum and harp are predicated of
good, but of spiritual good, as may appear from several passages
in the Word. Spiritual good is what is called the good of faith,
and is charity; but celestial good is what is called the good of
love, and is love to the Lord. There are two kingdoms of the
Lord in the heavens; one is called His celestial kingdom, and
in it are they who are in love to the Lord, and the other is
called the spiritual kingdom, and in it are they who are in
charity towards the neighbour. These kingdoms are most distinct, but still they act in unity in the heavens: of these distinct
kingdoms, or the celestial and spiritual things, see what has
been frequently said above. Formerly, in the Churches, various
kinds of musical instruments were made use of, as drums, psalteries, pipes, harps, decachords, and several others, some of
which belonged to the class of celestials, but some to the class

of spirituals, and when they are mentioned in the Word, they involve celestial and spiritual things, insomuch, that it may thence be known what kind of good is treated of, whether it be a spiritual or celestial. Drums and harps belonged to the class of spirituals, wherefore it is here said, as to spiritual good. That harp is predicated of things spiritual, and that stringed instruments signify spiritual things, but wind-instruments, celestial things, may be seen, n. 418, 419, 420.

4139. "And hast not permitted me to kiss my sons and my daughters"—that this signifies disjunction in a free state according to the faith of that good, appears from the signification of kissing, as being conjunction from affection, see n. 3573, 3574, 3800, hence, not to permit to kiss is disjunction; and from the signification of sons, as being truths, and of daughters, as being goods, of which we have occasionally spoken above, thus denoting disjunction as to truths and goods. That it was in a free state according to the faith of that good, is implied, of which state see above, n. 4136, 4137.

4140. "Now thou hast acted foolishly in doing"—that this signifies indignation, appears from the affection contained in these words.

4141. "Let God have my hand to do with you evil"—that this signifies a state of indignation if he had the power, appears from the signification of hand, as being power, see n. 878, 3387 That it is a state of indignation in which these words were spoken, and which is thence signified, is manifest.

4142. "And the God of your father in the night past said unto me"—that this signifies that it was not permitted by the Divine, may appear without explication, for it was forbidden him in a dream to speak to Jacob from good even to evil, as also follows.

4143. "Saying, Take heed to thyself from speaking with Jacob from good even to evil"—that this signifies a forbidding of communication, appears from the signification of speaking from good even to evil, as being no communication any longer, see above, n. 4126, thus a forbidding of communication.

4144. "And now going thou hast gone"—that this signifies that from proprium he separated himself, appears from the signification of going thou hast gone, as being to be separated. That it was of proprium, is evident.

4145. "Because desiring thou hast desired to the house of thy father"—that this signifies desire of conjunction with Good Divine directly influent, appears from the signification of father's house in this passage, that is, of Isaac and Abraham, as being good directly influent; that house denotes good, see n. 2233, 2234, 3652, 3720; that father also denotes good, see n. 3703; that Isaac is the good of the rational principle, see n. 3012, 3194, 3210; and moreover Abraham with Isaac repre-

sents Good Divine directly influent, and Laban collateral good,
or that which is not directly influent, n. 3665, 3778. Collateral
good, or that which is not directly influent, is that which was
called middle good, for this good derives much from worldly
things, which appear as goods, but are not goods; whereas
good directly influent is what comes immediately from the
Lord, or mediately through heaven from the Lord, and is Good
Divine separate from such worldly good as was just now mentioned. Every man who is regenerated is first in middle good,
in order that it may serve for introducing genuine goods and
truths, but after it has served this use, it is separated, and he is
brought to good which is directly influent. Thus the man who
is regenerated is perfected by degrees. For example: he who
is regenerated at first believes, that the good which he thinks
and does is from himself, and also that he merits somewhat, for
he does not yet know, and if he knows he does not comprehend,
that good can flow-in from any other source, neither can he conceive otherwise than that he must be recompensed, because he
does it from himself. Unless he believes this at first, he would
in no wise do good. By this means, however, he is initiated
both into the affection of doing good, and into knowledges concerning good, and concerning merit; and when he is thus
brought into the affection of doing good, he then begins to
think and to believe otherwise, namely, that good flows-in from
the Lord, and that he merits nothing by the good which he does
from proprium; and at length, when he is in the affection of
willing and doing good, he utterly rejects merit, yea, holds it
in aversion, and is affected with good from good: when he is
in this state, then good flows-in directly. Take another example from conjugial love. The good which precedes and
initiates, is beauty, or agreement of manners, or external application of the one towards the other, or equality of circumstances, or a desired condition of life. These goods are middle
goods, the first of conjugial love. Afterwards comes conjunction of minds, in that the one party wills as the other, and
perceives delight in doing what pleases the other. This is
another state, and now former things, although they are present,
still are not regarded. Lastly succeeds unition as to celestial
good and spiritual truth, namely, that the one believes as the
other, and is affected with the same good as the other, and
when this state exists, then each is together in the heavenly
marriage, which is that of good and truth, thus in conjugial
love, for conjugial love is nothing else, and in this case the
Lord inflows into the affections of each as into one affection.
This good is what inflows directly, whereas the former goods,
which inflowed indirectly, served as means of introducing to
this.

4146. " Wherefore hast thou stolen my gods ?"—that this

signifies indignation on account of a state of lost truth, appears from what was said and shown above, n. 4111, of the teraphim which Rachel took away.

4147. Verses 31, 32. *And Jacob answered, and said unto Laban, Because I feared; because I said, Perchance thou wilt snatch away thy daughters from being with me. With whom thou findest thy gods, he shall not live before our brethren. Search for thyself what is with me, and take to thyself: and Jacob knew not that Rachel had stolen them.* Jacob answered, and said unto Laban, Because I feared; because I said, Perchance thou wilt snatch away thy daughters from being with me, signifies a state, that in case separation was made by the freedom of that good, it would be injured as to the affections of truth: with whom thou findest thy gods, he shall not live before our brethren, signifies that the truth was not his, but that his truth did not subsist in its good: search for thyself what is with me, and take to thyself, signifies that all things of that good were separated: and Jacob knew not that Rachel had stolen them, signifies that they were of the affection of interior truth.

4148. "Jacob answered, and said unto Laban, Because I feared; because I said, Perchance thou wilt snatch away thy daughters from being with me"—that this signifies a state, that in case separation was made by the freedom of that good, it would be injured as to the affections of truth, appears from what goes before, in treating of separation by freedom on the part of the good signified by Laban, to which this is a reply. These words, all and singular, in the internal sense, involve heavenly arcana, which cannot be explained for the reason mentioned above, n. 4136. That a state is signified, in case separation was made by the freedom of that good, is evident; and that in this case the affections of truth would be injured, is signified by the words, "Perchance thou wilt snatch away thy daughters from being with me;" for daughters, in the present case Rachel and Leah, signify the affections of truth, as has been frequently shown above. How this case is, may better appear from what now follows.

4149. "With whom thou findest thy gods, he shall not live before our brethren"—that this signifies that the truth was not his, and that his truth did not subsist in its good, appears from the signification of gods, in the present case teraphim, as being truths, see n. 4111, but truths not of the good signified by Laban, but of the affection represented by Rachel. Since gods here signify those truths, it is therefore said that Rachel stole them, and they are further treated of in what follows; a circumstance which would not have been recorded, unless it had involved some arcana that are manifest only in the internal sense. Now as those truths which are here treated of, were not of the good signified by Laban, but of the affection of truth represented by Rachel, therefore the above words, "With whom thou findest thy gods, he shall not live before our brethren," signify, that the truth was not his, and that his truth did not subsist in its good. With this arcanum the case is as follows. Every spiritual good has its own truths, for where such good is, there are truths. Good considered in itself is one, but it becomes various by truths. Truths may be compared to the fibres which compose some organ of the body; according to the form of the fibres is the organ, consequently its operation, which operation is effected by the life which flows in through the soul, and the life is from the good which is from the Lord. Hence it is that good, although one, is yet various in every individual, and so various, that it is never altogether alike in one person as in another. Hence also it is, that the truth of one person can in no wise subsist in the good of another; for all truths, with every individual who is in good, communicate with each other, and constitute a certain form; wherefore, one person's truth cannot be transferred to another, but in case it is transferred, it passes into the form of him who receives it, and puts on another appearance. This arcanum, however, is of too deep a nature to admit of a brief explanation. Hence it is that the mind of one person is in no case altogether like that of another, but as is the number of mankind, so also is the variety of affections and thoughts whereby they are distinct from each other. Hence also it is that the universal heaven consists of angelic forms, which are in a perpetual variety, and which, being arranged into a celestial form by the Lord, act in unity; for a one in all cases is composed, not of idealities, but of varieties in form, which constitute a one according to the form. Hence it is manifest what is meant by the expression, that his truth did not subsist in its good.

4150. "Search for thyself what is with me, and take to thyself"—that this signifies that all things of that good were separated, appears from the sense of those words, which is, that nothing which is thine is with me, that. is, that nothing of the good signified by Laban is in the good which is Jacob; consequently, that all things of that good were separated.

4151. "And Jacob knew not that Rachel had stolen them" —that this signifies that they were of the affection of interior truth, appears from the representation of Rachel, as being the affection of interior truth, see n. 3758, 3782, 3793, 3819; and from the signification of stealing, as being to take away what is dear and holy, see n. 4112, 4113, 4133. Above, by Rachel stealing the teraphim or gods of Laban was signified a change of the state represented by Laban as to truth, see n. 4111. The change of state is further described in this and the following verses, and was from this ground, that the good represented by

Laban, after that it was separated from the good which is Jacob, came into another state by separation; for the truths which
appeared to him as his own, when the goods were conjoined,
were perceived as if taken away. This is the reason why Laban complained about them, and why he searched in the tents,
and did not find them; for the truths which were signified by
teraphim in a good sense, see n. 4111, were not his, but were
of the affection of truth which is Rachel. How this case is,
cannot appear except from those things which come to pass in
another life, for the things which in that life come to pass near
a man, appear to him as if they were in him. The case is
nearly the same with spirits in another life. When the societies
of spirits, which are in middle good, are in society with the
angels, it then appears to them altogether as if the truths and
goods of the angels are their own, nor do they know any other;
but when they are separated, they then perceive that it is not
so. On this account they complain, believing that they were
taken away by those with whom they have been in society.
This is what is signified, in the internal sense, by teraphim in
this and the following verses. In general, the case is, that no
one has any good or truth which is his own, but that all good
and truth flows in from the Lord, as well immediately as mediately through the angelic societies; but that still it appears
as if good and truth is man's own, and this because they may
be appropriated to him, until he comes into the state to know,
and afterwards to acknowledge, and at length to believe, that
they are not his, but the Lord's. It is also known from the
Word, and thence in the Christian world, that all good and all
truth is from the Lord, and that nothing of good is from man;
yea, the doctrinals of the Church, which are derived from the
Word, teach that man cannot even endeavour after good from
himself; thus, cannot will it, consequently, not do it, for doing
good is from willing good. They teach further, that the all of
faith is from the Lord, so that man cannot believe the least
thing, unless it flow in from the Lord. This the doctrinals of
the Church teach, and it is also taught in public preaching;
but that few, yea, very few, believe that it is the case, may
appear from the fact, that mankind in general suppose the all
of life to be in themselves, and scarce any suppose that it inflows. The all of the life of man consists in the faculty of being
able to think, and of being able to will, for if the faculty of
thinking and willing be taken away, nothing of life remains;
and the very essential of life consists in thinking what is good,
and in willing what is good, also in thinking what is true, and
in willing that which he thinks to be true. Now as these things
according to the doctrinals which are derived from the Word,
are not of man, but of the Lord, and flow in from the Lord
through heaven, hence they who have any strength of judg-

ment, and power of reflection, might be enabled to conclude that the all of life comes by influx. The case is the same with what is evil and false. It is agreeable to the doctrines derived from the Word, that the devil is continually endeavouring to seduce man, and that he is continually inspiring evil, whence also it is said, when any one has committed any enormous crime, that he has suffered himself to be seduced by the devil. This also is true, but few if any believe it; for as all good and truth is from the Lord, so every thing evil and false is from hell, that is, from the devil, for hell is the devil. Hence it may appear, that as all good and truth, so also every thing evil and false flows in, consequently also the thinking and willing evil; and as these things also flow in, it may be concluded by those who have any strength of judgment and power of reflection, that the all of life inflows, although it appears as if it were in man. That this is the case has been frequently shown to the spirits who have come fresh from the world into another life but some of them have said, that if every thing evil and false inflows, then nothing of evil and the false can be imputed to them, and that they are not in fault, because it came from another source. But they received for answer, that they appropriated it to themselves by this, that they believed themselves to think from themselves and to will from themselves, whereas if they had believed as the case really is, they would then not have appropriated those things to themselves: for they would then also have believed that all good and truth is from the Lord, and if they had believed this, they would have suffered themselves to be led by the Lord, and would thereby have been in another state; and then the evil which had entered into the thought and will would not have affected them, for there would not have come forth evil but good, according to the Lord's words in Mark, chap. vii. 15. Many, however, can know this, but few can believe. They who are evil can also know it, but still they do not believe, for they will to be in proprium, and this they love to such a degree, that when it is shown them that every thing inflows, they come into anxiety, and with the greatest earnestness request that they may be allowed to live in their proprium, urging, that if it were to be taken away from them, they could live no longer; thus they believe who also know. These observations are made in order to show how the case is with the societies which are in middle good, when they are conjoined to others, and when they are separated from them, namely, that when they are conjoined, they know no other than that goods and truths are their own, when yet they are not their own.

4152. Verses 33, 34, 35. *And Laban came into the tent of Jacob, and into the tent of Leah, and into the tent of both the handmaids, and he found not: and he went forth from the tent*

of Leah, and came into the tent of Rachel. And Rachel took
the teraphim, and placed them in the straw of the camel, and
sat upon them : and Laban handled all the tent, and found not.
And she said to her father, Let there not be anger in the eyes
of my lord because I cannot rise from before thee, because the
way of women is upon me : and he searched, and did not find
the teraphim. Laban came into the tent of Jacob, and into the
tent of Leah, and into the tent of both the handmaids, and he
found not, signifies that in their holy things there were not such
truths : and he went forth from the tent of Leah, and came into
the tent of Rachel, signifies the holiness of that truth : and
Rachel took the teraphim, signifies interior natural truths
which are from the Divine : and placed them in the straw of
the camel, signifies in scientifics : and sat upon them, signifies
that they were interior : and Laban handled all the tent, and
found not, signifies that therein was not what was his property -
and she said to her father, signifies to good : Let there not be
anger in the eyes of my lord because I cannot rise from before
thee, signifies that they cannot be revealed : because the way
of women is upon me, signifies that as yet she was amongst
uncleannesses : and he searched, and did not find the teraphim,
signifies that they were not his.

4153. "Laban came into the tent of Jacob, and into the
tent of Leah, and into the tent of both the handmaids, and
found not"—that this signifies that in their holy things there
were not such truths, appears from the signification of tent, as
being what is holy, see n. 414, 1102, 2145, 2152, 3210, 3312,
4128, in the present case, holy things, because mention is made
of tents, namely, those of Jacob, Leah, and the handmaids.
That those truths were not therein, is signified by the teraphim,
that they were not found there. That teraphim in a good sense
denote truths, see above, n. 4111. Jacob represents the good
of the natural principle ; Leah, the affection of external truth ;
and the handmaids, external affections, as shown above : and
as the truths which are here treated of were not external but
internal, therefore they were not found in their tents, that is,
holy things ; but they were in the tent of Rachel, that is, in the
holiness of the affection of interior truth, for Rachel represents
the affection of interior truth.

4154. " And he went forth from the tent of Leah, and came
into the tent of Rachel "—that this signifies the holiness of that
truth, appears from what has been just now said above. The
case with truths is as with goods, that they are exterior and
interior ; for there is an internal man and an external. The
goods and truths of the internal man are called internal goods
and truths, and the goods and truths of the external man are
called external goods and truths. The goods and truths of the

internal man are of a threefold degree, such as are in the three heavens. The goods and truths of the external man are also of a threefold degree, and correspond to the internal; for there are mediating goods and truths between the internal and external man, for without mediating goods and truths there is no communication. There are goods and truths proper to the natural man, which are called external goods and truths; and there are also sensual goods and truths, which are of the body, and thus are outermost. These goods and truths of a threefold degree appertain to the external man, and correspond to as many goods and truths of the internal man, as was said, on which subject, by the Divine Providence of the Lord, we shall speak elsewhere. The goods and truths of every degree are most distinct from each other, and are not in the least confounded. Those which are interior are component, and those which are exterior are composite. These, although they are most distinct amongst themselves, still do not appear to man as distinct; the sensual man sees no other than that all interior principles, yea, even internal, are merely sensual, for he sees from the sensual, and thus from the outmost; and from things outmost it is altogether impossible to see things interior, but from this interior it is possible to see the outmost. He who is a natural man, that is, who thinks from scientifics, knows no other than that the natural things, from which he thinks, are inmost, when yet they are external. The interior man, who judges and concludes from analytical principles discoverable from natural scientifics, in like manner believes that those things are the inmost of man, because they appear to him as inmost, but still they are beneath things rational, and thus in respect to genuine rational principles, they are exterior or inferior. Thus it is with the apprehension of man. These latter things, of which we are now speaking, are of the natural or external man in a threefold degree; but those things which are of the internal man, are also in a threefold degree, as was said, such as exist in the three heavens. From what has been now said, it may appear how the case is with the truths which are signified by teraphim, in that they were not found in the tents of Jacob, of Leah, and of the handmaids, but in the tent of Rachel, that is, in the holiness of the affection of interior truth. Every truth which is from the Divine is in a holiness, for it cannot be otherwise, because truth which is from the Divine is holy. It is called holy from the affection, that is, from the love, which inflows from the Lord, and causes man to be affected with truth.

4155. "And Rachel took the teraphim"—that this signifies natural interior truths which are from the Divine, appears from the representation of Rachel, as being the affection of interior truth, concerning which, see above; and from the signification of teraphim, as being truths which are from the Divine, see

n. 4111, or interior truths, the quality of which, and their residence, was shown above, n. 4145.

4156. "And placed them in the straw of the camel"—that this signifies in scientifics, appears from the signification of the straw of the camel, as being scientifics, see n. 3114. They are called straw, as well because they are food for camels, as because they are respectively gross and inordinate; wherefore also scientifics are signified by the entwistings of trees and of a forest, see n. 2831. That camels denote the common scientifics, which are of the natural man, see n. 3048, 3071, 3143, 3145. That scientifics are respectively gross and inordinate, and therefore are signified by straw, and also by things entwisted, as was observed, does not appear to those who are in scientifics alone, and in consequence of them pass for men of erudition. Such persons believe, that in proportion as a man is knowing, or in proportion to the science he possesses, in the same proportion he is wise. But that the case is otherwise, was made very manifest to me from those in another life, who, during their abode in the world, had been in scientifics alone, and had thence acquired the name and reputation of being learned, for at times they are more stupid than others who have had no skill in the sciences. The cause of this was discovered, namely, that scientifics are indeed the means of becoming wise, but that they are likewise the means of becoming insane. To those who are in the life of good, scientifics are the means of becoming wise, but to those who are in the life of evil, they are the means of becoming insane; for by scientifics they confirm not only the life of evil, but also the principles of the false, and this arrogantly, and with persuasion, because they believe themselves to be more wise than others, and thus they destroy their rational principle. He does not possess the rational principle, who can reason from scientifics, and occasionally to appearance more sublimely than others, it being only the lumen of infatuation which produces his dexterity; but he possesses the strength of the rational principle, who can discern that good is good, and truth truth, consequently that evil is evil, and the false false. He, however, who regards good as evil, and evil as good, also who regards truth as false, and the false as truth, can in no wise be called rational, but rather irrational, however he may appear to talk rationally. With him who sees clearly that good is good, and that truth is truth, and on the other hand, that evil is evil, and the false false, light inflows from heaven, and enlightens his intellectual principle, and causes the reasons, which he sees in his understanding, to be so many rays of that light. The same light also illuminates scientifics, so that they confirm, and moreover, arranges them into order and into a celestial form. But they who are contrary to good and truth, as all are who are in the life of evil, do not admit that heavenly light, but are delighted only with their lumen of infatuation; the nature of which lumen is, that it sees as one who in the dark beholds spotted streaks on a wall, and thence by phantasies makes images of every kind, which yet are not images, for when daylight comes, it appears that they are only spotted streaks. Hence it may be manifest, that scientifics are the means of becoming wise, and also are the means of becoming insane, that is, that they are the means of perfecting the rational principle, and are the means of destroying the rational principle. They, therefore, who have destroyed the rational principle by scientifics, in another life are more stupid than those who have been unskilled in the sciences. That scientifics are respectively gross, is manifest from this, that they belong to the natural or external man, and the rational principle, which is cultivated by them, to the spiritual or internal man. How far these principles differ and are distant from each other as to purity, may be known from what was said and shown concerning the two memories, n. 2469 to 2494.

4157. "And sat upon them"—that this signifies that they were interior, thus underneath her in the camel's straw, appears from this, that camel's straw, as was just now said above, signifies scientifics. The truths, which are signified by teraphim, were not scientifics, but in them; for in regard to truths of a threefold degree, spoken of above, n. 4154, the case is this, that the interior are in the exterior, for so they repose themselves in order.

4158. "And Laban handled all the tent, and did not find"— that this signifies that there was not therein what was his property, appears from the series of things treated of in the internal sense, thus without further explication.

4159. "And she said to her father"—that this signifies to good, appears from the signification of father, as being good, see n. 3703; and from the representation of Laban, who is here the father, as denoting middle good, spoken of above.

4160. "Let there not be anger in the eyes of my lord because I cannot rise from before thee"—that this signifies that they cannot be revealed, may also appear from the series of things treated of in the internal sense, consequently without further explication; for to rise would be to discover, consequently, to reveal the truths which are signified by teraphim. Thus, not to be able to rise, signifies that they could not be revealed.

4161. "Because the way of women is upon me"—that this signifies that as yet she was amongst uncleannesses, appears from the signification of the way of women, as denoting uncleannesses, and also that hence those things were unclean upon which she sat, Levit. xv. 19 to 31, thus that she was among uncleannesses. Interior truths are said to be among unclean-

nesses, when they are among scientifics which do not as yet
correspond, or are discordant. Such uncleannesses are removed
when man is cleansed, that is, when he is regenerated.

4162. "And he searched and did not find the teraphim"—
that this signifies that they were not his, or, that those truths
were not Laban's, appears from the signification of searching
and not finding. These words, in the external historical sense,
involve, that indeed they were Laban's, but were hidden; but
in the internal sense, that they were not his. That teraphim
are truths from the Divine, see n. 4111. How it is, that those
truths were not of the good signified by Laban, but of the affection of interior truth, may appear from what was said above,
n. 4151. Hence then it is manifest, what arcanum lies concealed in the circumstances here recorded concerning the teraphim. The reason why teraphim signify truths from the Divine,
is, because they who were of the ancient Church distinguished
the Divine of the Lord by various names, and this, according
to the diverse circumstances which appeared in effects, as, by
the name of the God Schaddai, from temptations, in which the
Lord fights for man, and after which He confers benefits upon
him, see n. 1992, 3667. His providence, to prevent man's entering of himself into the mysteries of faith, they called cherubim,
see n. 308. Truths Divine, which they received by answers,
they called teraphim. The rest of the Divine Attributes they
also called by particular names, but they who were wise among
them, by all those names meant none but the only Lord;
whereas the simple made to themselves so many representative images of that Divine; and when Divine worship began
to be turned into idolatry, they framed to themselves so many
gods. Hence came so many idolatries, even among the Gentiles, who increased the number. But as in ancient times
Divine things were understood by those names, some were retained, as Schaddai, and also cherubim, likewise teraphim, and
in the Word those names signify such things as have been
spoken of. That teraphim signify Truths Divine, which were
from answers, is manifest in Hosea, chap. iii. 4.

4163. Verses 36, 37, 38, 39, 40, 41, 42. *And Jacob was
angry, and chode with Laban ; and Jacob answered, and said
unto Laban, What is my transgression, what is my sin, that
thou hast pursued after me ? Whereas thou hast handled all
my vessels, what hast thou found of all the vessels of thine
house ? Set it here before my brethren and thy brethren, and
let them judge between us both. These twenty years have I been
with thee, thy sheep and thy goats have not been abortive, and
the rams of thy flocks have I not eaten. That which was torn
have I not brought to thee, I have indemnified it, of my hand
hast thou required it, stolen by day, and stolen by night. I have
been, in the day the heat devoured me, and cold in the night,*

*and my sleep was driven away from mine eyes.   These to me
twenty years I have served thee in thy house, fourteen years in
thy two daughters, and six years in thy flock, and thou hast
changed my reward ten manners.   Unless the God of my father,
the God of Abraham, and the dread of Isaac, had been with me,
thou wouldest now have sent me away empty ; my misery, and
the weariness of my hands, God hath seen, and hath judged in
the past night.*   Jacob was angry, and chode with Laban, signifies the zeal of the natural principle : and Jacob answered,
and said to Laban, What is my transgression, what is my sin,
that thou hast pursued after me? signifies that he did not separate himself from a principle of evil: whereas thou hast
handled all my vessels, what hast thou found of all the vessels
of thine house? signifies that no truths of good had been his
property, but that all were given : set it here before my brethren and thy brethren, and let them judge between us both,
signifies that judgment is from what is just and equitable :
these twenty years have I been with thee, signifies proprium :
thy sheep and thy goats have not been abortive, signifies his
state as to good and the good of truth : and the rams of thy
flock have I not eaten, signifies the truth of good that he took
nothing of his : that which was torn have I not brought to thee,
signifies that evil without its fault was with that good : I indemnified it, signifies that good was thence derived : of my
hand hast thou required it, signifies that it was from himself :
stolen by day and stolen by night, signifies evil of merit in like
manner : I have been, in the day the heat devoured me, and cold
in the night, and my sleep was driven away from mine eyes,
signifies temptations : these to me twenty years I have served
in thy house, signifies proprium : fourteen years in thy two
daughters, signifies the first period that he might acquire to
himself thence the affections of truth : and six years in thy flock,
signifies that next he might acquire good : and thou hast
changed my reward ten manners, signifies his state to himself,
when he applied those goods to himself : unless the God of my
father, the God of Abraham, and the dread of Isaac, had been
with me, signifies unless the Divine and the Divine Human :
thou wouldest now have sent me away empty, signifies that he
would have claimed all things to himself : my misery and the
weariness of my hands God hath seen, and hath judged in the
past night, signifies that all things were from Himself by His
own proper power.

4164. "And Jacob was angry, and chode with Laban"—
that this signifies zeal of the natural principle, appears from the
signification of being angry or wrathful, and thence chiding, as
being zeal ; and from the representation of Jacob, as being
good of the natural principle, concerning which, see above.
The reason why to be angry or wrathful, and thence to chide,

denotes zeal, is, because in heaven or with the angels there is no such thing as anger, but instead of anger, zeal. Anger differs from zeal in this, that there is evil in anger, but good in zeal; or that he who is in anger, intends evil to another with whom he is angry, but he who is in zeal, intends good to another towards whom he has zeal; wherefore also he who is in zeal can in an instant be good, and in the very act be good towards others, but not so he who is in anger. Although zeal in the external form appears like anger, still in the internal form it is altogether unlike.

4165. "And Jacob answered, and said unto Laban, What is my transgression? what is my sin, that thou hast pursued after me?"—that this signifies that he did not separate himself from a principle of evil, appears from the signification of transgression and sin, as being evil. That to pursue denotes that for the sake of which he separated himself, is evident; thus, that he did not separate himself from a principle of evil.

4166. "Whereas thou hast handled all my vessels, what hast thou found of all the vessels of thine house?"—that this signifies that no truths had been his property, but that all were given, appears from the signification of vessels of the house, as denoting own proper truths; that vessels denote truths, see n. 3068, 3079, 3316, 3318. Hence, that vessels of the house denote own proper truths, is evident. To handle them, and not to find, denotes that none had been his, consequently, that all were given. How this case is, may be seen, n. 4151.

4167. "Set it here before my brethren and thy brethren, and let them judge between us both"—that this signifies that judgment is from what is just and equitable, appears from the signification of brethren, as being goods, see n. 2360, 3803, 3815, 4121. Hence it follows, that my brethren and thy brethren denote what is just and equitable. That judging between us both denotes judgment, is manifest. The reason why my brethren and thy brethren denote what is just and equitable, is, because the subject here treated of is the natural principle; for in the natural principle that is properly called just and equitable, which in the spiritual principle is called good and true. There are in man two planes, on which are founded the celestial and spiritual things which come from the Lord. The one plane is interior, the other is exterior. The planes themselves are nothing else than conscience. Without planes, that is, without conscience, it is impossible for any thing celestial and spiritual from the Lord to be fixed, but it flows through as water through a sieve, wherefore they who are without such a plane, or without conscience, do not know what conscience is, yea, neither do they believe that there is any spiritual and celestial principle. The interior plane, or interior conscience, is where good and truth in a genuine sense is, for good and truth influent from the Lord is its active principle; but the exterior plane is the exterior conscience, and is where justice and equity in a proper sense is, for what is just and equitable, moral and civil, which also flows-in, is its active principle. There is also an outmost plane, which also appears as conscience, but is not conscience, namely, doing what is just and equitable for the sake of self and the world, that is, for the sake of self-honour or reputation, and for the sake of worldly wealth and possessions, also, for fear of the law. These three planes are what rule man, that is, by which the Lord rules man. By the interior plane, or by the conscience of spiritual good and truth, the Lord rules those who are regenerated. By the exterior plane, or by the conscience of justice and equity, that is, by the conscience of moral and civil good and truth, the Lord rules those who are not as yet regenerated, but who are capable of being regenerated, and also are regenerated in another life, if not in the life of the body. By the outermost plane, which appears like conscience, and yet is not conscience, the Lord rules all the rest of mankind, even the wicked. The latter, without such rule, would rush headlong into every species of wickedness and madness, which also they do, when loosed from the bonds of that plane; and they who do not suffer themselves to be ruled by those bonds, are either mad, or are punished according to the laws. These three planes act as one with the regenerate, for one flows into the other, and the interior disposes the exterior. The first plane, or the conscience of spiritual good and truth, is in the rational principle of man; but the second plane, or the conscience of moral and civil good and truth, that is, of what is just and equitable, is in his natural principle. From these considerations then it appears, what is meant by the just and equitable, which are signified by brethren, namely, just, by my brethren, and equitable, by thy brethren; for it is called just and equitable, inasmuch as the subject treated of is the natural man, of whom those principles are properly predicated.

4168. "These twenty years have I been with thee"—that this signifies proprium, appears from the signification of twenty, as being the good of remains, see n. 2280; but remains, when they are predicated of the Lord, are nothing else but His proprium, see n. 1906. Twenty years signify states of proprium. That years denote states, see n. 487, 488, 493, 893. The things contained in the words of Jacob to Laban, in the supreme sense, treat of the proprium in the natural principle, which the Lord acquired to Himself by His own proper power, and, indeed, of the various states of that proprium.

4169. "Thy sheep and thy goats were not abortive"—that this signifies his state as to good and the good of truth, appears from the signification of sheep, as being good, of which we shall

speak presently; and from the signification of goat, as being the
good of truth, concerning which, see n. 3995, 4006. By good,
simply expressed, is meant the good of the will, but by good
of truth is meant the good of the understanding. The good of
the will consists in doing good from good, but the good of the
understanding in doing good from truth. These goods appear
as one to those who do good from truth, but still they differ
much from each other; for to do good from good is to do it
from a perception of good, which perception has place with
none but the celestial; whereas to do good from truth, is to do
it from science and intellect thence derived, but without perception that it is so, the person being only instructed so by
others, or concluding so from himself by his intellectual faculty,
which may be fallacious truth. Nevertheless if it has good for
its end, then what is done from that truth becomes good. That
sheep signify goods, may appear from several passages in the
Word, of which I shall adduce only the following: "He was
afflicted, and He opened not His mouth; He is led as cattle to
the slaughter, and as a *sheep* before the shearers, and He opened
not His mouth," Isaiah liii. 7; speaking of the Lord, where He
is compared to a sheep, not from truth, but from good. So in
Matthew, "Jesus said unto the twelve whom He sent forth, Go
not into the way of the nations, and into a city of the Samaritans enter ye not; go ye rather to *the lost sheep of the house of
Israel*," x. 5, 6. The nations to which they should not go denote those who are in evils; that nations denote evils, see n.
1259, 1260, 1849; the cities of the Samaritans denote those
who are in falses; sheep denote those who are in goods. So in
John, "Jesus after His resurrection said unto Peter, Feed My
lambs; a second time He said, Feed *My sheep;* a third time
He said, Feed *My sheep*," xxi. 15, 16, 17. Lambs denote those
who are in innocence; sheep, as first mentioned, denote those
who are in good from good; sheep mentioned a second time,
denote those who are in good from truth. So in Matthew,
"When the Son of Man shall come in His glory, He shall set
the sheep on the right hand, the goats on the left; and shall say
to them on the right hand, Come ye blessed of My Father, possess as an inheritance the kingdom prepared for you from the
foundation of the world; for I was an hungered, and ye gave
Me to eat; I was athirst, and ye gave Me to drink; I was a
sojourner, and ye gathered Me; I was naked, and ye clothed
Me; I was sick, and ye visited Me; I was in prison, and ye
came to Me: inasmuch as ye have done it unto one of the least
of these My brethren, ye have done it unto Me," xxv. 31 to 40.
That sheep in this passage denote the good, that is, those who
are in good, is very evident. All the kinds of the goods of
charity are contained in the internal sense of these words, of
which, by the Divine Mercy of the Lord, we shall speak else-

where. Goats specifically signify those who are in faith and in no charity. In like manner in Ezekiel, "Ye, My flock, saith the Lord Jehovih, behold I judge between cattle and cattle, between the *rams of the sheep*, and between the goats," xxxiv. 17. That goats specifically denote those who are in a faith not from charity, may appear from the signification of goats, as being, in a good sense, those who are in the truth of faith, and thence in some charity, but in an opposite sense, those who, being in a faith not from charity, reason concerning salvation from the principle that faith saves. This also appears from what the Lord says of the goats in the passage above cited from Matthew. They, however, who are in no truth of faith, and at the same time in no good of charity, are carried into hell without such judgment, that is, without a conviction that they are in what is false.

4170. "And the rams of thy flock have I not eaten"—that this signifies the truth of good that he took nothing of his, appears from the signification of rams, as being truths of good (for sheep signify goods, hence rams, as being of sheep, signify truths of good); and from the signification of eating, as being to appropriate to self, see n. 3168, 3513, 3596, 3832, thus to take, for what is appropriated from another, is taken from him.

4171. "The torn have I not brought to thee"—that this signifies that evil without its fault was with that good, appears from the signification of torn, as being death occasioned by another, thus evil without its fault. The evils attendant on man have several origins. The first origin is from the hereditary, by continual derivations from grandfathers and great-grand fathers to the father, and from the father, in whom thus evils are accumulated, into the man's self. Another origin is from the actual, namely, what man acquires to himself by a life of evil. This evil, man takes partly from the hereditary, as from an ocean of evils, and puts into act, partly he superadds several things from himself, whence comes the proprium which man acquires to himself. But this actual evil, which man makes his proprium, has also divers origins, in general two; firstly, that he receives evil from others without his own fault: secondly, that he receives from himself, thus, with his own fault. What a man receives from others without his own fault, is what in the Word is signified by torn; but what he receives from himself, thus, with his own fault, in the Word is signified by carcase. Hence it is, that as in the ancient Church, so also in the Jewish, it was forbidden to eat what died of itself, or a carcase, and also what was torn, on which subject it is thus written in Moses, "Every soul which eateth *a carcase*, and *what is torn*, amongst him who is born in the land and a stranger, shall wash his garments, and bathe himself in waters, and shall be unclean even until the evening, and shall be clean; and if he hath not

washed, and hath not bathed his flesh, he shall bear his iniquity," Levit. xvii 15, 16. Again, "A *carcase* and *what is torn*
he shall not eat, to pollute himself therewith: I am Jehovah,"
Levit. xxii. 8; where what is torn denotes evil derived from
what is false, which is brought in by the wicked, who are the
wild beasts in the forest which tear in pieces, for the infernals,
in the Word, are compared to wild beasts. Again, "Ye shall
be men of holiness unto Me, therefore ye shall not eat *flesh
torn in the field*, ye shall cast it forth to the dogs," Exod. xxii.
31. And in Ezekiel, "The prophet to Jehovah, My soul hath
not been polluted, and a *carcase* and *what is torn* I have not
eaten from my childhood heretofore, and the flesh of abomination hath not come into my mouth," iv. 14. Again, "The
priests shall not eat any *carcase*, or *what is torn*, of bird and of
beast," chap. xliv. 31; speaking of the Lord's kingdom, which
is the new land there described. From these passages it may
appear what is meant in the internal sense by that which is torn.
In order, however, to make the meaning more evident, let us
take an example. He who leads a life of good, or who does
well to another from a principle of good-will, in case he suffers
himself to be persuaded by another who is in evil, that a life of
good contributes nothing to salvation, because all are born in
sins, and because no one can will good of himself, consequently
cannot do good, and that, on this account, a saving means has
been provided, which is called faith, and thus that he may be
saved by faith without a life of good, and this although he has
received faith at his dying hour: such a person, who has lived
a life of good, if he suffers himself to be persuaded, and afterwards is careless about his life, and also despises a life of good,
is said to be torn; for torn is predicated of the good into which
a false principle is insinuated, which causes good to be no
longer alive. Take also another example. Suppose a person
to have accounted the conjugial principle in the beginning to
be heavenly, but afterwards to suffer himself to be persuaded,
either singly or together with his conjugial partner, that it is
only for the sake of order in the world, and with a view to the
education and distinct care of children, and also with a view
to inheritance; and, moreover, that the bond of marriage is
nothing more than that of a contract, which may be dissolved
or relaxed by each party, if with consent, and thus after he has
received such persuasion, has no thought of marriage as being
heavenly; if in consequence of this he gives himself up to the
free indulgence of his appetites, the conjugial principle then
becomes what is called torn: and so in other instances. That
the wicked are they who tear in pieces, and this, by reasonings
from things external, into which reasonings internal things cannot be insinuated because of the life of evil, may appear from
these words in Jeremiah, "A lion out of the forest hath smitten

the great ones, a wolf of the deserts hath devastated them, a leopard watcheth over their cities, *every one going forth of them shall be torn in pieces*, because their transgressions are multiplied, their backslidings are made strong," v. 5, 6. And in Amos, "Edom persecuted his brother with the sword, and destroyed his companions, and *tore in pieces for ever* with his anger, and keepeth his fury continually," i. 11, 12.

4172. "I indemnified it"—that this signifies that good was thence derived, appears from the signification of indemnifying, as being to render good, here good thence derived. In regard to evil of fault and evil not of fault, which are signified by carcase and what is torn, as mentioned above, the case is this. Evil of fault, or evil which man has contracted to himself by actual life, and has also confirmed in thought even to faith and persuasion, cannot be amended, but remains to eternity : whereas evil not of fault, which man has not confirmed in thought, and has not inwardly persuaded himself to, does indeed remain, but only sticks to externals, but does not penetrate the interiors, and pervert the internal man. It is such evil whereby good comes ; for the internal man, which has not yet been affected and has not yet consented, can see it in the external man as being evil, and thus it may be removed. And as the internal man can see it, therefore he can at the same time see good more clearly, for from the opposite good appears more clearly than from that which is not opposite ; moreover, he is afterwards more sensibly affected with good. This then is what is meant by good thence derived.

4173. "Of my hand hast thou required it"—that this signifies that it was from himself, appears from the signification of hand, as being ability, see n. 878, 3387, thus that it was from Himself; for what is from His own power, is from Himself.

4174. "Stolen by day and stolen by night"—that this signifies evil of merit in like manner, appears from the signification of stolen or theft, as being evil of merit. Evil of merit exists when man attributes good to himself, and imagines that it is from himself, and therefore is willing to merit salvation. This evil it is, which in the internal sense is signified by theft. In regard to this evil, the case is as follows. In the beginning, all who are reformed suppose that good is from themselves, and thence, that by the good which they do, they merit salvation ; for to imagine that by the good which they do they merit salvation, is a sure consequence of imagining good to be from themselves, since the one imagination coheres with the other. Those, however, who suffer themselves to be reformed, do not confirm this imagination in thought, or persuade themselves that it is so, but it is successively dissipated ; for so long as man is in the external man, as all are in the beginning of reformation, he cannot do otherwise than think so, since he thinks only from

the external man. But when the external man with his concupiscences is removed, and the internal begins to operate, that is,
when the Lord through the internal man flows in with the light
of intelligence, and enlightens thence the external man, he then
begins to think otherwise, and does not attribute good to himself, but to the Lord. Hence it is manifest what the evil of
merit is, which is here meant, by which good comes, in like
manner as by the evil not of fault spoken of above. Nevertheless, if man, when he arrives at adult age, confirms it in thought,
and altogether persuades himself that he merits salvation by
the good which he does, this evil remains rooted, and cannot
be amended, for he claims to himself that which is the Lord's,
and thus does not receive the good which continually flows in
from the Lord; but instantly as it flows in, makes it self-derived,
and considers it as his own property, and consequently defiles
it. These are the evils which in a proper sense are signified by
thefts, see n. 2609.

4175. "I have been, in the day the heat devoured me, and
the cold in the night, and my sleep was driven away from mine
eyes"—that this signifies temptations, appears from the signification of heat and cold, as being the too much of love, and
the nothing of love, thus the two extremes; (day signifies a
state of faith or truth, which then is at the height; and night,
a state of no faith or truth, see n. 221, 935, 936;) and from the
signification of sleep driven away from mine eyes, as being continually, or without rest; and as such things are in temptations,
therefore these words signify temptations in general. The reason why heat signifies the too much of love, is, because spiritual fire and heat is love, and on the other hand spiritual cold
is no love. The very life of man is nothing but love, for without
love he has nothing at all of life; yea, if he reflects, he may
know, that all vital fire and heat which is in the body is from
this source. Cold, however, does not signify the privation of
all love, but the privation of spiritual and celestial love, and
the privation of this is what is called spiritual death. When
man is deprived of this love, he is inflamed with self-love and
the love of the world, which love is respectively cold, and also
becomes cold with man, not only while he lives in the body,
but also when he comes into another life. While he lives in the
body, if self-love and the love of the world is taken away from
him, he grows cold to such a degree, that he has scarcely any
thing of life; and the same happens if he is forced to think
holily of things celestial and Divine. In another life, when he
is among infernals, he is in the fire or heat of lusts, but if he
approaches heaven, this fire and heat is turned into cold, the
more intense the nearer he approaches, with an increase of
torment in the same degree. This cold is meant by the gnash-
ing of teeth, which is the lot of those who are in hell; see

Matt. viii. 12; chap. xiii. 42, 50; chap. xxii. 13; chap. xxiv. 51; chap. xxv. 30; Luke xiii. 28.

4176. "These twenty years have I served thee in thine house"—that this signifies proprium, appears from the signification of twenty, as being the good of remains, see n. 2280, which good, when it is predicated of the Lord, is what He acquired to Himself, n. 1906, thus His proprium; and from the signification of serving, as being (when it is predicated of the Lord) His own proper power, see n. 3975, 3977.

4177. "Fourteen years in thy two daughters"—that this signifies the first period, that he might acquire to himself thence the affections of truth, appears from the signification of fourteen or of two weeks, as being a first period; for week in the Word signifies nothing else than an entire period, great or small, see n. 2044, 3845; in like manner two weeks, when they are named as one, for a number being doubled and multiplied into itself does not take away the signification. Hence it is evident what is here meant by fourteen or two weeks. And from the signification of two daughters, in the present case Rachel and Leah, as being the affections of truth, see n. 3758, 3782, 3793, 3819; moreover, that daughters denote affections, see n. 2362.

4178. "And six years in thy flock"—that this signifies that next he might acquire good, appears from the signification of six, as being combat and labour, see n. 720, 737, 900, here, what remained of combat and labour, thus, what was next; and from the signification of flock, as being good, see n. 343, 2566, 3518.

4179. "And thou hast changed my reward ten manners"—that this signifies His state to Himself, when He applied those goods to Himself, appears from the signification of reward, when it is predicated of the Lord, as being from Himself, see n. 3996, 3999, thus, when He applied goods to Himself; and from the signification of changing it, as being the state of that good, which is signified by Laban, to Himself. That ten manners denote very much change, see n. 4077.

4180 "Unless the God of my father, the God of Abraham, and the dread of Isaac, had been upon me"—that this signifies unless the Divine and the Divine Human, appears from the signification of the God of a father, when it is predicated of the Lord, as being the Divine as to good; (that father is Divine Good, and son Divine Truth, see n. 2803, 3704, in the present case, the Divine Good of each essence;) and from the signification of the God of Abraham, as being the Divine Itself which is called the Divine Essence; (that Abraham represents the Lord as to the Divine Itself, see n. 2011, 3439;) and from the signification of the dread of Isaac, as being the Divine Human. The expression dread is used, because it is Divine

Truth which is meant, for Divine Truth has with it fear, dread, and terror, with those who are not in good, but not so Divine Good; this terrifies no one. In like manner, in what follows in this chapter, "Jacob sware into the dread of his father Isaac," verse 53; for Laban, as he was then separated from Jacob, that is, middle good separated from Good Divine, was in such a state, that he willed to bring in evil, as is evident from what is said of Laban. Therefore, such being then his state, it is said, the dread of Isaac. That the dread of Isaac signifies the God of Isaac, may be evident to every one, and also that the expression is used in reference to the above state. That Isaac represents the Lord's Divine Human, and this as to the Divine Rational, see n. 1893, 2066, 2072, 2083, 2630, 3012, 3194, 3210, 3973. In regard to this circumstance, that Divine Truth, which is from the Lord, has dread along with it with those who are not in good, but not so Divine Good, the case is this. The Holy which is from the Lord has in it Divine Good and Divine Truth. These continually proceed from the Lord; hence the light which is in the heavens, and hence the light which is in human minds; consequently hence wisdom and intelligence, for these are in that light. This light, however, of wisdom and intelligence, affects all according to reception. They who are in evil do not receive Divine Good, for they are in no love and charity, all good being of love and charity; but Divine Truth may be received even by the wicked, yet only by their external man, not by the internal. The case in this respect is like that of the heat and light which flow from the sun. Spiritual heat is love, thus good, but spiritual light is faith, thus truth. When heat from the sun is received, then trees and flowers vegetate, produce leaves, flowers, fruits or seeds; this comes to pass in the time of spring and summer; but when heat from the sun is not received, but only light, then nothing vegetates, but all the vegetative principle is torpid, as comes to pass in the time of autumn and winter. So also it is with the spiritual heat and light which comes from the Lord. If man is like spring or summer, he then receives the good of love and charity, and produces fruits; but if he is like autumn and winter, he then does not receive the good of love and charity, consequently he does not produce fruits, but still he can receive light, that is, know those things which are of faith or truth. Similar to this is the effect of winter light, for it in like manner exhibits colours and beauties, and renders them conspicuous, but with this difference, that it does not penetrate towards the interiors, because there is no heat therein, hence there is no vegetation. When, therefore, good is not received but only light, there is then, as in objects wherein heat is not received, only an image and symmetry of form proceeding from the light; in consequence whereof there is cold within, and

where there is cold within, there all things are torpid, and there
is as it were a corrugation and horripilation when the light
shines thereon.   These are the things which in living creatures
cause fear, dread, and terror.   By this comparison it may in
some sort be comprehended how the case is in regard to fear,
dread, and terror with the wicked, namely, that those things
are not from Divine Good, but from Divine Truth, and that
they prevail, when they do not receive Divine Good, and ye
receive Divine Truth; also, that Divine Truth without Divine
Good does not penetrate towards the interiors, but only sticks
in the extremes, that is, in the external man, and for the most
part in his sensual principle; and that hence man sometimes
appears beautiful in the external form, when yet there is filthiness in the internal.   Hence also it may appear what is the
quality of faith with the generality of men, which they say is
saving without good works, that is, without willing what is
good and acting what is good.   Since Divine Truth proceeds
from the Divine Human but not from the Divine Itself, there
fore the Divine Human is here signified by the dread of Isaac,
for, as was said, it is the Divine Truth which terrifies, but not
the Divine Good.   That Divine Truth proceeds from the Lord's
Divine Human, but not from the Divine Itself, is an arcanum
not hitherto discovered.   In respect to it the case is this.
Before the Lord came into the world, the Divine Itself flowed
into the universal heaven, and as heaven at that time consisted
for the most part of celestial [angels], that is, of those who
were in the good of love, that influx, through the Divine Omnipotence, produced the light which was in the heavens, and
thence the wisdom and intelligence.   But after mankind
removed themselves from the good of love and charity, then
that light could no longer be produced through heaven, con
sequently, neither could wisdom and intelligence, so as to
penetrate to the human race, wherefore it was of necessity,
in order to their salvation, that the Lord came into the world,
and made the Human in Himself Divine, that He Himself
as to the Divine Human might become Light Divine, and
thus might illuminate the universal heaven and the universal
world.   He had been light itself from eternity, for that light
through heaven was from the Divine Itself; and the Divine
Itself was what took the human and made this Divine, and
when this was made Divine, then He could from it illuminate
not only the celestial heaven, but also the spiritual heaven, and
likewise the human race, which received and receive Divine
Truth in good, that is, in love to Him and charity towards their
neighbour, as is evident in John, " As many as received Him,
to them gave He power to be the sons of God, believing on
His name, who were born not of bloods, nor of the will of the
flesh, nor of the will of man, but of God," i. 12.   From what

has been now said, it may appear what is signified by the following words in John, "In the beginning was the Word, and the Word was with God, and God was the Word; this was in the beginning with God: all things were made by Him, and without Him was not any thing made which was made; in Him was life, and the life was the light of men; it was the true light, which enlightens every man that cometh into the world," i. 1, 2, 3, 4, 9. The Word in this passage signifies Divine Truth. But that the Lord as to each essence is Divine Good, but that from Him proceeds Divine Truth, see n. 3704; for Divine Good cannot be received by man, nor even by an angel, but only by the Lord's Divine Human, which is meant by these words in John, "No one hath seen God at any time, the only-begotten Son, who is in the bosom of the Father, He hath made Him manifest," i. 18. Divine Truth, however, may be received, yet of a quality such as the man who receives is capable of admitting; in this truth may dwell Divine Good, with a difference according to reception. Such are the arcana which are presented to the angels, when these words are read by man "Unless the God of my father, the God of Abraham, and the dread of Isaac, had been with me." Hence it is manifest how much of heavenliness there is in the Word, and in all and singular its parts, although nothing of this appears in the sense of the letter; and hence also it is manifest what angelic wisdom is in comparison of human wisdom; and that angels are in the deepest arcana, when man does not even know that any arcanum is contained therein. But the arcana which have been mentioned are only very few, for in these arcana the angels see and perceive innumerable, yea, respectively indefinite arcana, which cannot in any wise be uttered, because human speech is not adequate to express them, nor the human mind capable of receiving them.

4181. "Thou wouldest now have sent me away empty"— that this signifies that he would have claimed all things to himself, appears from the signification of sending away empty, as being to take all away from him, thus to claim all to himself.

4182. "My misery and the weariness of my hands God hath seen, and hath judged in the night past"—that this signifies that all things were from Himself by His own proper power, appears from the signification of misery and weariness of the hands in this passage, as being temptations; and as the Lord by temptations and victories united the Divine to the human, and made this latter also Divine, and this by His own proper power, therefore these same words signify these things. That the Lord by temptations and victories united the Divine to the human, and made this latter Divine by His own proper ability, see n. 1661, 1737, 1813, 1921, 2776, 3318. That hand denotes ability, see n. 878, 3387, consequently my hands denote own proper ability. God hath seen, and hath judged, signifies the Lord's Divine, namely, that the Divine which was in Himself, and which was His, did it.

4183. Verse 43. *And Laban answered, and said unto Jacob, The daughters are my daughters, and the sons my sons, and the .flock my flock, and all that thou seest, this is mine. And for my daughters, what shall I do for them to-day, or for their sons whom they have borne?* Laban answered, and said unto Jacob, signifies an obscure state of perception: The daughters are my daughters, and the sons my sons, and the flock my flock, signifies that all the affections of truth, all truths and goods, were his: and all that thou seest, this is mine, signifies every thing perceptive and intellectual: and for my daughters, what shall I do for them to-day, or for their sons whom they have borne? signifies that he durst not claim those things to himself.

4184. "Laban answered, and said unto Jacob"—that this s gnifies an obscure state of perception, appears from the signification of answering and saying, as being perception. That to say, in the historicals of the Word, denotes to perceive, may be seen, n. 1898, 1919, 2080, 2862, 3509, 3395; that the state of perception is obscure, appears from what Laban here says, namely, that the daughters, the sons, and the flocks were his, when yet they were not his; and in the internal sense, that middle good claimed to itself all goods and truths. Respecting what is here said by Laban, see above, n. 3947, 4113.

4185. "The daughters are my daughters, and the sons my sons, and the flock my flock"—that this signifies that all the affections of truth, all truths and goods, were his, appears from the signification of daughters, in the present case Rachel and Leah, as being the affections of truth, see n. 3758, 3782, 3793, 3819. And from the signification of sons, as being truths, see n. 489, 491, 533, 1147, 3373. And from the signification of flock, as being goods, see n. 343, 1565, 2566. That he claimed those things to himself as his own, is evident, for he said, the daughters are my daughters, and the sons my sons, and the flock my flock.

4186. "And all that thou seest, this is mine"—that this signifies every thing perceptive and intellectual, appears from the signification of seeing, as being to perceive and understand, see n. 2150, 3863, thus that every thing perceptive and intellectual of truth and good was his. How this case is, was shown above, and illustrated by what passes in another life, namely, that spirits, especially of a middle sort, when they are in any angelic society, know no other at the time, than that the affections of good and truth, which flow-in from the society, are theirs, for such is the communication of affections and thoughts in another life, and so far as they are conjoined with that society, so far they suppose it to be so. The same spirits, when they are separated thence, are indignant, and when they come into a state of indignation, they come also into an obscure state (concerning which see n. 4184), in which, because they have no interior perception, they claim to themselves the goods and truths of the angelic society, which they had by the communication above mentioned. It is this state which is described in this verse. Moreover, it has been given me to know by much experience, how the affections of good and truth are communicated to others. Spirits of the above sort have been with me, and when they were conjoined by any thing of affection, they knew no other at the time, than that mine were theirs; and I have been informed that the case is the same with all men. For every man has spirits attendant upon him, who, as soon as they come to the man, and enter into his affection, know no other than that all things which are the man's, that is, all things of his affection and thought, are theirs. Thus spirits are conjoined to man, and by means of them man is governed by the Lord, n. 2488. Of such spirits, some experimental account will be given in what follows, at the close of the chapters.

4187. "And for my daughters, what shall I do for them to day, or for their sons whom they have borne?"—that this signifies that he durst not claim those things to himself, appears from the signification of daughters, as being the affections of truth, and of sons, as being truths, see n. 4185. That he durst not claim those things to himself, is signified by his saying, What shall I do for them to-day? and is evident from what goes before, namely, that God said to him in a dream, "Take heed to thyself, lest peradventure thou speak with Jacob from good even to evil," verse 24.

4188. Verses 44, 45, 46. *And now go, let us establish a covenant, I and thou, and let it be for a witness between me and between thee. And Jacob took a stone, and set it up for a statue. And Jacob said to his brethren, Gather together stones; and they took stones, and made an heap, and did eat there upon the heap.* Now go, let us establish a covenant, I and thou, and let it be for a witness between me and thee, signifies conjunction of the Divine Natural with goods of works; in which goods they are who are aside (*a latere*) or Gentiles: and Jacob took a stone, and set it up for a statue, signifies such truth and worship thence derived: and Jacob said to his brethren, signifies those who are in the good of works: Gather together stones; and they took stones, and made an heap, signifies truths from good: and did eat there upon the heap, signifies appropriation from good Divine.

4189. "Now go, let us establish a covenant, I and thou"— that this signifies conjunction of the Divine Natural with the goods of works, in which they are who are aside, or Gentiles, appears from the signification of covenant, as being conjunction, see n. 665, 666, 1023, 1038, 1864, 1996, 2003, 2021 ; and from the representation of Laban in the present case, who is I, as denoting the goods of works, whereof we shall speak presently ; and from the representation of Jacob. who is thou, as being the Divine Natural. The reason why Laban in the present case signifies the goods of works, in which they are who are aside, or Gentiles, is because Laban now being separated from Jacob, that is, middle good from Good Divine of the natural principle, can no longer represent middle good ; but as he served as a middle good, therefore he represents some good. and indeed a good aside, or a good collateral. That Laban, before he was thus conjoined with Jacob, represented good collateral, may be seen, n. 3612, 3665, 3778, consequently good *a latere*. The quality of this good will be explained in what follows. The case of Laban is similar to that of Lot and Ishmael. Lot, so long as he was with Abraham, represented the Lord as to the sensual external man, see n. 1428, 1434, 1547, 1597, 1598, 1698 ; but when he was separated from Abraham, he represented those who are in external worship, yet still in charity, n. 2317, 2324, 2371, 2399, also several states of the Church successively, n. 2422, 2459. In like manner Ishmael, so long as he was with Abraham, represented the Lord's first rational [principle], see n. 1893, 1949, 1950, 1951 ; but after wards, when he was separated, he represented the spiritual, r 2078, 2691, 2699, 3263, 3268. This also is the case with Laban. The reason is, because notwithstanding separation was made, still there remains conjunction, but not that which before existed. Hence it is, that Laban, in this passage and in what now follow, represents the goods of works, such as have place with those who are aside, that is, with the Gentiles ; the Gentiles are said to be aside or in collateral good, because they are out of the Church. They who are in good and truth within the Church are not in a collateral line, but in a direct line, for they have the Word, and by the Word direct communication with heaven, and by heaven with the Lord ; but not so the Gentiles, for these have not the Word, neither do they know the Lord. Hence it is that they are said to be aside. Those Gentiles, however, are meant who are in goods of works, that is, in externals in which inwardly is the good of charity. These are what are called goods of works, but not good works, for good works may be given without goods within, but not so the goods of works.

4190. " And Jacob took a stone, and set it up for a statue" —that this signifies such truth and worship thence derived, appears from the signification of stone, as being truth, see n. 643, 1298, 3720 ; and from the signification of statue, as being worship thence derived or from truth, see n. 3727. Hence it is evident that these words signify such truth, and worship thence

derived. By such truth is meant such as prevails among the
Gentiles ; for the Gentiles, although they know nothing of the
Word, nor consequently of the Lord, still are in possession of
external truths such as the Christians have ; as, that the Deity
is to be worshipped holily, that festivals are to be observed, that
parents are to be honoured, that men ought not to steal, or to
commit adultery or murder, or to covet what is another's. Thus
they are in possession of such truths as are contained in the
decalogue, which also are a rule of life for those within the
Church. They who are wise among them, not only observe the
same in external form, but also in internal, for they think that
such forbidden evils are not only contrary to their religion, but
also to the common good, thus, contrary to what is internally
due to man, consequently, contrary to charity, although they
do not so well know what faith is. In their obscurity they have
somewhat of conscience, against which they are not willing to
act, yea, some of them are not able to act against it. Hence it
may appear that the Lord rules their interiors, which are in obscurity, and thus that He imparts to them a faculty of receiving
interior truths, which also they do receive in another life : see
what was shown concerning the Gentiles, n. 2589 to 2604.
Occasionally it has been given me to converse with Christians
in another life on the state and lot of the Gentiles out of the
Church, in that they receive the truths and goods of faith more
easily than Christians who have not lived according to the
Lord's precepts ; and that Christians think cruelly of them, in
supposing that all who are out of the Church are damned, and
this, in consequence of a received canon, that out of the Lord
there is no salvation ; and that this is true, but that the Gentiles, who have lived in mutual charity, and have done what is
just and equitable from a kind of conscience, in another life receive faith, and acknowledge the Lord, more easily than they
who are within the Church, and have not lived in such charity.
Also, that Christians are in falsity in supposing that they alone
have heaven, because they have the book of the Word, written
on paper but not in their hearts, and that they know the Lord,
and yet do not believe Him Divine as to His Human, yea, ac
knowledge Him only as a common man as to His other essence,
which they call the human nature ; and on this account, when
they are left to themselves and their knowledges, do not even
adore Him ; and thus, that they are the people who are out of
the Lord, to whom there is no salvation.

4191. " And Jacob said to his brethren"—that this signifies
those who are in the goods of works, appears from the representation of Jacob, as being the Lord's Divine Natural (concerning which, see above) ; and from the signification of brethren,
as being goods, see n. 3815, 4121, here, those who are in the
goods of works. that is, the Gentiles, as was shown above, n.

4189; for all who are in good are conjoined with the Lord's Divine, and by reason of conjunction are called by the Lord brethren, as in Mark, " Jesus looking round about on them who sat about Him, said, Behold My mother, and *My brethren;* for whosoever shall do the will of God, he is *My brother*, and My sister, and My mother," iii. 32 to 35. All conjunction is by love and charity, as may appear evident to every one, for spiritual conjunction is nothing else but love and charity. That love to the Lord is conjunction with Him, is manifest; and that so likewise is charity towards the neighbour, appears from the Lord's words in Matthew, " Inasmuch as ye have done it to one of the least of these My brethren, ye have done it unto Me," xxv. 40; speaking of the works of charity.

4192. "Gather together stones; and they took stones, and made an heap"—that this signifies truths from good, appears from the signification of stones, as being truths, see above, n. 4190; and from the signification of heap, as being good. The reason why heap signifies good, is, because formerly, before they built altars, they made heaps, and ate together upon them, as a testimony that they were joined together in love. Afterwards, however, when the representatives of the ancients were accounted holy, instead of heaps they built altars, and these also of stones, but arranged in a more orderly manner, Joshua xxii. 28, 34. Hence the same is signified by a heap as by an altar, namely, the good of love, and by its stones the truths of faith.

4193. "And they did eat together there upon the heap"— that this signifies appropriation from Good Divine, appears from the signification of eating together, as being communication, conjunction, and appropriation, see n. 2187, 2343, 316? 3513, 3596, 3832; and from the signification of heap, as being good, see just above, n. 4192, in the present case, Good Divine.

4194. Verses 47, 48, 49, 50. *And Laban called it Jega Sahadutha; and Jacob called it Galeed. And Laban said, This heap is a witness between me and between thee to-day; therefore he called the name thereof Galeed: and Mizpah, because he said, Let Jehovah look between me and between thee, because we shall lie concealed a man from his companion. If thou afflictest my daughters, and if thou takest women over my daughters, no man is with us; see, God is a witness between me and between thee.* Laban called it Jegar Sahadutha, signifies its quality on the part of the good represented by Laban: and Jacob called it Galeed, signifies its quality on the part of the good of the Divine Natural: and Laban said, This heap is a witness between me and between thee to-day; therefore he called the name thereof Galeed, signifies that thus it shall be to eternity, hence its quality again: and Mizpah, because he said, Let Jehovah look between me and between thee, signifies presence of the Lord's Divine Natural : because we shall lie concealed a man from his companion, signifies separation in respect to those things which are of the Church : if thou afflictest my daughters, and takest women over my daughters, no man is with us, signifies the affection of truth that they should remain within the Church : see. God is a witness between me and between thee, signifies confirmation.

4195. " Laban called it Jegar Sahadutha"—that this signifies its quality on the part of the good represented by Laban, appears from the signification of calling, and of calling a name, as being quality, see n. 144, 145, 1754, 2009, 2724, 3421. Jegar Sahadutha signifies the heap of testimony in the idiom of Syria, whence Laban came. Such heaps in old time were for a sign, or a witness, and afterwards for worship : in the present case, for a sign and for a witness, for a sign that the boundary was there, and for a witness that a covenant was there established, and that none of them should pass it to do evil to another, as also appears from the words of Laban, "This heap is a witness, and the statue a witness, if I shall not pass this heap to thee, and if thou shalt not pass this heap to me, and this statue for evil," verse 52. Hence it is evident what is involved in Jegar Sahadutha, or heap of testimony. But in the internal sense, it signifies the quality of good derived from truths on the part of Laban, in other words, on the part of those who are in goods of works, that is, of the Gentiles.

4196. " And Jacob called it Galeed "—that this signifies quality on the part of the good of the Divine Natural, appears from the representation of Jacob, as being the Lord's Divine Natural, of which frequent mention has been made above. Galeed signifies a heap and a witness, or a heap-witness, in the Hebrew idiom, or that of Canaan, whence Jacob came. What a heap-witness is in the internal sense, shall be explained in what follows.

4197. " And Laban said, This heap is a witness between me and between thee to-day ; therefore he called the name thereof Galeed "—that this signifies that so it shall be to eternity, hence its quality again, appears from the signification of heap, as being good, see above, n. 4192 ; and from the signification of witness, as being confirmation of good by truth, of which we shall speak presently ; and from the signification of to-day, as being eternity, see n. 2838, 2998 ; and from the signification of calling a name, as being quality, see n 144, 145, 1754, 2009, 2724, 3421. The quality itself is contained in the name Galeed ; for in old time the names imposed contained quality, see n. 340, 1946, 2643, 3422. Hence it is evident what is signified by the words, " Laban said, This heap is a witness between me and between thee to-day ; therefore he called the name thereof Galeed," namely, testification of the conjunction of the good

here signified by Laban with Good Divine of the Lord's Natural, consequently, conjunction of the Lord by good with the
Gentiles, for this good is now represented by Laban (see n.
4189). The truths of that good are what testify of conjunction
but their good, so long as they live in the world, is aside
because they have not Divine Truths. Nevertheless, they who
are in that good, that is, who live in mutual charity, although
they have not Divine Truths directly from the Divine fountain,
that is, from the Word, still have not a closed good, but such
as may be opened, and also is opened in another life, when they
are instructed in the truths of faith and concerning the Lord.
The case is otherwise with Christians. Such of them as are in
mutual charity, and especially such as are in love to the Lord,
while they live in the world, are in direct good, because in
Divine Truths, wherefore they enter.into heaven without such
instruction, if in their truths there have not been falses, which
must first be separated. Christians, however, who have not
lived in charity, shut heaven against themselves, and very
many of them to such a degree, that it cannot be opened; for
they know truths and deny them, and also harden themselves
against them, if not in mouth, still in heart. The reason why
Laban called the heap in his own idiom first Jegar Sahadutha,
and afterwards in the idiom of Canaan, Galeed, when yet each
expression has nearly the same signification, is for the sake of
application, and thence of conjunction. To speak in the idiom,
or lip, of Canaan, is to apply himself to the Divine, for Canaan
signifies the Lord's kingdom, and, in a supreme sense, the Lord
(see n. 1607, 3038, 3705), as is evident in Isaiah, "In that day
there shall be five cities in the land of Egypt *speaking with
the lips of Canaan*, and swearing to Jehovah Zebaoth; in that
day there shall be an altar to Jehovah in the midst of the land
of Egypt, and a statue at the border thereof to Jehovah, and it
shall be *for a sign* and *for a witness* to Jehovah Zebaoth in
the land of Egypt," xix. 18, 19, 20. That witness denotes confirmation of good by truth, and of truth from good; and that
hence testimony denotes good from which truth is derived, and
truth which is from good, may appear from the Word in other
passages. That witness denotes confirmation of good by truth,
and of truth from good, appears from the following passages:
" Joshua said to the people, *Ye are witnesses to yourselves*, that
ye have chosen Jehovah to serve him: and they said, [We are]
witnesses. And now remove ye the gods of the stranger who
is in the midst of you, and incline your heart to Jehovah God
of Israel. And the people said to Joshua, We will serve Jehovah our God, and will obey His voice. And Joshua made a
covenant with the people in this day, and set for them a statue
and judgment in Shechem. And Joshua wrote those words
in the book of the law of God, and took a great *stone*, and set

It up there under an oak, which was in the sanctuary of Jehovah. And Joshua said unto all the people, *Behold this stone shall be to you for a witness*, because it hath heard all the sayings of Jehovah which He spake with you; and *it shall be to you for a witness*, lest ye deny your God," Joshua xxiv. 22, 23, 24, 25, 26, 27. That witness in this passage denotes confirmation, is evident, and indeed the confirmation of a covenant, consequently of conjunction, for a covenant signifies conjunction, see n. 665, 666, 1023, 1038, 1864, 1996, 2003, 2021; and as conjunction with Jehovah or the Lord exists only by good, and as no conjoining good exists but what has its quality from truth, it hence follows that witness is confirmation of good by truth. Good, in the above passage, is conjunction with Jehovah or the Lord by their choosing Him to serve Him; truth, by which confirmation was made, was the stone. That stone is truth, see n. 643, 1298, 3720: in a supreme sense, stone is the Lord Himself, because from Him is all truth, wherefore also He is called the stone of Israel, Gen. xlix. 24; and it is also said, Behold this stone shall be to us for a witness, because it hath heard all the sayings of Jehovah which He spake with us. So in the Apocalypse, " *I will give to my two witnesses* to prophesy a thousand two hundred and sixty days, clothed in sackcloth. These are the two olives, and the two candlesticks which stand before the God of the earth. And if any one shall desire to hurt them, fire shall go forth from their mouth, and shall devour their enemies. These have the power of shutting heaven. But when they shall have finished their *testimony*, the beast which cometh up out of the abyss shall make war with them, and shall overcome them, and shall kill them. But after three days and a half the Spirit of life from God entered into them, that they stood upon their feet," chap. xi. 3, 4, 5, 6, 7, 11. That the two witnesses in this passage are good and truth, that is, good in which is truth, and truth which is from good, each confirmed in hearts, is evident from its being said that the two witnesses are two olives and two candlesticks. That oil is such good, may be seen, n. 886; two olives denote celestial and spiritual good; celestial good is that of love to the Lord, and spiritual good is that of charity towards the neighbour; candlesticks are the truths of those goods, as will appear, when, by the Divine Mercy of the Lord, we come to treat of candlesticks. That these things, namely, goods and truths, have the power of shutting and opening heaven, may be seen in the preface to chap. xxii. of Genesis. The beast out of the abyss or hell killing them, signifies the vastation of good and truth within the Church; and the Spirit of life from God entering into them, that they stood upon their feet, signifies a new Church. That as heaps in old time were set for witnesses, so afterwards were altars, appears from Joshua, "The Reubenites and Gadites

said, See the figure of the altar of Jehovah, which our fathers
have made, not for burnt-offering, and not for sacrifice, but *it
is a witness between us and between you:* and the sons of Reuben and the sons of Gad called the *altar, that it is a witness
between us,* that Jehovah is God," xxii. 28, 34.   Altar denotes
the good of love, and, in a supreme sense, the Lord Himself,
see n. 921, 2777, 2811; witness, in the internal sense, is confirmation of good by truth.   Since witness signifies the confirmation of good by truth, and of truth from good, therefore, in a
supreme sense, it signifies the Lord, because He Himself is
Divine Truth confirming; as in Isaiah, "I will establish for
you a covenant of eternity, the true mercies of David; behold
I have given him a witness to the people, a prince and com-
mander to the people," lv. 4.   And in the Apocalypse, "And
from Jesus Christ, who *is the faithful witness,* the first-begotten
from the dead, and the prince of the kings of the earth," i. 5.
Again, "These things saith the *faithful and true witness,* the
beginning of the creature of God," iii. 14.   The command in
the representative Church, that every truth shall stand on the
mouth of two or three witnesses, Numb. xxxv. 30; Deut. xvii
6, 7; chap. xix. 15; Matt. xviii. 16, is founded on the Divine
Law, that one truth does not confirm good, but several truths,
for one truth without connection with others is not confirming,
but when there are several in connection, for from one another
may be seen.   One does not produce any form, thus not any
quality, but several connected in a series; for as one tone does
not produce any tune, still less any harmony, so neither does
one truth.   These are the considerations on which the above
law is founded, although in its external form it appears founded
in the state of civil society, but the one is not contrary to the
other; as in the case of the precepts of the decalogue, of which,
see n. 2609.   That *testimony* denotes good from which truth is
derived, and truth from which good is derived, follows of consequence from the above, and also is evident from the fact, that
the ten commandments of the decalogue written on the tables
of stone are called by one expression the testimony, as in
Moses, "Jehovah gave to Moses, when He had left off speaking
with him in Mount Sinai, the *two tables of testimony,* tables of
stone, written with the finger of God," Exod. xxxi. 18.   Again,
"Moses came down from the mountain, and *the two tables of
testimony* were in his hand, tables written on the two sides
thereof," Exod. xxxii. 15.   And as those tables were placed in
an ark, the ark is called the ark of testimony, of which it is
thus written in Moses, "Jehovah said unto Moses, *Thou shalt
give into the ark the testimony* which I shall give to thee,"
Exod. xxv. 16, 21.   Again, "Moses took and *gave the testimony
into the ark,*" Exod. xl. 20.   Again, "I will meet with thee,
and speak with thee from above the propitiatory from between

the two cherubs, which are *over the ark of testimony*," Exod.
xxv. 22. Again, " A cloud of incense covered the propitiatory,
which is *over the testimony*," Levit. xvi. 13. Again, " The rods
of the twelve tribes were left in the tent of the assembly, *before
the testimony*," Numb. xvii. 4. That hence the ark was called
the ark of testimony, besides the passage above cited, Exod.
xxv. 22 ; see also Exod. xxxi. 7; Apoc. xv. 5. The precepts of
the decalogue were on this account called a testimony, because
they had relation to a covenant, thus to a conjunction between
the Lord and man, which cannot exist unless man keeps those
precepts, not only in the external form, but also in the internal.
What the internal form of those precepts is, may be seen, n.
2609. Good, then, confirmed by truth, and truth derived from
good, is signified by testimony. This being the case. the tables
were also called tables of the covenant, and the ark, the ark of
the covenant. Hence it is evident what is signified in the
Word by testimony, in a genuine sense, as in Deut. iv. 45 :
chap. vi. 17, 20 ; Isaiah viii. 16 ; 2 Kings xvii. 15 ; Psalm xix
7 ; xxv. 10; lxxviii. 5; xciii. 5; cxix. 2, 24, 59, 79, 88, 138,
167 ; cxxii. 4; Apoc. vi. 9; chap. xii. 17; chap. xix. 10.

4198. " And Mizpah, because he said, Let Jehovah look
between me and between thee"—that this signifies the presence
of the Lord's Divine Natural in the good which is now repre
sented by Laban, appears from the signification of looking or
speculating, as being presence, for he who looks at another, or
from an high place of observation (*speculum*) sees him, is present with him in vision. Moreover seeing, when it is predicated
of the Lord, is foresight and providence, see n. 2837, 2839.
3686, 3854, 3863, thus also presence, but by foresight and
providence. As concerns the Lord, He is present with every
one, but according to reception ; for from the Lord alone is the
life of every one. They who receive His presence in good and
truth, are in the life of intelligence and wisdom ; but they who
receive His presence not in good and truth, but in evil and the
false, are in the life of insanity and folly, yet still in the faculty
of being intelligent and wise. That they still have this faculty,
may appear from the fact, that in an external form they know
how to feign and pretend what is good and true, and thereby
captivate men, which would not be the case unless they had
the above faculty. The quality of presence is signified by Mizpah, in the present case, the quality with those who are in goods
of works, or with the Gentiles, who are here represented by
Laban ; for the name Mizpah, in the original tongue, is derived
from looking.

4199. " Because we shall lie concealed a man from his com
panion"—that this signifies separation in respect to those things
which are of the Church, appears from the signification of lying

concealed in this passage, as being separation; and from the signification of a man from a companion, as being those who are within the Church, and those who are without. These are said to lie concealed, because they are separated as to good and truth, thus in respect to those things which are of the Church.

4200. "If thou afflictest my daughters, and takest women over my daughters, no man is with us"—that this signifies that the affections of truth should remain within the Church, appears from the signification of the daughters, Rachel and Leah, as being the affections of truth, see n. 3758, 3782, 3793, 3819; and from the signification of women, as being affections of truth not genuine, thus which are not of the Church. (The affections of truth constitute the Church, thus to take women over them signifies that there should be no other affections than of genuine truth.) And from the signification of no man with us, as being when a man shall be concealed from his companion, that is, when they are separated (see just above, n. 4199). Hence it is manifest that the above words signify, that the affections of genuine truth should remain within the Church, and not be defiled with truths not genuine.

4201. "See, God is a witness between me and between thee"—that this signifies confirmation, here, from the Divine, appears from the signification of witness, as being confirmation, see just above, n. 4197.

4202. Verses 51, 52, 53. *And Laban said to Jacob, Behold this heap, and behold the statue which I have set up between me and between thee. This heap is a witness, and the statue a witness, if I shall not pass this heap to thee, and if thou shalt not pass this heap and this statue to me, for evil. The God of Abraham and the God of Nahor judge between us, the God of their father; and Jacob sware into the dread of his father Isaac.* Laban said to Jacob, Behold this heap, and behold the statue which I have set up between me and between thee, signifies conjunction: this heap is a witness and the statue a witness, signifies confirmation: if I shall not pass this heap to thee, and if thou shalt not pass this heap and this statue to me, for evil, signifies a limit as much as can inflow from good: the God of Abraham and the God of Nahor judge between us, signifies the Divine into each: the God of their father, signifies from the Supreme Divine: and Jacob sware into the dread of his father Isaac, signifies confirmation from the Divine Human, which is called dread in that state.

4203. "Laban said to Jacob, Behold this heap, and behold the statue which I have set up between me and between thee" —that this signifies conjunction, appears from what has been said above; for the heap and the statue were for a sign and a

witness that a covenant was established, that is, that friendship
was established, thus, in the internal sense, that conjunction
was established.

4204. "This heap is a witness and the statue a witness"—
that this signifies confirmation, appears from the signification
of witness, as being confirmation, namely, of good by truth
which is a statue, and of truth from good which is a heap, see
above, n. 4197.

4205. "If I shall not pass this heap to thee, and if thou
shalt not pass this heap and this statue to me, for evil"—that
this signifies a limit as much as can inflow from good, appears
from the signification of passing here, as being to flow-in; and
from the signification of heap, as being good, see n. 4192; and
from the signification of statue, as being truth, see n. 3727,
3728, 4090. That each, as well the heap as the statue, were
for a sign or a witness, see the same passages, in the present
case, for a sign of a limit. Since the subject treated of is conjunction, it results from the series, that in the internal sense a
limit is denoted, as much as can flow-in from good. That con
junction is effected by good, and that good flows-in according
to reception, was said above. Reception of good, however,
can only exist according to truths, for truths are what good
flows into, good being the agent, and truth the recipient, wherefore all truths are recipient vessels, see n. 4166. Since truths
are what good flows into, truths are what limit the influx of
goods. This is here meant by the limit as much as can flow
from good. How this is, it may be expedient briefly to explain.
Truths with man, whatever they be, and of whatever quality,
enter into his memory by affection, that is, by a certain delight
of love. Without affection, or without the delight which is of
love, nothing can enter with man, because his life is in them.
Those truths which have entered, are reproduced when a similar
delight recurs, together with several other truths which have
associated or conjoined themselves. Also, when the same truth
is reproduced by a man himself or by another man, then also
the affection or delight which had been that of the love when
it entered, is in like manner excited, for they cohere in conjunction. Hence it may appear how the case is with the affection of truth. The truth which has entered with the affection
of good, is reproduced when a similar affection recurs, and so
is the affection when a similar truth recurs. Hence also it is
manifest, that no truth with genuine affection can possibly be
implanted and interiorly rooted, unless man be in good, for the
genuine affection of truth comes from the good of love to the
Lord and of charity towards the neighbour. This good flows-in
from the Lord, but it is not fixed except in truths, for truths
are the hospice of good, for they are in agreement together.
Hence also it is evident, that such as the truths are in their

quality, such is the reception of good.   Truths with the Gentiles, who have lived in mutual charity, are such, that good influent from the Lord may find a hospice in them, but during their abode in the world, not so much so as with Christians who have truths from the Word, and live thence in spiritual charity, see n. 2589 to 2604.

4206.   " The God of Abraham and the God of Nahor judge between us"—that this signifies the Divine into each, that is, into the good which those have who are within the Church, and into the good which those have who are out of the Church, appears from the signification of the God of Abraham, as being the Lord's Divine having respect to those who are within the Church; and from the signification of the God of Nahor, as being the Lord's Divine having respect to those who are out of the Church.   Hence it is evident, that those words signify the Divine into each.   The reason why the God of Abraham denotes the Lord's Divine having respect to those who are within the Church, is, because Abraham represents the Lord's Divine, consequently, that which comes directly from the Lord, see n. 3245, 3778 : hence they who are within the Churrh are specifically meant by the sons of Abraham, John viii. 39.   The reason why the God of Nahor denotes the Lord's Divine having respect to those who are out of the Church, is, because Nahor represents the Church of the Gentiles, and his sons those therein who are in a brotherhood, see n. 2863, 2864, 3052, 3778, 3868; therefore also in the present case Laban, who is the son of Nahor, represents lateral good, such as the Gentiles have from the Lord.   The reason why such various principles of the Lord are represented, is, not because there are various principles in the Lord, but because His Divine is variously received by men. The case here is like that of the life of man.   This life flows into and acts upon the various bodily organs of sense and motion, and upon the various members and viscera, and in every case exhibits a variety, for the eye is affected in one manner, the ear in another, the tongue in another; in like manner, the motion of the arm and hand differs from that of the loins and feet, and the action of the lungs differs from that of the heart, also the action of the liver from that of the stomach, and so in other cases; yet still it is one life which acts so variously in all these instances.   Not that the life itself acts diversely, but that it is diversely received, for it is the form of each part of the body according to which the action is determined.

4207.   "The God of their father"—that this signifies from the Supreme Divine, appears from the signification of God the Father, as being the Supreme Divine, for Father in the Word, whenever it occurs, in the internal sense signifies good, see n. 3703; and that the Lord's Father, or the Father when named by the Lord, is the Divine Good which is in Himself, see n.

3704. Divine Good is the Supreme Divine, but the Divine Word is what is from the Divine Good, and is also called the Son. Moreover by father is here meant Therah, who was the father of both Abraham and Nahor; and that he represents the common stock of the Church, may be seen, n. 3778. Hence Abraham, in a respective sense, represents the genuine Church, and Nahor, the Church of the Gentiles, as was said just above, n. 4206.

4208. "And Jacob sware into the dread of his father Isaac" —that this signifies confirmation from the Divine Human, which is called dread in that state, appears from the signification of swearing, as being confirmation, see n. 2842, 3375; and from the signification of the dread of Isaac, as being the Lord's Divine Human, see n. 4180; that oaths were made by the Lord's Divine Human, see n. 2842. The reason why it is here said, the God of Abraham, the God of Nahor, the God of their father or Therah, and the dread of Isaac the father of Jacob, is, because the sons of Therah acknowledged so many gods, for they were idolaters, see n. 1353, 1356, 1992, 3667; and it was peculiar in that house, that every family worshipped its own god. Hence it is here said, the God of Abraham, the God of Nahor, the God of their father, and the dread of Isaac. It was, however, enjoined to the family of Abraham to acknowledge Jehovah for their God; but still they did not acknowledge Him otherwise than as another god, by whom they might distinguish themselves from the Gentiles; thus they acknowledged Him in name alone: on which account also they so often turned aside to other gods, as may appear from the historical parts of the Word. The reason was, because they were only in externals, not knowing, neither desirous to know, what internals were. The very rituals of their Church were respectively to them no other than idolatrous, because they were separated from things internal, for every ritual of the Church separate from what is internal is idolatrous. Still the genuine principle of the Church might be represented by them, for representations do not respect person, but thing, see n. 665, 1097, 1361, 3147. In order, however, that a representative Church might exist, and thus there might be some communication of the Lord through heaven with man, it was needful they should be bound especially to acknowledge Jehovah, if not in heart, yet in mouth, for representatives with them did not go forth from internals, but from externals, and thus communicated themselves, otherwise than in a genuine Church, in which a communication is effected by internals; wherefore also their Divine worship did not at all affect their souls, that is, did not make them blessed in another life, but only prosperous in the world. It was on this account, namely, to keep them in externals, that so many miracles were wrought among them, which would not have been the case had they been in internals; and therefore they were so often compelled by punishments, by captivities, and by threats, to worship, when yet no one is compelled to internal worship by the Lord, but this worship is implanted by freedom, see n. 1937, 1947, 2174, 2875, 2876 to 2881, 3145, 3146, 3158, 4031. The principal external was, that they should confess Jehovah, for Jehovah was the Lord, Who was represented in all things of that Church: that Jehovah was the Lord, see n. 1343, 1736, 2921, 3035.

4209. Verses 54, 55. *And Jacob sacrificed a sacrifice in the mountain, and called his brethren to eat bread together: and they did eat bread together, and passed the night in the mountain. And in the morning Laban arose early, and kissed his sons and his daughters, and blessed them; and Laban went, and returned to his place.* Jacob sacrificed a sacrifice in the mountain, signifies worship from the good of love: and called his brethren to eat bread together, signifies appropriation of good from the Lord's Divine Natural: and they did eat bread signifies effect: and they passed the night in the mountain signifies tranquillity: and in the morning Laban arose early signifies the enlightenment of that good by the Lord's Divine Natural: and kissed his sons and his daughters, signifies the ac knowledgment of those truths and of the affections of the same and blessed them, signifies joy thence derived: and Laban went and returned to his place, signifies the end of representation by Laban.

4210. "Jacob sacrificed a sacrifice in the mountain"—that this signifies worship from the good of love, appears from the signification of sacrifice, as being worship, see n. 922, 923, 2186 and from the signification of a mountain, as being the good of love, see n. 795, 796, 1430. Sacrifice signifies worship, because sacrifices and burnt-offerings were the principals of all worship in the latter or Hebrew representative Church. They also sacrificed in mountains, as is likewise evident from the Word throughout, because mountains from their height signified those things which were high, as are the things of heaven, which are called celestial things, and hence in a supreme sense they signified the Lord, whom they called the Highest: from appearance they so supposed, for the things which are interior appear as being higher, as in the case of heaven with man, which is interiorly in him, but yet man supposes that it is on high. Hence it is, that wherever in the Word the expression high is used, in the internal sense it signifies what is interior. In the world, man must needs conclude that heaven is on high, as well from the fact that the visible which is round about on high is called heaven, as because man is in time and place, and thus thinks from the ideas thereof; and also from this, that few know what interior is, and still fewer that there is neither place nor time therein. Hence it is, that the expressions used in the Word are according to the ideas of man's thought. If they had not been according to such ideas, but according to angelic ideas, then man would not have had the least perception thereof, but every one would have wondered what was meant, and whether there was any meaning, and thus would have rejected it as something which contained nothing in accord with his understanding.

4211. "And called his brethren to eat bread together"— that this signifies appropriation of good from the Lord's Divine Natural, appears from the signification of brethren, as being those who were now in covenant, that is, joined together in friendship, and in the internal sense, those who are in good and truth; (that these are called brethren, see n. 367, 2360, 3303, 3459, 3803, 3815, 4121, 4191;) and from the signification of eating together, as being appropriation, see n. 3168, 3513, 3832; (that eating together and feasting with the ancients signified appropriation and conjunction by love and charity, see n. 3596 ;) and from the signification of bread, as being the good of love, see n. 276, 680, 1798, 3478, 3735, and in a supreme sense the Lord, see n. 2165, 2177, 3478, 3813. Since bread in a supreme sense signifies the Lord, it therefore signifies every thing holy which is from Him, that is, every thing good and true, and as there is not any other good, which is good, but that of love and charity, therefore bread signifies love and charity. Sacrifices formerly had no other signification; wherefore they were called by one expression, bread, see n. 2165, and also the flesh of the sacrifices was eaten, in order to represent a heavenly feast, that is, conjunction by the good which is of love and charity. This now is what is signified by the sacred supper, for this supper succeeded in the place of sacrifices, and of feasts on what was sanctified; and this sacred supper is an external of the Church, which has in it an internal, and by the internal conjoins the man, who is in love and charity, with heaven, and by heaven with the Lord; for in the sacred supper also, to eat signifies to appropriate; the bread, celestial love; and the wine, spiritual love; and this in such a sort, that when man is in holiness while he eats, nothing else is perceived in heaven. The reason why it is said, appropriation of good from the Lord's Divine Natural, is, because the subject treated of is the good of the Gentiles, for the good of the Gentiles is now represented by Laban, see n. 4189. Man's conjunction with the Lord is not with His essential Supreme Divine, but with His Divine Human, for man cannot have any idea at all of the Lord's Supreme Divine, since it so far transcends his idea, that the idea totally perishes and becomes none: of His Divine Human, however, he can have an idea; for every one is conjoined by thought and affection, where the subject conjoined with is capable of being apprehended by some idea, but not where it cannot be so appre

hended.   While the Lord's Human is the subject of thought,
then, if there be holiness in the idea, the holiness is thought of,
which from the Lord fills heaven, thus also heaven is thought
of, for heaven in its complex has relation to one man, and this
from the Lord, see n. 684, 1276, 2996, 2998, 3624 to 3649.
Hence it is, that conjunction cannot exist with the Lord's Supreme Divine but with His Divine Human, and by the Divine
Human with His Supreme Divine.   Hence it is that it is said
in John, "No one hath seen God at any time, except the only-
begotten Son," i. 18, and that no passage is given to the Father
but by Him; also, that He is the Mediator.   This may be manifest from this consideration, that all those within the Church,
who say that they believe in the Supreme Being, and despise
the Lord, are such as believe nothing at all, not even that there
is a heaven or a hell, and worship nature; and also, if they are
willing to be instructed by experience, it will appear that the
wicked, yea, the most wicked, say the same.   But men think
variously of the Lord's Human, and one man differently from
another, and one more holily than another.   They who are
within the Church, can think that His Human is Divine, and
also that He is one with the Father, as He Himself saith that
the Father is in Him, and He in the Father; but they who are
out of the Church cannot do this, as well because they do not
know any thing of the Lord, as because they take their idea of
the Divine Being from no other source than from images which
they see with their eyes, and from idols which they can touch.
Still, however, the Lord conjoins Himself with them by the
good of charity and obedience in their gross idea.   Hence it is
that it is here said that they have appropriation of good from
the Lord's Divine Natural; for the conjunction of the Lord
with man is according to the state of his thought, and thence
of his affection.   Those who are in the most holy idea of the
Lord, and at the same time in the knowledges and affections of
good and truth, as those may be who are within the Church,
are conjoined with the Lord as to His Divine Rational; but
those who are not in such holiness, nor in such an interior idea
and affection, are conjoined with the Lord as to His Divine
Natural: they whose holiness is of a still grosser kind, are
conjoined to the Lord as to His Divine Sensual.   The latter
conjunction is what is represented by the brazen serpent, which
was a means of revival from the bite of serpents to those who
looked upon it, see Numb. xxi. 9.   In this conjunction are those
of the Gentiles, who worship idols, and yet live according to
their religious principles in charity.   From these considerations
then it may appear, what is meant by the appropriation of good
from the Lord's Divine Natural, which is signified by Jacob's
calling the brethren to eat bread together.

4212. " And they did eat bread"—that this signifies effect

namely, friendship, in an external sense, and conjunction by good and truth in the natural [principle], in a supreme sense, may appear without explication.

4213. " And passed the night in the mountain"—that this signifies tranquillity, appears from the signification of passing the night, as being to have peace, see n. 3190, thus tranquillity. That they who entered into a covenant should pass the night in one place, was also a ritual, because passing the night in one place signified that there was no longer any hostility; in the internal sense, that there was tranquillity and peace, for they who are joined together as to good and truth, are in tranquillity and peace; wherefore it is here said, in the mountain, because mountain signifies the good of love and charity, see n. 4210, for the good of love and charity gives peace. What peace and tranquillity is, may be seen, n. 92, 93, 1728, 2780, 3170, 3696, 3780.

4214. " And in the morning Laban arose early"—that this signifies the enlightenment of that good by the Lord's Divine Natural, appears from the signification of arising in the morning early, as being enlightenment, n. 3458, 3723; and from the representation of Laban, as being good such as the Gentiles are in, n. 4189: that the enlightenment of this good from the Lord's Divine Natural is here meant, is evident from the series. As regards enlightenment, it is all from the Lord, and by the good in man; such also as the good is, such is the enlightenment. Most persons believe that those are enlightened, who can reason about good and truth, and about the evil and false, and that they are in a state of enlightenment so much the greater, the more subtilly and acutely they can talk on such subjects, and at the same time confirm them by many scientifics, and likewise give an appearance of probability to what they say by comparisons, especially by such as are from things of sense, and by other persuasives. Such persons however may still be in no enlightenment, although they have an imaginative and a perceptive faculty. This faculty is two-fold, one which comes from the light of heaven, another which comes from the lumen of infatuation; both appear similar in the external form, but in the internal they are altogether different. That which is from the light of heaven is in good, that is, exists in those who are in good; these from good can see truth, and know as in clear day whether it be so, or be not so. That which is from the lumen of infatuation is in evil, that is, exists in those who are in evil. The reason why these latter can reason on such subjects is, because they have some faculty of knowing them, but are in no affection of doing; that this is not to be in enlightenment, every one may comprehend. As to the lumen of infatuation in another life, the case is this: those who have been in such lumen in the world, are in the same in another life, and reason there on good and truth, and on evil and the false, and this, much more perfectly and excellently than in the life of the body, for their thoughts are not then withdrawn and impeded by cares relating to the body and the world, nor are so terminated therein as during their abode in the body and the world. It is however instantly apparent, not to them, but to good spirits and angels, that their reasonings are those of the lumen of infatuation, and that the light of heaven, which flows-in, is instantly changed into such a lumen, and that in this case the light of heaven is either suffocated, as when the light of the sun falls upon some opaque body and becomes black, or is reflected, as is the case with those who are in the false; or is perverted, as when the light of the sun falls upon dirty and filthy objects, and causes dirty colours and offensive odours. So it is with those who are in the lumen of infatuation, and believe themselves to be more enlightened than others, because they can reason intelligently and wisely, and yet live in evil. Who these are, and what is their quality, appears from every particular of their discourse, while they do not feign a sem blance of good with a view to deceive. They who deny or despise the Lord, and within themselves ridicule those who confess Him, are among them. They who love adulteries, and laugh at those who believe marriages holy and not to be vio lated, are also among them. They who believe the precepts and doctrinals of the Church to be for the sake of the vulgar, that they may be kept thereby in restraint, and themselves make light of those precepts and doctrinals, are in like manner among them. Those who attribute all things to nature, and believe those to be simple and of weak judgment who assert a Divine therein, are in like manner also among them. Those who ascribe all and singular things to their own proper prudence, and say that there is a Supreme Being, which in general or in the universal governs something, but nothing in particular or in singular, and have confirmed themselves in this opinion, are also such; and so in other cases. Such persons are in the lumen of infatuation also in another life, and also reason acutely among their like, but when they approach to any heavenly society, that lumen is instantly extinguished, and becomes dark, consequently their thought is obscured so that they cannot so much as think, for they are there touched lightly by the light of heaven, which, as was said, is either suffocated with them, or reflected, or perverted, wherefore they cast themselves headlong thence into hell, where such a lumen prevails. From these considerations it may appear what is the nature of true enlightenment, that it is from the good which comes from the Lord, and what false enlightenment, that it is from the evil which comes from hell.

4215. "And kissed his sons and his daughters"—that this

signifies the acknowledgment of those truths, and of the affections of the same, appears from the signification of kissing, as being conjunction from affection, see n. 3573, 3574, consequently acknowledgment, for where there is conjunction by good and truth, there is acknowledgment of the same; and from the signification of sons, as being things true or truths, see n. 489, 491, 533, 1147, 2623, 3773; and from the signification of daughters, that is, of Rachel and Leah, as being the affections of the same, that is, of truths, see n. 3758, 3782, 3793, 3819. That to kiss signifies conjunction from affection, is from correspondence; for there is a correspondence of heaven with all the organs and members of the body, concerning which see the relations at the close of each chapter. There is a correspondence of the internals with all things of the face, hence the disposition shines forth from the countenance, and the interior disposition or the mind from the eyes. There is also a correspondence of the thoughts and affections with the actions and gestures of the body. That there is the same with all the voluntary actions and gestures is a known thing, and also with the involuntary ones; for humiliation of heart produces a bending of the knees, which is an external gesture of the body; humiliation still greater and more interior produces prostration to the earth; gladness of the disposition and joy of the mind produces singing and joyful exclamation; sadness and internal mourning produces weeping and lamentation; but conjunction from affection produces kissing. Hence it is evident, that such external acts, since they correspond, are signs of things internal, and that an internal is in them as in signs, from which internal they receive their quality. With those, however, who are willing by externals to assume a semblance of internals, such externals also are for signs, but signs of simulation, of hypocrisy and deceit, as is the case with kissing; for every one by kissing is desirous to signify that he loves another from his heart, knowing that kissing is from this ground, and that it is a sign of conjunction from affection, and being willing thereby to persuade his neighbour that he loves him for the sake of good in him; when yet it is for the sake of himself, and of self honour and gain, thus not for the sake of good, but for the sake of evil, for he who regards himself as an end, not as an end intermediate to good, and is willing to be conjoined with another as to that end, is in evil.

4216. "And blessed them"—that this signifies joy thence arising, appears from the signification of blessing, as being to wish things prosperous, see n. 3185, thus to testify joy when one departs.

4217. "And Laban went and returned to his place"—that this signifies an end of the representation by Laban, appears from the signification of returning to his place, as being to go

back again to a former state ; that place denotes state, see n.
2625, 2837, 3356, 3387, 3404; hence it is that these words signify an end of the representation by Laban.   From what has
been shown above, it may appear, that all and singular the
things in the Word contain things interior ; and that the inte
rior things are such as are adequate to the perception of the
angels attendant on man : as for example, when the term bread
is used in the Word, the angels do not know what material
bread is, but what spiritual bread is, thus, instead of bread they
perceive the Lord, Who Himself teaches in John that He is
the bread of life, chap. vi. 33, 35 ; and as they perceive the
Lord, they perceive those things which are from the Lord, consequently, His love towards the universal human race, and
therewith they perceive at the same time the reciprocal love of
man to the Lord, for these things cohere in one idea of thought
and affection.   In a way not unlike this the man thinks, who
is in a holy state, when he receives the bread of the sacred
supper, for he thinks on such occasion not of bread, but of
the Lord and of His mercy, and of those things which relate
to love to Him and to charity towards the neighbour, because
he thinks of repentance and amendment of life, but this with a
variety according to the holiness in which he is, not only as to
thought, but also as to affection.   Hence it is evident, that
bread, as mentioned in the Word, does not suggest the idea of
any bread to the angels, but suggests the idea of love, togethe
with the innumerable things which relate to love.   In like man
ner wine, when it is read in the Word, and also is received in
the sacred supper.   On such occasions, the angels do not think
at all of wine, but of charity towards the neighbour ; and this
being the case, and this the ground of man's connection with
heaven, and by heaven with the Lord, therefore bread and wine
were made symbols, and they unite the man who is in what is
holy with heaven, and by heaven with the Lord.   The case is
the same with singular the things in the Word ; and therefore
the Word is the uniting medium between man and the Lord,
and unless such a uniting medium existed, it would be impossible for heaven to flow-in with man, for without a medium
there could be no unition, but heaven would remove itself from
man ; and if heaven were removed, it would be impossible for
any one any longer to be led to good, not even to corporeal
and worldly good, but all restraints, even external ones, would
be broken.   The Lord governs the man, who is in good, by the
internal restraints of conscience, but if a man be in evil, the
Lord governs him only by the external restraints ; and if these
were broken, every one would become insane, as he is who is
without fear of the law, without fear of death, and without fear
of the loss of honour and gain, and thence of reputation,
these being external restraints ; thus the human race would

perish. Hence it may appear why the Word exists, and what is its quality. That the Church of the Lord, where the Word is, is like a heart and lungs ; and that the Church of the Lord, where the Word is not, is like the rest of the viscera, which live from the heart and lungs, may be seen above, n. 637, 931, 2054, 2853.

A CONTINUATION OF THE SUBJECT CONCERNING THE GRAND MAN AND CONCERNING CORRESPONDENCE.

4218. *IN the preceding parts of this work, at the end of the chapters, relations have been given of what it was granted me to see and perceive in the world of spirits and in the heavens of angels ; and lastly, the* GRAND MAN *was treated of, and correspondence. In order that it may be fully known how the case is with man, and that he is in connection with heaven, not only as to his thoughts and affections, but also as to his organic forms both interior and exterior, and that without such connection he could not subsist even for a moment, it is allowed me in this part to continue what was begun at the end of the preceding chapters, concerning correspondence with the* GRAND MAN.

4219. *That it may be known in general how the case is with the* GRAND MAN, *it is to be observed, that the universal heaven is the* GRAND MAN, *and that heaven is named the* GRAND MAN, *because it corresponds to the Lord's Divine Human ; for the Lord is the only Man, and so much as an angel and spirit, or a man on the earth, has from Him, so far they also are men. Let not any one believe that man is man from the fact of having a human face and a human body, and brains, and viscera, and members. These things are common to him with brutes, wherefore also they die and become a carcase ; but man is man in that he is capable of thinking and willing as a man, thus of receiving those things which are Divine, that is, which are of the Lord ; by these things man distinguishes himself from beasts and savages ; and also becomes a man in another life in regard to his quality, according as those things have been appropriated to him by reception in the life of the body.*

4220. *They who in the life of the body had received the Divine things which are of the Lord, that is, who had received His love towards the universal human race, consequently, who had received charity towards the neighbour, and reciprocal love to the Lord, they, in another life, are gifted with intelligence and wisdom, and with happiness ineffable, for they become angels, thus truly men. They, however, who in the life of the body had not received the Divine things which are of the Lord, that is, had not received love towards the human race, still less*

*reciprocal love to the Lord, but have only loved, yea, worshipped
themselves, and consequently have had for an end those things
which regard self and the world, they, in another life, after
passing a short career therein, are deprived of all intelligence,
and become most stupid, and are amongst the stupid infernals.*

4221. *In order that I might know that this is the case, it
has been given me to discourse with such as have so lived, and
also with one whom I was likewise acquainted with in the life
of the body. He, during his life, did whatever good he did to
his neighbour for the sake of himself, that is, for the sake of
self-honour and self-gain ; he despised others, and even hated
them ; he confessed God indeed with his mouth, but yet did not
acknowledge Him in heart. When it was given me to speak
with him, there exhaled from him a kind of corporeal sphere,
his speech was not like that of spirits, but of a man yet alive ;
for the speech of spirits is distinguished from human speech in
this, that it is full of ideas, or that a spiritual principle is in
it, thus a vitality inexpressible, but in the present case it was
not so. Such a sphere exhaled from him, and was perceived in
singular the things which he spoke. He appeared there among
the vile, and it was said, that they who are such, become successively so gross and stupid as to thoughts and affections, that no
one in the world is more so. They have a place under the but-
tocks, where their hell is. Hence also, before, a certain one
appeared, not in appearance like a spirit, but like a grossly corporeal man, in whom there was so little of the life of intelligence which is properly human, that he might be called stupidity
in effigy. Hence it appeared manifest of what quality they become, who are in no love to the neighbour, or the public, still
less towards the Lord's kingdom, but only in self-love, regarding
themselves alone in every thing, yea, adoring themselves as gods,
and thus also being willing to be adored by others, this being
their intention in whatever they do.*

4222. *As concerns the correspondence of the* Grand Man
*with the parts of man, it exists with all and singular, with his
organs, members, and viscera, and this in such a sort, that there
is not any organ and member in the body, nor any part in an
organ and member, nor even any particle of a part, with which
there is not a correspondence. It is a known fact, that every
particular organ and member in the body consists of parts, and
of parts of parts ; as in the case of the brain ; this in general
consists of what is properly called the cerebrum, of the cerebellum, of the medulla oblongata, and the medulla spinalis, the
latter being a continuation or a kind of appendix. The cerebrum, again, properly so called, consists of several members,
which are its parts, of the membranes which are called the dura
mater and the pia mater, of the corpus callosum, of the corpora
striata, of ventricles and cavities, of smaller glands, of septa, in*

general, of the cineritious substance and medullary substance, moreover of sinuses, blood-vessels, and plexuses. The case is the same with the bodily organs of sense and of motion and with the viscera, as is well known from anatomical observations. All these things in general and in particular correspond most exactly to the GRAND MAN, *and therein, to so many heavens as it were; for the Lord's heaven is in like manner distinguished into lesser heavens, and these into still lesser, and these into least, at length into angels, of whom each individual is a small heaven corresponding to the largest. These heavens are most distinct among themselves, each particular one belonging to its general heaven, and the general heavens to the most general or the whole, which is the* GRAND MAN.

4223. *But with regard to correspondence the case is this, that the above-mentioned heavens correspond indeed to the real organic forms of the human body, wherefore it was said, that those societies, or those angels, belong to the province of the brain, or the province of the heart, or the province of the lungs, or the province of the eye, and so forth; but still they principally correspond to the functions of those viscera or organs. The case herein is like that of the organs and viscera themselves, in that the functions constitute one with their organic forms; for it is not possible to conceive of any function except from forms, that is, from substances, substances being the subjects from which functions exist. For example, sight cannot be conceived without the eye, nor respiration without the lungs, the eye being the organic form from which and by which sight exists, and the lungs the organic form from which and by which respiration exists; so also in other cases. Functions therefore are what the heavenly societies principally correspond to, and this being the case, organic forms also are what they correspond to, for the one is indivisible and inseparable from the other, insomuch that whether we say function or organic form by which and from which the function exists, it is the same thing. Hence it is that there is a correspondence with the organs, members, and viscera, because with the functions; wherefore, when the function is produced, the organ also is excited. This is the case also in all and singular the things which a man does. When he wills to do this or that, and to act thus or otherwise, and makes it the subject of his thought, then the organs move themselves agreeably thereto, thus according to the intention of the function or use; for it is use which rules in forms. Hence also it is manifest that before the organic forms of the body existed, use was, and that use produced and adapted them to itself, but not vice versa; but when the forms are produced, or the organs adapted, uses thence proceed, and in this case it appears as if the forms or organs are prior to the use, when yet it is not so; for use flows in from the Lord, and this through heaven, according to the order and*

*according to the form in which heaven is arranged by the Lord,
thus according to correspondences. Hereby man exists, and
hereby he subsists. Hence it is further evident from what
ground it is, that man as to all and singular things corresponds
to the heavens.*

*4224. Organic forms are not only those which appear to the
eye, and which can be discovered by microscopes, but there are
also organic forms still purer, which cannot possibly be discovered by any eye, whether naked or assisted. The latter forms
are of an interior kind, as the forms which are of the internal
sight, and finally those which are of the intellect, which latter
are inscrutable, but still they are forms, that is, substances; it
not being possible for any sight, not even intellectual, to exist,
but from something. It is also known in the learned world,
that without substance, which is a subject, there exists not any
mode, or any modification, or any quality which manifests itself actively. Those purer or interior forms which are inscrutable, are what form and fix the internal senses, and also produce
the interior affections. With those forms the interior heavens
correspond, because they correspond with the senses thereof, and
with the affections of these senses. But inasmuch as several
things have been discovered to me concerning those forms, and
their correspondence, they cannot be clearly expounded unless
they are severally and specifically treated of, wherefore also in
the following work, by the Divine Mercy of the Lord, it is allowed me to continue what was begun in the foregoing part concerning the correspondence of man with the GRAND MAN, to the
intent that man may know, not from any ratiocination, still
less from any hypothesis, but from experience itself, how the
real case is with him, and with his internal man which is called
his soul, and lastly with his conjunction with heaven, and by
heaven with the Lord, consequently, what is the ground whence
man is man, and by what he is distinguished from the beasts;
and moreover, how man separates himself from that conjunction, and conjoins himself with hell.*

*4225. It is expedient previously to observe, who are within
the GRAND MAN, and who are out of that man. All who are
in love to the Lord, and in charity towards the neighbour, and
do good to him from the heart according to the good appertaining to him, and who have a conscience of what is just and equitable, are within the GRAND MAN, for they are in the Lord,
consequently in heaven; but all who are in self-love and the
love of the world, and thence in concupiscences, and do good
only for the sake of laws, of self-honour, and worldly wealth,
and for the sake of reputation thence derived, thus who interiorly are merciless, in hatred and revenge against their neighbour
because of themselves and the world, and delighted with his hurt
when he does not favour them, are out of the GRAND MAN, for*

they are in hell.   Such persons do not correspond with any or gans and members in the body, but with various corruptions and diseases therein induced, concerning which also, by the Divine Mercy of the Lord, I shall speak from experience in what follows.   They who are out of the GRAND MAN, *that is, out of heaven, cannot possibly enter it, for they are contrary lives; yea, if by any means they do enter, as is the case sometimes with such as in the life of the body have had the art to feign themselves angels of light, when they come thither (which is permitted occasionally in order that their quality may be known), they are admitted only to the first entrance, that is, to those who as yet are simple, and not fully instructed, on which occasion, they who enter as angels of light can scarcely stay there a moment, because the life of love to the Lord and of charity towards the neighbour prevails there; and as nothing there corresponds to their life, they can scarce respire.   That spirits and angels also respire, may be seen, n. 3884 to 3893.   Hence they begin to be tormented, for respiration is according to freedom of the life, and what is wonderful, they can scarce at length move, but become like those who are in heaviness, the interiors being seized with anguish and torments, wherefore they cast themselves down headlong, and this to hell, where they get their respiration and faculty of motion: hence it is that life in the Word is represented by mobility.   They who are in the* GRAND MAN *are in freedom of respiration, when in the good of love; but still they are distinguished according to the quality and quantity of good.   Hence, there are so many heavens, which in the Word are called mansions, John* xiv. 2 *; and every one in his own heaven is in his own life, and has influx from the universal heaven, every one therein being the centre of all influxes, hence in the most perfect equilibrium, and this according to the stupendous form of heaven, which is from the Lord alone; thus, with all variety.*

4226. *Sometimes spirits recently deceased, who interiorly have been evil during their lives in the world, but exteriorly have borrowed an appearance of good by the works which they have done for others for the sake of themselves and the world, have complained that they were not admitted into heaven, they having no other opinion of heaven, than as a place into which they might be admitted by favour.   But answer was made them, that heaven is denied to no one, and if they were desirous of it they might be admitted.   Some also were admitted to the heavenly societies which were nearest to the entrance, but when they came thither, by reason of the contrariety and repugnance of the life, they perceived, as was said, a cessation of respiration, an agony and torment as it were infernal, and cast themselves down thence, saying afterwards, that heaven to them was hell, and that they in no wise believed that heaven was such a place.*

4227. *There are several of each sex, who have been such in the life of the body, that wherever it was in their power, they sought by art and deceit to subdue to themselves the minds of others with a view to rule over them, especially with the powerful and the rich, that they might be the only ones to rule under their name; and who have acted covertly, and removed others, especially the well-disposed, and this by various methods, not indeed by blaming them, because probity defends itself, but by other methods, by perverting their counsels, calling them simple and also evil, and by attributing misfortunes to them, if any come to pass, besides other things of a similar nature. They who have been such in the life of the body, are also such in another life, for his own life follows every one. By living experience from spirits of this sort, when they have been with me, I have found it to be so, because they acted then in the same manner, but still more cunningly and ingeniously, for spirits act more subtly than men, being loosed from the ties of the body, and the bonds of the gross modes of sensations. They were so subtle, that sometimes I did not perceive that they had an intention or end of domination; and when they were discoursing among themselves, they were cautious lest I should hear and perceive them; but it was told me by others who heard them, that their designs were wicked, and that by magical arts, thus by aid from a diabolical crew, they studied to compass their end. They made light of murdering the upright; they accounted the Lord, under Whom they said they were willing to rule, as vile, regarding Him only as another man, who had worship paid Him by ancient custom, as with other nations, which made men gods, and worshipped them, and which they durst not contradict, because they were born in that worship, and would thereby suffer in their reputation. Concerning these spirits I can say this, that they obsess the thoughts and will of men who are like them, and with such insinuate themselves into their affection and intention, so that they cannot in any wise know, without the Lord's Mercy, that such spirits are present, and that they are in the society of such. These spirits correspond to the corruptions of the purer blood of man, which blood is called the animal spirit, which the corruptions enter without order, and wherever they diffuse themselves, they are like poisons which induce cold and torpor in the nerves and fibres, from which break forth the most grievous and fatal diseases. When such act in consort, they are known by this, that they act in a quadruped manner, to use the expression, and that they are seated on the hinder part of the head under the cerebellum to the left; for they who act under the occiput, operate more clandestinely than others, and they who act on the hinder part are desirous to bear rule. They reasoned with me about the Lord, and said, that it is wonderful He does not hear prayers when they pray, and thus does not aid them in their supplications;*

but it was given me to answer, that they could not be heard, because they have for an end such things as are contrary to the salvation of mankind, and because they pray for themselves against all others, and when they thus pray that heaven is closed, for they who are in heaven attend only to the ends of those who pray. These things indeed they were not willing to acknowledge, but still they could answer nothing. There were men of this sort, and these in consort with women, who said, that from the women they could conceive several designs, because they were quicker and more cunning in their views of such things. They are much delighted in the consort of those who have lived in whoredom. Such for the most part apply themselves to secret and magical arts in another life, for there are very many magical arts in another life, which are altogether unknown in the world, and spirits of the above sort apply themselves thereto, as soon as they come into another life, and learn to fascinate those among whom they are, especially those under whom they are desirous to have rule; nor do they abhor wicked and abominable practices. Concerning their hell, what its quality is, and where they are when in the world of spirits, I shall speak elsewhere. From these considerations it may be manifest, that every one's own particular life remains with him after death.

4228. The subject concerning the GRAND MAN and correspondence, will be continued at the close of the following chapter, where correspondence with the senses in general will be treated of.

END OF VOLUME FOURTH.